THE ESSENTIAL ELLEN WILLIS

Other Books by Ellen Willis
Published by the University of Minnesota Press

Beginning to See the Light: Sex, Hope, and Rock-and-Roll

No More Nice Girls: Countercultural Essays

Out of the Vinyl Deeps: Ellen Willis on Rock Music

The Essential Ellen Willis

ELLEN WILLIS

Nona Willis Aronowitz, Editor

With Contributions from Spencer Ackerman,
Stanley Aronowitz, Irin Carmon, Ann Friedman,
Cord Jefferson, and Sara Marcus

University of Minnesota Press
Minneapolis | London

This book is published with assistance from the Margaret S. Harding Memorial Endowment honoring the first director of the University of Minnesota Press.

Published by the University of Minnesota Press
111 Third Avenue South, Suite 290
Minneapolis, MN 55401-2520
http://www.upress.umn.edu

Library of Congress Cataloging-in-Publication Data

Willis, Ellen, author.
　　The Essential Ellen Willis / Ellen Willis; Nona Willis Aronowitz, editor; with contri-
　butions from Spencer Ackerman, Stanley Aronowitz, Irin Carmon, Ann Friedman, Cord
　Jefferson, and Sara Marcus.
　　Includes bibliographical references.
　　ISBN 978-0-8166-8120-4 (hc)
　　ISBN 978-0-8166-8121-1 (pb)
　　1. American essays.　I. Aronowitz, Nona Willis, 1984– editor of compilation.　II. Title.
　AC8.W665 2014
　081—dc23

2014001752

Printed in the United States of America on acid-free paper

The University of Minnesota is an equal-opportunity educator and employer.

20　19　18　17　16　15　14　　　　　　　　　　　　10　9　8　7　6　5　4　3　2　1

CONTENTS

ix ACKNOWLEDGMENTS

xi INTRODUCTION: TRANSCENDENCE   NONA WILLIS ARONOWITZ

The Sixties Up from Radicalism

3 INTRODUCTION   SARA MARCUS

5 Up from Radicalism: A Feminist Journal (*US Magazine*, 1969)

20 Dylan (*Cheetah*, 1967)

36 The Cultural Revolution Saved from Drowning (*The New Yorker*, September 1969)

40 Women and the Myth of Consumerism (*Ramparts*, 1970)

43 Talk of the Town: Hearing (*The New Yorker*, February 1969)

The Seventies Exile on Main Street

49 INTRODUCTION   IRIN CARMON

51 Beginning to See the Light (*Village Voice*, 1977)

59 Janis Joplin (*The Rolling Stone Illustrated History of Rock 'n' Roll*, 1980)

64 Classical and Baroque Sex in Everyday Life (*Village Voice*, May 1979)

67 Memoirs of a Non–Prom Queen (*Rolling Stone*, August 1976)

70 The Trial of Arline Hunt (*Rolling Stone*, 1975)

89 Abortion: Is a Woman a Person? (*Village Voice*, March and April 1979)

94 Feminism, Moralism, and Pornography (*Village Voice*, October and November 1979)

101   The Family: Love It or Leave It *(Village Voice, September 1979)*

115   Tom Wolfe's Failed Optimism *(Village Voice, 1977)*

121   The Velvet Underground *(Stranded by Greil Marcus, 1979)*

132   Next Year in Jerusalem *(Rolling Stone, April 1977)*

The Eighties   Coming Down Again

173   INTRODUCTION   ANN FRIEDMAN

175   Toward a Feminist Sexual Revolution *(Social Text, Fall 1982)*

200   Lust Horizons: Is the Women's Movement Pro-Sex? *(Village Voice, June 1981)*

209   The Last Unmarried Person in America *(Village Voice, July 1981)*

213   Teenage Sex: A Modesty Proposal *(Village Voice, October 1986)*

216   Sisters under the Skin? Confronting Race and Sex
       (Village Voice Literary Supplement, June 1982)

229   Radical Feminism and Feminist Radicalism *(Social Text, Summer 1984)*

256   Escape from New York *(Village Voice, July 1981)*

276   Coming Down Again: After the Age of Excess *(Village Voice, January 1989)*

288   The Drug War: From Vision to Vice *(Village Voice, April 1986)*

292   The Drug War: Hell No, I Won't Go *(Village Voice, September 1989)*

297   The Diaper Manifesto: We Need a Child-Rearing Movement
       (Village Voice, July 1986)

305   To Emma, with Love *(Village Voice, December 1989)*

The Nineties   Decade of Denial

309   INTRODUCTION   CORD JEFFERSON

311   Selections from "Decade of Denial" *(Don't Think, Smile!, 2000)*

323   Ending Poor People As We Know Them *(Village Voice, December 1994)*

327   What We Don't Talk about When We Talk about *The Bell Curve*
       (Don't Think, Smile!, 2000)

334   Rodney King's Revenge *(Don't Think, Smile!, 2000)*

339   Million Man Mirage *(Village Voice, November 1995)*

343   Monica and Barbara and Primal Concerns *(New York Times, March 1999)*

346   Villains and Victims *(Don't Think, Smile!, 2000)*

358   'Tis Pity He's a Whore *(Don't Think, Smile!, 2000)*

366   Is Motherhood Moonlighting? *(Newsday, March 1991)*

368   Say It Loud: Out of Wedlock and Proud *(Newsday, February 1994)*

370 Bring in the Noise (*The Nation*, April 1996)

375 Intellectual Work in the Culture of Austerity (*Don't Think, Smile!*, 2000)

The Aughts Our Politics, Ourselves

391 INTRODUCTION SPENCER ACKERMAN

393 Why I'm Not for Peace (*Radical Society*, April 2002)

401 Confronting the Contradictions (*Dissent*, Summer 2003)

405 The Mass Psychology of Terrorism (*Implicating Empire*, edited by Stanley Aronowitz et al., 2003)

416 Dreaming of War (*The Nation*, September 2001)

420 Freedom from Religion (*The Nation*, February 2001)

429 Our Mobsters, Ourselves (*The Nation*, March 2001)

437 Is There Still a Jewish Question? Why I'm an Anti-Anti-Zionist (*Wrestling with Zion*, edited by Tony Kushner and Alisa Solomon, 2003)

444 Ghosts, Fantasies, and Hope (*Dissent*, Fall 2005)

450 Escape from Freedom: What's the Matter with Tom Frank (and the Lefties Who Love Him)? (*Situations*, 2006)

464 Three Elegies for Susan Sontag (*New Politics*, Summer 2005)

Coda Selections from "The Cultural Unconscious in American Politics: Why We Need a Freudian Left"

473 INTRODUCTION STANLEY ARONOWITZ

477 The Cultural Unconscious in American Politics: Why We Need a Freudian Left

ACKNOWLEDGMENTS

Doing the research for *Out of the Vinyl Deeps* was mostly a solitary project (not counting a crucial assist from Georgia Christgau), but putting together *The Essential Ellen Willis* was a far more crowd-sourced process. Thank you to Robert Christgau, Richard Goldstein, Donna Gaines, Ann Snitow, Alice Echols, Devon Powers, Rosalyn Baxandall, Alix Shulman, and Rick Perlstein for your suggestions of what to include. Thanks to the archivists at the Radcliffe Institute for organizing Mom's work in such an intuitive way, and thanks to Laura Sikes Jambon for the "artifacts" photographs.

I was incredibly lucky to include the voices of Ann Friedman, Cord Jefferson, Spencer Ackerman, Irin Carmon, Sara Marcus (whose realtalk partly inspired this collection), and my dad, Stanley Aronowitz, whose essays render this collection much more vivid and relevant. I'm grateful to Doug Armato at the University of Minnesota Press for "getting" this project and for his merciful edit when we needed to cut fifty thousand words. Thanks also to Danielle Kasprzak, who was ever patient when the project dragged on longer than intended. And thank you, Meredith Kaffel, for handling business so I didn't have to.

INTRODUCTION: TRANSCENDENCE
Nona Willis Aronowitz

When a collection of my mom Ellen Willis's rock criticism, called *Out of the Vinyl Deeps,* was released in the spring of 2011, it fell into open arms. Veteran music writers rediscovered forty-year-old writings, while brand-new cultural critics reblogged her photos and quotes on Tumblr. It was a multigenerational outpouring of appreciation, a sense that this collection really did fill a void, really had revised the lineup of Important Rock Writers.

But something wasn't quite right. People who were just picking her up labeled her a "rock critic" first and foremost, even though she'd written about music for really only the first seven years of her career. Many fans were completely unaware that after and during her stint as the first pop music critic at the *New Yorker* she was a contributing columnist for *Rolling Stone,* a longtime *Village Voice* staffer, a feminist activist—the take-to-the-streets kind—and eventually a professor who invented a new and still unrivaled cultural reporting program at New York University. One reviewer wrote that she "left the profession" after *The New Yorker* to "pursue academia."[1] My mother would be mortified.

Cultural critic Sara Marcus came to her defense in the *Los Angeles Review of Books* shortly after *Out of the Vinyl Deeps* was published: "All you goobers care about is Dylan, Dylan, Dylan, I want to grumble, when Willis went on to become one of the most ecstatic, intellectually astute, and readable thinkers ever to come out of the radical feminist underground."[2] She ended her long essay by calling for an Essential Ellen Willis anthology that would put together all her work on sex, politics, feminism, and culture in one volume, "not walled off from each other in ghettos, but occupying a brilliant landscape together, expansive, joyful, alive." At that moment, it was clear the narrative needed tweaking again, in order to put Mom's work in context of an incredibly daring, restless forty-year career.

Ellen Willis was born in 1941 in the Bronx, to a police lieutenant and a college-educated housewife, and was raised in suburban Queens. Her adult life started out relatively conventional for a studious, introspective, middle-class woman: she got married to a nice Jewish boy from Columbia while majoring in English at Barnard and eventually moved to Berkeley with him to study comparative literature. But by twenty-four, she was a divorced grad-school dropout living in a tiny apartment in the East Village who knew she wanted "some kind of writing job," although at first she wasn't sure how to make that happen in prefeminist New York City. She managed to score a staff writer position at *Fact* magazine (the ad was in the "help wanted male" section), but eventually, with the help of her downtown neighborhood—and boyfriend and rock critic Robert Christgau—she began to craft her personal Venn diagram: rock music, women's lib, and grand, deliberately non-Washington politics.

Mom would have a hard time crafting her "brand" nowadays. She was intellectual but not academic. She was a journalist but not primarily an "objective" reporter. She poached from her life and detailed her thought processes without devolving into memoir. It's not that the identities of "rock critic" and "feminist writer" aren't valuable, but my mother refused to devote herself exclusively to either; she used both more as touchstones, as lenses through which to see the world. One of the most astounding things about her was how many facets of culture she engaged herself in, depending on the pulse of the decade. In the sixties, she reported on rock music and counterculture for *The New Yorker,* while also immersing herself in the burgeoning women's liberation movement (she founded the radical feminist group Redstockings along with Shulamith Firestone). As the backlash of the 1970s set in, she wrote about sex, abortion, marriage, and religion. She tackled parenting, drugs, race, and cultural backlash in the eighties; political psychodramas in the nineties; war, class, and the cultural unconscious in the aughts.

But even if she isn't easily categorized, she still had a crystalline worldview, one that was highly influenced by both her secular Jewish upbringing in New York, where she lived for most of her life, and her rebellion against those old models. She continually used the word "transcendent," which aptly describes the way she sidestepped any neat category. It was also one of her highest compliments, a code word for a portal into political and emotional freedom, a description for an idea, large or small, that helps us plod through the inertia and our endless rationalizing about the forces that govern us and the decisions we make about our lives. She was a liberationist in the old-school sense of the word, a way that was neither Ayn Rand nor Allen Ginsberg. She went further than the language of "justice" and "equality"—those could veer quickly into the Judeo-Christian concepts of sacrifice and self-seriousness. She cared about pleasure, fun, consciousness, intellectual fulfillment. She employed a strong sense of irony, but she always had enough optimism to imagine a different set of rules, an attitude, as she's often quoted as writing, that's "as spiritually necessary and proper as it is intellectually suspect." The Ellen Willis philosophy of "transcendence," nurtured since the midsixties, needs its own separate space, unmoored from its particular time and era. This collection is that space.

Once I decided to put together this volume and started rereading everything, including pieces that hadn't been collected or even published, I couldn't help but see parallels to present-day questions. Her 1969 account of a New York state legislature's abortion hearing that was all male, save one nun, immediately recalls Sandra Fluke's ordeal. "Abortion: Is a Woman a Person?" (1979) evokes the Personhood maelstrom of the past few years. "Is Motherhood Moonlighting?" (1989) proposes actual solutions to the endless modern-day angst of *The Atlantic,* "Why Women Still Can't Have It All." "Don't Think, Smile!" and its assault on nineties leftist lily-livers bring to mind Obama's infuriating postelection bargains. And 1999's "Intellectual Life in the Culture of Austerity" echoes what *Mother Jones* recently called the "Great Speedup"—the toll that a low-wage economy takes on our emotional and intellectual lives. Mom saw right through the roaring nineties and warned of "growing economic insecurity, a long-term decline in real wages, and fewer social benefits and public services." Sound familiar?

These analogs depressed me a little (an infinite loop of mean mommies, Limbaugh book covers, *New Yorker* cartoons of the Clintons), but they also convinced me of her work's ongoing relevance. It's for this reason that rather than frame this book with an introduction by a long-revered literary titan I handed over the mike to my own generation. Ann Friedman, Irin Carmon, Spencer Ackerman, Cord Jefferson, and Sara Marcus inhabit distinct cultural corners, but they're all fierce, unapologetic, accessible, and genuinely intellectually curious—in other words, Willis-like. Their responses to her work reassured me that in a world where deadlines come by the hour and writing two thousand blog-words a day is the norm there's still a place for journalism that's ruminative and not reactive. Frank and not accommodating.

Even though this anthology tells a holistic story, it is separated by decades, because it's clear Mom thought of her own work this way (the three collections she published during her lifetime were all roughly ten years apart). The Sixties: Up from Radicalism is the shortest section of the book, when my mother was just starting to realize post-Berkeley that her own voice was valuable, that her own unconventional beauty was palatable to a new counterculture, that her own private desire for a liberating alternative needn't be so private after all. Although the lion's share of my mother's sixties writing was about rock music—the visceral id to the left's ego—to me, the heart of the section is the deeply personal and previously uncollected "Up from Radicalism: A Feminist Journal." It baldly chronicles my mom's transformation from an introverted, highly intelligent coed who was terrified to challenge the "rules" to a furious and fully conscious woman who had never seen so clearly. (It also reveals Wilhelm Reich's very early influence on Mom's way of thinking.)

But even though her perspective was profoundly shaped by the sixties and all its possibilities, Mom hit her stride just as she was grappling with the aftermath of that utopian moment, the maestros of which had failed to keep up the momentum. (She also was single and lived alone for much of the 1970s, a factor that retrospectively seems to have influenced some of her highly personal writing during this period, either directly or obliquely.) In The Seventies: Exile on Main Street she dives headfirst into feminist debates about sex, porn, and abortion, pointing out the strain of conservatism in the mainstream wing of the women's movement. In The Eighties: Coming Down Again she struggles to be the radical voice of reason amid a superstorm of conservatism on the right and hopelessness on the left. She has a child—me—and forms the kind of nuclear family she could have scarcely pictured a decade earlier. Yet she rewrites the rules within those boundaries, an experience that pushes her to overlay her definition of "family" on to that of the Reaganites and relish the asymmetry. And in The Nineties: Decade of Denial, during which she started NYU's Cultural Reporting and Criticism Program and employed the phrase *cultural conversation,* she uses the scandalous court dramas consuming the nation— Monicagate, the O. J. Simpson trial, the Anita Hill hearing—as a way of confronting the most painful crannies of our national identity.

Although each section has several new pieces, much of this work has been collected elsewhere—except the essays in The Aughts: Our Politics, Ourselves. Ellen Willis was hardly afraid of the Internet and wrote quicker pieces for *Slate* and *Salon* that weighed in on contemporary political debates, but the majority of her work became increasingly lengthy and complex (and therefore appeared in more and more obscure publications). She became preoccupied with war in the wake of 9/11, a realization that led me to ask the *Guardian*'s national security reporter Spencer Ackerman to write the section's intro, and she pondered how the legacy of psychoanalysis permeates our domestic and foreign policy. She spent much of the 2000s skewering the left, which was now unrecognizable from the one she and her peers had cultivated. And she was obsessed with *The Sopranos,* a show that distilled her very worst fears about politics and culture: that people don't really change or transcend age-old cultural traps because it requires far too much soul searching and honesty to do so.

Willis tackles this same "cultural unconscious" in the Coda, which comprises several unpublished chapters of a book on psychoanalysis and American politics that she never finished because of an aggressive relapse of lung cancer in 2006. It should be taken exactly as it is: a first draft. I'm sure my mother would be discomfited by the fact that the material has been published in such a raw state, and I considered this long and hard. But ultimately I decided it was more important to unveil these ideas rather than to wait for an editing process that would never come. My mother had been working on this book for the better part of a decade, and as my father, Stanley Aronowitz, points out in his introduction, the idea of producing a tome rather than a collection of essays scared the shit out of her. This trepidation probably also explains why these pages are so tonally different from her journalism; she might have assumed (wrongly, if you ask me) that a trenchant topic like psychoanalysis deserved a more straight-faced approach. My hunch is that she would have injected more zingers and Willis-isms in the final edit.

The reader may notice that other than the more scholarly Coda this collection is weighted toward revealing Ellen Willis the woman, my way of cutting through the forced pigeon-holing of "rock critic" or "radical leftist" or "feminist writer." Much of the new, uncollected material—"Up from Radicalism"; "To Emma, with Love"; "The Diaper Manifesto"—is personal or confessional, while a few of her more theoretical, academic essays—"Feminism without Freedom" and "Race and the Ordeal of Liberal Optimism"—didn't make the cut. As I re-read the essays, I realized the quest to be an intellectually rich and full person, someone who wasn't necessarily happy all the time but always thinking and questioning and wondering how things could be better, was such a dominant theme regardless of topic that I couldn't help but arrange the anthology around this impulse.

I was reassured by this decision when I reread 1977's "Next Year in Jerusalem," ostensibly a failed conversion story but really a strikingly honest account of a radical, feminist, liberationist writer challenging, then reaffirming, her own contributions and loyalties. Amid broad discussions about feminism and religion and politics and sex, Mom reveals through her personal epiphanies why her writing, and good writing in general, is so important. She had a way of dissecting current events and sociological categories that not only illuminated the root of the immediate problem but also clarified its significance in a larger continuum. "In a communication crisis, the true prophets are the translators," Mom wrote of Bob Dylan in 1967. She could have been writing about herself.

NOTES

1. Audra Schroeder, "Out of the Vinyl Deeps: Ellen Willis on Rock Music," *The Austin Chronicle,* July 15, 2011. http://www.austinchronicle.com/music/2011-07-15/out-of-the-vinyl -deeps-ellen-willis-on-rock-music/.

2. Sara Marcus, "Cherry Bomb," *Los Angeles Review of Books,* September 19, 2011. http:// blog.lareviewofbooks.org/post/10397541163/cherry-bomb.

The Sixties
Up from Radicalism

INTRODUCTION
Sara Marcus

Ellen Willis often wrote about the legacy of the sixties, unwilling to let its meaning and memory be defined by those who would dismiss its most transformative ambitions as utopian nonsense. She didn't properly hit her stride as a writer until the last three years of the '60s, but she took up a wealth of material in that short span of time, and the pieces included in this part of the book show a sophisticated young writer starting to work out many of the themes and concerns that would occupy her for the rest of her life.

From the start, her music writing placed rock and folk in an expanded social context, mingling economics and archetypes, advertisers and amplifiers. In "Dylan"—her first published piece of music criticism, and the one that got her hired at the *New Yorker*—she turns a literary-critical eye on one of the most enigmatic figures in pop, dissecting his protean mythologies and shifting styles. Her lively report on Woodstock, written two years after the Dylan piece, does not anatomize myths so much as unveil the machinery behind them: in "The Cultural Revolution Saved from Drowning," she draws aside the beaded curtain of counterculture idealism to reveal the festival as an outsize concert-promotion gambit gone haywire, a human disaster narrowly averted by the unsung efforts of locals, volunteers, and the Hog Farm commune.

It was in her discovery of the women's liberation movement that Willis's sixties really acquired its center of gravity. After watching from the margins of multiple New Left factions, she found in the newly resurgent feminism an activist and intellectual home base, a process she narrates vividly in the intimate timeline "Up from Radicalism," published here for the first time since it appeared in *US Magazine* in 1969. Leaving the rigid, vanguardist world of mostly male politicos, she embraced a new movement, one that proceeded from the facts of women's lives and feelings as it formulated its political program. Suddenly, things that directly affected her life but had seemed external to politics—things like pleasure, consumption, sex, self-worth—came into focus as absolutely crucial to societal transformation.

With her characteristic blend of idealism and realism, she began to write on topics that we are still struggling with almost a half-century later: unrealistic beauty standards plugged by mass media; the things women must do to win men's attention; the intractable inequality that seems to haunt sexual liberation; the extreme difficulty of balancing career and family. She could connect with a range of audiences. For the readers of *The New Yorker,* she broke down the basics of women's lib; for the activist *Ramparts* crowd, she challenged leftist ideas about the (female) consumer as corporate dupe, and she insisted on a movement based on more than what anybody does or doesn't buy: "We must recognize that no individual decision, like rejecting consumption, can liberate us." In the twenty-first century, when artisanal locavorism often stands in for political action and women buy liberation in a lipstick tube because it's in such short supply everywhere else, we would all do well to heed Willis's words.

SARA MARCUS is the author of *Girls to the Front: The True Story of the Riot Grrrl Revolution.* Her criticism and essays have been published in *Bookforum, Artforum, The Nation,* the *Los Angeles Review of Books, Slate, Salon,* and *Rolling Stone.* She is currently a doctoral student in English at Princeton University.

Up from Radicalism
A Feminist Journal

This journal should really start at the beginning of my life, because that's when the struggle starts. Black kids find out they're Black, little girls find out they're female. By the time I was six or so, I must have discovered the awful truth, because I made a big point of despising boys—on the grounds that they were stupid and unadventurous. But when I playacted with my girl friends, I always wanted a boy's part. And my model was my father, who drew me diagrams of magnets and the digestive system, not my mother, who intruded on my life of the mind by making me dry the dishes. Later on things got more complicated. On one level I was determined to prove that except for a little accident of hormones, I was a perfectly good man: I was going to be a famous writer/actress/scientist. Domestic chores were contemptible (I would have servants, since I couldn't have a wife) and children—who needed them? Women were pretty contemptible too, except those happy few of us who were really men.

At the same time, without any feeling of absurdity, I worked obsessively at making myself a desirable object. I followed all the rules—build up their egos, don't be aggressive, don't flaunt your brains, be charming, diet, dance, be with it, wear a girdle, never kiss goodnight on the first date—until I learned that breaking them a little, or better yet appearing to break them, attracted the more imaginative boys. When I finally abandoned the sexual double standard it was less because I realized it was unfair (I always knew that) than because the game had changed—men now wanted experienced women. And if you had to pretend you weren't a virgin, there wasn't much point in being one.

At twenty, I graduated from a prestige college with honors, ready to make my way as a quasi-man among men. And I received my diploma as a woman—I was married. I might as well start there.

1962

I got married against my better judgment. At some point before the wedding there is a mysterious break between my rational and motor faculties. Though I am having more and more doubts, I keep behaving as if nothing is happening inside my head. Finally I make a half-hearted attempt to postpone the date and when that doesn't work I just abdicate and, as I put it to myself, let the current flow. Obviously something in me is anxious to get married, even if I'm not. Afterward I think maybe that's how it works for everybody. After all, I have too much pride to admit how I feel, so who knows what other wives are thinking?

We move to Berkeley and I start graduate school. I'm going mainly because of all those vocational conferences at Barnard that transmitted the message: better take typing and shorthand. Anything but that! I hate studying, but cling to the status of student.

I am still pretty militant about housework—I insist that we split it half and half, with the result that nothing much gets done—but I act very domestic when other people are around. No one is going to think I'm a henpecking wife.

1963

I can't decide what to do about school or about my marriage, and I get very depressed. Try the psychotherapy clinic at the U.C. health center. But the therapist they assign me is a woman; I know right away I just can't level with another woman; the distrust is too strong. So I talk around my problems, hoping something will happen anyway. Maybe it does—I muster enough decisiveness to quit school. Okay. But what do I do now?

Kennedy is dead. I am very disturbed; I've been caught up in the patriotic idealism myth more than I like to admit, and my husband has applied for a government job overseas. I want some kind of writing job. In college I published a couple of magazine articles and a handbook of advice for freshman girls. After three months of looking—the women in the employment agencies keep telling me to make my hair lie down more—I find a job in San Francisco, writing promotion copy for textbooks at $75 a week.

1964

I decide I should get involved in the civil rights movement. I have all the Jewish-leftist tropisms, I've marched for integration and against the bomb but I've never done anything serious. I put on a SNCC button and go to CORE meetings. But I never feel very welcome, and I never think of anything illuminating to say.

Free Speech erupts. I am an enthusiastic partisan, but don't join the sit-in. I'm not a student anymore; I won't be a hanger-on.

I read Wilhelm Reich, A. S. Neill and Paul Goodman and decide I'm an anarchist. If it is the suppression of sexuality by the authoritarian family that destroys the natural communal impulses of children and perpetuates oppressive institutions, then the system is against the best interests of the rulers as well as the ruled, and what we need is not violent revolution but a mass transformation of consciousness. We have to start on our own, building decentralized people's institutions. I become very interested in communities. Richard Alpert comes to S.F. and lectures on the LSD community at Millbrook. He talks about how the drug dissolves people's ego hangups and helps them live cooperatively, and it's really convincing until he explains how the women at Millbrook are earth-goddesses. He doesn't say who does the community's shitwork, but I have my suspicions.

I am much more taken with the arrangement at the cooperative Sierra Club Lodge, where my husband and I spend a weekend. It's very cheap because every guest does a chore. Dishwashing, my choice, is an assembly-line operation, done in 15 minutes. That's the answer to the housework problem—economy of scale.

1965

We move again. My husband's name is coming up for his overseas job and he will be training in Washington. I'm uncomfortable about Vietnam, but also poor and anxious to travel.

The only work I can get in D.C. is typing, and we're not in great financial need, so I decide to stay home and write. But my husband hints that if I'm not going to do anything, i.e., make money, I ought to pay more attention to the housework. I decide I'd rather type.

My husband is assigned to an African post. I start wondering what I'll do there. All the references to wives in the agency brochures assume that they are raising children and/or doing charity work and being good hostesses at parties and charming assets to their husbands' careers. Obviously the government expects two bodies for the price of one. Well it's not getting mine. I absolutely intend to make my own independent money. But how? Let's face it, Africa is not the place for a literary career. One afternoon we visit an official who has just come back from "our" post. I ask if there are jobs available on the English-language newspapers. He says there probably are. "But," he adds, "it's up to the Embassy. If they don't want you to work, you don't work."

We have more fights about housework, especially cooking. I want to eat in restaurants all the time. My husband thinks it's a disgusting extravagance. I insist that we have more than enough money, what are we saving it for? Which doesn't stop me from feeling guilty. (It's his money.) (Good wives cook.) (It isn't as if he never helps me.) (Why am I being nasty and causing trouble over something so trivial?)

I think I'm looking forward to going overseas and that I've accepted my marriage because . . . life is like that, as they say . . . and I like my husband, which is something. But on some level I feel a confrontation approaching. If I go to Africa it's a commitment, I can't pick up and go home. I get very moody. Write poems about suicide, murder, and mental breakdowns. Fantasize. Become ridiculously infatuated with another man. And finally have this vision of myself as another Carol Kennicott, keeping my hair long, singing radical folk songs to admiring bureaucrats, writing a mediocre novel coyly fictionalizing my situation, my husband beginning to hate me as he realizes. No. Life is not like that. I make the break and move to New York.

1966–1967

I register at the Barnard alumnae placement service. The director tells me I won't be able to get anything above the secretarial level. So do the first half-dozen employment agency "counselors" I meet. It gets so bad I actually send away for some graduate school catalogues.

Then in the *Times* help wanted male section, I find an ad for a staff writer on a small magazine. The publisher tells me he wants someone with more experience, but I can have another editorial job. He remarks that his editor gets along better with women. I ask why he doesn't list the staff writer in the help-female section. "It never occurred to me," he says. The pay is terrible, but I get a prestigious title and a pep talk about my potential.

I have my first tentative skirmishes with men. I'm pretty rusty. All those years in the provinces, I'm still quoting poets I read in college. Besides, marriage has given me an illusory sense of power. A married woman can flirt with men, tell them her troubles, presume on their friendship, and by the rules they can't demand that she follow through. If she wants a man (especially a single man) it is not only acceptable, but almost expected, for her to make the first move. In no other situation does she have so much freedom. Furthermore the status marriage confers insulates her somewhat from rejection and humiliation. Whatever another man might think of her or do to her, at least one man has certified her Class A merchandise. Propped up by marriage, I've been dealing with men from a position of (relative) strength. Now that I'm on my own I begin to see the point, for women, of the European system of institutionalized adultery.

I realize I'm suspicious of men. Something else to feel guilty about. It's so unliberated, the old double-standard hangup, fear of being used, fear of being a conquest—conquest, for Christ's sake—so I'm fucked up, by Dear Abby and a countersexualrevolutionary childhood. The important thing is not to show it. Men don't want neurotic chicks. Don't think, just do whatever you want—only what I want is affected by the vibrations I'm getting, or afraid of getting. What I don't want is for this or that promising guy to think I'm cold, naive, straight, not turned on by him, or conversely desperate, undiscriminating, overinvolved, etc. What I really want is to choose the movement myself, but I've learned at least this much; if you're too picky about details you end up with nothing. I remember all this from before I was married. But as a post-adolescent I wasn't expected to be cool about it. Now I'm what men like to call a big girl.

I find I can't keep myself from playing roles. The emotionless decadent, looking for diversion from boredom, is a favorite. Corny, but it works by my criteria: maximum pleasure, minimum anxiety.

I run into B., a classmate of mine years ago. He is a reporter and his first major magazine piece has attracted a lot of attention and three book offers. He is very cocky. His aggressiveness puts me so uptight that I go into my blasé-bohemian rap (if I do sleep with you, it won't matter). He tells me that his real commitment is to a girl from out of town (don't expect anything, baby). Great start.

I soon learn why W., my immediate boss, gets along better with women. No man would put up with his total intolerance of self-assertion. I stay twice as long as any of my male predecessors. I'm afraid of ending up a *Time* researcher.

One of my duties is to criticize W.'s manuscripts. His prose is clichéd, awkward and wordy, but if I make too many suggestions he sulks and rejects them. After a decent probation I approach him about a writing assignment. He tells me he doesn't have time to teach me to write. Later he agrees to let me do a profile if he can dictate the slant.

Finally I try a minor power play. Our publisher is hungry for new young writers and I've found one—B. I point him out to W. He tells me to keep my friends out of the office because they might steal his ideas. B. convinces me the time has come to go over W.'s head to the publisher, who likes his work. Given W.'s authority complex, I'm pretty sure to lose my job—if our boss has to choose between us, he's not going to choose me. Still, no man would let someone shit on him this way—why should I?

After the big blowup, B. helps me stave off *Time* Inc. by getting me some freelance assignments. I am amazed when my stuff is actually accepted, and then chagrined at my defeatism. Why does B. have to tell me 25 times that my writing is good before I'll believe it? Why did I accept W.'s opinion of me, even while I was fighting it?

A friend is hired as editor of a new magazine and asks me to join the staff as an associate editor. When I meet the publisher he tells me he hopes I won't mind answering the phones sometimes; all the girls in the office help out.

Even while I was a government wife, I never stopped identifying with the left. This schizophrenia was possible partly because of the lingering Kennedy mystique, but mostly because my political involvements had always been so tenuous. No organization ever seemed to be doing what I wanted to do, whatever that was. And things are no different now. I try joining a radical group. Its ideas are pretty close to mine but its practice turns out to be telling Puerto Ricans in the Ave. D housing project how the corporations are oppressing them. One go-round is enough; it doesn't take any black power polemicist to make me feel like a patronizing fool.

I'm becoming disenchanted with quasi-religious utopianism. The hippies aren't making much headway. Sexual freedom, the end of ego games and communal cooperation can't be willed into existence. Psychic liberation is difficult, maybe impossible, even for the dedicated. And most people aren't about to give up their hard-won equilibrium and whatever little they have in the way of money, security or power for—not happiness, but an ideal of happiness that might or might not be attainable.

Anyway, this approach is impossibly parochial in the face of the urgent conflict between U.S. imperial power and the rest of the world, not to mention the black colony at home. Vietnam can't wait for the president of Boeing to drop out of the rat race; kids in the ghetto need all the ego they've got.

I'm into Marxist theory more than ever before. In international terms, it offers the only cogent explanation of what's going on. But there's something essential missing: Marxists don't understand the political and human significance of sex. When they consider sexual problems at all it's only to dismiss them as the affliction of a decadent bourgeoisie, to be swept away by the emerging proletariat. But no proletarian revolution has yet been able to sweep them away.

What we need is an analysis that can connect the politics of nations with the politics of our own bodies. A large order. Marcuse's attempt is the best, and he concludes that nothing can be done.

1968

It's getting better—if not for the country, at least for me. I'm reviewing rock and working on a book. My combine with B. has miraculously survived and prospered after a series of passionate and/or hysterical adjustments.

February: *Ramparts* prints a sketchy, rather condescending article on "woman power," which mentions the new radical women's movement, the first I've heard of it.

April: J., a recent acquaintance, mentions in passing that she belongs to a feminist group, but I don't take it up. Why?

A young girl, a friend of some friends, comes to town to get an abortion and stays with me. Doctor is a well-known, respected abortionist. Charges her $700, which she has to borrow. I'm disturbed to learn she was given no antibiotics. Next day she starts hurting. Neither of us wants to face trouble, so we wait. But the pain gets worse. I waste an hour calling private doctors, leery of a police hassle at Bellevue. Her fever shoots up and I call an ambulance, panicked that I may have waited too long. The doctor, if you can call him that, lets her have it. While he's examining her and giving her shots and sticking tubes in her and she's yelling, in terrible pain and scared to death, he starts in, "YOU WENT TO A QUACK, RIGHT?," keeping at it until she says yes, and then "That was a stupid thing to do, wasn't it? How much did it cost you?" and on and on. She asks him if she's going to die. The prick won't say no. When he's through I ask how she is. He gives me his nastiest you-East-Village-sluts-are-all-alike look and says, "She's very sick," loud enough for her to hear, and strides out of the ward. The nurse reassures me. She's full of penicillin and it's going to be all right.

She spends a week in the hospital. When she's ready to go home one of the doctors gives her a prescription for birth control pills, but the clinic pharmacist won't give her all the pills at once. She has to come back every month. Regulations. I argue: there's no point to this, it's harassment. "Don't be smart, lady," he says.

August: Chicago, screwing the Democrats. Under siege, my political confusion disappears. But when the battle's over I get depressed about the we-are-making-the-revolution-now machismo-mongering and we-are-the-people bullshit. We've yet to become the people. Am I the people? Are the Yippies me? I don't know.

September: from Chicago, B. and I go west. On our way I read about the women's liberation protest against the Miss America contest. I'm dubious—won't people think they're just ugly, jealous women? But I remember what it's like to be examined and compared at a party. And I'm proud that women are in the papers for fighting.

J. and husband and kids have moved to San Francisco and we're staying at their place. She gives me a copy of *Notes from the First Year,* a journal published by the New York radical women's group. It disturbs me. Too much "Get off my back, whitey." All our problems aren't caused by men—are they? The tone strikes me as frighteningly bitter, especially about sexual relationships. Either I've been remarkably lucky, or they've been unlucky . . . or maybe I let men who give me a hard time off the hook too easily.

J. and I talk about communes. To me, the communal family, with domestic work shared equally by both sexes, is the only solution to child-rearing without slavery. Having the sole responsibility for a vulnerable, dependent life, never being able to act on impulse, makes women dull and desperate. Why should we have to choose between being fully, freely human and having a share in raising the next generation? J. envisions a sanctuary for radicals and a center for political activity. I think just making a commune work is a difficult enough political project.

I go with J. to a women's meeting. It's somewhat chaotic, a dozen different subjects are discussed, but what impresses me most is just the fact of women getting together and talking. And though I am a stranger, I feel included. There's none of the prickly suspicious aloofness that brings me down whenever I go to a political meeting. No sense that I have to pass some initiation to be accepted. Or that anyone looks at me as raw material to "organize."

I resolve to join the New York group when I get home. *Notes* scares me, but by now I recognize that I'm resisting.

November: the women behind *Notes* are nothing like my fantasies of anti-sex fanatics. They seem no different from other women, except friendlier. Most are young; perhaps half are married.

The basic activity of the group is consciousness-raising, the loosely applied formula for which is sharing of personal experience: generalization: analysis. Ideally, analysis of an issue should give rise to appropriate action; the action then becomes part of the experience to be analyzed. But the movement is growing so fast, it's hard to maintain continuity. Already I feel like a veteran. New women keep coming in, women who are just discovering their oppression, asserting for the first time their independence from husbands and lovers, overwhelmed that here they are listened to, respected. They want to talk about everything, their jobs, their husbands, their childhoods, their abortions, their attitudes toward other women. So we talk. Sometimes it's great, sometimes it's bullshit, but I learn something at every meeting.

For a while I feel that now I understand and love all other women. It's a great high until I realize that it's mostly a defense against the fear and antagonism of a lifetime, a compound of superiority ("Oh, I'd rather be friends with men, they're much more stimulating!" Translation: I'm not like them, I've made it out of the ghetto) and sexual competitiveness. Revise: I'm starting to be interested in other women. To feel warmth and sympathy. To recognize a new loyalty. To realize other women are not the enemy. To understand as a gut reality the phenomenon of rulers setting the ruled against each other.

Also: I stop using certain expressions.

1) "Personal," as in don't blame the social system for your personal inadequacies. True, we all have our idiosyncrasies. We each cope with certain situations better than with others. A. is better than I am at the sexual game, I am better at the work game. But the situations themselves are common to all of us. And they all have a common denominator, namely the subordination of women to men. That is politics, not personality.

2) "Extreme case." W. is an extreme case—most bosses aren't like that. A rapist is an extreme case. But oddly enough, we've all run into our share of extreme cases. A lyncher is an extreme case. In all probability some lower-class, right-wing nut. Decent people don't approve of lynching. But their racism produces the lynchers. And sexism produces martinets, rapists and wife-beaters.

December: one night someone says the main obstacle to our liberation is that we've swallowed sexist ideology; we must stop feeling guilty about being "unfeminine," refuse to play our traditional roles. This touches off an emotional argument. It's not a matter of brainwashing, the opposition insists. There are consequences for stepping out of our roles. If you refuse to be a domestic servant and your man calls you bitchy and unloving, the whole culture backs him up. It won't help to find another man. Most men won't accept our individual attempts at self-liberation—why should they? They are organized, we aren't. Names do hurt us: they're warnings. If we step out of line too often, the penalties are loneliness, sexual deprivation and in most cases the economic and spiritual dead end of menial jobs. Unless we can manage to please a man, even the one significant human activity reserved for women—bringing up children—is available to us only at an exorbitant cost.

So if women are "brainwashed" it's because facing their powerlessness is too painful. If we can't change things, it doesn't help to stew about them. And we can only change things together. As we build a movement, as we organize to attack the institutions that keep us down, our psychic defenses will go too. Guilt is fear.

Fear. . . . What about my fear of sexual exploitation? Isn't it just a residue of traditional morality propaganda? Isn't it my father's disapproval I'm unconsciously worried about? That's what I've always assumed, but as soon as I say it I know it's not true. I'm afraid of something real. But what? How does it work?

We talk. And again, there's the exhilaration of finding out it's not just me. Everyone understands exactly what I mean. All of us bohemian-radical-freaks who consort with men who espouse the sexual revolution agree that something is not quite kosher about the sexual revolution. *Notes* hinted the same thing, and because I wasn't ready to assimilate it, I got angry. If you can't change things, it doesn't help to stew. . . .

There can be no sexual revolution in a vacuum. Our sexual status, like our economic and political status, has improved somewhat since the Victorian era, but the rhetoric of emancipation has far outstripped the social reality. The "liberated woman," like the "free world," is a fiction that obscures real power relations and defuses revolution. How can women, subordinate in every other sphere, be free and equal in bed? Men want us to be a little free—it's more exciting that way. But women who really take them at their word put them uptight and they show it—by their jokes, their gossip, their obvious or subtle putdowns of women who seem too aggressive or too "easy." By denying that these attitudes still predominate, the s.r. propaganda has undermined our main defense against them, which was to insist, as a prerequisite to sex, that men love us or accept responsibility for us—or at least hang around long enough so that we can know what we're getting into. Now that all this is unhip we are under pressure to sleep with men on their terms, because if we won't, other women will. Not that there's anything wrong with casual pleasure. It must be nice to be able to be casual. But we've never had that option. On the contrary, to avoid both the humiliation of being treated as an object and the frustration of celibacy, we have to be supersensitive game players. It's nerve-wracking and not much fun, except for a few real adepts (the femme fatales). Many women just give up, let men treat them like shit, and call it freedom or innate feminine altruism. A few decide that men aren't worth the hassle. But most of us try to hang in there.

For the first time I understand what is ultimately wrong with the "change your head" line. Up against the wall, Beatles.

1969

January: the Mobilization-sponsored counter-inaugural activities in Washington are to include a women's liberation action. The theme will be Give Back the Vote: we will destroy our voter registration cards to dramatize the futility of the 80-year suffrage struggle in gaining freedom for women.

Mobe's ad in the *Guardian* calls for an end to the war and freedom for Black and Spanish people.[1] No mention of women's liberation. Women in another group want to ask men to destroy their voter cards. Apparently they have interpreted the action as a simple protest against electoral politics, rather than a specifically feminist rejection of appeasement by ballot.

I get the funny feeling that we're being absorbed. Will we get the chance to deliver our message, or are we just there to show our support for the important (i.e., male-oriented) branches of the left? Our group decides to confront this issue with a speech attacking male chauvinism in the movement.

Dave Dellinger introduces the rally with a stirring denunciation of the war and racism.

"What about women, you schmuck?" I shout.

"And, uh, a special message from women's liberation," he adds.

Our moment comes. M. from the Washington group gets up to speak. This isn't the protest against movement men, which is second on the agenda, just fairly innocuous radical rhetoric—except that it's a good-looking woman talking about women. The men go crazy. "Take it Off!" "Take her off the stage and fuck her!" They yell and boo and guffaw at unwitting double entendres like "We must take to the streets." When S., who is representing the New York group, comes to the mike and announces that women will no longer participate in any so-called revolution that does not include the abolition of male privilege, it sounds like a spontaneous outburst of rage.

By the time we get to the voter card business, I am shaking. If radical men can be so easily provoked into acting like rednecks, what can we expect from others? What have we gotten ourselves into?

Meanwhile Dellinger has been pleading with us to get off the stage, "for your own good." Why isn't he telling them to shut up?

Just yesterday many of the women present were arguing against S.'s statement on the grounds that in spite of their chauvinism movement men are basically our allies, and we shouldn't embarrass them in front of the straight press! As it turns out, none of the above-ground papers so much as mentions the women's action. Even the *Guardian* mysteriously neglects to report the second speech.

The whole fiasco has forced me to do some thinking. Without realizing it, I've held two contradictory views of women's liberation. On the one hand I recognize the Black analogy and the need for separate groups free from male bias and male control. I know that socialist revolutions have not eliminated male supremacy, that Soviet women still bear the burden of domestic responsibility, that machismo still flourishes in Cuba. But until now I've also assumed that women's liberation was part of the radical movement, that one of our essential functions, in fact, was to bring masses of women into the left. Washington has destroyed that illusion. How can it be good for women to join a movement whose ideology, history and practice have been created by their oppressors? We need not only separate groups but a separate movement, free of preconceptions, which will build an analysis of women's oppression that is rooted in our day-to-day experience and base on that analysis our own revolutionary program. It is also clear that a genuine alliance with male radicals will not be possible until sexism sickens them as much as racism. This will not be accomplished through persuasion, conciliation, or love, but through independence and solidarity: radical men will stop oppressing us and make our fight their own when they can't get us to join them on any other terms.

Most of the women in New York's counter-inaugural delegation have come to the same conclusions. We decide to form an action group based on a militantly independent radical feminist consciousness.

Many women violently disagree with this approach, insisting that capitalism is the only enemy, that male supremacy is a symptom, that only ruling class men benefit from it. This contradicts my experience and common sense: all men benefit from having women to relieve them of menial, repetitive, domestic tasks, cater to their needs and build up their egos. Anyway, the ideology of male supremacy does not stem from capitalism but from the patriarchal family, the oldest, most pervasive class structure in existence. The family is the basic institution that oppresses women, defining their roles as domestics and breeders, controlling their sexuality, and forcing them into economic dependence.

February: the state is holding another of its "expert" hearings on abortion reform, in which (mostly male) doctors, lawyers, politicians and clergymen go before an all-male legislative committee to decide whether in certain special circumstances the government should stop forcing women to have babies. The witnesses this time are fourteen men and a nun.

Feminists, both liberal and radical, organize a protest: these phony experts have no right to control our bodies and our lives. Forced child-bearing is slavery. We want total repeal of the law and free abortion clinics. Half a dozen women's liberationists, including me, plan to disrupt the hearing and demand that the forum be turned over to women, the only experts on abortion.

I volunteer to make up a leaflet, I write it, type it, letter it, mimeograph it, amazed the whole time at my self-confidence. In other political organizations I would have worried over a job like this for days and called a dozen people to ask what I should say. But this time I'm doing it for myself, writing from the memory of pregnancy scares, of the doctor who wouldn't prescribe pills for me because I was unmarried and underage and then bawled me out for wasting his time, of my friend screaming in the hospital. I'm writing from anger. Nobody needs to tell me a thing.

At the hearing, I am nervous. I have deep feminine inhibitions against being nasty and making myself conspicuous. But as the testimony proceeds—a decrepit judge is advocating legal abortion for women who have "done their social duty" having four children—my adrenalin rises. Then a member of our cadre gets up and shouts, "Okay, now let's hear from the real experts!" When she finishes talking, I start, and I have never felt less inhibited in my life. In another minute, most of the women in the room are angrily demanding to testify.

"Won't you act like ladies?" a legislator pleads, but no one is listening.

March: we give our new group a name—Redstockings—and plan our first action. As a follow-up to the abortion demonstration, we will hold our own hearing, at which women will testify about their abortions. About a dozen women agree to speak. Many others refuse because they are afraid of static from employers or families.

One problem in setting up the hearing is to make sure it's understood as politics rather than soap opera. A poor man can tell how it feels to go hungry, and everyone will take for granted the political context. But if a women speaks frankly about her sexual/reproductive life—which is as central to her oppression as the poor man's economic life—the standard response is pornographic enjoyment of what are considered highly intimate revelations. As a result we are inhibited about discussing sex with each other, let alone in public. At one meeting we got onto men's attitudes toward women's sexual pleasure and a woman said, "Let's get serious" (by which she meant let's discuss capitalism). We also have to contend with the widespread assumption that women's concerns in general are "personal," "subjective." Women have been excluded from the larger society and defined as private creatures. The very idea of male-female relations as a political question confounds most people: politics takes place between groups of men, in the "world." It is because of this prejudice that our consciousness raising method—an attempt to define our political reality that has had its analogues in the black movement and the Chinese revolution—is so often dismissed as "group therapy."

There are two ways to get over this obstacle: to confront the audience with the spurious personal-political distinction and to have at our disposal a thorough knowledge of the politics of abortion. We spend a couple of meetings discussing abortion prohibition as a sexual punishment, motherhood as women's "social duty," the white middle class monopoly on relatively safe abortions, male authoritarianism and misogyny in the medical profession, the taboo on the idea that a normal, healthy woman might not want children, reprisals against women who speak out. But we agree that although the witnesses will have this context in mind, they will not talk theory. They will talk about themselves.

It works, in fact it's more effective than we had hoped. The testimony is honest and powerful and evokes strong reactions from the audience—empathy, anger, pain. Women stand up to give their own testimony. One woman decries "the atmosphere of hostility toward men." A man yells, "Lesbians!," another remarks that women talk too much, and another sneers at "sob stories." A hint of defensiveness creeps into the women's replies. But then a feminist in the audience walks up to the mike and speaks, controlling but not concealing her rage: "Yes, I have to admit I'm hostile to men. Men have exploited us; why shouldn't we be hostile? Is an oppressed group supposed to love its oppressors?"

Afterward a Black guy says he's never been to such a supercharged meeting except where Blacks were speaking to white people.

We're hoping the idea will catch on and become the equivalent, for the women's movement, of the Vietnam teach-ins.

April: consciousness-raising has one terrible result. It makes you more conscious. I can't walk in the street anymore. I used to be fairly oblivious to the barrage of comments from men on my anatomy and what they'd like to do with it. I didn't even realize that I generally stare straight ahead because if I catch the wrong man's eye he'll think I'm encouraging him.

So what's wrong, a male friend wants to know, with men digging you? Don't you like to look at attractive men? Sure, I even like to look at attractive women. But most men who ogle us on the street, especially the ones who feel the need to say something, or even touch, aren't digging us. They're showing hatred and contempt. The message: baby, you're just a collection of sexual parts walking down the street for my benefit. I can say anything I want and you can't object because I'm stronger than you and you're scared.

Think of a Black man in a southern town. A white man makes a jocular, insulting comment and he can't answer back. A white woman passes and he knows he'd better point his eyes elsewhere. Straight ahead, and stay out of trouble. That's powerlessness.

How I'd love to be able to say, "Shut up, motherfucker, or I'll beat the shit out of you!" Sometimes I curse them or give them the finger, if the street is crowded.

I stop to buy a hot dog and the counterman talks baby talk to me, in the manner of countermen. He calls me "dear" (cf. "boy"). I conceive an experiment in self-liberation. I say, with a propitiatory smile, "You know, you don't have to talk to me as if I'm five years old." The counterman is enraged. He raves, not to me, but to the other (male) customers. "See? You act nice to somebody and look what you get! Try to be nice!" And then he turns to me with the crusher: "You'll never get married if you act like that!" I guess I should make some consciousness-raising comeback like "Tried it once—didn't like it." But I don't have the heart. I feel like an idiot. A certified crank. No sense of humor.

Another discovery: a lot of men, especially working-class men, won't get out of the way for a woman on the street. They walk in a straight line and expect you to move. I develop a policy of confrontation. I walk straight too and bump into them. They don't quite understand what's happening and mutter something like "Lady, watch where you're going."

I go to a dinner party. As usual, when dinner is over the men relax while the women clear the table. This time I actually ask two men to help. They make no sign that they've heard me. I cart off my share of dishes and sit down, and one of these same guys asks (honest!), "So what are you into in women's liberation?" "I'm into being pissed off at men who don't clear the table," I reply. He says nothing and composes his face into a blank: ask a serious question and what do you get?

After a Redstockings meeting, some of us are sitting in the coffeehouse around the corner. Two men come over uninvited and openly listen to our conversation, ignoring our suggestions that they get lost. Men at a nearby table are staring at us. They can't stand the spectacle of women together without men and not looking for men. Finally one of them (Black, with an Afro and hippie glasses) stands up and says, "What are you hens chattering about?" We talk back, of course, but they've done what they wanted, ruined our conversation. We won't give them the satisfaction of leaving, but they've won anyway. For the first time I have some really specific violence fantasies.

What used to be called my private life is affected too. I can't switch off my new awareness and see my relationship with B. as strictly individual, human, free of class considerations. He checks out on the obvious things: respect for my work, absence of domestic servant hangups and Don Juanism, etc. But he definitely prefers to be the leader in any situation, whether it involves men (a concomitant of male dominance is competition among males) or women; he is the kind of person who when he's going somewhere with a group walks two steps ahead and chooses the route. B. plans most of our social life, and most of our friends are his friends. (When I don't like friends of his, I try to get to know them better and conquer my dislike; when he doesn't like friends of mine he either refuses to see them or acts like a martyr about it.) We have always had something of a mentor-neophyte relationship. B. got me out of my job and into free-lancing and convinced me to stick with journalism; he even encouraged me to join the women's movement when I was procrastinating.

B.'s assumption of dominance clashes with my increasing need to assert myself and we fight. Sometimes we work it out, sometimes we won't. But I know there is a limit to how far I can challenge him before he finds being with me intolerable. And here is where the ugly fact of power comes in. B. can find any number of women who will accept him the way he is; I've never known a man who could accept me the way I now want to be. And sometimes when I fight with B. I get terribly frightened. For my commitment to heterosexual sex is very basic and I want, need love and companionship. I still find it possible to confront B.'s chauvinism and at the same time appreciate what is individual and human about us. But how will I feel when I've been in the movement five years instead of six months?

Some feminists advocate complete separatism. I'd like to believe they are crazy. . . .

The abortion reform bill is unexpectedly killed. The bill was a farce, but that only makes the Assembly's action more shocking and disgusting. Key man in this spirited affirmation of the compulsory pregnancy system is Assemblyman Martin Ginsberg, who was crippled by polio as a child. He argues that if we allow women to abort deformed fetuses, the next step is murdering deformed children like him. After which 14 assemblymen, spontaneously or by design, withdraw their support for the bill, reversing the result.

My first reaction is simply that I want to kill him. A man who is more concerned about his own hypothetical death than about the real deaths of thousands of women is unsalvageable.

Fanon says that an oppressed individual cannot feel liberated until he kills one of the oppressors.

Women? Killing? The idea seems ludicrous. But the anger is there, and it's real, and it will be expressed. We have begun and we can't go back.

US Magazine, 1969

NOTE

1. [*Editor's note*: Mobe refers to the Spring Mobilization Committee to End the War in Vietnam, which later became the National Mobilization Committee to End the War in Vietnam.]

Dylan

I.

Nearly two years ago, Bob Dylan had a motorcycle accident. Reports of his condition were vague, and he dropped out of sight. Publication of his book, *Tarantula,* was postponed indefinitely. New records appeared, but they were from his last album, *Blonde on Blonde.* Gruesome rumors circulated: Dylan was dead; he was badly disfigured; he was paralyzed; he was insane. The cataclysm his audience was always expecting seemed to have arrived. Phil Ochs had predicted that Dylan might someday be assassinated by a fan. Pete Seeger believed Dylan could become the country's greatest troubadour, if he didn't explode. Alan Lomax had once remarked that Dylan might develop into a great poet of the times, unless he killed himself first. Now, images of James Dean filled the news vacuum. As months passed, reflex apprehension turned to suspense, then irritation: had we been put on again? We had. Friends began to admit, with smiles, that they'd seen Bobby; he was rewriting his book; he was about to sign a contract with MGM Records. The new rumor was that the accident had been a cover for retreat. After *Blonde on Blonde,* his intensive foray into the pop demimonde, Dylan needed time to replenish his imagination. According to a less romantic version, he was keeping quiet till his contracts expired.

The confusion was typical. Not since Rimbaud said "*I* is another" has an artist been so obsessed with escaping identity. His masks hidden by other masks, Dylan is the celebrity stalker's ultimate antagonist. The original disparity between his public pose as rootless wanderer with southwestern drawl and the private facts of home and middle-class Jewish family and high school diploma in Hibbing, Minnesota, was a commonplace subterfuge, the kind that pays reporters' salaries. It hardly showed his talent for elusiveness; what it probably showed was naïveté. But his attitude toward himself as a public personality was always clear. On an early recording he used the eloquent pseudonym "Blind Boy Grunt." "Dylan" is itself a pseudonym, possibly inspired by Dylan Thomas (a story Dylan now denies), possibly by a real or imaginary uncle named Dillon, who might or might not be the "Las Vegas dealer" Dylan once claimed was his only living relative.

In six years Dylan's stance has evolved from proletarian assertiveness to anarchist angst to pop detachment. At each stage he has made himself harder to follow, provoked howls of execration from those left behind, and attracted an ever-larger, more demanding audience. He has reacted with growing hostility to the possessiveness of this audience and its shock troops, the journalists, the professional categorizers. His baroque press conference inventions are extensions of his work, full of imaginative truth and virtually devoid of information. The classic Dylan interview appeared in *Playboy,* where Nat Hentoff, like a housewife dusting her furniture while a tornado wrecks the house, pursued the homely fact through exchanges like: "Do you have any unfulfilled ambitions?" "Well, I guess I've always wanted to be Anthony Quinn in *La Strada*. . . . I guess I've always wanted to be Brigitte Bardot, too; but I don't really want to think about *that* too much."

Dylan's refusal to be known is not simply a celebrity's ploy, but a passion that has shaped his work. As his songs have become more introspective, the introspections have become more impersonal, the confidences of a no-man without past or future. Bob Dylan as identifiable persona has been disappearing into his songs, which is what he wants. This terrifies his audiences. They could accept a consistent image—roving minstrel, poet of alienation, spokesman for youth—in lieu of the "real" Bob Dylan. But his progressive self-annihilation cannot be contained in a game of let's pretend, and it conjures up nightmares of madness, mutilation, death. The nightmares are chimerical; there is a continuing self, the Bobby Dylan friends describe as shy and defensive, hyped up, careless of his health, a bit scared by fame, unmaterialistic but shrewd about money, a professional absorbed in his craft. Dylan's songs bear the stigmata of an authentic middle-class adolescence; his eye for detail, sense of humor, and skill at evoking the archetypal sexual skirmishes show that some part of him is of as well as in the world. As further evidence, he has a wife, son, and house in Woodstock, New York. Instead of an image, Dylan has created a magic theater in which the public gets lost willy-nilly. Yet he is more—or less—than the sum of his illusions.

Many people hate Bob Dylan because they hate being fooled. Illusion is fine, if quarantined and diagnosed as mild; otherwise it is potentially humiliating (Is he laughing at me? Conning me out of my money?). Some still discount Dylan as merely a popular culture hero (How can a teenage idol be a serious artist? At most, perhaps, a serious demagogue). But the most tempting answer—forget his public presence, listen to his songs—won't do. For Dylan has exploited his image as a vehicle for artistic statement. The same is true of Andy Warhol and, to a lesser degree, of the Beatles and Allen Ginsberg. (In contrast, James Dean and Marilyn Monroe were creatures, not masters, of their images.) The tenacity of the modern publicity apparatus often makes artists' personalities more familiar than their work, while its pervasiveness obscures the work of those who can't or won't be personalities. If there is an audience for images, artists will inevitably use the image as a medium—and some images are more original, more compelling, more relevant than others. Dylan has self-consciously explored the possibilities of mass communication just as the pop artists explored the possibilities of mass production. In the same sense that pop art is about commodities, Dylan's art is about celebrity.

This is not to deny the intrinsic value of Dylan's songs. Everyone interested in folk and popular music agrees on their importance, if not their merit. As composer, interpreter, most of all as lyricist, Dylan has made a revolution. He expanded folk idiom into a rich, figurative language, grafted literary and philosophical subtleties onto the protest song, revitalized folk vision by rejecting proletarian and ethnic sentimentality, then all but destroyed pure folk as a contemporary form by merging it with pop. Since then rock-and-roll, which was already in the midst of a creative flowering dominated by British rock and Motown, has been transformed. Songwriters have raided folk music as never before for new sounds, new images, new subject matter. Dylan's innovative lyrics have been enthusiastically imitated. The folk music lovers who managed to evolve with him, the connoisseurs of pop, the bohemian fringe of the literary community, hippies, and teenagers consider him a genius, a prophet. Folk purists and political radicals, who were inspired by his earlier material, cry betrayal with a vehemence that acknowledges his gifts.

Yet many of Dylan's fans—especially ex-fans—miss the point. Dylan is no apostle of the electronic age. Rather, he is a fifth-columnist from the past, shaped by personal and political nonconformity, by blues and modern poetry. He has imposed his commitment to individual freedom (and its obverse, isolation) on the hip passivity of pop culture, his literacy on an illiterate music. He has used the publicity machine to demonstrate his belief in privacy. His songs and public role are guides to survival in the world of the image, the cool, and the high. And in coming to terms with that world, he has forced it to come to terms with him.

II.

By 1960 the folk music revival that began in the fifties had expanded into an all-inclusive smorgasbord, with kitschy imitation-folk groups at one end, resurrected cigar-box guitarists and Ozark balladeers at the other. Of music that pretended to ethnic authenticity, the most popular was folk blues—Lead Belly, Sonny Terry and Brownie McGhee, Lightnin' Hopkins. The response to blues was in part a tribute to the ascendancy of rock-and-roll—Negro rhythms had affected the consciousness of every teenager in the fifties. But blues, unlike rock, was free of identification with the dominant society. Its sexuality and rebelliousness were undiluted, and it was about people, not teen-agers. Besides, the Negro, always a dual symbol of suffering and life force, was gaining new political importance, and folk blues expressed the restlessness of activists, bohemians, déclassé intellectuals. Since younger Negro performers were not interested in preserving a genre they had abandoned for more distinctly urban forms, white city singers tried to fill the gap. Patronized unmercifully by blues purists, the best of them did not simply approximate Negro sounds but evoked personal pain and disenchantment with white culture.

At the same time there was a surge of folk composing. The Weavers, in the vanguard of the revival, had popularized the iconoclastic ballads and talking blues of Woody Guthrie, chronicler of the dust bowl and the Depression, the open road, the unions, the common man[1] as intrepid endurer. Pete Seeger, the Weavers' lead singer in the early days and the most prestigious folk musician in the country, had recorded albums of topical songs from the thirties and forties. With the emergence of the civil rights movement, freedom songs, some new, some updated spirituals and union chants, began coming out of the South. Northern musicians began to write and perform their own material, mainly variations on the hard-traveling theme and polemics against racism, the bomb, and middle-class conformity. Guthrie was their godfather, Seeger their guru, California songwriter Malvina Reynolds their older sister. Later, they were to acquire an angel—Joan Baez, who would record their songs and sing them at racial demonstrations and peace rallies; an organ—*Broadside,* a mimeographed magazine founded in 1962; and a sachem—Bob Dylan.

Gerde's Folk City, an unassuming, unbohemian cabaret in Greenwich Village, was the folk fans' chief New York hangout. On Monday, hootenanny night, blues interpreters like Dave Van Ronk, bluegrass groups like the Greenbriar Boys, the new topical songwriters—Tom Paxton, Phil Ochs, Len Chandler— would stop in and perform. Established singers came because Gerde's was part of the scene, because they enjoyed playing to the aficionados who gathered after midnight. The young ones came for a showcase and for contact with musicians they admired.

When Bob Dylan first showed up at Gerde's in the spring of 1961, fresh-skinned and baby-faced and wearing a schoolboy's corduroy cap, the manager asked him for proof of age. He was nineteen, only recently arrived in New York. Skinny, nervous, manic, the bohemian patina of jeans and boots, scruffy hair, hip jargon and hitchhiking mileage barely settled on nice Bobby Zimmerman, he had been trying to catch on at the coffeehouses. His material and style were a cud of half-digested influences: Guthrie-cum-Elliott; Blind Lemon Jefferson-cum-Lead Belly-cum-Van Ronk; the hillbilly sounds of Hank Williams and Jimmie Rodgers; the rock-and-roll of Chuck Berry and Elvis Presley. He was constantly writing new songs. Onstage, he varied poignancy with clownishness.

His interpretations of traditional songs—especially blues—were pretentious, and his harsh, flat voice kept slipping over the edge of plaintiveness into strident self-pity. But he shone as a comedian, charming audiences with Charlie Chaplin routines, playing with his hair and cap, burlesquing his own mannerisms, and simply enjoying himself. His specialty was composing lightly sardonic talking blues—chants to a bass-run guitar accompaniment, a favorite vehicle of Woody Guthrie's: "Them Communists were all around / in the air and on the ground / . . . I run down most hurriedly / and joined the John Birch society."

That fall, *New York Times* folk music critic Robert Shelton visited Gerde's and gave Dylan an enthusiastic review. Columbia Records signed him and released a mediocre first album in February 1962. It contained only two Dylan compositions, both nonpolitical. Dylan began publishing his topical songs in *Broadside.* Like his contemporaries, he was more propagandist than artist, his syntax often barbarous, his diction crude. Even so, his work stood out—it contained the most graphic descriptions of racial atrocities. But Dylan also had a gentler mood. Road songs like "Song to Woody" strove—not too successfully—for Guthrie's expressive understatement and simple, traditional sound.

In May 1962, *Broadside* published a new Dylan song, "Blowin' in the Wind." Set to a melody adapted from a spiritual, it combined indignation with Guthriesque simplicity and added a touch of original imagery. It received little circulation until nearly a year later, when Peter, Paul, and Mary heard Dylan sing it at a coffeehouse. Their recording of the song sold a million copies, inspired more than fifty other versions, and established topical song as the most important development of the folk revival. The relative subtlety of the lyric made the topical movement aesthetically self-conscious. It did not drive out direct political statements—Dylan himself continued to write them—but it set a standard impossible to ignore, and topical songs began to show more wit, more craftsmanship, more variety.

"Blowin' in the Wind" was included on Dylan's second album, *The Freewheelin' Bob Dylan,* which appeared in May 1963. This time, nearly all the songs were his own; five had political themes. It was an extraordinary record. The influences had coalesced; the voice, unmusical as ever, had found an evocative range somewhere between abrasion and sentimentality; the lyrics (except for "Masters of War," a simplistic diatribe against munitions makers) were vibrant and pithy. The album contained what may still be Dylan's best song—"It's a Hard Rain's A-Gonna Fall," a vivid evocation of nuclear apocalypse that owed much to Allen Ginsberg's biblical rhetoric and declamatory style. Its theme was modern, its spirit ancient. At first hearing, most of the *Freewheelin'* songs sounded less revolutionary than they were: so skillfully had Dylan distilled the forms and moods of traditional music that his originality took time to register.

Freewheelin' illuminated Dylan's America—or rather, two Americas. "Hard Rain" confronted the underside, "where the executioner's face is always well-hidden," "where black is the color and none is the number," a world of deserted diamond highways, incipient tidal waves, clowns crying in alleys, children armed with guns and swords, "10,000 whisperin' and nobody listenin'" and occasional portents of redemption: "I met a young girl, she gave me a rainbow." The satirical "Talking World War III Blues" toured the country's surface: hot dog stands, parking meters, Cadillacs, rock-and-roll singers, telephone operators, cool females, officious doctors. Dylan's moral outrage coexisted with a grudging affection for American society and its foibles. If there was "Masters of War," there was also "I Shall Be Free": "My telephone rang, it would not stop, it was President Kennedy callin' me up. / He said my friend Bob, what do we need to make this country grow? / I said my friend John, Brigitte Bardot."

For a time the outrage predominated. Dylan's output of bitter protest increased and his humor receded. He was still learning from Woody Guthrie, but he often substituted despair for Guthrie's resilience: his finest ballads chronicled the disintegration of an unemployed miner's family; the killing of a Negro maid, punished by a six-month sentence; the extremity of a penniless farmer who shot himself, his wife, and five kids. At the same time his prophetic songs discarded the pessimism of "Hard Rain" for triumph in "The Times They Are A-Changin'" and vindictiveness in "When the Ship Comes In": "Then they'll raise their hands, say we'll meet all your demands, and we'll shout from the bow, your days are numbered."

It was Dylan's year. Stimulated by the wide acceptance of his work, inspired by his ideas and images, topical songwriters became more and more prolific. Dylan songs were recorded by dozens of folk singers, notably Joan Baez (at whom he had once sneered, "She's still singing about Mary Hamilton. Where's that at?"). No folk concert was complete without "Hard Rain," or "Don't Think Twice," or a protest song from Dylan's third album, *The Times They Are A-Changin'.* The college folk crowd imitated Dylan; civil rights workers took heart from him; masochistic journalists lionized him. And in the attenuated versions of Peter, Paul, and Mary, the Chad Mitchell Trio, even Lawrence Welk, his songs reached the fraternity house and the suburb.

Then Dylan yanked the rug: he renounced political protest. He put out an album of personal songs and in one of them, "My Back Pages," scoffed at his previous moral absolutism. His refrain—"Ah, but I was so much older then, I'm younger than that now"—seemed a slap at the thirties left. And the song contained scraps of uncomfortably private imagery—hints of aesthetic escapism?

Folk devotees were shocked at Dylan's apostasy. Folk music and social protest have always fed on each other, and the current revival had been political all along. For children of Depression activists growing up in the Eisenhower slough, folk music was a way of keeping the faith. When they converged on the Weavers' Town Hall hootenannies, they came as the anti-McCarthy resistance, pilgrims to the thirties shrine. The Weavers were blacklisted for alleged Communist connections; Pete Seeger had been *there,* singing for the unions, for the Spanish Republic. It didn't matter what they sang—in the atmosphere of conspiratorial sympathy that permeated those performances, even "Greensleeves" had radical overtones. Later, as the left revived, folk singing became a badge of involvement, an expression of solidarity, and most important, a history-in-the-raw of struggle. Now, Dylan's defection threatened the last aesthetically respectable haven for believers in proletarian art.

Dylan had written personal songs before, but they were songs that accepted folk conventions. Narrative in impulse, nostalgic but restless in mood, their central image the road and its imperative, they complemented his protest songs: here was an outlaw, unable to settle for one place, one girl, a merely private life, committed to that symbolic onward journey. His new songs were more psychological, limning characters and relationships. They substituted ambition for the artless perfection of his best early songs; "It Ain't Me, Babe," a gloss on the spiritual possessiveness of women, took three stanzas to say what "Don't Think Twice, It's All Right" had suggested in a few phrases: "I'm thinkin' and wonderin', walkin' down the road / I once loved a woman, a child I'm told / gave her my heart but she wanted my soul."[2] Dylan's language was opening up—doves sleeping in the sand were one thing, "crimson flames tied through my ears" quite another. And his tone was changing: in his love songs, ingenuousness began to yield to self-possession, the spontaneity of the road to the gamesmanship of the city. They were transitional songs, full of half-realized ideas; having rejected the role of people's bard, Dylan had yet to find a new niche.

III.

In retrospect, Dylan's break with the topical song movement seemed inevitable. He had modeled himself on Woody Guthrie, whose incessant traveling was an emotional as well as economic necessity, whose commitment to radical politics was rooted in an individualism as compulsive as Dylan's own. But Guthrie had had to organize or submit; Dylan had other choices. For Guthrie, the road was habitat; for Dylan, metaphor. The closing of the iron mines had done to Hibbing what drought had done to Guthrie's Oklahoma, but while Guthrie had been a victim, Dylan was a bystander. A voluntary refugee from middle-class life, more aesthete than activist, he had less in common with the left than with literary rebels—Blake, Whitman, Rimbaud, Crane, Ginsberg.

The beauty of "Hard Rain" was that it exploited poetry while remaining a folk lyric, simple, repetitive, seemingly uncontrived. Now Dylan became self-consciously poetic, adopting a neo-Beat style loaded with images. Though he had rejected the traditional political categories, his new posture was if anything more scornful of the social order than before. "It's Alright, Ma (I'm Only Bleeding)" attacked both the "human gods" who "make everything from toy guns that spark to flesh-colored Christs that glow in the dark" and their acquiescent victims. "Gates of Eden," like "Hard Rain," descended into a surreal netherworld, the menace this time a psychic bomb, the revolt of repressed instinct.

As poetry these songs were overrated—*Howl* had said it all much better—and they were unmusical, near-chants declaimed to a monotonous guitar strum. Yet the perfunctory music made the bohemian commonplaces work—made them fresh. Perhaps it was the context: though few people realized it yet, the civil rights movement was losing its moral force; the Vietnam juggernaut was becoming the personal concern of every draftable man; a new generation of bohemians, more expansive and less cynical than the Beats, was about to blossom. The time was right for a reaffirmation of individual revolt.

But Dylan had also been exposed to a very different vision: in May 1964, he had toured an England transformed by mod fashion and the unprecedented excitement over the Beatles and the Rolling Stones. When his new record came out the following spring, its title was *Bringing It All Back Home.* On the album jacket a chiaroscuro Dylan, bright face emerging from ominous shadows, stared accusingly at the viewer. In black suit and striped shirt, he perched on a long divan, hugging a cat, behind him a modish, blank-faced beauty in scarlet lounging pajamas. The room, wreathed in light and dominated by a baroque mantelpiece, abounded with artifacts—*Time,* a movie magazine, a fallout shelter sign, folk and pop records (including earlier Dylan), a portrait, a candlestick, a few mysterious objects obscured by the halo.

Most of side one was devoted to "Gates of Eden" and "It's Alright, Ma." But the most arresting cut on the side was "Mr. Tambourine Man," a hymn to the psychedelic quest: "Take me disappearing through the smoke-rings of my mind. . . . take me on a trip upon your magic swirling ship." Drug-oriented bohemians loved it; it was another step away from the sober-sided politicals. It was also more like a folk song than anything Dylan had written since giving up politics, a spiritual road song with a lilting, singable melody.

The other side was rock-and-roll, Dylan on electric guitar and piano backed by a five-man band. It was not hard rock. There was no over-dubbing, and Dylan played his amplified guitar folk-style. But the beat was there, and the sound, if not overwhelming, was big enough to muffle some of the lyrics. These dispensed a new kind of folk wisdom. Chaos had become a condition, like the weather, not to analyze or prophesy but to gripe about, cope with, dodge: "Look out, kid, it's somethin' you did / God knows when but you're doin' it again." The message was pay attention to what's happening: "Don't follow leaders, watch the parkin' meters."

One rock song, "Subterranean Homesick Blues," was released as a single. As Dylan's pop debut, it was a modest success, hovering halfway up the *Cash Box* and *Billboard* charts. That summer, Dylan cut "Like a Rolling Stone," the most scurrilous and—with its powerful beat—the most dramatic in a long line of non–love songs. It was a number-one hit, as "Blowin' in the Wind" had been two years before—only now it was Dylan's own expressive snarl coming over radio and jukebox.

"Like a Rolling Stone" opened Dylan's first all-rock album, *Highway 61*

Revisited. More polished but less daring than *Bringing It All Back Home,* the album reworked familiar motifs. The title song, which depicted the highway as junkyard, temple, and battlefield, was Dylan's best face-of-America commentary since "Talking World War III Blues." The witty and scarifying "Ballad of a Thin Man," which derided the rationalist bewildered by the instinctual revolt, was an updated "Times They Are A-Changin'," with battle lines redrawn according to pop morality. Dylan did not hail the breakdown of sanity he described but merely kept his cool, mocking Mr. Jones (the pop equivalent of Mr. Charlie) for committing squareness: "The sword-swallower he comes up to you and then he kneels / . . . and he says here is your throat back, thanks for the loan / and something is happening but you don't know what it is, do you, Mr. Jones?" "Desolation Row" was Dylan's final tribute to the Götterdämmerung strain in modern literature—an eleven-minute freak show whose cast of losers, goons, and ghosts wandered around in a miasma of sexual repression and latent violence underscored by the electronic beat.

The violent hostility of traditionalists to Dylan's rock-and-roll made the uproar over "My Back Pages" seem mild. Not only orthodox leftists but bohemian radicals called him a sellout and a phony. At the July 1965 Newport Folk Festival he appeared with his electric guitar and was booed off the stage. Alan Lomax, America's foremost authority on folk songs, felt Dylan had chucked his artistry for a big audience and forsaken a mature culture for one that was evanescent and faddish. Tom Paxton, dean of the new crop of topical songwriters, commented: "'Where it's at' is a synonym for 'rich.'"

Defiantly, Dylan exacerbated the furor, insisting on his contempt for message songs and his indifference to causes, refusing to agonize over his wealth or his taxes ("Uncle Sam, he's my *uncle!* Can't turn your back on a member of the family!"). In one notorious interview he claimed he had written topical songs only to get published in *Broadside* and attract attention. Many former fans took the bait. Actually, Dylan's work still bristled with messages; his "opportunism" had absorbed three years of his life and produced the finest extensions of traditional music since Guthrie. But the purists believed in it because they wanted to. Their passion told less about Dylan than about their own peculiar compound of aristocratic and proletarian sensibilities.

Pure folk sound and idiom, in theory the expression of ordinary people, had become the province of middle-class dissidents who identified with the common man but whose attitude toward common men resembled that of White Russian expatriates toward the communized peasants. For them popular music—especially rock-and-roll—symbolized the displacement of the true folk by the masses. Rock was not created by the people but purveyed by the communications industry. The performer was incidental to engineer and publicity man. The beat was moronic, the lyrics banal teenage trivia.

These were half-truths. From the beginning, there was a bottom-up as well as top-down movement in rock-and-roll: neighborhood kids formed groups and wrote songs; country singers adopted a rhythm-and-blues beat. Rock took a mechanized, acquisitive society for granted, yet in its own way it was protest music, uniting teenagers against adults' lack of sympathy with youthful energy and love and sex. The mediocrity of most performers only made rock more "authentic"—anyone could sing it—and one of the few remaining vindications of the American dream—any kid from the slums might become a millionaire. (The best singers, of course, were fine interpreters; Elvis Presley and Chuck Berry did not have golden voices, but neither did Lead Belly or Woody Guthrie.) Rock-and-roll was further from the grass roots than traditional music, but closer than any other kind of pop. If folk fans did not recognize this, the average adult did, and condemned the music for its adolescent surliness and its sexuality, covert in the lyrics, overt in the beat and in the intense response to idols.

But it remained for the British renaissance to prove that the mainstream of mass culture could produce folk music—that is, antiestablishment music. The Beatles, commercial without apology, delighted in the Americanized decadence of their environment. Yet their enthusiasm was subversive—they endorsed the reality of the culture, not its official myths. The Rolling Stones were iconoclastic in a different way: deliberately ugly, blatantly erotic, they exuded contempt for the public while making a fortune. Their cynicism, like Lead Belly's violence or Charlie Parker's heroin, was part of their charisma. Unlike traditional folk singers, they could cheerfully censor their lyrics for Ed Sullivan without seeming domesticated—the effect was more as if they had paraded a sign saying "Blank CBS." British rock was far superior to most early rock-and-roll.[3] Times had changed: electronic techniques were more sophisticated, radio stations and record companies less squeamish about sexual candor, and teen culture was merging into a more mature, less superficial youth culture with semi-bohemian tastes. Most important, the British groups successfully assimilated Negro music, neither vitiating rhythm-and-blues nor imitating it, but refining it to reflect their own milieu—white, urban, technological, materialistic, tough-minded.

Most folk fans—even those with no intrinsic objections to rock, who had perhaps listened to it when they were teenagers and not obliged to be serious—assumed that commercial exploitation automatically gutted music. Yet the Stones were creating blues as valid as the work of any folk singers, black or white. After *Bringing It All Back Home*, the contradiction could no longer be ignored, and those not irrevocably committed to the traditional folk ethos saw the point. Phil Ochs praised *Highway 61*; Joan Baez cut a rock-and-roll record; more and more folk singers began to use electronic instruments. Folk-rock generated an unaccustomed accord between the folk and pop worlds. In *Crawdaddy!* Richard Fariña lauded "this shift away from open-road-protest-flat-pick-style to more Nashville-Motown-Thameside, with the strong implication that some of us had been listening to the AM radio." Malvina Reynolds pronounced the new rock-and-roll "a wonder and delight." By November 1966, folk-rock had received the final imprimatur—Pete Seeger recorded an album backed by three members of the Blues Project.

Folk-rock was never a form, but a simpleminded inspiration responsible for all sorts of hybrids. At first it was mostly rock versions of Dylan folk songs, social protest rock, and generational trauma rock, a weekend-hippie version of the classic formula, children against parents. Then, self-styled musical poets Simon and Garfunkel began imitating Dylan's apocalyptic songs ("The words of the prophets are written on a subway wall"), starting a trend of elaborate and, too often, sophomoric lyrics. The Lovin' Spoonful invented the "good-time sound," a varying mixture of rock, blues, jug, and old pop. Donovan wrote medieval fantasies and pop collages like "Sunshine Superman" and "Mellow Yellow." And there was acid-rock, the music of new bohemia.

Psychedelic music, like folk-rock, was a catch-all label; it described a variety of products shaped by folk, British rock, Chicago blues, jazz, Indian music. Psychedelic lyrics, heavily influenced by Dylanesque imagery, used the conventions of the romantic pop song to express sexual and mystical rather than sentimental love and focused on the trip—especially the flight—the way folk music focused on the road. The Byrds, who had started folk-rock moving with their hit record of "Mr. Tambourine Man," launched the California psychedelic sound with "Eight Miles High," which picked up on the Beatles' experiments with Indian instrumentation and was ostensibly about flying over the London airport (it was banned anyway by right-thinking disc jockeys). Though the Byrds were from Los Angeles, the scene soon shifted north, and a proliferation of underground rock groups—some, like Jefferson Airplane, the Grateful Dead, and Country Joe and the Fish, quickly surfaced—made San Francisco the new center of avant-garde pop, superseding Britain.

The California groups came closest to making the term *folk-rock* say something. For hippie culture, bastard of the Beat generation out of pop, was much like a folk culture—oral, naive, communal, its aphorisms ("Make love, not war," "Turn on, tune in, drop out") intuited, not rationalized. Pop and Beat, thesis and antithesis of the affluent society, contained elements of synthesis: both movements rejected intellect for sensation, politics for art, and Ginsberg and Kerouac glorified a grassroots America that included supermarkets and cars as well as mountains and apple pie. The hippies simplified the Beats' utopian anarchism and substituted psychedelic drugs for Zen and yoga; they also shared the pop enthusiasm for technology and the rainbow surface of affluence—their music was rock, their style mod. Like Dylan, they bridged old culture and new—they were still idealists—and they idolized him. But he did not consider himself their spokesman. At twenty-five, he was too old ("How can I be the voice of their generation? I'm not their generation") and, though he did not admit it publicly, too well read. While "Mr. Tambourine Man" was becoming the hippie anthem, he was saying "LSD is for mad, hateful people" and making fun of drugs in "Memphis Blues Again." Dylan was really at cross-purposes with the hippies.

They were trying to embody pop sensibility in a folk culture. He was trying to comprehend pop culture with—at bottom—a folk sensibility.

IV.

It is a truism among Dylan's admirers that he is a poet using rock-and-roll to spread his art: as Jack Newfield put it in the *Village Voice,* "If Whitman were alive today, he too would be playing an electric guitar." This misrepresentation has only served to discredit Dylan among intellectuals and draw predictable sniping from conscientious B-student poets like Louis Simpson and John Ciardi. Dylan has a lavish verbal imagination and a brilliant sense of irony, and many of his images—especially on the two *Blonde on Blonde* records—are memorable. But poetry also requires economy, coherence, and discrimination, and Dylan has perpetrated prolix verses, horrendous grammar, tangled phrases, silly metaphors, embarrassing clichés, muddled thought; at times he seems to believe one good image deserves five others, and he relies too much on rhyme. His chief literary virtue—sensitivity to psychological nuance—belongs to fiction more than poetry. His skill at creating character has made good lyrics out of terrible poetry, as in the prerock "Ballad in Plain D," whose portraits of the singer, his girl, and her family redeem lines like: "With unseen consciousness I possessed in my grip / a magnificent mantelpiece though its heart being chipped."

Dylan is not always undisciplined. As early as *Freewheelin'* it was clear that he could control his material when he cared to. But his disciplines are songwriting and acting, not poetry; his words fit the needs of music and performance, not an intrinsic pattern. Words or rhymes that seem gratuitous in print often make good musical sense, and Dylan's voice, an extraordinary interpreter of emotion though (or more likely because) it is almost devoid of melody, makes vague lines clear. Dylan's music is not inspired. His melodies and arrangements are derivative, and his one technical accomplishment, a vivacious, evocative harmonica, does not approach the virtuosity of a Sonny Terry. His strength as a musician is his formidable eclecticism combined with a talent for choosing the right music to go with a given lyric. The result is a unity of sound and word that eludes most of his imitators.

Dylan is effective only when exploiting this unity, which is why his free-verse album notes are interesting mainly as autobiography (or mythology) and why *Tarantula* is unlikely to be a masterpiece. When critics call Dylan a poet, they really mean a visionary. Because the poet is the paradigmatic seer, it is conventional to talk about the film poet, the jazz poet. Dylan is verbal, which makes the label even more tempting. But it evades an important truth—the new visionaries are not poets. Dylan is specifically pessimistic about the future of literature. Far from Desolation Row, "The Titanic sails at dawn / . . . Ezra Pound and T. S. Eliot fighting in the captain's towers / while calypso singers laugh at them and fishermen hold flowers." The infamous Mr. Jones, with his pencil in his hand, his eyes in his pocket, and his nose on the ground, is a literary man. With the rock songs on *Bringing It All Back Home,* Dylan began trying to create an alternative to poetry. If Whitman were alive today, he might be playing electric guitar; then again, he might be writing advertising copy.

In May 1966, Dylan recorded *Blonde on Blonde,* a double album cut in Nashville with local musicians. Formally, it was his finest achievement since *Freewheelin',* but while the appeal of the *Freewheelin'* songs was the illusion of spontaneous folk expression, the songs from *Blonde on Blonde* were clearly artifacts, lovingly and carefully made. The music was rock and Nashville country, with a sprinkling of blues runs and English-ballad arpeggios. Thematically, the album was a unity. It explored the subworld pop was creating, an exotic milieu of velvet doors and scorpions, cool sex ("I saw you makin' love with him, / you forgot to close the garage door"), zany fashions ("it balances on your head just like a mattress balances on a bottle of wine, / your brand-new leopard-skin pillbox hat"), strange potions ("it strangled up my mind, / now people just get uglier and I have no sense of time"), neurotic women ("she's like all the rest / with her fog, her amphetamine, and her pearls").

The songs did not preach: Dylan was no longer rebel but seismograph, registering his emotions—fascination, confusion, pity, annoyance, exuberance, anguish—with sardonic lucidity. Only once, in "Just like a Woman," did his culture shock get out of control: "I can't stay in here / ain't it clear / that I just can't fit." Many of the songs were about child-women, bitchy, unreliable, sometimes vulnerable, usually one step ahead: "I told you as you clawed out my eyes / I never really meant to do you any harm." But there were also goddesses like Johanna and the mercury-mouthed, silken-fleshed Sad-Eyed Lady of the Lowlands, Beatrices of pop who shed not merely light but kaleidoscopic images.

The fashionable, sybaritic denizens of *Blonde on Blonde* are the sort of people despised by radicals as apologists for the system. Yet in accepting the surface that system has produced, they subvert its assumptions. Conservative and utopian ideologues agree that man must understand and control his environment; the questions are how, and for whose benefit. But pop culture defines man as a receiver of stimuli, his environment as sensory patterns to be enjoyed, not interpreted (literature and philosophy are irrelevant) or acted upon (politics is irrelevant). "If you want to understand me, look at my surface," says Andy Warhol. And "I like my paintings because anybody can do them." The bureaucrat defends standardization because it makes a complex society manageable. Yet he thinks of himself as an individualist and finds the idea of mass-produced, mechanized art incomprehensible, threatening—or a put-on. The pop artist looks at mass culture naively and sees beauty in its regular patterns; like an anthropologist exhibiting Indian basket-weaving, Warhol shows us our folk art—soup cans. His message—the Emperor has no clothes, but that's all right, in fact it's beautiful—takes acceptance of image for essence to its logical extreme. *Blonde on Blonde* is about this love of surface.

Dylan's sensitivity to pop comes straight out of his folk background. Both folk and pop mentalities are leery of abstractions, and Dylan's appreciation of surface detail represents Guthriesque common sense—to Dylan, a television commercial was always a television commercial as well as a symbol of alienation. From the first, a basic pragmatism tempered his commitment to the passionate excesses of the revolutionist and the *poète maudit* and set him apart from hipster heroes like James Dean. Like the Beats, who admired the total revolt of the hipster from a safe distance, Dylan is essentially nonviolent. Any vengefulness in his songs is either impersonal or funny, like the threats of a little boy to beat up the bad guys; more often, he is the bemused butt of slapstick cruelty: "I've got a woman, she's so mean / sticks my boots in the washing machine / sticks me with buckshot when I'm nude / puts bubble gum in my food."

Dylan's basic rapport with reality has also saved him from the excesses of pop, kept him from merging, Warhol-like, into his public surface. *John Wesley Harding,* released after twenty months of silence, shows that Dylan is still intact in spirit as well as body. The songs are more impersonal—and in a way more inscrutable—than ever, yet the human being behind them has never seemed less mysterious. For they reveal Dylan not as the protean embodiment of some collective nerve, but as an alert artist responding to challenge from his peers. If Dylan's first rock-and-roll songs were his reaction to the cultural changes the new rock represented, *John Wesley Harding* is a reaction to the music itself as it has evolved since his accident. The album is comprehensible only in this context.

As Dylan's recovery advanced, he began making the papers again. He signed a new contract with Columbia—the defection to MGM never came off—and the company announced that he was recording. Dylan was still revered, his near-mythic status only solidified by his long absence from the scene. But whether he could come back as an active performer was another question. Shortly after the appearance of *Blonde on Blonde,* three important albums—the Beatles' *Revolver,* the Stones' *Aftermath,* and the Beach Boys' *Pet Sounds*—had all set new standards of musical ambition and pretension. Ever since, the "serious" rock groups had been producing albums that said, in effect, "Can you top this?"—a competition that extended to album covers and titles. In the spring of 1967 the Beatles released *Sgt. Pepper's Lonely Hearts Club Band,* possibly the most elaborate rock album ever made and certainly the most celebrated. It was reported that Dylan had listened to the first few cuts of *Sgt. Pepper* and snapped "Turn that off!"; perhaps the new developments in rock—which he had done so much to inspire—had left him behind. On the other hand, perhaps he was leaving rock behind. Many of Dylan's associates—notably Tom Wilson, his former A&R man—had always insisted that Dylan was much more sophisticated musically than he let on. And in May a New York *Daily News* reporter quoted Dylan as saying he was at work on "two new sounds."

By Christmas the Stones were first in the pretensions sweepstakes: *Their*

Satanic Majesties Request, with its 3-D cover, was almost a parody of the whole art-rock phenomenon. How was Dylan going to top *that*? Everyone waited for a revolutionary masterpiece or an extravagant flop. What we got was *John Wesley Harding* in a plain gray jacket with a polaroid snapshot of Dylan and three Indians in the country. The first sound to greet the eager listener was the strumming of an acoustic guitar. The first line of the first song was "John Wesley Harding was a friend to the poor." Dylan had done it again.

The new melodies are absurdly simple, even for Dylan; the only instruments backing his guitar, piano, and harmonica are a bass, a drum, and in two songs an extra guitar; the rock beat has faded out and the country and English ballad strains now dominate. The titles are all as straight as "John Wesley Harding": most are taken from the first lines of the songs. The lyrics are not only simple but understated in a way that shows Dylan has learned a trick or two from Lennon–McCartney, and they are folk lyrics. Or more precisely, affectionate comments on folk lyrics—the album is not a reversion to his early work but a kind of hymn to it. Nearly all the songs play with the clichés of folk music. The title song, for instance, seems at first hearing to be a second-rate "Jesse James" or "Pretty Boy Floyd." It starts out with all the catch phrases about the benevolent outlaw, then goes into the story: "It was down in Cheney County the time they talk about / With his lady by his side he took a stand." But the next line goes right out of it again: "And soon the situation there was all but straightened out." You never learn what happened in Cheney County or why it wasn't *entirely* straightened out, and the song ends with more stock lines about the bandit's elusiveness and the helplessness of the law. It is not about John Wesley Harding, but about a familiar formula: and this, friends, is how you write the generic outlaw song.

Several of the songs are folk-style fantasies. "Frankie Lee and Judas Priest" is both a folk ballad (based on another stock situation, the gambler on the road) and one of Dylan's surrealist dream songs; "As I Walked Out One Morning" describes a run-in with an Arthurian enchantress as if she were a revenue agent or the farmer's daughter. This juxtaposition of the conventional and the fantastic produces an unsettling gnomic effect, enhanced in some cases by truncated endings: in "The Drifter's Escape," the drifter's trial for some unknown offense ends abruptly when lightning strikes the courthouse and he gets away in the confusion; "All along the Watchtower" ends with a beginning, "Two riders were approaching, the wind began to howl." The aura of the uncanny that these songs create is probably what Dylan meant when he remarked, years ago, that folk songs grew out of mysteries.

But some of the album is sheer fun, especially "Down along the Cove," a jaunty blues banged out on the piano, and "I'll Be Your Baby Tonight," a thirties-type pop tune that rhymes "moon" with "spoon" for the benefit of those pundits who are always crowing over the demise of "Tin Pan Alley pap." And "Dear Landlord," the best cut musically, is further evidence that Dylan has—well, the only word for it is—mellowed: "Now each of us has his own special gift and you know this was meant to be true, / And if you don't underestimate me I won't underestimate you." In the end, what this album is about is Dylan's reconciliation with his past, with ordinary people, and even—warily, ambivalently—with his archenemies, the landlords of the world.

Of course, being Bob Dylan, he has turned this reconciliation into a rebellion. His sudden removal of the mask—see, it's me, a songwriter, I just want to write nice songs—and the apparent step backward could be as traumatic for the public as his previous metamorphoses; Dylan is still in the business of shaking us up. *John Wesley Harding* does not measure up to *Blonde on Blonde.* It is basically a tour de force. But it serves its purpose, which is to liberate Dylan—and the rest of us—from the *Sgt. Pepper* straitjacket. Dylan is free now to work on his own terms. It would be foolish to predict what he will do next. But I hope he will remain a mediator, using the language of pop to transcend it. If the gap between past and present continues to widen, such mediation may be crucial. In a communications crisis, the true prophets are the translators.

Cheetah, 1967

NOTES

The version of "Dylan" printed here is the anthologized essay Willis included in *Beginning to See the Light.* This version first appeared in *Cheetah* in 1967, and Willis later added footnotes for the anthologized version. Other than the footnotes, they are identical. An earlier, shorter version called "The Sound of Bob Dylan" was also published in *Commentary* in 1967.

1. When I wrote this piece (and a few others in the book), I had not yet stopped using *man, he,* etc., as generic terms applying to both sexes. In the interest of historical accuracy I've left these locutions intact, though they grate on me aesthetically as well as politically. For the same reason I have not changed *Negro* to *black.*

2. Here as elsewhere in this prefeminist essay I refer with aplomb if not outright endorsement to Dylan's characteristic bohemian contempt for women (which he combined with an equally obnoxious idealization of female goddess figures). At the time I did not question the idea that women were guardians of oppressive conventional values; I only thought of myself as an exception. *I* was not possessive; I understood men's need to go on the road because I was, spiritually speaking, on the road myself. That, at least, was my fantasy; the realities of my life were somewhat more ambiguous.

3. This statement now strikes me as absurd, a confusion of aesthetic sophistication and self-consciousness with merit in some absolute sense. It makes even less sense when applied to the best midsixties British rock versus the best early rock-and-roll. Precisely because they had a more spontaneous, direct relation to their material and their audience, performers like Elvis Presley, Chuck Berry, Little Richard, and Jerry Lee Lewis got to places that the Beatles, the Stones, and the Who never even tried to reach. The reverse is also true, of course.

The Cultural Revolution Saved from Drowning

You have to give the producers of the Woodstock Music and Art Fair this much credit: they are pulling off a great public relations coup. They have apparently succeeded in creating the impression that the crisis in Bethel was a capricious natural disaster rather than a product of human incompetence, that the huge turnout was completely unexpected (and, in fact, could not have been foreseen by reasonable men), and that they have lost more than a million dollars in the process of being good guys who did everything possible to transform an incipient fiasco into a groovy weekend. Incredibly, instead of hiding from the wrath of disappointed ticket-buyers and creditors they are bragging that the festival was a landmark in the development of youth culture and have announced that they plan to hold it again next year. But before history is completely rewritten, a few facts, semifacts, and strong inferences are in order.

For at least a month before the festival, it was obvious to everyone involved in the music scene—industry people, writers for both the straight and the underground press, radicals, and hippies—and also to the city fathers of Wallkill, New York, that the crowd was going to be enormous and the facilities inadequate. The four under-thirty backers of Woodstock Ventures seemed to be motivated less by greed than by sheer hubris: the ambitiousness of the project was meant to establish them as *the* pop producers, kingpins of the youth market. Their promotion was pervasive. On July 18th, a month before the festival, the *Times* reported that the management expected as many as two hundred thousand people and had already sold fifty thousand tickets. At that time, they were planning to hold the festival in Wallkill, on a three-hundred-acre site—half the size of the grounds in Bethel—linked to civilization by three country roads. When a Concerned Citizens Committee warned that Wallkill's water supply could not accommodate the anticipated influx and that festival officials had not made realistic plans to cope with traffic, health, or security, the producers vowed to fight the town's attempt to exclude them and implied that the opposition came from antiyouth rednecks. When the change of site was announced, just twenty-four days before the scheduled opening of the fair, there was a lot of speculation that it would never come off at all. An experienced promoter told me, "It'll happen, but only because they've got so much money tied up in it. They can't afford to back out. But they'll never finish their preparations in three weeks. Monterey took three months. It's going to be complete chaos." Alfred G. Aronowitz, of the *Post,* one of the few journalists to cast a consistently cold eye on the four young entrepreneurs, wrote witty on-location reports giving them the needle and adding to the general pessimism. Meanwhile, back on St. Marks Place, Woodstock was rapidly evolving into this year's thing to do. A "Woodstock Special" issue of the underground weekly *Rat,* published the week of the festival, featured a page of survival advice that began, "The call has been put out across the country for hundreds of thousands to attend a three-day orgy of music and dope and communal experience." I left for Bethel in much the same spirit that I had gone to Chicago at the time of the Democratic Convention. I was emotionally prepared for a breakdown in services and a major riot. If I enjoyed the festival, that would be incidental to participating in a historic event. The actual number of people who showed up was a surprise. The only other real surprise was that there was no riot. The extra numbers could not excuse the flimsiness of the water pipes (they broke down almost immediately), the paucity of latrines (about eight hundred for an expected two hundred thousand people) and garbage cans, or the makeshift medical facilities (the press tent had to be converted into a hospital). One kid reportedly died of a burst appendix—an incident that in 1969 should at least inspire some questions.

Although it is possible that the fair lost money, many knowledgeable people are inclined to doubt that the loss was anywhere near the one and a half million dollars Woodstock Ventures is claiming. The corporation should open its books to the public. The thousands of ticket-holders who were turned away from the site because of traffic jams (while other thousands of contributors to the traffic jams got in free) deserve some consideration. So far, the management has said nothing about refunds, and there has been talk of setting up a group suit to demand the money. One complication is that since no tickets were collected there is no way of distinguishing those who made it from those who didn't, but rumor has it that the state may sidestep this problem by suing the producers on the ground that they had no serious intention of taking tickets at the fairgrounds.

If the festival succeeded in spite of the gross ineptitude of its masterminds, it was mostly because three hundred thousand or more young people were determined to have a good time no matter what. The accounts of the peacefulness and generosity of the participants are all true, but they have tended to miss the point. The cooperative spirit did not stem from solidarity in an emergency—the "we all forgot our differences and helped each other" phenomenon that attends power blackouts and hurricanes—so much as from a general refusal to adopt any sort of emergency psychology. The widespread conviction that the Lord (or the Hog Farm, or the people of Monticello, or someone) would provide removed any incentive to fight or to hoard food, and the pilgrims simply proceeded to do what they had come to do: dig the music and the woods, make friends, reaffirm their lifestyle in freedom from hostile straights and cops, swim naked, and get high. Drug dealing was completely open; kids stood on Hurd Road, the main thoroughfare of the festival site, hawking mescaline and acid. But the most exhilarating intoxicants were the warmth and fellow-feeling that allowed us to abandon our chronic defenses against other people. As for the music, though rock was the only thing that could have drawn such a crowd, it was not the focal point of the festival but, rather, a pleasant background to the mass presence of the hip community. Few of us got close enough to see anything, and as the music continued for seventeen hours at a stretch our adrenaline output naturally decreased. (On Sunday, a boy who had driven in from California commented, "Wow, I can't believe all the groups here, and I'm not even listening to them." "It's not the music," said another. "It's—all this!") The sound system was excellent, and thousands listened from camps in the woods, dozing and waking while the music went on till dawn. Everyone was so quiet you felt almost alone in the dark, but you couldn't move very far without stepping on someone's hand or brushing against a leg.

The festival site was like the eye of a storm—virtually undisturbed by the frantic activity behind the scenes. Once the nuisance of getting there was over with (I eventually got a ride in a performers' police-escorted caravan) and the Lord had provided (I just happened to bump into some friends with a leak-proof tent and plenty of food), I found the inconveniences trivial compared to the pleasures. But then I did not have to sleep out in the mud for two nights, and by Sunday I couldn't help suspecting that some of the beautiful, transcendent acceptance going around was just plain old passivity. It was a bit creepy that there was such a total lack of resentment at the fair's mismanagement, especially among those who had paid from seven to eighteen dollars. People either made excuses for Woodstock Ventures ("They couldn't help it, man; it was just too big for them") or thought of the festival as a noble social experiment to which crass concepts like responsible planning were irrelevant. For the most part, they took for granted not only the discomforts but the tremendous efforts made by the state, the local communities, and unpaid volunteers to distribute cheap or free food and establish minimum standards of health and safety. No one seemed to comprehend what the tasks of mobilizing and transporting emergency food, water, and medical personnel, clearing the roads, and removing garbage meant in terms of labor and money. Ecstatic heads even proclaimed that the festival proved the viability of a new culture in which no one worked and everything was free. And in the aftermath anyone who has dared to complain has been put down as a crank. It should be possible to admit that the people created a memorable gathering without embracing those who botched things up. (A letter writer in the *Village Voice* went as far as to say, "Woodstock Ventures should be congratulated and not chastised for giving us smiles, peace, music, and good vibrations." All those paying customers might disagree about being "given" music; personally, I don't see why Woodstock Ventures should get credit for my smiles.) But maybe it isn't. And maybe there is a lesson here about the political significance of youth culture. From the start, the cultural-revolutionary wing of the radical movement saw Woodstock as a political issue. The underground papers made a lot of noise about businessmen profiting from music that belonged to the community, and some movement people demanded and received money to bring political groups to the festival and set up an enclave called Movement City as a center for radical activity. If the festival staff had been foolish enough to try to restrict the audience to paid admissions, the movement might have had something to do. As it was, Movement City was both physically and spiritually isolated from the bulk of the crowd. It was not the activists but a hundred-odd members of the Hog Farm, a Santa Fe–based pacifistic commune, who were the most visible community presence, operating a free kitchen, helping people recover from bad acid trips, and setting up a rudimentary communication system of oral and written survival bulletins. A few radicals talked hopefully of liberating the concessions or the stage area. Abbie Hoffman interrupted the Who's set on Saturday night to berate the crowd for listening to music when John Sinclair, a Michigan activist, had just been sentenced to a long prison term for giving some marijuana to a cop. Peter Townshend hit Hoffman with his guitar, and that is more of a commentary on the relation of rock to politics than all of *Rat*'s fuzzy moralizing.

What cultural revolutionaries do not seem to grasp is that, far from being a grass-roots art form that has been taken over by businessmen, rock itself comes from the commercial exploitation of blues. It is bourgeois at its core, a mass-produced commodity, dependent on advanced technology and therefore on the money controlled by those in power. Its rebelliousness does not imply specific political content; it can be—and has been—criminal, fascistic, and coolly individualistic as well as revolutionary. Nor is the hip lifestyle inherently radical. It can simply be a more pleasurable way of surviving within the system, which is what the pop sensibility has always been about. Certainly that was what Woodstock was about: ignore the bad, groove on the good, hang loose, and let things happen. The truth is that there can't be a revolutionary culture until there is a revolution. In the meantime, we should at least insist that the capitalists who produce rock concerts charge reasonable prices for reasonable service.

The New Yorker, September 1969

Women and the Myth of Consumerism

If white radicals are serious about revolution, they are going to have to discard a lot of bullshit ideology created by and for educated white middle-class males. A good example of what has to go is the popular theory of consumerism.

As expounded by many leftist thinkers, notably Marcuse, this theory maintains that consumers are psychically manipulated by the mass media to crave more and more consumer goods, and thus power an economy that depends on constantly expanding sales. The theory is said to be particularly applicable to women, for women do most of the actual buying, their consumption is often directly related to their oppression (e.g., makeup, soap flakes), and they are a special target of advertisers. According to this view, the society defines women as consumers, and the purpose of the prevailing media image of women as passive sexual objects is to sell products. It follows that the beneficiaries of this depreciation of women are not men but the corporate power structure.

First of all, there is nothing inherently wrong with consumption. Shopping and consuming are enjoyable human activities and the marketplace has been a center of social life for thousands of years.

The locus of oppression resides in the production function: people have no control over which commodities are produced (or services performed), in what amounts, under what conditions, or how these commodities are distributed. Corporations make these decisions and base them solely on their profit potential.

As it is, the profusion of commodities is a genuine and powerful compensation for oppression. It is a bribe, but like all bribes it offers concrete benefits— in the average American's case, a degree of physical comfort unparalleled in history. Under present conditions, people are preoccupied with consumer goods not because they are brainwashed but because buying is the one pleasurable activity not only permitted but actively encouraged by our rulers. The pleasure of eating an ice cream cone may be minor compared to the pleasure of meaningful, autonomous work, but the former is easily available and the latter is not. A poor family would undoubtedly rather have a decent apartment than a new TV, but since they are unlikely to get the apartment, what is to be gained by not getting the TV?

The confusion between cause and effect is particularly apparent in the consumerist analysis of women's oppression. Women are not manipulated by the media into being domestic servants and mindless sexual decorations, the better to sell soap and hair spray. Rather, the image reflects women as they are forced by men in a sexist society to behave. Male supremacy is the oldest and most basic form of class exploitation; it was not invented by a smart ad man. The real evil of the media image of women is that it supports the sexist status quo. In a sense, the fashion, cosmetics, and feminine hygiene ads are aimed more at men than at women. They encourage men to expect women to sport all the latest trappings of sexual slavery—expectations women must then fulfill if they are to survive. That advertisers exploit women's subordination rather than cause it can be clearly seen now that *male* fashions and toiletries have become big business. In contrast to ads for women's products, whose appeal is use this and he will want you (or if you don't use this, he won't want you), ads for the male counterparts urge, You too can enjoy perfume and bright-colored clothes; don't worry, it doesn't make you feminine. Although advertisers are careful to emphasize how *virile* these products are (giving them names like Brut, showing the man who uses them hunting or flirting with admiring women—who, incidentally, remain decorative objects when the sell is aimed directly at men), it is never claimed that the product is *essential* to masculinity (as makeup is essential to femininity), only *compatible* with it. To convince a man to buy, an ad must appeal to his desire for autonomy and freedom from conventional restrictions; to convince a woman, an ad must appeal to her need to please the male oppressor.

For women, buying and wearing clothes and beauty aids is not so much consumption as work. One of a woman's jobs in this society is to be an attractive sexual object, and clothes and makeup are tools of the trade. Similarly, buying food and household furnishings is a domestic task; it is the wife's chore to pick out the commodities that will be consumed by the whole family. Appliances and cleaning materials are tools that facilitate her domestic function. When a woman spends a lot of money and time decorating her home or herself, or hunting down the latest in vacuum cleaners, it is not idle self-indulgence (let alone the result of psychic manipulation) but a healthy attempt to find outlets for her creative energies within her circumscribed role.

There is a persistent myth that a wife has control over her husband's money because she gets to spend it. Actually, she does not have much more financial authority than the employee of a corporation who is delegated to buy office furniture or supplies. The husband, especially if he is rich, may allow his wife wide latitude in spending—he may reason that since she has to work in the home she is entitled to furnish it to her taste, or he may simply not want to bother with domestic details—but he retains the ultimate veto power. If he doesn't like the way his wife handles his money, she will hear about it. In most households, particularly in the working class, a wife cannot make significant expenditures, either personal or in her role as object-servant, without consulting her husband. And more often than not, according to statistics, it is the husband who makes the final decisions about furniture and appliances as well as about other major expenditures like houses, cars, and vacations.

Consumerism as applied to women is blatantly sexist. The pervasive image of the empty-headed female consumer constantly trying her husband's patience with her extravagant purchases contributes to the myth of male superiority: we are incapable of spending money rationally: all we need to make us happy is a new hat now and then. (There is an analogous racial stereotype—the black with his Cadillac and magenta shirts.) Furthermore, the consumerism line allows Movement men to avoid recognizing that they exploit women by attributing women's oppression solely to capitalism. It fits neatly into already existing radical theory and concerns, saving the Movement the trouble of tackling the real problems of women's liberation. And it retards the struggle against male supremacy by dividing women. Just as in the male movement, the belief in consumerism encourages radical women to patronize and put down other women for trying to survive as best they can, and maintains individualist illusions.

If we are to build a mass movement we must recognize that no individual decision, like rejecting consumption, can liberate us. We must stop arguing about whose lifestyle is better (and secretly believing ours is) and tend to the task of collectively fighting our own oppression and the ways in which we oppress others. When we create a political alternative to sexism, racism, and capitalism, the consumer problem, if it is a problem, will take care of itself.

Ramparts, 1970

Editor's note: Although this essay was technically published in the seventies, it appears in this chapter because it was written in 1969—a distinction and parameter Willis used in her previous essay collections.

Talk of the Town
Hearing

In each of the past three years, the New York State Legislature has defeated proposals to liberalize the state's eighty-six-year-old criminal-abortion statute, which permits an abortion only when the operation is necessary to preserve a pregnant woman's life. Now a reform bill introduced by State Assemblyman Albert H. Blumenthal, of New York County, appears likely to pass. It would amend "life" to "health," and give relief to women who are physically or mentally unequipped to care for a child or who risk bearing a deformed child, to victims of rape and incest, and to the very young. A second bill is also pending. Sponsored by Assemblywoman Constance Cook, of the 125th Assembly District, it would repeal the abortion law entirely and make abortion available on the same basis as any other medical treatment. The repeal bill has received little public attention. Newspapers that mention it at all tend to treat it as a quixotic oddity. Most people do not know that the Cook bill exists, and some legislators, when asked for their support, have professed not to have heard of it. A number of women's organizations, however, are very much aware of the repeal proposal and are determined to spread the word. These groups are part of a revived—and increasingly militant—feminist movement. They include the National Organization for Women (NOW), the radical October Seventeenth Movement (a split-off from NOW), and Women's Liberation, a collective label for radical feminist groups formed by women activists who found that men on the left too often expected them to type, make coffee, and keep quiet. Whatever their ideological differences, feminists have united on the abortion issue. They oppose Blumenthal's reforms—or any reforms—and demand total repeal. Abortion legislation, they assert, is class legislation, imposed on women by a male-supremacist society, and deprives women of control over their bodies. They argue that women should not have to petition doctors (mostly male) to grant them as a privilege what is really a fundamental right, and that only the pregnant woman herself can know whether she is physically and emotionally prepared to bear a child.

Last Thursday, the Joint Legislative Committee on the Problems of Public Health convened in the Public Health Building, at 125 Worth Street, to hear a panel of expert witnesses—doctors, lawyers, and clergymen selected for their knowledge of medical, legal, and social problems connected with abortion—who were to comment on the law and suggest modifications. About thirty women, including City Councilman Carol Greitzer, came to the hearings to demonstrate against reform and for repeal, against more hearings and for immediate action, and against the committee's concept of expertise. "The only real experts on abortion are women," read a leaflet distributed by Women's Liberation. "Women who have known the pain, fear, and socially imposed guilt of an illegal abortion. Women who have seen their friends dead or in agony from a post-abortion infection. Women who have had children by the wrong man, at the wrong time, because no doctor would help them."[1] The demonstrators, about half of them young women and half middle-aged housewives and professionals, picketed outside the building until the proceedings began, at 10 a.m. Then they filed into the hearing room. The eight members of the Joint Committee—all male— were lined up on a platform facing the audience. The chairman, State Senator Norman F. Lent, announced that the purpose of the meeting was not to hear public opinion but, rather, to hear testimony from "experts familiar with the psychological and sociological facts." Of the fifteen witnesses listed on the agenda, fourteen were men; the lone woman was a nun.

The first witness, the chairman of the Governor's commission on abortion reform, began enumerating the commission's recommendations. Suddenly, a young, neatly dressed woman seated near the front stood up. "OK, folks," she said. "Now it's time to hear from the real experts. I don't mean the public opinion you're so uninterested in. I mean concrete evidence from the people who really know—women. I can tell you the psychological and sociological effect the law has had on *me*—it's made me *angry*! It's made me think about things like forcing doctors to operate at gunpoint."

It took several minutes for Senator Lent to collect himself and try to restore order. By that time, several other women were on their feet, shouting.

"Where are the women on your panel?" one woman said.

"I had an abortion when I was seventeen. You don't know what that's like," another said.

"Men don't get pregnant. Men don't rear children. They just make the laws," said a third.

Senator Lent began, "If you girls can organize yourselves and select a spokesman—"

"We don't want a spokesman! We all want to testify!" a woman cried.

"But wait a minute, dear—" the Senator began.

"Don't call me 'dear'! Would you call a black person 'boy'?" the woman shouted.

The committee quickly adjourned the hearing and announced that there would be a closed executive session in an upstairs room.

Senator Seymour Thaler, who has been long associated with hospital reform, and who is himself a proponent of the Cook bill, was furious with the women. "What have you accomplished?" he called out. "There are people here who want to do something for you!"

"We're tired of being done for! We want to *do,* for a change!" one of the women replied.

Upstairs, police barred the door and the women stood outside shouting. "We are the experts!" Women's Liberation sent in a formal request to testify, and the committee replied that two women might speak after the other witnesses had finished. The women were not satisfied ("It's a back-of-the-bus compromise!" "They just want to stall us till the newspapermen go home!"), but half a dozen members of Women's Liberation decided to stick it out. All of them were under thirty, and half were married. Two had had illegal abortions; one had had a child and given it up for adoption; one had a friend who had nearly died because she hesitated to go to the hospital after a badly done seven-hundred-dollar operation.

As it turned out, the women waited for seven hours, sitting on the floor in the corridor, because the authorities, afraid of further disruption, would not let them into the hearing room. Finally, three women were permitted to speak. They talked about their experiences and demanded a public hearing that would be devoted entirely to the expert testimony of women.

The legislators would not agree to this. "Why do you assume we're against you?" one senator asked. "Four of the witnesses were for repeal. They said the same things you've been saying."

"There's a political problem you're overlooking," said the last of the women to speak. "In this society, there is an imbalance in power between men and women, just as there is between whites and blacks. You and your experts may have the right ideas, but you're still men talking to each other. *We* want to be consulted. Even if we accepted your definition of an expert—and we don't— couldn't you find any female doctors or lawyers?"

"I agree with you about the law," Senator Thaler said. "But you're just acting out your personal pique against men."

"Not personal pique—*political grievance!*" the final speaker replied.

"All I can say," Senator Thaler declared, in conclusion, "is that you're the rudest bunch of people I've ever met."

The meeting broke up, and everyone began drifting out. "Well, we're probably the first women ever to talk about our abortions in public," one woman said. "That's something, anyway."

The New Yorker, February 1969

NOTE

1. [*Editor's note*: As revealed in "Up from Radicalism," Willis is actually quoting from her leaflet—a clever way to slip in her own convictions about abortions in an ostensibly reported piece.]

The Seventies
Exile on Main Street

INTRODUCTION
Irin Carmon

The world had changed only so much for her. The world has changed only so much for us.

Reading the Ellen Willis of the seventies feels too painfully like having our latter-day lives described. Such are the spasms of a revolution, which doesn't necessarily happen in linear fashion, which sometimes goes backward before it goes forward, and which requires all too much work in between.

Willis, for whom the seventies are in part a hangover from the instantly mythologized sixties, doesn't shrink from living in her time, even when it offers cruel backlash, and even when her own desires and doubts defy her ideals. "The worst insult you could throw at those of us who had been formed by the sixties was to imply that we were living in the past; not to be totally wired into the immediate moment meant getting old, which we hoped we would die before," she writes in "Beginning to See the Light."

Signs of the incomplete work of liberation were and are everywhere. Women were having sex with fewer consequences but with the lingering side effects of inequality, where "freedom for women is defined solely as sexual freedom, which in practice means availability on men's terms." Willis hears it in the music she loves, diagnosing the precise contradiction of liberatory yet misogynistic music: "Male performers perpetuated the mythology that made women the symbol of middle-class respectability and kicked over the pedestal without asking who had invented it in the first place." Janis Joplin, she realizes, "sang out of her pain as a woman, and men dug it. Yet it was men who caused the pain, and if they stopped causing it, they would not have her to dig." The temptation is to blame sex and culture, rather than the power structure that still informs them, a temptation Willis resists.

Retreat—from pop culture, from sex, from bodily autonomy—is not an option. She rejects separatism and also, implicitly, essentialism: "For me feminism meant confronting men and male power and demanding that women be free to be themselves everywhere, not just in a voluntary ghetto." That means refusing to apologize or equivocate, as in the terrifyingly relevant "Abortion: Is a Woman a Person?" Willis lays out her case against forced pregnancy and asserts, "In 1979 it is depressing to have to insist that sex is not an unnecessary, morally dubious self-indulgence but a basic human need, no less for women than for men." (It's depressing in 2014, too.) But it never means the abdication of self-criticism—of herself, of the movement, of the female-led forays into pop culture that left her cold—and it does mean hurtling honestly into the unknown, as in the religious odyssey of "Next Year in Jerusalem."

Desire, and ultimately sexual freedom, in Willis's utopia, is not about decadence or novel ways to organize the same exhausted battles; it comes with a responsibility for justice and self-knowledge. In the meantime, there is backlash and imperfect middle ways, and there is porn. A fierce civil libertarian, Willis was mostly unwilling to allow her visceral critique of pornography to triumph over her commitment to free speech—and the prescient suspicion that what would be wielded against obscenity would also be wielded against liberation.

"I imagine that in utopia, porn would wither away along with the state, heroin, and Coca-Cola," she writes. In the meantime, we have the desire and the unfinished work. And her writing to make sense of it all.

IRIN CARMON is a national reporter for MSNBC.com, where she covers gender and politics, and a visiting fellow at the Yale Law School's Program for the Study of Reproductive Justice.

Beginning to See the Light

On November 7, I admitted I was turned on by the Sex Pistols. That morning I had gone from my shrink to my office and found that a friend who takes an interest in my musical welfare had sent me a package of British punk singles and albums. He had been urging me to listen to the stuff, and I had been resisting; I was skeptical about punk, in both its British and American versions. The revolt against musical and social pretension, the attempts to pare rock to its essentials, the New York bands' Velvetesque ironic distance had a certain déjà vu quality: wasn't all that happening five years ago? When I had first heard "God Save the Queen" on the radio, my main reaction had been, "They sound like Mott the Hoople—what's the big deal?" And the Ramones bored me; I felt they were not only distanced but distant, apologists for coldness as a worldview. I had dutifully gone to see them at CBGB's and bought their first album, hoping to be interested in what they were trying to do, but duty goes only so far. I was also put off by the heavy overlay of misogyny in the punk stance.

In October I had gone to an art show opening in Queens and had run into another punk evangelist, Bob Christgau. He argued that people who put down the punk bands as "fascist" were really objecting to their lack of gentility. The English bands, he said, were overtly antifascist, and after all it was in England that fascism was a serious threat, not here. I wasn't so sure, I said, either that fascism wasn't a threat here or that the punk rockers were incapable of flirting with it.

I wasn't referring to the swastikas or sadomasochistic regalia that some punk bands affected to prove they were shocking, though I felt that to use Nazi symbolism for any purpose was both stupid and vicious. I meant that sexism combined with anger was always potentially fascistic, for when you stripped the gentility from the relations between the sexes, what too often remained was male power in its most brutal form. And given the present political atmosphere, that potential was worrisome. The American right was on the move; the backlash against feminism was particularly ominous. Jimmy Carter, with his opposition to abortion, his fundamentalist religion, and his glorification of the traditional (i.e., male-dominated) family, was encouraging cultural reaction in a way that was all the more difficult to combat because he was a Democrat and supposedly a populist. Closer to home, I found it deeply disturbing that so many liberal and leftist men I knew considered Mario Cuomo[1] some sort of working-class hero— that they were at best willing to ignore, at worst secretly attracted to, Cuomo's antifeminist attitudes. The punk rockers were scarcely defenders of the family, or of tradition, but like pseudopopulist politicians they tended to equate championing the common man with promoting the oppression of women. That the equation was as inherently contradictory as "national socialist" was unlikely to deter men from embracing it.

The following week I went hiking in the Blue Ridge Mountains. At the inn where I was staying I took a lot of more or less friendly kidding about being from New York, to which I responded with more or less friendly defensiveness; no, there had been no looting in my neighborhood during the blackout, and yes, I walked around at night by myself. Back in the city, in the early morning, my clock radio clicked on to wake me up. I lay in bed drifting. The deejay delivered a commercial about a *Voice* article on punk rock: "A cult explodes and a movement is born!" Then came the news: the West German commandos had made their triumphant raid on the terrorists at Mogadishu. I lay in bed confused. Were the punk rockers the terrorists or the raiders?

Some friends of mine were giving a Halloween costume party. I decided to go as a punk. I wore a black T-shirt that read in yellow letters "Anarchy in Queens" (I would love to be able to say I found it somewhere, but in fact I had it made up), a huge safety-pin earring, pasty white makeup, green food coloring on my teeth, and fake vomit that I had bought in a magicians' supply store.

Around the same time I was beginning to emerge from a confusing and depressing period in my life. I had a problem I needed to face, a painful and scary choice to make, and I had been refusing to think about it. In such circumstances, music was my enemy. It had a way of foiling my attempts at evasion; when I was least prepared, some line or riff or vocal nuance would invariably confront me with whatever I was struggling to repress. And so I had simply stopped listening. I told myself that the trouble was I was tired of old music, and there was no new music that excited me. I wondered if I were coming to the end of an era—was rock and roll no longer going to be important in my life?

Then I gave up trying to censor my thoughts. Immediately there were plenty of records I needed to hear: *Blood on the Tracks*; *Loaded*; *Heat Treatment* and *Howlin' Wind*; *Astral Weeks*; *Exile on Main St.*; *The Bessie Smith Story, Volume 4*, which includes "Send Me to the 'Lectric Chair" and "Empty Bed Blues." I realized with a shock that although I'd listened to "Send Me to the 'Lectric Chair" hundreds of times over the years, I had never really heard it before. It was a fierce, frightening song: a woman described how she had killed her lover, reeling off the brutally graphic details with almost casual defiance, saying in effect, "I lost my temper and I blew it and I'm sorry now but it's too late so fuck it." Bessie had concentrated more intensity in that one song than Janis Joplin had achieved in her whole career. I played it over and over.

And now I had all these punk-rock records, by the Sex Pistols, the Clash, Slaughter and the Dogs, the Unwanted, Wire, the Adverts, Johnny Moped, Eater, X-Ray Spex, the Buzzcocks, Chelsea, the Rezillos. I liked them; they made most of what passed for rock these days sound not only genteel but out of focus. And I was knocked out by the Sex Pistols. How could I have denied that they had a distinctive sound? I knew I might react differently if I saw them live, or if I could hear more than about 1 percent of their lyrics, but for the moment—as had so often happened in the past—my conceptual reservations were overwhelmed by the immediate, angry force of the music. WE DON'T CARE!— but they cared about not caring.

Later I listened to my Ramones album and found that it moved me more than it had before. It seemed that the British had done it again—beamed my culture back at me in a way that gave it new resonances. The last time (when "swinging London" was prosperous and euphoric) they had done this by achieving an aesthetic distance—based on their detachment from America's racial history— that was also a kind of innocence. This time (when England was in deep economic and political trouble) they were doing it by ignoring—or more precisely smashing—the distance the American punk bands had taken uninnocent pains to achieve. It was not that groups like the Sex Pistols and the Clash had no irony of their own, that their punk persona was not a calculated creation. But the passion with which they acted out that persona reflected England's unambiguously awful situation; the Ramones were stuck with the American dilemma, which is that the system is bad enough to piss us off, and not bad enough so that we can make up our minds what to do about it.

Months before my capitulation to the Sex Pistols I was talking to an editor and we got on the subject of pop music. I said that I still felt involved with the increasingly distinct subgenre of contemporary rock and roll, but there wasn't that much of it around, and what there was was often disappointing. The editor asked what sort of music I was talking about. "Well, the bands that play CBGB's . . . Graham Parker . . . Springsteen . . ." "Patti Smith?" "Yes." The editor shook her head. "All these people," she said, "are still caught up in the past, in the myth of the sixties." "I disagree," I said, feeling a bit prickly because I'd had this argument before. "It's just that they *acknowledge* the sixties, instead of trying to pretend all that stuff never happened."

The argument bothered me. Talk about irony: the worst insult you could throw at those of us who had been formed by the sixties was to imply that we were living in the past; not to be totally wired into the immediate moment meant getting old, which we hoped we would die before. The thing was, I really felt not guilty. In the past couple of years, especially, the sixties had seemed very distant to me. When I thought of the person I had been in 1967, or even 1970, she was almost as much of a stranger as my college-student self. I rarely played music that had been popular in the sixties; most of it lacked a certain dour edge that felt necessary in this crabbed decade. It was nevertheless true that many of my favorite records had been made by veterans of the sixties, just as it was true that I was still interested in my past, felt a continuing need to understand and absorb it. Was this need regressive?

I had once raised the question in a letter to Greil Marcus, and he had replied:

> Well, we're caught in our own trap. We promoted and got across a myth of the '60s and now we're paying for it—having it thrown back on us as some sort of strange aberration that we all caught a disease from—i.e., it wasn't a real era, wherein real things happened, it was some giant anomaly. Well, it can seem like that, because so much of such intensity happened so fast. . . . more happened in rock and roll in six months of '65 than in all of the '70s. . . . More happened politically in 1968—in terms of stuff we will live with and think about all our lives with great emotion and puzzlement—than since. Etc.

That was part of the problem—too much had happened to assimilate all at once. Culturally and politically, the seventies had been at best dull, at worst grim, yet for me the retreat into work and introspection had its positive side; it was a chance to consolidate what I'd learned, live down some of the egregious silliness I'd been party to. How else was I to figure out where I was heading? Feminism, drugs, Vietnam, the flowering of pop culture had changed me. They were no longer "the sixties"; they were part of my luggage.

Yet what was finally most insidious about the whole "You're caught in the myth of the sixties" business was not its denial that the sixties were real—and therefore consequential—as well as mythical, but its use of *the sixties* as a dismissive label with which to quarantine certain ideas and attitudes. What, for instance, did it really mean to relegate Patti Smith or the Ramones to the sixties? True, seventies rock and roll had roots in the sixties, but then so did disco, which editors and other cultural arbiters agreed was quintessential seventies music: the original disco audience—middle-class blacks who retained a black cultural identity rather than imitating whites—had been created by the civil rights movement and black nationalism. The difference was that rock and roll, as a musical language, was always on some level about rebellion, freedom, and the expression of emotion, while disco was about cooling out as you move up, about stylizing and containing emotion.[2] I knew I was supposed to consider the first set of concerns as outdated as the miniskirt. Yet owing to the parlous state of New York's economy, I was, for the first time ever, somewhat downwardly mobile; I aspired to have less control over my feelings, not more; liberation was still a potent idea for me, not because I was clinging to the utopian sixties but because I was still oppressed as a woman—and still angry about it—in the conservative seventies. In short, though I had nothing against disco, rock and roll had a lot more to do with my life. And I couldn't help suspecting that "You're still living in the sixties" was often nothing more than code for "You refuse to admit that what really matters to you is to stake out a comfortable position in the upper middle class." Well, not only did I refuse to admit that: I didn't even think it was true.

I was grappling with my uncensored thoughts, finding them no less scary and painful, the night I went to see Ms. Clawdy at the Women's Coffee House. Ms. Clawdy is a singer-songwriter from Oakland. In the early seventies she managed and wrote songs for an all-female rock-and-roll band called Eyes; later she sang with another women's band, Rosie and the Riveters; now she performs alone, accompanying herself on the piano. She has a local following, particularly though not exclusively in the San Francisco Bay Area's lesbian/feminist/alternative-women's-culture community, but she is unknown outside California. I've rooted for Ms. Clawdy for years, not only because she is good but because of what she is good at. Her music successfully combines two of my main passions: feminism and rock and roll. The Women's Coffee House gig was her first performance in New York, and to see it I had passed up Graham Parker at the Palladium.

For those of us who crave music by women who will break out of traditional molds, write and sing honestly about their (and our) experience, and create art so powerful that men and the society in general will have to come to terms with it whether they want to or not, the seventies have offered scant comfort. Though many women performers give me pleasure, few have touched those specifically feminist yearnings. There is the Joy of Cooking, whose music endures but whose lyrics seem dated and sentimental now; Joni Mitchell's *Blue,* ditto; some of Yoko Ono's stuff; great songs here and there like Helen Reddy's "Summer of '71," Carly Simon's "You're So Vain," Patti Smith's "Redondo Beach" . . . give me an hour and I'll think of a dozen more examples, but that only proves my point.

As a woman who has made a significant contribution to what I've called contemporary rock and roll, Patti Smith stands alone. Her best songs are as good as any in rock and roll, and she is capable of an electrifying live performance. But she is erratic; in concerts she has a habit of generating enormous energy, then diffusing it with rambling, pointless raps. I've always wondered if she were afraid of her considerable power. I'm also uncomfortable with her androgynous, one-of-the-guys image; its rebelliousness is seductive, but it plays into a kind of misogyny—endemic to bohemian circles and, no doubt, to the punk-rock scene—that consents to distinguish a woman who acts like one of the guys (and is also sexy and conspicuously "liberated") from the general run of stupid girls.

So Patti Smith may be a rock-and-roll hero, but she is not quite a feminist heroine. Ms. Clawdy, on the other hand . . . I watched her with an avidity that came from discovering someone who was distinctively herself yet fit my generic fantasy. Her style was at once functional and matter-of-factly sensual; her plump, womanly body was encased in red mechanic's overalls. She was funny, ironic, passionate, self-deprecating without being masochistic, vulnerable without being pathetic, and political in the best sense—that is, willing to tell the truth about the conditions of her life. I enjoyed her funny songs—especially a discourse on compulsive eating called "Ice Cream Cone"—but I liked her best at her most serious. Of her newest songs the one that most compelled me was "The Dark Side," which she introduced by noting that Chairman Mao had urged revolutionary artists to emphasize the bright side of life and that she hadn't followed his advice. But my favorite was still her signature song, "Night Blindness." Whenever she sang it I heard something new. This time, the lines that got to me were "We all need love, it's worth any price you pay / That's what my mother said, and she lives alone today."

I had gone to the show with a woman friend, and afterward we were so high that we ran down the street, shouted, and hugged. Some weeks later, I had dinner with Ms. Clawdy, aka Ella Hirst, and we talked about the possibilities for an alternative women's culture. I had once been attracted to the idea but had long since become convinced that it was unworkable and even reactionary. It was, I believed, inseparable both in theory and in practice from political ideas I had rejected: that sexual and cultural separatism were a solution to the oppression of women or an effective strategy for ending that oppression. For me feminism meant confronting men and male power and demanding that women be free to be themselves everywhere, not just in a voluntary ghetto. Separatists argued that a consistent feminist had to break all sexual and emotional ties with men, yet it seemed to me that not to need men for sex or love could as easily blunt one's rage and pain and therefore one's militance; I also had the feeling that there was a lot of denial floating around the separatist community—denial that breaking with men did not solve everything, that even between women love had its inescapable problems. I suspected that a culture based on separatist assumptions was unlikely to be angry enough, or truthful enough, to be revolutionary.

I had arrived at these conclusions not by thinking about the issue abstractly, but by trying to answer a specific question: why did I like so little of the women's-culture music I had heard? The feminist music scene had two main tendencies. One was a women's version of political folk music, which replicated all the virtues (simplicity, intimacy, community) and all the faults (sentimentality, insularity, heavy rhetoric) of the genre. Some of it was fun to listen to, but the idiom was too well worn to promise anything exciting or original. The other tendency actively turned me off: it was a slick, technically accomplished, rock-influenced but basically conventional pop. I believed that this music could be a commercial success; supposedly the product of a dissident culture, it struck me as altogether compatible with the MOR blandness of most white pop music.

What disturbed me most about both brands of women's-culture music was that so much of it was so conventionally feminine. Years ago Ella Hirst had told me that she thought most female performers did not have a direct line to their emotions, the way men did—they were too busy trying to please. It seemed to me that too many of the women's-culture people had merely switched from trying to please men to trying to please other women.

A couple of years ago I had gone to see the feminist folk-rock group the Deadly Nightshade at a lesbian bar in Boston. They sang "Honky Tonk Women" with rewritten, nonsexist lyrics. Someone in the audience sent them an outraged note, attacking them for singing an antiwoman song. The lead singer read the note aloud and nervously and defensively complained that the writer hadn't been listening. The incident had helped me understand why I wasn't enthusiastic about the group. They did not have the confidence, or the arrogance, to say or feel "If you don't like it, tough shit." It was not that I thought performers should be indifferent to the response of their audience. I just thought that the question they ought to ask was not "How can I make them like me?" but "How can I make them hear me?"

Ella protested that I was harder on these women, who were at least trying to create an alternative system of values, than on traditional female performers. She had a point. Why did the Deadly Nightshade's wimpiness bother me more than Linda Ronstadt's sex-kitten routine? For the same reason, probably, that the radical left's offenses against women always incensed me more than everyone else's.

But rock and roll, as always, posed a more troublesome paradox. Listening to the Sex Pistols, trying to figure out if "Bodies" was really an antiabortion song, I discovered that it was something even worse. It was an outburst of loathing for human physicality, a loathing projected onto women because they have babies and abortions and are "a fucking bloody mess," but finally recoiling against the singer himself: "I'm not an animal!" he bellowed in useless protest, his own animal sounds giving him the lie. It was an outrageous song, yet I could not simply dismiss it with outrage. The extremity of its disgust forced me to admit that I was no stranger to such feelings—though unlike Johnny Rotten I recognized that the disgust, not the body, was the enemy. And there lay the paradox: music that boldly and aggressively laid out what the singer wanted, loved, hated—as good rock and roll did—challenged me to do the same, and so, even when the content was antiwoman, antisexual, in a sense antihuman, the form encouraged my struggle for liberation. Similarly, timid music made me feel timid, whatever its ostensible politics. What I loved most about Ms. Clawdy was that I could have liberating form and content both; I could respond as a whole person. Listening to most rock and roll was like walking down the street at night, automatically checking out the men in my vicinity: this one's okay; that one could be trouble, watch out. Listening to most feminist music was like taking a warm bath. Ms. Clawdy did not make me wary—but that didn't mean she let me relax.

The other day, I was sitting on a bench in front of the laundromat on my corner. While I waited for my wash, I thought about the choice I still had to make. For some reason I happened to glance upward, and my eyes hit a stop sign. I laughed; if my life had to be a series of metaphors, I ought to pick some better ones. Like, say, the last verse of "Night Blindness": "I never thought that anyone would know me like you do. / If I let you make me happy you could make me unhappy too. / I told my friend, she said she knows just how I feel / But I have to take a chance and find out if it's real."

Village Voice, 1977

NOTES

1. A candidate for mayor of New York in 1997.

2. While this is all true as far as it goes, it is a bit beside the point. Despite its base in minority subcultures (black and gay), disco is a mass cultural phenomenon and so inevitably embodies the spirit of the times in a more immediate and central way than rock and roll, which has become a somewhat abstracted comment on itself and (like jazz in the fifties) an essentially bohemian taste. In any case, seventies rock and roll is obsessed with its formal tradition, a concern that links it to the past in a special way. Finally, there are distinctions to be made: Bruce Springsteen is far more tied into the sixties than the punk and new wave bands. (For elucidation of these last two points, see my essay from *Stranded* on the Velvet Underground.)

Janis Joplin

Janis Joplin was born in 1943 and grew up in Port Arthur, Texas. She began singing in bars and coffeehouses, first locally, then in Austin, where she spent most of a year at the University of Texas. In 1966 she went to San Francisco and got together with a rock band in search of a singer, Big Brother and the Holding Company. The following summer Big Brother performed at the Monterey Pop Festival; Janis got raves from the fans and the critics and from then on she was a star. *Cheap Thrills,* Big Brother's first major album (there had been an early record on a small-time label), came out in July 1968. By then there were tensions between Janis and the group, and she left soon afterward.

With her new backup band she made another album, *I Got Dem Ol' Kozmic Blues Again MaMa!* But the band never quite gelled, and in the spring of 1970 Janis formed another, Full-Tilt Boogie. They spent most of the summer touring, then went to Los Angeles to record an album, *Pearl.* It was Janis's last. On October 4th, 1970, she died of an overdose of heroin.

The hippie rock stars of the late sixties merged two versions of that hardy American myth, the free individual. They were stars, which meant achieving liberation by becoming rich and famous *on their own terms*; and they were, or purported to be, apostles of cultural revolution, a considerably more ambitious and romantic vision of freedom that nevertheless had a similar economic foundation. Young Americans were in a sense the stars of the world, drawing on an overblown prosperity that could afford to indulge all manner of rebellious and experimental behavior. The combination was inherently unstable—Whitman's open road is not, finally, the Hollywood Freeway, and in any case neither stardom nor prosperity could deliver what they seemed to promise. For a fragile historical moment rock transcended those contradictions; in its aftermath our pop heroes found themselves grappling, like the rest of us, with what are probably enduring changes in the white American consciousness—changes that have to do with something very like an awareness of tragedy. It is in this context that Janis Joplin developed as an artist, a celebrity, a rebel, a woman, and it is in this context that she died.

Joplin belonged to that select group of pop figures who mattered as much for themselves as for their music; among American rock performers she was second only to Bob Dylan in importance as a creator/recorder/embodiment of her generation's history and mythology. She was also the only woman to achieve that kind of stature in what was basically a male club, the only sixties culture hero to make visible and public women's experience of the quest for individual liberation, which was very different from men's. If Janis's favorite metaphors—singing as fucking (a first principle of rock and roll) and fucking as liberation (a first principle of the cultural revolution)—were equally approved by her male peers, the congruence was only on the surface. Underneath—just barely—lurked a feminist (or prefeminist) paradox.

The male-dominated counterculture defined freedom for women almost exclusively in sexual terms. As a result, women endowed the idea of sexual liberation with immense symbolic importance; it became charged with all the secret energy of an as yet suppressed larger rebellion. Yet to express one's rebellion in that limited way was a painfully literal form of submission. Whether or not Janis understood that, her dual persona—lusty hedonist and suffering victim—suggested that she felt it. Dope, another term in her metaphorical equation (getting high as singing as fucking as liberation) was, in its more sinister aspect, a painkiller and finally a killer. Which is not to say that the good times weren't real, as far as they went. Whatever the limitations of hippie rock star life, it was better than being a provincial matron—or a lonely weirdo.

For Janis, as for others of us who suffered the worst fate that can befall an adolescent girl in America—*unpopularity*—a crucial aspect of the cultural revolution was its assault on the rigid sexual styles of the fifties. Joplin's metamorphosis from the ugly duckling of Port Arthur to the peacock of Haight-Ashbury meant, among other things, that a woman who was not conventionally pretty, who had acne and an intermittent weight problem and hair that stuck out, could not only invent her own beauty (just as she invented her wonderful sleazofreak costumes) out of sheer energy, soul, sweetness, arrogance, and a sense of humor, but have that beauty appreciated. Not that Janis merely took advantage of changes in our notions of attractiveness; she herself changed them. It was seeing Janis Joplin that made me resolve, once and for all, not to get my hair straightened. And there was a direct line from that sort of response to those apocryphal burned bras and all that followed.

Direct, but not simple. Janis once crowed, "They're paying me $50,000 a year to be like me." But the truth was that they were paying her to be a personality, and the relation of public personality to private self—something every popular artist has to work out—is especially problematic for a woman. Men are used to playing roles and projecting images in order to compete and succeed. Male celebrities tend to identify with their mask making, to see it as creative and—more or less—to control it. In contrast, women need images simply to survive. A woman is usually aware, on some level, that men do not allow her to be her "real self," and worse, that the acceptable masks represent men's fantasies, not her own. She can choose the most interesting image available, present it dramatically, individualize it with small elaborations, undercut it with irony. But ultimately she must serve some male fantasy to be loved—and then it will be only the fantasy that is loved anyway. The female celebrity is confronted with this dilemma in its starkest form. Joplin's revolt against conventional femininity was brave and imaginative, but it also dovetailed with a stereotype—the ballsy, one-of-the-guys chick who is a needy, vulnerable cream puff underneath—cherished by her legions of hip male fans. It may be that she could have pushed beyond it and taken the audience with her; that was one of the possibilities that made her death an artistic as well as human calamity. There is, for instance, the question of her bisexuality. People who knew Janis differ on whether sexual relationships with women were an important part of her life, and I don't know the facts. In any case, a public acknowledgment of bisexual proclivities would not necessarily have contradicted her image; it could easily have been passed off as more pull-out-the-stops hedonism or another manifestation of her all-encompassing need for love. On the other hand, she could have used it to say something new about women and liberation. What makes me wonder is something I always noticed and liked about Janis: unlike most female performers whose act is intensely erotic, she never made me feel as if I were crashing an orgy that consisted of her and the men in the audience. When she got it on at a concert, she got it on with everybody.

Still, the songs she sang assumed heterosexual romance; it was men who made her hurt, who took another little piece of her heart. Watching men groove on Janis, I began to appreciate the resentment many black people feel toward whites who are blues freaks. Janis sang out of her pain as a woman, and men dug it. Yet it was men who caused the pain, and if they stopped causing it they would not have her to dig. In a way, their adulation was the cruelest insult of all. And Janis's response—to sing harder, get higher, be worshiped more—was rebellious, acquiescent, bewildered all at once. When she said, "Onstage I make love to 25,000 people, then I go home alone," she was not merely repeating the cliché of the sad clown or the poor little rich girl. She was noting that the more she gave the less she got and that, honey, it ain't fair.

Like most women singers, Joplin did not write many songs; she mostly interpreted other people's. But she made them her own in a way few singers dare to do. She did not sing them so much as struggle with them, assault them. Some critics complained, not always unfairly, that she strangled them to death, but at her best she whipped them to new life. She had an analogous adversary relationship with the musical form that dominated her imagination, the blues. Blues represented another external structure, one with its own contradictory tradition of sexual affirmation and sexist conservatism. But Janis used blues conventions to reject blues sensibility. To sing the blues is a way of transcending pain by confronting it with dignity, but Janis wanted nothing less than to scream it out of existence. Big Mama Thornton's classic rendition of "Ball and Chain" carefully balances defiance and resignation, toughness and vulnerability. She almost pities her oppressor. Her singing conveys, above all, her determination to survive abuse. Janis makes the song into one long frenzied, despairing protest. Why, why, *why,* she asks over and over, like a child unable to comprehend injustice. The pain is overwhelming her. There are similar differences between her recording of "Piece of My Heart" and Erma Franklin's. When Franklin sings it, it is a challenge: no matter what you do to me, I will not let you destroy my ability to be human, to love. Joplin seems rather to be saying, surely if I keep taking this, if I keep setting an example of love and forgiveness, surely he has to understand, change, give me back what I have given.

Her pursuit of pleasure had the same driven quality; what it amounted to was refusal to admit of any limits that would not finally yield to the virtue of persistence—*try just a little bit harder*—and the magic of extremes. This war against limits was largely responsible for the electrifying power of Joplin's early performances; it was what made *Cheap Thrills* a classic, in spite of unevenness and the impossibility of duplicating on a record the excitement of her concerts. After the split with Big Brother, Janis retrenched considerably, perhaps because she simply couldn't maintain that level of intensity, perhaps for other reasons that would have become clear if she had lived. My uncertainty on this point makes me hesitate to be too dogmatic about my conviction that leaving Big Brother was a mistake.

I was a Big Brother fan. I thought they were better musicians than their detractors claimed, but more to the point, technical accomplishment in itself was not something I cared about. I thought it was an ominous sign that so many people did care, including Janis. It was, in fact, a sign that the tenuous alliance between mass culture and bohemianism—or, in my original formulation, the fantasy of stardom and the fantasy of cultural revolution—was breaking down. But the breakdown was not as neat as it might appear. For the elitist concept of "good musicianship" was as alien to the holistic, egalitarian spirit of rock and roll as the act of leaving one's group the better to pursue one's individual ambition was alien to the holistic, egalitarian pretensions of the cultural revolutionaries. If Joplin's decision to go it alone was influenced by all the obvious professional/commercial pressures, it also reflected a conflict of values within the counterculture itself—a conflict that foreshadowed its imminent disintegration. And again, Janis's femaleness complicated the issues, raised the stakes. She had less room to maneuver than a man in her position, fewer alternatives to fall back on if she blew it. If she had to choose between fantasies, it made sense for her to go with stardom as far as it would take her.

But I wonder if she really had to choose, if her choice was not in some sense a failure of nerve and therefore of greatness. Janis was afraid Big Brother would hold her back, but if she had thought it was important enough, she might have been able to carry them along, make them transcend their limitations. There is more than a semantic difference between a group and a backup band. Janis had to relate to the members of Big Brother as spiritual (not to mention financial) equals even though she had more talent than they, and I can't help suspecting that that was good for her not only emotionally and socially but aesthetically. Committed to the hippie ethic of music-for-the-hell-of-it—if only because there was no possibility of their becoming stars on their own—Big Brother helped Janis sustain the amateur quality that was an integral part of her effect. Their zaniness was a salutary reminder that good times meant silly fun—remember "Caterpillar"?—as well as Dionysiac abandon; it was a relief from Janis's extremism and at the same time a foil for it. At their best moments Big Brother made me think of the Beatles, who weren't (at least in the beginning) such terrific musicians either. Though I'm not quite softheaded enough to imagine that by keeping her group intact Janis Joplin could somehow have prevented or delayed the end of an era, or even saved her own life, it would have been an impressive act of faith. And acts of faith by public figures always have reverberations, one way or another.

Such speculation is of course complicated by the fact that Janis died before she really had a chance to define her post–San Francisco, post–Big Brother self. Her last two albums, like her performances with the ill-fated Kozmic Blues Band, had a tentative, transitional feel. She was obviously going through important changes; the best evidence of that was "Me and Bobby McGee," which could be considered her "Dear Landlord." Both formally—as a low-keyed, soft, folkie tune—and substantively—as a lyric that spoke of choices made, regretted, and survived, with the distinct implication that compromise could be a positive act—what it expressed would have been heresy to the Janis Joplin of *Cheap Thrills.* "Freedom's just another word for nothing left to lose" is as good an epitaph for the counterculture as any; we'll never know how—or if—Janis meant to go on from there.

Janis Joplin's death, like that of a fighter in the ring, was not exactly an accident. Yet it's too easy to label it either suicide or murder, though it involved elements of both. Call it rather an inherent risk of the game she was playing, a game whose often frivolous rules both hid and revealed a deadly serious struggle. The form that struggle took was incomplete, shortsighted, egotistical, self-destructive. But survivors who give in to the temptation to feel superior to all that are in the end no better than those who romanticize it. Janis was not so much a victim as a casualty. The difference matters.

The Rolling Stone Illustrated History of Rock 'n' Roll, 1980

Classical and Baroque Sex in Everyday Life

There are two kinds of sex, classical and baroque. Classical sex is romantic, profound, serious, emotional, moral, mysterious, spontaneous, abandoned, focused on a particular person, and stereotypically feminine. Baroque sex is pop, playful, funny, experimental, conscious, deliberate, amoral, anonymous, focused on sensation for sensation's sake, and stereotypically masculine. The classical mentality taken to an extreme is sentimental and finally puritanical; the baroque mentality taken to an extreme is pornographic and finally obscene. Ideally, a sexual relationship ought to create a satisfying tension between the two modes (a baroque idea, particularly if the tension is ironic) or else blend them so well that the distinction disappears (a classical aspiration). Love-making cannot be totally classical unless it is also totally baroque, since you can't abandon all restraints without being willing to try anything. Similarly, it is impossible to be truly baroque without allowing oneself to abandon all restraints and so attain a classical intensity. In practice, however, most people are more inclined to one mode than to the other. A very classical person will be incompatible with a very baroque person unless each can bring out the other's latent opposite side. Two people who are very one-sided in the same direction can be extremely compatible but risk missing a whole dimension of experience unless they get so deeply into one mode that it becomes the other.

Freud, the father of the sexual revolution, was a committed classicist who regarded most baroque impulses as infantile and perverse. Nevertheless, the sexual revolution, as it is usually defined, has been almost exclusively concerned with liberating those impulses from the confines of an exaggeratedly classical puritanism. The result, to my mind, has been an equally distorting cultural obsession with the baroque. Consider, for example, that quintessential expression of baroque angst (a contradiction in terms, the product of Jewish guilt; Christian guilt is classical all the way), Lenny Bruce's notorious monologue about fucking a chicken. Or, come to think of it (puns are baroque), Portnoy's adventures with liver. I mean seriously (classically, that is), is fucking chickens and livers what sex is all about?

Curiously, contemporary sexual "experts" never mention this crucial polarity. This is because they have a vested interest in what might be called establishment or middlebrow baroque—really an attempt to compromise with pro-classical traditionalists who insist that sex should be somehow worthwhile, not just fun. Thus the basic axiom of establishment baroque is that consensual sex in any form is wholesome and good for you; a subsidiary premise is that good sex depends on technical skill and is therefore an achievement. Kinsey, with his matter-of-fact statistical approach to his subject, was a pioneer of establishment baroque. Masters and Johnson belong in this category, as do all behavior therapists. The apotheosis of multiple orgasm is an establishment baroque substitute for the old-fashioned classical ideal of coming together. Real baroque sex has no ideals. Much as I hate to admit it, what I have in mind here is a sort of middlebrow baroque project—to report on the two kinds of sex in everyday life.

Time: Night is classical; so are sunrise and sunset. High noon and half an hour before dinner (or during dinner) are baroque.

Location: Outdoors is classical, except for crowded nude beaches. The back seat of a car is classical if you're a teen-ager, baroque otherwise. The shower is classical; the bathtub is baroque.

Number: Two is classical. One or three or more is baroque.

Lighting: Total darkness is ultraclassical except when it's a baroque variation. Dim lights and candlelight are classical. Floodlights and fluorescent lights are definitely baroque.

Clothing: The only truly classical outfit is nothing. Clothing evokes fantasy and fantasies are baroque. Black lace underwear is of course the classic baroque outfit. Red is baroque, as is anything see-through. Frilly white nightgowns are a baroque impulse with classical content.

Food: Eating in bed is baroque, although artichoke hearts and sour cream are more classical than potato chips and pizza. Tongues, tastes, and flavors are inherently baroque. Comparing sex with food is usually middlebrow baroque, except when a classicist, quarreling with the baroque idea that getting off is getting off no matter how you do it, points out that "Steak and hamburger may both be protein but they still taste different." Putting food anywhere but in your mouth is superbaroque.

Drugs: Wine and marijuana are classical. Cocaine and Quaaludes are baroque.

Music: Comparisons between sex and music are classical even if the music itself is baroque. Rock-and-roll is a good mixture of both sensibilities. My favorite classical sex song is Rod Stewart's "Tonight's the Night"; my favorite baroque sex song is "Starfucker." Rock-and-roll is usually more classical than disco.

Pornography: Porn is basically a baroque phenomenon. Much of it (*Hustler,* most X-rated movies) is belligerently anticlassical and therefore a form of inverted puritanism. Some of it *(Playboy)* is pure middlebrow baroque. Many porn classics (like *Fanny Hill*) have a fairly large classical element. The larger the classical element, the likelier that a piece of pornography will be judged to have redeeming social value. If it is classical enough, it stops being porn altogether and becomes art, but this is a very subjective and relative matter. *Lady Chatterley's Lover* was once considered pornographic because it used certain baroque words, but by contemporary standards it is cornball classical. (Actually, Lawrence seems to have intended a classical celebration of the joy of the baroque, and he might have pulled it off if it weren't for all that solemn phallic worship and particularly those ridiculous flowers. One thing he did accomplish, though: he made "fuck" into a classical word without sacrificing its baroque connotations.) Pornography also becomes art when it is so baroque it is classical, like *The Story of O.*

Sex manuals: *Love without Fear* is echt-classical. The *Kama Sutra* is baroque with classical trappings (all that religious overlay). *The Joy of Sex,* with its sections headed "Starters," "Main Courses," and "Sauces and Pickles," is middlebrow baroque except for its rather classical illustrations.

Devices: All technology is baroque, including contraceptives, vibrators, and air conditioning.

Sexism: Classical sexism is the mystique of yin and yang, masculine strength and feminine surrender, noble savage and earth mother, D. H. Lawrence, Norman Mailer. Baroque sexism is the objectification of women, black garter belts and six-inch heels, Larry Flynt, Helmut Newton.

Feminism: Classical feminism is a vision of total equality, the transcendence of artificial social roles, love and respect for one's partner as an individual. Baroque feminism asserts women's right to be baroque, traditionally a male prerogative; rejects preconceptions about what is natural and moral; insists that anything goes for either sex so long as it feels good.

National characters: The Italians are classical. So are the French, though they pretend otherwise. The Communist countries and Sweden are middlebrow baroque. As a rule, wildly baroque countries exist only in their conquerors' imagination. Americans have classical leanings, but the world headquarters of baroque is New York City. In Manhattan you can eat a chicken and the waiter won't even notice.

Village Voice, May 1979

Memoirs of a Non-Prom Queen

There's a book out called *Is There Life after High School?* It's a fairly silly book, maybe because the subject matter is the kind that only hurts when you think. Its thesis—that most people never get over the social triumphs or humiliations of high school—is not novel. Still, I read it with the respectful attention a serious hypochondriac accords the lowliest "dear doctor" column. I don't know about most people, but for me, forgiving my parents for real and imagined derelictions has been easy compared to forgiving myself for being a teenage reject.

Victims of high school trauma—which seems to have afflicted a dispropor-tionate number of writers, including Ralph Keyes, the author of this book—tend to embrace the ugly duckling myth of adolescent social relations: the "innies" (Keyes's term) are good-looking, athletic mediocrities who will never amount to much, while the "outies" are intelligent, sensitive, creative individuals who will do great things in an effort to make up for their early defeats. Keyes is partial to this myth. He has fun with celebrity anecdotes: Kurt Vonnegut re-ceiving a body-building course as a "gag prize" at a dance; Frank Zappa yelling "fuck you" at a cheerleader; Mike Nichols, as a nightclub comedian, insulting a fan—an erstwhile overbearing classmate turned used-car salesman. In con-trast, the ex–prom queens and kings he interviews slink through life, hiding their pasts lest someone call them "dumb jock" or "cheerleader type," perpetu-ally wondering what to do for an encore.

If only it were that simple. There may really be high schools where life ap-proximates an Archie comic, but even in the Fifties, my large (5,000 students), semisuburban (Queens, New York), heterogeneous high school was not one of them. The students' social life was fragmented along ethnic and class lines; there was no universally recognized, schoolwide social hierarchy. Being an athlete or a cheerleader or a student officer didn't mean much. Belonging to an illegal sorority or fraternity meant more, at least in some circles, but many socially active students chose not to join. The most popular kids were not necessarily the best looking or the best dressed or the most snobbish or the least studious. In retrospect, it seems to me that they were popular for much more honorable reasons. They were attuned to other people, aware of subtle social nuances. They projected an inviting sexual warmth. Far from being slavish followers of fashion, they were self-confident enough to set fashions. They suggested, initiated, led. Above all—this was their main appeal for me—they knew how to have a good time.

True, it was not particularly sophisticated enjoyment—dancing, pizza eating, hand holding in the lunchroom, the usual. I had friends—precocious intellectuals and bohemians—who were consciously alienated from what they saw as all that teenage crap. Part of me identified with them, yet I badly wanted what they rejected. Their seriousness engaged my mind, but my romantic and sexual fantasies, and my emotions generally, were obsessively fixed on the parties and dances I wasn't invited to, the boys I never dated. I suppose what says it best is that my "serious" friends hated rock & roll; I loved it.

If I can't rationalize my social ineptitude as intellectual rebellion, neither can I blame it on political consciousness. Feminism has inspired a variation of the ugly duckling myth in which high school wallflower becomes feminist heroine, suffering because she has too much integrity to suck up to boys by playing a phony feminine role. There is a tempting grain of truth in this idea. Certainly the self-absorption, anxiety and physical and social awkwardness that made me a difficult teenager were not unrelated to my ambivalent awareness of women's oppression. I couldn't charm boys because I feared and resented them and their power over my life; I couldn't be sexy because I saw sex as a mine field of conflicting, confusing rules that gave them every advantage. I had no sense of what might make me attractive, a lack I'm sure involved unconscious resistance to the game girls were supposed to play (particularly all the rigmarole surrounding clothes, hair and cosmetics); I was a clumsy dancer because I could never follow the boy's lead.

Yet ultimately this rationale misses the point. As I've learned from comparing notes with lots of women, the popular girls were in fact much more in touch with the reality of the female condition than I was. They knew exactly what they had to do for the rewards they wanted, while I did a lot of what feminist organizers call denying the awful truth. I was a bit schizy. Desperate to win the game but unwilling to learn it or even face my feelings about it, I couldn't really play, except in fantasy; paradoxically, I was consumed by it much more thoroughly than the girls who played and played well. Knowing what they wanted and how to get it, they preserved their sense of self, however compromised, while I lost mine. Which is why they were not simply better game players but genuinely more likable than I.

The ugly duckling myth is sentimental. It may soothe the memory of social rejection, but it falsifies the experience, evades its cruelty and uselessness. High school permanently damaged my self-esteem. I learned what it meant to be impotent; what it meant to be invisible. None of this improved my character, spurred my ambition, or gave me a deeper understanding of life. I know people who were popular in high school who later became serious intellectuals, radicals, artists, even journalists. I regret not being one of those people. To see my failure as morally or politically superior to their success would be to indulge in a version of the Laingian fallacy—that because a destructive society drives people crazy, there is something dishonorable about managing to stay sane.

Rolling Stone, August 1976

The Trial of Arline Hunt

Jewel's is one of a cluster of singles bars on Union Street near San Francisco's fashionable Pacific Heights district. The canopy over the door is stamped with the bar's motto, "Where Incredible Friendships Begin." At the entrance a sign warns that "blue jeans, T-shirts, collarless jerseys, tank shirts, transvestites, etc." are "taboos." The doorman wears a suit. Inside, the middlebrow, stained-glass-and-wood-paneling decor seems a perfunctory attempt to disguise the stark functionalism of the place, which is dominated by two bars, one sitdown and one standup, surrounded by lots of space. Unlike Hal's Pub across the street, Jewel's serves no food, not even coffee. A few small tables are tucked in the corners like afterthoughts. A slick rock band plays but there is rarely much room to dance. Jewel's attracts a mixed crowd—salesmen, secretaries, students, some freaks, a few blacks, an occasional young executive. The "taboos" are not strictly enforced but most patrons dress neatly, the women in pantsuits, the men in neo-mod suits or sport jackets or turtlenecks and styled hair. There are always more men and they set the tone, a compound of sexual bravado and joking belligerence. On a busy night Jewel's is so crowded that forced proximity becomes a kind of intimacy. Men overflow into the street, cruising the women who walk by.

September 18, 1974—a Wednesday—was not a busy night. It was raining and Jewel's was almost empty when two young women from the neighborhood came in and sat down at the bar. Arline Hunt and her roommate and best friend, Bobbie Richards, were both office workers in their early twenties. Arline was small and slim and had dark hair and a puckish, wry little smile. She wore a navy knit shirt with a collar and long sleeves, navy bell-bottoms, clunky shoes, a long silver chain, and dangling earrings. From a distance she gave an impression of sophistication; up close her candid, friendly face suggested a college freshman. Bobbie, dressed in jeans and a sweater, looked like a fair, even younger version of Arline. They often dropped in for a few drinks at one or another of the bars on Union Street. That night they ordered beers and chatted with the bartender.

An hour or so later, a man walked in and sat next to Arline. Fred Dumond, the thirty-two-year-old owner of an agency for temporary typists, was a familiar figure on the dating bar strip. Fred was well put together, if a bit packaged-looking—a shortish but muscular body, hair styled in a shag cut, brown leather jacket over turtleneck jersey—and he projected a kind of self-confidence some would call glib. He had a reputation for being a ladies' man; the word people used was "swinger" or sometimes, less kindly, "operator." He ordered a bottle of Schlitz and started a conversation with Bobbie while Arline was in the ladies' room. When Arline came back, Fred began to focus on her with a caustic banter that made her laugh. He joked about the way people's profiles revealed their characters—take Barbra Streisand's, for instance. He talked about a car he wanted to buy and made sarcastic jokes about his split with his wife. Arline asked him questions. They all drank more beer. Fred kept bantering and Arline continued to be amused. Around 10:30, Bobbie had to leave; she was expecting a phone call from her boyfriend. Arline got up to go with her but Bobbie told her to stay if she felt like it. Fred urged her to have another drink; he would take her home. She decided to stay awhile and told Bobbie, "I'll be home in half an hour."

It took Bobbie twenty minutes to walk back to the apartment she shared with Arline and a third woman, Joanne Kovacs. They were all close friends from high school in the semirural town of Shelton, California. Their apartment was cheerful and unpretentious, with Arline's charcoal drawings on the walls and *Cosmo* and *Mademoiselle* on the coffee table and beer in the refrigerator and a cat named Minestrone and Bobbie's tropical fish tank.

Bobbie received her phone call and went to bed. She was not, she recalls, at all worried about Arline. "It never occurred to me that there might be anything wrong. Fred seemed like a nice guy, friendly, even though I wasn't too impressed with him. He wasn't really our type of person. He made me think of a high-school greaser who had grown up and gotten neat clothes and a haircut. I didn't get the feeling that Arline was interested in him or that he was coming on strong to her. She was just enjoying a nice conversation. She likes to draw people out, to joke around with people. She is a very compassionate person and he was telling her about his problems. Later she told me, 'He looked sad, I thought he was lonely.' It was nothing unusual for her."

But then, around 3:00 a.m., the telephone rang again, waking Bobbie up. It was Arline. "Bobbie," she said, "I have just been raped." Bobbie heard a man's voice in the background yell, "That's a hell of a thing to say!" She heard Arline reply, "That's a hell of a thing to do!"

"I could tell she was really upset. I was really frightened—you know how you always have visions of murder. I said, 'Arline, where are you?' She said,

'Somewhere on Geary.' I asked her, 'Are you okay?' She whispered, 'I don't know, I'm scared, Bobbie, I think he's sick.' I know her, I knew she was petrified. I told her, which was asinine, 'Try to find out where you are.' So she said to him, 'What's this address?' and the phone went bang. From the way the guy hung up I thought, If Arline gets out of there alive, she's lucky. I woke Joanne and told her Arline was in trouble and then I called the police. They said they'd do what they could, but Geary was an awfully long road."

Bobbie and Joanne turned out the lights and sat by the kitchen window with a flashlight. They thought Fred might take Arline home; if they spotted him, they would call the police again. They sat and waited.

Number 2211 Geary Boulevard is part of a huge, bleak beehive of a luxury apartment complex owned by the Christian Science Church. Fred Dumond lived on the twelfth floor in apartment 1209. His next door neighbors, in apartment 1210, were John and Maureen Hollis, a solidly middle-American married couple in their fifties, the parents of grown children. Both of them worked as administrators in the church.

On September 18 the Hollises went to bed, as usual, at 10:00 p.m. Around 2:30 they woke up to the sounds of a woman screaming, which they later described as "terrifying" and "blood-curdling." "It was screaming at the top of the voice saying, 'Help me, please help me,'" said John Hollis. "I jumped out of bed," his wife recalled. "The phone was on my side of the bed and I called security and I said, 'I think there's a murder being committed.'" At first, dazed and sleepy, she couldn't tell where the sounds were coming from; they simply filled the room. But then she was sure: they were coming from next door, through the common wall that separated the bedroom of apartment 1209 from her own. She could also hear bumping noises and a man's voice. "I couldn't stand it. I went into the living room and I could still hear them in there. I was just terrified."

The screams continued—they went on, intermittently, for fifteen or twenty minutes altogether—and when there was no response from the building's security office, John Hollis made a second urgent call. Then he got dressed and went outside to see if there were lights in the windows of any of the apartments near his. He stood in front of the building and peered upward. There was a light in the bedroom of apartment 1209. He turned and saw a young woman standing about ten feet away.

"I've been raped," she said.

He took her to the security office, where the guards finally called the police.

When patrolman Martin Atkins and his partner, Robert Mitchell, arrived at 2211 Geary, Arline was laughing hysterically. "It's a nervous reaction," she apologized. "You can check with my psychiatrist." The two policemen questioned her, called for another radio car to take her to Pacific Hospital, and went up to 1209 to arrest the suspect. Patrolman Atkins knocked several times. When he got no response, the security man opened the door. They walked past a bathroom to the left of the front door and a kitchen on the right, into the living room, and then into the bedroom, which was off to the left of the living room, right next to the bathroom. Fred was lying in bed, apparently asleep, dressed in jockey shorts. There was a splatter of what looked like bloodstains on the sheet. Patrolman Mitchell shook him awake. Atkins told him he was under arrest for rape and advised him of his rights. Fred Dumond said, "You've got to be kidding."

Pacific Hospital boasts a model program for the treatment and counseling of rape victims. The project, initiated by a psychiatric nurse and a sociologist in 1972, has been an education for all concerned. "The emergency staff used to be into the whole phenomenon of blaming the victim," says Joan Christiansen, assistant nursing director in charge of emergency services. "She was either drinking, or being seductive, or walking around at 3:00 a.m. Since we've had the program there has been a total change in attitude. Rape is a *crisis*. Different women react differently—some are upset, some calm, some in a state of shock—but every victim's life is disrupted in four ways: physically, emotionally, socially, sexually." At Pacific, nurses trained in counseling skills try to ease these disruptions by helping the rape victim to express her feelings and cope with specific problems, such as whether to press charges.

When Arline Hunt arrived in Pacific's emergency room, a nurse met her and saw her through the hospital routine. After receiving her consent, a gynecology resident examined her genitals for injuries, took smears for sperm and for a gonorrhea culture, gave her a prophylactic shot of penicillin and morning-after pills. The nurse told her to be sure and get a follow-up examination, since rape victims often get vaginal and urinary infections.

At 5:00 a.m., a counselor came and listened to Arline's story. Her report described Arline as "attractive, neatly dressed, cooperative, coherent, responding, pretty verbal." After the interview Arline tried to call her roommates, forgot her own telephone number, and had to look it up. By the time the police took her home she didn't feel like talking at all. Her period had started earlier that day and she was bleeding heavily. She hadn't had a chance to clean up at the hospital—the doctor had explained that washing might destroy evidence—and she felt, as she put it later, "filthy and disgusting." There was only one thing she wanted to do: take a shower.

> . . . A few years ago, I signed up with a computer dating service. Dozens of men I knew absolutely nothing about had my address and phone number. They came to my apartment to pick me up, I went to theirs for drinks or dinner. It didn't occur to me till years later how dangerous this was. Anything could have happened. . . .
>
> . . . We met in a bar. Like it or not, it's one of the few ways to meet men in this city. I liked him; there weren't any suspicious vibes. He did make a couple of jokes about my tits, but I put it down to normal

male obnoxiousness. He drove me home and I let him in because he said he had to use the bathroom. . . .

. . . As I was unlocking the hall door, a man came up behind me. I tried to slam the door on him, but couldn't. I was so embarrassed about acting paranoid that I apologized. I could have gone to a ground floor apartment and rung the bell or yelled, but I was afraid of being hysterical and paranoid and making a scene for nothing. So I just started walking casually upstairs. He followed me and pulled a knife. . . .

. . . While he was raping me I started getting the strangest feeling that all this was somehow familiar. I realized that it wasn't so different from times I'd fucked guys I didn't really want to fuck because I couldn't think of a graceful way to refuse. . . .

—fragments from a consciousness-raising session on rape

When Arline talks about September 18 her voice takes on a sardonic edge, as if she were describing not only her own horror but the folly of the human condition.

"We stayed for a couple of hours after Bobbie left, maybe more. I liked him. He was funny; he was making me laugh. And he seemed to need someone to talk to. But I didn't want to go out with him. He asked me and I said no, it's been nice talking to you but this is it. I was trying to explain without being too blunt. He wasn't my type. He was bragging about his money and that stuff doesn't impress me.

"A friend of his came in and bought us a few beers. Then I said I had to leave. I got my coat and umbrella and gave him my pocketbook so I could put my coat on. We went outside and he hailed a cab—I assumed he was going to take me home. I asked him for my pocketbook. He said, 'Wait a minute.' We got in and he gave the cabdriver his address. I said, 'Hey, I've got to go home, I've got to work tomorrow,' and I told the driver to go to my place. Fred said, 'No, we'll work this out later.' He gave his address again, and I gave mine again. The cabdriver just kept going to 2211 Geary. I thought well, this guy is being childish. He's playing a little game. We got out in front of his building and I said, 'Can I have it back now?' and he went inside, and I followed him up in the elevator. I couldn't leave without my pocketbook—it had my money, my keys, my identification, my Valium. Just everything I needed. And he was just ignoring me. I figured he'll have his fun, he'll have his little joke, and when he gets tired of it he'll give me my pocketbook. I wasn't scared at all. It didn't occur to me. I meet a lot of guys who play these dumb games and it's annoying but they're not rapists. You can't go around suspecting everybody.

"I followed him into his apartment and he slammed the door and stood in front of it. I said, 'Okay, stop playing games, can I please have my pocketbook so

I can get a cab and go home?' And he said, 'You are not going anywhere.' I said, 'What do you mean?' All of a sudden it was like he was a totally different person. The change in him was incredible. He said, 'You are not going anywhere. Go in the bedroom and take your clothes off.' I thought, I can't take this seriously. I felt sick. Sick and weak. I said, 'I promise I won't tell anybody about this if you'll just let me leave right now.'

"He pulled me into the bathroom and pushed me down on the side of the tub and went to the toilet and urinated. I was disgusted. I stood up and he pushed me down again. I picked up my umbrella and tried to use it against him, but he just pulled it away from me and started laughing. I still had my coat on. He pushed me into the bedroom and made a phone call to some guy. I don't remember what they said. Then I started to feel really faint. I didn't want to lie down, or it would be all over. So I asked him for a glass of water. He said, 'All right, but don't try anything.' He went into the kitchen and I ran over to the phone and dialed the operator. [The kitchen was between the bedroom and the door.] But he got back too quickly and hung up the phone and said, 'Don't you do that again.' And then he pushed me over to the bed.

"He pushed me down on the bed and I got back up again and he pushed me down again. I started screaming at the top of my lungs and he was saying, 'Shut up, they are making me do this.' And I said 'Who?' and he said, 'I can't tell you, but if you go out of here, they are going to get you anyway.' And so I started to scream again because at this point I didn't know what was happening and I didn't care. I just wanted somebody to hear me or something to happen. Then he started pulling down my pants—they were stretchy with an elastic waist— and I was fighting him but finally he pulled them off, and my underpants. I tried to push my fingers in his neck, and I tried to get him in the groin but it didn't work. He stuck his fingers into my throat so I couldn't scream.

"I saw there was no point resisting. I was afraid of what he might do. I knew he was crazy. He had a violent temper, he kept yelling at me to shut up. And he was strong. I was afraid he would try to strangle me with my necklace or rip my earrings out, so I took them off. I took my top off.

"I told him I had my period and he said, 'I don't care,' and ripped out my Tampax and threw it on the floor. He pinned my hands above my head. Then he got on top of me and had sexual intercourse and stuck his finger in the back part of me.

"After he stopped, I got off the bed. I saw my Tampax on the floor and I picked it up and said, 'You're disgusting!' and threw it down again. He was still lying in bed. I dialed the operator and said, 'There's been a rape at this number.' He grabbed the receiver and slammed it down. Then I called Bobbie. I felt almost fearless at that point.

"I got dressed and got my pocketbook and umbrella out of the bathroom and ran out. He was yelling at me that I was stupid, I was the stupidest woman he'd ever seen. I ran down twelve flights of stairs."

A woman who grows up in a big city learns early that her purse is a third arm, *never* to be relinquished, least of all to a man she has just met at a bar. Perhaps Arline Hunt had not been in San Francisco long enough to abandon the sheltered, upper-middle-class mentality of Shelton for urban war-zone smarts. Perhaps, on the other hand, something in her simply refused to live that way.

"I can't ask myself why did I do this or that. Why did I give him my pocketbook, why didn't I scream in the cab. Because I know I wouldn't have done anything different—I don't mean now, knowing what I know, but then. I guess," she says—that sardonic tone again—"I'm trusting, naive, dumb or whatever."

A friend and occasional lover, an advertising writer named Gary, put it another way. "There's something almost Zen about Arline: whatever will be will be, don't expect much and don't demand anything, just go along with whatever's happening. Arline never asks, 'What are we doing tonight?' She just comes in and sits down and asks for a beer. I would say Arline has a deflated opinion of herself, but she doesn't get bent out of shape. She likes to get fucked up and have a good time."

When Arline went off to her parents' alma mater, a small college in Kansas—ending up there because she hadn't felt like shopping around for schools—she expected to hate it. But she met some good people and had good times. She smoked grass, and took speed to stay up all night writing her C papers, and experimented with acid, which made her laugh and laugh, magnifying the laughter to freaky proportions. After two years she quit and went home.

When she moved to San Francisco in 1973 it was without any great enthusiasm. She had been living with her parents for the last year, working at dull clerical jobs, and she was anxious to get away. The city itself did not excite her, but in the city she would have her friends.

People, relationships—what else really mattered? She hated her job as a clerk in a textbook company. She thought about finding something she would really like doing, perhaps something connected with art—she had been painting and drawing since childhood. Gary urged her to promote herself, to put together a portfolio and try to get a job designing greeting cards or place mats, but she never did.

So what it came down to was people and a good time. People who were sincere and not out for what they could get. People, she never failed to emphasize, who had an absurd sense of humor and could make her laugh.

Not that Arline's life was all fun and games. For one thing, there was Graham. Graham was Arline's first lover. They met when she was sixteen; he was out of high school and engaged. She thought he was an aggressive bastard and didn't understand what was driving her to sleep with him. She hated it: it was uncomfortable, she was just doing it to please him, and she felt guilty besides.

All through college Arline went out with lots of men, but she didn't have sex again until the summer she returned to Shelton. She fell in love with a young Englishman and agreed to marry him, but by the following winter she had changed her mind. Shortly afterward she ran into Graham at a party. He was married by then, with two kids.

"I still thought he was obnoxious," she recalls. "I don't know why I went out with him, but I did—I had to give a fake name to my parents. I got used to him. He was always the hard-ass guy, but in another way he wasn't, not really."

The relationship turned into an intense love affair. For the first time Arline really enjoyed sex. She was also miserable, crazy, dependent. They talked about running away and living together; then Graham began avoiding her. When she confronted him, he admitted that he couldn't leave his children. After that there were many goodbyes that didn't stick. Once, soon after Arline had moved to San Francisco, he came down for a disastrous visit. "I had said I would see him, but no sex. He completely forced it; it was scary. He was always too aggressive and demanding. My roommates didn't approve of him coming. I kept telling them not to worry, nothing was going to happen. So when he forced me I couldn't scream. I didn't want anyone to know. I just cried." As usual she forgave him and the affair dragged on.

It was around the same time that the trouble at work began. The company provided a small lunchroom where most of the employees—the office staff and the men who worked in the shipping department—ate at noon. One day Arline was sitting at a table playing cards with a group of people when she saw one of the shippers staring at her. "I was frozen, I couldn't look up. I had to stop playing. My body was uncontrollable. After that I tried sitting with my back to them. It just kept growing, a horrible feeling of anxiety. I was afraid to light a cigarette 'cause my hands were shaking. I started eating in the room I work in but it's glassed in and the shippers work outside and they would just naturally look in. Before, there were always times when I would be nervous but it never affected me in such a physical way. Maybe part of it is living in the city."

In August 1974, Arline began seeing a psychiatrist. Along with once-a-week therapy he prescribed Valium. At the time of her encounter with Fred Dumond she was taking five milligrams once or twice a day.

On September 19, at nine in the morning, Arline went to court to swear out her complaint. Bobbie went with her. They hadn't slept. Arline was still in shock and spacey from pills, and she and Bobbie had noticed for the first time a bruise on each of her wrists. Trying to answer questions, she broke down. James Delaney, the assistant district attorney who would be handling her case, told her, to her relief—she was afraid of seeing Fred in court—that she didn't need to hang around for the arraignment. At home she kept trying to erase the night, to pretend it never happened. "It was too weird, too sickening. I couldn't remember things . . . even now it's almost like it happened to someone else. But it was *there*."

Arline's parents were on vacation; when they came back the following week she called her mother. Arline says she never really considered not telling her parents, though she was apprehensive about their reaction. Her father, a biologist, and her mother, a housewife constantly involved with community projects, were high-energy achievers and Arline felt they disapproved of her for not using her abilities. They were also conservative and religious and emotionally reserved, all of which made communication difficult. Her mother would have none of Arline's attempt to explain that in her world Fred's behavior was not so extraordinary as to arouse suspicion. "How could you not know something was happening? Why didn't you tell the taxi driver this man had your pocketbook?" It was Arline's first exposure to an attitude that would soon become familiar.

On October 10, Arline had to appear for a probable cause hearing, at which a judge would decide whether the prosecution had enough of a case to present to a grand jury. The decision went in Arline's favor, but the hearing was traumatic. Fred Dumond attended but did not testify. He watched impassively as his lawyer, Burton C. Scott of the prestigious local firm of Frazier, Frazier and Santini, a man with a reputation for toughness and a glass eye that made his stare frightening, introduced Arline to the art of cross-examination.

"He was trying to catch me on every detail, twisting everything I said. In a situation like that you're not thinking, 'I'm gonna get raped, I'd better plan my strategy for the trial.' You're just thinking about wanting to get out of there. Times and sequences aren't on your mind.

"I was freaking out, one of the policemen was telling me to calm down. The lawyer brought up my psychiatrist and my pills. I may have my problems, but I'm not crazy. Then he asked me how I knew I was penetrated. I said, 'I could feel it.' He said, 'Oh, so you've felt that sensation before.' The D.A. objected to that one."

Bobbie also testified briefly. "It was brutal. The defense lawyer was trying to confuse Arline, make her feel stupid. He scared her to death. And all these old men up for other cases were standing around, watching and laughing, and Arline having to say, 'Well, if you want to be explicit, he put his penis inside me.'"

Arline considered dropping the case, but decided she had to go through with it: "I couldn't see letting him get away with it. I couldn't see just letting a sick person like that out on the street." She felt a rage at the thought that Dumond might get off. Her friends, trying to prepare her for the worst, were warning her how difficult it was to get rape convictions. Bobbie had seen the TV documentary *A Case of Rape*: the rapist had been acquitted and the victim and her husband had ended up getting divorced. "At first I couldn't face that possibility. The unfairness of it. I didn't know what I'd do. After a while I resigned myself. I knew the way things were run, he'd probably be acquitted. I already felt defeated." Gary told her she ought to look on the whole thing as a learning experience about the real world.

The case went to the grand jury, and Arline had to tell her story once more. Months passed; the trial was postponed twice, aggravating her anxiety and depression. She got scared walking around the neighborhood. She lost weight. Her psychiatrist doubled her dose of Valium. The atmosphere in the apartment was funereal; nothing much was funny these days. At this low point she decided to call her brother in Los Angeles and tell him the whole story.

He hadn't heard it before. Arline's parents had, after the initial shock, been sympathetic and concerned; they supported, even admired, her decision to prosecute. Yet they were obviously still touchy about the subject, for they hadn't said a word to anyone, including their three other children. Arline did not have much contact with her only brother, who was older and married, but she identified with him because he too had refused to do the expected: after going to graduate school in physics, he had decided he didn't like it and was driving a school bus. His wife was a student and a feminist. At her suggestion Arline got in touch with the Women's Law Commune in Berkeley; a lawyer there promised to check on the D.A.'s investigation to make sure all leads were being pursued.

In February, Arline met a computer programmer named David at a bar called Storey's, and they started going out. "My feelings about sex hadn't changed," she says. "I knew Dumond was really sick, that all men weren't like that. One thing I was secure in was his sickness." But she was upset when David made skeptical noises about her story, when he too wanted to know, come on now, really, *why* did you go up there in the first place. . . .

Three days before the trial, Arline and Bobbie had dinner at Hal's Pub. Bobbie, facing the door, saw two men walk in. "Arline," she said, "put your head down on the table and don't look up. Dumond and his friend are here." They both put their heads down. When they looked up again a few minutes later, the men were gone.

> Q: *Would you describe your clothing, Miss Hunt? You describe having underpants on under your slacks. Did you have anything on underneath your sweater?*
> A: No.
> Q: *You had no bra on, did you?*
> A: No.
> Q: *Have you ever been raped before?*
> A: No, I haven't.
> Q: *Did you ever scratch this man?*
> A: I tried to put my finger in his throat.
> Q: *Did you ever scratch this man?*
> A: No.
> Q: *How long were you fighting him?*
> A: I don't know.
> Q: *According to your testimony there was a struggle the whole time, was there not?*
> A: My fingernails are not long enough to be able to harm anybody.
> Q: *Did you ever bite him?*
> A: No.

Q: *Did you ever land a kick?*

A: Did I what?

Q: *Did you land a kick, did you ever really kick him?*

A: I tried to.

Q: *And during this whole time you were not able to inflict an injury on him, is that so?*

A: He was stronger than I was, and I couldn't.

Q: *During this struggle, Miss Hunt, were you injured? Did you get any cuts—*

A: I got bruises on my wrists where he held them above my head.

Q: *Did you show them to the doctor at the hospital?*

A: No, because I didn't notice them until the next day, and other people did notice them.

Q: *Did you see him put his penis inside?*

A: No, I didn't see it.

Q: *And didn't you tell the district attorney when he asked you on direct examination that you don't think that he had a climax?*

  (Delaney objects and is overruled.)

A: I didn't know. I didn't say I didn't think.

Q: *All right. You didn't know. So would it be fair to say you didn't feel what you might have felt was a climax, would that be a fair statement?*

A: I don't know what he had. I don't know if he had a climax or not.

Q: *When were you finally able to get out of that apartment?*

A: I don't know the time.

Q: *What time did you call your girlfriend Bobbie from the apartment?*

A: I told you I thought it was probably around 3:00, 2:30 or 3:00, something like that.

Q: *Would it refresh your memory if I told you that you said earlier that it was somewhere around 3:30?*

A: I don't know the exact time. I told you that before.

Q: *If it was somewhere around 3:00, is it your testimony from the time you got there at about 1:00 until about 3:00, you were on the bed struggling, two hours?*

A: I don't know how long it was.

Q: *How long did it take him to urinate in the bathroom?*

A: Do you think I had a watch on and I was looking at it?

  (Delaney objects and is overruled.)

Q: *Was it more than five minutes?*

A: I don't know.

  (Before the judge in a closed hearing):

Q: *Have you ever tried to injure yourself?*

A: No, I haven't.

Q: Have you ever tried to commit suicide?

A: No, I haven't.

Q: You hesitated. Is there any reason why you hesitated, Miss Hunt?

A: Only because I think this is a little bit personal and doesn't per-
tain to what's going on.

—excerpts from the cross-examination of Arline Hunt

Jim Delaney knew that *People v. Dumond* would be a stinker. Arline Hunt had gone to a man's apartment from a dating bar, and her pocketbook story (witnessed only by an anonymous cabbie the police had been unable to find) was hard to believe if you didn't know her. It also helped to know that rapes originating in these dating bars were becoming more and more common, becoming a pattern. Women were starting to be more aware of the risks, but there would always be people who took chances; a recent rash of hitchhiking murders in the Bay Area had not stopped thousands of women from hitchhiking.

It was also damaging that Arline had taken off her shirt and jewelry—though Delaney's wife had told him that having an earring torn out was one of her own big fears ever since it had happened to a friend of hers taking off a sweater. Finally, the doctor who examined Arline hadn't found any sperm, nor had he noticed her bruises, which weren't, in any case, impressive injuries.

Still, Delaney wasn't entirely pessimistic. The Hollises had agreed to testify. John was actually flying in from Chicago, where he was working on a temporary assignment. Maureen was not happy to be living alone at 2211 Geary, with Fred Dumond still next door; she worried that if she testified he might try to get even in some way. But she felt it was her duty to come forward. Besides being ultra-respectable, they were simply nice, obviously morally concerned people—ideal witnesses from a credibility standpoint. Delaney hoped they could convince a jury that Arline had been screaming for twenty minutes in the next apartment.

The trial of Fred Louis Dumond for rape, including a lesser charge of assault with intent to rape, began on March 3, 1975. The presiding judge was Andrew P. Blackburn, a highly respected jurist with a reputation—even among liberals who disliked his hard-nosed law-and-order stance—for meticulous fairness. Philip Pacetta, another attorney from Frazier, Frazier, had taken over the defense from Scott, who had a prior commitment. The three-woman nine-man jury was predominantly white, middle-aged, and working-class.

Arline and Bobbie arrived together. They were, according to Gary, "a mess—emaciated, untogether, out of control of the situation." For the fourth time Arline faced having to re-create the details of September 18. "Usually I could just not think about it. Going through it all, again and again—that was the worst part." At the grand jury hearing a jury member had said, "Just tell the story—you don't have to relive it."

Delaney put Arline on the stand first. Her direct testimony went quickly;

most of the day and part of the next were devoted to cross-examination. Pacetta was a younger, less formidable man than Scott, not so inclined to verbal brutality, and Judge Blackburn kept him more or less under control. The prosecution won a crucial point when Blackburn refused to admit Arline's psychiatrist and tranquilizers as evidence of mental instability; after allowing Pacetta to pursue the question *voir dire* (without the jury present), he ruled that it was prejudicial and irrelevant: "I find that no issue arises by reason of the young lady drinking beer and taking Valium at the same time such as would affect her memory or her ability to recall events or would cause her to imagine things that never took place. . . . I find in the second place that the lady has never had any history of imagining things." Still, the interrogation was an ordeal.

"I felt the lawyer was trying to make a fool of me. He wanted exact times, situations, positions, over and over again. I would forget things and he would trip me up. He would bring up discrepancies from the minutes of the probable cause hearing. Most of these things were irrelevant little details, but to the jury it would look like I was lying. There was a rip in my pants; I hadn't noticed it till after probable cause. The lawyer tried to make me say I'd testified that they weren't ripped. I just hadn't noticed it. He kept trying to make me admit to lies: 'Isn't it a fact that you were kissing?' He even brought up seeing Dumond in Hal's Pub. As if we were there to meet him. As if we had a date."

Bobbie sat in the courtroom, living Arline's misery. Two old men sitting next to her were snoring. She could hear others making cracks about Arline, snickering when she had to talk about her period, agreeing that, boy, she had sure screwed up her story now. "She was on trial," Bobbie said flatly. "If you hated the guy and wanted to murder him, you wouldn't want to go through it—except for principle. She would get confused. *What time? What time?* It was six months ago and there were obviously things she wanted to block out. She was on the verge of breaking down half the time."

Arline was finally dismissed and the remaining prosecution witnesses took up the rest of the second day. Delaney had some small successes: He got Officer Atkins to testify that he had noticed Arline's bruises and mentioned them to Delaney at the September 19 complaint hearing; and he established that the hospital's negative sperm report was inconclusive. The examining physician testified that menstrual blood could flush out sperm and that because of Arline's flow he had been unable to see whether seminal fluid was present or not. He had simply taken his sample from the area where it was most likely to accumulate. Delaney asked if his findings meant that Arline's vagina contained no sperm. He answered, "No. . . . I can only say that in the sample I took, there was no sperm."

But the crucial witness was John Hollis. He recounted what he had heard and done and made as good an appearance as Delaney had hoped. On cross-examination, however, there was a brief skirmish that would prove significant:

Q: And isn't it a fact, Mr. Hollis, that on this particular night you told the security guard that you thought the noises were coming from the eleventh floor?

A: No, I don't recall that I said they were coming from the eleventh floor. I said since sound does travel, that was the reason I went out to see if there was any question, but the light was on in the room next to my bedroom.

The following morning, the defense began by calling the supervisor of security for 2211 Geary Boulevard. Pacetta had him read into the record an entry from the security office log for September 19: "2:35 . . . received call from tenant in apartment 1210 complaining about a loud noise and screaming coming from the 11th floor (he thinks)." Next, Fred's friend took the stand and testified that at Jewel's "Arline and Fred were talking, and all of a sudden she put her arms around him and pulled him close to her and whispered something." The third witness was Fred Dumond.

There was some disagreement among courtroom staffers, journalists, and other observers about Dumond's effectiveness as a witness. Some were impressed with his suntanned good looks, his sophisticated, expensive suit, and his calm confidence. Others thought he was a bit too smooth and sure of himself, that he was, as one veteran trial watcher put it, "a real con man." There were rumors about Dumond's behavior with women he had interviewed at his agency. He had two felony convictions—one for receiving stolen TV sets, the other for stealing from an employer—that Delaney was permitted to introduce for the purpose of impeaching his credibility. Even his lawyer didn't like him; Fred had been upset about Pacetta's taking over his case and relations between them had been strained. Months after the trial, Pacetta would comment that Fred had presented himself as "shallow" and "a swinger." In fact, Pacetta argued, it was just this image that made him credible: Why would a ladies' man like him have to rape anybody?

Fred's account contradicted Arline's in nearly every particular. She said he hadn't bought any of her drinks; he claimed he had. He swore that she never gave him her pocketbook. They were not arguing in the cab but kissing. At his apartment they petted on the couch in the living room, then moved to the bedroom, kissing, fondling, undressing. At one point Arline went to the bathroom, and he heard the toilet flush. After she came back, he put his fingers in her vagina and noticed that she was menstruating. (Obviously what she had flushed was her Tampax.) He was disgusted and asked her to leave. She got angry and upset. They argued; there was some "fairly loud" but not "excessively loud" yelling. Arline called her roommate and accused him of rape. He got furious and hung up the phone. He said, "Get the hell out of my house—you are a nut." She yelled at him some more, then left.

Delaney's cross-examination worried one point and another, but he was unable to ruffle Dumond's cool. He began their last exchange by asking, "Did you hear her scream at all?"

> A: Scream, no.
> *Q: Did you hear anybody scream?*
> A: I don't recall hearing—hearing screaming at that point.
> *Q: Arline never screamed?*
> A: She was talking in a rather hysterical voice, but she wasn't
>   screaming, no.
> *Q: Did you hear her scream "Help me, help me, God help me?"*
> A: No. I didn't. She never said that.

Dumond stepped down and, after a last minor witness, the defense rested.

On the fourth and last day of the trial Delaney introduced a rebuttal witness: Maureen Hollis. She testified that when she first awakened, she had thought the sounds might be coming from the eleventh floor. But after a few minutes, she had been quite certain they came from next door. She described them as "blood-curdling screams and shrieks."

Then came closing arguments. In his summation Pacetta used the phrase "dating bar" fourteen times. He reminded the jury that Arline had been having a good time at Jewel's; that she had not protested to the cabdriver or anyone else that Fred had her pocketbook; that he had not forced her to go home with him; that she had taken off some of her clothing; that she had not seen the defendant penetrate or felt him climax; that no sperm was found; that the security report specified the eleventh floor. He suggested that Arline's testimony was confused and inconsistent, that she had spent more time at Fred's than her story accounted for. If Fred was going to rape her, Pacetta wondered, would he take her to his own home? Let her call her roommate? Bring her a glass of water? Go to sleep afterward? In short, did this attractive, well-dressed young man look like a rapist?

Delaney argued that Arline had no reason to be afraid of Fred before he slammed the door; that she had taken off her things out of fear; that she didn't have to *see* the penetration to know it happened; that she wasn't concentrating on the defendant's climax but on her own anguish; that the sperm report wasn't definitive; that no one had kept track of time that night; that it could have been almost 2:00 before they got to the apartment; that no one, let alone a terrified woman who had just been raped, could remember everything; did the jurors recall every detail of, say, their last accident? On the contrary, it was the defendant's memory ("we did this for fifteen minutes, this for twenty") that was too good to be believed. Why, if Arline was lying, would she make up something as far out as the story about watching him urinate? Or admit taking off clothes? In fact, why would she subject herself to all this—a complaint session, a probable cause hearing, and now this trial? Who was more believable: this woman who had nothing to gain except the mortification of testifying about these indignities committed upon her, or this man with a criminal record, on trial for rape— this man who professed to be so repelled by Arline's bleeding, yet went to sleep on the bloodstained sheets? But all this aside, one thing could not be explained away: the screaming the Hollises had heard. Not mere loud argument, but "terrifying," "blood-curdling" screams.

One argument Delaney didn't make had the courtroom habitués shaking their heads. Was it likely that this man-of-the-world, who had so many women falling all over him that he didn't have to rape anybody, would get so upset about a girl having her period? Whatever had happened up there, that, they agreed, sounded farfetched. Later, Phil Pacetta would argue, with the characteristic ironic undertone that made his out-of-court defenses of Dumond sound more like insults, "He had wined her and dined her, investing all that time in a potential score—and at the last minute he finds out she's bleeding. Why should he get involved with a woman who's bleeding all over the place? He felt that *she* was out to rape *him*!"

At Delaney's suggestion Arline stayed away from the courtroom the day Fred testified. "I'm glad I wasn't there. I would have freaked out when he told that story. When I heard what it was, I thought, he's got to be kidding. I was really happy because I figured he didn't have much of a chance. I called my mother and asked her if she would believe what he said. She said, 'I'm prejudiced but it sounds fishy to me.'

"I couldn't tell much about the jury. There was one older woman who kept giving me scrutinizing looks; I didn't know if she was just concentrating or what. But I honestly thought that they couldn't believe his story."

The jury went out at 3:00 p.m. and deliberated for four hours. Since the court session was over for the day, the judge ordered the verdict sealed. In the morning the foreman announced it: "Not guilty." Judge Blackburn told the jurors to be seated and asked the clerk to poll them. This was a routine procedure on a guilty verdict; it was rarely done for an acquittal. Something was up. One by one, the jurors confirmed their verdict: not guilty. Judge Blackburn directed the clerk to affirm the verdict. Then, with barely controlled anger, he began:

"It is almost impossible in this county to get a conviction of rape. . . . I am reluctantly coming to the conclusion, whether it is the permissive society or what we are living in, at least as far as jurors are concerned, rape is no longer a crime. And when we have a trial, instead of trying the defendant, you make the poor girl the defendant. . . . You have seen television programs, girls don't report rape for the humiliation involved in it, the degradation they go through in the trial. . . . They are made the defendant, and they walk out of this courtroom with one thought in their mind: in our courts there is no justice for the victims of rape. And I can't say that I disagree with them.

"How many countless rapes are committed and never hit the courtroom because of the way jurors treat rape victims. I don't know, but it has gotten to be almost a national scandal. . . . And if you jurors believe the girls who are victims of this kind of violent sexual assault aren't entitled to the protection of our juries, just like the defendants are, then it is a sick society.

"Now I am coming to this case. You had two responsible citizens of this state, irreproachable of integrity and principles, who testified before you that they heard screaming there for twenty minutes. Can it be, ladies and gentlemen, that you believed the screaming, terrified girl, with blood-curdling calls, consented to the advances of this defendant? Can you disbelieve those people? And can you believe a defendant who stood with two convictions, one that he was a thief and the other that he dealt in stolen property? . . . Believe him and disbelieve them? Well, that's what you have done. . . .

"I wish I could say to you that you performed your jury service in the highest traditions of this state, and I can't."

He ended by summarily dismissing them from jury duty for the rest of their terms.

The day the verdict came down, Arline was at work. When she didn't hear from Jim Delaney, she called his office. She had to pry the information out of him. Did they come to a decision? Yes. What was it? Well, it's gonna be in the paper tomorrow. What does that mean? What do you think? Not guilty. Arline began to cry. Then Delaney told her about the judge's speech.

Blackburn's rebuke transformed *People v. Dumond* from a routine rape case— a "swearing contest," in courthouse parlance—to a controversial one. Local feminists were delighted; most defense lawyers were outraged at what they regarded as an attempt to intimidate juries. An exception was Philip Pacetta, who not only defended Blackburn's right to speak but when asked if he agreed with the judge's comments said: "The record speaks for itself."

The jurors themselves were, for the most part, disturbed and angry. One woman juror called Blackburn's action "a rape of the jury system" and wrote a letter of protest to the chief justice of the California Supreme Court demanding that Blackburn apologize to the jurors in open court. A male juror declared, "To be blunt, I think the judge is nuts."

To Arline, Blackburn's statement was a boost. It showed that at least she wasn't a joke, soothed her fears that people were laughing at her and thinking she was a liar. It made her feel a little less defeated. Then she read an article in an underground paper that quoted one juror as saying, "I thought just the way the others did. She was as guilty as he was. If she hangs around a place like that, she deserves everything she gets." The casual cruelty of the remark—"someone's torn ego using me as a punching bag"—was only part of what outraged her. If she "deserved what she got," that implied that she "got" something, which meant that this juror hadn't believed Fred Dumond when he denied having sex with her: "Some fine upstanding citizen, to condone perjury and then sit in judgment of me!" That perception, as the comments of other jurors would confirm, was essentially accurate. Whatever one thought of the propriety of Blackburn's outburst (or, for that matter, of the verdict itself), his target was well chosen.

In some ways Arline Hunt had been more fortunate than most rape complainants. The police had treated her considerately—although, according to a source at the courthouse, they were privately incredulous at her story—and so had Pacific Hospital. The Women's Law Commune agreed that the D.A. had conducted an excellent investigation. Opinions on Delaney's role in court were mixed. "Delaney is a type," said a local journalist. "A San Francisco old boy, hale and hearty. I wouldn't call him any kind of hero. I doubt that he really cared about the case before Blackburn made it into a big thing." Gary complained that Delaney smiled too much. "He wasn't as distressed as he should have been. I didn't feel that Arline had a good relationship with him. She was a docile client and he was none too aggressive." Delaney himself worried that he was not aggressive enough in cross-examining Fred. "He was such a smooth bastard: I was in a dilemma as to whether there was anything I could do to break his story or whether badgering would just solidify it." But there were other people— Arline was one—who felt he had tried very hard to win.

The trial itself, unpleasant as it was, could have been much worse. Arline was not, for example, subjected to an inquisition on her sexual experience. And another judge might have allowed the defense to bring up her psychiatric treatment. Except for Pacetta's emphasis on dating bars and bralessness, the trial had probably been as fair as the adversary system—with its built-in potential for harassing witnesses and confusing the jury with side issues—allowed.

The basic problem was that the jury reflected the nature of the jury pool, which in San Francisco as elsewhere is mainly drawn from the most conservative segment of the population. Transients are grossly underrepresented, young people and the conspicuously educated almost always challenged. Moreover, most states make it easier for women to be excused from serving, though the effect of such policies on rape trials is not as obvious as it might appear: not only are most female jurors conservative, elderly housewives who tend to disapprove of sexually active single women, but many women seem to feel a defensive need to blame the rape victim in order to reassure themselves that "it could never happen to me." In any case, the three women on Fred Dumond's jury—all of them over fifty—were as actively in favor of acquittal as most of the men. During a recess a court official overheard two of the women jurors talking in the corridor; they agreed that by going to a bar and not wearing a bra, Arline Hunt was "asking for it." And one woman, acting as a technical adviser to the male jurors, assured them that it was impossible to remove a Tampax by force—a patent absurdity.

What was decisive, for the majority of jurors, was simply that Arline had gone to a man's apartment—no one took the pocketbook story seriously—and was therefore fair game. They had surprisingly little trouble rationalizing the screams: "You hear screaming—maybe it's serious, maybe not. She was half in the bag. Sometimes you entice a person and then get scared." "The screaming didn't carry any weight—I think the words were put in [the witness's] mouth. There weren't any marks on her." "Women scream for many reasons." "It came from the eleventh floor." "It was overdramatized, there wasn't enough evidence. No blood in the hall or anything like that." Few of the jurors seemed to care much whether Fred's story was true and some were explicitly skeptical; the man who had called Blackburn "nuts" said flatly, "He didn't impress me. I couldn't say I believed him any more than I believed her."

Two of the men fought for conviction, but Donald Peterson, a thirty-two-year-old laborer and bartender, was the only juror who would admit to doubts about the verdict. "I was for conviction," Peterson said, "but it looked to me like we weren't going to convict. And there was a little doubt—no physical evidence, gaps in time, the stuff about the Tampax. Assault I could have gone with, but to put a guy away for fifteen years for rape. . . . I felt sorry for her. She ran into a dude who wouldn't take no for an answer. The women were impressed with him but to me he looked like a real rat bastard. I meet a lot of guys like him where I work, and if he took out my sister, I'd be waiting up. Yeah, I believe she really screamed. But that kid would have had to have her arms broken before *they* would believe her. Except for one guy, who was trying to tell them, 'You're trying the girl, not the guy.' I had second thoughts then. I still do."

Shortly after the trial, Fred Dumond dissolved his business, was evicted from his apartment—probably at the instigation of the Hollises—and disappeared. At Arline Hunt's apartment something like normality began to reassert itself. Then in early June, Arline quit her job. She had been feeling much better—or so Bobbie had thought—but now her depression deepened again. She felt that a man she was seeing was putting her off, that a girlfriend was rejecting her. One day she was talking on the phone to her married sister in Michigan and began to feel that her sister wanted to hang up. When she got off the phone she was crying. While Bobbie was in the bathroom, she took every pill in the house, then told Bobbie what she had done. She spent a month in the private psychiatric hospital with which her doctor is affiliated. After her release, she began looking for another job.

Rolling Stone, 1975

Editor's note: All names, places, dates, and other identifying details have been changed to protect the anonymity of participants in the case discussed. Shortly after "The Trial of Arline Hunt" was published in *Rolling Stone,* Willis ran into then–*New Yorker* editor William Shawn in the hallway. Upon complimenting the piece, he remarked that he "could never publish something like that." At that moment, Willis knew her *New Yorker* days were over.

Abortion
Is a Woman a Person?

If propaganda is as central to politics as I think, the opponents of legal abortion have been winning a psychological victory as important as their tangible gains. Two years ago, abortion was almost always discussed in feminist terms—as a political issue affecting the condition of women. Since then, the grounds of the debate have shifted drastically; more and more, the right-to-life movement has succeeded in getting the public and the media to see abortion as an abstract moral issue having solely to do with the rights of fetuses. Though every poll shows that most Americans favor legal abortion, it is evident that many are confused and disarmed, if not convinced, by the antiabortionists' absolutist fervor. No one likes to be accused of advocating murder. Yet the "pro-life" position is based on a crucial fallacy—that the question of fetal rights can be isolated from the question of women's rights.

Recently, Garry Wills wrote a piece suggesting that liberals who defended the snail-darter's right to life and opposed the killing in Vietnam should condemn abortion as murder. I found this notion breathtaking in its illogic. Environmentalists were protesting not the "murder" of individual snail-darters but the practice of wiping out entire species of organisms to gain a short-term economic benefit; most people who opposed our involvement in Vietnam did so because they believed the United States was waging an aggressive, unjust, and/or futile war. There was no inconsistency in holding such positions and defending abortion on the grounds that women's welfare should take precedence over fetal life. To claim that three very different issues, each with its own complicated social and political context, all came down to a simple matter of preserving life was to say that all killing was alike and equally indefensible regardless of circumstance. (Why, I wondered, had Wills left out the destruction of hapless bacteria by penicillin?) But aside from the general mushiness of the argument, I was struck by one peculiar fact: Wills had written an entire article about abortion without mentioning women, feminism, sex, or pregnancy.

Since the feminist argument for abortion rights still carries a good deal of moral and political weight, part of the antiabortionists' strategy has been to make an end run around it. Although the mainstream of the right-to-life movement is openly opposed to women's liberation, it has chosen to make its stand on the abstract "pro-life" argument. That emphasis has been reinforced by the movement's tiny left wing, which opposes abortion on pacifist grounds and includes women who call themselves "feminists for life." A minority among pacifists as well as right-to-lifers, this group nevertheless serves the crucial function of making opposition to abortion respectable among liberals, leftists, and moderates disinclined to sympathize with a right-wing crusade. Unlike most right-to-lifers, who are vulnerable to charges that their reverence for life does not apply to convicted criminals or Vietnamese peasants, antiabortion leftists are in a position to appeal to social conscience—to make analogies, however facile, between abortion and napalm. They disclaim any opposition to women's rights, insisting rather that the end cannot justify the means—murder is murder.

Well, isn't there a genuine moral issue here? If abortion *is* murder, how can a woman have the right to it? Feminists are often accused of evading this question, but in fact an evasion is built into the question itself. Most people understand "Is abortion murder?" to mean "Is the fetus a person?" But fetal personhood is ultimately as inarguable as the existence of God; either you believe in it or you don't. Putting the debate on this plane inevitably leads to the nonconclusion that it is a matter of one person's conscience against another's. From there, the discussion generally moves on to broader issues: whether laws defining the fetus as a person violate the separation of church and state; or conversely, whether people who believe an act is murder have not only the right but the obligation to prevent it. Unfortunately, amid all this lofty philosophizing, the concrete, human reality of the pregnant woman's dilemma gets lost, and with it an essential ingredient of the moral question.

Murder, as commonly defined, is killing that is unjustified, willful, and malicious. Most people would agree, for example, that killing in defense of one's life or safety is not murder. And most would accept a concept of self-defense that includes the right to fight a defensive war or revolution in behalf of one's independence or freedom from oppression. Even pacifists make moral distinctions between defensive violence, however deplorable, and murder; no thoughtful pacifist would equate Hitler's murder of the Jews with the Warsaw Ghetto rebels' killing of Nazi troops. The point is that it's impossible to judge whether an act is murder simply by looking at the act, without considering its context. Which is to say that it makes no sense to discuss whether abortion is murder without considering why women have abortions and what it means to force women to bear children they don't want.

We live in a society that defines child rearing as the mother's job; a society in which most women are denied access to work that pays enough to support a family, child-care facilities they can afford, or any relief from the constant, daily burdens of motherhood; a society that forces mothers into dependence on marriage or welfare and often into permanent poverty; a society that is actively hostile to women's ambitions for a better life. Under these conditions the unwillingly pregnant woman faces a terrifying loss of control over her fate. Even if she chooses to give up the baby, unwanted pregnancy is in itself a serious trauma. There is no way a pregnant woman can passively let the fetus live; she must create and nurture it with her own body, in a symbiosis that is often difficult, sometimes dangerous, always uniquely intimate. However gratifying pregnancy may be to a woman who desires it, for the unwilling it is literally an invasion—the closest analogy is to the difference between lovemaking and rape. Nor is there such a thing as foolproof contraception. Clearly, abortion is by normal standards an act of self-defense.

Whenever I make this case to a right-to-lifer, the exchange that follows is always substantially the same:

> RTL: If a woman chooses to have sex, she should be willing to take
> the consequences. We must all be responsible for our actions.
> EW: Men have sex, without having to "take the consequences."
> RTL: You can't help that—it's biology.
> EW: You don't think a woman has as much right as a man to enjoy
> sex? Without living in fear that one slip will transform her life?
> RTL: She has no right to selfish pleasure at the expense of the
> unborn.

It would seem, then, that the nitty-gritty issue in the abortion debate is not life but sex. If the fetus is sacrosanct, it follows that women must be continually vulnerable to the invasion of their bodies and loss of their freedom and independence—unless they are willing to resort to the only perfectly reliable contraceptive, abstinence. This is precisely the "solution" right-to-lifers suggest, usually with a touch of glee; as Representative Elwood Rudd once put it, "If a woman has a right to control her own body, let her exercise control before she gets pregnant." A common ploy is to compare fucking to overeating or overdrinking, the idea being that pregnancy is a just punishment, like obesity or cirrhosis.

In 1979 it is depressing to have to insist that sex is not an unnecessary, morally dubious self-indulgence but a basic human need, no less for women than for men. Of course, for heterosexual women giving up sex also means doing without the love and companionship of a mate. (Presumably, married women who have had all the children they want are supposed to divorce their husbands or convince them that celibacy is the only moral alternative.) "Freedom" bought at such a cost is hardly freedom at all and certainly not equality—no one tells men that if they aspire to some measure of control over their lives, they are welcome to neuter themselves and become social isolates. The don't-have-sex argument is really another version of the familiar antifeminist dictum that autonomy and femaleness—that is, female sexuality—are incompatible; if you choose the first, you lose the second. But to pose this choice is not only inhumane; it is as deeply disingenuous as "Let them eat cake." No one, least of all the antiabortion movement, expects or wants significant numbers of women to give up sex and marriage. Nor are most right-to-lifers willing to allow abortion for rape victims. When all the cant about "responsibility" is stripped away, what the right-to-life position comes down to is, if the effect of prohibiting abortion is to keep women slaves to their biology, so be it.

In their zeal to preserve fetal life at all costs, antiabortionists are ready to grant fetuses more legal protection than people. If a man attacks me and I kill him, I can plead self-defense without having to prove that I was in danger of being killed rather than injured, raped, or kidnapped. But in the annual congressional battle over what if any exceptions to make to the Medicaid abortion ban, the House of Representatives has bitterly opposed the funding of abortions for any reason but to save the pregnant woman's life. Some right-to-lifers argue that even the danger of death does not justify abortion; others have suggested "safeguards" like requiring two or more doctors to certify that the woman's life is at least 50 percent threatened. Antiabortionists are forever worrying that any exception to a total ban on abortion will be used as a "loophole": better that any number of women should ruin their health or even die than that one woman should get away with not having a child "merely" because she doesn't want one. Clearly this mentality does not reflect equal concern for all life. Rather, antiabortionists value the lives of fetuses above the lives and welfare of women, because at bottom they do not concede women the right to an active human existence that transcends their reproductive function. Years ago, in an interview with Paul Krassner in *The Realist,* Ken Kesey declared himself against abortion. When Krassner asked if his objection applied to victims of rape, Kesey replied—I may not be remembering the exact words, but I will never forget the substance—"Just because another man planted the seed, that's no reason to destroy the crop."[1] To this day I have not heard a more eloquent or chilling metaphor for the essential premise of the right-to-life movement: that a woman's excuse for being is her womb. It is an outrageous irony that antiabortionists are managing to pass off this profoundly immoral idea as a noble moral cause.

The conservatives who dominate the right-to-life movement have no real problem with the antifeminism inherent in their stand; their evasion of the issue is a matter of public relations. But the politics of antiabortion leftists are a study in self-contradiction: in attacking what they see as the violence of abortion, they condone and encourage violence against women. Forced childbearing does violence to a woman's body and spirit, and it contributes to other kinds of violence: deaths from illegal abortion; the systematic oppression of mothers and women in general; the poverty, neglect, and battering of unwanted children; sterilization abuse.

Radicals supposedly believe in attacking a problem at its roots. Yet surely it is obvious that restrictive laws do not keep women from seeking abortions; they just create an illicit, dangerous industry. The only way to drastically reduce the number of abortions is to invent safer, more reliable contraceptives, ensure universal access to all birth control methods, eliminate sexual ignorance and guilt, and change the social and economic conditions that make motherhood a trap. Anyone who is truly committed to fostering life should be fighting for women's liberation instead of harassing and disrupting abortion clinics (hardly a nonviolent tactic, since it threatens the safety of patients). The "feminists for life" do talk a lot about ending the oppression that drives so many women to abortion; in practice, however, they are devoting all their energy to increasing it.

Despite its numerical insignificance, the antiabortion left epitomizes the hypocrisy of the right-to-life crusade. Its need to wrap misogyny in the rhetoric of social conscience and even feminism is actually a perverse tribute to the women's movement; it is no longer acceptable to declare openly that women deserve to suffer for the sin of Eve. I suppose that's progress—not that it does the victims of the Hyde Amendment much good.

Village Voice, March and April 1979

NOTE

1. A reader later sent me a copy of the Kesey interview. The correct quotation is "You don't plow under the corn because the seed was planted with a neighbor's shovel."

Feminism, Moralism, and Pornography

For women, life is an ongoing good cop–bad cop routine. The good cops are marriage, motherhood, and that courtly old gentleman, chivalry. Just cooperate, they say (crossing their fingers), and we'll go easy on you. You'll never have to earn a living or open a door. We'll even get you some romantic love. But you'd better not get stubborn, or you'll have to deal with our friend rape, and he's a real terror; we just can't control him.

Pornography often functions as a bad cop. If rape warns that without the protection of one man we are fair game for all, the hard-core pornographic image suggests that the alternative to being a wife is being a whore. As women become more "criminal," the cops call for nastier reinforcements; the proliferation of lurid, violent porn (symbolic rape) is a form of backlash. But one can be a solid citizen and still be shocked (naively or hypocritically) by police brutality. However widely condoned, rape is illegal. However loudly people proclaim that porn is as wholesome as granola, the essence of its appeal is that emotionally it remains taboo. It is from their very contempt for the rules that bad cops derive their power to terrorize (and the covert approbation of solid citizens who would love to break the rules themselves). The line between bad cop and outlaw is tenuous. Both rape and pornography reflect a male outlaw mentality that rejects the conventions of romance and insists, bluntly, that women are cunts. The crucial difference between the conservative's moral indignation at rape, or at *Hustler,* and the feminist's political outrage is the latter's understanding that the problem is not bad cops or outlaws but cops and the law.

Unfortunately, the current women's campaign against pornography seems determined to blur this difference. Feminist criticism of sexist and misogynist pornography is nothing new; porn is an obvious target insofar as it contributes to larger patterns of oppression—the reduction of the female body to a commodity (the paradigm being prostitution), the sexual intimidation that makes women regard the public streets as enemy territory (the paradigm being rape), sexist images and propaganda in general. But what is happening now is different. By playing games with the English language, antiporn activists are managing to rationalize as feminism a single-issue movement divorced from any larger political context and rooted in conservative moral assumptions that are all the more dangerous for being unacknowledged.

When I first heard there was a group called Women Against Pornography, I twitched. Could I define myself as Against Pornography? Not really. In itself, pornography—which, my dictionary and I agree, means any image or description intended or used to arouse sexual desire—does not strike me as the proper object of a political crusade. As the most cursory observation suggests, there are many varieties of porn, some pernicious, some more or less benign. About the only generalization one can make is that pornography is the return of the repressed, of feelings and fantasies driven underground by a culture that atomizes sexuality, defining love as a noble affair of the heart and mind, lust as a base animal urge centered in unmentionable organs. Prurience—the state of mind I associate with pornography—implies a sense of sex as forbidden, secretive pleasure, isolated from any emotional or social context. I imagine that in utopia, porn would wither away along with the state, heroin, and Coca-Cola. At present, however, the sexual impulses that pornography appeals to are part of virtually everyone's psychology. For obvious political and cultural reasons nearly all porn is sexist in that it is the product of a male imagination and aimed at a male market; women are less likely to be consciously interested in pornography, or to indulge that interest, or to find porn that turns them on. But anyone who thinks women are simply indifferent to pornography has never watched a bunch of adolescent girls pass around a trashy novel. Over the years I've enjoyed various pieces of pornography—some of them of the sleazy Forty-second Street paperback sort—and so have most women I know. Fantasy, after all, is more flexible than reality, and women have learned, as a matter of survival, to be adept at shaping male fantasies to their own purposes. If feminists define pornography, per se, as the enemy, the result will be to make a lot of women ashamed of their sexual feelings and afraid to be honest about them. And the last thing women need is more sexual shame, guilt, and hypocrisy—this time served up as feminism.

So why ignore qualitative distinctions and in effect condemn all pornography as equally bad? WAP organizers answer—or finesse—this question by redefining pornography. They maintain that pornography is not really about sex but about violence against women. Or, in a more colorful formulation, "Pornography is the theory, rape is the practice." Part of the argument is that pornography causes violence; much is made of the fact that Charles Manson and David Berkowitz had porn collections. This is the sort of inverted logic that presumes marijuana to be dangerous because most heroin addicts started with it. It is men's hostility toward women—combined with their power to express that hostility and for the most part get away with it—that causes sexual violence. Pornography that gives sadistic fantasies concrete shape—and, in today's atmosphere, social legitimacy—may well encourage suggestible men to act them out. But if *Hustler* were to vanish from the shelves tomorrow, I doubt that rape or wife-beating statistics would decline.

Even more problematic is the idea that pornography depicts violence rather than sex. Since porn is by definition overtly sexual, while most of it is not overtly violent, this equation requires some fancy explaining. The conference WAP held in September was in part devoted to this task. Robin Morgan and Gloria Steinem addressed it by attempting to distinguish pornography from erotica. According to this argument, erotica (whose etymological root is "eros," or sexual love) expresses an integrated sexuality based on mutual affection and desire between equals; pornography (which comes from another Greek root, "porne," meaning prostitute) reflects a dehumanized sexuality based on male domination and exploitation of women. The distinction sounds promising, but it doesn't hold up. The accepted meaning of erotica is literature or pictures with sexual themes; it may or may not serve the essentially utilitarian function of pornography. Because it is less specific, less suggestive of actual sexual activity, "erotica" is regularly used as a euphemism for "classy porn." Pornography expressed in literary language or expensive photography and consumed by the upper middle class is "erotica"; the cheap stuff, which can't pretend to any purpose but getting people off, is smut. The erotica-versus-porn approach evades the (embarrassing?) question of how porn is *used*. It endorses the portrayal of sex as we might like it to be and condemns the portrayal of sex as it too often is, whether in action or only in fantasy. But if pornography is to arouse, it must appeal to the feelings we have, not those that by some utopian standard we ought to have. Sex in this culture has been so deeply politicized that it is impossible to make clear-cut distinctions between "authentic" sexual impulses and those conditioned by patriarchy. Between, say, *Ulysses* at one end and *Snuff* at the other, erotica/pornography conveys all sorts of mixed messages that elicit complicated and private responses. In practice, attempts to sort out good erotica from bad porn inevitably come down to "What turns me on is erotic; what turns you on is pornographic."

It would be clearer and more logical simply to acknowledge that some sexual images are offensive and some are not. But logic and clarity are irrelevant—or rather, inimical—to the underlying aim of the antiporners, which is to vent the emotions traditionally associated with the word "pornography." As I've suggested, there is a social and psychic link between pornography and rape. In terms of patriarchal morality both are expressions of male lust, which is presumed to be innately vicious, and offenses to the putative sexual innocence of "good" women. But feminists supposedly begin with different assumptions—

that men's confusion of sexual desire with predatory aggression reflects a sexist system, not male biology; that there are no good (chaste) or bad (lustful) women, just women who are, like men, sexual beings. From this standpoint, to lump pornography with rape is dangerously simplistic. Rape is a violent physical assault. Pornography can be a psychic assault, both in its content and in its public intrusions on our attention, but for women as for men it can also be a source of erotic pleasure. A woman who is raped is a victim; a woman who enjoys pornography (even if that means enjoying a rape fantasy) is in a sense a rebel, insisting on an aspect of her sexuality that has been defined as a male preserve. Insofar as pornography glorifies male supremacy and sexual alienation, it is deeply reactionary. But in rejecting sexual repression and hypocrisy—which have inflicted even more damage on women than on men—it expresses a radical impulse.

That this impulse still needs defending, even among feminists, is evident from the sexual attitudes that have surfaced in the antiporn movement. In the movement's rhetoric pornography is a code word for vicious male lust. To the objection that some women get off on porn, the standard reply is that this only shows how thoroughly women have been brainwashed by male values—though a WAP leaflet goes so far as to suggest that women who claim to like pornography are lying to avoid male opprobrium. (Note the good-girl-versus-bad-girl theme, reappearing as healthy-versus-sick, or honest-versus-devious; for "brainwashed" read "seduced.") And the view of sex that most often emerges from talk about "erotica" is as sentimental and euphemistic as the word itself: lovemaking should be beautiful, romantic, soft, nice, and devoid of messiness, vulgarity, impulses to power, or indeed aggression of any sort. Above all, the emphasis should be on *relationships,* not (yuck) *organs.* This goody-goody concept of eroticism is not feminist but feminine. It is precisely sex as an aggressive, unladylike activity, an expression of violent and unpretty emotion, an exercise of erotic power, and a specifically genital experience that has been taboo for women. Nor are we supposed to admit that we, too, have sadistic impulses, that our sexual fantasies may reflect forbidden urges to turn the tables and get revenge on men. (When a woman is aroused by a rape fantasy, is she perhaps identifying with the rapist as well as the victim?)

At the WAP conference lesbian separatists argued that pornography reflects patriarchal sexual relations; patriarchal sexual relations are based on male power backed by force; ergo, pornography is violent. This dubious syllogism, which could as easily be applied to romantic novels, reduces the whole issue to hopeless mush. If all manifestations of patriarchal sexuality are violent, then opposition to violence cannot explain why pornography (rather than romantic novels) should be singled out as a target. Besides, such reductionism allows women no basis for distinguishing between consensual heterosexuality and rape. But this is precisely its point; as a number of women at the conference put it, "In a patriarchy, all sex with men is pornographic." Of course, to attack pornography, and at the same time equate it with heterosexual sex, is implicitly to condemn not only women who like pornography, but women who sleep with men. This is familiar ground. The argument that straight women collaborate with the enemy has often been, among other things, a relatively polite way of saying that they consort with the beast. At the conference I couldn't help feeling that proponents of the separatist line were talking like the modern equivalents of women who, in an era when straightforward prudery was socially acceptable, joined convents to escape men's rude sexual demands. It seemed to me that their revulsion against heterosexuality was serving as the thinnest of covers for disgust with sex itself. In any case, sanitized feminine sexuality, whether straight or gay, is as limited as the predatory masculine kind and as central to women's oppression; a major function of misogynist pornography is to scare us into embracing it. As a further incentive, the good cops stand ready to assure us that we are indeed morally superior to men, that in our sweetness and nonviolence (read passivity and powerlessness) is our strength.

Women are understandably tempted to believe this comforting myth. Self-righteousness has always been a feminine weapon, a permissible way to make men feel bad. Ironically, it is socially acceptable for women to display fierce aggression in their crusades against male vice, which serve as an outlet for female anger without threatening male power. The temperance movement, which made alcohol the symbol of male violence, did not improve the position of women; substituting porn for demon rum won't work either. One reason it won't is that it bolsters the good girl–bad girl split. Overtly or by implication it isolates women who like porn or "pornographic" sex or who work in the sex industry. WAP has refused to take a position on prostitution, yet its activities— particularly its support for cleaning up Times Square—will affect prostitutes' lives. Prostitution raises its own set of complicated questions. But it is clearly not in women's interest to pit "good" feminists against "bad" whores (or topless dancers, or models for skin magazines).

So far, the issue that has dominated public debate on the antiporn campaign is its potential threat to free speech. Here too the movement's arguments have been full of contradictions. Susan Brownmiller and other WAP organizers claim not to advocate censorship and dismiss the civil liberties issue as a red herring dragged in by men who don't want to face the fact that pornography oppresses women. Yet at the same time, WAP endorses the Supreme Court's contention that obscenity is not protected speech, a doctrine I—and most civil libertarians—regard as a clear infringement of First Amendment rights. Brownmiller insists that the First Amendment was designed to protect political dissent, not expressions of woman-hating violence. But to make such a distinction is to defeat the amendment's purpose, since it implicitly cedes to the government the right to define "political." (Has there ever been a government willing to admit that its opponents are anything more than antisocial troublemakers?) Anyway, it makes no sense to oppose pornography on the grounds that it's sexist propaganda, then turn around and argue that it's not political. Nor will libertarians be reassured by WAP's statement that "We want to change the definition of obscenity so that it focuses on violence, not sex." Whatever their focus, obscenity laws deny the right of free expression to those who transgress official standards of propriety—and personally, I don't find WAP's standards significantly less oppressive than Warren Burger's. Not that it matters, since WAP's fantasies about influencing the definition of obscenity are appallingly naive. The basic purpose of obscenity laws is and always has been to reinforce cultural taboos on sexuality and suppress feminism, homosexuality, and other forms of sexual dissidence. No pornographer has ever been punished for being a woman hater, but not too long ago information about female sexuality, contraception, and abortion was assumed to be obscene. In a male supremacist society the only obscenity law that will not be used against women is no law at all.

As an alternative to an outright ban on pornography, Brownmiller and others have advocated restricting its display. There is a plausible case to be made for the idea that antiwoman images displayed so prominently that they are impossible to avoid are coercive, a form of active harassment that oversteps the bounds of free speech. But aside from the evasion involved in simply equating pornography with misogyny or sexual sadism, there are no legal or logical grounds for treating sexist material any differently from (for example) racist or anti-Semitic propaganda; an equitable law would have to prohibit any kind of public defamation. And the very thought of such a sweeping law has to make anyone with an imagination nervous. Could Catholics claim they were being harassed by nasty depictions of the pope? Could Russian refugees argue that the display of Communist literature was a form of psychological torture? Would proabortion material be taken off the shelves on the grounds that it defamed the unborn? I'd rather not find out.

At the moment the First Amendment issue remains hypothetical; the movement has concentrated on raising the issue of pornography through demonstrations and other public actions. This is certainly a legitimate strategy. Still, I find myself more and more disturbed by the tenor of antipornography actions and the sort of consciousness they promote; increasingly their focus has shifted from rational feminist criticism of specific targets to generalized, demagogic moral outrage. Picketing an antiwoman movie, defacing an exploitative billboard, or boycotting a record company to protest its misogynist album covers conveys one kind of message, mass marches Against Pornography quite another. Similarly, there is a difference between telling the neighborhood news dealer why it pisses us off to have *Penthouse* shoved in our faces and choosing as a prime target every right-thinking politician's symbol of big-city sin, Times Square.

In contrast to the abortion rights movement, which is struggling against a tidal wave of energy from the other direction, the antiporn campaign is respectable. It gets approving press and cooperation from the city, which has its own stake (promoting tourism, making the Clinton area safe for gentrification) in cleaning up Times Square. It has begun to attract women whose perspective on other matters is in no way feminist ("I'm antiabortion," a participant in WAP's march on Times Square told a reporter, "but this is something I can get into"). Despite the insistence of WAP organizers that they support sexual freedom, their line appeals to the antisexual emotions that feed the backlash. Whether they know it or not, they are doing the good cops' dirty work.

Village Voice, October and November 1979

The Family
Love It or Leave It

When I talk about my family, I mean the one I grew up in. I have been married, lived with men, and participated in various communal and semicommunal arrangements, but for most of the past six years—nearly all of my thirties—I have lived alone. This is neither an accident nor a deliberate choice, but the result of an accretion of large and small choices, many of which I had no idea I was making at the time. Conscious or not, these choices have been profoundly influenced by the cultural and political radicalism of the sixties, especially radical feminism. The sense of possibility, of hope for great changes that pervaded those years affected all my aspirations; compromises that might once have seemed reasonable, or simply to be expected, felt stifling. A rebellious community of peers supported me in wanting something other than conventional family life; feminist consciousness clarified and deepened my ambivalence toward men, my skepticism about marriage. Single women were still marginal, but their position was dignified in a way it had never been before: it was possible to conceive of being alone as a choice rather than a failure.

For me the issue was less the right to be alone, in itself, than the right to take as much time and room as I needed to decide what kind of life I wanted, what I could hold out for. Intimate connections are important to me. I want a mate, or so I believe, and possibly a child. Before the counterculture existed I was attracted to the idea of communal living and I still am. Yet obviously other priorities have intervened: I haven't found what I supposedly want on terms I can accept. The psychologist in me suggests that I don't want it as wholeheartedly as I think, the feminist retorts that it's not my fault if a sexist society keeps offering me a choice between unequal relationships and none, and I'm sure they're both right. Anyway, I wouldn't take back the choices I've made. I would not wish to be a different person, or to have been shaped by a different time.

Still, I can't help being uneasy about the gap between the lessons I learned during that time and the rules of the game in this one. As the conservative back-lash gains momentum, I feel a bit like an explorer camped on a peninsula, who looks back to discover that the rising tide has made it into an island and that it threatens to become a mere sandbar, or perhaps disappear altogether. If there is one cultural trend that has defined the seventies, it is the aggressive resurgence of family chauvinism, flanked by its close relatives, antifeminism and homophobia. The right's impassioned defense of traditional family values—the common theme of its attacks on the Equal Rights Amendment, legal abortion, gay rights, sexual permissiveness, child care for working mothers, and "im-moral" (read unattached female) welfare recipients—has affected the social at-mosphere even in the liberal, educated middle class that produced the cultural radicals. The new consensus is that the family is our last refuge, our only de-fense against universal predatory selfishness, loneliness, and rootlessness; the idea that there could be desirable alternatives to the family is no longer taken seriously. I've also noticed a rise in the level of tension between married and single people. Over the years family boosters have subjected me to my share of hints that I'm pathetic, missing out on real life, or that the way I live is selfish and shallow, or both; I've indulged an unworthy tendency to respond in kind, flaunting my independence and my freedom from the burdens of parenthood while implying that I see through their facade of happiness to the quiet despera-tion beneath. Lately these exchanges have become edgier; sometimes they ex-plode into fights. As I said, I'm uneasy.

Of course, "family" is one of those concepts that invite stretching. One might reasonably define a family as any group of people who live under the same roof, function as an economic unit, and have a serious commitment to each other—a definition that could include communes and unmarried couples of whatever sex-ual preference. But the family as it exists for most people in the real world—in a social and historical context—is nothing so amorphous or pluralistic. It is an [institution, a set of laws, customs, and beliefs] that define what a family is or ought to be, the rights and duties of its members, and its relation to society. This institution embraces only households of people related by birth or marriage. It is rooted in the assumption of male authority over dependent women and children, the sexual double standard, and the traditional exchange of the hus-band's financial support for the wife's domestic and sexual services. It defines the pursuit of individual freedom as selfish and irresponsible ("narcissistic" in current jargon), the subordination of personal happiness to domestic obliga-tions as the hallmark of adulthood and the basis of morals. Above all, the family is supposed to control sex and legitimize it through procreation; family morality regards sensual pleasure for its own sake as frivolous, sexual passion as dan-gerous and fundamentally antisocial. In a family-centered society prevailing attitudes toward people who live differently range from pity to indifference to hostile envy to condemnation. Women who step outside the home into the world become fair game for economic and sexual exploitation; children who have no parents, or whose parents cannot or will not give them adequate care, get minimal attention from a community that regards them as aliens in a land where only citizens have rights.

On the left, family chauvinism often takes the form of nostalgic declarations that the family, with its admitted faults, has been vitiated by modern capitalism, which is much worse (at least the family is based on personal relations rather than soulless cash, etc., etc.). Christopher Lasch's *The Culture of Narcissism* is the latest polemic to suggest that radicals who criticize the family are beating a dead (and presumably mourned) horse. True, capitalism has eroded patriarchal authority; the family has been drastically altered by modern developments from industrialism to women's participation in the labor force to the hedonism implicit in mass culture. (Personally, I prefer the present system, with its admitted faults, to one that allowed women no rights at all.) But it is perverse to deny that the family and its ideology continue to shape our lives. Most of us have been brought up by parents or other relatives. It is in the family that children discover their sexuality and learn how women and men are supposed to behave, toward the world and each other. The family is still the main source of women's oppression and the main focus of feminist politics, which is probably why male leftists are so inclined to premature announcements of its demise.

Whether or not they work outside the home, most women base their lives on marriage and motherhood; since job discrimination ensures that women earn roughly half as much as men and lack of public child-care facilities is a further deterrent to single motherhood, women's employment has not ended their dependence on marriage, nor has it relieved them of the chief responsibility for housework and child rearing. Though families who conform to the classic patriarchal pattern are now in the minority, most domestic-relations laws define the obligations of husband and wife in terms of their traditional roles. So does the government. Nixon vetoed federally funded child care on the grounds that the state should not usurp the prerogative of the family, code for "Mothers should stay home where they belong and if they don't, it's their children's tough luck." The Carter administration's response to the poverty of families dependent on a female breadwinner was to suggest that federal job programs employ *men,* the assumption being that women should be married to men who can support them. Despite all the activism of the past ten years, our society still regards wife beating as a private domestic matter, condones rape within marriage, hesitates to condemn men for raping independent or sexually active women, restricts women's access to contraception and abortion, discriminates against homosexuals, and even throws them in jail. In most states it is still legal to punish a spouse by using evidence of sexual "immorality" as a weapon in contested divorces and child-custody disputes. Social prejudice against single people remains pervasive: we are immature, unreliable, and incapable of deep attachments, we don't own property, we like loud music, our sexual activities are offensive, and if too many of us are allowed in we'll ruin the neighborhood. (The stereotype goes double for homosexuals.) Unmarried couples and groups also encounter various forms of discrimination, from difficulty in renting apartments, obtaining mortgages, and buying insurance to ordinances that limit or ban communal housing to tax laws that allow only the legally married to file joint returns. Nor do "illegitimate" children have equal legal rights.

The relation of capitalism to the family is in fact far more dialectical than analyses like Lasch's suggest. When families were economically self-sufficient, they provided jobs for those who could work and took care of those who could not. In an industrial economy, where workers must find buyers for their labor, anyone who cannot command a living wage faces a grim existence; even the white middle-class man at the height of his earning power may find that a technological advance, an economic downturn, or an illness has made him unemployable. While government services like unemployment insurance and social security purport to fill the gaps, in practice they offer a bare minimum of protection against disaster and do nothing to alleviate the day-to-day anxiety of coping with a hostile system. For most people the only alternative to facing that anxiety alone is to be part of a family. At least in theory, family members are committed to each other's survival; small, unstable, and vulnerable as the contemporary nuclear family may be, it is better than nothing.

Capitalists have an obvious stake in encouraging dependence on the family and upholding its mythology. If people stopped looking to the family for security, they might start looking to full employment and expanded public services. If enough parents or communal households were determined to share child rearing, they might insist that working hours and conditions be adapted to their domestic needs. If enough women refused to work for no pay in the home and demanded genuine parity on the job, our economy would be in deep trouble. There is a direct link between the conservative trend of American capitalism and the backlash on so-called cultural issues. During the past decade, the loss of the Vietnam War, the general decline in American influence, and the growing power of the oil industry have led to an intensive corporate drive to increase profits by reducing social services, raising prices faster than wages, and convincing the public to have "lower expectations"; in the same period blatant family chauvinism has become official government policy. Under the circumstances it is not surprising that most people are less inclined to demand change—with all the risk and uncertainty such demands entail—than to cling to what they have and defend it against attack. These days "my family first" is only a slightly less insular version of the "me first" psychology the insecurity of capitalism provokes. Both are based on the dismaying knowledge that if you and your family are not first, they are all too likely to be last. People who are

clinging are never eager to share their branch, nor do they look kindly on anyone who insists it's rotten wood.

Like most educated white middle-class women of my generation, I did not
grow up worrying about economic survival. My central problems had to do with
the conflict between a conservative upbringing and the "sexual revolution,"
between traditional definitions of femininity and a strong desire for worldly
achievement and independence. For me the cultural revolt began in the late
fifties with the libertarian campaign against obscenity laws and conventional
sexual morality. I was for it, but I was also suspicious, and no wonder: quite
aside from my own internal conflicts, the sexual freedom movement was full
of contradictions. The libertarians did not concern themselves with the quality of sexual relationships or the larger social and emotional causes of sexual
frustration. They were less influenced by feminism than their counterparts
in the twenties; in theory they advocated the sexual liberation of women, but
in practice their outlook was male-centered and often downright misogynist.
They took for granted that prostitution and pornography were liberating. They
carried on about the hypocrisy of the sexual game—by which they meant men's
impatience with having to court women and pay lip service to their demands
for love, respect, and commitment. No one suggested that men's isolation of
sex from feeling might actually be part of the problem, rather than the solution.

Around the same time, more radical ideas were beginning to surface. While
I was in high school, I was fascinated by the Beats and their rejection of the
"square" institution of marriage. Later I began to read and learn from radical Freudians like Paul Goodman, Norman Mailer, Herbert Marcuse, and—
especially—the original radical Freudian, Wilhelm Reich. Where Freud contended that civilization required instinctual repression, Reich argued that what
Freud took to be civilization, in some absolute sense, was a specific, changeable
social structure—authoritarian, patriarchal, class-bound. In Reich's view the in-
cestuous fantasies, perverse impulses, and sadistic aggression that dominated
the Freudian unconscious were themselves the product of repression—the
child's response to the frustration of its natural sexual needs. He claimed that
when his patients managed to overcome their neurotic sexual inhibitions they
became spontaneously decent, rational, and cooperative; the problem, from the
conservative moralist's standpoint, was that they also developed a sense of independence and self-respect that made them question arbitrary authority, compulsive work, passionless marriage, and conventional moral and religious ideas.
The function of sexual repression, Reich concluded, was to instill in children
the submissive attitudes demanded by patriarchal "civilization." Thus a truly
revolutionary program could not be limited to economic issues, but must include demands for sexual liberation, the emancipation of women, and the transformation of the family. (Unsurprisingly, Goodman, Mailer, and other cultural
radicals heavily influenced by Reich's work did not pick up on his feminism.)

To my mind, Reich's most revolutionary assertion was also his simplest (some would say most simpleminded): that natural sexuality is the physical manifestation of love. He insisted that the perception of tenderness and sensuality as separate, even antagonistic phenomena was the collective neurosis of an antisexual culture, that pornography, prostitution, rape, and other forms of alienated sex were the by-products of ascetic moralism, the underside of patriarchy, the social equivalent of the Freudian unconscious. These ideas have encountered near-universal resistance; the belief in an intrinsic split between lust and love is one of our most deeply ingrained and cherished prejudices. Most people agree that untrammeled pursuit of sexual pleasure is one thing, socially responsible relationships quite another; debate is usually over the proper ratio of license to repression. Though all democratic thought is based on the premise that freedom is compatible with civilization, that under the right conditions people are capable of self-regulation, even dedicated democrats hesitate to apply this premise to sex and family life. Radicals criticize the conservative assumption that people are innately acquisitive, violent, and power-hungry; yet most swallow the parallel idea that the sexual drive is innately solipsistic. Sex, they assume, is different. Why? It just is. Everybody knows *that*.

What everybody knows is not necessarily wrong. But it seems clear to me that if there were no inherent opposition between freedom and responsibility, pleasure and duty, "mere" sex and serious love, the patriarchal family would create it. I believe that sexual love in its most passionate sense is as basic to happiness as food is to life and that living and sleeping with a mate one does not love in this sense violates fundamental human impulses. Which is to say that since passion is by definition spontaneous—we can behave in ways that inhibit or nurture it, but finally we feel it or we don't—a marital arrangement based on legal, economic, or moral coercion is oppressive. But the whole point of marriage is to be a binding social alliance, and it cannot fulfill that function unless mates are forced or intimidated into staying together. Traditional patriarchal societies dealt with this contradiction by refusing to recognize passionate love as a legitimate need. For men it was seen as an illicit disruptive force that had nothing to do with the serious business of family; for women it was usually proscribed altogether. The modern celebration of romantic love muddled the issue: now we want marriage to serve two basically incompatible purposes, to be at once a love relationship and a contract. We exalt love as the highest motive for marriage, but tell couples that of course passion fades into "mature" conjugal affection. We want our mates to be faithful out of love, yet define monogamy as an obligation whose breach justifies moral outrage and legal revenge. We agree that spouses who don't love each other should not have to stay together, even for the sake of the children; yet we uphold a system that makes women economic prisoners and condone restrictive adversary divorce laws. We argue that without the legal and moral pressure of marriage lovers won't make the effort required to live intimately with someone else; but by equating emotional commitment with the will to live up to a contract, we implicitly define passion as unserious, peripheral to real life.

Another equally insoluble conflict is built into the nuclear family. Children are a twenty-four-hour-a-day responsibility, yet parents have legitimate needs for personal freedom, privacy, and spontaneity in their lives. The brunt of this conflict falls on mothers, but even if fathers shared child care equally, the basic problem would remain. Child rearing is too big a job for one or even two people to handle without an unnatural degree of self-sacrifice, destructive for both generations.

A different kind of family structure could solve or ease these problems. In matrilineal societies mothers, children, and their blood relatives were the ongoing social unit; the permanence of sexual relationships apparently became an issue with the rise of patriarchy. In traditional patriarchies the extended family at least gave parents some relief from responsibility for their offspring. The logical postpatriarchal unit is some version of the commune. Groups of people who agreed to take responsibility for each other, pool their economic resources, and share housework and child care would have a basis for stability independent of any one couple's sexual bond; children would have the added security of close ties to adults other than their biological parents (and if the commune were large and flexible enough, parents who had stopped being lovers might choose to remain in it); communal child rearing, shared by both sexes, would remove the element of martyrdom from parenthood.

I realize that the kind of change I'm talking about amounts to a social and psychic revolution of almost inconceivable magnitude. Yet to refuse to fight for love that is both free and responsible is in a sense to reject the possibility of love itself. I suspect that in a truly free society sexual love would be at once more satisfying and less terrifying, that lovers would be more spontaneously monogamous but less jealous, more willing to commit themselves deeply yet less devastated if a relationship had to end. Still, there is an inherent, irreducible risk in loving: it means surrendering detachment and control, giving our lovers the power to hurt us by withdrawing their love, leaving, or wanting someone else. The marriage contract appeals to our self-contradictory desire to negate that risk, nullify that power. I don't mean to suggest that people who reject marriage are less afflicted with this desire than anyone else; remaining single can be an excellent way of distancing oneself from love, or avoiding it altogether. But I am convinced that contrary to its myth, the institution supports our fear of love rather than our yearning for it. We can embrace marriage, hoping to transcend its contradictions, or reject it, hoping to find something better; either way we are likely to be disappointed.

Until recently I had no doubt which route I preferred. I had married at twenty, left three years later, and though I did not rule out marrying again if I had some specific practical reason, the idea bothered me the way the thought of signing a loyalty oath always had. It was not the public, ceremonial aspect of marriage

I objected to—I thought the decision to share one's life with a lover was worth celebrating—but the essence of marriage, the contract. Whatever two people's private view of their relationship, however they might adapt the ceremony, in getting legally married they officially agreed to be bound by the rules of a patriarchal institution—one of which was that the state defined the circumstances in which they could be unbound. Besides, most people made endless assumptions about married couples and treated them accordingly; it wasn't so easy to get married and pretend you weren't.

I was also put off by the marriages I observed; domestic life as most of my peers lived it made me feel claustrophobic. What disturbed me was the degree of emotional repression most "successful" (that is, stable and reasonably contented) marriages seemed to involve. Given the basic contradictions of the family, it inevitably provoked conflicts that had to be submerged. But the conditions of contemporary middle-class marriage—the prevalence of divorce and infidelity, the emergence of feminism, the nagging ambivalence about whether we were supposed to enjoy life or be Adults—tended to bring those conflicts into the open, requiring a whole extra layer of evasions to keep them at bay. While some couples had managed to fight out the battle of the sexes to a real understanding instead of a divorce, most successful marriages I knew of were based on a sexist détente: the husband had made it clear that he would not give up certain prerogatives and the wife pretended not to hate him for it. Add a bit of sexual and emotional boredom in an era when not to be madly in love with your spouse was a social embarrassment, and it was not surprising that so many "happy" couples radiated stifling dependence or low-level static. No, I would think, with a fair amount of smugness, better alone than trapped.

But the year I turned thirty-five, an odd thing happened: I had a persistent fantasy about getting married. It was—on the surface at least—a fantasy of triumph. At the time of my actual marriage, I had felt that my life was totally out of control. I was a scared kid making a promise I suspected I wouldn't keep, at a conventional wedding I didn't want, in a dress I'd been talked into getting. A rabbi I hardly knew presided over the traditional Jewish ritual, in which the bride gets to say precisely nothing. Since then I had, as they say, come a long way, but it had been a rocky trip. While I had rebelled against the idea that a woman needs a man to run her life, I had struggled with an undertow of conviction that such rebellion was disastrous hubris. On the level of social reality this made perfect sense; if feminism had taught me anything, it was that the liberated woman was a myth, that women who deviated from prescribed feminine behavior always paid a price. But the connection between the personal and the political is usually more convoluted than it seems. In fact, my conflict had less to do with the real social consequences of nonconformity than with an unconscious fear that I could not, after all, be female and yet competent to make my way through the world. In my relationships I had found it hard to draw the essential line between the power men have over women and the power all lovers have over each other—but I had begun to understand that what I was really fighting, more often than not, was the power of my own worst impulses to give in, give up, and be dependent.

That year, I felt the struggle was paying off. Some balance had shifted; emotionally I was on my own in a way I had not been before. And so my marriage fantasy was a kind of exorcism. Now that I was strong enough to love a man and preserve my identity, confident enough to make a choice that wouldn't be easy to get out of, I would do it over again and do it right—I would get to talk, play rock-and-roll, wear what I pleased. By marrying I would beat the system, give the lie to all the old farts who insisted that women could not have autonomy and love too. As the noted feminist Mick Jagger was to put it a couple of years later, American girls want everything—and I was no exception.

Though I sensed an underside to all this, I was too proud of my psychic victory to realize I was doing yet another version of the liberated woman tap dance, one that contained its own negation. These days the formula is familiar: women, we are told (often by women themselves) are now free enough so that they can choose to be sex objects/wear six-inch heels/do the housework without feeling oppressed. The unspoken question, of course, is whether women can refuse to be sex objects/wear six-inch heels/do the housework without getting zapped. When women start answering, in effect "We've made our point—let's not push our luck," it is a sure sign of backlash. And in retrospect it seems clear that my sudden interest in marriage (it's just a silly fantasy, I kept telling myself) was an early sign that the backlash was getting to me. As it intensified, I found myself, in moments of rank self-pity, thinking about marriage in a very different spirit. Okay (I would address the world), I've fought, I've paid my dues. I'm tired of being a crank, of being marginal. I want in!

As a single woman, and a writer who will probably never make much money, I feel more vulnerable now than I ever have before. My income has not kept up with inflation. I am approaching the biological deadline for maternity, confronting the possibility that the folklore of my adolescence—if a woman doesn't settle down with a man before she's thirty, forget it—may turn out to apply to me after all. I am very conscious of the sustenance I have always gotten (and mostly taken for granted) from the family I grew up in: the intense bonds of affection and loyalty; the acceptance born of long intimacy; the power of "we," of a shared slant on the world, a collective history and mythology, a language of familiar jokes and gestures. In some ways I have re-created these bonds with my closest friends, but it is not quite the same. The difference has to do with home being the place where when you have to go there they have to take you in—and also being (as the less-quoted next line of the poem has it) something you haven't to deserve. I have friends who would take me in, but on some level I think I have to deserve them.

Around the time I began having these feelings, but before I had quite faced them, I broke a long-standing taboo and had a love affair with a married man. At night I would sit in my kitchen arguing with myself, debates that usually began with the reflection that what I was doing was selfish, irresponsible, and an egregious breach of female solidarity. But goddammit, I would protest, I refuse to define it that way! I really believe there's such a thing as a basic human right to love whom you love and act on it.

But if you're hurting another woman? Making her unequal struggle with this whole fucked-up system more difficult?

Well, the fact is, it hurts if your mate wants someone else! That's an inescapable part of life—no matter what the almighty contract says!

Oh, yeah, right—life is unfair. And the children?

Silence, more coffee.

I never did resolve that argument; it just settled undigested in my stomach. Afterward, I had to admit I could not come up with a handy moral, except perhaps that there is no such thing as a free lunch. Morals aside, there was the matter of all those unacknowledged illusions about what I could get away with—humiliating perhaps, humbling certainly. At odd moments an old image would float into my mind. Once, as a bus I was riding in pulled out of a station, a silly-looking dog danced alongside, coming dangerously close to the wheels and yapping its lungs out. The bus rolled on.

Recently a friend reminded me that in the early, heady days of feminist activism I had said to her, "We're not going to see the results of this revolution in our lifetime; we're making it for the women who come after us." A judicious and sensible comment, but I'm not sure I ever really meant it. The reason feminism touched me so deeply was that I wanted the revolution for myself; I can't help being disappointed and angry that it is turning out to be every bit as difficult as I claimed to believe. Reaction is always temporary, I know that—what I'm afraid of is that it won't end in time to do me any good. But I also realize that kind of pessimism feeds the reaction and is in fact part of it. For all the external pressures that have contributed to the retrenchment of the erstwhile dissident community, in a sense reaction was built into its passionate optimism. The mentality that currently inspires sixties veterans to say things like "We didn't succeed in abolishing the family. This proves we were wrong—the family is necessary" is of a piece with the counterculture's notorious impatience. Our ambitions outstripped both the immediate practical possibilities and our own limitations. People turned themselves and each other inside out; terrible bitterness between women and men came to the surface; everything seemed to be coming apart, with no imminent prospect of our finding a better way to put it back together. A lot of people were relieved when the conservative mood of the seventies gave them an excuse to stop struggling and stretching themselves to uncertain purpose; a lot of men were particularly relieved when the backlash gave them support for digging in their heels against feminism. Some former rebels have turned against their past altogether, dismissing their vision as adolescent extravagance, reducing a decade of history to the part of it that was—inevitably—foolish and excessive. Many more have responded to the reaction with confusion and malaise. If women must reconcile their raised consciousness with the limits of a conservative time, men are torn between their more regressive impulses and their desire to be (or be thought) good guys. Increasingly, both sexes tend to define feminism and related cultural questions not as public issues calling for political action but as a matter of private "life styles" and "options." This sort of individualism is not only a retreat from sixties radicalism but in very real ways an extension of it—a more modest liberal version of the counterculture's faith that simply by dropping out of the system we could have the world and have it now.

That we did not manage in a few years to revolutionize an institution that has lasted for thousands, serving indispensable functions as well as oppressive ones, is hardly something to be surprised at or ashamed of. Rather, what needs to be repudiated is the naive arrogance implicit in slogans like "abolish the family" and "smash monogamy," in the illusion of so many counterculturists that revolution meant moving in with a bunch of people and calling it a commune. Far from being revolutionary, the cultural left was basically apolitical. That so much of its opposition was expressed in terms of contempt for capitalism and consumerism only confirms how little most sixties radicals understood the American social system or their own place in it. There is a neat irony in the fact that leftists are now romanticizing the family and blaming capitalism for its collapse, while ten years ago they were trashing the family and blaming capitalism for its persistence. Ah, dialectics: if an increasingly conservative capitalism has propelled the seventies backlash, it was a dynamic liberal capitalism that fostered the sixties revolt. The expansion of the American economy after World War II produced two decades of unprecedented prosperity, which allowed masses of people unprecedented latitude in making choices about how to live. Just as more and more people could afford to buy houses, cars, and appliances, they could choose to work less—or at less lucrative occupations—and still earn enough to survive without undue hardship, especially if they didn't have kids to support. As a result a growing minority—particularly among the children of the upper middle class—felt free to question the dominant social arrangements, to experiment and take risks, to extend student life with its essentially bohemian values into adulthood rather than graduate to professional jobs, nuclear families, and the suburbs.

What most counterculture opposition to capitalism amounted to was this minority's anger at the majority for refusing to make the same choice. Even the organized left, which should have known better, acted as if the way to change American society was for each person individually to renounce the family, material comfort, and social respectability. That most people were doing no such thing was glibly attributed to sexual repression, greed, and/or "brainwashing" by the mass media—the implication being that radicals and bohemians were sexier, smarter, less corrupt, and generally more terrific than everyone else. Actually, what they mostly were was younger and more privileged: it was easy to be a self-righteous antimaterialist if you had never known anxiety about money; easy to sneer at the security of marriage if you had solicitous middle-class parents; easy, if you were twenty years old and childless, to blame those parents for the ills of the world. Not that radicals were wrong in believing that a sexually free, communal society was incompatible with capitalism, or in perceiving connections between sexual repression, obsessive concern with material goods, and social conformity. But they did not understand that, psychology aside, most people submit to the power of institutions because they suffer unpleasant consequences if they don't. It made no sense to talk of abolishing the family without considering the genuine needs it served and organizing against the social pressures that inhibited us from satisfying those needs in other ways. In the seventies the left itself would provide the best illustration of that truth: it was when economic conditions worsened, around the time most sixties rebels were reaching an age where anxieties about the future were not so easy to dismiss, that radicals began to change their line on the family.

But if the political myopia of the counterculture was partly a matter of class and age, it was even more a matter of sex. Like every other segment of society, the counterculture was dominated by men, who benefited from the male privileges built into the family structure and so did not care to examine it too closely. While they were not averse to freeing themselves from their traditional obligations in the family, they had no intention of giving up their prerogatives. To support a woman, promise permanence or fidelity, or take responsibility for the children one fathered might be bourgeois, but to expect the same woman to cook and clean, take care of the kids, and fuck on command was only natural. Despite an overlay of radical Freudian rhetoric, their sexual ethos was more or less standard liberal permissiveness; they were not interested in getting rid of the roles of wife and whore, only in "liberating" women to play either as the occasion demanded.

It remained for the women's liberation movement to begin to understand the family in a political way. Radical feminists exposed the hypocrisy of a "cultural revolution" based on sexual inequality, attributed that inequality to the historic, institutionalized power of men as a group over women as a group, and called for a mass movement to end it. Feminism became the only contemporary political movement to make an organized effort to change, rather than simply drop out of the patriarchal family.

Feminist consciousness-raising and analysis produced a mass of information about the family as an instrument of female oppression. But on those aspects of family chauvinism that did not directly involve the subordination of women, the movement had little to say. (There were individual exceptions, notably Shulamith Firestone in *The Dialectic of Sex*.) Radical feminists tended to be skeptical of the counterculture's vision of a communal utopia. Many defended the nuclear family, arguing that it was not marriage, only traditional marital sex roles that oppressed women; at the other extreme were factions that challenged the value of heterosexuality and even sex itself.

In a sense, radical feminism defined itself in opposition to the psychological explanations of behavior so prevalent on the left. Most early women's liberationists had come out of a left-counterculture milieu where they were under heavy pressure to go along with the men's notion of sexual freedom. As soon as feminism surfaced, the left began to resist it by arguing that the conventional pattern of male-female relationships was the result of capitalist conditioning, that men were not oppressors but fellow victims. As feminists pointed out, this argument ignored the advantages men's privileged status conferred, their reluctance to give up those advantages, and the day-to-day social and economic constraints that kept women in their place. In effect it absolved men of all responsibility for their actions and implied that women could remedy their condition simply by straightening out their heads.

Vital as it was to combat the left's mushy, self-serving psychologism, radical feminists have tended to fall into the opposite error of dismissing psychology altogether. This bias has been particularly limiting when applied to the crucial subject of sex. Feminists have been inclined to blame women's sexual problems solely on men's exploitative behavior and lack of consideration for women's needs, whether emotional or specifically erotic. The criticism is accurate so far as it goes. But it is impossible to understand female—or for that matter male—sexuality without acknowledging the impact of growing up in a culture that despite its surface permissiveness is deeply antisexual. A distorted, negative view of sex is basic to patriarchal psychology: since girls learn to regard their genitals as a badge of inferiority, boys to equate theirs with dominance and aggression, sexual pleasure gets tangled up with sadistic and masochistic feelings and hostility between the sexes. At the same time, both sexes have a powerful emotional investment in traditionally masculine and feminine behavior because they associate it with their sexual identities and with sex itself.

Just as a real sexual revolution must be feminist, a genuinely radical feminism must include a critique of sexual repression and the family structure that perpetuates it. Yet the two questions remain distinct in most people's mind—a distinction that contributes to the backlash, since it allows people to succumb to family chauvinist attitudes without confronting their antifeminist implications. As it so often does, the right has a clearer grasp of the problem than its opposition, which is one reason "pro-family" reactionaries have been more politically effective than feminists who protest that they're not against the family, they just want women to have equality within it. The issue of family chauvinism is at the core of the conflict between feminist and antifeminist women, as well as the antagonism that smolders even in sophisticated feminist circles between wives who feel that single women do not support them or understand their problems and single women who feel that wives are collaborating with the system. While feminists have rightly emphasized the common oppression of married and single women and the ways men have pitted us against each other, this kind of analysis ignores the fact that the family has its own imperatives: just as women can ally with men to defend the interests of a class or race, they can share their husbands' family chauvinism. Women in a patriarchy have every reason to distrust male sexuality and fear their own. Under present conditions heterosexuality really is dangerous for women, not only because it involves the risk of pregnancy and of exploitation and marginality, but because it is emotionally bound up with the idea of submission. And so long as women are economically dependent on their husbands, they cannot afford to countenance the idea that men have a right to anything so unpredictable as passion. As a result, women are as likely as men—if not more so—to see the family as our only alternative to unbridled lust and rapine.

To regard marriage and singleness simply as "options," or even as situations equally favorable to men and oppressive to women, misses the point. The institution of the family and the people who enforce its rules and uphold its values define the lives of both married and single people, just as capitalism defines the lives of workers and dropouts alike. The family system divides us up into insiders and outsiders; as insiders, married people are more likely to identify with the established order, and when they do, they are not simply expressing a personal preference but taking a political stand. The issue, finally, is whether we have the right to hope for a freer, more humane way of connecting with each other. Defenders of the family seem to think that we have already gone too far, that the problem of this painful and confusing time is too much freedom. I think there's no such thing as too much freedom—only too little nerve.

Village Voice, September 1979

Tom Wolfe's Failed Optimism

My deepest impulses are optimistic, an attitude that seems to me as spiritually necessary and proper as it is intellectually suspect. In college and for some time afterward, my education was dominated by modernist thinkers and artists who taught me that the supreme imperative was courage to face the awful truth, to scorn the soft-minded optimism of religious and secular romantics as well as the corrupt optimism of governments, advertisers, and mechanistic or manipulative revolutionaries. I learned that lesson well (thought it came too late to wholly supplant certain critical opposing influences, like comic books and rock-and-roll). Yet the modernists' once-subversive refusal to be gulled or lulled has long since degenerated into a ritual despair at least as corrupt, soft-minded, and cowardly—not to say smug—as the false cheer it replaced. The terms of the dialectic have reversed: now the subversive task is to affirm an authentic postmodernist optimism that gives full weight to existent horror and possible (or probable) apocalyptic disaster, yet insists—credibly—that we can, well, overcome. The catch is that you have to be an optimist (an American?) in the first place not to dismiss such a project as insane.

A subtheme of the sixties utopianism was the attempt—often muddled, at times self-negating—to arrive at some sort of honest optimism. This concern was also implicit in the antiutopian sensibility first self-consciously articulated by the pop artists. Pop sensibility—loosely defined as the selective appreciation of whatever is vital and expressive in mass culture—did more than simply suggest that life in a rich, capitalist, consumption-obsessed society had its pleasures; the crucial claim was that those pleasures had some connection with genuine human feelings, needs, and values and were not—as both conservative and radical modernists assumed—mere alienated distraction. Pessimists like

Herbert Marcuse argued that advanced capitalism destroyed the autonomous self and with it the possibility of authentic pleasure, let alone happiness; pop implied a more sanguine view of the self as guerrilla, forever infiltrating territory officially controlled by the enemy, continually finding new ways to evade and even exploit the material and psychic obstacles that the social system continually erected. I shared this view; I doubted that either Marx or Freud would quarrel with the proposition that a human being who had the urge to build a castle, and found that the only material available was shit, would soon learn how to build shit castles—and how to use the unique properties of shit to advantage. Pop was about the ways in which the spirit of the people invaded the man's technology: restrict us to three chords, a back beat, and two minutes of air time, and we'll give you—rock-and-roll.

The pop stance was honest up to a point. But its commitment to making the most of the existing reality excluded painful or dangerous questions about systemic change. Not that pop optimism was devoid of political content: it was by definition populist (while modernist pessimism was, at least in part, an aristocratic vote of no-confidence in the lower orders), and it gleefully offended upper bourgeois pieties about art, taste, and the evils of consumerism. Nor did the pop sensibility deny or defend the various forms of oppression that at once hedged our pleasures and made them possible; its very celebration of human resilience implied an awareness of such barriers to fulfillment. But it took that tension for granted. The price of pop optimism was a deeper fatalism; in a way Andy Warhol's silk-screened electric chair was more chilling than anything in *One Dimensional Man.* Those of us who were unwilling to pay that price looked for ways to integrate the pop impulse with political and cultural radicalism and with the parallel experience of the immanence of the spirit—best described as religious—that had become a mass phenomenon because of a technological achievement called LSD. Yet pop remained central, if only because mass culture was the bloodstream in which other influences had to circulate if they were to have much effect.

I had no more than an inkling of the importance of all this when, in the fermenting mid-sixties, I first came across *The Kandy-Kolored Tangerine-Flake Streamline Baby.* The book—particularly the title piece and the one on Las Vegas, neither of which I'd read in their original *Esquire* incarnations—made a strong impression on me. Tom Wolfe had pulled off the remarkable feat of not only describing but embodying pop consciousness—an essentially alliterate phenomenon—in print. The baroque extravagance of his prose mirrored the cultural styles he was writing about; his narrative voice captured the single-minded vision, the manic enthusiasm, the confident, idiosyncratic genius of their inventors. He even played around with his own mass art, journalism, borrowing not only from fiction but from advertising and pulp jargon. His introduction laid out assumptions that had already begun to affect my view of the world: "Here was this incredible combination of form plus money in a place nobody ever thought about finding it. . . . Suddenly classes of people whose styles of life had been practically invisible had the money to build monuments to their own styles. . . . Stock car racing, custom cars—and, for that matter, the jerk, the monkey, rock music—still seem beneath serious consideration, still the preserve of ratty people with ratty hair and dermatitis. . . . Yet all these rancid people are creating new styles all the time and changing the life of the whole country in ways that nobody even bothers to record, much less analyze. . . . The new sensibility—*Baby baby baby where did our love go?*—the new world, submerged so long, invisible and now arising, slippy, shiny, electric—Super Scuba-man!—out of the vinyl deeps."

In comparison, Wolfe's second collection, *The Pump House Gang,* fell curiously flat. It was full of repetitious variations on the proliferation-of-styles theme, which in 1968 was no longer either new or neglected, and Wolfe's enthusiasm seemed forced, his rhetorical devices mechanical, as if he himself were bored with it all. Most of the pieces had been written two or three years earlier, and the gap showed. A lot had happened to overshadow, or at least complicate, all that churning of the vinyl deeps—the Vietnam escalation, black power, the burgeoning of radical and bohemian dissidence. Wolfe was not unaware of those events; on the contrary, he devoted a page of introduction to defensive ridicule of intellectuals' avidity for disaster: "War! Poverty! Insurrection! Alienation! O Four Horsemen, you have not deserted us entirely. The game can go on." He recalled that during a symposium on the sixties, a few years ago, the other panelists had been so obsessed with gloomy maunderings that he had been moved to protest. "'What are you talking about?' I said. 'We're in the middle of a . . . Happiness Explosion!'" Elsewhere in the introduction Wolfe announced the imminent spontaneous demise of the class structure, already accomplished in New York.

Though I did not expect incisive radical analysis from Tom Wolfe, anymore than I expected it from Mick Jagger, I did think a touch of the Stones'—or even the Beatles'—irony was in order. By indulging in mindless yea-saying, Wolfe betrayed the tension at the core of pop, converting it to a more sophisticated version of the traditional American booster mentality, whose purpose was, as it had always been, cosmetic. It was this betrayal, I suspected, that made *The Pump House Gang* so lifeless. There was some truth in Wolfe's complaint; intellectuals did have an emotional investment in apocalypse, for reasons that rightly offended his populism. But it was hard to take seriously a populism that willfully ignored certain discomfiting facts. Such as that the ratty-haired dermatitic kids whose creativity Wolfe so admired, and who populated the lower ranks of the class structure he so jauntily pronounced dead, were providing most of the bodies for the war.

Still, the book contained one piece that confounded all these judgments— "The Pump House Gang," Wolfe's account of the La Jolla surfers who hung out and hung loose on the beach, creating a hedonistic subculture based on physical perfection, daring, contempt for the straight life, mystical rapport with the ocean, above all youth and a horror of age. The story paid Wolfe's usual loving attention to surface minutiae, but it also had an underside. There was the *mysterioso* Pacific, which had somehow drowned this fantastic surfer, who should have been . . . *immune*; there was the ineluctable aging process, which would sooner or later consign the Pump House Gang to the cruel obsolescence they themselves had decreed. The piece made me shiver; it hovered on the edge of a metaphorical wave that suggested both the danger and the lure of the American ride. It also suggested Wolfe was basically too talented and too honest to practice the complacency he preached.

That suggestion was justified, and then some, by *The Electric Kool-Aid Acid Test*. I think *Acid Test* is a great book, certainly the best to come out of the sixties. Again Wolfe uses his reportorial gifts to get down a sensibility based largely on a revolt against the supremacy of words. But there is something more: *Acid Test* is about the whole sticky problem of optimism, of how to pursue the elusive synthesis. What makes the book so powerful—and so brave—is the way Wolfe allowed the Pranksters' vision to challenge and stretch his own. Ken Kesey and his friends created a wondrous new style, rooted in American history, myth, technology, and popular culture, but their aim was not aesthetic—it was messianic. If Wolfe's pop sympathies were engaged by the style, his antiutopianism must have been equally offended by the aim. Yet the two could not be separated, for they were complementary aspects of a central unifying impulse—to live out and spread the psychedelic experience. If Wolfe was really to do his job—report accurately on what the Pranksters' trip was about—he could not take them seriously on one level, dismiss them as silly hippies on another. Like everyone else he had in some sense to choose: was he on the bus or off?

For Wolfe, getting on did not mean taking acid—apparently he did not—or abdicating his particular role in the Pranksters' movie, which was to be a reporter. *Acid Test* always keeps the proper critical distance; it carefully documents the Pranksters' confusions, fuck-ups, and ultimate failure. But Wolfe does not hold himself aloof from the pain of that failure. From his first meeting with Kesey at the beginning of the book to the "WE BLEW IT!" litany at the end, he never shirks the recognition that there was a real chance to blow.

Wolfe has never risked or achieved so much since; in the seventies his writing has increasingly reflected and served the decade's characteristic failures of imagination and will. On its own terms, Wolfe's first seventies book, *Radical Chic & Mau-Mauing the Flak Catchers,* is successful, even brilliant; his demolition of rich liberals and of the charades that so often pass for left-wing politics in this country is maliciously accurate and irresistibly funny. Yet the terms themselves represent a retreat from the complex blend of identification and objectivity that informs the best of his earlier work to a more conventional stance as critic of manners and mores. And the pieces are a moral retreat as well. Like the *Pump House Gang* introduction, they offer specific truths in the service of a larger lie. Their underlying assumption is that political action is inherently ridiculous and irrelevant, nothing more than a ritual designed—like, say, a demolition derby—to meet the psychological needs of its participants. But while Wolfe has always regarded demolition derbies and most other American rituals with tolerance if not positive fondness, the very idea of social conscious pisses him off, and he takes a mean-spirited pleasure in discrediting it.

In his most recent work Wolfe's wit has declined as his crankiness has increased. *The Painted Word* parlays a slight and dubious thesis into a long and boring polemic. And *Mauve Gloves & Madmen, Clutter & Vine,* Wolfe's latest and weakest anthology, hits a note of asperity that suggests nothing so much as the curmudgeonly irritation of an old tory. The title piece is a heavy-handed, son-of-radical-chic exposé of that ungrateful wretch, the rich West Side writer who finances his rich West Side existence with jeremiads about repression and recession. "The Intelligent Co-Ed's Guide to America," a frankly conservative attack on radical intellectuals cum defense of American democracy, could have been lifted, minus a few exclamation points, from the pages of *Commentary*.

Then there is "The Me Decade and the Third Great Awakening," in which Wolfe attempts to graft his standard happiness-is-postwar-prosperity number to a report on the popularity of various therapeutic/sexual/religious invitations to self-fulfillment. The result has an oddly schizophrenic quality. On the one hand, the current preoccupation with "me" is a product of leisure and money, hence to be applauded as further evidence against the disaster mongers. On the other hand, it is not lower-class kids who show up at Esalen and EST but West Side writers who are bored with Martha's Vineyard, and anyway, all that silly self-absorption—all that psychic muckraking—what is it, really, but a form of internal disaster mongering? Wolfe does not try to reconcile these opposing trains of thought; he just scatters cheap shots in all directions and ends up saying less about middle-class narcissism than any random Feiffer cartoon.

The one memorable piece in *Mauve Gloves* is "The Truest Sport: Jousting with Sam and Charlie," a day-in-the-life account of Navy bomber pilots flying missions over North Vietnam. Wolfe's greatest strength is his ability to write from inside his subjects, even when they are inarticulate, and since that skill requires empathy rather than spleen, he has always written best about people he admires. He admires the bomber pilots. They are prototypical American heroes—not eccentric offshoots of the genre, like Kesey, but the real thing: men who do much and say little, who master rather than submit to machines, who test their skills to the limit, keep their cool in the face of death, and enjoy a mystical confrontation with the universe denied ordinary mortals.

A few years ago, Wolfe wrote about the same brand of heroism in his *Rolling Stone* series on the Apollo 17 astronauts. But astronauts are one thing, bomber pilots quite another. The real suspense of "The Truest Sport" is not whether Dowd and Flint will make it back from their deadly trip over Haiphong harbor, but whether Wolfe can compel his readers—most of whom, he knows, are inclined to regard Vietnam bomber pilots as war criminals—to see these men as complex human beings who are in certain ways admirable, more admirable perhaps than you or I. Improbably, he succeeds, at least with me. "The Truest Sport" is an impressive tour de force. It has, however, one rather disturbing flaw: the Vietnamese are as invisible to Wolfe as they were to the pilots.

What bothers me is not that Wolfe didn't write an antiwar tract but that the issue of whether the war was right or wrong, the bombings necessary or criminal, is not even an implicit issue in the piece. What matters to Wolfe is that he prefers the pilots' stoic style to that of whiny, bad-sport peaceniks who never put their lives on the line but whose influence on the conduct of the war—particularly the restrictions placed on bombing raids—made the pilots' task more difficult and dangerous. I wish I could believe that Wolfe's use of the sporting metaphor (it is one of the pilots who compares the bombing missions to jousting) is at least a bit ironic. But I'm afraid the truth is that Wolfe simply refuses to entertain the possibility that there are times when style is beside the point.

The continuing inability of someone as intelligent and perceptive as Tom Wolfe to confront unpleasant political realities in any serious way—even to admit that, like it or not, they exist—strikes me as not just obtuse but neurotic. It comes, I think, from Wolfe's failure to resolve the contradiction between his populist faith in human possibility and his essentially conservative political instincts. The cultural excitement of the sixties allowed Wolfe to avoid facing that conflict; it was possible then to nourish the illusion that politics didn't matter, that the real action was elsewhere. For all the prominence of political movements, it was the idea of cultural revolution—whether in its right-wing (pop) or left-wing (psychedelic) versions—that dominated the sixties imagination; Kesey was antipolitical, in his way a class American individualist, and Wolfe loved the way the Pranksters' anarchism befuddled the straight left. But the times changed, abruptly and rudely exposing the fragility of that idea—and of the prosperity on which it had depended. Cultural revolution had been a side effect of expanding American empire; thanks to the Vietnamese, the expansive days were over. The vaunted postscarcity economy, which would make all that nasty conflict between classes academic, had failed to arrive; if you believed the projections of ecologists, it never would. And in the absence of a political spark the happiness explosion was fizzling out.

Deprived of cultural fireworks to celebrate, Wolfe diverted his energy to attacking the left—to, as it were, killing the bearer of bad news. But the repressed always returns. At this point, Wolfe's optimism, such as it is, denies rather than affirms. The voice he raises against his archenemies, the disaster mongers, is the strident, defensive, I'm-all-right-Jack voice of official rationalization, a negative voice worthy of the archenemies themselves. It is, one might say, the sound of the . . . old sensibility . . . once again having the last whine. For the time being.

Village Voice, 1977

The Velvet Underground

I'll Let You Be in My Dream

A change of fantasy: I have just won the first annual Keith Moon Memorial Essay Contest. (This year's subject was "Is Ecstasy Dead?") The prize is a fallout shelter in the bowels of Manhattan, reachable only through a secret entrance in CBGB's basement. It is fully stocked: on entering the contest I was asked to specify my choice of drugs (LSD), junk food (Milky Way), T-shirt ("Eat the Rich"), book *(Parade's End),* movie *(The Wizard of Oz),*[1] rock-and-roll single ("Anarchy in the U.K."), and rock-and-roll album. The album is *Velvet Underground,* an anthology culled from the Velvets' first three LPs. (My specially ordered version of this collection is slightly different from the original; for "Afterhours," a song I've never liked much, it substitutes "Pale Blue Eyes," one of my favorites.) The songs on *Velvet Underground* are all about sin and salvation. As luck would have it, I am inspecting my winnings at the very moment that a massive earthquake destroys a secret biological warfare laboratory inside the Indian Point nuclear power plant, contaminating New York City with a virulent, radioactive form of Legionnaires' disease. It seems that I will be contemplating sin and salvation for a long time to come.

I Love the Sound of Breaking Glass

In New York City in the middle sixties the Velvet Underground's lead singer, guitarist, and auteur, Lou Reed, made a fateful connection between two seemingly disparate ideas—the rock-and-roller as self-conscious aesthete and the rock-and-roller as self-conscious punk. (Though the word *punk* was not used generically until the early seventies, when critics began applying it to un-regenerate rock-and-rollers with an aggressively lower-class style, the concept goes all the way back to Elvis.) The Velvets broke up in 1970, but the aesthete-punk connection was carried on, mainly in New York and England, by Velvets-influenced performers like Mott the Hoople, David Bowie (in his All the Young Dudes rather than his Ziggy Stardust mode), Roxy Music and its offshoots, the New York Dolls and the lesser protopunk bands that played Manhattan's Mercer Arts Center before it (literally) collapsed, the antipunk Modern Lovers, the archpunk Iggy Stooge/Pop. By 1977, the same duality had surfaced in new ways, with new force, under new conditions, to become the basis of rock-and-roll's new wave.

There are important differences, both temperamental and musical, that di-vide today's punks and punkoids from the Velvets and other precursors and from each other; American punk (still centered in New York) and its British counterpart are not only different but in a sense opposed. Yet all this music belongs to a coherent genre, implicitly defined by the tension between the term *punk* and the more inclusive *new wave,* with its arty connotations. If the Velvets invented this genre, it was clearly anticipated by the Who: Pete Townshend, after all, is something of an aesthete, and Roger Daltrey something of a punk. It was not surprising that the impulse to make music that united formal ele-gance and defiant crudity should arise among working-class Englishmen and take shape among New York bohemians; each environment was, in its own way, highly structured and ridden with conflict. And as a vehicle for that impulse, rock-and-roll had unique advantages: it was defiantly crude, yet for those who were tuned in to it, it was also a musical, verbal, and emotional language rich in formal possibilities.

The Who, the Velvets, and the new wave bands have all shared this concep-tion of rock-and-roll; their basic aesthetic assumptions have little to do with what is popularly known as "art rock." The notion of rock-as-art inspired by Dylan's conversion to the electric guitar—the idea of making rock-and-roll more musically and lyrically complex, of combining elements of jazz, folk, clas-sical, and avant-garde music with a rock beat, of creating "rock opera" and "rock poetry"—was from the rock-and-roll fan's perspective a dubious one. At best it stimulated a vital and imaginative eclecticism that spread the values of rock-and-roll even as it diffused and diluted them. At worst it rationalized a form of cultural upward mobility, concerned with achieving the appearance and pre-tensions of art rather than the reality—the point being to "improve" rock-and-roll by making it palatable to the upper middle class. Either way, it submerged rock-and-roll in something more amorphous and high-toned called rock. But from the early sixties (Phil Spector was the first major example) there was a countertradition in rock-and-roll that had much more in common with "high" art—in particular avant-garde art—than the ballyhooed art-rock syntheses: it involved more or less consciously using the basic formal canons of rock-and-roll as material (much as the pop artists used mass art in general) and refining, elaborating, playing off that material to produce what might be called rock-and-roll art. While art rock was implicitly based on the claim that rock-and-roll was or could be as worthy as more established art forms, rock-and-roll art came out of an obsessive commitment to the language of rock-and-roll and an equally obsessive disdain for those who rejected that language or wanted it watered down, made easier. In the sixties the best rock often worked both ways: the special virtue of sixties culture was its capacity for blurring boundaries, transcending contradictions, pulling off everything at once. But in the seventies the two tendencies have increasingly polarized: while art rock has fulfilled its most philistine possibilities in kitsch like Yes (or, for that matter, Meat Loaf), the new wave has inherited the countertradition, which is both less popular and more conscious of itself *as* a tradition than it was a decade ago.

The Velvets straddled the categories. They were nothing if not eclectic: their music and sensibility suggested influences as diverse as Bob Dylan and Andy Warhol, Peter Townshend and John Cage; they experimented with demented feedback and isolated, pure notes and noise for noise's sake; they were partial to sweet, almost folk-like melodies; they played the electric viola on "Desolation Row." But they were basically rock-and-roll artists, building their songs on a beat that was sometimes implied rather than heard, on simple, tough, pithy lyrics about their hard-edged urban demimonde, on rock-and-roll's oldest metaphor for modern city life—anarchic energy contained by a tight, repetitive structure. Some of the Velvets' best songs—"Heroin," especially—redefined how rock-and-roll was supposed to sound. Others—"I'm Waiting for the Man," "White Light/White Heat," "Beginning to See the Light," "Rock & Roll"—used basic rock-and-roll patterns to redefine how the music was supposed to feel.

The Velvets were the first important rock-and-roll artists who had no real chance of attracting a mass audience. This was paradoxical. Rock-and-roll was a mass art, whose direct, immediate appeal to basic emotions subverted class and educational distinctions and whose formal canons all embodied the perception that mass art was not only possible but satisfying in new and liberating ways. Insofar as it incorporates the elite, formalist values of the avant-garde, the very idea of rock-and-roll art rests on a contradiction. Its greatest exponents—the Beatles, the Stones, and (especially) the Who—undercut the contradiction by making the surface of their music deceptively casual, then demolished it by reaching millions of kids. But the Velvets' music was too overtly intellectual, stylized, and distanced to be commercial. Like pop art, which was very much a part of the Velvets' world, it was antiart art made by antielite elitists. Lou Reed's aesthete-punk persona, which had its obvious precedent in the avant-garde tradition of artist-as-criminal-as-outlaw, was also paradoxical in the context of rock-and-roll. The prototypical rock-and-roll punk was the (usually white) working-class kid hanging out on the corner with his (it was usually his) pals; by middle-class and/or adult standards he might be a fuck-off, a hell-raiser, even a delinquent, but he was not really sinister or criminal. Reed's punk was closer to that bohemian (and usually black) hero, the hipster: he wore shades, took hard drugs, engaged in various forms of polymorphous perversity; he didn't just hang out on the corner, he lived out on the street, and he was a loner.

As white exploitation of black music, rock-and-roll has always had its built-in ironies, and as the music went further from its origins, the ironies got more acute. Where, say, Mick Jagger's irony was about a white middle-class English bohemian's (and later a rich rock star's) identification with and distance from his music's black American roots, his working-class image, and his teenage audience, Lou Reed's irony made a further leap. It was not only about a white middle-class Jewish bohemian's identification with and distance from black hipsters (an ambiguity neatly defined when Reed-as-junkie, waiting for his man on a Harlem street corner, is challenged, "Hey white boy! Whatchou doin' up-town?") but about his use of a mass art form to express his aesthetic and social alienation from just about everyone. And one of the forms that alienation took pointed to yet another irony. While the original, primal impulse of rock-and-roll was to celebrate the body, which meant affirming sexual and material pleasure, Reed's temperament was not only cerebral but ascetic. There was nothing resembling lustiness in the Velvets' music, let alone any hippie notions about the joys of sexual liberation. Reed did not celebrate the sadomasochism of "Venus in Furs" any more than he celebrated heroin; he only acknowledged the attraction of what he saw as flowers of evil. Nor did he share his generation's enthusiasm for hedonistic consumption—to Reed the flash of the affluent sixties was fool's gold. Like Andy Warhol and the other pop artists he responded to the aesthetic potency of mass cultural styles; like Warhol he was fascinated by decadence— that is, style without meaning or moral content; but he was unmoved by that aspect of the pop mentality, and of rock-and-roll, that got off on the American dream. In a sense, the self-conscious formalism of his music—the quality that made the Velvets uncommercial—was an attempt to purify rock-and-roll, to purge it of all those associations with material goodies and erotic good times.

Though it's probable that only the anything-goes atmosphere of the sixties could have inspired a group like the Velvets, their music was prophetic of a leaner, meaner time. They were from—and of—hardheaded, suspicious New York, not utopian, good-vibes California. For all Lou Reed's admiration of Bob Dylan, he had none of Dylan's faith in the liberating possibilities of the edge— what he had taken from *Highway 61 Revisited* and *Blonde on Blonde* was the sound of the edge fraying. Like his punk inheritors, he saw the world as a hostile place and did not expect it to change. In rejecting the optimistic consensus of the sixties, he prefigured the punks' attack on the smug consensus of the seventies; his thoroughgoing iconoclasm anticipated the punks' contempt for all authority—including the aesthetic and moral authority of rock-and-roll itself.

Throughout this decade rock-and-roll has been struggling to reclaim its identity as a music of cultural opposition, not only distinct from but antagonistic to its own cultural conglomerate, rock. The chief accomplishment of the punks has been to make that antagonism explicit and public in a way that is clearly contemporary—that is, has nothing to do with "reviving" anything except the spirit of opposition itself. What is new in rock-and-roll—what is uncomfortable and abrasive and demanding—is the extent to which it insists on a defensive stance; the authentic late seventies note is nothing so much as cranky. Though the British punk movement was in some respects a classic revolt of youth—a class-conscious revolt, at that—its self-mocking nihilism is a classic crank attitude, while the American new wave makes up in alienated smart-assism for what it lacks in shit-smearing belligerence. The power and vitality of the crank posture are attested to by the way it makes less discordant sensibilities sound corny, even to those of us who might prefer to feel otherwise. Bruce Springsteen may still pull off a credible mélange of fifties teenage-street-kid insurgency, sixties apocalyptic romance, and early/mid-seventies angst, but he is an anomaly; so is Graham Parker, whose stubborn and convincing faith in traditional rock-and-roll values recalls John Fogerty's. Patti Smith, on the other hand, is a transitional figure, half cranky messiah, half messianic crank. The rock-and-rollers who exemplify the current aesthetic do so with wide variations in intensity, from Johnny Rotten (maniacal crank) to Elvis Costello (passionate crank) to Nick Lowe or Talking Heads (cerebral cranks) to the Ramones (cranks of convenience). (The Clash, one convolution ahead, is boldly anti- or postcrank—the first eighties band?) The obvious core of their crankiness is their consciousness of themselves as a dissident minority, but it's more complicated than that. Real, undiluted rock-and-roll is almost by definition the province of a dissident minority (larger at some times than at others); it achieved its cultural hegemony in the sixties only by becoming rock—by absorbing competing cultural values and in turn being absorbed, making a new rebellion necessary. What is different now is that for the first time in the music's twenty-five-year history, rock-and-rollers seem to accept their minority status as given and even to revel in it. Which poses an enormous contradiction, for real rock-and-roll almost by definition aspires to convert the world.

In some ways the crankiness of current rock-and-rollers resembles the disaffection of an earlier era of bohemians and avant-gardists convinced they had a vision the public was too intractably stupid and complacent to comprehend. But because the vision of rock-and-roll is inherently populist, the punks can't take themselves seriously as alienated artists; their crankiness is leavened with irony. At the same time, having given up on the world, they can't really take themselves seriously as rock-and-rollers, either. They are not only antiart artists but antipeople populists—the English punks, especially, seem to abhor not only the queen, America, rich rock stars, and the uncomprehending public, but humanity itself. The punks' working-class-cum-lumpen style is implicitly political; it suggests collective opposition and therefore communal affirmation. But it is affirmation of a peculiarly limited and joyless sort. For the new wave's minimalist conception of rock-and-roll tends to exclude not only sensual pleasure but the entire range of positive human emotions, leaving only what is hard and violent, or hard and distanced, or both: if the punks make sex an obscenity, they make love an embarrassment.

In reducing rock-and-roll to its harshest essentials, the new wave took Lou Reed's aesthete-punk conceit to a place he never intended. For the Velvets the aesthete-punk stance was a way of surviving in a world that was out to kill you; the point was not to glorify the punk, or even to say fuck you to the world, but to be honest about the strategies people adopt in a desperate situation. The Velvets were not nihilists but moralists. In their universe nihilism regularly appears as a vivid but unholy temptation, love and its attendant vulnerability as scary and poignant imperatives. Though Lou Reed rejected optimism, he was enough of his time to crave transcendence. And finally—as "Rock & Roll" makes explicit—the Velvets' use of a mass art form was a metaphor for transcendence, for connection, for resistance to solipsism and despair. Which is also what it is for the punks; whether they admit it or not, that is what *their* irony is about. It may be sheer coincidence, but it was in the wake of the new wave that Reed recorded "Street Hassle," a three-part, eleven-minute antinihilist anthem that is by far the most compelling piece of work he has done in his post-Velvets solo career. In it he represents nihilism as double damnation: loss of faith that love is possible, compounded by denial that it matters. "That's just a lie," he mutters at the beginning of part three. "That's why she tells her friends. 'Cause the real song—the real song she won't even admit to herself."

The Real Song, or I'll Never Be Your Mirror

If the Velvets suggested continuity between art and violence, order and chaos, they posed a radical split between body and spirit. In this way too they were closer to the Who than to any other contemporaries. Like the Velvets the Who were fundamentally ascetic; they too saw the world as hostile—particularly the world as organized by the British class system. Their defiance was cruder than the Velvets', their early music as hard and violent as any to come out of the new wave. But they were not cranks; they were determined to convert the world, and Townshend's guitar smashing expressed his need to break through to his audience as well as his contempt for authority, including the authority of rock-and-roll itself. That need to connect also took another form: even before Townshend discovered Meher Baba, the Who's music had a side that could only be called religious. If it seemed, at first, surprising that the same band could produce music as uncompromising in its bitterness as "Substitute" and as miraculously transcendent as the "You are forgiven!" chorus of "A Quick One," it was no contradiction; on the contrary, it was precisely Townshend's sense of the harshness of life, the implacability of the world, that generated his spiritual hunger.

The same can be said of Lou Reed, except that *spiritual hunger* seems too self-important a phrase to apply to him; the Velvets' brand of spirituality has little in common with the Who's grand bursts of mystical ecstasy or Townshend's self-conscious preoccupation with the quest for enlightenment. It's impossible to imagine Lou Reed taking up with a guru, though he might well write a savagely funny (and maybe chillingly serious) song about one. The aesthete-punk and his fellow demimondaines are not seeking enlightenment, though they stumble on it from time to time; like most of us they are pilgrims in spite of themselves. For Townshend moral sensitivity is a path to spiritual awareness; for Reed awareness and the lack—or refusal—of it have an intrinsically moral dimension. While he is not averse to using the metaphors of illusion and enlightenment—sometimes to brilliant effect, as in "Beginning to See the Light" and "I'll Be Your Mirror"—they are less central to his theology than the concepts of sin and grace, damnation and salvation. Some of his songs ("Heroin," "Jesus," "Pale Blue Eyes") explicitly invoke that Judeo-Christian language; many more imply it.

But *theology* too is an unfairly pretentious word. The Velvets do not deal in abstractions but in states of mind. Their songs are about the feelings the vocabulary of religion was invented to describe—profound and unspeakable feelings of despair, disgust, isolation, confusion, guilt, longing, relief, peace, clarity, freedom, love—and about the ways we (and they) habitually bury those feelings, deny them, sentimentalize them, mock them, inspect them from a safe, sophisticated distance in order to get along in the hostile, corrupt world. For the Velvets the roots of sin are in this ingrained resistance to facing our deepest, most painful, and most sacred emotions; the essence of grace is the comprehension that our sophistication is a sham, that our deepest, most painful, most sacred desire is to recover a childlike innocence we have never, in our heart of hearts, really lost. And the essence of love is sharing that redemptive truth: on the Velvets' first album, which is dominated by images of decadence and death, suddenly, out of nowhere, comes Nico's artless voice singing, "I'll be your mirror / . . . The light on your door to show that you're home. / When you think the night has seen your mind / That inside you're twisted and unkind / . . . Please put down your hands, 'cause I see you."

For a sophisticated rock-and-roll band with a sophisticated audience this vision is, to say the least, risky. The idea of childlike innocence is such an invitation to bathos that making it credible seems scarcely less difficult than getting the camel of the Gospels through the needle's eye. And the Velvets' alienation is also problematic: it's one thing for working-class English kids to decide life is shit, but how bad can things be for Lou Reed? Yet the Velvets bring it off— make us believe/admit that the psychic wounds we inflict on each other are real and terrible, that to scoff at innocence is to indulge in a desperate lie—because they never succumb to self-pity. Life may be a brutal struggle, sin inevitable, innocence elusive and transient, grace a gift, not a reward ("Some people work very hard / But still they never get it right," Lou Reed observes in "Beginning to See the Light"); nevertheless we are responsible for who and what we become. Reed does not attempt to resolve this familiar spiritual paradox, nor does he regard it as unfair. His basic religious assumption (like Baudelaire's) is that like it or not we inhabit a moral universe, that we have free will, that we must choose between good and evil, and that our choices matter absolutely. If we are rarely strong enough to make the right choices, if we can never count on the moments of illumination that make them possible, still it is spiritual death to give up the effort.

That the Velvets are hardly innocents, that they maintain their aesthetic and emotional distance even when describing—and evoking—utter spiritual nakedness, does not undercut what they are saying; if anything, it does the opposite. The Velvets compel belief in part because, given its context, what they are saying is so bold: not only do they implicitly criticize their own aesthetic stance—they risk undermining it altogether, ending up with sincere but embarrassingly banal home truths. The risk is real because the Velvets do not use irony as a net, a way of evading responsibility by keeping everyone guessing about what they really mean. On the contrary, their irony functions as a metaphor for the spiritual paradox, affirming that the need to face one's nakedness and the impulse to cover it up are equally real, equally human. If the Velvets' distancing is self-protective (hence in their terms damning), it is also revelatory (hence redeeming); it makes clear that the feelings being protected are so unbearably intense that if not controlled and contained they would overwhelm both the Velvets and their audience. The Velvets' real song is how hard it is to admit, even to themselves.

That song in its many variations is the substance of *Velvet Underground.* This album can be conceived of—nonlinearly; the cuts are not at all in the right order—as the aesthete-punk's *Pilgrim's Progress,* in four movements. ("Sha la la, man, whyn't you just slip away?" I can hear Lou Reed say to that.)

One: Worldly Seduction and Betrayal

"Sunday Morning," a song about vague and ominous anxiety, sums up the emotional tone of this movement: "Watch out, the world's behind you." "Here She Comes Now" and "Femme Fatale," two songs about beautiful but unfeeling women (in the unlovable tradition of pop—not to mention religious—misogyny, Lou Reed's women are usually demonic or angelic icons, not people), sum up its philosophy: "Aah, it looks so good / Aah, but she's made out of wood." These songs underscore the point by juxtaposing simple, sweet, catchy melodies with bitter lyrics sung in flat, almost affectless voices (in "Sunday Morning," Reed's voice takes on a breathiness that suggests suppressed panic). "White Light/ White Heat," a song about shooting speed, starts out by coming as close as any Velvets song does to expressing the euphoria of sheer physical energy; by the end of the trip the music has turned into bludgeoning, deadening noise, the words into a semiarticulate mumble.

Two: The Sin of Despair

"Heroin" is the Velvets' masterpiece—seven minutes of excruciating spiritual extremity. No other work of art I know about has made the junkie's experience so powerful, so horrible, so appealing; listening to "Heroin" I feel simultaneously impelled to somehow save this man and to reach for the needle. The song is built around the tension between the rush and the nod—expressed musically by an accelerating beat giving way to slow, solemn chords that sound like a bell tolling; metaphorically by the addict's vision of smack as a path to transcendence and freedom, alternating with his stark recognition that what it really offers is the numbness of death, that his embrace of the drug ("It's my wife and it's my life") is a total, willful rejection of the corrupt world, other people, feeling. In the beginning he likens shooting up to a spiritual journey: he's gonna try for the Kingdom; when he's rushing on his run he feels like Jesus's son. At the end, with a blasphemous defiance that belies his words, he avows, "Thank your God that I'm not aware / And thank God that I just don't care!" The whole song seems to rush outward and then close in on itself, on the moment of truth when the junkie knowingly and deliberately chooses death over life—chooses damnation. It is the clarity of his consciousness that gives the sin its enormity. Yet the clarity also offers a glimmer of redemption. In the very act of choosing numbness the singer admits the depths of his pain and bitterness, his longing for something better; he is aware of every nuance of his rejection of awareness; he sings a magnificently heartfelt song about how he doesn't care. (A decade later, Johnny Rotten will do the same thing in an entirely different way.) A clear, sustained note runs through the song like a bright thread; it fades out or is drowned out by chaotic, painful distortion and feedback, then comes through again, like the still small voice of the soul. Reed ends each verse with the refrain, "And I guess that I just don't know." His fate is not settled yet.

Three: Paradise Sought, Glimpsed, Recollected

This movement consists of four songs about world-weary sophistication and the yearning for innocence. "Candy Says" defines the problem: "I've come to hate my body and all that it requires in this world / . . . I'd like to know completely what others so discreetly talk about." "Jesus" is a prayer: "Help me in my weakness, for I've fallen out of grace." In "I'm Set Free" the singer has his illumination, but even as he tries to tell about it, to pin it down, it slips away: "I saw my head laughing, rolling on the ground / And now I'm set free to find a new illusion." In "Pale Blue Eyes" the world has gotten in the way of the singer's transcendent love: "If I could make the world as pure and strange as what I see / I'd put you in the mirror I put in front of me."

Musically these songs are of a piece. They are all gentle, reflective. They all make use of the tension between flat, detached voices and sweet melodies. They all have limpid guitar lines that carry the basic emotion, which is bitter-sweet: it is consoling to know that innocence is possible, inexpressibly painful that it always seems just out of reach. In "Pale Blue Eyes" a tambourine keeps the beat or, rather, is slightly off where the beat ought to be, while a spectacular guitar takes over completely, rolling in on wave after wave of pure feeling.

Four: Salvation and Its Pitfalls

"Beginning to See the Light" is the mirror held up to "Heroin." I've always been convinced that it's about an acid trip, perhaps because I first really heard it during one and found it utterly appropriate. Perhaps also because both the song and the acid made me think of a description of a peyote high by a Beat writer named Jack Green: "A group of us, on peyote, had little to share with a group on marijuana; the marijuana smokers were discussing questions of the utmost profundity and we were sticking our fingers in our navels & giggling." In "Beginning to See the Light" enlightenment (or salvation) is getting out from under the burden of self-seriousness, of egotism, of imagining that one's suffer-ings fill the universe; childlike innocence means being able to play. There is no lovelier moment in rock-and-roll than when Lou Reed laughs and sings, with amazement, joy, gratitude, "I just wanta tell you, *everything* is all right!"

But "Beginning to See the Light" is also wickedly ironic. Toward the end, carried away by euphoria, Reed cries, "There are problems in these times / But ooh, none of them are mine!" Suddenly we are through the mirror, back to the manifesto of "Heroin": "I just don't care!" Enlightenment has begotten spiri-tual pride, a sin that like its inverted form, nihilism, cuts the sinner off from the rest of the human race. Especially from those people who, you know, work very hard but never get it right. Finally we are left with yet another version of the spiritual paradox: to experience grace is to be conscious of it; to be conscious of it is to lose it.

Coda: I'd Love to Turn You On

Like all geniuses, Lou Reed is unpredictable. In "Street Hassle" he does as good a job as anyone of showing what was always missing in his and the Velvets' vision. As the song begins, a woman (or transvestite?) in a bar is buying a night with a sexy young boy. This sort of encounter is supposed to be squalid; it turns out to be transcendent. Reed's account of the odd couple's lovemaking is as ten-der as it is erotic: "And then sha la la la la he entered her slowly and showed her where he was coming from / And then sha la la la la he made love to her gently, it was like she'd never ever come." Of course, in part two he almost takes it all back by linking sex with death. Still.

What it comes down to for me—as a Velvets fan, a lover of rock-and-roll, a New Yorker, an aesthete, a punk, a sinner, a sometime seeker of enlightenment (and love) (and sex)—is this: I believe that we are all, openly or secretly, struggling against one or another kind of nihilism. I believe that body and spirit are not really separate, though it often seems that way. I believe that redemption is never impossible and always equivocal. But I guess that I just don't know.

Stranded by Greil Marcus, 1979

NOTES

Originally published in *Stranded: Rock and Roll for a Desert Island,* edited by Greil Marcus. New York: Knopf, 1979. The anthology was a compilation of critics' responses to the question "What rock-and-roll album would you take to a desert island?"

1. On second thought, I'd rather have *Gone With the Wind,* or maybe *The Harder They Come.*

Next Year in Jerusalem

Genesis

In the spring of 1975, my brother Michael, then 24, was on his way home from his third trip through Asia when he arrived in Israel, planning to stay a few weeks before heading back to New York. On April 28th, he wrote to our parents: "I've been staying at, of all things, an Orthodox Jewish yeshiva—when I got to Jerusalem I went to visit the Wailing Wall and got invited—they hang around there looking for unsuspecting tourists to proselytize. It's sort of a Jewish Jesus-freak type outfit—dedicated to bringing real Judaism to backsliding Jews. I haven't been especially impressed by the message, but it's been a really interesting week." On June 4th, he wrote me, "I've had my lack of faith shaken."

I appreciated the ironic turn of phrase. Then its meaning hit. I read on: "I've read and talked about it enough to realize that the arguments for the existence of G-d (a spelling which shows how superstitious I'm becoming)—and the Jewish version of it at that—are very plausible and intellectually if not emotionally convincing. . . . It's frightening, because while I can convince myself of the possibility and even probability of the religion, I don't like it—its 613 commandments, its puritanism, its political conservatism, its Jews-first philosophy. On the other hand, if it is the truth, not to follow it means turning your back on the truth." He was postponing his return till the end of July.

I called my parents. My mother thought I was being an alarmist—Mike couldn't be serious about religion; it was too removed from the way he'd been brought up. "He's spelling God 'G-d,'" I said. There is a religious law that you cannot destroy paper on which you have spelled out "God."

Two weeks later they got another letter: "I haven't written because I'm having trouble describing what's happening. I feel more and more that I'm trapped into a religion whose truth I can't deny. . . . I've never given much thought to the existence of God—my LSD experiences had (same as with Ellen) left me with the idea that there was 'something' there, but I never thought it was knowable or explainable (& if it was explainable certainly more in terms of mystical experience & Buddhism than the 'God of our Fathers' of Judaism). But my time here has really forced me to come to terms with what that 'something' might be. . . . I'm not Jesus-freaking out—I haven't come to this through any blinding moment of illumination or desire to be part of a group—it's been an intellectual process (which I've been fighting emotionally all the way), and I'd like nothing better than to reject it—I just don't think I'll be able to.

"The final shock in this letter is that I may not leave here at the end of July. If I accept this as the truth, I have to take time to learn about it."

The "truth" Mike proposed to accept was Judaism in its most extreme, absolutist form: the God of the Old Testament exists; He has chosen the Jewish people to carry out His will; the Torah (the Five Books of Moses and the Oral Law elaborating on them) is literally the word of God, revealed to the Jews at Mt. Sinai; the creation, the miracles in Egypt, and other biblical events actually happened; the Torah's laws, which are based on 613 *mitzvot* (commandments) and govern every aspect of one's existence, must be obeyed in every detail; they are eternal, unchangeable.

My parents had the same first impulse: "Let's go to Israel and bring him home." My father was already out of his chair and about to leave the house to go buy plane tickets when they looked at each other and decided they were overreacting. My own reaction was a kind of primal dread. In my universe, intelligent, sensible people who had grown up in secular homes in the second half of the 20th century did not embrace biblical fundamentalism—let alone arrive at it through an "intellectual process." My brother was highly intelligent, had always seemed sensible. What was going on?

My father is a retired police lieutenant; my mother is a housewife. They married during the Depression and now live in a house with a paid-up mortgage in a modestly middle-class section of Queens, New York. They are college educated, literary minded and politically liberal. I am the oldest of their three children; my sister, a graduate student in linguistics, is in the middle; Mike is the youngest. Mike and I were born in December, nine years apart almost to the day. The coincidence of birthdays is one of many similarities. If the prospect of Mike's becoming an Orthodox Jew was frightening, it was not simply because he was my brother, someone I loved. I felt an almost mystical identification with Mike. Our baby pictures were identical, and though Mike was now taller and thinner than I, we had the same fair skin, curly brown hair, and astigmatic, sleepy green eyes. We were (not that I really believed in that stuff—still—)

cliché Sagittarians: analytical, preoccupied with words and ideas. We were inclined to repress feelings; our intellectual confidence coexisted with emotional
insecurity and a tendency to depressions.

I was fascinated with the notion that Mike was what I might have become
had I been a man, the lastborn instead of the first—a child of the Seventies
rather than the Sixties. I wondered how much the differences between us had
to do with our circumstances rather than our basic natures. For there were
differences, of course. Mike was much more reserved than I; he rarely talked
about his feelings, his problems or his relationships. I was more worldly, more
willing to compete in and compromise with a hostile system. My friendships
were central to my life; he was, or seemed to be, a loner.

The qualities we shared were more pronounced in Mike, the opposing tendencies more hidden. Next to him I always felt a bit irrational and uncool. Picture a recurrent family scene: my father and I are sitting in the kitchen, having a
passionate political argument. My brother is listening, not saying a word. Suddenly I put myself in his place, become self-conscious. I hear all the half-truths
and rhetorical exaggerations that in the emotion of the moment I have allowed
to pass my lips. I realize, with chagrin, that my father and I have had, and my
brother has listened to, the same argument at least half a dozen times before. I
am sure Mike thinks we are ridiculous.

I was disturbed and mystified by what I saw as my brother's swing from a
skepticism more rigorous than my own to an equally extreme credulity. How
could anyone familiar with the work of a certain Viennese Jew possibly believe
in God the Father? What puzzled me even more was Mike's insistence that he
was being reluctantly convinced by irresistible arguments. It seemed to me that
his critical intelligence could only be in the way.

On acid I had, as Mike observed, experienced the *something* that Westerners
have most commonly called "God"—the source of all truth, beauty, goodness.
Unlike Mike, I had felt that I knew what it was. "So this is what it's all about," I
had marveled. "It's so simple. So obvious. And I've known it all the time. I just
didn't know I knew." But when I came down it was less obvious. The ecstasy—a
word that didn't quite convey a feeling as natural as a spring thaw, as comfortable as coming home—gradually slipped away. "All God is," I would try to explain, "is reality—the simple, wonderful reality behind the abstract concepts
and ingrained habits of perception that keep us from ever really experiencing it." And I would sound hopelessly abstract even to myself. Soon, whatever
clouded the doors of perception in ordinary life began to invade my acid trips as
well. I tried to fight that process—doggedly pursuing the right mood, the right
situation—and only made things worse; finally, frustrated and demoralized, I
stopped tripping. The entire experience had a permanent, profound effect on
the way I saw myself and the world. I knew that connecting with Reality—I
couldn't call it God; to me that word meant an old man with a white beard—was

the crucial business of life, the key to freedom, sanity, happiness. I knew that if I could make the connection I would think: "How silly of me to have forgotten!" But I didn't know how to proceed.

This problem was not, of course, peculiar to me. It had been plaguing spiritual seekers for thousands of years. Many had tried, far more eloquently than I, to express what they agreed was inexpressible. Recognizing the inadequacy of intellectual analysis, religions tried to evoke the crucial connection through myths, rituals, rules of conduct. But in the end religion, like language, tried to express the truth in concrete form and so inevitably distorted it. If all religions were inspired by a common Reality, each reflected the particular cultural, political and psychological limitations of the people who invented and practiced it. Which posed another problem. If you understood that your religion was only an imperfect approach to the truth, you remained outside it, an observer, a critic. If, on the other hand, you truly believed—worshipped an omnipotent God, accepted Jesus as your savior, surrendered to a guru—you were confusing a set of metaphors for reality with Reality itself. And that put you back on square one. Or did it?

On my second acid trip I had had a joyous vision of the birth of Christ. In one part of my mind I had become an early Christian, experiencing the ecstasy of grace, redemption, the washing away of sin. But on a deeper level I had remained aloof, thinking, "Remember, you are a Jew." For the first time I had had a wistful inkling of what it must be like to be committed to a powerful myth. Maybe if you had faith that Jesus would save you, He would. Maybe the point was simply to stop listening to that observer/critic inside my head, to surrender my will, to have faith, and what I had faith in didn't matter any more than whether I took a train or a bus to my destination.

"Suppose you had faith in Hitler?" my observer/critic, that irrepressible crank, could not help objecting. Still, part of what had messed up my acid trips was doubt, whispering like the serpent: What if the straight world is right, and what you think is Reality is a seductive hallucination? I couldn't assent to the experience without reservation, following wherever it led: it might lead to insanity. So I tried to compromise. I wanted to tap the ecstasy whenever I wanted and be "normal" the rest of the time. It was, I suppose, the same impulse that makes sinners go to church on Sunday, with much the same result.

I was aware of the link between my skepticism and my Jewishness. It was, after all, the Jew who was the perennial doubter, the archetypal outsider, longing for redemption while dismissing the claims of would-be redeemers as so much snake oil. But what did any of this have to do with the kind of Jewishness my brother was talking about?

Mike had grown up in the economic and cultural slough of the Seventies. Though he had always been an excellent student, he had never liked school; he had found college as boring and meaningless as high school and elementary school before that. Since graduating from the University of Michigan in 1970, with a B.A. in Chinese, he had spent nearly half his time traveling. Recurrent asthma had kept him from being drafted. Between trips he would come back to New York and drive a cab to make money for the next trip. He had never had a job he liked. During his last stay in New York he had begun writing articles about Asia, and he had gone back with the idea of doing more. He had had a few pieces in newspapers, but no major breakthrough, and one major disappointment: an article he'd worked hard on was first accepted by a magazine, then sent back.

Mike was also depressed about Cambodia and Vietnam. In 1973 he had spent almost two months in Cambodia and had come away convinced that as much as the people hated the corrupt Lon Nol government, they did not want the Americans to leave and permit a Communist takeover. As Mike saw it, they wanted to be left alone to farm while the Khmer Rouge made them take sides and shot those who chose incorrectly; they were religious Buddhists, while the Communists were anti-religious and would make young men work instead of becoming monks; in short, they wanted to return to their traditional, pre-war way of life, which the Communists would permanently destroy. Those premises had led Mike to what seemed an unavoidable conclusion: the Americans should not withdraw. For someone who had shared the American left's assumptions about the war, it was a disturbing reversal. If he had been wrong about Cambodia, he thought, perhaps he had been wrong about Vietnam. This past fall, a return trip to Cambodia and two weeks in Vietnam had reinforced his doubt.

When Mike arrived in Jerusalem, he had been traveling for seven months. He was going home to uncertain writing prospects, another cab job or something similar, no close friends, isolation in a political atmosphere that took for granted the assumptions he had discarded, and a general ambiance of post counterculture aimlessness. It took no great insight to suspect that what traditional Judaism offered—absolute values to which Mike could dedicate his life; a new and exciting subject to study; a close-knit religious community; a stable, secure social structure—was considerably more attractive. Anyway, I didn't believe that people ever made profound spiritual changes for purely intellectual reasons. There had to be feelings Mike wasn't acknowledging. Not that this proved anything about the validity of Judaism. A believer could argue that Mike had been drifting because he hadn't found God, that his unhappiness was, in fact, God's way of leading him to the truth. Still, I worried that he was succumbing to an authoritarian illusion in an attempt to solve (or escape from) his problems.

In answer to my request for more details, Mike sent a seven-page, single-spaced typed letter. I chewed it over, making notes in the margin. Much of it was devoted to debunking evolution. The marvelous complexity and interdependence of everything in the universe—so the argument ran—show planning and purpose and could not have come about through the random process of natural selection. Plants and animals are perfectly constructed machines; the brain has been compared to a computer. When you see a computer your obvious conclusion is that someone built it according to a plan. ("Rampant anthropomorphism" I scribbled.) Every detail of creation is purposeful. For example, ready-to-eat fruits (like apples) have tempting, bright colors; vegetables that require cooking (like potatoes) are drab. ("What about toadstools?") No one has ever seen a mutation that changed one species into another. How does evolution explain something like a poisonous snake, whose survival advantage depends on a combination of traits, each useless alone? Did its poison come first, and did it then wait around millions of years for the ability to inject or vice versa? And why did creation stop; why aren't new things constantly coming into being? ("Human chauvinism!" I wrote. "Who says creation stopped—new life forms take eons—we can't even see plants grow.")

As for the God-given nature of the Torah, when you study it in Hebrew, along with the commentaries that have been written on virtually every word, it is hard to believe that such depth and complexity could have been achieved by human beings; Judaism is such a restrictive religion that the Jews would never have accepted it if the entire people hadn't witnessed the revelation; biblical prophecies predict the Jewish exile, the return to Israel and other historical events. The prophecies were impressive, I had to admit: "Ye will be torn away from the land whither thou goest . . . and God will scatter you among the nations . . . thou wilt find no ease and there will be no resting place for the sole of thy foot. . . . And then God thy God will return . . . and gather thee together. . . ." And so on. I began to get a headache.

Finally, my brother came to the subject I had been anticipating and dreading: women. Orthodox Judaism enshrined as divine law a male supremacist ideology I had been struggling against, in one way or another, all my life. It was a patriarchal religion that decreed separate functions for the sexes—man to learn, administer religious law and exercise public authority: woman to sanctify the home. For Mike to accept it would be *(face it!)* a betrayal. Already I had had the bitter thought: "You want to go back in time, find a community where mamma will still take care of you. You're just like the rest." Under the anger was fear that my sense of special connection with my brother was an illusion. *If I were a man . . . if he were a woman . . .* there was an unbridgeable gap in that *if.*

From a secular viewpoint, Mike conceded, Judaism gave men the better deal, but from a religious viewpoint it wasn't so clear. For one thing, God-fearing men, though they had the power to oppress women, would not do so. And if our purpose on earth was not to do interesting work or have a good time but to come close to God, then women had certain advantages: they had fewer commandments to perform, fewer opportunities to sin and by having children could approach God more easily.

"Power to oppress is oppressive," I wrote in the margin. "Power corrupts the saintliest man. Exemption from responsibilities is implicit insult." Yet I realized that, after all, my objections were beside the point. This God, if He really existed, had chosen to create a hierarchy of sexes. Doubtless He had some purpose in mind, some spiritual test, perhaps a lesson in conquering pride. It might seem unfair, but it had to be for the best in the end . . . and I could never believe in such a God, never, it violated my surest sense of what Reality was about. When you connected there were no hierarchies, divisions, roles; all that was part of the husk that fell away. "I am the vanguard of the revolution!" I had shouted, high on acid, climbing up a mountain trail followed by two men who were truly my equals, our battle-of-the-sexes fright masks discarded somewhere down the road. There would be misunderstandings later, but that was another story.

No, I couldn't believe in the Jewish God. He had been invented by men seeking a rationale for their privileges. He had been invented by people seeking to reduce an ineffable Reality to terms they could understand—to a quasi-human "creator" with a "plan" and a "purpose," standing outside the universe and making it the way a carpenter made a table.

In August, my parents visited Mike in Jerusalem. He was still living and studying at Yeshivat Aish HaTorah. A yeshiva is a school where Jews study Torah; this one also functioned as a small religious community. It occupied modest quarters—a communal study room, a few classrooms, a library, an office for the rabbi—in the Jewish section of the Old City; several nearby apartments served as dormitories. Aish HaTorah (the name means "Fire of the Torah") is an English-speaking yeshiva headed by Noach Weinberg, a rabbi from New York. Most of its students—there were around 25 at the time—were young Americans; most had been tourists passing through. Mike was taking courses in Chumash (the Five Books of Moses), the Mishna (the written codification of the Oral Law), halacha (Jewish law), Biblical Hebrew, and "48 Ways to Gain Knowledge" (talks by the rabbi on Jewish ideas about learning). His weekday schedule began at seven in the morning, with an hour of prayer before breakfast. Ordinarily, he had classes and study hours from 9 to 1, then lunch and 20 minutes of afternoon prayer, classes and study from 3 to 7:30, dinner, evening prayer from 8:30 to 9, and more classes till 10. He usually studied till around 11:30. During mother and dad's visit, he was taking some time off in the afternoon and evening.

My parents had both, in their individual ways, been struggling to come to terms with Mike's "conversion." My mother considered herself in some sense religious; she believed in God, even believed that the Torah might be God-given. But she couldn't see that God required us to observe all those regulations. Wasn't it enough to be a good person? Characteristically, she focused on practical concerns. Was Mike happy? Would religion give him what he badly needed—something satisfying to do with his life?

My father was the son of an Orthodox rabbi, but for all his adult life he had equated rationalism and religious tolerance with enlightenment. Clarence Darrow, defending Scopes and evolution against Bryan and the fundamentalist know-nothings, had been his intellectual hero. To have a child of his reject those values was a painful shock. But he had been forced by his respect for Mike's mind—and no doubt by the logic of his own belief in tolerance—to reexamine his attitudes. He went to Jerusalem prepared to listen.

The trip was reassuring. Mike seemed happier, more relaxed, more sure of himself. He was enjoying his studies. "He was different," my father told me. "There was a step up in emotional vibration. I'd never seen him so enthusiastic before." I remained skeptical; Mike's enthusiasm might be some sort of manic facade. I was still working on my reply to his long letter, debating whether to mention my qualms about his motives. From one point of view, Mike was doing something incredibly brave, even heroic: in quest of truth as he saw it he was breaking with the values and assumptions of his family, his peers, American society and the entire post-Enlightenment West. For me to bring up psychology would be to add whatever clout I had to the enormous pressure of conventional wisdom that Mike was probably having trouble enough resisting. And then there was my old religious question: even if Judaism confused its central metaphor with absolute truth, would it work for Mike if he believed? Judaism, I reminded myself, was a spiritual discipline that had been practiced for over 3,000 years; psychotherapy had existed for less than a hundred, with inconclusive results.

For three years I had been seeing a Reichian therapist. I was seeking relief from specific emotional problems, but my larger spiritual problem lurked in the back of my mind. What, after all, were emotional problems but forms of—or metaphors for—disconnection? The Reichian method is based on the premise that muscular tensions hold back repressed emotions which the therapist can elicit by attacking the bodily "armor" directly, bypassing the treacherous intellect. I believed this approach worked; it had helped me a lot. Yet I could claim no miracles, only that I had come—slowly, undramatically—to feel better, see more clearly. For all I knew, my brother would get further with Judaism.

Still—suppose Mike was really being trapped, not by arguments but by his emotions? Suppose by bringing up my worries I could help him—by which I meant save him. For despite my theoretical conviction that we all had to seek the truth in our own way, I hoped, with guilty passion, that Mike would get off this particular path, would wake up one morning, ask, "What am I doing here?" and come home. I decided to say what I had to say. For me, Freud was far closer than Darwin to the heart of the matter.

The Mirror

In America most of the time I was unhappy and bored. I couldn't find what I wanted to do or people I wanted to be with. You were supposed to be very hip and inside I wasn't. I didn't identify with hip people or enjoy being around them. I couldn't figure out where I fit in. Traveling was my escape. I would go through a lot of rottenness and boredom for the sake of some periods of happiness—experiences that really took me out of myself, like trekking in the Himalayas.

When I came to Israel from Jordan I was very tired out and I wanted to go home. I didn't have much money left. There was a girl I really wanted to go back and see though I had no reason to believe she would want to see me. I was really homesick. But I felt a responsibility to see something new. I went with the guy from the yeshiva looking for an interesting experience. Reb Noach gave me the usual pitch: "Stay here for a week. If you haven't seen a yeshiva you haven't seen Israel." We had a big political argument—I said things looked bad for Israel and the only reasonable thing to do was give back the occupied land and make peace. We had a talk about the moral imperative proof of God. Reb Noach asked where I got my concept of good. I said, "From my parents."

That week I realized Judaism was much more interesting than I'd thought. When I read Jewish philosophy I realized my mind was Jewish. I felt that for the first time I had found people who thought the way I did, who were really logical and consistent. But the idea of God was very alien to me. Then I read a pamphlet about Torah and science. I started reading the arguments about evolution. Suddenly I had a flash: "This whole theory is ridiculous!" It had a tremendous effect. I felt that my mind had been playing tricks on me. I'd been accepting this theory without really looking into it—just like Cambodia. Logically, you knock down the theory of evolution and you're stuck with—God created the world.

I left to do some traveling and went to Safed. I was sitting down looking at a map and two English guys, students of this Hassid who was up from Tel Aviv for the weekend, invited me to meet him. I went and we started talking. He had pure charisma. I related to Reb Noach as a good person, but this Hassid was someone with power. He said that people go all around the world looking into this and that and they know it's not true—then they're hit with Judaism and they leave because they're afraid it's true. It had a big effect on me because of my realization about evolution and because I'd been asking myself why I was leaving. I knew I was scared to stay and check it out.

The English guys kept telling me there are no coincidences, it wasn't an accident that I was there at the same time the Hassid happened to be visiting. I started getting scared—was all this really true? I felt lousy about myself: I had always prided myself on being open-minded. Now I had no logical reasoning for leaving, just an emotional desire to go home. I felt totally wiped out.

When I got back to the yeshiva I started reading Torah with the Hirsch commentaries. There was a daily Chumash [Five Books] class. I was learning some Hebrew and could feel the power of the Torah much more than in translation. And the prophecies—I kept trying to find arguments against the prophecies and couldn't come up with any.

After two or three weeks I was in doubt—what was I going to do? One day I was reading the prophecies at the end of Deuteronomy and I had this cold shiver—I realized that I really believed all this. My first reaction was to compromise—I would go home, read, then decide. Or I would take a few years and travel and then come back. Finally I realized my whole life would have to change.

The first time I went to Southeast Asia I had a lot of asthma trouble. I'd almost feel like I was having a heart attack. Sometimes my pills wouldn't work and I was afraid they would just stop working. When I got into religion I realized— how can I expect a pill to work? God controls what goes on. Your life can be snuffed out at any moment. That had a strong part in keeping me here. It wasn't that I started believing in God to conquer a fear of death. Intellectually believing doesn't do that anyway. But I realized I couldn't compromise and say two years from now I'll come back, because there's no assurance of anything.

I went and cancelled my plane ticket. It was painful. I was afraid my family would reject me, think I was crazy. My mind was telling me one thing. My emotions still wanted to go home.

Around Thanksgiving Mike came to New York for a month. Seeing him was a relief. His skullcap and newly grown beard made him look less boyish, but he was still wearing jeans. I felt no distance between us, no sense that he was in any way not himself. I hugged him, wondering if the Orthodox prohibition against men touching women they weren't married to applied to sisters.

Mike stayed with our parents. So that he could observe the dietary laws, mother bought him his own dishes and silverware and pots, boiled her cooking utensils and took them to a mikva (ritual bath), cleaned the oven and left it on at the hottest setting for two hours, served him kosher food, cooked him meat and dairy dishes separately in the new pots. Mike prayed three times a day, said blessings over his food and grace after meals, washed his hands on rising in the morning and before eating bread. Since the complicated Sabbath laws could only be fully observed in an Orthodox environment, he spent weekends with religious families.

He had been home several weeks when we had The Talk. We had already had a number of talks, but it was this one that sank in. We were having lunch at a kosher cafeteria on 47th Street, patronized largely by Hassidim and other ultra-Orthodox Jews in the diamond business. It was crowded with men in traditional black suits. I was insisting that it was impossible to prove the existence or the nature of God. The ultimate Reality was by definition ungraspable by reason; Mike's belief had to be based on intuition, not logic. "It's both." Mike said. "First, you have to have an intuition that logic is real—that logic tells you something about the way the world is. Then if an idea is illogical—if it's inconsistent with what you know—you intuitively know it's wrong. Like the complexity of the world is inconsistent with the idea that it all happened at random, by natural selection."

"Not necessarily. In an infinite universe even the most unlikely combination of events can happen . . ."

"It's possible. But it's not probable. And when you take all the proofs together—the depth of Torah, the prophecies—maybe you can explain any one of them away, but you can't explain them all as coincidence. It just gets too improbable. Reasoning can tell you what's most probable, and when you have an overwhelming probability your intuition tells you it has to be true."

"Well, my intuition tells me the world wasn't created in six days."

Mike explained that the length of the six days of creation was open to question, since the Sun wasn't created till the fourth day; that there was no problem with the idea of a biological evolution guided by God rather than natural selection, or of humanlike beings existing before Adam, so long as you accepted Adam as the first true man in the spiritual sense—made "in the image of God." I was struck by the way he argued. He sounded like me in the early days of feminism talking to women who were unconvinced. It had been one of those rare times when I felt both sure of my ground and sure it was in the other person's interest to see things my way. That confidence had made me a good organizer; now, on the receiving end, I felt defensive.

I wasn't sure why. I did not find Mike's anti-evolution argument persuasive, but I was not, in any case, a dogmatic evolutionist. On acid I had had the strong impression that it was somehow in the nature of Reality to ceaselessly order itself into complex patterns; even before that I had been inclined to believe there was some unknown organizing principle in the universe. Once I had confessed to a friend, "I don't think the universe is absurd." "You don't?" she said. "No. I think it's basically logical." There was a pause. "Maybe," my friend said, "you *need* to see logic in it." Maybe. Either way, there was no need to assume a God with personality, a will or a purpose.

"But it's possible," Mike said. "You have to admit it's logically possible."

"It's based on a naive analogy. A chair is made by a person, so the world has to be made by a superperson."

"You're assuming the secular view of reality—that we created God, not the other way around. The Jewish perspective is like a mirror image. It's not God who's like a human being; it's human beings who are made in God's image. Our way of making things is *something like* God's way. We don't get the idea of God from having parents—our relationship with our parents is meant to give us an idea of how to relate to God."

"Reality isn't a being with a personality," I said. "It's just—Reality."

"You had a mystical experience that showed you there's a spiritual reality. Judaism says that on top of this experience, which all religions share, we have a revelation that tells us what that reality is, what it wants from us."

"The idea that it wants something contradicts my experience," I insisted.

"Not your experience. Just your interpretation of it."

"But I didn't interpret it. I just had it. That's what made it unique."

"Of course you interpreted it. You've grown up with a whole view of reality that says we're free, we can do what we want. So naturally you see God as something impersonal, instead of a God who says, 'You have to do what I want, not what you want.'"

I shook my head, but I felt the presence of the serpent. Had I experienced Reality, or just another deceptive metaphor?

"I don't do whatever I want," I said. "I try to do what's right."

"But you decide what's right."

"Not me, my ego. The part of me that's attuned to Reality decides. Reality defines what good is." Pretty mushy, my observer/critic remarked.

"All right. But in practice you don't really believe that you're required to live a certain way except for obvious things, like not killing. Judaism says God gave us a law, this is what it is, we have to obey it."

"I believe," I began, aware that I was entering a mine field of rhetoric, "I feel I *know,* from my—experience"—*or was it just an interpretation?*—"that when we're in touch with Reality what's right and what we really want are the same. To love and be loved, to have a just, decent society. To figure out how to make that truth work in practice—to struggle toward it—that's what life is about. Freedom isn't doing whatever we please; it's a basic ethical value. It means taking responsibility for the struggle. Not looking to some authority to get us off the hook."

"But it doesn't work. Look at what's happening in the world; look at what Western 'enlightenment' has accomplished. Total chaos, and it's getting worse."

It was the classic conservative line. Your utopian dreams are unrealistic, against human nature. Look at the evidence. Bloody wars; repressive governments; nuclear threat; ecological destruction. And what revolution—be honest, now—what revolution has really succeeded by your standards? I was on familiar terms with this litany. Though I considered myself a radical, had been a leftist and feminist activist, I struggled perpetually with doubts (again). And if I believed, finally, in my obligation to defy a pessimism that amounted to self-fulfilling prophecy—what was that but a leap of faith?

"In a Torah community," Mike was saying, "there's no crime, the family isn't falling apart. People are serious about being good people because they're living for God, not just themselves."

"Intuitively, I can't see it," I said. "This cosmic dictator idea of God. I just don't see it."

"But you have to ask why. There are powerful emotional reasons for not seeing it. You'd have to admit that God controls your life, that you're not free. You'd have to submit to a lot of restrictions you don't like. You'd have to change. No one wants to change."

True.

"You have an incredibly complex and organized universe. Everything in it works together perfectly. The most obvious explanation is that a creator planned it that way. Everyone intuitively saw that—everyone believed in God—until evolution gave them an excuse not to. Or take the prophecies. You can explain them as a bunch of improbable coincidences but why resist the obvious answer—that they come from God, who knows the future?"

"It was the Bible predicting the return that gave the Zionists the idea in the first place," I objected.

"But it would never have happened if it weren't for the Nazis," Mike said. "Another coincidence?"

I had no answer. The prophecies had bothered me from the start. And Mike had a point: why was it so important to me to explain them away? During my first session with my Reichian shrink he had poked my jaw muscles and asked drily, "Do you ever lose an argument?" With a shock I saw that I wasn't winning this one. Mike's premises were not only far more sophisticated than I had thought; they were the basis of a formidably comprehensive, coherent world view. All along Mike had been asking me questions I couldn't answer. How did I explain the creation of the world? How did I explain the strange history of the Jews—their unremitting persecution and unlikely survival, their conspicuous role in world affairs? How did I explain the Torah itself, with its extraordinary verbal intricacy, the meanings upon meanings the rabbis had found in phrases, words, even letters; the consistency with which their analyses hung together after the 1,500 years or more that they had spent hunting down contradictions? I knew that "comprehensive and coherent" did not necessarily mean "true." "I don't know" was an honorable answer. But it did not win arguments.

I was suffering from acute mental vertigo. What a phony I was—glibly assuring Mike that his transformation had to be based on intuition rather mere argument, while all along my confidence in my own intuition had rested on the assumption that I had the better arguments. The last thing I wanted was to be left with only fragile, fallible intuition as a shield against a system of ideas that neatly reversed everything I believed. Like a mirror image.

I understood now what Mike had meant when he said he felt trapped, understood how his skepticism could turn against itself. My own skepticism told me that however sure I was of my perceptions, I could be wrong. Therefore, since I could not prove Judaism was false, I had to admit that it could be true. And the thought of admitting any such thing threw me into a panic. Which of course was the best possible evidence for Mike's suggestion that I rejected Judaism simply because I did not care to accept it. I wanted nothing so much as to forget the whole question, and for that very reason I was bound by all my standards of intellectual honesty and courage to pursue it.

I was overwhelmed with superstitious paranoia. This was exactly how Mike had been drawn in, Mike who was so much like me. Mike was the one person in the world who could have gotten me to listen seriously to this argument. And he had stopped off in Israel mainly because of me: I had been there earlier that year, with a group of journalists, and had written him that it was interesting. From his point of view, none of this was coincidental.

During the next few days my panic intensified. The one aspect of my life that I had never seriously doubted was my obligation to make my own choices and my own mistakes and if need be suffer the consequences. Since the only certainty was that the way to Reality was uncertain, I had no alternative. Now I saw that this certainty was as uncertain as any other. And so for the first time I faced a choice that was truly absolute, that included no tacit right to be wrong—the spiritual equivalent of a life-or-death decision in war. If the Jewish God existed and I willingly rejected Him, I would be making the ultimate, irretrievable mistake. Contrary to the common impression, Jewish theology included a system of reward and punishment that operated in both this life and the next. The eternal punishment for rejecting Torah was called *karait*—"cutting off"—which meant, I assumed, what I would call total alienation from Reality. Only it was much more vivid and terrifying when you envisioned it as a punishment rather than an impersonal consequence, as losing the love, incurring the wrath of the ultimate parent.

And if I gave up my precious freedom, a renunciation that felt like death, for what I saw as an alien, joyless, shackled existence—and it turned out that the serpent had betrayed me again, that there was no God of Wrath or God of Love after all? And how could I ever know for sure? It seemed to me that whatever I did I was in trouble.

I had shed another layer of innocence. I would never again feel smug about Patty Hearst, Ronnie Davis, the legions of post-acid freaks who had joined mystical cults. I understood. It could happen to me. For the first time I wished I had never taken drugs, never seen beyond the scientific rationalism that might be narrow but was surely safe. I envied my father's faith in evolution. I envied everyone around me, going peacefully about their lives, taking for granted—if they thought about it at all—that Mike's brand of religion was eccentric fanaticism, nothing to do with them. I especially envied non-Jews. The 613 *mitzvot* were reserved for the Chosen People. Others had only to obey certain basic moral laws—mostly obvious things—like not killing.

I had frustrating conversations with friends who found it hard to believe that someone so sensible and intelligent could be wondering if she ought to become an Orthodox Jew.

"Maybe it's right for him; that doesn't mean it's right for you."

"If it's true, then it has to be right for me."

"You couldn't live that way."

"That's not the point. The point is, is it true?"

"Maybe it's true for him."

"You don't understand. Judaism claims to be absolute truth. Either it's true for everybody, or it's not true at all."

"Nobody has a monopoly on the truth."

"That's the secular point of view. . . . From the Jewish point of view there is an absolute truth, I can know it, I just don't want to accept it."

"Well, why should you accept it if you don't want to?"

"Because if it's true, then all my ideas are wrong, I'm living the wrong way, I'm totally blowing it."

"Who's to say there's only one way to live?"

"*But don't you see?* You say, 'We're free to decide how to live.' Religious Jews say, 'No, you're not free.' So you say, 'We're free to reject that argument.' It's circular reasoning!"

"Why are you getting so upset?"

Then I talked to a woman who understood. She had grown up Catholic and lost her faith. It seemed that losing your faith and losing your lack of faith had much in common. At some point you were suspended between two competing, self-consistent realities, knowing you had to go back or forward, with no one to help you and no net. And once you were out there, you realized that skeptic and believer were mirror images, reflecting a vision of logic in the universe.

Judaism teaches that God's rewards and punishment operate on the principle of *mida k'neged mida*—measure for measure. For example, a friend of Mike's had asked to borrow 100 Israeli pounds; Mike had lent the money, but grudgingly; shortly afterward he had 100 pounds stolen from his wallet, though there was more money in it.

During my panic I had become obsessed with the thought that this principle might explain a central irony in my own life. I had come of age at a time when sexual liberation did not yet mean groupies and massage parlors, when it was still a potent metaphor for liberation in general. At the core of my feminism was rage at the suppression of female sexuality and a romantic vision of sexual freedom as joyous, unreserved acceptance of my body, my femaleness, my partner in love. Though I hated the way this vision had been perverted, co-opted and turned against women, I believed no less in the vision itself.

The irony, of course, was the contrast between ideal and reality. Part of that reality was historical: feminism had transformed women's consciousness without, as yet, transforming society, leaving a gap between what many of us demanded of a relationship and what most men were willing to give. Yet there were ways of making the best of this situation while I tended to make the worst of it. At 34, with a marriage and two quasi-marriages behind me, I felt, all too often, like an awkward teenager. My distrust of men fed a prickliness that provoked rejection that confirmed my distrust; worse, I was still afflicted, on some level, with the adolescent notion—no doubt the result of all those real and symbolic fights in the back seat—that to give in to sexual pleasure was to lose a power struggle. In general I thought of myself fairly sane, but my conflicts about sex and men felt out of control—and thinking in those terms was undoubtedly part of the problem. For the sexual dilemma was the same as the spiritual one: to try harder was not only useless but self-defeating.

I had come to see my predicament as a sort of cosmic mockery, deflating my utopian pretensions. But from the Jewish standpoint, what could be a neater measure-for-measure punishment for refusing my ordained role as wife and mother? The symmetry was perfect: feminist consciousness had inspired both my sexual aspirations and the defensiveness that undermined them. It was the message one might expect from a cranky, conservative-Freudian God, out to show me that feminism was the problem rather than the solution, that all this emancipation claptrap violated my true nature and would deny me the feminine fulfillment I really craved.

Another mirror image, more powerful than the rest, it exposed my most private pain, doubt and vulnerability. I knew then that I had to go to Israel and confront my terror at its source—to put myself in my brother's place and see if I reached the same conclusions. I also knew that I had to write about the process. I was not sure these imperatives were compatible. When I decided not only to write about my trip but to write about it on assignment—which meant committing myself to come home and deliver a manuscript—I felt a bit like Ulysses tying himself to the mast. The difference, of course, was that I could cut myself loose if I chose. And in its perverse way, my very need to hedge was evidence of my good faith. At least it would have to do.

First Encounters

I left New York on March 22nd, 1976, on an overnight flight packed with Jewish tour groups. Here and there I saw religious men in beards and yarmulkes (skullcaps). At dawn they began getting up to form a minyan (ten-man quorum) for morning prayer. The Israeli flight attendants gave them dirty looks for blocking the aisles.

We arrived around noon. I wandered outside, past clumps of armed teenage soldiers, looking for Mike. I was beginning to wonder if we had missed each other when a tall, thin boy wearing a yarmulke approached me.

"Are you Ellen?"

Chaim was a student at my brother's yeshiva; he had come to meet me because Mike had a bad cold. He explained that we would stop first at Rabbi and Rebbetzin Weinberg's, where I would leave my bags, then go to find Mike. We took a cab into Jerusalem, talking sketchily about the experiences that had brought each of us here, and caught the bus for Kiryat Zanz, a religious neighborhood nestled in a rocky hillside. In contrast to the gorgeous landscape, the rows of identical low apartment buildings were dreary, housing project modern. Block 5 Building 2 housed the Weinbergs and their nine children.

The rebbetzin invited us into an apartment that conveyed a sense of busy warmth. It was crammed with books and artifacts—menorahs, vases of flowers, bright fabrics, pictures of wise men, a colored-glass chandelier.

Dinah Weinberg is a striking woman. Slim, fair, blue-eyed, in her late 30s, she looks like a picture-postcard of the ideal Jewish matriarch—one part strength and competence, one part motherliness, one part a modest, almost austere beauty accentuated by the kerchief that covers her head. (When an Orthodox woman marries, her hair becomes private, seen only by her husband.)

I immediately craved her approval without quite knowing why. We sat in the kitchen chatting about my brother while children wandered in and out. I mentioned that I wanted to find out more about women's role in Judaism.

"Good!" the rebbetzin said. "People misunderstand it."

"Suppose I don't want children," I began, "or anyway no more than one or two . . ."

Mrs. Weinberg's reply threw me. "If someone gave you money, would you turn it down?"

"I don't get the comparison." Money buys freedom; children take it away: the instant I had the thought it seemed unbearably crass.

"Children are a blessing," said the rebbetzin firmly. The conversation had taken a depressing turn. I could no more imagine having nine children than contemplate climbing Mt. Everest.

"I don't want to devote all my time to children," I said. "I want to write."

"You can do both. A Jewish woman shouldn't spend all her time with her children. We can do much more."

"If I had a bunch of kids I wouldn't have any time and energy to spare."

"The Almighty wants us to use our talents. He wouldn't punish you by not letting you write. You'd find the time."

Well, maybe so. I wasted so much time, after all. No doubt a disciplined person could raise half a dozen kids in the time I spent day-dreaming, reading junk, sleeping late. But I would never be that person; I knew my limitations. Or was that just an excuse for laziness?

The rebbetzin kissed me goodbye, and Chaim and I took a bus to the walled Old City. The Jewish Quarter, which had been largely destroyed by the Jordanians in 1948, was still being rebuilt; the smell of dust and the sound of drilling were pervasive. Mike emerged from his dorm looking pale and tired from his cold. We walked over to Yeshivat Aish HaTorah, which was on a side street called Misgav Ladach tucked beside a huge construction site. To the northeast the yeshiva overlooked some of the most spectacular sights in Jerusalem—the Mount of Olives, the Valley of Kidron and the golden Dome of the Rock. It was a short walk from the Western Wall ("Wailing Wall"), the sacred remnant of King Solomon's Temple.

We found the rabbi in his office. Like his wife, Noach Weinberg has a compelling presence. He is in his mid-40s, but with his white beard, black suit and air of authority he seems older. He regarded me with a friendly smile and eyes that suggested he had my number but liked me anyway. I thought he looked like God the Father in His more jovial aspect. After we had been introduced he told Mike that a kid who had been staying at the yeshiva was about to leave.

"You know why they leave?" he said to me. "They leave because they're scared they'll like it." He shook his head. "Insanity! Do you know how Jews define sin? Sin is temporary insanity."

For instance, he explained, he had a bad habit of wasting time; who in his right mind would want to waste time?

"What about more serious sins?" I said.

Reb Noach raised his eyebrows. "Wasting time," he said, "is very serious. It's a kind of suicide."

For the first few days I stayed with one of Mike's teachers, Shimon Haskel, and his wife Chaya. I began to unwind from my trip and settle in. I was feeling close to Mike, and we talked more openly than ever before about our family, our childhoods, our fears and hang-ups. Mike told me that I seemed so confident he had always been afraid of me: I told him that I'd felt he was Mr. Cool, secretly putting me down.

"But now," said Mike, "I'm not afraid of you anymore." I was pleased with the change in him. He was not only more confident but more willing to face his emotional problems—the split between intellect and feeling, the distance from other people, the lack of joy. He was obliged to face them, for they were also religious problems. It was a commandment to be happy; unhappiness in effect denied God's love, dismissed His gifts.

Mike was also absorbed in his work. He found the yeshiva completely different from all the schools he had hated. Both teachers and students were deeply involved in learning; they had no doubt that what they were doing was important. Universities, Mike felt, were dead; Aish HaTorah was alive. For several hours every morning he studied Gemara (the voluminous rabbinical commentaries on the Mishna; Mishna and Gemara together constitute the Talmud). In the afternoon and evening he studied Rambam (Maimonides). Somehow he found the time to talk with new people, listening to their problems, answering questions, and out of this had come another project: he was writing a group of papers arguing various proofs of God's existence and the Torah's divinity. His persuasiveness and intellectual skills had made him something of a star at the yeshiva.

Aish HaTorah is a yeshiva for *ba'al teshuvas*—delinquent Jews who have "returned." It is the fourth such yeshiva that Noach Weinberg has started in the past decade. Recently, others have picked up on Reb Noach's vision and started their own yeshivas in Jerusalem and Tel Aviv.

In America, the most conspicuous Jewish evangelizers of Jews have been Hassidim. Hassidism, a tendency within Judaism that stresses joy, prayer and mystical experience, began in the last century as a revolt by poor and uneducated Jews against the elitist intellectualism of the yeshivas of Eastern Europe, particularly Lithuania. The *ba'al teshuva* yeshiva movement in Israel comes from the latter tradition, that of the *misnagdim*—rationalist opponents of Hassidism—who emphasize learning Torah as the highest value and chief means of approaching God. A yeshiva like Aish HaTorah operates on the premise that the best weapon against unbelief is rational argument. It follows that the crucial first step is to get people to listen. Boys are urged to come for a day, an hour, a meal, a bed. (No one has to pay unless he can afford to; the school is supported mostly by contributions.) A beginner's program runs for three months and then repeats; a student can start at any point. Those who stay can advance as fast as their ability allows to study the Talmud and biblical commentaries.

There was a major hitch in my plan to replicate Mike's experience: I could not go to Aish HaTorah. Orthodox education is sexually segregated, and opportunities for women are limited. Learning is a religious obligation only for men; among tradition-minded Jews the issue of whether women should study Torah and Talmud, and if so how much, is controversial. None of the women's schools in Jerusalem offers a comprehensive intellectual and religious experience like Aish HaTorah's. Nor do they cater to transients. Still, I decided to check out a couple of schools and visit a student Mike knew.

Lorie Bernstein was 19 and the product of a rich Long Island suburb; her divorced parents owned clothing stores. Mike had first met her at the airport on his way back from New York. During the cab ride into Jerusalem she had told him that she had been a Hassid for a while but had reverted to existentialism; Mike had urged her to give Judaism another try. Since then she had become a fervent *ba'al teshuva*. When I introduced myself she hugged me excitedly. She was small and bouncy, with dark hair tucked in a bun; she wore a long-sleeved blouse, a long skirt and gold-rimmed, blue-tinted glasses.

I had found Lorie just as she was about to do some errands in Mea Shearim, an old, poor, fanatically pious community noted for its anti-Zionists (they believe there cannot be a legitimate Jewish state until the coming of the Messiah), its Hassids in medieval caftans, and its signs demanding that female tourists conform to Torah standards of modest dress. We walked there together. Lorie stopped several times to give coins to beggars, all the while keeping up a passionate monologue.

"God gives us so much, you just have to do something back. I love doing *mitzvot* and helping people. A few *agurot* mean nothing to you, but you're giving someone food, making him happy. This religion is so beautiful!" She was bubbly, breathless; energy rolled off her in waves. "Whether there's a God or not, the Torah helps you live up to your potential—it's like tripping—you get an awareness of everything you do. I really have to think about food now—what's milk, what's meat, my mother-love side and beast side? Every day I have to thank God for all kinds of things. Thank God I'm awake. (Think of all the people who aren't awake.) Thank God for commanding me to wash. Whenever I wash I'm aware of my hands and how wonderful they are. Thank God for clothing the naked. How many people think every day about how they have clothes and other people don't? There's even a prayer for the bathroom—thank God for my ducts and orifices, that they're working properly."

I asked her how she felt about Judaism's view of women.

"I'm *dying* to get married and have children. Right now I'm doing *teshuva,* repentance. What could possibly be more important than having children?"

I mumbled something about wanting to write.

"Writing!" Lorie said scornfully. "I used to write, I used it to get rid of energy. What's writing compared to creating a human being, a soul?"

"It happens to be what I want to do."

"What you *want*! I used to be that way. The most important thing was to be authentic—to do what I really wanted to do, even if I hurt someone. My ideal was Meursault in *The Stranger*. Life was meaningless so why pretend it wasn't? Anyway," she said, "most things you think you want to do you don't really want to do. *Other* people want you to do them. The only thing I really miss is getting high. I *love* getting high—I love it! If there was one thing that could get me off religion it would be that."

On the other side of the street—we were now in Mea Shearim—two touristy looking girls passed by, transgressing the modesty laws by wearing jeans. "If I weren't with you," Lorie said, "I'd go over and yell at them."

"I don't think it does much good to yell at people," I said, feeling resentful about the anti-writing remarks.

"You can't tell," said Lorie. "Sometimes one little thing can change you around. What got me to join the Hassidim was that someone told me how low their divorce rate was. If I just explained about modesty—why it's not good to wear pants . . ." She stopped. "I'm being too heavy, aren't I? I'm sorry. I get carried away when I meet a new person."

We walked past stalls selling fruits and vegetables, down a narrow, cobbled back street, to visit a friend of Lorie's who might help place some students with families for Shabbos. Leah, a vivacious, middle-aged Hassidic housewife, insisted on serving us vegetable soup, bread and cream cheese. She supervised the washing ritual, showing me how to pour from the two-handled cup, how to cup my hands, making me do it over until I got it exactly right, while Lorie bounced up and down, protesting, "Leah! You'll discourage her! You've got to start out easy!"

I began hanging around Lorie's school, sitting in on classes—which mostly centered on Hebrew texts and made me feel as if I'd stumbled into the middle of a foreign-language movie with inadequate subtitles—and talking with Lorie and her friends. There was Frieda from Brooklyn, strong, blunt, a scrapper, a woman with a vision: she intended to start a *ba'al teshuva* organization in the States. There was Cindy who had identified with black people so intensely that she still spoke with a trace of a pseudo-Southern accent, who had decided to convert to Christianity and had joined a black church, but then—*boruch Hashem!*—praise God!—had realized where she belonged. There was Sarah, who had been born Protestant in Chicago and had converted after investigating every philosophy there was and deciding that only Judaism made sense.

But at the psychological center of my life in Jerusalem were the rabbi and the rebbetzin. Noach Weinberg, the youngest son of a Hassid, grew up on New York's Lower East Side; Dinah came from Long Island. They met and married in the late Fifties, and emigrated to Israel in 1961. Reb Noach was determined to do something to reverse the Jewish drift away from Torah. For six years he studied with this goal in mind and in 1967 he started his first yeshiva. Aish HaTorah has been going since 1973. Reb Noach runs the school, teaches and makes periodic fundraising trips to the States. The rebbetzin mothers their children, runs their household, studies, teaches, does charity work, and acts as counselor and friend to the yeshiva students and other young people who seek her out. During Aish HaTorah's first year she was also its chief administrator.

On Monday nights a group of women met at Rebbetzin Weinberg's for her class on the 613 *mitzvot*. The rebbetzin was currently discussing the *mitzva* to do good. Doing good, in Jewish terms, involves a constant struggle between the two sides of our nature: the *yeitzer tov* (good inclination), which arises from the soul and desires to serve God, and the *yeitzer hara* (evil inclination), which stems from the body and craves unlimited material, sexual and egotistical satisfactions.

"What's the difference between a war against people and the war against the *yeitzer hara*?" the rebbetzin asked. "A people war has an end—there's no end to the *yeitzer hara* war. A people war doesn't go on 24 hours a day. In a people war, you win something limited. If you win the *yeitzer hara* war, you have everything. And if you lose . . ."

It was an incongruous image for a Jewish mother of nine but I couldn't help thinking of Joan of Arc.

"You have to develop a strategy. For instance, suppose you know that when you meet a certain person you're going to talk *lashon hara*."

Lashon hara, slander, is an important sin, the subject of a formidable body of law. It is forbidden to say anything disparaging about someone—whether or not it is true—or to say anything that could be construed as disparaging, or to listen to such talk. It is even forbidden to praise someone in front of an enemy who might be tempted to argue. The Haskels had a sign in their kitchen that said, "Is that *lashon hara*?"

"You should try to avoid the person," said the rebbetzin. "But if you can't, then you should think, how can I avoid the bad conversation? Is there some other way I can make her feel good?"

"Why not take the direct approach," one of the women asked, "and just say, 'Let's not talk *lashon hara*'?"

"Not everyone can take that," said the rebbetzin. "You might just put her on the defensive."

To be good, Mrs. Weinberg summed up, was to emulate the Almighty, to become as perfect an image of Him as possible. To be Infinitely patient, to return insult with kindness—and without self-congratulation. How to do this? "Know the 613 *mitzvot*. There is no other way."

It occurred to me that if Talmudic logic had made Mike realize how Jewish his thinking was, Jewish ethics made me realize how Jewish my feelings were. I was beginning to understand Jewish guilt. Unlike Christian guilt, which assumed one's inherent depravity, it came from the idea that one could and should attain perfection. Jews who took their religion seriously had no need to feel guilty. They knew the 613 *mitzvot* were the way, and if they backslid they could catch themselves and carry on. For Jews like me it was different; secular enlightenment was the brew that provoketh the desire but taketh away the performance. We still craved perfection, and so we pursued utopian politics, utopian sex, utopian innocence. But we had no law to guide or reassure us. With the law, one could have patience with one's shortcomings. Without it, if we were not there we were nowhere at all. "To live outside the law you must be honest"—Bob Dylan, a Jew, said that.

Since the Haskels had three little children and another guest in their crowded apartment, I moved in with Chaya's stepsister, Abby Ginsberg, and her roommate, Sharon Weitz. They shared a large apartment—inherited from Abby's parents, who had gone back to the States—on Shimoni Street in Rasco, an attractive residential neighborhood that was not predominantly religious. Like the Haskels they were from the Midwest. Abby was studying at Hebrew University, Sharon at a seminary. Both women were more religious than their families.

I felt immediately comfortable with Sharon and Abby, in part because their sense of female identity did not seem radically different from my own. They had not grown up isolated from secular life. They had gone to public high school, dated, worn pants; they had not married at 18; they were serious about learning; the man Abby was seeing pitched in with the cooking and played blues on his guitar. Unlike Lorie, they were not reacting against their past; because their religious commitment had deepened gradually rather than come through sudden conversion, they had none of the *ba'al teshuva*'s dogmatic intensity.

"Of course I feel a conflict between Judaism and feminism," Sharon said. "It's harder to accept if you've been exposed to Western ideas than if you grew up in Mea Shearim. But if you're committed to Judaism, other principles have to adjust. To me a Jewish life offers so many satisfactions . . ." She smiled and shrugged. Intellectually she knew where she stood, but emotionally she was still struggling. "The thing I really care about," said Abby "is being able to learn. If I thought the *halacha* wouldn't allow me to learn—then I might have a problem."

Abby was ebullient; Sharon had a quieter warmth. They were ten years younger than I, but I often felt as if our ages were reversed. They projected a balance, an un-self-conscious maturity symbolized for me by the way they cooperated in maintaining their cheerful apartment. The Shimoni Street place was just an ordinary middle-class apartment, conventionally furnished by the absent parents, serving as a way station for two young, transient students. But Abby and Sharon made it feel like home. They were, for one thing, enthusiastic cooks. Almost every afternoon I would come back to find them in the kitchen discussing recipes; since Abby was experimenting with vegetarianism they were always trying new concoctions—cheese-and-spinach soufflés, vegetable pies, fruit salads.

Often Abby's friend, Joshua, would be there too. He was leaving for the States in a few weeks, right after Passover; in the meantime he and Abby were trying to figure out how they felt about each other. Orthodox Jews do not play sexual games: a man and a woman are either compatible or they aren't, and if they decide they are they get married. So Josh was at Shimoni Street several nights a week. He and Abby would study and argue points of *halacha,* and then we would all help with the dinner and eat together, talking and joking about the events of the day, what this or that teacher said, my latest argument with Lorie. I would go to bed and read, or write in my notebook, and when I padded to the kitchen or the bathroom at 2 or 3 a.m. I would, as often as not, hear the pacific murmur of one of Josh and Abby's marathon conversations.

Truth and Consequences

"The first commandment," said Reb Noach, "is to know there is a God." We were resuming a conversation we had started a few days earlier. "The disease of Western thought," he had said then, "is: 'There is no absolute truth.' But it's intuitively obvious that either something is true or it isn't. Listen—'There is no absolute truth.' 'Are you sure?' 'Yes.' 'Are you absolutely sure?'" I could afford to laugh. I believed something was true or it wasn't; I just didn't think we could know for sure which was which. "They call us fanatics. But a fanatic is someone who won't listen to reason. I say, let's reason together. Let's find a premise on which we can both agree and reason from there. The purpose of reason," he had concluded, "is to get someone to the point where his intuition will say, 'Yes, you're right.'"

"*Know* there is a God," Reb Noach repeated. "Not 'Have faith.' Understand! Reason! But reason can only tell you what you already know. It's a servant, like your hand." He held his hand out. "Hand! Come to my nose!" The hand did not move. "What's this? Revolution? Don't be silly! No, your hand acts on what you really want, not on what you say you want. Reason will tell you what you really know—what are your perceptions. Not other people's, not society's."

For the next hour or so, Reb Noach tried to persuade my intuition. If my father on his deathbed asked me to say a mourner's prayer for him, would I? Of course. If he asked me to say a bunch of nonsense syllables, would I? Probably not. Why not? What's the difference? Well, I think religious ritual is meaningful, worthy of respect; that doesn't mean it represents absolute truth. If someone ran in front of my car and I hit him, wouldn't I feel guilty, even if I couldn't possibly have stopped in time? Yes, I would. What did that tell me? "Even if it's not technically my fault, someone has suffered because of me. It's irrational, but I'd think, 'If I'd just done something different—taken the bus, stayed home . . .'"

"The reason you would feel guilty," Reb Noach said, "is that it really would be your fault. If you hadn't done something wrong, God wouldn't have chosen you as the instrument of someone's death."

I appreciated Reb Noach's technique. I realized that I had, on occasion, used it myself. (Don't you and your husband both work? Suppose you lived with your sister, and you both worked, and she wanted you to cook dinner every night because she was tired—would you do it? Why not? Well, then, what's different about doing it for a man?) But my intuition was unconvinced. I still couldn't see the ultimate Reality as a being who cared, willed, intervened in our lives and—might as well bring it up—decreed separate functions for men and women.

"You don't think men and women are basically different?"

"*Basically,* no," I said. "*Basically,* I think we're all human beings."

"One of the craziest ideas in this crazy modern world," said Reb Noach, "is that men and women are the same. Men and women are two different species!"

I insisted that whatever the differences—and who could tell at this point which were inherent, which imposed by a patriarchal culture?—they did not require women to devote themselves to as many babies as chose to make their appearance. Reb Noach shook his head.

"Children are the greatest pleasure," he said, "but people today are so decadent they prefer their material comforts to children."

"It's not just material comfort!" I protested. "People have a right to some freedom—some time for themselves . . ."

"Decadence, Ellen. I'd have 50 children, a hundred. Every child is a lesson in love!"

"My parents aren't decadent! They've worked hard to bring up three children—to educate us all . . ."

Suddenly I found myself weeping.

"Ellen!" The rabbi's voice vibrated through me, alarmed, caring, soothing as a touch. "I'm not condemning *people*! Who knows who's better than who? I'm talking about actions. Mistakes, Ellen."

I wasn't sure why I was crying—except that if my middle-class family-centered parents could by any standard be accused of decadent behavior, then I was completely hopeless. My loss of control took me by surprise. I suppose it was my first overt symptom of culture shock.

How long was it since I'd landed at the airport—eight days? Nine? It felt much longer. My sense of time had changed, along with my perspective. I was, in crucial ways, an outsider—a reporter, at that—in a strange culture. Yet because I was Jewish, I was also family. Whatever anyone might think of me, whether I was religious or not, so long as I was living in the Orthodox community I was on some basic level accepted as part of it. And so I began, almost imperceptibly at first, to identify with that community and feel weirdly estranged from the secular world. I found myself thinking of non-religious people as "they." When I had an errand in downtown Jerusalem I felt assaulted by its frenetic, noisy, garish urbanness, by the crowds of Israelis who milled along Jaffa Road without a care for the subtleties of Jewish law.

Even the ever-present political tension began to seem part of that other world. A deep belief that God controls events tends to cool political fervor, and only a minority of Orthodox Israelis fit the stereotype of the militant religious nationalist; Mike and his friends were critical of the rabbinical establishment for what they saw as its readiness to bend the Torah to the demands of the state. I had arrived in Israel at a volatile time: Palestinian students had been demonstrating in the Old City; Israeli Arabs were protesting the expropriation of Arab land in the Galilee. I read about it all in the *Jerusalem Post,* feeling, absurdly, that Israeli politics had been much more vivid to me when I was in New York.

A religious universe enveloped me. I was surrounded by people who believed and, more important, lived that belief every minute. Conversation among Orthodox Jews never strays far from questions of ethics, points of law, one's religious activities; even small talk is inescapably religious: "I'm feeling better, *boruch Hashem!*"; "I ran into so-and-so on Shabbos"; "She's going to have a *milchig* [dairy] wedding." Orthodox life has its own special rhythm. There is the daily rhythm of prayer and the weekly rhythm of preparations for Shabbos: rushing to clean and cook before Friday sundown, when all work must be suspended; setting lights to go on and off automatically; taking turns showering, hoping the hot water won't run out; dressing up; lighting the Sabbath candles. There is Shabbos itself: making *kiddush* (blessing and sharing wine); washing and breaking bread and sitting down to the traditional European-Jewish Friday night chicken dinner; the men going off to *shul* Saturday morning, coming home to a meal of *cholent,* a stew that is made before Shabbos and left simmering on the stove; studying, walking, visiting or napping in the afternoon; the light supper and finally the *havdalah* ("division") ceremony with which Shabbos ends.

Although the process was less dramatic, my immersion in Jewish life was having a far more potent effect on me than my confrontation with Jewish ideas. I could argue with ideas, but I could not, without being an abrasive nuisance, refuse to adapt, in important respects, to the customs of my hosts. On the most superficial level this meant not washing Abby and Sharon's dairy dishes in the meat sink, but it also meant shifting mental gears to participate in conversations that took a religious outlook for granted. Living with Orthodox Jews was like being straight at a party where everyone else is stoned; after a while, out of sheer social necessity, you find yourself getting a contact high.

There was, for instance, the afternoon I spent talking with Lorie and Frieda. Frieda had recruited Lorie for her *ba'al teshuva* organization; they were planning to go back to New York in July to get the project moving. I started giving advice. If they wanted young, educated women to take Judaism seriously, I argued, their organization would have to engage women's minds the way Aish HaTorah had engaged Mike's. That meant . . . and then I heard myself: I was telling them how to seduce me.

I had always thought of Orthodox Judaism as a refuge for compulsives: not only did its ubiquitous requirements and prohibitions seem to preclude spontaneity, but since the *halacha,* like any body of law that applies basic principles to specific situations, was open to interpretation, it provided endless opportunities for what outsiders would call hairsplitting. For example, it's Shabbos and Sharon and Abby have a problem: they have, as usual, left a kettle of boiling water on a burner they lit Friday afternoon, and now the flame has gone out. Is it permitted to switch the kettle to another lit burner? If the water has cooled off, heating it up again would violate the rule against cooking on Shabbos. If it's still hot, moving it should be okay. But it must have cooled off slightly. How hot does it have to be? Under the kettle, covering both burners, is a metal sheet, there as a reminder not to turn the flames up or down; does this make both flames one fire, which would mean that switching the kettle is allowed in any case? Abby, Sharon and Josh debated this issue for half an hour—it remained unresolved, and they did not move the kettle.

I understood now that to call this sort of behavior compulsive was to assume that religious observance was a distraction from life, while for believers it was the whole point; secular concerns were the distraction. If doing *mitzvot*—all of them, not just those you understood or liked—was the way to serve God, to connect with Reality, then it was crucial to do them exactly right. For the people around me Torah was not a straitjacket but a discipline, shaping and focusing their energies toward the only meaningful end. It was an arduous discipline, but one that was no more inherently compulsive than my own search for the precise adjective, or the care with which feminists analyzed the minutiae of sexual relationships.

And what was so sacred, anyway, about the arcane customs of my hyper-urban, freelance existence? For all that I was so attached to it, I had to admit that it was, in the context of human history, more than a little strange. Sociologists liked to talk about how rootless and mobile Americans were, but most Americans at least had families. Despite my reluctance to assume the burdens of motherhood in a sexist society, it disturbed me to think that I would very likely never have children: I felt that child rearing, like working and loving, was one of the activities that defined humanness. Even my work—my excuse for so much of what I did or didn't do—sometimes struck me as ridiculous. What was the point of sitting home scratching symbols on paper, adding my babblings to a world already overloaded with information? And what of my belief in the supreme importance of connecting with Reality? Orthodox Jews acted on their version of that belief; did I? Well, there was my therapy. It occupied all of 45 minutes of my week—less time than it took me (speaking of compulsive rituals) to read the Sunday *Times.* Did I really have my priorities straight?

If my traumatic talk with Mike had shocked me into realizing that Judaism was a plausible intellectual system, living in Jerusalem was making me realize that Judaism was a plausible way of life. And that realization slid relentlessly into the next: that it was plausible even for me. My rapport with Abby and Sharon weakened my defenses against this frightening idea. I experienced Shimoni Street as a kind of halfway house. Much as I admired the rebbetzin, she was too unlike me to be a model. Lorie, in an entirely different way, was also from another world. But Abby and Sharon had the psychology of modern intellectual women. If they found Orthodox life exalting and full of purpose—if they had been exposed to the freedoms I had, yet did not feel deprived—perhaps I did not need those freedoms as much as I thought.

Yet even as I was drawn into the Orthodox subculture, I also resisted it. My resistance took an embarrassing form, it surfaced as a spoiled brat yelling, "I won't!" If I had come to Israel to experience Judaism, it made sense for me to try to observe Jewish law. I had resolved, for instance, to eat only kosher food during my stay. For a month this would scarcely be a major deprivation; I had stuck to reducing diets that required much more discipline. Yet I found that I couldn't keep away from the junk-food stands on Jaffa Road; I stuffed myself with suspect brands of chocolate; under my modest dresses I was puffing out at a disquieting rate. Then there was the synagogue issue. Though communal prayer was not required of women, I felt that I should, at least once, attend services at an Orthodox *shul*. But I was afraid to face what I saw as the total humiliation of sitting upstairs in the women's section. Some journalist, I mocked myself. Lucky no one ever sent you to cover a war.

I began to realize that I was depressed. The weather, still wintry and raw, depressed me. The city itself depressed me, which was a surprise. On my first trip to Israel I had reacted very differently. I was not thinking about religion then; I was preoccupied with politics, war history, the tragic clash of nationalism. But I had been awed by the radiance of Jerusalem. Perhaps it was just the combination of natural beauty and antiquity, but whatever holiness was, the city breathed it. Standing before the massive stones of the Western Wall, submerged in a crowd of people praying, I had felt the pain and ecstasy of millions of pilgrims course through me.

A friend had arranged for several members of our group to have Friday night dinner with a religious family, and all evening I felt the way I had at the Wall. Everything had a preternatural clarity and significance. When our host said the blessings over the bread and wine, I marveled that I had been so obtuse as not to see. Blessing one's food—appreciating the miracle of food—what could be more fitting? And the whole idea of the Sabbath, one day a week when you were forbidden ordinary distractions and had to be alone with yourself and Reality . . . I imagined myself back in New York City, spending a Saturday without writing, eating in a restaurant, taking the subway; a whole day with the phone off the hook and the record player silent. A fantasy, of course, I could never live that way, didn't even want to, and yet I felt a pang: isn't this what it's all about, the acid peace, the connection you say you want, getting rid of all the noise?

Now, though I remembered those feelings, I couldn't re-create them. I went to the Wall, saw weathered stone spattered with pigeon droppings, left quickly because of the cold wind. And Shabbos, with all its restrictions, was simply oppressive, like a tight girdle. "Last time," said Mike, "you could be open to it because you weren't seriously thinking about it as a possibility."

It was during Shabbos, the second since I'd arrived, that my depression hit full force. A friend of Mike's had invited us for the weekend. He and his wife were warmly hospitable and I struggled guiltily against my gloom. I felt suffocated by domesticity, by the children calling for mommy, the men leaving for *shul* and the women staying home, the men sitting at the table and the women carting away the dishes. I wanted to tear off my itchy, constricting stockings. I wanted to write in my notebook, turn on lights, eat without going through half an hour of ritual first.

The next day I went to El Al to confirm my return reservation. The flight I was booked on left April 22nd, but my excursion ticket was good for two extra weeks if I wanted them and I figured it was time to decide. I was always superstitious about switching flights; now, looking over the timetable, I felt irrationally certain that if I changed my plans I would end up staying in Israel. Something would trap me here. When Lorie first came to Jerusalem she had dreamed she was in prison, supervised by a mean lady; she had wanted to get out, but by the time they were ready to let her go, a month later, she loved it and wanted to stay. On the strength of that dream Lorie had decided to stay a month and, sure enough she was still here . . . This is ridiculous, I lectured myself. If you want to go you'll go; if you want to stay you'll stay; and if God is really controlling your life it's useless to second-guess Him. I debated staying at least a few extra days, but that would mean going through another Shabbos. I decided to stick with my original flight.

As soon as I left the office, a new wave of paranoia hit: God would punish me for my rotten attitude toward Shabbos. My plane would crash or be attacked by terrorists. *Mida k'neged mida*—measure for measure. Later that day, I realized I couldn't leave on April 22nd: it was the last day of Passover, and I had been invited to Reb Noach's. The prospect of having to change my reservation after all solidified my conviction that I would never make it back to the States. I had received a sign. There were no coincidences.

When I told Mike about my scheduling mix-up, he looked as if I'd punched him in the jaw. "You're leaving early," he said. "I thought you had six weeks."

"I planned on staying a month. I'm just doing what I was going to do all along."

"It's not just that. You want to leave because you're depressed. You're reacting exactly the same way I did."

My gut contracted.

"Mike, I'm not you. We may be alike in a lot of ways, but we're two different people." Under the panic I had to remember that, hold on to that. "If I want to go home I'm going home, and I'm not going to feel guilty about it."

"But you can't postpone these questions . . ." He shook his head. "When you first came, you were really relating to what was going on. Now I feel as if you've withdrawn."

"Do you really have to go back?" the rebbetzin asked. I had come over for another talk with Reb Noach.

"Theoretically," I said, "I could throw over my entire life and stay. But I don't want to."

"Do you think it's important to find out if there's a God?"

"Well . . ." *Leave me alone! Get off my back!*

"If there is, and we don't find out, are we culpable?"

I don't have to listen to this! It's brainwashing, that's what it is!

"I can find out in New York," I said.

"If I offered you a $200,000 business deal," Reb Noach put in, "you wouldn't say, 'I can make the same deal in America.' You'd say, 'Let's talk.'"

"I have a whole life to get back to," I insisted. "I like my life."

"Then you *won't* really try to find out," said the rebbetzin.

"I didn't say that."

"Well, will you?"

"I don't know," I said, feeling miserable.

I was not in the best mood to face Reb Noach. During our talks, he had been going through the proofs of God one by one. His theme this time was: "A design must have a designer." I had by now had this argument with several people. I still didn't buy it. Finally, Reb Noach said, "Ellen, think for a minute: is there a reason you don't want to believe the proofs?"

"Well, I can't deny that," I said. "I don't want to change my whole world view. But . . ."

"Look at it objectively! If you accept one proof it doesn't mean changing your whole world view."

"But I don't accept it. I don't see that the order in the universe has to be created by a personal God."

"There seems to be a wall here," said Reb Noach. "I don't want to pursue this unless you want to."

He started on another tack. "Why was the world created? For our pleasure. What is the one thing we are capable of doing? Seeking pleasure. So how can we go wrong? Insanity! Tell me—what's the opposite of pleasure?"

"Pain," I said.

"No! No! The opposite of pleasure is *comfort*. Pleasure *involves* pain. Decadence is opting for comfort. For example, what's more important, wisdom or money? Ask most people, they'll say 'wisdom.' 'Okay, stay here six months and I'll give you wisdom.' 'I can't—I have a job, a girlfriend, I'm supposed to take a vacation in the Greek islands.' 'Stay six months and I'll give you $20,000.' 'Fine!' 'What about your job, your girlfriend?' 'They'll wait.'

"The soul wants wisdom; the body wants money. The soul wants pleasure; the body wants comfort. And what's the highest pleasure? The aim of the soul? God, Ellen. That's real happiness—ecstasy, Ellen! Find out what you're living for! Take the pain—pleasure only comes with a lot of pain. I'm your friend—I'm with you. Give up your life of striving for success, for identity, your name up there . . ."

Unfair! "Do you really think I write just to get my name in print?"

"I think you do it to have an identity. To be 'a writer.'"

"I do like having that. But would you believe that I write mainly because I enjoy it, and I'm good at it, and"—defiantly—"I think it's useful work!"

"Shakespeare's okay," said Reb Noach, "but unless you know the real meaning of life, you're a zombie, a walking dead man. Find out what you're living for, Ellen. Clarity or death!"

There began to be moments—usually early in the morning, before I forced myself to get up and face the day—when I was more inclined than not to believe that it was all true, that I was only resisting because I couldn't stand the pain of admitting how wrong I was. *What about the prophecies* . . . and the way modern history seemed almost a conspiracy to drive the Jews back to Israel . . . and the Bible. . . . Mike and I had been going over Genesis, along with the Rashi commentary, and I had had a sudden vision, like an acid flash, of a Garden, and a Presence . . . and my personality, my Sagittarian compulsion to aim straight at the cosmic bull's-eye. . . . *"The blessing and curse of being a Jew,"* said Reb Noach, *"is that Jews are thirsty for God, for the absolute. A Jew can never have peace. Whatever he does he'll be the best at, whether it's being a radical or being a criminal. It's all misplaced searching for God. Every Jew is a neurotic. . . ."*

And if I became religious, what would I do? Insanity, decadence, call it what you please, I could never be a traditional Jewish mother. But maybe I didn't have to be. Actually only men were subject to a specific *mitzvah* to marry and have children. And not everyone took the Weinbergs' hard line on procreation—according to one rabbi I'd met, a psychologist, the *halacha* permitted contraception when necessary to preserve a woman's health, including her emotional health. Nor were the role divisions in the family absolute, no law actually forbade women to work outside the home, or men to share housework. Even within the bounds of Judaism I could be a feminist of sorts, crusading for reforms like equal education, perhaps contesting the biased *halachic* interpretations of male rabbis. And my experience would put me in a unique position to reach women like me and bring them back.

In private I could have this fantasy, even take it seriously. Which would not stop me, an hour or a minute later, from getting into a furious argument with a man. It was one thing to consider the abstract possibility that women's role in Judaism was not inherently oppressive, another to live in a culture that made me feel oppressed. Once when Mike and I were dinner guests of another of his teachers I complained, "You know, it makes me feel like a servant when you sit there like a lump while I help serve and clean up."

"It isn't customary for the men to help," Mike said, "and if I got up I'd make everybody uncomfortable, including the women." He had a point—when in Rome and all that—but it was a point he was not exactly loath to make. The fact was that for Mike, moving from Western secular society to Orthodox Judaism had meant an increase in status and privilege; for me it meant a loss.

One night Mike and I got together with Dick Berger, one of his best friends at the yeshiva. Mike was very high on Dick, who, he said, was an unusually perceptive person with a gift for sensing someone's emotional blocks. He had been encouraging Mike to get more connected to his feelings. I had met Dick once and he had told me a little about himself. He had been a newspaper reporter in Pittsburgh, had written an unpublished novel, had been into psychedelics and Transcendental Meditation. Later he had told Mike that he felt I had seen him only as material for my article. I didn't think that was true, but I worried about it anyway. I hated it when people claimed to know my motives better than I did, but I always worried that they were right.

The conversation that night was pleasant enough until Dick and I got into an argument about men sharing child care. Dick suggested that 3,000 years of tradition shouldn't be tampered with, and I started getting angry in a way I knew from experience led to no good. Then he really pushed the wrong button.

"You're so emotional! Can't we talk about this objectively?"

"You're hardly being objective. It's in your interest as a man to think what you think."

"I'm feeling detached," Dick insisted. "By that I mean attached to my basic essence. You're reacting out of your conditioning in Western culture."

"You're reacting out of your male-supremacist prejudices, only you have 3,000 years of tradition on your side."

"But I'm not being aggressive and hostile—you are!"

"You can afford to be 'objective' and 'detached'! You're happy with the system—I'm the one who's being oppressed by it! Why shouldn't I be hostile— what right do you have to demand that we have this conversation on your terms . . ." My sentence went hurtling off into the inarticulate reaches of un-God-like rage.

Another time, another friend of Mike's: Harvey, a tall, dark, intense South African. "I'm not here because I want to be," he said. "I want freedom and money and the pleasures of the body. I was happy in my non-religious life—I miss it. But once you know there's a God . . ."

We started arguing about design and evolution. "Either there's a God," Harvey said, "or all this harmony and purpose is a coincidence."

"Those aren't the only possibilities . . ."

"And there are vast odds against coincidence. If you had a dart board that had lots of red and just a little white, where do you think your dart would hit?"

"That's a silly analogy," I said.

"What if you had to lay money on it?"

"I'm not going to play this game! It's ridiculous! It's irrelevant!"

"Answer me," the prosecutor insisted. "Would you bet on white or red?"

"I'm not Pascal!" I yelled. "And I'm not about to change my entire life because of some abstract intellectual decision about what the odds are on there being a God!"

"The Torah isn't only a carrot, you know. It's a stick, as well. There's punishment—you get cut off . . ."

And I'm not going to play your guilt game, either! You men are not going to cram your sexist religion down my throat!

There it was, the dirty little secret: I might be persuaded to return to Judaism—but not by a man. After one of our encounters, Reb Noach had declared, "You are emotionally committed to rebelling against the male sex!" He was right, of course, and in principle I agreed that one ought to be wary of such a priori commitments. But whenever I clashed with a man I seemed to end up with a renewed conviction that my rebellion was a matter of simple sanity. Men with their obnoxious head trips! Men with their "objectivity": "Let's discuss this rationally—should I remove my foot from your neck or shouldn't I?"

Exodus

> And it shall be when thy son asketh thee in time to come, saying, What is this? That thou shall say unto him, By strength of hand the Lord brought us out from Egypt, from the house of bondage.
>
> —*Exodus 13:14*

> You know her life was saved by rock & roll.
>
> —*Velvet Underground*

Mike and I were walking in Mea Shearim talking about happiness. My revised departure date was nearly two weeks away, time for plenty of changes, but I knew that I would not, at least for the present, become an Orthodox Jew. My decision had involved no epiphany, no cathartic moment of truth; my doubts remained and perhaps always would. But to put it that way was looking at it backward. The fact was that only a compelling, inescapable moment of truth could have made me religious. Nothing less could shake my presumption in favor of a life that made me happy.

From Mike's point of view, I was refusing to accept the truth because of a strong emotional resistance; though he too had resisted, his unhappiness with secular life had made it easier to give up. On the other hand, he kept suggesting, I might be a lot less happy than I thought.

"Dick sees you as a very unhappy person," Mike said. "And Reb Noach thinks you're really unhappy."

I felt a twinge of resentment—who were these people, who hardly knew me, to call me unhappy?—mixed with anxiety. Was I fooling myself? I didn't think so. I was not perfectly happy, or as happy as I wanted to be, but in spite of my unresolved problems I was happier than not. Having problems, even serious ones, was not the same as being unhappy. I knew the difference because I had experienced it. For about seven years, beginning the year I started college, I had suffered from a severe depression. At the time I hadn't called it that, I didn't know what to call it. I wasn't especially sad; I just had this puzzling sense that nothing was quite real, that my life was, as I put it to myself, all procedure and no substance. Most of my activities, however theoretically enjoyable, secretly disappointed me. Reading my favorite poets, camping in Yosemite, marching on CORE picket lines, making love, somehow I nearly always felt like a spectator. When I got married I knew I was making a mistake but felt powerless to act on that knowledge; no matter how a movie may horrify you, you don't yell "No!" at it or smash the projector. I was conscious that all was not well, but then I thought, perhaps everyone felt this way, perhaps this was just the way life was. In the beginning that thought jibed neatly with the spirit of the time—the tail end of the silent Fifties.

My depression had begun gradually, for no obvious reason, and ended the same way. But over the years my memories of descent and recovery had crystallized around a few symbolic events. The first occurred when I was a Barnard freshman infatuated with a Columbia sophomore, an old friend from high school. One day I ran into him on the street and casually suggested—we were friends, right?—getting together some time. He looked uncomfortable and mumbled a non-answer. To my surprise I felt almost no pain. I noted that fact with detached interest. How sensible, I thought. Why cry over a situation I have no power to change? Four years later, when I was living in Berkeley, I heard Bob Dylan for the first time and was an instant fanatic. Dylan's voice got straight through to me, and what it said was, No, this is not just the way life is. Then a friend lent me Wilhelm Reich's classic, *Character Analysis*. I had never heard of Reich, and the book was a revelation: among other things, it contained a precise description of my emotional state. Other people had been in the same condition and been cured! I was not hopeless! It took me a while to pick up on these messages but eventually I left my husband, returned to New York, became a journalist, decided I thought I was really a radical and fell in love. Somewhere along the line I noticed that my strange remoteness was gone.

I had had bouts of depression since then—the worst one had driven me to my therapist—and in occasional moments of stress I had reverted to staring at the movie. But I felt certain that I would never again lose myself in so terrible a way. In retrospect, it was clear that what had done me in were my conflicts about growing up female—conflicts I still felt. The difference was that I had decided to engage and struggle with life rather than withdraw from it. And making that decision—as often as necessary—was what happiness was about. I agreed with the Jewish insistence that happiness was a choice. Yet how I had gained the strength to choose remained a mystery, part of the larger mystery of how one connected with Reality. Like the inexplicable, ineffable liberation I'd experienced on acid, my emergence from despair had ultimately depended on what religious people call the grace of God.

Not that external circumstances were irrelevant. Things might have been very different if it had not been for the Sixties—and especially for rock & roll. Rock had been a major factor in my recovery; it had had the power to move me when almost nothing else did. I had been an ardent rock & roll fan in high school. (Sometimes I thought this was why my depression hadn't hit until I arrived at Barnard where—this was 1958—you were still supposed to dance to Lester Lanin.) But by the early Sixties I had largely abandoned pop for folk music. Still, when Dylan released his first rock album I was excited. I felt he had brought it all back home in more ways than one. After my marriage broke up in 1965 I started listening to AM radio again. The Sixties renaissance had begun; the pop charts were dominated by the Beatles and Stones and their epigoni, by Motown and folk rock. My new love was not only obsessed with the music but self-conscious about its cultural significance and its influence on our lives in a way that was new to me. I began to make my own connections. My first serious article was a long essay on Dylan.

Mike had once been a rock fan, but since becoming religious he had come to see rock as a drug, an escapist distraction. He also considered my writing a suspect activity; he and Dick Berger agreed that journalism, like traveling, was a way of observing life rather than participating in it.

"Do you think you would have gotten more out of being here if you had just come and gotten involved instead of having to think about your article?" Mike asked.

"I don't know," I said. "But if I hadn't decided to write an article I probably wouldn't have come."

Without the protection of my writer's role—my license to observe—I might not have had the courage to come. But more important, my overwhelming urge to write about a subject that touched every major issue in my life had routed a powerful impulse to repress, sit tight, let inertia take over; my decision to face up to my spiritual crisis was inseparable from my compulsion to observe and analyze it, to pursue every last connection. Anyway, writing was not just observing—it was sharing one's observations, a social act. It was also hard work. My identity as a writer might, as Reb Noach had suggested, be a prop for my ego, but it also had something to do with taking my work seriously. I had not begun thinking of myself as "a writer" until I had changed my attitude from

"Right now I'm writing, maybe next year I'll study psychology" to "I'm going to stop playing games and commit myself to being the best writer I can be." Now, looking back on that change, I saw it as another crucial step toward happiness.

Clarity or death! Reb Noach insisted, and if there was one bit of clarity that emerged from all my confusion it was the conviction that my happiness was not illusory. As I tried to explain that conviction to Mike, I felt suddenly disgusted with my current funk. No wonder Dick and Reb Noach thought I was unhappy. I was a mess. I had gained ten pounds and developed a cold. I was sleeping later and later. If I had a serious talk with someone it exhausted me so much I would run back to the security of Shimoni Street and take a nap. "When we act out of fear of pain we're choosing death," Reb Noach was always saying. "The Torah says, 'Choose life!'" I had been running from the pain of uncertainty and conflict, had even thought, "I can't stand any more of this—I'm going to kill myself." How absurdly self-important!

Perhaps it was sheer determination to prove Mike wrong but my mood slowly began to change. I began, finally, to respond to the beauty of Jerusalem, to the hills and the peculiar atmospheric sparkle I had noticed nowhere else. I felt as if I'd been let out of prison.

Passover was approaching. I had deliberately scheduled my trip so that I would be in Israel for the week-long holiday. The Passover Seder—which was supposed to be celebrated on each of the first two nights—was the one Jewish ritual my family regularly observed. Most years we had our Seders with my mother's sister's family; my uncle, who was observant though not Orthodox, presided at the ceremony. For the rest of us Passover was less a religious occasion than a family party, a spring version of Thanksgiving. Still, it was impossible to retell the Exodus story year after year and be unaffected by it. It was, after all, a story about escaping oppression for freedom, and I was fond of thinking of it in contemporary political and psychological terms; to me the Seder's concluding invocation—"Next year in Jerusalem!"—expressed hope for both kinds of liberation. To Orthodox Jews, however, Passover meant something very different—as I had learned attending Lorie's classes, the traditional definition of the freedom the Exodus represented was a mirror image of my own.

Passover commemorates a historical event—the deliverance of the Jewish people from slavery in Egypt, the prelude to the revelation of the Torah. But for the religious Jew it is also an ongoing reality. The Haggadah (the account of the Exodus read at the Seder) says, "In every generation each individual is bound to regard himself as if he personally had gone forth from Egypt." According to tradition, Egypt represents materialism, hedonism, amorality. To relive the Exodus is to affirm one's liberation from bondage to the Pharaoh within—the *yeitzer hara*—and one's readiness to live in true freedom, that is, under God's law. This theme is made concrete in the central symbol of Passover, the *matzah*—unleavened bread. Because the fleeing Jews did not have time to let their bread rise, it is forbidden during Passover to eat or possess bread or any food made with leaven: symbolically, leaven represents the expansion of the *yeitzer hara*.

Reb David, a young teacher at Aish HaTorah, and his wife Ruth had invited Mike and me for the first Seder. In the morning we went over to help with last-minute preparations. Ruth put me to work hemming her older son's new holiday pants. Later I played with the kids, who had been sent out on the porch with a bowl of nuts to crack. A week ago their noise, mess and bickering would have driven me further into myself; now I was actually having fun.

The Seder began at around eight. The idea of the ceremony is to teach everyone—especially the children present—as much about the Exodus and its meaning as possible. Reb David went over each page of the Haggadah, asking questions, discussing various rabbis' interpretations, and by the time we reached the end of the first part—which we had to do before we could eat—it was almost midnight. After dinner we carried on for two more hours. The Seder ended—I had wondered about this beforehand—with the traditional words: "Next year in Jerusalem."

Later in the week, Mike and I were guests at the Weinbergs', along with several vacationing students of both sexes. I was very conscious of the rebbetzin, who seemed continually busy—though her admiring female guests competed with each other for jobs, there was always more to do—and continuously serene. Occasionally one of the kids gave her a hard time, balking at some little chore. Long after the average parent would have been shrieking with frustration, the rebbetzin would calmly repeat her request—or else, with no visible resentment, she would do the task herself.

Feeling guilty about my own lack of patience and selflessness, a lack I was sure was obvious to everyone, I slinked around trying to be inconspicuous. Finally the rebbetzin cornered me.

"I think," she began, "that you think you have to hide your femininity to be taken seriously."

For a moment I was speechless. "Why do you think that?"

"Well, for instance, the way you dress, the way you wear your hair."

Oh, if that's all she means, I thought. She doesn't realize, I'm only looking this way because I've been depressed. I knew I had been neglecting my appearance. Most days I stuck my long hair under a scarf so I wouldn't have to bother with it, and I couldn't wear anything with a waistline because I'd gained so much weight. On the other hand, the baggy dress I had on was actually quite fashionable in New York, and besides, since my normal jeans-and-T-shirt wardrobe was *halachically* unacceptable, what was I supposed to wear, and anyway, wasn't this the same old oppressive business of always judging a woman by her looks? . . . Nice try, but it won't do, I admitted. Face it: she's right.

The big lie of male supremacy is that women are less than fully human; the basic task of feminism is to expose that lie and fight it on every level. Yet for all my feminist militance I was, it seemed, secretly afraid that the lie was true—

that my humanity was hopelessly at odds with my ineluctably female sexuality—while the rebbetzin, staunch apostle of traditional femininity, did not appear to doubt for a moment that she could be both a woman and a serious person. Which was only superficially paradoxical, for if you were absolutely convinced that the Jewish woman's role was ordained by God, and that it was every bit as important spiritually as the man's, how could you believe the lie?

I was too much the product of Western libertarian values to travel the rebbetzin's route to self-acceptance, and so far I had not succeeded in finding my own . . .

On my last night in Jerusalem I went back for a final visit with the Weinbergs. Reb Noach was talking to a young visitor named Ron. Ron was explaining that he had come to Israel to get his head straight, figure out what to do with his life. Did he want to take over his father's diamond-polishing business, or what?

"Come to our yeshiva," Reb Noach said. "Find out what Judaism has to say about these questions. For instance, why are we here? What are we here for?"

"To serve God?"

"No. The world was created to give man pleasure. The Torah tells us how to get it. The Almighty didn't want us wandering around like chickens with their heads chopped off."

Ron was obviously interested, and Reb Noach began urging him to come to Aish HaTorah for a week.

"I can't," said Ron. "I've committed myself to work on my kibbutz till the end of July. And my girlfriend is there."

"Don't worry about the kibbutz. They can get someone to take your place. What are you there for? You won't find the answers to your questions on a kibbutz."

"I can't come now," said Ron. "But I promise in three months I'll be back."

"Come now," Reb Noach persisted. "Who knows what could happen in three months? A man should never say, 'When I have time I'll study.'"

"I can't," said Ron, "but my mind is really blown by your concern."

I made my goodbyes. Reb Noach gave me some parting advice: "Jews say, whatever else you do, be happy. Even if you're a lawbreaker, just fulfill that one commandment."

In the morning Mike went with me to the airport. We stood there awkwardly, unable to say most of what we felt. For the first time since this long trip had begun, I had the old flash that he was my male mirror image.

Judaism teaches the conventional patriarchal idea that men have more of a bent for abstract reasoning, women for intuitive understanding. I believe that this split is social, not biological—that in a society where men rule and women nurture, it makes sense for men to develop their intellect at the expense of their emotions and for women to do the opposite. Still, I agree that although the difference is probably not innate, and certainly not absolute—I, for one, am more cerebral than most of the men I know—it does exist. And at the moment Mike and I were a study in contrasting male and female sensibilities. I was leaving Israel, with all the intellectual questions unresolved, because in the end I trusted my feelings and believed in acting on them. Though I might use logic as a weapon against uncertainty, I did not, finally, have Mike's faith that it would lead me to the truth.

Mike had been 24 when he became religious. I had been 23 when I came out of my deadly depression. It seemed to me that both changes represented the same basic decision to be happy. But mine had been a purely intuitive decision, to allow myself to feel; his had presented itself as an intellectual decision, to go where his logic led. Perhaps our paths were equally valid. Perhaps not. As I kissed my brother goodbye I still did not know whether my refusal to believe was healthy self-assertion or stubborn egotism; the Jews, the Bible tells us, are a stiff-necked people.

I arrived exhausted at Kennedy, retrieved my baggage, slogged through customs and went outside to wait for my parents to pick me up. Only then did I allow myself a moment of enormous relief. I had made it after all. No crash, no bomb, no hijacker, no unexplained delay. I was here in New York, body and soul intact. And then I thought, so what? Suddenly I was quite unable to understand what I had been so anxious to come back to. The airport was bleak and sterile. The weather was unseasonably cold, and a freaky windstorm was making everyone run for cover. I huddled in the doorway of the terminal watching the cars go by like an endless procession of anti-American clichés. When my parents drove up I felt another surge of relief, but on the way back to their house my confusion returned. Where did I belong? What did I want?

The following evening my father drove me home to my apartment in Manhattan. The windstorm had blown away the smog, and from the expressway we had an unusually clear view of the harbor and the skyline. It was dusk, the lights of the city were beginning to blink on, and I was seized with an almost religious tenderness for New York and its special beauty. Yet at the same time, staring at those glittering lights, I saw something else: the temptations of Egypt. My eyes filled, and I thought—groping for irony I could not quite reach—

How does it feel
To be on your own
With no direction home,
Like a complete unknown?

Rolling Stone, April 1977

The Eighties
Coming Down Again

INTRODUCTION
Ann Friedman

If the seventies were the hangover after the heady days of revolution, the eighties were when sobriety really began to set in. Drug experimentation had led to a wasteful national war on narcotics and, on a personal level, very real addictions. The sexual revolution had trailblazed uneasy relationship terrain that didn't necessarily leave women more fulfilled. Racial equality remained surprisingly elusive, even in most activist spheres. Pregnancy was becoming almost as heavily regulated as abortion. And parenting? Virtually neglected by earlier iterations of the feminist movement.

Countercultural activists and writers of previous decades had made the case that these issues were even worth talking about. As Ellen Willis explained in a *Fresh Air* interview with Terry Gross in 1989, in the sixties and seventies, sexism was "reflexive, taken for granted"—until feminists loudly called it out. But those of us who came of age in a post-Vietnam, post-*Roe* world know all too well that identifying a problem is not the same thing as addressing it. By the eighties, the shake-up had occurred. It was time for the fallout.

The sexual revolution exploded the old rules for men, but a decade later women had yet to claim similar freedoms—to say nothing of the sexual rights of teenagers. Radicals had marched for equality without so much as caulking their own racial divisions. Feminist ideals had motivated women to shoulder-pad up and join the workforce but fell short of explaining how they could find balance and fulfillment at home. Even some of the most basic (and enduring) sloganeering about reproductive rights would have to be reconsidered. "It's less a matter of 'the right to control our bodies' than the freedom to accept and relish our bodies, to explore our capacity for pleasure," Willis writes in "To Emma, with Love."

As society grappled with its freshly hatched notions of gender and freedom, personal sexual dynamics changed in unexpected ways. In "Toward a Feminist Sexual Revolution," Willis writes, "As many men see it, they need women sexually more than women need them, an intolerable imbalance of power." Willis chronicled the backlash in real time and on a personal level. "What is devastating about AIDS," she writes in "Emma," "is not only that it kills people, but that it threatens to kill desire."

The personal seemed to be further and further from the mainstream political discussion, and the "pro-family" politics of conservatism began to tighten its grip on the country. This was the beginning of the culture-war dynamic that would eventually bring us legal fights over racial diversity in college admissions and legislative wars over access to emergency contraception and transvaginal ultrasounds. These are the sorts of fights that the nonpoliticized still claim are minor points, mere quibbles. We can all name a handful of female CEOs. We've all eaten brunch next to a cute interracial couple. Most of our friends are on birth control. The mainstream perception is that the fight is mostly over.

Before most of her contemporaries felt the first snaps of the backlash, Willis had already spotted this complacency. She not only looked forward, urging the left to provide a counternarrative about the possibilities of freedom and pleasure, but she looked back, examining where exactly the revolution went wrong. "Radical movements by definition focus attention on the gap between present and future, and cast their participants, for the present, in the negative role of opposition. Fighting entrenched power means drawing battle lines, defining the enemy," Willis writes in 1989's "Coming Down Again," a meditation on the decade's cultural detox (or was it discipline?). Given entrenched and intersecting oppressions of class and race and gender, we are all somebody's enemy. A sobering reality. But, she points out, this means the reverse is also true: we are all allies. An intoxicating truth.

ANN FRIEDMAN is a magazine writer and Internet enthusiast in California. She is a columnist for *New York* magazine's website and the *Columbia Journalism Review*.

Toward a Feminist Sexual Revolution

It's perhaps some indication of the complex, refractory nature of my subject that this is the third version of my preface to the article that follows—itself the third revision of what began as a talk at a feminist conference in 1981. At that time, feminists were just beginning to engage in a passionate, explosive debate—or rather, a series of overlapping, intertwined debates—about sex. The arguments crystallized around specific issues: pornography; the causes of sexual violence and how best to oppose it; the definition of sexual consent; the nature of women's sexuality and whether it is intrinsically different from men's; the meaning of heterosexuality for women; the political significance of "fringe" sexualities like sadomasochism and, more generally, the relation of sexual fantasy to action, sexual behavior to political practice (in the early '80s, when feminists used the term *political correctness* it was to refer sarcastically to the anti-pornography movement's efforts to define a "feminist sexuality"). Each of these issues, in turn, became a focus of deeply felt disagreement over the place of sexuality and sexual morality in a feminist analysis and program. In one way or another, they raise the question of whether sexual freedom, as such, is a feminist value, or whether feminism ought rather to aim at replacing male-defined social controls over sex with female-defined controls.

While there has always been tension among feminists with differing sexual attitudes, it was only with the eruption of these debates that the differences came to the surface and defined political factions, creating a serious intramovement split. In my view, the reason for this development (or at least its catalyst) was the rise of the new right. The women's liberation movement had emerged in a liberal political and social climate; like the rest of the left it had devoted much of its energy to making a radical critique of liberalism. So long as sexual liberalism appeared to be firmly entrenched as the dominant cultural ideology, feminists put a high priority on criticizing the hypocrisies and abuses of the male-dominated "sexual revolution." But as liberalism fell apart, so did the apparent feminist consensus on sex. Confronted with a right-wing backlash bent on reversing social acceptance of non-marital, non-procreative sex, feminists like me, who saw sexual liberalism as deeply flawed by sexism but nonetheless a source of crucial gains for women, found themselves at odds with feminists who dismissed the sexual revolution as monolithically sexist and shared many of the attitudes of conservative moralists.

Since the mid-'80s, the intensity of the sex debates has waned, not because the issues are any closer to being resolved, but because the two sides are so far apart they have nothing more to say to each other. "Pro-sex" feminists (as we came to be labeled) can claim some victories: we succeeded in countering the prevailing public assumption that the anti-pornography movement's sexual conservatism was *the* feminist position and the porn debate a conflict between "feminists" and "First Amendment absolutists"; we were instrumental in defeating ordinances that defined pornography as a form of sex discrimination, enshrining feminist sexual conservatism as public policy; and we largely won the battle for the hearts and minds of feminist academics, journalists, and other intellectuals. Yet on the level of the unexamined, semi-conscious attitudes that permeate popular culture and politics, the equation of sexual liberalism with sexism and violence against women is, if anything, more widespread than it was ten years ago. This, of course, reflects the accelerating intensity of the anti-sexual backlash during the Reagan-Bush years. But it also points up a fundamental failure on the part of the "pro-sex" camp: the failure to put forward a convincing alternative analysis of sexual violence, exploitation, and alienation.

These issues were of vital concern to an earlier wave of sexual liberationists. From the 1930s through the 1960s, sexual radicalism was anchored in a radical psychoanalytic tradition whose paradigmatic figure is Wilhelm Reich and whose basic assumptions derive from Freud's libido theory. For radical Freudians the sexual impulse is a biologically given energy, a dynamic force that pushes toward gratification; sexual desire blocked from expression or awareness does not disappear but takes indirect forms, leaving its imprint both on individuals' feelings, fantasies, and behavior, and on social institutions. From this premise, sexual radicals argued that the patriarchal family's suppression and manipulation of children's sexual desires produced adults whose sexuality was distorted by unconscious rage; that the need to repress and control this rage led people to perpetuate and defend the very system that produced it; and that nonetheless it continually leaked out in all manner of anti-social and sadistic behavior.

With the advent of radical feminism, radical Freudianism came into political disrepute; the sexual politics of both feminist and gay liberation movements were informed by a deep (and well-founded) distrust of any kind of biologically based theory, as well as anger at the sexist and homophobic history of psychoanalysis. This anti-Freudianism, combined with the impact on social theory of structuralist and post-structuralist discourse—in particular the influence of Jacques Lacan, Michel Foucault, and structural anthropology—gave rise to a major shift in the way most contemporary sexual radicals understand and talk about sex. At the heart of this shift is a sweeping, social constructivist rejection of any concept of a "natural" sexual drive, and of the idea that the biological dimension of sexuality, if it can be said to exist at all, in any way determines or shapes our actual experience.

I do not share this view. On the contrary, I believe we can't understand sex as an emotional, moral, or social issue, let alone formulate a politics of sexual liberation, without some recourse to the idea of sexual satisfaction as a biological need. While I'm convinced that a radical Freudian understanding of sex is "truer"—that is, has more explanatory power—than a social constructivist position, my essay does not attempt to make that argument. Rather, it explores the possibility that a version of the Reichian paradigm might resolve the seeming contradiction between a sexual liberationist politics and a feminist critique of male sexual aggression. Constructivist libertarians concur in the assumption on which this project rests: that sexual freedom is a basic human value and cannot be ceded or compromised. Yet to abstract sex from biology—from our bodily species-life—calls this premise into question. The idea that sex is wholly a social construction removes it from the realm of necessity and makes our sexual choices a matter of ethics and taste. But if libidinal gratification is not a need, on the same bedrock level as the need for self-preservation, why is a sexually free society necessarily preferable to a sexually restrictive one, particularly if sexual freedom appears to conflict with other social goods? At this historical moment, the greatest threat to the very idea of sexual liberation as a possibility is AIDS: those of us who still reject the imposition of a repressive sexual morality stand accused of pushing death. But that argument loses its force if sexual repression is itself deeply inimical to human well-being and even survival; if indeed repression fosters, rather than curbs, sexual and social irresponsibility and violence.

The radical Freudian analysis of sex is embedded in its psychosocial analysis of the family—specifically, of how children are inducted into the established social order, a crucial issue for feminists. In contemporary feminist discourse, however, these are two quite separate discussions. For the most part, feminists who look to psychoanalysis for an explanation of masculine and feminine character formation have adopted the perspective of object relations theory, in which sexual desire, per se, is not a central category. At the same time, feminist sexual liberationists have examined the varieties of desire—particularly "deviant," which is to say dissident, desire—and their representation, exploring their complex relation to (among other things) gender, race, class, heterosexual dominance, and erotophobia, but displaying little interest in their origins. Again, this lacuna is understandable: for both women and homosexuals, inquiry into the process of sexual development has always been linked with assumptions of pathology. Yet only by analyzing that process can we understand how sexual morality in a patriarchal culture becomes a primary instrument of social control. This question, finally, is the central concern of my essay, which I offer not only as an entry in the debate between feminist sexual radicals and conservatives, but as an invitation to further discussion of what sexual radicalism means.

The traditional patriarchal family maintains sexual law and order on two fronts. It regulates the relations between the sexes, enforcing male dominance, female subordination, and the segregation of "masculine" and "feminine" spheres. It also regulates sexuality per se, defining as illicit any sexual activity unrelated to reproduction or outside the bounds of heterosexual, monogamous marriage. Accordingly, the new right's militant defense of traditional family values has a dual thrust: it is at once a male-supremacist backlash against feminism and a reaction by cultural conservatives of both sexes against the "sexual revolution" of the '60s and '70s.

There is, of course, an integral connection between sexism and sexual repression. The suppression of women's sexual desire and pleasure, the denial of reproductive freedom, and the enforcement of female abstinence outside marriage have been primary underpinnings of male supremacy. Conversely, a restrictive sexual morality inevitably constrains women more than men, even in religious subcultures that profess a single standard. Not only is unwanted pregnancy a built-in punishment for female participation in sex (assuming the prohibition of birth control and abortion on the one hand, and lesbianism on the other) and therefore a powerful inhibitor; it is visible evidence of sexual "delinquency," which subjects women who break the rules to social sanctions their male partners never have to face. Still, it is important to recognize that the right's opposition to sexual permissiveness—as expressed in its attacks on abortion, homosexuality, "pornography" (defined as any sexually explicit material), sex education, and adolescents' access to contraception and abortion without parental consent—has consequences for both sexes. Gays and teenagers are obvious targets. But the success of the "pro-family" agenda would also impinge on the lives of adult heterosexual men, who would have to contend with the unwanted pregnancies of their wives and lovers, women's increased sexual fears and inhibitions, restrictions on frank discussion and public legitimation of sex and sexual fantasy, and a general chilling of the sexual atmosphere. While some men are willing to accept such constraints on their own freedom in order to reassert certain traditional controls over women, many are not.

The dual focus of right-wing sexual politics, on feminism and on sex itself, has serious implications for feminist theory and strategy. It means that feminists cannot define their opposition solely in terms of defending female autonomy against male power, nor can they ignore the fact that conflict over sexual morality cuts across gender lines. If the women's movement is to organize effectively against the right, it will have to develop a political theory of sexuality and in particular an analysis of the relation between feminism and sexual freedom. Such an analysis would help feminists to identify and avoid responses to sexual issues that unwittingly undercut feminist aims. It would clarify many disagreements among women who regard themselves as feminists. It would also enable feminists to seek alliances with male opponents of the right's sexual politics—alliances that are undoubtedly necessary if the battle is to be won—on the basis of a clear understanding of mutual interests, differences that need to be resolved to achieve a working coalition, and issues on which it is possible to agree to disagree. The intensity of debate on sex among feminists and gay activists reflects a visceral comprehension—if not always an articulate understanding—of how much is at stake.

At present, the right has its feminist opponents at an enormous disadvantage: it has a coherent ideology and program whose anti-feminist and anti-sexual aspects reinforce each other. In contrast, feminists are ambivalent, confused, and divided in their views on sexual freedom. While there have been feminist sexual libertarians in both the 19th century and contemporary movements, for the most part women's liberation and sexual liberation have developed as separate, often antagonistic causes. The sexual libertarian movement that began in the 1950s was conspicuously male-dominated and male-supremacist. Though it advocated a single standard of freedom from sexual guilt and conventional moral restrictions, it displayed no insight into the social reasons for women's greater inhibition and conformity to moral norms. On the contrary, women were blamed—often in virulently misogynist terms—for adhering to the sexual prohibitions men and a patriarchal society had forced on them. At the same time male libertarians intensified women's sexual anxieties by equating repression with the desire for love and commitment, and exalting sex without emotion or attachment as the ideal. From this perspective liberation for men meant rebelling against the demands of women, while liberation for women meant the opportunity (read obligation) to shuck their "hangups" about casual sex.

The question that remained unasked was whether men had sexual hangups of their own. Was the rejection of any link between sexual desire and emotional involvement really an expression of freedom—or merely another form of repression? To what extent did men's demand for "pure" sex represent a predatory disregard of women as people—an attitude that could only reinforce the conventionally feminine sexual reluctance, passivity, and unresponsiveness that men found so frustrating? There was also the touchy issue of whether sex as conventionally initiated and orchestrated by men was pleasurable for women. In theory there was much concern with female orgasm and the need for men to satisfy women; in practice that concern often translated into a demand that women corroborate men's ideas about female sexuality and protect men's egos by acting satisfied whether they were or not. A conservative popular Freudianism neatly co-opted the idea that women had a right to sexual fulfillment by preaching that such fulfillment could be achieved only through "mature" acceptance of the feminine role. In effect women were told that to actively assert their sexual needs would make satisfaction of those needs impossible; if they were submissive and yet unsatisfied it meant they weren't submissive in their hearts. For women trapped in this logic, the theoretical right to orgasm became a new source of pain, inadequacy, and self-blame. Finally, the sexual revolution did not seriously challenge the taboo on lesbianism (or homosexuality in general).

At its inception, the women's liberation movement was dominated by young women who had grown up during or since the emergence of sexual libertarian ideology; many radical feminists came out of the left and the counterculture, where that ideology was particularly strong. Unsurprisingly, one of the first issues to surface in the movement was women's pent-up rage at men's one-sided, exploitative view of sexual freedom. From our consciousness-raising sessions we concluded that women couldn't win no matter how they behaved. We were still oppressed by a sexual double standard that while less rigid was by no means obsolete: women who took too literally their supposed right to sexual freedom and pleasure were regularly put down as "easy," "aggressive," or "promiscuous." Heterosexual women still lived in fear of unwanted pregnancy; in 1968 abortion was illegal—except in the most dire circumstances—in every state. Yet at the same time men were demanding that women have sex on their terms, unmindful of the possible consequences, and without reference to our own feelings and needs. In addition to suffering sexual frustration from the inhibitions instilled by repressive parents, fear of pregnancy, and men's sexual judgments and exploitative behavior, we had to swallow the same men's humiliating complaints about how neurotic, frigid, and unliberated we were. Unfortunately, the movement's efforts to make political sense of this double bind led to confusions in feminist thinking about sex that are still unresolved.

At least in theory, organized feminism from the '60s to the present has been united in endorsing sexual freedom for women, including the right to express our sexual needs freely, to engage in sexual activity for our own pleasure, to have sex and bear children outside marriage, to control our fertility, to refuse sex with any particular man or all men, to be lesbians. Almost as universally, feminists have regarded male sexuality with suspicion if not outright hostility. From the beginning radical feminists argued that freedom as men defined it was against women's interests; if anything men already had too much freedom, at women's expense. One faction in the movement strongly defended women's traditional demands for marriage and monogamy against the anti–nuclear family, sexual liberationist rhetoric of the counterculture. Proponents of this view held that the sexual revolution simply legitimized the age-old tendency of men in a male-supremacist society to coerce, cajole, or fool women into giving them sex without getting anything—love, respect, responsibility for the children, or even erotic pleasure—in return.[1] At the other extreme were feminists who argued that under present conditions, any kind of sexual contact with men, in marriage or out, was oppressive, and that the issue for women was how to resist the relentless social pressure to be with a man.[2] Later, lesbian separatists elaborated this argument, claiming that only women were capable of understanding and satisfying women's sexual needs.

The idea that in the interest of equality women's sexual freedom must be expanded and men's restricted has a surface common-sense logic. Yet in practice it is full of contradictions. For one thing, the same social changes that allow greater freedom for women inevitably mean greater freedom for men. Historically, a woman's main protection from sexual exploitation has been to be a "good girl" and demand marriage as the price of sex—in other words, relinquish her sexual spontaneity to preserve her bargaining power. Furthermore, this traditional strategy will not work for individual women if most women "scab" by abandoning it, which implies the need for some form of social or moral pressure to keep women in line. (If one assumes that women will voluntarily decline to take advantage of their increased freedom, then demanding it makes no sense in the first place.) In practice, relaxing social condemnation of female "unchastity" and permitting women access to birth control and abortion allay social concern about men's "ruining" or impregnating respectable women, and so invariably reduce the pressure on men—both from women and from other men—to restrain their demands for casual sex. Thus the feminist critique of male sexuality tends to bolster the familiar conservative argument that a morality restricting sex to marriage is in women's interest—indeed, that its purpose is to protect women from selfish male lust.

Another difficulty is that judgments of men's heterosexual behavior necessarily imply judgments about what women want. Dissenters within feminist groups immediately challenged the prevailing judgments, arguing with monogamists that they wanted to sleep with more than one man, or that they didn't want the state messing in their sex lives, and arguing with separatists that they enjoyed sex with men. As a result, assumptions about what women want were soon amended to authoritative pronouncements on what women *really* want/ought to want/would want if they were not intimidated/bought off/brainwashed by men. The ironic consequence has been the development of feminist sexual orthodoxies that curtail women's freedom by setting up the movement as yet another source of guilt-provoking rules about what women should do and feel.

That irony is compounded by another: the orthodoxies in question dovetail all too well with traditional patriarchal ideology. This is most obviously true of polemics in favor of heterosexual monogamy, but it is no less true of lesbian separatism, which in recent years has had far more impact on feminist thinking. There have been two overlapping but distinct tendencies in lesbian feminist politics: the first has emphasized lesbianism as a forbidden erotic choice and lesbians as an oppressed sexual minority; the other—aligning itself with the separatist faction that surfaced in the radical feminist movement before lesbianism as such became an issue—has defined lesbianism primarily as a political commitment to separate from men and bond with women.[3] The latter tendency has generated a sexual ideology best described as neo-Victorian. It regards heterosexual relations as more or less synonymous with rape, on the grounds that male sexuality is by definition predatory and sadistic: men are exclusively "genitally-oriented" (a phrase that is always used pejoratively) and uninterested in loving relationships. Female sexuality, in contrast, is defined as tender, nonviolent, and not necessarily focused on the genitals; intimacy and physical warmth are more important to us than orgasm. The early pre-lesbian separatists argued that celibacy was a reasonable alternative to sleeping with men, and some suggested that the whole idea of a compelling sexual drive was a male invention designed to keep women in their place; women didn't need sex, and men's lust was less for pleasure than for power.[4] In short, to the neo-Victorians men are beasts who are only after one thing, while women are nice girls who would just as soon skip it. The inescapable implication is that women who profess to enjoy sex with men, especially penile-vaginal intercourse itself, are liars or masochists; in either case victims of, or collaborators with, oppression. Nor are lesbians automatically exempt from criticism; gay women whose sexual proclivities do not conform to the approved feminine stereotype are assumed to be corrupted by heterosexism.

Though neo-Victorianism has been most militantly promoted by lesbian separatists, in modified form—i.e., allowing that men (some men at least) can change their ways and be good lovers—it has also had wide appeal for heterosexual feminists. (Conversely, lesbians have been among its loudest critics; this is not a gay-straight split.) Its most popular current expression is the anti-pornography movement, which has seized on pornography as an all-purpose symbol of sex that is genitally oriented, hence male, hence sadistic and violent, while invoking the concept of "erotica" as code for sex that is gentle, romantic, relationship-oriented—in a word, feminine. Clearly, this conventional view of female as opposed to male sexuality is consistent with many women's subjective experience. Indeed, there are probably few women who don't identify with it to some degree. But to take that experience at face value is to ignore its context: a patriarchal society that has systematically inhibited female sexuality and defined direct, active physical desire as a male prerogative. Feminist neo-Victorians have made the same mistake—only with the sexes reversed—as male libertarians who criticize female sexual behavior while adopting stereotypical male sexuality as the standard for judging sexual health and happiness. In the process they have actively reinforced the larger society's taboos on women's genital sexuality. From a conservative perspective, a woman who has assertive genital desires and acts on them is "bad" and "unwomanly"; from the neo-Victorian perspective she is "brainwashed" and "male-identified."

Overtly or implicitly, many feminists have argued that sexual coercion is a more important problem for women than sexual repression. In the last few years, the women's movement has increasingly emphasized violence against women as a primary—if not *the* primary—concern. While sexual violence, coercion, and harassment have always been feminist issues, earlier feminist analyses tended to regard physical force as one of several ways that men ensure women's compliance to a sexist system, and in particular to their subordinate wife-and-mother role. The main function of sexual coercion, in this view, is to curb women's freedom, including their sexual freedom. Rape and the tacit social tolerance of it convey the message that, simply by being sexual, women are "provocative" and deserve punishment, especially if they step out of their place (the home) or transgress society's definition of the "good" (inhibited) woman. Similarly, sexual harassment on the street or on the job, and exploitative sexual demands by male "sexual revolutionaries," punish women for asserting themselves, sexually and otherwise, in the world.

The current feminist preoccupation with male violence has a very different focus. Rape and pornography, redefined as a form of rape, are regarded not as aspects of a larger sexist system but as the foundation and essence of sexism, while sexual victimization is seen as the central fact of women's oppression. Just as male violence against women is equated with male supremacy, freedom from violence is equated with women's liberation.[5] From this standpoint the positive aspect of freedom—freedom for women to *act*—is at best a secondary concern, and freedom for women to assert an active genital sexuality is, by the logic of neo-Victorianism, a contradiction in terms.

Whatever its intent, the effect of feminists' emphasis on controlling male sexuality—particularly when that emphasis is combined with a neo-Victorian view of women's nature and the conviction that securing women's safety from male aggression should be the chief priority of the women's movement—is to undercut feminist opposition to the right. It provides powerful reinforcement for conservative efforts to manipulate women's fear of untrammeled male sexuality, intimidating women into stifling their own impulses toward freedom so as to cling to what little protection the traditional roles still offer. The convergence of neo-Victorian and pro-family ideology is most striking in the recent attempts by so-called "feminists for life" to argue that abortion is "violence against women" and a way for men to escape responsibility for their sexual behavior. While this argument did not come from within the feminist movement but from anti-abortion pacifists seeking to justify their position to feminists, it is perfectly consistent with neo-Victorian logic. No tendency in organized feminism has yet advocated outlawing abortion, but one does occasionally hear the argument that feminists should spend less energy defending abortion and more on educating women to understand that the real solution to unwanted pregnancy is to stop sleeping with men.[6]

Neo-Victorians have also undermined feminist opposition to the right by equating feminism with their own sexual attitudes, in effect reading out of the movement any woman who disagrees with them. Since their notion of proper feminist sexuality echoes conventional moral judgments and the anti-sexual propaganda presently coming from the right, their guilt-mongering has been quite effective. Many feminists who are aware that their sexual feelings contradict the neo-Victorian ideal have lapsed into confused and apologetic silence. No doubt there are also thousands of women who have quietly concluded that if this ideal is feminism, then feminism has nothing to do with them.

In short, feminists are at a theoretical impasse. If a feminist politics that advocates restrictions on male sexuality leads inexorably to the sexual repression of women and the strengthening of anti-feminist forces, such a politics is obviously untenable. But how can women support sexual freedom for both sexes without legitimizing the most oppressive aspects of male sexual behavior? I believe our hope for resolving this dilemma lies in reexamining certain widely shared assumptions about sex, male versus female sexuality, and the meaning of sexual liberation.

The philosophy of the "sexual revolution" as we know it is an extension of liberalism: it defines sexual freedom as the simple absence of external restrictions—laws and overt social taboos—on sexual information and activity. Since most people accept this definition, there is widespread agreement that we are already a sexually emancipated society. The easy availability of casual sex, the virtual lack of restrictions (at least for adults) on sexual information and sexually explicit material, the accessibility (for adults again) of contraception, legal abortion, the proliferation of massage parlors and sex clubs, the ubiquity of sexual images and references in the mass media, the relaxation of taboos against "deviant" sexual practices—all are regularly cited as evidence that this culture has largely overcome its anti-sexual history. At the same time, sexual liberalism has clearly not brought nirvana. Noting that "liberated" sexuality is often depressingly shallow, exploitative, and joyless, many men as well as women have concluded that sexual liberation has been tried and found wanting, that it is irrelevant or even inimical to a serious program for social change.

This is a superficial view. In the first place, this society is far from endorsing, even in principle, people's right to consensual sexual relations, of whatever sort they prefer, as a basic liberty. (Skeptics are invited to imagine public reaction to a proposed constitutional amendment guaranteeing freedom of sexual association.) There is strong and stubborn resistance to legalizing—let alone accepting as socially and morally legitimate—all sexual acts between consenting adults; children have no recognized sexual rights at all, and adolescents virtually none.[7] But a more basic problem with this premature disillusionment is that it focuses on the quantity and variety of sexual activity, rather than the quality of sexual experience. Ultimately, the premise of sexual libertarian movements is that a gratifying sexual life is a human need whose denial causes unnecessary and unjustified suffering. Certainly, establishing people's right to pursue sexual happiness with a consenting partner is a condition for ending that suffering. Yet as most of us have had occasion to discover, it is entirely possible to "freely" participate in a sexual act and feel frustrated, indifferent, or even repelled. From a radical standpoint, then, sexual liberation involves not only the abolition of restrictions but the positive presence of social and psychological conditions that foster satisfying sexual relations. And from that standpoint, this culture is still deeply repressive. Most obviously, sexual inequality and the resulting antagonism between men and women are a devastating barrier to sexual happiness. I will argue in addition that sexual liberalism notwithstanding, most children's upbringing produces adults with profoundly negative attitudes toward sex. Under these conditions, the relaxation of sexual restrictions leads people to try desperately to overcome the obstacles to satisfaction through compulsive sexual activity and preoccupation with sex. The emphasis on sex that currently permeates our public life—especially the enormous demand for sexual advice and therapy—attests not to our sexual freedom but to our continuing sexual frustration. People who are not hungry are not obsessed with food.

It is in this context that we need to examine the male sexual pattern feminists have protested—the emphasis on conquest and dominance, the tendency to abstract sex from love and social responsibility. Sexual liberalism has allowed many men to assert these patterns in ways that were once socially taboo, and to impose them on reluctant women. But to conclude from this fact that male sexual freedom is inherently oppressive is to make the uncritical assumption that men find predatory, solipsistic sexual relations satisfying and inherently preferable to sex with affection and mutuality. As I have noted, some feminists argue that male sexuality is naturally sadistic. Others grant that men's predatory tendencies are a function of sexism, but assume that they are a simple, direct expression of men's (excessive) freedom and power, the implication being that anyone who has the opportunity to dominate and use other people sexually will of course want to take advantage of it.

This assumption is open to serious question. If one pays attention to what men consciously or unwittingly reveal about their sexual attitudes—in their fiction and confessional writing (see *Portnoy's Complaint* and its epigoni), in their political polemics (see George Gilder's *Sexual Suicide*), in sociological and psychological studies (see *The Hite Report on Male Sexuality* or Lillian Rubin's *Worlds of Pain*), in everyday interaction with women—the picture that emerges is far more complicated and ambiguous. Most men, in fact, profess to want and need mutual sexual love, and often behave accordingly, though they have plenty of opportunity to do otherwise. Many men experience both tender and predatory sexual feelings, toward the same or different women, and find the contradiction bewildering and disturbing; others express enormous pain over their inability to combine sex with love. Often men's impulses to coerce and degrade women seem to express not a confident assumption of dominance but a desire to retaliate for feelings of rejection, humiliation, and impotence: as many men see it, they need women sexually more than women need them, an intolerable imbalance of power.[8] Furthermore, much male sexual behavior clearly reflects men's irrational fears that loss of dominance means loss of maleness itself, that their choice is to "act like a man" or be castrated, embrace the role of oppressor or be degraded to the status of victim.

None of this is to deny men's objective social power over women, their reluctance to give up that power, or their tendency to blame women for their unhappiness rather than recognize that their own oppressive behavior is largely responsible for women's sexual diffidence. My point is only that the behavior that causes women so much grief evidently brings men very little joy; on the contrary, men appear to be consumed with sexual frustration, rage, and anxiety. With their compulsive assertions of power they continually sabotage their efforts to love and be loved. Such self-defeating behavior cannot, in any meaningful sense, be described as free. Rather it suggests that for all the unquestionable advantages men derive from "acting like a man" in a male-supremacist society, the price is repression and deformation of spontaneous sexual feeling.

The idea that untrammeled male sexuality must inevitably be oppressive is rooted in one of our most universal cultural assumptions: that the sexual drive itself (that is, "pure" passion unanchored to the "higher" purposes of marriage and procreation) is inherently anti-social, separate from love, and connected with aggressive, destructive impulses. (In providing a modern, secular rationale for this idea, Freud reinforced—even as he demystified—traditional Judeo-Christian morality.) Sexual liberals have promoted the competing assumption that sex is simply a healthy, enjoyable biological function with no intrinsic moral connotations. But this bland view not only violates most people's sense that their sexuality is not an isolated "function," that it is bound up with their emotions, their values, their very being; it also evades the question of sexual destructiveness. In practice, sexual liberals often refuse to acknowledge the hostile, alienated, and exploitative impulses that attend contemporary sexual "freedom." As a result, people who experience their own sexuality as corrupted by those impulses, or who feel victimized by the sexual behavior of others, tend to fall back on some version of the old conservative idea.

There is, however, another possibility, advanced by a minority of utopians, romantics, and cultural radicals: that sexual desire, tenderness, and empathy are aspects of a unified erotic impulse; that the splitting of this impulse and the attendant perversion of sexual desire into exploitative, solipsistic lust are an artificial social product. This thesis has been most systematically and convincingly elaborated in Wilhelm Reich's radical critique of Freud.[9] In essence, Reich argued that parental condemnation of infantile genital desires and sensations forces the child to split (bad) sex from (good) love. The child reacts to this thwarting of its sexual expression with frustration, rage, and a desire for revenge. These feelings modify the sexual impulse itself; the child's sexuality becomes sadistic. If the sadistic feelings are also forbidden they turn inward, producing guilt and masochism. People's guilt at their own overt or repressed sadism, along with their observation of other people's anti-social behavior, prompts the conviction that sex is inherently destructive. Yet that conviction rests on a piece of circular reasoning: repression creates the destructiveness that is then cited as proof of the eternal need for repression. In this way, sexual repression becomes the self-perpetuating basis of a sadomasochistic psychology[10] that is in turn crucial to the maintenance of an authoritarian, hierarchical social order.

Reich contended that people with an anti-sexual upbringing tend to uphold established authority—even when the practical conditions for rebellion exist—because that authority fulfills several functions: it reinforces people's inner controls over their sadistic impulses and protects them from the uncontrolled sadism of others; it invites people to express sadistic feelings vicariously by identifying with authority; and it permits people to vent those feelings directly on whoever is below them in the social hierarchy. In this way the anger that should inspire social rebellion is transformed into a conservative force, impelling people to submit masochistically to their oppressors while bullying their "inferiors." Yet even for ruling classes, Reich maintained, power is at best a substitute for genuine fulfillment.

Reich's concept of a basic erotic unity shattered by genital repression has radical implications for feminist sexual politics. I have tried to show how efforts to control male sexuality undermine women's struggle for freedom and equality, and vice versa. To take the argument a step further, if the sexual impulse is intrinsically selfish and aggressive, there are two possible explanations for why men's sexuality, far more than women's, has displayed these characteristics. One is that sexual desire, per se, is inherently male; the pitfalls of this idea have been discussed at length. The other is that women have simply not been allowed to be as selfish and exploitative as men; to adopt this notion puts feminists in the position of agreeing with conservatives that liberating women from the feminine role would destroy the social cement that keeps civilization going. If, on the other hand, sexual destructiveness can be seen as a perversion that both reflects and perpetuates a repressive system, it is possible to envision a coherent feminist politics in which a commitment to sexual freedom plays an integral part.

Similarly, if parents, by rejecting their children's genitality, atomize the erotic impulse and direct infantile sexuality into a sadistic mode, the source of the difference between "masculine" and "feminine" sexual patterns seems clear. While boys are permitted, indeed encouraged, to incorporate their sadistic impulses into their sexual identities and to express them in socially approved ways, girls' aggression is no more tolerated than their genitality. Like men, women experience a split between lust and love, but the lustful component of their sexuality is subjected to severe inhibition. Women who do not suppress their lustful feelings altogether—or sublimate them into disembodied romanticism or mother love—usually feel free to express them only in the relatively safe and socially validated context of marriage or a quasi-marital commitment: what looks like women's superior ability to integrate sex and love is only a more hidden form of alienation.

I want to argue, then, that male and female children develop masculine and feminine sexual psychologies through a systematic (though largely unconscious) process of parental intimidation, in which sexual repression and sexism function symbiotically. But before I go on, I ought to note that its controversial premises aside, my thesis has another difficulty. Like psychoanalysis itself, my argument invokes a model of family that is in rapid decline in this country and arguably has never applied to large sections of the American (let alone the world's) population: the "ideal" nuclear family, in which the parents provide a traditional model of sexual roles and attitudes toward sex, and dispense strict but loving parental discipline. Freud and Reich developed their theories in the context of Victorian middle-class family life. I grew up in the '40s and '50s, when the male breadwinner/dependent wife pattern was still hegemonic (if far from universal), and my ideas about sexual character formation have been strongly influenced by insights from my own psychotherapy. How, then, can I presume to generalize beyond these culturally specific milieus?

My presumption starts with the idea that whatever their differences, all patriarchal cultures uphold—indeed are defined by—certain basic institutional norms. One is male supremacy and its psychic concomitants, masculine and feminine identity. Another is the underlying denigration (often masked by surface acceptance) of genital sexuality. The third is familialism, a system in which children belong legally and socially to their parents (with varying ties to other biological kin), while the society as a whole has only the most minimal responsibility for their welfare—which means that they depend for survival on parental love and, particularly when very young, are subject to virtually unlimited parental control. In my view, the cultural ingredients of the repressive symbiosis I'm about to describe are precisely these ubiquitous norms. Furthermore, while the patriarchal family has taken many forms and served a variety of social and economic functions in different times and places and among different social groups, its constant essential task has been to care for and socialize children, thereby perpetuating its norms from one generation to the next. Granted that this process too has been subject to countless variations, produced by historical, class, racial, religious, and other cultural differences, surely it must also have crucial common elements. And my speculation is that the nuclear household reveals, or at least suggests, such commonalities, for precisely the same reason it inspired psychoanalysis in the first place: the family in its mom-dad-kids configuration, stripped of extended family relationships and preindustrial socioeconomic baggage, confined within a privatized domestic environment and devoted almost exclusively to its bedrock purpose, can make its psychic dynamics uniquely visible.

In the contemporary American context, this analysis implies that the sexual psychology of the iconic white middle-class suburban family of the '50s still has something to do with our own reality despite three decades of massive social change that includes black rejection of the presumed superiority of white middle-class culture, feminism, gay liberation, the normalization of women (particularly mothers) in the work force, sexual liberalism, easy divorce, the weakening of parental authority, and the rising incidence of single motherhood (which among the urban black poor amounts to the virtual demise of the patriarchal family in any form). Just as the new right charges, all such changes destabilize and threaten to undermine the process of "normal" sexual character formation. Yet this remains a sexist and sex-negative culture, and, as the condition of millions of poor children attests, a dogmatically familialist one.

To understand how sexism and sexual repression converge in the child's mind, it is necessary, in my view, to rethink two Freudian concepts that most feminists have either rejected or interpreted in purely symbolic terms—castration anxiety and penis envy. My contention is that children subjected to the three social conditions I've enumerated develop a quite literal belief in the reality or threat of an attack on their genitals as pleasure-giving organs, as well as an artificial valuation of the penis as an indicator of social power and worth.[11] From infancy children absorb two sets of messages about their sexual organs. As soon as they discover genital desire and pleasure, they learn that such feelings are forbidden. Masturbation and interest in their own, their parents', or other children's genitals provoke parental anxiety and discomfort if not outright displeasure. Their frustrated desire excites aggressive, vengeful feelings and fantasies that are even more taboo, so that their infantile experience of genitality is thoroughly permeated with a sense of danger. Meanwhile, they have been learning—by observing the behavior of their parents, their siblings, and the world at large—about the social differences between the sexes. At some point, they come to understand that there are two classes of people, one superior and dominant, one inferior and subordinate, distinguished by the presence or absence of the penis. It seems entirely reasonable that children's efforts to piece together all this disturbing information about sex and gender should lead them to the terrible conclusion that girls have been physically mutilated and socially devalued for bad sexual desires, and that boys risk being punished for their badness in similar fashion.

This perceived catastrophe drastically alters the child's relation to the world. The child already knows that its parents have the fearful power to deprive it of love, protection, even life, but that knowledge is typically leavened by confidence in the parents' love. The apparent evidence of female castration convinces the child, far more effectively than normal parental discipline could do, that even the most loving parents are willing to use their power in a truly terrifying way. This in turn suggests to the child that its badness must be utter depravity; the other logical possibility—that the parents are not really loving at all, but capriciously, monstrously cruel—is too frightening to contemplate. The child may at first deny the evidence, or its full import, or its irrevocability, but eventually the bad news sinks in and becomes a traumatic blow to the child's lingering hopes of beating the system. In accepting the awful truth, the child undergoes a kind of conversion to the parents' sexual values. After that, though he or she may still rebel, it will be with a sense of moral illegitimacy.

Since the child's sexual desires do not go away, but continue to evoke anxiety and guilt, its only choice is to repress the whole complex of feelings, especially the traumatic discovery with which they are connected; this ensures that the infantile interpretation of sexual difference will remain impervious to rational correction. But the impact of the trauma, and the degree of sexual repression it generates, are not the same for both sexes. For one thing, their earlier experience has been different: from the beginning, girls' sexual and aggressive impulses are restricted more severely. In addition, there is an enormous emotional difference between fear of mutilation and the conviction that one has already been mutilated. The boy's fear of castration is softened by the knowledge that so far he has been bad and gotten away with it; the girl imagines that her defiance has provoked terrible retribution. The boy fears a punishment that, bad as it is, is specific and limited; the girl's speculation on what might happen to her if she persists in incurring parental wrath is limited only by her imagination and capacity for terror. The boy feels impotent, humiliated by his parents' ability to frighten him into submission; the girl suffers, in addition, the far more devastating humiliation of consignment to an inferior class. Furthermore, her terror and humiliation are compounded by other intensely powerful emotions: violation, grief, despair.

The children's subsequent experience will reinforce these sexual differences. The boy will see that within prescribed limits he can safely express his "bad" impulses toward women outside the family, with greater or lesser freedom depending on the women's social status. Given this outlet, his fear will actually stimulate his sexual aggression: by "acting like a man" he can continually assure himself that he is not a woman, while maintaining vigilant control over these castrated beings who must surely hate him and covet his precious organ. The girl, in contrast, will observe that male power often expresses itself in sexual hostility and aggression; she will see that men punish rebellious women with contempt, rejection, and violence. When she grasps the concept of rape she will understand it as a reenactment of her original violation. All this will add to her terror and give it concrete form. In the interest of survival she must at all costs suppress her bitterness, hatred, envy, vengefulness, and predatory lust and accept her subordination. She must desperately direct her energies toward being *good*.

The castration trauma can be seen as the pivotal event of an ongoing process of acculturation in which parents prepare their children to "freely" embrace a masculine or feminine identity—that is, to see conventional sexual behavior and attitudes as the only tenable alternative and to repress feelings that do not fit the mold. In large part, parents accomplish this simply by acting out their own masculine and feminine patterns in relation to the child. That parents unconsciously assume toward their children their entire complex of cultural attitudes toward men, women, and sexuality would explain the common observation that in relating to a child of the other sex, heterosexual parents undercut their sexual prohibitions with covert seductiveness, while in relating to a child of the same sex, they augment the prohibitions with covert hostility based on competitiveness and, no doubt, defenses against forbidden homosexual feelings. Since the parents have internalized the cultural atomization of the erotic, their seductiveness—split off from acceptably sexless parental love—will have a predatory aspect, accentuated by the power differential between adult and child.

This configuration suggests a particular view of another Freudian construction, the Oedipus complex. Though children undoubtedly feel a spontaneous erotic attraction to their parents (especially, given the present system of child-rearing, their mothers), there is no reason to believe that intense, exclusive heterosexual desire for one parent and jealous hatred of the other necessarily follow, even for boys, while Freud himself acknowledged that the Oedipus complex in girls required further explanation. On the contrary, it seems likely that parents instigate the Oedipal triangle, encouraging the other-sex child's fantasies with their seductiveness (while at the same time their disapproval inhibits the child's sexual explorations in general), and provoking or exacerbating same-sex rivalry with their own hostile, competitive behavior.

If the castration trauma terrorizes children into foreclosing certain psychic possibilities (accepting sexual desire as good and natural, seeing male-female difference as a morally neutral fact), the function of the Oedipal situation, as I will try to show, is to channel their response to the trauma in socially approved directions, beginning, most obviously, with heterosexuality. Under "normal" circumstances the child, in coping with the desire, fear, rage, guilt, and disappointment the triangle generates, will eventually come to identify with the prescribed sexual roles because they represent the path of least resistance, offering the least risk of punishment, the most relief from guilt, and the most compensatory satisfactions. If something goes wrong (if, for instance, a child remains unconvinced that conformity offers any rewards worth having; if disappointment with the parent of the other sex is too overwhelming, or conversely the attraction is too strong; if fear of the same-sex parent is excessive or insufficient; if the parents are truly cruel or neglectful; if actual incest occurs) he or she may balk at the final giving over to conventional masculine/feminine identity. In adult life the recalcitrant child may prefer homosexuality or some other form of "deviance"; develop a sexual personality defined by overt emotional conflict and "maladjustment"; or withdraw from the sexual arena altogether. In practice, of course, these choices overlap and form a continuum, from a decisive commitment to masculinity or femininity, with more or less successful repression of conflicting desires, to total refusal, generally disastrous to the individual concerned, to be conscripted into the sexual culture.

What follows is an attempt to outline the paradigmatic "successful" working out of the Oedipus complex for both sexes. The discussion assumes two heterosexual parents in the home, with the mother as primary caretaker—even now the situation of most young children. As I've suggested, families that diverge significantly from this model should logically produce a wider, less predictable range of sexual psychologies, a prospect of major concern to social conservatives. But there is a complication to keep in mind. Sexual acculturation has never been more than relatively successful, even in societies enforcing rigid adherence to traditional patriarchal standards. However, through the imposition of psychic repression and guilt, "illicit" sexual desire and rage continually threaten to break through, which is why internal controls must be reinforced by external social sanctions. The system's failures, its "bad" and "deviant" products, do not really contradict the norm, only invite its enforcement. Similarly, individual families or even familial cultures that deviate from the norm do not exist in a vacuum. They are situated in a dominant culture that affects both parental behavior and attitudes and children's perceptions of how families are supposed to work, as well as a cultural history that has shaped the parents' emotional makeup. For a child brought up by a single parent with a conventional sexual identity in a conventional environment, a fantasy of the missing parent may in crucial respects substitute for the actual person; even if the child has never met the absent parent, and if the caretaking parent does not have lovers on whom the child's imagination can focus, he or she may construct a workable fantasy out of parental and social messages about what mothers or fathers are like. (Conversely, in a standard nuclear family whose emotional undercurrents are greatly at odds with the facade of normality, the child's experience and consequent path may be far less typical.) As for urban black cultures stigmatized as deviant because of (among other things) their "matriarchal structures" and "absent fathers," the resulting differences in sexual patterns fit comfortably within the dominant culture's images of badness and otherness. What I'm proposing is that the psychology perpetuated by the "ideal" Oedipus conflict defines a sexual norm that, however attacked and eroded, still exerts a powerful influence on most people's behavior and unconscious predispositions. In fact, I would question whether people whose childhood experience departed so radically from the paradigm that it has no emotional resonance for them can function in this culture even as deviants.

In the "normal" case, the mother's role in the family ensures that from the beginning boys and girls get different signals about sex. To the boy, the mother conveys a complex and contradictory message of affection, seduction, and rejection. In the context of her maternal love and his infantile dependence, her seductiveness, with its admixture of aggression, makes her an embodiment of erotic power that is both irresistible and scary; at the same time her disapproving rejection of his sexual response frustrates and confuses him. His father, on the other hand, is more clearly censorious, more emotionally distant (since he is less involved in the child's day-to-day care), and much more powerful: the mother, so potent a figure in relation to the boy, is obviously subject to the father's control. It is also clear that father has claimed mother for himself, and that the sexual prohibitions he enforces on the rest of the family do not apply to him.

The boy's discovery of his mother's "castration" puts all this in a new light: mother belongs to the deprived class, therefore she must envy and hate his maleness. This explains both the predatory element in her desire—which he interprets now as a potential attack on his penis, stemming from a wish to appropriate the prized object—and, in part, her sexual rejection. He is outraged at his mother's betrayal in condemning the "badness" she has encouraged—and of which she is equally guilty, as her penisless condition attests. But he also understands her behavior as a means of protecting both of them from his father. For father is obviously responsible for mother's punishment, and by far the greater threat to his own manhood.

In response to this threat, the boy represses his guilty desire and his rage at his father. He accepts his father's moral authority and adopts him as a model, a strategy that is at once a form of appeasement and of acceptable competition. But he can allow himself to feel considerable anger at his less dangerous mother. By deprecating her (she is after all "only a woman") he takes revenge, reduces the danger still further, comforts himself for his loss, and compensates for the humiliation of having to submit to his father. Yet he also idealizes her: out of guilt and the need to renounce their sexual bond (and also as a way of negating his father's victory), he denies her seductive attitude and transforms her into the pure woman who rejects men's bad impulses for their own good.

The mother is more unambiguously hostile to her daughter's sexuality. Besides seeing the girl as a rival and a doubly taboo sexual object, she feels freer to exercise power over a (mere) girl. We can also assume that she identifies more with a daughter, and that the girl's naive desire threatens to undermine her own hard-won inhibitions. Finally, it is mother's job to enforce the sexual double standard. The likely result is that the girl will blame her mother for her mutilation, while her father's seductiveness gives rise to the hope that he, as the real authority in the family, will rescind the punishment. Disillusioned with mother (her first love), she diverts her passion to father and imagines that he will side with her because she is willing to be "bad" with him in defiance of spiteful mother (who, as the girl sees it, wants her child to share her own deprived state). Also, since she has not yet accepted her inferior status as irrevocable or deserved, she believes that she is worthy of her father, while her mother is clearly not his equal. Her moment of awful truth comes when she understands that her father will neither restore her penis nor choose her over her mother. Though he has encouraged her badness, he nonetheless condemns it and stands with his wife, the good woman, against her. She realizes now that the powerful man she counted on to protect her may abandon or turn on her instead.

With this realization, her perception of the aggressiveness in her father's desire translates into a threat of rape, or even death. With horror and panic she imagines that having alienated her mother and failed to win her father she is an outcast, alone, powerless, contemptible. Her only recourse is to devote herself to appeasing her parents in the hope of regaining some sense of a secure place in the world, and, despite her humiliating demotion, some kind of self-respect. She adopts her mother's sexual righteousness, not only out of fear and guilt but because she has begun to believe that her mother punished her out of love, to warn her and keep her from inciting her father to rape and murder. On one level the girl's loyalties revert to a pre-Oedipal pattern, in which father was if anything an unwelcome rival for mother's attention: she sees herself and her mother as fellow victims of male power. Yet she does not completely suppress her desire for her father, who continues to be seductive as well as rejecting. Rather, she represses the self-willed aggression at the core of her "badness" and, again taking her mother as a model, expresses her sexual response in an indirect, muted—i.e., feminine—way. Thus she propitiates her father while simultaneously placating and competing with her mother.

In the girl's case, the most dangerous emotion is not her Oedipal desire, in itself, but her subversive wish to reject her female destiny. She can admit (much more readily than the boy can admit of his mother) that she is sexually attracted to her father and craves his sexual approval; what she cannot afford to recognize is her fury at not getting satisfaction, at being forced into passivity with the threat of violence. Like the boy, she is often able to express a modicum of anger at mother, who is less powerful and, she surmises, has already done her worst; such anger usually takes the form of competitiveness, disparagement of mother's inferior feminine traits, and complaints about being dominated, unloved, or misunderstood. But it is a superficial, ambivalent anger, for the daughter's deepest feelings of rage and betrayal must remain buried if she is to do what she has to do: be a woman.

For both sexes, the incentive to identify with the same-sex parent and embrace a conventional sexual role is not only fear of punishment but the prospect of psychic and social rewards. For the boy the rewards are greater, more direct, and more obvious. He will be able to express his aggressive impulses, his needs for both autonomy and power, in a wide range of non-sexual activities in the larger world (which activities and how wide a range will depend on his position in the class and racial hierarchy, but his opportunity will always exceed that of women in comparable social categories). He will have authority over women, the power to punish them if they forget their place, and a gratifying feeling of superiority. He will have considerable leeway in demanding and taking sexual pleasure, which, however morally dubious, even in his own eyes, is nonetheless a prerogative and an imperative of manhood.

For the girl, the male-dominated world outside the home promises little in the way of power, material reward, or self-esteem. Direct, aggressive pursuit of sexual gratification or personal power over men is taboo. Given these strictures, the role of good woman has significant advantages.[12] It allows her to exercise a certain amount of power by withholding sex and manipulating men's desire. It enables her to marry: with luck her husband will provide indirect access to the resources of the male world, a vicarious outlet for her impulses to worldly participation and power, disguised sexual fulfillment in the form of romantic ecstasy, and (if she is really lucky) actual sexual satisfaction within permissible bounds. Marriage carries with it the privilege of motherhood, which will become her greatest and most socially legitimate source of power, as well as a source of erotic pleasure. Finally, goodness offers her a means to retrieve her shattered pride. If she is good, men will respect her; in fact, she can claim moral superiority to men with their animal urges. In the name of morality she can, if she chooses, crusade against vice, bully "bad" women, and even make men feel guilty—another socially acceptable way to vent aggression and exercise power.

Since the sexual formations of women and men are complementary, each sex to a large extent meets the expectations (positive and negative, overt and repressed) of the other; the child's experience with the other-sex parent "works" when applied to other heterosexual objects (which is why, just by "acting naturally," each new generation of parents re-creates that experience with its children). In adult life, the masculine man displaces most of his feelings about his mother to his relations with other women, carrying with him the emotional contradictions of his childhood. His experience ensures that women can do nothing right, that he will always feel cheated: sexual rejection or reserve evokes the primal disappointment, while ready acceptance (let alone active seduction) revives the castration fear. To complicate matters, he assumes that marriage and procreation legitimize his lust (father is allowed to fuck mother), yet to marry a woman and have children with her defines her as good, hence sexually taboo. His unconscious confusions reinforced by social mores, he treats "good" women with "respect"; the rage their reserve provokes he directs—in the form of sexual predation and contempt—toward the "bad" women who respond to him, thereby transgressing their prescribed role and challenging his authority. He tends, in other words, to arrange his sex life on the principle that he wouldn't want to join any club that would have him as a member. When he marries he demands his wife's sexual compliance, yet cannot tolerate any display of "excessive" sexual enthusiasm, initiative, or self-assertion. Then, finding domestic sex boring and his wife's "goodness" inhibiting, he sleeps with (or has fantasies of) more exciting women to whom he need recognize no loyalty or commitment. He

feels guilty about his own "bad" desires, yet also proud of them since they confirm his manhood. He considers the "good" woman morally superior to himself,
yet has a deep conviction that all women are secretly bad, that their goodness is
a hypocritical facade. If he transgresses the bounds of respectful behavior with
the good woman, he rationalizes that he could only get away with it because she
was really bad all along. At its extreme this is the psychology of the rapist and
the wife-beater.

The same double binds ensure that the woman's claim to goodness, hence
her safety and legitimacy, is never secure. In the first place, she knows on some
level that her goodness *is* phony—that deep down she is indeed lustful, angry,
rebellious—and she feels guilty about it. As a result she will often accept the
judgment of the rapist or wife-beater that she somehow asked for or deserved
punishment. Furthermore, the requirements of goodness are contradictory.
The good woman must defer to men, do their will; she must also curb her sexual desire; yet part of what men will is that women not only sleep with them but
desire them. Her father wanted her to desire him, but when she went too far
(and how far was that? where did she cross the line?) love turned into rejection
and threat. As she grows up she will encounter the same dilemma: the boys
demand that she be attractive and sexy, but if she goes too far they label her
easy; if, on the other hand, she goes too far in the other direction—too aloof, too
indifferent—they condemn her as a cold bitch or a sexual failure. In marriage
the good woman must not refuse her husband but must not demand too much.
Always she must walk the elusive line between being too good, therefore bad,
and not good enough. The line shifts with history and circumstance, the particular man or his particular mood; the more freedom women achieve the more
tenuous the line becomes. The anxiety this uncertainty provokes functions actively as a means of social control; women can never stop trying to be *better,* to
escape an inescapable taint. Given this impossible situation, it is no wonder that
so many feminists are more preoccupied with their fears of male violence than
with their hopes for sexual freedom. Indeed, women's quest for security—futile
by the very nature of the system—not only discourages women from demanding
freedom but often moves them to defend rigid standards of sexual morality and
resist any blurring of the line between good and bad women. In doing so, they
shore up the very system that punishes them. Finally, the only way women will
ever break out of this trap is to end the association between sex and badness.

Sexual liberals have tried to dismiss that association as an unenlightened
remnant of our puritanical past. But since the cultural unconscious cannot be
erased by fiat, they have succeeded mainly in damaging their credibility. In a
sense, sexual liberalism creates its owns backlash. Men scoff at the idea of the
good woman—and find that they are terrified by the specter of the bad woman,
self-willed, demanding, perhaps insatiable. Women try to be free—and end up
being punished. Both sexes equate sexual freedom with a license to be bad—
and feel guilty. The power imbalance between the sexes remains. As a result,

the symbiosis of sexism and sexual repression continues to re-create a complex of patriarchal emotions that increasingly conflict with our rational ideas and aspirations and with the actual conditions of our lives. It is in fact the social instability and psychological tensions this conflict produces that have made people so receptive to "pro-family" ideology. The right proposes to resolve the conflict by changing social reality to conform to our most conservative emotions. Feminist politics, in contrast, often seem to embody the conflict instead of offering an alternative solution. Nor is this any wonder, if such a solution must include a fundamental transformation in people's sexual psychology. Yet however overwhelming and frightening, it is precisely this issue that we must somehow begin to address.

The first step, I believe, is simply to affirm the validity, in principle, of sexual liberation as a feminist goal. This in itself will clarify many confusions and contradictions in current feminist thinking, and indicate practical political directions. For instance, my analysis suggests that crusading against pornography as a symbol of male violence will impede feminism rather than advance it; that focusing *primarily* on issues of women's safety (like rape) may be more problematic and less effective than focusing on issues of women's sexual freedom (like abortion rights); that it is important for feminists to defend people's (including men's) freedom to engage in consensual sexual activity, including acts we may find distasteful. In short, it is a losing proposition for feminists to compete with the right in trying to soothe women's fears of sexual anarchy. We must of course acknowledge those fears and the legitimate reasons for them, but our interest as feminists is to demonstrate that a law-and-order approach to sex can only result in a drastic curtailment of our freedom. In the long run, we can win only if women (and men) want freedom (and love) more than they fear its consequences.

Social Text, Fall 1982

NOTES

Editor's note: This essay was reprinted in the 1992 collection, *No More Nice Girls,* with the first section appearing as a preface.

1. Some radical feminists argued that there was nothing wrong with marriage, per se, only with sex roles within marriage. (In a sense this position was an early version of Betty Friedan's "pro-family" feminism, minus the sentimental glossing over of male power.) Others maintained that while sexual freedom in the context of women's liberation was an ultimate goal, for now it was in our interest to resist the sexual revolution. See, for example, Shulamith Firestone, *The Dialectic of Sex* (New York: Morrow, 1970), 160–63. Another version of this argument was advanced by Kathie Sarachild, an influential theorist in the early movement, in "Hot and Cold Flashes," *The Newsletter,* vol. I, no. 3 (May 1, 1969). "We women can use marriage as the 'dictatorship of the proletariat' in the family revolution. When male supremacy is completely eliminated, marriage, like the state, will wither away."

2. Of the early radical feminist groups taking a female separatist position, the most influential were The Feminists in New York City and Cell 16 in Boston.

3. For a lucid exposition of this distinction I am indebted to Alice Echols's "The New Feminism of Yin and Yang," in *Powers of Desire: The Politics of Sexuality,* ed. Ann Snitow, Christine Stansell, and Sharon Thompson (New York: Monthly Review Press, 1983).

4. The best-known exponents of these views were Ti-Grace Atkinson, of The Feminists, and Dana Densmore, of Cell 16.

5. The following is a good example of this kind of thinking: ". . . if we are going to destroy the effects of pornography in our lives. . . . We must each be able to visualize on a grand scale what it is that we want for ourselves and for our society. . . . Would you try now to think of what it would be like to live in a society in which we are not, every minute, bombarded with sexual violence? Would you try to visualize what it would be like to go to the movies and not see it, to be able to walk home and not be afraid of it. . . . If we set that as our goal and demand nothing less, we will not stop fighting until we've achieved it." Kathleen Barry, "Beyond Pornography: From Defensive Politics to Creating a Vision," in *Take Back the Night: Women on Pornography,* ed. Laura Lederer (New York: Morrow, 1980), 312.

6. The June 1981 issue of the feminist newspaper *off our backs* published two letters to the editor on this theme. One of the writers, while affirming her unequivocal stand in favor of legal abortion, protests, "Why are we fighting so hard to make it 'safe' to fuck with men? . . . Why don't we focus on eliminating the need for abortion and birth control?" The other letter states, "Compulsory pregnancy results from compulsory penetration. . . . So I'm getting impatient to know when we will really take control over our bodies and not let ourselves be penetrated?" and goes on to assert "the inescapable fact that since I did not allow men to have control over my body, I could not then turn around and claim control over my baby's body."

7. In the ongoing debate over "the epidemic of teenage pregnancy" and whether it is best dealt with by providing teenagers with contraceptives or giving them lectures on chastity, birth control advocates have argued that access to contraception does not increase teenage sexual activity. So far as I know, no "responsible" organization has dared to suggest that adolescents have sexual needs and should have the right to satisfy them.

8. Shere Hite's *Hite Report on Male Sexuality* (New York: Knopf, 1981) includes many revealing comments from men on this particular theme: see her chapters on "Men's View of Women and Sex" and "Rape, Paying Women for Sex, and Pornography."

9. Reich's basic argument is laid out in *The Function of the Orgasm* (New York: Farrar, Straus, and Giroux, 1973), *The Sexual Revolution* (New York: Farrar, Straus, and Giroux, 1974), and *The Mass Psychology of Fascism* (New York: Farrar, Straus, and Giroux, 1970).

10. Sadomasochism as a consensual sexual practice has recently been a subject of controversy in the women's movement, and among anti-pornography activists "sadomasochism" has become something of a code word for any form of sexuality condemned by neo-Victorian standards. To avoid confusion, I want to make clear what I mean by *sadomasochistic psychology*: an emotional attitude consisting of the impulse to dominate, hurt, or revenge oneself on others, along with a reactive guilt manifested in the impulse to submit to others and seek their protection, while embracing pain and suffering as evidence of one's moral purity. In my view—and Reich's—this attitude is the inner emotional analogue of social hierarchy. In a sense, psychic sadism and masochism are perversions of the impulses to assertive, autonomous activity and emotional giving, respectively—impulses that are inevitably corrupted by social inequality and coercion.

From this perspective, sadomasochism is a universal cultural attitude, expressed in a myriad of sexual and nonsexual, overt and unconscious, acted and fantasized, public and private, harmful and harmless ways. The neo-Victorian attitude, compounded of sentimentalized feminine eroticism and punitive moralism, is itself rooted in sadomasochism.

11. Feminist theorists who agree on the importance of female "castration" as a determinant of feminine psychology have tended to adopt a Lacanian perspective, attributing significance to the phallus as cultural metaphor, rather than the penis as anatomical fact. See especially Juliet Mitchell, *Psychoanalysis and Feminism* (New York: Random House, 1974), and Gayle Rubin, "The Traffic in Women," in *Toward an Anthropology of Women,* ed. Rayna R. Reiter (New York: Monthly Review Press, 1975).

12. Accordingly, this role is not equally available to all women: men of dominant classes and races have typically regarded women of subordinate classes and races as "bad" by cultural definition, and therefore fair game for sexual and economic exploitation. For an excellent analysis of how black women have been systematically denied "good woman" status, see bell hooks, *Ain't I a Woman: Black Women and Feminism* (Boston: South End Press, 1981).

Lust Horizons
Is the Women's Movement Pro-Sex?

My nominations for the questions most likely to get a group of people, all of whom like each other and hate Ronald Reagan, into a nasty argument: Is there any objective criterion for healthy or satisfying sex, and if so what is it? Is a good sex life important? How important? Is abstinence bad for you? Does sex have any intrinsic relation to love? Is monogamy too restrictive? Are male and female sexuality inherently different? Are we all basically bisexual? Do vaginal orgasms exist? Does size matter? You get the idea. Despite the endless public discussion of sex, despite the statistics of "experts" and the outpourings of personal testimony about our sexual desires, fantasies, and habits, we have achieved precious little clarity—let alone agreement—about what it all means. At the same time there is no subject on which people are more passionately, blindly, stubbornly opinionated.

What is especially disconcerting, to those of us who believe that an understanding of sexuality is crucial to a feminist analysis, is that feminists are as confused, divided, and dogmatic about sex as everyone else. This sense of an intractably resistant, perennially sore subject pervades two recent anthologies that in other ways could hardly be more disparate. *Women—Sex and Sexuality,* a collection of articles from the feminist academic journal *Signs,* is a sober mix of theoretical essays, reviews, reports on research, and historical documents. The theory section is the most consistently interesting: most of the essays, including some I violently disagree with, raise provocative questions or make points worth mulling. (I particularly recommend Judith Walkowitz on the politics of prostitution, Rosalind Petchesky on reproductive freedom, Ann Barr Snitow on sex in women's novels, Alix Kates Shulman on the genesis of radical feminist ideas about sex—I should add that the last two and I belong to the same women's group.) Otherwise the book is uneven, with valuable information and insights weighed down by reviews that are little more than summaries and research that borders on the trivial. Stilted academic prose is an intermittent problem, though less so than in most scholarly collections.

The sex issue of *Heresies*—a journal that was started by feminist artists and has put out 12 issues, each devoted to a single theme and edited by a different collective—is more fun to read. It is lively, raunchy, irreverent; it intersperses theoretical articles ("Pornography and Pleasure," "A Herstorical Look at Some Aspects of Black Sexuality," "Narcissism, Feminism, and Video Art") with stories, poems, satire, cartoons, and witty graphics. The *Signs* anthology defines its subject in the most inclusive terms; *Heresies* sticks to the aspect of sex feminists have had the most trouble discussing—desire ("Where do our desires come from? How do they manifest themselves in their infinite variations? And what, if anything, do they tell us about what it means to be a woman?"). The editors of *Women—Sex and Sexuality* see the movement's lack of any coherent sexual theory as healthy eclecticism: "Since female sexuality exists within specific contexts, within matrices of the body and the world, no single perspective, no single discipline, can do justice to it." The *Heresies* collective simply admits it couldn't agree on much; divergent editorials by individual (but anonymous) editors are scattered throughout the issue.

The failure of feminists to get a grip, so to speak, on this all-important subject is particularly disappointing, given our (naive?) hopes at the beginning. In "Sex and Power: Sexual Bases of Radical Feminism," her contribution to the *Signs* collection, Alix Kates Shulman explains the premise of radical feminist consciousness raising: "The so-called experts on women had traditionally been men who, as part of the male-supremacist power structure, benefited from perpetuating certain ideas. . . . We wanted to get at the truth about how women felt. . . . Not how we were *supposed* to feel but how we really did feel." As it turned out this was easier said than done, especially when the feelings in question were sexual. To challenge male "expertise" on what good sex is or ought to be, what women feel or ought to feel, is only a prerequisite to understanding "how we really feel." Women's sexual experience is diverse and often contradictory. Women's sexual feelings have been stifled and distorted not only by men and men's ideas but by our own desperate strategies for living in and with a sexist, sexually repressive culture. Our most passionate convictions about sex do not necessarily reflect our real desires; they are as likely to be aimed at repressing the pain of desires we long ago decided were too dangerous to acknowledge, even to ourselves. If feminist theory is to be truly based in the reality of women's lives, feminists must examine their professed beliefs and feelings with as much skepticism as they apply to male pronouncements. Otherwise we risk simply replacing male prejudices and rationalizations with our own. But what criteria do we apply to such an examination? How do we distinguish between real and inauthentic feelings?

An influential strain in early radical feminist thought assumed that women had a kind of collective wisdom, drawn from their experience, that would spontaneously emerge as the existence of a movement encouraged women to believe change was possible and to admit the truth of their situation, instead of fatalistically acquiescing (or pretending to acquiesce) in male supremacist lies. In practice, what this tended to mean was a faith in authenticity by consensus—particularly when the consensus of a feminist group seemed to dovetail with the traditional complaints and demands (the "individual struggles") of "apolitical" women. Not coincidentally, the consensus among proponents of this view was that women really want marriage and monogamy, albeit on equal terms that do not now exist. (To the extent that lesbianism was discussed, it was assumed either that lesbians were exceptions or that lesbianism was a response to male oppressiveness, rather than a positive choice.) The "free love" ideology of male leftists and bohemians was, they argued, nothing but a means of exploiting women sexually while avoiding commitment and responsibility; the "sexual revolution" had not benefited women, but merely robbed us of the right to say no. If some women nonetheless preferred "free love," it was only because marriage under present conditions was also oppressive. The opposite possibility was not considered: that women really want free love—on equal terms that do not now exist—and prefer to let the state police their sexual relationships only because the present male-defined and -dominated "sexual revolution" has so little to do with either genuine love or genuine freedom.

For another faction in the movement—which also surfaced right at the beginning—the standard of authenticity became one's degree of antagonism toward men and male attitudes, particularly sexual attitudes. By this standard, marriage and "free love" are equally repugnant. Heterosexual relations are by definition a violation of women's true feelings; the only authentic choices are lesbianism or celibacy. Here there was some confusion, for separatists tended to talk as if lesbianism and celibacy were at once freely chosen alternatives and necessary responses to men's oppressive behavior. But this contradiction was resolved by an implicit biological determinism: men are inherently violent and predatory; women are inherently loving and nurturing; and the essence of men's oppressiveness is their insistence on imposing their maleness—especially their male sexuality on unwilling women. (Adrienne Rich's article in *Women—Sex and Sexuality,* "Compulsory Heterosexuality and Lesbian Existence," is a classic example of this line of reasoning. Her premise is that both men and women desire women; this has impelled men to erect the whole structure of patriarchal relations for the specific purpose of ensuring their access to women's vaginas. Where homosexual men fit into this analysis is unclear.) This wing of the movement has been primarily responsible for putting a feminist imprimatur on certain familiar ideas—that men are too genitally oriented, that women are more interested in nongenital forms of eroticism, that the supposedly irrepressible sex drive is a male problem (or a male myth), that women can take sex or leave it.

These apparently opposed perspectives meet on the common ground of sexual conservatism. The monogamists uphold the traditional wife's "official" values: emotional commitment is inseparable from a legal/moral obligation to permanence and fidelity; men are always trying to escape these duties; it's in our interest to make them shape up. The separatists tap into the underside of traditional femininity—the bitter, self-righteous fury that propels the indictment of men as lustful beasts ravaging their chaste victims. These are the two faces of feminine ideology in a patriarchal culture: they induce women to accept a spurious moral superiority as a substitute for sexual pleasure, and curbs on men's sexual freedom as a substitute for real power.

In one form or another, sexual conservatism still permeates the movement. In their introduction the editors of *Women—Sex and Sexuality,* Catharine Stimpson and Ethel Spector Person, approach the issue of sexual freedom with cautious equivocation, but quickly betray an underlying conservatism. They ask, "Is female sexuality like male sexuality, or does it obey laws of its own?" then note that researchers with an "egalitarian bias," who prefer "to see the sexualities as essentially identical," have found support in recent scientific studies. But "such a belief can be only apparently feminist. Too often, egalitarians masculinize the model of sexuality. They believe that male sexuality most accurately embodies a human sexuality that neither cultural nor psychological constraints have corrupted." Perhaps. On the other hand, some egalitarians, including me, are inclined to believe that while "uncorrupted" male and female sexuality would be pretty much alike, cultural and psychological constraints have corrupted the sexuality of both sexes in different ways. But in the next sentence we see what all this has been leading up to: "They also tend to esteem a pure and unfettered sexuality as an invariant key to self-validation and autonomy." Translation: to be "egalitarian" is to legitimize unfettered male lust—for both sexes, yet. It's safer if female sexuality is different—maybe we don't want to be unfettered.

Person, a psychoanalyst, elaborates on this theme in an article called "Sexuality as the Mainstay of Identity: Psychoanalytic Perspectives." First, she reminds us that Freud's libido theory—the concept of sexual excitation as energy that presses for release and if not satisfied directly (in orgasm) will seek indirect or disguised outlets—is unproven. True, but it hasn't been disproved either. On the contrary, it remains the most plausible explanation for a whole range of phenomena, from the way sexual excitement feels, to the obvious correlation between sexual inhibition and certain neurotic symptoms or character traits, to the centrality of sexual restrictions in patriarchal morality. Anyway, one would think that whatever their hostility to other aspects of Freud's thought, feminists would welcome the libido theory, since it supports the claim that men's suppression of women's genital sexuality is an intolerable denial of our needs. But the assumption that women have genital needs is precisely what's unacceptable from Person's point of view. She argues that sexual activity and orgasm are indispensable to men's mental health, but not to women's; specifically, men need sex to feel like men, while in women "gender identity and self-worth can be consolidated by other means."

This argument reinforces a social stereotype while completely ignoring social reality. In this culture, where women are still supposed to be less sexual than men, sexual inhibition is as integral to the "normal" woman's identity as sexual aggression is to a man's; it is "excessive" genital desires that often make women feel "unfeminine" and unworthy. In rejecting the idea that an active, autonomous sexuality is a necessary aspect of female autonomy in general, Person also rejects the possibility that the systematic social inhibition of female sexuality is a way of inhibiting our self-assertion in other areas—that this indeed may be the chief social function of our antisexual training. She notes the "evidence in the clinical literature that masturbation in adolescent girls is related to high self-esteem and to the subsequent pursuit of career goals," but quickly dismisses the obvious inference: "It is unlikely that masturbation itself is so beneficial; more likely some general assertiveness plays a role in the exploration of both sexuality and role experimentation."

From her dubious hypothesis Person reaches the following conclusions: "Many women have the capacity to abstain from sex without negative psychological consequences. (The problem for women is that they are often denied the legal right of sexual refusal.)" "One ought not dictate a tyranny of active sexuality as critical to female liberation." "Given a current liberal climate of thinking about sexuality there is a danger, not so much in an anti-erotic attitude, but in too much insistence on the expression of sexuality as the sine qua non of mental health and self-actualization." I hope that in the current conservative climate Person is having second thoughts, but I'm not counting on it. She goes on to say that a "neutral" discussion of sexuality must weigh not only the advantages of sexual activity but "the adaptive advantages of the capacity for abstinence, repression, or suppression." No doubt about it—when one must endure abstinence, repression, or suppression, the capacity to adapt does come in handy. But somehow I always imagined that feminism was about rebelling, not adapting.

It has been years since feminist sexual conservatism (a contradiction in terms, really) has had to face any sustained or organized opposition, but that is beginning to change. Both of these collections—particularly *Heresies*—reflect the early, tentative stirrings of a revived feminist debate on sexuality, which is in turn a response to the right-wing backlash. The right does have a coherent perspective on sex, one that unites a repressive sexual morality with the subordination of women. Since feminists are at best ambivalent about sexual freedom, they have not been able to make an effective counterattack. Indeed, the movement's attacks on sexual exploitation and violence, male irresponsibility, pornography, and so on have often reinforced right-wing propaganda by giving the impression that feminists consider the loosening of controls over sexual behavior a worse threat to women than repression. While liberals appeared to be safely in power, feminists could perhaps afford the luxury of defining Larry Flynt or Roman Polanski as Enemy Number One. Now that we have to cope with Jerry Falwell and Jesse Helms, a rethinking of priorities seems in order.

Which is why I'm grateful for *Heresies'* sex issue. Both the content of individual pieces and an overall feistiness of style and tone assume that the purpose of women's liberation is to liberate women, not defend our superior capacity for abstinence. (The issue does include an article by a woman extolling the joys of celibacy, but even she admits to masturbating. This may technically be celibacy, but abstinence it ain't.) As one of the anonymous editorials puts it, "The work in this magazine encourages us to reflect on our individual and collective relationship to our desires for and of the flesh. . . . In a system where Women make love but do not fuck, where Women request but do not demand, women who actively strategize for their own pleasure are confused. . . . If we are not Women as we have been designed, then who are we? Many of us fear for our feminine identity . . . . As we proceed in this project of creating a feminist understanding of our sexual choices, our changing desires and our erotic possibilities, we prepare the way for a sexual politics that has pleasure as its goal." In "Pornography and Pleasure," Paula Webster argues that the antipornography movement "has chosen to organize and theorize around our victimization, our Otherness, not our subjectivity and self-definition. In focusing on what male pornography has done to us, rather than on our own sexual desires, we tend to embrace our sexually deprived condition and begin to police the borders of the double standard. . . . Indeed, I am convinced that pornography, even in its present form, contains important messages for women. As Angela Carter suggests, it does not tie women's sexuality to reproduction or to a domesticated couple or exclusively to men. It is true that this depiction is created by men, but perhaps it can encourage us to think of what our own images and imaginings might be like."

In short, *Heresies #12* is, among other things, a forum for dissidents in the sex debate, and it tacitly acknowledges that role by publicizing a recent intramovement skirmish. Last year NOW, on the advice of its lesbian caucus, passed a resolution specifically excluding from its definition of lesbian rights certain forms of sexual expression that had been "mistakenly correlated with Lesbian/Gay rights by some gay organizations and by opponents of Lesbian/Gay rights seeking to confuse the issue": pederasty, pornography, sadomasochism (all of which were alleged to be issues of violence or exploitation, not of sexual preference), and public sex ("an issue of violation of the privacy rights of nonparticipants"). While the impetus for the resolution seems to have been opposition to the "boy love" movement, its effect is to endorse the moralistic rhetoric and the conventionally feminine sexual politics of the antiporn campaign; it also has disturbing overtones of homophobic and/or self-hating insistence that "lesbians are respectable too."

The resolution inspired a letter of protest that has been circulating as a petition in feminist, lesbian, and gay circles and has collected about 150 signatures.

My women's group (a hotbed of sexual dissidence) had a somewhat different point of view, so we wrote our own letter. All three documents are reprinted in *Heresies* under the headline, "News Flash: People Organize to Protest Recent NOW Resolution on Lesbian and Gay Rights."

Lesbians have been conspicuous on both sides of the clash between sexually conservative and libertarian feminists. On the one hand, it is lesbian separatists who have most militantly embraced a saccharinely romantic, nice-girl's view of female sexuality as the proper feminist outlook, while disparaging sexual attitudes deemed too aggressive or too bluntly lustful as "male-identified" (movementese for "unfeminine"). Other lesbians—impelled in part by the recognition that it's hardly in lesbians' interest to encourage moralistic attacks on unconventional sexual behavior—retort that feminists have no business setting up standards of politically correct sexuality and that women who do so are, like all bigots, fearfully condemning what they don't understand.

A recent focus of this argument within the lesbian feminist community has been the issue of sadomasochism (i.e., consensual sexual practices involving dominance and submission rituals and the infliction of pain or humiliation). The prevailing lesbian feminist line has been that S-M, like pornography, is a male trip, a form of violence rather than sex, a re-creation of oppressive patriarchal, heterosexual patterns; lesbians don't have S-M relationships, and if they do it's because they are victims of heterosexist brainwashing. Dissenters have argued that lesbians do indeed have such relationships, that S-M is as legitimate a sexual taste as any other, and that its despised practitioners are an oppressed sexual minority.

Pat Califia carries on this debate in *Heresies.* In "Feminism and Sadomasochism," she argues that S-M is not a form of sexual assault but a fantasy—"a drama or ritual"—enacted by mutual consent: "The participants are enhancing their sexual pleasure, not damaging or imprisoning one another. A sadomasochist is well aware that a role adopted during a scene is not appropriate during other interactions and that a fantasy role is not the sum total of her being."

What then is the function and meaning of the drama? Why the desire to act out in bed roles that in other contexts would be distasteful? Califia's explanations are less than satisfying. She suggests that S-M involves a quest for "intense sensations" and "pleasure from the forbidden," that a sadist may encourage a masochist "to lose his inhibitions and perform an act he may be afraid of, or simply acknowledge shame and guilt and use it to enhance the sex act rather than prevent it." But she doesn't pursue these observations further, and in the end we learn little more than that S-M turns her on. For Califia this is enough; commenting on the term *vanilla*—S-M jargon for non-S-M people—she says, "I believe sexual preferences are more like flavor preferences than like moral/political alliances." To the question of whether sadomasochism will survive the revolution, she replies, "My fantasy is that kinkiness and sexual variation will multiply, not disappear, if terrible penalties are no longer meted out for being sexually adventurous."

Can it possibly be that simple? Here is Califia's list of the activities she enjoys: "Leathersex, bondage, various forms of erotic torture, flagellation (whipping), verbal humiliation, fist-fucking, and watersports (playing with enemas and piss)." "There are many different ways to express affection or interest," she asserts. "Vanilla people send flowers, poetry, or candy, or they exchange rings. S-M people do all that, and may also lick boots, wear a locked collar, or build their loved one a rack in the basement."

Does the need to act out fantasies of debasing oneself or someone else really require no further explanation? Does it have nothing to do with buried emotions of rage or self-hatred? Nothing to do with living in a hierarchical society where one is "superior" to some people and "inferior" to others, where men rule and women serve? Can the need to connect sexual pleasure with pain and humiliation be unrelated to the fact that our sexual organs and their function are still widely regarded as bad, contemptible, and embarrassing, a reproach to our higher spiritual natures? Is it irrelevant that our first erotic objects were our all-powerful parents, who too often hurt and humiliated us by condemning our childish sexuality?

Puritanism is not the only obstacle to a feminist understanding of sex. If self-proclaimed arbiters of feminist morals stifle honest discussion with their dogmatic, guilt-mongering judgments, sexual libertarians often evade honest discussion by refusing to make judgments at all. I think that to read women out of the movement because of their sexual habits is outrageous, and that to label any woman's behavior as "male" is a sexist absurdity. I also think it's dangerous to assume that certain kinds of behavior will disappear "after the revolution" (as dangerous as assuming that "the revolution" is a discrete event, which will someday be over once and for all). But I don't believe our sexual desires are ever just arbitrary tastes. Rather, I see sadomasochism as one way of coping with this culture's sexual double binds, which make it painfully difficult for people to reconcile their sexual needs with dignity and equality. To be sure, the same can be said of many more conventional sexual practices: what, after all, is the ritual of male pursuit and female ambivalence (or, increasingly these days, the opposite) but a disguised and therefore respectable form of sadomasochistic theater? Probably none of us is free of sadomasochistic feelings; no doubt the hostility sadomasochists inspire is in large part horror at being directly confronted with fantasies most of us choose to repress, or to express only indirectly. The issue is whether such fantasies, expressed or denied, are themselves the product of thwarted desire. The very idea that "the forbidden" offers special pleasures suggests that the answer is yes.

Another source of controversy among feminists, lesbians, and gays is the claim of "man-boy love" advocates that theirs is yet another unconventional

sexual taste, entirely consensual and beneficial to all concerned, that is unfairly maligned by puritanical homophobes as child molesting. This one is
much stickier, for the question is not only whether sexual attraction between
adults and children (most adult-child sex takes place between men and girls)
is comparable to a yen for chocolate, but whether, given the vulnerability of
children to the power of adults, such relationships can ever be truly consensual.
I don't think they can. Adults can too easily manipulate children's needs for
affection, protection, and approval; children are too inexperienced to understand all the implications of what they're agreeing to (or even, in some cases,
initiating). And it seems to me that what attracts adults to children is precisely
their "innocence"—which is to say their relative powerlessness. There is the
question, though, of where to draw lines. At what age does a child become a
young person, and when does protecting children from exploitation become a
denial of young people's sexual autonomy? Some 15-year-olds are more mature
than many adults will ever be. And I agree that the public's readiness to equate
all adult-child sex with child molesting comes in part from a need to deny that
kids have active sexual desires. Still, in this instance I would rather err on the
side of restrictiveness, for if children cannot rely absolutely on adult protection,
they have no ground under their feet.

The "I'm O.K., you're O.K." brand of sexual libertarianism is a logical extension of the feminist and gay liberationist demand for the right to self-definition.
But the further this principle is extended, the sharper are its contradictions.
Though self-definition is the necessary starting point for any liberation movement, it can take us only so far. To me it is axiomatic that consenting partners
have a right to their sexual proclivities, and that authoritarian moralism has
no place in a movement for social change. But a truly radical movement must
look (to borrow a phrase from Rosalind Petchesky) beyond the right to choose,
and keep focusing on the fundamental questions. Why do we choose what we
choose? What would we choose if we had a real choice?

Village Voice, June 1981

The Last Unmarried Person in America

The great marriage boom of '84 began shortly after Congress passed the historic National Family Security Act. Though most of its provisions merely took care of old, long overdue business—abolishing divorce, enabling local communities to prosecute single people as vagrants, requiring applicants for civil service jobs to sign a monogamy oath, making the interstate sale of quiche a federal offense, and so on—two revolutionary clauses cleared the way toward making a reality of what had until then been an impossible dream: universal marriage.

The child purity provision, popularly known as the Down-There Amendment, prevents premarital sex by allowing parents to marry a child to a suitable mate as soon as he or she shows signs of prurient interests—"After all, it's better to marry than to burn," as President Ray Gun so eloquently observed. (An amendment that would have included the unborn in this provision was defeated on the grounds that it cast aspersions on fetal innocence.) Another landmark is the act's legalization of homosexual marriage. This was the most controversial aspect of the bill, splitting the pro-family movement into two camps—the purists, who insisted that homosexuality was a sin, period, and the pragmatists, who pointed out that denying homosexuals the sacrament of marriage discouraged their impulses toward decent respectability, kept dens of iniquity like Greenwich Village in business, and played into the hands of feminists who claimed that women didn't really want to get married anyway. In the end a compromise was reached: homosexuals who swore not to have sex would be permitted to marry, and those who declined to take advantage of this privilege would be deported to Saudi Arabia.

The week after President Gun signed the bill into law, we interviewed a number of the happy couples who had been standing on line at City Hall for up to three days waiting to apply for marriage licenses. The heterosexuals all insisted the Family Security Act had nothing to do with their decision to tie the knot. "It was a totally spontaneous thing," said one radiant young woman. "We were ready to make a commitment."

"My landlord was going to double my rent," her radiant young fiancé explained. "He feels, and I can't say I really blame him, that single men attract quiche-eaters to the area. It got me thinking, and I realized that I really wanted to settle down."

"It was so cute the way he proposed," the young woman broke in. "He came over one afternoon while I was sewing scarlet S's on my clothes—it was the day before the deadline, and I'd been procrastinating, as usual. He kissed me and said, 'Why spend your time doing that, when you could be sewing on my buttons instead?'"

We talked next to a pair of radiant young lesbians who proclaimed this the happiest day of their lives. To our delicate inquiry as to whether it would bother them not to have sex, one of the women replied coldly, "That is a bigoted, heterosexist question. Why do straight people always assume we're dying for sex? We think sex is dirty just like you do."

"We're getting married for love," her fiancee declared, "and for children."

"Do you plan to adopt," we asked, "or to be artificially inseminated?"

"Don't be ridiculous! We're going to have our own. The idea that women need men to have babies is patriarchal propaganda. Do you still believe that fairytale about God being Jesus's father?"

On June 30, after a month in which clergymen and government officials worked around the clock to meet the demand for weddings, riots erupted in two cities where laboratory equipment needed for blood tests broke down from overuse, and the last shipment of degenerate sex fiends was dispatched to the Middle East, the president announced proudly that the goal for which all Americans were praying had been achieved: everyone in the 50 states and the District of Columbia was married. The next day our newspaper received an indignant phone call.

"Tuesday here," said a voice that sounded like a cross between a purr and a bark. "I'm calling you guys because you have a reputation for being open-minded. Didn't your editor come out for allowing divorce to save the lives of the children?"

"Not divorce," we said. "Just separation."

"Okay. But you agree that what's going on is just a little excessive?"

"Look, Mr.—Mrs.?—ah, Tuesday," we said nervously, "why exactly are you calling?"

"*Mrs.*, my ass!" our caller exclaimed. "*That's* why I'm calling. The president is a liar! As he knows perfectly well, since his Secret Service thugs argued with me for five hours yesterday, I'm as single as the day I was born. And I have no plans to get married, either."

This *was* news. Minutes later we were on our way to an exclusive interview with Ruby Tuesday, the last unmarried person in America. We caught up with Ruby, who makes her home in an empty car of the Lexington Avenue IRT, at the Union Square station. She was a striking-looking woman. It wasn't the green hair so much as the fact that instead of the one scarlet S required by law—a requirement we had naively imagined was obsolete—she wore a see-through satin jumpsuit made entirely of scarlet S's sewn together.

"Come on in," she said. "Have a quiche. It's okay—I make my own."

She was still shaking her head at the chutzpah of the president and the Secret Service. "To think that I *voted* for the guy. He promised to get the government off my back—what did I know? This thing has, whadayucall it, *radicalized* me. Do you know what these fuckers wanted to do? Get some poor slob who couldn't stand the plumbing in Saudi Arabia to come back and marry me, and have Jerry Falwell do it on TV, right before the president's announcement. The Soviets would shit, they said. Ha!"

"We take it you don't agree with that analysis?"

"Listen, don't get me wrong. I'm no Communist! No way! But what could be more communistic than trying to get everybody to *live* with each other? Besides, I'm Jewish."

We asked Ruby why she had such strong objections to marriage.

"It's taken me 15 years to get this car just the way I like it," she said. "Why should I share it with some asshole?"

"Don't you feel a need for intimacy? Community? Commitment?"

"Nah."

"Would you call yourself a narcissist?"

Ruby raised her eyebrows. "I know you're just doing your job," she said, "but let's not get insulting. I'm as kinky as the next one, but some things I won't do even for money."

We apologized. "Would you mind telling us your sexual preference?"

"Hm. Well, sometimes I can really get into plain old-fashioned fucking. Then again there's nothing quite like having your ass licked and your cunt sucked at the same time."

"Actually, what we meant was, do you prefer men or women?"

"Yes," said Ruby enthusiastically.

We decided to take another tack, and asked her how the public was reacting to her refusal to perform what most of us considered a patriotic duty, necessary to end our humiliating dependence on Japanese moral fiber. Ruby rolled her eyes.

"I've done without moral fiber all my life, and I've never felt better," she said. "But try to convince people of that nowadays! I have to admit I'm not too popular. Everybody's paranoid about me. The wives think I'm after their husbands and the husbands think I'm after their wives. I don't believe in homewrecking, but what am I supposed to do? There's nothing but husbands and wives *left*."

"Are you now or have you ever been a feminist?"

"I'm for equal pay for equal work," said Ruby with conviction, "and anybody who doesn't like it can get fucked. About all the other stuff, I don't know. I went to a meeting of Women Against Pornography once, but that was mostly to meet girls."

"Aren't you worried about getting picked up on a vagrancy rap?"

"Nah. They can't touch me. I looked it up: the Supreme Court decided I can't be busted unless I do something, like ask a child for directions. And only two justices have been assassinated since then."

"But the Family Security Act overrules that decision. It says, 'Congress finds that the rotten Supreme Court decision allowing dangerous marriage-dodgers to stalk our streets is full of shit!'"

Ruby shook her head stubbornly. "It won't stick, until they kill at least one more justice."

"When that happens, will you go under—er, into hiding?"

"The fuck I will! This used to be a free country! They'll have to drag me away."

The rhinestones on Ruby's eyelashes gleamed defiantly. We noticed that she was looking us up and down. "Are you married?" she demanded.

"Of course we're married," we said. What was she driving at?

"So they managed to intimidate you," said Ruby, giving us a pitying look.

"Not at all!" we said hotly. "We got married because we wanted to! We needed intimacy and community and commitment!"

"Bullshit," said Ruby, continuing to look at us in a way we were beginning to find unnerving. "Are you really going to tell me that getting a deportation order had nothing to do with it?"

We turned bright red. "How did you know?" we said finally. "We haven't told a soul."

"Oh, I can always tell when I'm turning somebody on," said Ruby, smiling indulgently. "You know, I find you quite attractive, too."

Feeling a little weak, we made an attempt to pull ourselves together and act professional. "Thank you for your time," we said loftily. "We'll be going now."

"Stay here tonight," Ruby said. "You won't regret it."

"Well—we'd like to, but—no. No, we just can't do it."

"Why not?"

"It's too risky. Suppose the National News Council found out?"

"I'm very discreet. The only thing you have to worry about is the picket line outside. But a bag over your head should take care of that."

"No—no, really—" By this time Ruby was stroking our back and kissing our ear. Our heart thumped. "Have another quiche," she whispered.

Village Voice, July 1981

Teenage Sex
A Modesty Proposal

What else is new? The Schools Chancellor and the Board of Education President, those liberal do-gooders, want to make sex education compulsory and give out contraceptives in the high schools; outraged board members, parents, and bishops denounce this blatant promotion of Teenage Sex. The so-called compromise: no contraceptives will be dispensed, only prescriptions, and local boards can choose whether or not to teach baby-killing. Meanwhile, in New York City alone, some teenager commits a sexual act every two-and-a-half seconds.

Let's face it: everyone agrees that TS is evil, but no one has the guts to *do* anything about it. The liberals, of course, are hopeless. "We don't like Teenage Sex any more than you do," they whine. "But we can't turn back the clock. Sex is all over TV, in the streets, the schools, the parking lots, the closets, and bathtubs of America." So, they argue, we should concentrate on preventing pregnancy and VD. Give 'em sex education, birth control, even counseling to help them "manage sex responsibly" and (God forgive us!) "have good relationships." And now our estimable Board President assures us that giving out contraceptives "tends to make youngsters less promiscuous and not more promiscuous." Sure, and if you put foxes in chicken coops they'll help sit on the eggs.

These boneheads miss the essential point: if you think you can't stop evil, that's all the more reason to punish it. Allowing teenagers to have sexual pleasure without paying for it through the nose violates the most basic principle of civilized society, to wit, "For every illicit sex act a baby, a disease, and a partner who hates you in the morning." (That goes double for girls. I'm all for equal rights, but a slut is a slut.)

Conservatives understand this principle, but for some reason they're reluctant to admit it. Instead they blather on about the need to provide kids with moral values. They want schools to give lectures on chastity. Give me a break! Does anybody seriously think that if Nancy Reagan went around making a personal appeal to every high school kid in the city to just say no, the TS rate would go down one iota? Have lectures ever stopped your kids? Did they stop you?

It's time to move beyond toothless moralizing and merely negative policies like depriving kids of sex information and birth control; time, in short, to make war on TS. And the fact is, there's only one strategy that can work: making the very idea of sex so frightening that no sane teenager could enjoy it. I call this practical strategy "benign terrorism." Here are 12 suggestions for implementing it.

Define TS as child abuse. When an adult has sex with a child, it is called child abuse. Why is it any different when children abuse each other? Anyone caught committing TS should be tried as a child abuser. Pregnancy or venereal disease will of course be considered prima facie evidence of TS.

Start TS prevention at birth. Everyone used to understand that the best way to prevent Teenage Sex is to scare the shit out of children. But in recent years an unholy alliance of permissive doctors, secular humanists, condom companies, and pornography czars has obscured this basic truth with a relentless propaganda campaign. Parents have been told not to slap an infant's hand when it wanders down there, not to tell little kids to stop touching it or you'll cut it off (and older ones that they'll go blind or crazy), not to punish them for playing doctor, not to tell them sex is dirty and disgusting. We must counterattack with a high-powered media campaign designed to reach every parent with the message that the Victorians had the right idea. We must institute antisex programs in every school, nursery school, and day-care center.

Sex-segregate the schools. To prevent homosexuals from taking advantage of this reform, security guards should be stationed in bathrooms at all times. Teachers should observe students closely, and any students caught flirting should be branded "G" (see below).

Institute "pass laws" for teenagers. Under these laws, teenagers would be issued national identity cards, which they would have to carry at all times. They would be subject to a daily 4 p.m. curfew. In or out of the house they would have to be chaperoned at all times by a parent or other authorized adult. They would be forbidden to set foot in a car, since the automobile, from the teenager's point of view, is nothing but a mobile bed.

Register homosexuals and brand a "G" on their foreheads. The purpose of this measure is not to stigmatize sodomists but simply to alert parents, teachers, and others to when they need to be especially vigilant in supervising a same-sex group (as in sex-segregated schools, see above).

Institute random vaginal testing for the presence of sperm and the absence of virginity. The latter tests are sometimes unreliable, so no conclusions should be drawn before investigating a girl's history of athletic activity and tampon use.

Establish a special TS taskforce. Its duties would include running a 24-hour hotline to take TS reports; spot-checking cars, movie theaters, and apartment house stairwells for illicit or unsupervised teenagers; giving out rewards to teenagers for informing on their friends, and to parents for informing on their children and their children's friends.

Bring back the chastity belt. In addition to the traditional model, designers are currently working on chastity belts for the mouth. (While belts are eminently worth trying, we should be alert to the danger of organized crime making huge profits from an underground lock-picking industry.)

Lower the legal marriage age to 12, and make marriage compulsory for anyone who commits TS. These measures alone should go a long way toward solving our problem, since a wedding automatically turns Teenage Sex into Marital Commitment. However,

TS offenders whose partners cannot be found should be jailed until they get married or turn 21. Every offender is a serious danger to the entire teenage community. It is estimated that the teenager who gets caught will, on the average, have committed 384.5 previous offenses.

Impose the death penalty for contraceptive dealers who sell to minors. I know, I know, the Supreme Court, even under Rehnquist, probably isn't ready for this. First, we would need an effective educational campaign to make the public understand that TS is highly addictive, and that the birth-control peddler is guilty of nothing less than hopelessly hooking our nation's youth.

Now I come to my last and perhaps most controversial proposal:

Castrate second offenders. This may seem harsh, but facing up to the Teenage Sex crisis is not for the fainthearted. Let us talk frankly: the crux of the problem is male lust, for as we all know, girls are uninterested in sex until boys corrupt them. I would, however, exempt from this penalty any boy who has committed TS with a girl of bad reputation. For as we all know, a boy can only be as pure as the first little whore who gives in to him.

Village Voice, October 1986

Sisters under the Skin?
Confronting Race and Sex

Recently, at a feminist meeting, a black woman argued that in American society race is a more absolute division than sex, a more basic determinant of social identity. This started an intense discussion: if someone shook us out of a deep sleep and demanded that we define ourselves, what would we blurt out first? The black woman said "black woman." Most of the white women said "woman"; some said "lesbian." No one said "white person" or "white woman."

I'm not sure it makes sense to say that one social division is more absolute than another. I wonder if it isn't more a matter of different kinds of division. Most blacks and whites live in separate communities, in different social, cultural, and economic worlds, while most women and men share each other's daily, intimate lives and cooperate, even if unequally, in such elemental activities as fucking, procreating, and keeping a household going. On the other hand, a man and a woman can spend their lives together and have such disparate versions of their "common" experience that they might as well live on different planets. Do I feel more distant from black women than from white men? Everything else (class) being equal? (Except that it usually isn't.) In some ways yes, in some ways no. But whatever the objective truth, my sex feels more basic to my identity than my race. This is not surprising: in a sexist society it's impossible to take one's femaleness for granted; in a racist society whiteness is simply generic humanness, entirely unremarkable. Suppose, though, that a black revolution were to seriously challenge my racial privileges? Suppose I had to confront every day, every hour, the question of which side I'm on?

Such questions excite and disturb me. Like talk about sexuality, discussions of the racial-sexual nexus radiate danger and taboo—a sign that the participants are on to something. Lately such discussions, mostly initiated by black women, are happening more often. They raise the heartening possibility of connecting, and in the process revitalizing, the unhappily divergent discourses of feminism and black liberation. This could be the first step toward creating a new feminist radicalism, whose interracial, interclass bonds go deeper than lowest-common-denominator coalition politics.

One of the women at the meeting suggested that I read *Sally Hemings,* Barbara Chase-Riboud's controversial historical novel about Thomas Jefferson's black mistress. I found it a devastating study of the psychology of masters and slaves, the politics of romantic love, the relations between black and white women, and the institution of the family. Much of its power lies in the way the author merges the race and sex of each character into a seamless whole, bringing home the point that to abstract these categories is already to falsify experience. So long as whiteness and maleness remain the norm, white women can think of themselves as "women," black men as "blacks"; but black women, doubly the Other, must be constantly aware of their dual identity at the same time that they suffer from both racial and sexual invisibility. In forcing the rest of us to see them, they also present us with new and far less tidy pictures of ourselves.

This suggests that confronting the oppression of black women means more than taking in new information or taking up new issues. It also means questioning the intellectual frameworks that the (male-dominated) black and (white-dominated) feminist movements have set up. If race and sex are experientially inseparable, can we (should we) still analyze them separately? If all women are subject to male supremacy—yet black and white women play out their relations with men (both inside and outside their own communities) in different ways—do they still have a common core of female experience, a common political oppression *as women*? Theoretically, the different situations of black women and black men should raise the same sort of question. But in practice black women have tended to single out their relation to white women and feminism as the more painful, problematic issue. This subject is now bursting through a decade's sediment of sloganeering, ritualistic condemnations, and liberal apologies to inform some provocative new writing.

But first, I feel I have to say something about Angela Davis. Her *Women, Race, and Class* may have been inspired by all this ferment, but the kindest judgment I can make is that it misses the point. From Davis's orthodox Marxist perspective (still CP after all these years!), in which economic relations determine all, while sexual relations have no material status and sexism is merely a set of bad attitudes, the question of how racial and sexual politics interact loses its meaning: Davis strips racism of its psychocultural dimension and treats it strictly as a form of economic exploitation; she tends to ignore sexism altogether, except when invoking it as an excuse for white bourgeois feminists to undermine the struggles of black and working people. (For instance, she rightly condemns the racism of white suffragists outraged at the prospect that black men would get the vote before white women—but rationalizes the sexism that prompted black men to sell out women of both races by agreeing that the black male vote should have priority. Black men's "sexist attitudes," Davis argues, were "hardly a sound reason for arresting the progress of the overall struggle for Black liberation"—and never mind the effect on that struggle of denying the vote to half the black population.) Still, it would be a mistake to simply dismiss Davis's book as an anachronism. In more subtle and ambiguous forms, its brand of left antifeminism continues to influence women's thinking. Besides, Angela Davis is a public figure, and *Women, Race, and Class* will undoubtedly outsell both the books I'm about to discuss.

Gloria I. Joseph is black; Jill Lewis is white. In *Common Differences: Conflicts in Black and White Feminist Perspectives,* they attempt to explore their separate histories, confront misunderstandings, and move toward "collaborative struggle." The book has the flavor of an open-ended political conversation; for the most part the authors write separate chapters, each commenting from her own perspective on various aspects of sexual politics. The result is uneven, full of intellectual loose ends and contradictions, and both writers have an unfortunate penchant for clotted, obfuscatory prose. But *Common Differences* does help to clarify touchy areas of black-white conflict. Joseph's chapters—which taught me a lot, especially about black mothers and daughters—are a valuable counterweight (and an implicit rebuke) to the tendency of white feminist theorists to base their generalizations about the female condition on white women's experience. In discussing black women's lives, Joseph uses a time-honored feminist method: she records group discussions and individual comments, picks out common themes and contradictions, and tries to draw conclusions. The immediacy of this material exposes white feminist parochialism more effectively than any abstract argument.

Without denying the movement's shortcomings, Lewis sets out to debunk the stereotype of the spoiled, elitist "women's libber." The feminist movement, she maintains, deserves recognition as the only social movement to challenge the status of women as women. She argues that white feminists have been struggling toward a deeper understanding of race and class, and that even those sectors of the movement most narrowly oriented to white middle-class concerns "have engaged in and won concrete struggles that potentially open up new terrain for *all* women."

In their introduction, Joseph and Lewis agree that "as a political movement, women's liberation did and does touch on questions which in different ways affect *all* women's lives." But *Common Differences* is much more about difference than about commonality. In *Ain't I a Woman: Black Women and Feminism* bell hooks strides boldly beyond pluralism to the rockier ground of synthesis. While hooks also stresses the uniqueness of black women's experience and the ways it has been discounted, her aim is to enlarge the theoretical framework of feminism. To this end she analyzes black women's condition in a historical context, tracing the basic patterns of black female oppression to slavery and developing three intertwined themes: black men's sexism, white women's racism, and the effect of white men's racial-sexual politics on the relations between black and white women. Hooks is a contentious writer, and I don't always agree with her contentions, but *Ain't I a Woman* has an intellectual vitality and daring that should set new standards for the discussion of race and sex.

The central political question these books raise is why the contemporary feminist movement has been so white. Most critics of the movement have offered a simple answer: white feminists' racism has driven black women away. This indictment is true as far as it goes, but it already takes for granted facts that need explaining. Why, in the first place, was it primarily white women, rather than black women or both groups simultaneously, who felt impelled to mobilize against sexism? And why did so many politically conscious black women reject the movement (in some cases the very idea of feminism) out of hand, rather than insisting that it purge its theory and practice of racism, or organizing groups committed to a nonracist feminist politics? Antifeminist leftists have typically argued that sexual politics are inherently a white middle-class crotchet, irrelevant to women who are "really"—i.e., economically and racially—oppressed. Or else (this is Angela Davis's main strategy) they redefine feminism to mean women fighting together against racism and capitalism, and conclude that black and white working-class women have been the leaders of the *real* feminist struggle. Either way they imply that sexism is not a problem for black women, if indeed it is a problem at all.

Hooks, Joseph, and Lewis reject this idea. They assume that black women have a stake in women's liberation, and see white feminists' racism as part of a complex social history that has shaped black women's politics. Bell hooks argues that estrangement between black and white women goes all the way back to slavery. The terms of the conflict, as she sees it, were defined by white men who applied racism to a Victorian sexual (and class) ideology that divided women into two categories: good (chaste, delicate, to be protected and idealized) and bad (licentious, unrefined, to be exploited and punished). While the white upper-class southern woman represented the feminine ideal, black female slaves were stigmatized, in schizoid fashion, both as bad women—therefore deserving to be raped and beaten—and as nonwomen: in doing the same work as men, black women threatened the ideology of female inferiority, a contradiction resolved by defining them as neuter beasts of burden.

At the same time, the white woman's power to collaborate in oppressing blacks softened and obscured the reality of her own inferior position. She exercised this power most directly over female slaves, whom she often treated with the special viciousness of the insecure boss. No doubt the degraded status of black women also reminded her, subconsciously at least, of what can happen to any female who provokes men into dropping the mask of patriarchal benevolence. As hooks observes, the manifest cruelty of white women's own husbands, fathers, and brothers "served as a warning of what might be their fate should they not maintain a passive stance. Surely, it must have occurred to white women that were enslaved black women not available to bear the brunt of such intense antiwoman aggression, they themselves might have been the victims." As a result, the very identification that might have led white women to black women's defense probably had the opposite effect. White men's sexual pursuit of black women also exposed white women's humiliating position: they could neither prevent their husbands' behavior nor claim a comparable freedom for themselves. Instead they expressed their anger, salvaged their pride, and defended their own good-woman status by vilifying black women as seducers and sluts.

Hooks shows that what she calls the "devaluation of black womanhood" did not end with slavery but remains a potent source of black women's rage. Her account of how black women are systematically disparaged as whores, castrating matriarchs, and sexless mammies explains a crucial ingredient of black female hostility to the women's movement. Clearly, when white feminists ignored black female experience and in effect equated "woman" with "white woman," the insult had a double meaning for black women: it suggested that we were not only reinforcing white supremacy but trying to have it both ways by preserving our monopoly on femininity and its rewards (respect, status, financial support) while demanding the option of rejecting it. This perception of bad faith fueled the angry denunciations of feminism as "white women's business."

But envying white women's "femininity" is a trap for black women, as hooks is well aware. Idealization of the white woman's status has tended to divert black women from demanding sexual justice to attacking black men for their inability to support stay-at-home wives. Many black women have endorsed black male demands for female subservience in the hope that at last they would get a crack at the pedestal. At the same time, their envy of white women has been mixed with contempt, an emotion that led some black women to insist they didn't need a movement because they were already liberated. Another illusion in hooks's relentless catalogue: strength in adversity and the need to make a living are not the same thing as freedom.

Gloria Joseph emphasizes the painful collisions of black and female identity. As she says, "an individual cannot be two separate entities." Yet black women suffer from two modes of oppression and so are implicated, like it or not, in two social movements at once. At best this involves a double burden, at worst a continuing conflict of loyalties and priorities. Joseph shows that deep ambivalences permeate black women's thinking—on black men (distrust and antagonism mixed with solidarity, affection, and protectiveness), on sex ("a 'desirable no-no,' an 'attractive nuisance'"), on feminism itself (most of Joseph's respondents reject the movement but endorse its goals). Her argument suggests that black women have been slow to commit themselves to feminism—especially the more radical aspects of sexual politics—for fear of weakening their ties with the black community and the black struggle. Jill Lewis points out that white middle-class women could focus single-mindedly on feminism because "they did not have the stakes of *racial* unity or solidarity with White men that the Black women had with Black men" and because their privileges left them "free of the survival struggles that are priorities for minority and working-class women." If anything, class and racial privileges (particularly education) spurred their consciousness of sexual injustice by raising expectations that were thwarted purely because they were women.

Ironically, Joseph exemplifies the dilemma she describes: like many other black women who define themselves as feminists, she draws the line at calling black men oppressors. While Joseph and Lewis agree that black and white women are oppressed as women, they uncritically assume that male supremacy is a product of white culture, and that the concept does not really apply to male-female relations among blacks, except insofar as all white institutions and values shape black life. Lewis asserts that institutionalized sexism in America was imported by European immigrants, as if Native American, African, and other nonwhite cultures were free of male dominance. In fact, no anthropologist, feminist or otherwise, has ever come up with convincing evidence of a culture in which some form of male dominance does not exist.

Lewis and Joseph argue that because black men do not have the same worldly power as white men, "Male dominance as a salient problematic factor in male-female sexual relationships cannot be considered as a universal trait applicable to all men." But Joseph's own descriptions of black women's attitudes toward sex, men, and marriage—not to mention their struggles to bring up children alone—belie this view. Rather, her evidence confirms that despite black men's economic and social subordination to whites they share with all men certain male supremacist prerogatives, including physical and sexual aggression, the assumption of male superiority, and refusal to share responsibility for child rearing and housework. Joseph and Lewis also make the puzzling claim that sexist repression is more severe for white women because "Black women can be kept in their places via racism alone." Does racism alone account for black women's oppression as mothers, workers (including domestic workers), welfare recipients, prostitutes, victims of rape and sexual exploitation?

All this adds up to a bad case of conceptual confusion. You can't simultaneously agree that black women need feminism and deny the basic premise of feminism—that men have power over women. Women who engage in this form of doublethink still have a toe or two in the camp of left antifeminism; while rejecting crude economism of the Angela Davis variety, they assume that sexism is perpetuated not by men in general but by a white capitalist ruling class.

Hooks insists on the reality of black male sexism. Discussing the experience of female slaves, she angrily refutes the cliché that "the most cruel and dehumanizing impact of slavery . . . was that black men were stripped of their masculinity." This idea, she argues, merely reflects the sexist assumption that men's experience is more important than women's and that "the worst that can happen to a man is that he be made to assume the social status of woman." In fact, though all slaves suffered brutal oppression, "black men were allowed to maintain some semblance of their societally defined masculine role." Noting that American blacks came from African patriarchal cultures, hooks rejects the idea that black men learned sexism from whites and the myth (repeated once again by Angela Davis) that within the slave community men and women were equal. On the contrary, the slaves accepted the concept of male superiority, and black families maintained a sexual division of labor, with women doing the cooking, cleaning, and child care. Nor did slaveholders assign black men "women's work." Black women, however, were forced by their white masters to perform both "masculine" and "feminine" functions, working alongside black men at backbreaking labor in the fields, while also serving as houseworkers, breeders, and sexual objects.

Hooks implicitly links what she sees as black women's false consciousness about sexism with their political isolation: while the sexism of black male activists has forced black women to choose between asserting themselves as women and maintaining racial solidarity, the racism of white feminists has reinforced and justified that split. *Ain't I a Woman* describes how this combination of pressures undermined black women's efforts to participate in both 19th and 20th century feminist movements. In dissecting the rhetoric of the contemporary black and women's movements, hooks shows how sexism has been promoted as a cure for racism, sisterhood as a rationale for ignoring it. Black power advocates, confusing liberation with the assertion of their "manhood," embraced a white man's contention that a black matriarchy was the cause of their problems, and called on black women to advance the black cause by being submissive; some even suggested that sexual equality was a white racist idea, indicative of the white man's effeteness and decadence. Black Muslims tried to reverse the racist Victorian paradigm, defining black women as the feminine ideal and white women as devils (and establishing rigid patriarchal families).

Meanwhile the early radical feminists were claiming that the division between men and women was the most basic social hierarchy, and that since men had ruled every known political system, racism was basically a male problem ("men dominate women, a few men dominate the rest"—Redstockings Manifesto). This analysis, which I and most of my political cohort then subscribed to, has had a good deal of influence on the movement as a whole. It has two erroneous implications: that it's impossible for white women to oppress black men, and that racial conflict between black women and white women has no objective basis, but is (on both sides) an inauthentic antagonism that only serves the interests of men. Radical feminists understood, theoretically, that to build female unity white women had to oppose racism and change their own racist attitudes and behavior. We were sharply critical of liberal feminists who defined women's freedom in terms of professional careers and formal equality within a racist, class-stratified social system. Yet emotionally our belief that sex was a more basic division than race allowed us to evade responsibility for racism. It was tempting to imagine that simply by doing what we wanted most passionately to do—build a radical feminist movement—we would also be fighting racism; tempting, too, to play down how much we benefited from being white. For a while feminism seemed a way out of the classic bind of white middle-class radicals: we no longer had to see ourselves as privileged people wondering where we fit into the revolutionary struggle; we too were part of an oppressed class with a historic destiny.

Hooks's anger at this refusal to be accountable is well-deserved. But when she gets down to specifics, she tends to oversimplify and at times rewrite history. In her indictment of "white upper and middle-class feminists" (Abby Rockefeller aside, who are these upper-class feminists I keep hearing about?), the movement becomes a monolith. The political differences between liberals and radicals, the social conditions that allowed the former to co-opt and isolate the latter, the fierce intramovement debates about race and class are ignored or dismissed. White feminists' main aim, hooks charges, has been to join the male power structure; the movement has posed no threat to the system.

This is silly. The women's movement has been no more or less opportunistic than the black movement, the labor movement, or any other mass movement successful enough to attract power mongers. Feminists have not succeeded in making a revolution (neither, I believe, has the rest of the left), but—as Jill Lewis ably argues—we did create a new political arena and set a revolutionary process in motion. (Among other things, we established the political context in which a book like *Ain't I a Woman* can be written and read.) The best measure of our threat to the system is the virulence of the reaction against us.

Hooks also indulges in overkill when she tries to explain white feminists' appropriation of female experience in terms of two different, even contradictory forms of racism. My own view is that the right explanation is the obvious one: we were acting on the unconscious racist assumption that our experience was representative, along with the impulse to gloss over racial specificities so as to keep the "complication" of racism from marring our vision of female unity. Hooks makes these points, but she also argues that white feminists have shared the racist/sexist perception of black women as nonwomen. In the process she accuses white feminists of claiming that black women are oppressed only by racism, not sexism, and denying that black men can be oppressive. These charges are, to put it mildly, befuddling. If there was any point radical feminists insisted on it was that all women were oppressed because of their sex, and that all men had the power to oppress women. In response, antifeminist black women (along with black and white male leftists) made the arguments hooks now puts in our mouths, and denounced us as racists for attributing a "white problem" to black people. Inevitably, many white women have echoed these arguments, but it's perverse to blame feminists for them.

In fact, white feminists have generally been quite conscious of black women *as women*; it's their blackness we've had trouble with. Straightforward reactionary racism exaggerates differences and denies commonalities; liberal racism, more typical of white feminists, does the opposite. Since the denial of black women's "femininity" is such a central issue for hooks, she mistakenly assumes that protecting an exclusive claim to femininity is equally an issue for all white women. On the contrary, white feminists felt free to challenge received definitions of femininity because we took for granted our right to be considered women. And it was precisely because our claim to womanhood was not an issue for us that we were insensitive to black women's pain at being denied it by racial fiat. Many white feminists recognized that the division between white women and black women had something to do with good girls and bad girls. (Shulamith Firestone, in *The Dialectic of Sex,* discusses this idea at length.) What we didn't see was the asymmetry: we could decide to be bad, or play at being bad; black women had no choice.

Hooks's misperception of white feminists' psychology also leads her to argue that their analogies between women and blacks were designed "to evoke in the minds of racist white men an image of white womanhood being degraded" by association with black people, especially black men. Again, the "image of white womanhood" had much less resonance than hooks imagines, either for white feminists or for the white liberal and leftist men who were our immediate targets. The main reason that '60s feminists relied so heavily on comparisons between sexism and racism is that white male politicos recognized the race issue as morally legitimate, while dismissing feminism as "a bunch of chicks with personal problems." If anything, we were trying to evoke in these men the same guilt about sexism that they already felt about racism; since we hadn't yet experienced the drawbacks of liberal guilt, we craved its validation. We also hoped, naively enough, to convince black men to renounce their sexism and identify with the feminist cause.

Hooks takes a hard line on analogies between women and blacks. She argues that they always imply a comparison between white women and black men, that they make black women invisible, obscure the issue of white women's racial privilege, and divert attention from racism to white women's problems. Certainly racial-sexual analogies have been misused in all the ways hooks cites, but I don't see these misuses as either invariable or necessary. Many feminists have made analogies between women and blacks in full awareness that they are talking about two overlapping groups; what they mean to compare is two sets of oppressive relations, male-female and white-black. And though the dynamics and effects of racism and sexism differ in important ways, the parallels—legal, social, ideological—do exist. Which is why antiracist movements have been so instrumental in stimulating feminist consciousness and revolt.

Hooks refuses to recognize this. Scoffing at the idea that abolitionism inspired the first feminist wave, she says, "No 19th century white woman could grow to maturity without an awareness of institutionalized sexism." But of course 19th century white women—and for that matter my generation of white women—did exactly that. It is the essence of institutionalized sexism to pose as the natural order; to experience male dominance is one thing, to understand that it is political, therefore changeable, is quite another. For me and most feminists I know, that politicizing process was very much influenced by the civil rights and black power movements. Conversely, though feminism was not a miraculous antidote to our racist impulses and illusions, it did increase our understanding of racism.

Surely, the answer to exploitative comparisons between women and blacks is not to deny the organic link between antisexist and antiracist politics. Here hooks, too, gets trapped in contradictory thinking. She argues that the issues of racism and sexism cannot really be separated, yet she repeatedly singles out racism as an issue that is not only separate from sexism but prior to it. According to hooks, "American society is one in which racial imperialism supersedes sexual imperialism," and all black people, black men included, are absolutely lower on the social scale than any white woman. In other words, it is illegitimate for feminists to regard sexism as a category that can, at least theoretically, be abstracted from (and compared to) racism; but no comparable stricture applies to black liberationists.

Gloria Joseph agrees that, "In the end, it is a question of priorities, and given the nature of racism in this country, it should be obvious that the Black liberation struggle claims first priority." Most black feminists whose views I know about take a similar position. It is easy to see why: because racism is intertwined with, and in part defined by class oppression, black people as a group suffer an excruciating combination of economic hardship and social indignity that white middle-class women and even most white working-class women escape. (Of course this does not necessarily hold true for individuals—it can be argued that a middle-class educated black man is a lot better off than a white welfare mother from an Appalachian rural slum.) Besides, as hooks points out, women without the insulation of racial or class privilege are also the most vulnerable to sexist oppression: a white professional woman can buy liberation from housework by hiring a black maid; she can also (for the time being) buy the legal abortion Medicaid patients are denied.

Left antifeminists have often used this line of reasoning to suggest that sexual issues should wait until racism and poverty are abolished. Black feminists, by definition, have rejected that idea. But what then does it mean, in practical political terms, to say that despite the irreducibly dual character of black women's oppression, their sex is less immediate an issue than their race? Specifically, what does this imply for the prospect of an antiracist feminist movement, or, more modestly, "collaborative struggle"?

While hooks never really focuses on strategic questions, Joseph and Lewis often write as if black and white women are on fundamentally separate tracks. They refer, for instance, to "White feminism," a concept as self-contradictory as, say, "male socialism"; while one can speak of a feminism limited and flawed by white racist bias, it is *feminism* only to the extent that it challenges the subjection of women as a group. (The mechanical pluralism underlying the notion of separate-but-equal "White" and "Black" feminisms also impels the authors to capitalize "White." Though capitalizing "Black" may make sense as a polemical device for asserting black pride, racial self-assertion by white people is something else again.) But in discussing abortion, Jill Lewis endorses a specific approach to integrating feminism with race and class struggle. The strategy she describes has developed as a response to the abortion backlash, but the basic idea could be applied to almost any feminist issue. Since I think it's both appealing and fallacious, I want to discuss it in some detail.

Lewis argues that to "isolate" abortion as an issue and defend it in terms of freedom for women betrays a white middle-class bias: since black women suffer not only from being denied safe abortions but from sterilization abuse, inadequate health care, and poverty—all of which impinge on their reproductive choices—a radical approach to "reproductive rights" must address all these concerns. The trouble with this logic is that abortion is not just one of many medical or social services being rolled back by Reaganism; nor does the present opposition to abortion stem from the same sources or political motives as pressure toward sterilization. Abortion is first of all the key issue of the new right's antifeminist campaign, the ground on which a larger battle over the very idea of women's liberation is being fought. In essence, the antiabortionists are arguing that women who assert their free agency and refuse to be defined by their childbearing capacity are immoral. (In contrast, no one defends poverty or forced sterilization on principle.) So long as this moral attack on women is gaining ground, presenting abortion primarily as a health or social welfare measure is ineffective because it evades the underlying issue. Our choice right now is to defend abortion as a pivotal issue of women's freedom, or lose the battle by default. This is not to belittle the urgency of opposing sterilization abuse (which is, among other things, another expression of contempt for black femaleness) or demanding better health care. Nor is it to deny that all these issues are linked in important ways. My point is only that the reproductive rights strategy does not resolve the touchy question of priorities. Rather, while purporting to cover all bases, it submerges sexual politics in an economic and social welfare program.

Is this good for black women? Gloria Joseph points out that on the issue of abortion rights, "Black women have even more at stake, since it is they who suffer more from illegal and abusive abortions." They also suffer more from having unwanted children under horrendous conditions. If a sexual-political strategy offers the only real chance to preserve legal abortion and restore public funding, it is clearly in black women's interest. Since black women are faced with so many urgent problems, they may well have other priorities, but it doesn't follow that white women who concentrate on abortion are indulging a racist bias. On the contrary, they're doing a crucial job that will benefit all women in the end.

All this suggests that the question of whether racism is worse (or more basic, or more pressing) than sexism matters less than the fact that both are intolerable. I don't agree with the white feminists bell hooks castigates for dismissing racial differences on the grounds that "oppression cannot be measured." It's clear to me that in demonstrable ways, some oppressed people are worse off than others. But I do question whose interests are really served by the measuring. Once it's established that black women are the most victimized group, and that most black men are more victimized than most white women—then what?

In my experience, this kind of ranking does not lead to a politics of genuine liberation, based on mutual respect and cooperation among oppressed groups, but instead provokes a politics of *ressentiment,* competition, and guilt. Black men tend to react not by recognizing the sexual oppression of black women but by rationalizing their antifeminism as a legitimate response to white women's privilege. White women who are sensitive to the imputation of racism tend to become hesitant and apologetic about asserting feminist grievances. As for white women who can't see beyond their own immediate interests, attempts to demote them in the ranks of the oppressed do nothing but make them feel unjustly attacked and confirmed in their belief that sexual and racial equality are separate, competing causes. The ultimate results are to reinforce left antifeminism, weaken feminist militance, widen the split between the black and feminist movements, and play into the divide and conquer tactics of white men ("We can do something for blacks or for women, but not both, so you folks fight it out"). Black women, caught in the racial-sexual crossfire, stand to lose the most.

Insistence on a hierarchy of oppression never radicalizes people, because the impulse behind it is moralistic. Its object is to get the "lesser victims" to stop being selfish, to agree that their own pain (however deeply they may feel it) is less serious and less deserving of attention (including their own) than someone else's. Its appeal is that it allows people at the bottom of social hierarchies to turn the tables and rule over a moral hierarchy of suffering and powerlessness. But whatever the emotional comfort of righteousness, it's a poor substitute for real change. And we ought to know by now that effective radical movements are not based on self-abnegation; rather, they emerge from the understanding that unless we heal the divisions among us, none of us can win.

The logic of competing oppressions does not heal divisions but intensifies them, since it invites endless and absurd extension—for every person who has no shoes, there is always someone who has no feet. (One might ask, by this logic, what bell hooks has to complain about next to a woman from a dirt-poor Third World country who was sold to her husband and had her clitoris cut off at age four.) White women will not become committed allies of black women because they're told that their own suffering is unimportant. What white women must be convinced of is that it's impossible to have it both ways—that the privileges we cling to are an insuperable obstacle to the freedom and equality we long for. We need to learn this lesson again and again. Good books help.

Village Voice Literary Supplement, June 1982

Radical Feminism and Feminist Radicalism

I was a radical feminist activist in the late 60s. Today I often have the odd feeling that this period, so vivid to me, occurred fifty years ago, not a mere fifteen. Much of the early history of the women's liberation movement, and especially of radical feminism (which was not synonymous with the w.l.m. but a specific political current within it) has been lost, misunderstood or distorted beyond recognition. The left, the right and liberal feminists have all for their own reasons contributed to misrepresenting and trivializing radical feminist ideas. To add to the confusion, radical feminism in its original sense barely exists today. The great majority of women who presently call themselves "radical feminists" in fact subscribe to a politics more accurately labeled "cultural feminist." That is, they see the primary goal of feminism as freeing women from the imposition of so-called "male values," and creating an alternative culture based on "female values." Cultural feminism is essentially a moral, countercultural movement aimed at redeeming its participants, while radical feminism began as a political movement to end male supremacy in all areas of social and economic life, and rejected the whole idea of opposing male and female natures and values as a sexist idea, a basic part of what we were fighting. Though cultural feminism came out of the radical feminist movement, the premises of the two tendencies are antithetical. Yet on the left and elsewhere the distinction is rarely made.

Along with simply wanting to retrieve this history (my history), I think it's crucial for understanding what happened to the women's movement later, and what's happening now. In the first couple of years of its existence, radical feminism showed every sign of becoming a true mass movement. We had enormous energy and enthusiasm and used a variety of tactics—demonstrations and speakouts; tireless organizing among friends and coworkers, on street corners, in supermarkets and ladies' rooms; above all, a prodigious output of leaflets, pamphlets, journals, magazine articles, newspaper and radio and TV interviews. The movement exploded into public consciousness, pushed the National Organization for Women and other liberal feminist organizations way to the left, and grew so fast that existing groups didn't know what to do with the influx of new members. Organized radical feminist activism was most visible and prominent in New York City, Boston and Washington, D.C. and on the West Coast, but myriads of small groups inspired by radical feminist ideas sprang up all over the country.

It was radical feminism that put women's liberation on the map, that got sexual politics recognized as a public issue, that created the vocabulary ("consciousness-raising," "the personal is political," "sisterhood is powerful," etc.) with which the second wave of feminism entered popular culture. Radical feminists sparked the drive to legalize abortion and created the atmosphere of urgency in which liberal feminists were finally able to get the Equal Rights Amendment through Congress and most of the states. Radical feminists were also the first to demand total equality in the so-called private sphere—equal sharing of housework and child care, equal attention to our emotional and sexual needs. It's no exaggeration to say that the immense transformation in women's consciousness over the past fifteen years has been inspired by the issues radical feminists raised. One exasperating example of how easy it is to obliterate history is that Betty Friedan can now get away with the outrageous claim that radical feminist "extremism" turned women off and derailed the movement she built. Radical feminism turned women on, by the thousands.

Yet this movement collapsed as quickly as it had grown. By 1975 radical feminism had given way to cultural feminism. The women's liberation movement had become the women's movement, in which liberals were the dominant, not to say hegemonic force. Socialist and Marxist feminism, which had come out of other tendencies of the w.l.m. and segments of the left influenced by it, were theoretically confused and practically marginal.[1] Feminism had become a reformist politics, a countercultural community, and a network of self-help projects (rape crisis centers, battered women's shelters, women's health clinics, etc.).

How and why did this happen? Like other left social movements, feminism had to contend with the institutional and ideological power of American liberalism, which succeeded in marginalizing radical feminists while channeling the aspirations they aroused into demands for reform on the one hand, a cult of the individual "liberated woman" on the other. In addition, radical feminism had surfaced only a short time before the expansive prosperity and utopian optimism of the 60s succumbed to an era of economic limits and political backlash. The conservative retrenchment of the 70s had a critical negative impact, not only in strengthening political resistance to feminist demands but in constricting women's personal choices, making rebellion of any sort more difficult and risky, and undermining faith in the movement's more radical possibilities. Yet these external pressures, heavy as they were, do not wholly explain why radical feminism fell apart so easily and thoroughly. Contradictions within the movement, problems with its basic assumptions, played a crucial role. I joined New York Radical Women, the first women's liberation group in New York City, in 1968, about a year after it had started meeting. By that time the group was deeply divided over what came to be called (by radical feminists) the "politico-feminist split." The "politicos'" primary commitment was to the new left. They saw capitalism as the source of women's oppression: the ruling class indoctrinated us with oppressive sex roles to promote consumerism and/or keep women a cheap reserve labor force and/or divide the workers; conventional masculine and feminine attitudes were matters of bourgeois conditioning from which we must all liberate ourselves. I sided with the "feminists," who at some point began calling themselves "radical feminists." We argued that male supremacy was in itself a systemic form of domination—a set of material, institutionalized relations, not just bad attitudes. Men had power and privilege and like any other ruling class would defend their interests; challenging that power required a revolutionary movement of women. And since the male-dominated left would inevitably resist understanding or opposing male power, the radical feminist movement must be autonomous, create its own theory and set its own priorities. Our model of course was black power—a number of the early radical feminists had been civil rights activists.

Though new leftists immediately accused the radical feminists of being bourgeois and antileft, in fact nearly all of us considered ourselves leftists of one kind or another—socialists, anarchists, pacifists, new leftists of various stripes. When I joined women's liberation I had no ongoing, organizational ties with the left and my politics were a somewhat confused blend of cultural radicalism, populism and Marxism, but I certainly thought of myself as a leftist. With few exceptions, those of us who first defined radical feminism took for granted that "radical" implied antiracist, anticapitalist and anti-imperialist. We saw ourselves as radicalizing the left by expanding the definition of radical to include feminism. In accordance with that definition, we agreed that until the left embraced feminism, our movement should not work with leftist men or male-dominated left groups, except perhaps for ad hoc coalitions. Some feminists argued that it was also against women's interests to join left groups as individuals; others continued to work with men on various left issues and projects. Either way, we assumed that building an autonomous radical feminist power base would further the struggle for sexual equality in mixed left organizations, just as in other arenas. We took for granted the need for a radical, feminist left.

What we didn't do—at least not in any systematic way—was tackle the question of how to integrate a feminist perspective with an overall radical politics. At that stage of the movement it would have been premature. Our overriding priority was to argue, against pervasive resistance, that male-female relations were indeed a valid political issue, and to begin describing, analyzing and challenging those relations. We were really on uncharted territory, and trying to explore that territory while under very heavy pressure from the left and from the "politicos" in the w.l.m. to subordinate feminist questions to traditional leftist concerns. It's hard to convey to people who didn't go through that experience how radical, how unpopular and difficult and scary it was just to get up and say, "Men oppress women. Men have oppressed me. Men must take responsibility for their actions instead of blaming them on capitalism. And yes, that means you." We were laughed at, patronized, called frigid, emotionally disturbed man-haters and—worst insult of all on the left!—apolitical.

In retrospect I see that we were faced with an insoluble contradiction. To build a women's liberation movement we had to take male supremacy out of the context of social domination in general. Yet from the very beginning we ran into problems of theory and strategy that could only be resolved within a larger context. Radical feminists professed a radical skepticism toward existing political theories, directed as they were toward the study of "man," and emphasized "consciousness-raising"—the process of sharing and analyzing our own experience in a group—as the primary method of understanding women's condition. This process, so often misunderstood and disparaged as a form of therapy, uncovered an enormous amount of information about women's lives and insights into women's oppression, and was the movement's most successful organizing tool. Yet the emphasis on personal experience tended to obscure and mystify the fact that we all interpreted our experience through the filter of prior political and philosophical assumptions. (For that matter, the idea of basing one's theory on shared personal experience came from the Chinese revolution's "Speak pains to recall pains" via the black movement's "Tell it like it is.")

Many debates on feminist issues were really debates about differing overall world views. For example, when a group of radical feminists did consciousness-raising on sex, we discovered that most of the women who testified preferred monogamous relationships, and that pressure for more sexual freedom came mostly from men (at that point, heterosexuality was a more or less unchallenged assumption). There were a lot of arguments about how to interpret that material (did it represent these women's true desires, their objective interest given a sexist culture, or the psychology of the oppressed) and what to make of the minority who disagreed (was the difference in their situation or their emotional makeup, did they have false consciousness, or what). And to a large extent the differing positions that emerged depended on whether one viewed sexuality from a psychoanalytical perspective (my own ideas were very much influenced by Wilhelm Reich), a behaviorist perspective, a Simone de Beauvoirist existential humanist perspective or an orthodox Marxist rejection of psychological categories as unmaterialist. Despite its oppositional stance toward the existing left, radical feminism was deeply influenced by Marxism. While many w.l.m.

"politicos" tried to fit women's liberation into pre-existing Marxist categories, radical feminists appropriated certain Marxist ideas and assumptions (specifically, concepts of class interest, class struggle, and materialism) and applied them to male-female relations. Maoism, especially, was instrumental in shaping radical feminist ideas about the nature of power and oppression.

Though radical feminists did not deny being influenced by the ideas of other radical movements (on the contrary, we often pointed to those continuities as evidence of our own revolutionary commitment), we acted as if it were somehow possible for women to separate their ideas about feminism from their ideas about everything else. There was an unarticulated assumption that we could work out our differences solely within a feminist framework and ignore or agree to disagree on other political issues. Again, I think that assumption was necessary, in order to create a feminist framework to begin with, but it made for a very fragile kind of solidarity—and it also excluded large groups of women. The question of why the radical feminist movement was overwhelmingly white and mostly middle class is complex, but one reason is surely that most black and working-class women could not accept the abstraction of feminist issues from race and class issues, since the latter were so central to their lives.

At the same time, the narrowness of the movement's demographic base limited the value of generalizations about women and men based on feminists' personal experience. So another of the problems in interpreting data gleaned from consciousness-raising was, to what extent did it reveal patterns of male-female relations in general, and to what extent did it reflect the situation of women in particular social groups?

I don't want to be misunderstood—I think consciousness-raising did reveal a lot about male-female relations in general. In basic ways women's subordination crosses class, racial and cultural lines and it was a strength of radical feminism to insist on that reality. (We also insisted, rightly in my opinion, that male dominance had to be understood as a transhistorical phenomenon, though we didn't use that language. In effect we challenged historicism as an adequate conceptual framework for understanding politics—a challenge that's since arisen in other quarters.) I'll go further and claim that in accumulating detailed information about the interaction of men and women on a day-to-day level, the consciousness-raising process contributed important insights into the nature of power relations in general—not only sexism.

Still, our lack of attention to social differences among women did limit and distort both our analysis and our practice, and it's hard to see how that could have been avoided without reference to a politics about other forms of social domination. When the minority of radical feminists who were working class or from working-class backgrounds began to challenge class bias within the movement, the same problem arose: the movement had no agreed-on politics of class that we could refer to, beyond the assumption that class hierarchy was oppressive. And again the dilemma was that to turn our attention to building such a politics would conflict with the imperatives of the specifically feminist project that had just barely begun.

Very early in the game radical feminists tried to make an end run around this problem by advancing the thesis that women's oppression was not only the oldest and most universal form of domination but the primary form. We argued that other kinds of hierarchy grew out of and were modeled on male supremacy—were in effect specialized forms of male supremacy. This idea has a surface logic, given that all the hierarchical systems we know about have been ruled and shaped by men. But it's a false logic, I think, because it assumes that men in creating and maintaining these systems are acting purely *as men,* in accordance with peculiarly male characteristics or specifically male supremacist objectives. It implicitly denies that the impulse to dominate, or to use a more materialist formulation, an authoritarian response to certain conditions of life, could be a universal human characteristic that women share, even if they have mostly lacked the opportunity to exercise it. It's a logic that excludes women from history not only practically but ontologically, and it leads to an unrealistic view of women as a more or less undifferentiated underclass with no real stake in the power struggles of class, race and so on that go on among groups of men.

This notion of women's oppression as the primary oppression was very appealing for several reasons. It was a way of countering the left's insistence that class oppression was primary and women's liberation at best a subsidiary struggle—we could claim that on the contrary, all previous revolutions were mere reformist preludes to the real thing. It allowed white middle-class women to minimize the ways in which women participated in and benefited from race and class privilege. Most important, I think, it seemed to offer a resolution to the contradiction I've been talking about: it held out the possibility that a feminist theory could also be a general theory of social transformation. For all these reasons I fairly uncritically bought this thesis—helped to sell it, in fact.

By 1969, radical feminists were beginning to meet in their own small groups. The first group to publicly espouse a radical feminist line was Redstockings, a spinoff from New York Radical Women, which Shulamith Firestone and I started early in 1969. Shortly after that, the October 17th Movement, a radical split-off from NOW led by Ti-Grace Atkinson, changed its name to The Feminists and proclaimed itself a radical feminist organization. These groups, which were both very influential in the movement, developed distinctive and opposing political stances.

Redstockings' dominant political tendency was a kind of neo-Maoist materialism. In addition to the belief in personal experience as the bedrock of feminist theory, this perspective was grounded in two basic principles. One was a view of sexual class struggle as the direct exercise of power by men, acting in their economic, social and sexual self-interest, over women. In this view institutions were merely tools of the oppressor and had no political significance in and of themselves. The idea that systems (like the family or capitalism) are in some sense autonomous, that they operate according to a logic that in certain ways constrains the rulers as well as the ruled, was rejected as a mystification and a way of letting men off the hook. To say, for instance, that the family oppressed women was to evade the fact that our husbands and fathers oppressed us; to say that men's sexist behavior was in any way dictated by social or familial norms was to deny that men oppressed women by choice, out of self-interest. The other principle was that women's behavior was always and only a rational, self-interested response to their immediate material conditions, i.e., their oppression by men. When women appeared to consent to their oppression, it was because they saw that individual resistance would not get them what they wanted, but only invite the oppressor's anger and punishment. As we built a movement capable of winning real change, more and more women would feel free to speak up and act collectively in their own behalf. The "pro-woman line," as this position was called, was absolutely antipsychological. It rejected as misogynist psychological explanations for feminine submissiveness or passivity, since they implied that women collaborated in or were responsible for their oppression. Psychological explanations of men's behavior were regarded as yet another way to avoid blaming men for male supremacy.

The most articulate and systematic exponents of these ideas were Kathie Sarachild and Carol Hanisch, both former SNCC activists and founding members of New York Radical Women; Irene Peslikis, who wrote the classic article "Resistances to Consciousness"; and Pat Mainardi, author of "The Politics of Housework." I did not fully share these politics—I believed in the importance of the unconscious and thought the pro-woman line was simplistic—but I was profoundly influenced by them. They were quite effective in challenging my tendencies to over-psychologize everything when social explanations were staring me in the face, and to avoid confronting my painful personal relations with men by making abstract arguments about the system. The genius of the Redstockings brand of radical feminist materialism was its concreteness. It demanded that women examine their everyday lives and face the most immediate and direct sources of their pain and anger. For women who responded to that demand, the confrontations inspired a powerful and urgent desire to change things. Activism became a personal emotional necessity—always a more effective spur to organizing than abstract principle or moral sentiment—with specific and immediate as well as long-range goals. As a result the materialist version of radical feminism had by far the most impact on the larger society, in terms of changing women's view of themselves and the world and inspiring both individual rebellion and collective political action.

But the reductionism of the Redstockings line led to basic miscalculations. For one thing, it underestimated the difficulty of change. If, for instance, resistance to feminism or outright antifeminism among women comes solely from rational fears of the consequences of challenging male authority, then the way to combat it is simply to build a movement and convince women that sisterhood really is powerful—that organized and unified we can win. But suppose in addition to the rational fears and hopes, women suffer from deep unconscious convictions of their own powerlessness and worthlessness and the unlimited power of men? Suppose they unconsciously equate being a "good woman" in men's terms not only with survival but with redemption from utter degradation? If that's true, then the successes of a feminist movement may actually intensify women's fears along with their hopes, and provoke unbearable emotional conflict. And that can lead not only to various forms of female antifeminist backlash, but to feminists managing in various ways to sabotage their own movement— even to redefine feminism so that it embraces and glorifies traditional feminine values. Both these things have in fact happened, and are continuing to happen, and it's impossible to understand these developments or confront them politically without a psychological critique. I won't belabor the parallels with the over-optimism of classical Marxism and its inability to explain why large numbers of European workers supported fascism.

Similarly, the dismissal of institutions as "mere tools" was an obstacle to understanding how change takes place, or fails to. It became an excuse not to really study the institutions that affect women, especially the family. From Redstockings' perspective, the problem with the family was simply male supremacy: women were subordinated within marriage and at the same time forced to marry for economic security and social legitimacy; we were assigned the care of children, but denied control of our fertility. Left criticism of the family per se was dismissed as men's resistance to committing themselves to women and children, emotionally and financially.

This analysis was superficial. To begin with it ignored the way the fundamental premise of the family system—the definition of a man, a woman and their biological children as the basic social unit, with the corresponding assumption that the community as a whole has little if any responsibility for children— automatically puts women in an unequal position. Maternity is obvious; paternity must be acknowledged or proved in some formal way. So women in a familialist system need marriage to establish the father's social obligation to his children, and this in itself gives men power to set the terms of the marriage contract. When women seek to change those terms without challenging the family system itself, they run into a double bind. Women's demands for equality in the home come up against male resistance, and if they press their demands "too far," the probable result is not an equal marriage, but no marriage at all. (This is not abstract speculation; conflict over equality is clearly an element in today's high divorce rate.) Of course, the demands would not be possible in the first place if women had not already won enough economic and sexual independence to survive outside marriage. But for a women in a familialist society the price of freedom to live independently is all too likely to be "freedom" to support and rear children alone or be unwillingly childless. Furthermore, the economic inequality rooted in the patriarchal family system actually worsens as women are denied access to men's incomes and single motherhood itself becomes a barrier to economic advancement.

In short, feminism inevitably destabilizes the family, and so long as the family remains an unquestioned given of social relations, women are trapped into choosing between subordination and abandonment. This is the specter haunting contemporary sexual politics, as antifeminist women desperately try to restore the traditional bargain and feminists as desperately try to have it both ways. There's no way to understand, let alone resolve, this dilemma without an institutional analysis. The problem with our system of child rearing, which is absolutely basic to the oppression of women, is not only sexism but familialism— the equation of biological and social parenthood. Unless it's understood that way, the best we'll ever get is a jerry-built system of day-care centers designed to allow women to keep their shit jobs, and here and there the inspiring example of a "nurturing father" who expects the Medal of Honor for doing what mothers have always done.

But again, if it's impossible to understand women's condition without making a real critique of the family as an institution, the radical feminist strategy of isolating male supremacy from other forms of domination breaks down. The family has more than one political dimension: besides subordinating women, it's also a vehicle for getting children of both sexes to submit to social authority and actively embrace the values of the dominant culture. Among other things that means enlisting both women and men to uphold the family system and its sexual morality, in which sex for its own sake is bad and dangerous and must be subordinated to the "higher" purposes of heterosexual monogamous marriage and procreation. True, men have always had more license to be "bad" than women and have even been *required* to be "bad" to prove their manhood. But all this means is that men experience a conflict between their sexual desire and identity and their "higher" nature—not, as radical feminists have tended to assume, that men are free of sexual guilt and repression. This conflict and its manifestations—the perception of sex and love as separate or opposed, and sex as connected with violence—are integral to the patriarchal concept of masculinity, while femininity, on the other hand, requires the suppression of "bad" desires and a romanticized, spiritualized eroticism.

The sexual revolution loosened the grip of conservative sexual morality but did not basically change its psychic underpinnings. We all to some degree internalize familialist sexual ideology in its feminine or masculine version. To the extent that any of us rejects it, we are rejecting being a woman or a man as the culture defines it and defining ourselves as social, sexual deviants, with all the consequences that entails. We are all oppressed by having this ideology imposed on us, though some groups are particularly oppressed—women, youth, homosexuals and other sexual minorities. So there is a political fault line in the society dividing people who are in one way or another defending this ideology (and the practices that go with it) from people who are in one way or another rebelling against it. This line cuts across gender, and like class or racial difference creates real divisions among women that can't simply be subsumed in an antisexist politics. It also defies analysis strictly in terms of the "self-interest" of one class of people oppressing another. Ultimately the interest of sexual conservatives in suppressing sexual dissidence is their interest in obliterating possibilities they themselves have painfully relinquished. This interest is so powerful that there are few sexual dissidents—and I would call feminists and unapologetic gays dissidents by definition—who are not also conservative in some ways.

While ignoring all these complications, Redstockings' vision of direct confrontation between sexual classes put an enormous premium on unity among women. The idea was that if all women supported each other in demanding equality—if there were no women willing to "scab"—then men would have no choice but to accept the new order. This was the model of struggle put forward in *Fanshen,* William Hinton's account of revolution in a Chinese village, which circulated widely in the movement. It was inspiring reading, but America is not a Chinese village; Hinton's cast of characters, at least as he presented it, was divided by class, sex and age, but not by multiple ethnic and cultural antagonisms.[2] For all the reasons I've been laying out, I don't see universal sisterhood as a practical possibility. Fortunately, men are hardly a monolith—they are deeply divided along various social and political axes, disagree with each other on what "male self-interest" is, and don't necessarily support each other in the face of feminist demands. Feminist struggle will never be a matter of women as a united class confronting men as a united class, but rather of particular groups of women pressing on vulnerable points in the structure of male supremacy and taking advantage of divisions among men. Direct personal pressure on men to change their behavior will be more feasible in some communities than in others. Most early radical feminists operated in a social milieu that was middle-class, educated, culturally liberal and politically leftist. A degree of economic opportunity, access to birth control and the decline of rigidly familialist mores—along with the fact that most of us were young and as yet uninterested in having children—allowed us a certain amount of independence, therefore power, in dealing with "our" men, and we were also in a position to appeal to their proclaimed belief in democracy and equality.

Even under the best conditions, though, direct confrontation has built-in limits, because it requires a level of day-to-day militance that's impossible to sustain over the long haul. After a while even the most passionate feminists get tired, especially when they see how slow the progress is. As soon as they ease the pressure, men take advantage of it and start a backlash, which then touches off a backlash by *women* who feel they've struggled too hard for not enough result. That's part of the story of the 70s. I'm not saying that personally confronting men is not worth doing, or that our doing it hasn't had lasting effects, because it has. But I think it is basically a minority tactic, and one that flourishes in the exceptional moment, rather than *the* model of revolutionary struggle.

When applied beyond the realm of direct personal combat to feminist demands for changes in public policy, the pure class struggle paradigm becomes much more problematic. These demands operate on two levels. They are aimed at men as a group in that they attack the sexist assumptions embedded in social and economic institutions. But they are also aimed more specifically at men (and the occasional woman) with institutional power—corporate, legal, medical, religious or whatever—who by virtue of their positions represent other interests and ideological commitments besides male privilege. Such interests and commitments may have priority over sexist imperatives or even conflict with them. Thus the alliances and oppositions that form around feminist demands are rarely based strictly on gender or sexual class interest.

For instance, although legal abortion reduces women's subordination and dependence on men, men as a class have not closed ranks against it. Rather, the active political opposition has come from sexually conservative familialists of both sexes (most but not all of whom are opposed to feminism across the board). Many men have supported legal abortion on civil liberties or sexual libertarian grounds. Others have supported it on racist grounds, as an antiwelfare or population control measure. Male politicians have more often than not based their position on abortion on one simple criterion: what would get them reelected. The medical establishment supports freedom for doctors to perform abortions while opposing feminist demands that paramedicals be allowed to perform them. And so on. Most men have at worst been indifferent to or ambivalent about the abortion issue; most women, on the other hand, *have* seen abortion rights as in their female self-interest. Without this asymmetry, it is doubtful that feminists could have won legal abortion or kept it in the face of heavy pressure from the right. As it is, our biggest defeat on this issue, the ban on Medicaid funds for abortion, has clearly involved other factors besides sexism. The new right took advantage of middle-class women's apathy toward the poor, while mobilizing antiwelfare sentiment among people outside the hard-core familialist antiabortion constituency. Often a combination of racist, antipoor and sexist feelings motivated men to opposition in a way sexism alone had not ("Let those irresponsible women have their abortions, but not at my expense"). Battles over measures to combat economic discrimination against women involve similar complexities. Some men, putting economic class loyalty or opposition to corporate power or commitment to economic equality above their specifically male self-interest, support such measures (especially if they hope to get feminist support for their economic agenda); some women oppose them, whether on familialist grounds or because of *their* economic class loyalty and/or ideological belief in a free market economy.

I use examples of struggles for reform because feminists have never yet been in a position to make an active fight for basic structural changes in institutions.

Such a fight would be impossible for a feminist movement alone; to envision it presupposes the existence of a left capable of attacking state and corporate power. And in that context, the configuration of alliances and oppositions across gender lines would if anything be much more complicated than it is now.

The Feminists agreed with Redstockings that male domination was the primary oppression and that women and men were political classes. Beyond that the groups diverged. For one thing, The Feminists used the terms "sex role" and "sex class" interchangeably—they identified sexism with particular, complementary patterns of male and female behavior. Redstockings' view of sex roles, like its view of institutions, was that they reflected male power, but were not primary political categories. The Feminists' conflation of role and class provided a basis for rejecting the pro-woman line: if the female role, per se, defined women's oppression, then conforming to the role was upholding the oppression. The Feminists' attitude toward institutions was even more reductive than Redstockings', in the opposite direction. While Redstockings assumed that the sexist dimension of an institution could somehow be abstracted from the institution itself, The Feminists assumed that the primary institutions of women's oppression—which they identified as marriage and the family, prostitution, and heterosexuality—were entirely defined by sexism, that their sole purpose was to perpetuate the "sex-role system." Therefore, radical feminists must destroy them. (The Feminists had a penchant for words like "destroy" and "annihilate.") The Feminists also rejected consciousness-raising in favor of abstract theorizing, but never clearly laid out the philosophical or epistemological basis of their ideas.

For all the limitations of Redstockings' materialism, we at least knew that we had to base a feminist program on women's actual lives and feelings, and that the important thing was to understand women's behavior, not judge it from some utopian moral standpoint. The Feminists were idealist, voluntarist and moralistic in the extreme. They totally disregarded what other women said they wanted or felt, and their idea of organizing was to exhort women to stop submitting to oppression by being subservient or participating in sexist institutions like marriage. Once at an abortion demonstration in front of a legislative committee I had a huge argument with a member of the group who was yelling at the committee's female secretaries and clerks that they were traitors for not walking out on their jobs and joining us. The Feminists were the first radical feminist group to suggest that living or sleeping with men was collaborating with the system. They shocked the rest of the movement by making a rule that no more than a third of their membership could be married or living with a man.

The Feminists, and in particular their best-known theorist, Ti-Grace Atkinson, also developed a set of ideas about sex that will be familiar to anyone who has followed current movement debates. The first radical feminist to talk about heterosexual intercourse as an institution was probably Anne Koedt, a member of New York Radical Women who later joined The Feminists, in her essay "The Myth of the Vaginal Orgasm." Koedt was careful to distinguish between intercourse as an option and as an institutionalized practice defined as synonymous with "normal" sex. She also assumed that the point of sex was pleasure, the point of institutionalized intercourse was male pleasure, and the point of challenging that construct was equal pleasure and orgasm for women. Atkinson wrote an article elaborating on this idea of "the institution of sexual intercourse," but took it in a different direction. As she saw it the purpose of the institution was getting women to reproduce and the concept of sexual need or drive was mere ideology. What erotic pleasure was or whether it existed was unclear, especially in the present social context. In fact, heterosexual intercourse was so thoroughly corrupted by the sex-role system that it was hard to imagine a future for it even as an optional practice.

The Feminists' organizing manifesto condemned the institution of heterosexual sex very much in Atkinson's terms, and added that since sex was part of the marriage contract, marriage meant legalized rape. It also included the statement—tucked in inconspicuously, so it seemed a lot less significant than it does in retrospect—that in the context of freedom, physical relations between individuals of whatever sex would not necessarily emphasize genital contact. The implication was that any special interest in or desire for genital sex, heterosexual or otherwise, was a function of sexism. This was a mental leap that seems to me clearly grounded in unconscious acceptance of a traditional patriarchal assumption, namely that lust is male.

The Feminists' perspective on sex was a minority view within radical feminism, considered provocative but out on some weird edge. The predominant attitudes in Redstockings were more typical: we took for granted women's desire for genital sexual pleasure (the importance of fucking to that pleasure was a matter of debate) and focused our critique on the ways men repressed and frustrated women sexually. Though we theoretically defended women's right to be lesbian or celibate, there was a strong heterosexual presumption underlying Redstockings politics. It was tacitly assumed, and sometimes explicitly argued, that men's need for sexual love from women was our biggest weapon in both individual and collective struggle—and that our own need for *satisfying* sexual love from men was our greatest incentive for maintaining the kind of personal confrontation feminism required. We rejected sexual separatism as a political strategy, on materialist grounds—that simply refusing to be with men was impractical and unappealing for most women, and in itself did nothing to challenge male power. But beyond that we didn't really take it seriously as a personal choice, let alone an expression of militance. On the contrary, we thought of living without men as the bitter price we might have to pay for our militance in demanding equal relationships. Tension over these issues, among others, led an alienated minority to quit Redstockings and join The Feminists.

At that point lesbianism per se had not yet emerged as an issue, but there were pitfalls for lesbians in both groups' ideas. If you accepted Redstockings' assumption that the struggle for equality in heterosexual relationships was the nerve center of radical feminism, lesbians were by definition marginal to the movement. The Feminists offered a much more attractive prospect—by their logic lesbians were, simply by virtue of rejecting sexual relationships with men, a liberated vanguard. But there was a catch: the vanguard role was available only to lesbians willing to ignore or play down the element of sexual desire in their lesbian identity. As Alice Echols has pointed out, the convergence of homophobic and antisexual pressures from the movement eventually impelled the majority of lesbian feminists to accept this tradeoff and sanitize lesbianism by defining it as a political choice rather than an erotic one.[3] To complicate matters, many of the feminists who "converted" to lesbianism in the wake of lesbian separatism did so not to express a compelling sexual inclination but to embrace a political and cultural identity; some of these converts denied that lesbianism was in any sense a sexual definition, and equated their rejection of compulsory heterosexuality with "liberation" from sex itself, at least insofar as it was "genitally oriented." In this atmosphere, lesbians who see freedom to express their unconventional sexuality as an integral part of their feminism have had reason to wonder if the label "male identifier" is any improvement over "pervert."

Toward the end of 1969, Shulie Firestone and Anne Koedt started a third group, New York Radical Feminists, which rejected both the pro-woman line and The Feminists' arrogant vanguardism. Two of the group's theoretical principles have been important in the later history of the movement. One has to do with the meaning of male power. Most radical feminists assumed men wanted dominance for the sake of material benefits—by which they meant not only the economic, in the broad sense, benefits of the sexual division of labor, but the psychic benefits of having one's emotional needs catered to without any obligation to reciprocate. NYRF proposed in essence that men wanted to exercise power for its own sake—that it was intrinsically satisfying to the ego to dominate others. According to their formulation men do not defend their power in order to get services from women, but demand services from women in order to affirm their sense of power. The group's other important proposition was its entry in the ongoing debate about why women submit to their oppression. While Redstockings' answer was necessity and The Feminists' implicit answer was cowardice, NYRF insisted that feminine behavior was both enforced and internalized: women were trained from birth both to conform to the feminine role and to accept it as right and natural. This pass at an analysis of male and female behavior was incoherent, implicitly biologistic and sexist. Besides suggesting that men, by virtue of their maleness, had an inherent predilection for power, NYRF's formulation gave men credit for being active agents while implicitly defining women as passive recipients of social indoctrination. The social-learning model, applied to women, also posed the same problem as all behaviorist psychologies—it could not account for resistance to the system. Inevitably it implied its antinomy, moral voluntarism, since the very existence of a feminist movement meant that some women had in some sense transcended their conditioning.

All the disparate versions of radical feminist analysis shared two basic weaknesses that contributed to the movement's demise. First, commitment to the sex-class paradigm pinned women's hopes for radical change on a millennial unity of women across barriers of class, race, cultural values and sexual orientation. The gap between what radical feminism promised and what it could deliver without a more complex, multivalent theory and strategy was immense. That gap was all too soon filled by attempts at individual liberation through "overcoming female conditioning," fantasies of benevolent matriarchies, the equation of woman-bonding, an alternative women's community and/or a "politically correct lifestyle" with feminism, and moralizing about the iniquity of men and "male values." Underlying these individualist and countercultural revisions of radical feminism was an unadmitted despair of real change. That despair is expressed more overtly in the work of cultural feminist theorists like Andrea Dworkin, who has reified the sex-class paradigm, defining it as a closed system in which the power imbalance between men and women is absolute and all-pervasive. Since the system has no discontinuities or contradictions, there is no possibility of successful struggle against it—at best there can be moral resistance.

The movement's second major weakness was its failure to develop a coherent analysis of either male or female psychology—a failure so total that to me it indicates a willed ignorance rooted in terror. While there was a dissenting minority, radical feminists as a group were dogmatically hostile to Freud and psychoanalysis, and psychoanalytic thought—especially its concept of the unconscious and its emphasis on the role of sexual desire in human motivation—had almost no impact on radical feminist theory. Since I agree with Juliet Mitchell that psychoanalysis is not a defense of patriarchal culture but an analysis of it—though I don't subscribe to her Lacanian interpretation of Freud—I think radical feminists' closed-mindedness on the subject was an intellectual and political disaster.

As I've discussed elsewhere, I basically agree with Freud's model of how children develop a masculine or feminine psychology in response to parental suppression and channeling of infantile sexuality.[4] Of course, as a radical I also believe that the social context in which this takes place is subject to change: male superiority is not a biological fact, and the patriarchal family and sexual repression are not prerequisites of civilization. But Freud's sexism and pessimism are not sufficient to explain why most radical feminists were so blind to his subversive insights, while they had no comparable qualms about selectively criticizing and appropriating other male theorists, Marx, for instance. I believe—and I know this is the kind of circular argument that drives anti-Freudians crazy—that the movement's violent rejection of psychoanalysis was in part a response to its hitting too close to home. At a time when feminism itself was tearing off layers of protective skin and focusing our attention on feelings we'd spent our lives suppressing, it was not surprising that women should resist any further attack on their defenses. To analyze women's behavior psychoanalytically was to risk unmasking all our secret strategies for coping with the traumatic linking of our sexual organs to our class inferiority, and with the resulting unconscious feelings of irrevocable violation, shame, global terror and dangerous rage. And those cherished strategies would not necessarily pass political muster, since—if you accept Freud's basic assumptions—it's precisely through women's attempt to manage their unconscious conflicts that femininity is reproduced. For instance, one typical feminine strategy is to compensate for the humiliation of sexual "inferiority" with self-righteous moralism and asceticism. Whether this is rationalized as religious virtue or feminist militance, the result is to reinforce patriarchal values. As I see it, a psychoanalytic perspective is crucial to understanding and challenging such self-defeating tendencies in feminist politics, and for that reason it is anathema to feminists who confuse the interests of women with their own unconscious agenda.

Redstockings did not succeed in defining psychology as a nonissue. Most radical feminists recognized that there were aspects of male and female feelings and behavior that eluded pragmatic, common-sense explanation. But their attempts to acknowledge the psychological dimension have been fragmented and muddled. In general, the inheritors of the radical feminist movement have followed the path of New York Radical Feminists and endorsed some version of behaviorism, biological determinism or an ad hoc, contradictory mélange of both. Given the history of biologism as the enemy's weapon, most feminists who draw on it prefer to pretend it's something else, and behaviorist terminology can be useful for this purpose. The present "radical feminist" antipornography movement provides a good example. It claims that pornography conditions men to sexual sadism, which is the foundation and primary expression of their power over women, and conditions women to accept their victimization. But if you examine the argument closely, it doesn't hang together. If men have the power, create the pornography and define the values it embodies, conditioning might perhaps explain how some men transmit a sadistic mentality to others, but not how or why that mentality arose in the first place. And in fact it is clear from the rest of their rhetoric that antiporn theorists equate male sexuality, per se, with sadism. As for women, the antipornography movement explicitly defines authentic female sexuality as tender, romantic and nongenitally oriented, despite the suspicious resemblance of this description to the patriarchal stereotype of the good woman. It is only women who disagree with this view of their sexuality who are proclaimed to be victims of male-supremacist conditioning. (How antiporn activists have managed to avoid being conditioned is not explained.) In this case, the language of behaviorism serves not only to deflect charges of biologism, but to inflate the importance of pornography as a target and dismiss political opponents.

The disintegration of radical feminism took several forms. First of all radical feminist ideas caught the attention of large numbers of women, especially educated, upper-middle-class women, who had no radical perspective on other matters and often were uninterested in, if not actively hostile to, left politics as such. These women experienced sexual inequality in their own lives, and radical feminism raised their consciousness. But their awareness of their oppression as women did not make them radicals in the sense of being committed to overall social transformation, as the early radical feminists had naively assumed it would. Instead they seized on the idea of women's oppression as the primary oppression and took it to mean not that feminism was or should be inclusive of other struggles, but that left politics were "male" and could be safely ignored.

This idea became a prominent theme of cultural feminism. It also led to the development of a new kind of liberal feminism. Many women reacted to radical feminism with an intense desire to change their lives, or the social arrangements that immediately affected them, but had no intention of supporting changes that would threaten their (or their husbands') economic and social class status. Many of the same women were reluctant to explicitly attack male power—not only because of the personal consequences of militance, but because the whole subject of power is uncomfortable for people who are basically committed to the existing socioeconomic order. The result was a brand of politics best exemplified by *Ms.* magazine, which began publishing in 1972. The traditional reformism of organizations like NOW was economistic and hostile to the "personal" sexual and emotional issues radical feminists were raising. *Ms.* and the new liberals embraced those issues, but basically ignored the existence of power relations. Though they supported feminist reforms, their main strategy for changing women's lives was individual and collective self-improvement. They were partial to the argument that men and women are fellow victims of sex-role conditioning. But where the "politicos" in the early movement had blamed this conditioning on capitalism, the liberals blamed it vaguely on "society," or the media, or the schools, ignoring the question of who runs these institutions and on whose behalf. In terms of their political ethos and constituency, the difference between the *Ms.*-ites and NOW was roughly analogous to the difference between the McGovern and Humphrey wings of the Democratic Party, and *Ms.* was to radical feminism what the "new politics" Democrats were to the new left.

On one level *Ms.*-ism and cultural feminist anti-leftism were the inevitable and predictable distortions of a radical movement that reaches far beyond its founders. They were testimony to people's desire to have it both ways—to fight their oppression while holding on to their privileges—as well as their tendency to take refuge in simple if illusory solutions. But the specific forms the distortions took were inspired by the idea of sex as the primary division and reflected the inadequacy of the sex-class paradigm as the basis for a radical movement. Although the early radical feminists were appalled by these uses of our ideas, we can't avoid some responsibility for them.

Within the radical feminist movement itself, the original momentum almost immediately began giving way to a bitter, immobilizing factionalism. The first issue to create permanent rifts was equality in the movement. Partly out of rebellion against hierarchical structures (especially in the new left), partly because consciousness-raising required informality, radical feminists, like the w.l.m. as a whole, had chosen the putatively structureless small group as their main form of organization. Yet every group had developed an informal leadership, a core of women—I was part of that core in Redstockings—who had the most to do with setting and articulating the direction of the group. Women who felt excluded from equal participation challenged not only the existing leaders but the concept of leadership as a holdover from male-dominated organizations. Debates about group process, the oppressive behavior of some members toward others and leaders' alleged exploitation of the movement for personal ends began to dominate meetings, to the exclusion of any engagement with sexism in the outside world.

The problems of elitism, class bias, differences in power within the movement and opportunism were certainly real—they were much the same kinds of problems that had surfaced elsewhere on the left—but by and large the attempts to confront them were ineffective and in the long run disastrous. Obviously, there are inherent difficulties in trying to build a democratic movement. You can't create a perfect society in microcosm while the larger society remains the same, and you can't change the larger society if you spend all your time and energy trying to create a utopian microcosm. The goal should be to strike a balance—work on finding ways to extend skills, experience and confidence to everyone, but at the same time encourage people who already have these assets to use them for the movement's benefit, provided they are accountable for *how* they use them in the movement's name. What makes this so difficult is not only the leaders' desire for personal power or their resistance to being held accountable and sharing their skills, but the rage of those who find themselves at the bottom of yet another hierarchy. They tend to want instant redress, and since there's no way to instantly create a situation where everyone has equal power—because the differences come from years of differential opportunities—some people resort to the pseudo-solution of demanding that those who have the skills or other forms of social power not use them, either for the movement or for themselves. Which is a dead end in terms of creating an effective movement, as well as an unreasonable demand on individuals trying to live their lives within the present social system.

These issues come up in all egalitarian movements, but the premises of radical feminism made them especially intense. The assumption that women's oppression is primary, and that the differences among women can be worked out entirely within an antisexist context, shaped the movement's predominant view of women and class: that a woman's position in the class hierarchy derived solely from the men she was attached to, that women could oppress other women by virtue of their class status but not men, that class conflict among women was a product of false consciousness, and that any form of class striving or power-mongering was therefore "male-identified" behavior. For some women this category extended to any form of individual achievement, intellectual activity, articulateness or self-assertion, the assumption being that these could only derive from some unholy connection with male power. The implicit corollary was that traditionally feminine behavior was the only truly sisterly behavior. These ideas too became staples of cultural feminism. Of course, many radical feminists disagreed and pointed out that charges of pushiness and overachieving were always used by dominant groups to keep oppressed groups in their place. But since the dissenters were operating out of the same basic framework as their adversaries, they tended to adopt some version of the mirror-image position that since women's common interest transcended class differences, this democracy in the movement business must be a sexist plot to cut down feminist leadership and keep the movement weak.

Though this idea was literally absurd, there was a grain of emotional truth in it. Much of the opposition to elitism took the form of unworkable, mechanistic demands for an absolutely random division of labor, taking no account of differences in skill, experience or even inclination. (As usual, The Feminists carried this tendency the furthest, instituting a strict lot system for the distribution of all tasks. When the group decided that no member could talk to the media unless chosen by lot, Ti-Grace Atkinson quit.) These demands were often coupled with personal attacks on individuals that were little more than outbursts of fury and *ressentiment* against any woman who seemed to have achieved some measure of autonomy, recognition or influence. Some feminist leaders reacted with defiance, some quit the movement, and others—myself included—tried to respond to the criticism by echoing it and withdrawing from our leadership roles, in classic guilty liberal fashion. With all the accusations and breast-beating, there was relatively little honest effort to deal with the concrete problems involved in creating a movement that was both egalitarian and effective. The result was not democracy but paralysis. And part of the reason, I'm convinced, was unconscious fear that feminists' demands for freedom and power would provoke devastating retribution. The movement was stripping away our protective mask of feminine compliance, and its leaders were the most visible symbol of that.

During the same period, working-class women in the movement began talking to each other about their experience with class oppression and confronting middle-class feminists. This new application of the consciousness-raising process educated feminists about the workings of the class system on the level of personal relations, but it did not significantly change class relations in the movement or help to unify women across class lines. As I've noted, there was no way within the parameters of radical feminism to connect the struggle for internal democracy with active opposition to the class system per se. This split between internal and externally oriented politics was exacerbated by a total emphasis on class as a set of oppressive personal relations. It was assumed that the strategy of challenging men's sexist behavior could be applied with equal success to challenging women's class-biased behavior. But this assumption overlooked fundamental differences in the dynamics of class and sexual politics. While the basic institutions of sexist oppression are located in personal life, a realm in which men have a great deal of personal power, the basic institutions of class oppression are located in the public world of the political economy, where middle-class people (women, especially) have little power. That does not mean there is no personal aspect to class oppression, but it does suggest that personal politics are not the cutting edge of class struggle.

For some radical feminists, however, consciousness-raising about class led to a political identity crisis. I was one of those who became convinced that *women* were implicated in the class system and had real class interests, that women could oppress men on the basis of class and that class differences among women could not be resolved within a feminist context alone. Which meant that a feminist movement purporting to represent all women had to connect in some organic way to a workers' movement, and by extension to a black liberation movement and other movements of oppressed groups—in short, to a left. Some women reacted to this realization by going back to the existing left to promote feminism from within; some moved off in search of a socialist-feminist synthesis. My own experience left me with a lot of new questions and no answers. In the fall of 1969 I had moved to Colorado Springs to work in a G.I. organizing project, intending at the same time to start a radical feminist movement in the area. Obviously, I was already interested in somehow combining feminist and leftist organizing, less out of any abstract commitment to the idea than from the impulse to integrate different sides of my life and politics. Two radical feminists from New York, including Joyce Betries, who was working-class and had raised the class issue in Redstockings, came out to work with me, and we started a women's liberation group. Betries also began confronting the oppressive class relations between middle-class and working-class members of the project and between civilians and G.I.s. After going through this confrontation in a sexually mixed group, in which the women were also raising feminist issues, I had no doubt that the standard radical feminist line on class was wrong.

Unlike Betries, who became active in Youth Against War and Fascism, I continued to regard myself as a radical feminist. I still believed that male supremacy was a structure of domination at least as basic as class or race, and so far as I could tell neither the "male" left nor the socialist-feminists—who struck me as updated versions of 60s politicos—agreed. But I rejected the idea of the primacy of women's oppression and began reluctantly to reject the global sisterhood model of feminist revolution. I saw that the fate of feminism at any given time and place was bound up with the fate of the larger left, though I had no idea how to translate this perception into a political strategy. At this point—1971—our G.I. project had fallen apart along with the rest of the new left, radical feminism was doing the same, and the prospects for any kind of radical politics looked grim. If I felt confused and stymied, I was not alone.

The final blow to the radical feminist movement as a vital political force was the gay-straight split, which took place in the early 70s. Lesbian separatists added a crucial ingredient to existing female separatist ideology—a positive vision of community. While early separatism offered only the moral reward of revolutionary purity, lesbian feminism offered in addition the more concrete social and sexual benefits of a women's counterculture. It then defined that culture not simply as a strategy for achieving women's liberation or as a form of sustenance for its troops but as the meaning and purpose of feminism.

At a time when the enormous obstacles facing the movement were becoming apparent, this vision had an understandable appeal. And while it had particular advantages for women already committed to lesbianism (and oppressed as lesbians), it could not have been a transforming influence on the movement if it had not exerted a strong pull on the feelings of radical feminists generally. Not only did many women break with heterosexuality to join the lesbian feminist counterculture, and even more experiment with it; many feminists who remained practicing heterosexuals identified with that culture and its ideology and considered themselves failed or incomplete feminists. Others argued that sexual orientation was irrelevant; what mattered was whether a woman accepted the *values* of female culture. By this route, cultural feminism evolved into a politics that anyone could embrace, that had little to do with sexual separatism or lesbianism as a sexual practice. The "female values" cultural feminists proclaimed—either with openly biologistic arguments, as in Jane Alpert's influential article, "Mother Right," or with behaviorist window dressing—were none other than the traditional feminine virtues. Once again we were alleged to be loving, nurturing, in tune with nature, intuitive and spiritual rather than genital in our eroticism, while men were violent, predatory, alienated from nature, committed to a sterile rationalism and obsessed with genital sex. (There was some disagreement on whether men were hopeless cases or whether women could teach them female values and thereby "humanize" them.) Thus "radical feminism" came full circle, from challenging the polarization of the sexes to affirming it and embracing a reverse sexism.

Insofar as cultural feminists translated their ideas into political activism, their chief focus was male violence against women. Radical feminists had defined rape and other forms of male aggression as weapons for enforcing male dominance— for punishing "uppity" female behavior or simply reminding women who was boss. But their lack of attention to psychology had left a gap in their analysis: in discussing sexual violence as a more or less deliberate, instrumental choice, they ignored it as a sexual and emotional experience. The movement was inconsistent in its view of the relation between rape and sexuality. On the one hand it noted the continuity between rape and "normal" male sexual aggressiveness, and the resulting social tendency to rationalize rape as fun and games. Yet in reaction to this confusion, and to the related myth that men rape out of un-controllable sexual need, the radical feminist mainstream asserted that "rape is violence, not sex"—a tidy slogan that avoided disturbing "unmaterialist" questions about the nature of male desire, the relationship of pleasure to power. And the iconoclastic Feminists, who implicitly equated heterosexuality with rape, declined to recognize sexual pleasure as a motive in either.

Cultural feminists leaped into this psychological breach, rightly (and there-fore effectively) insisting on the reality of sexual violence as an erotic experi-ence, an end in itself. Unfortunately, they proceeded to incorporate this insight into their neo-Victorian caricature of men's sexual nature and to generalize it to all patriarchal relations. New York Radical Feminists had broken with ear-lier radical feminist thought to argue that men wanted power for its intrinsic satisfactions, not its concomitant rewards; cultural feminists spelled out the implication of this position—that all sexist behavior is an extension of the para-digmatic act of rape. From this standpoint sexual violence was the essence and purpose of male dominance, the paradigmatic "male value," and therefore femi-nism's central concern.

In the late 70s, cultural feminists' emphasis shifted from actual violence against women to representation of sexual violence in the media and then to pornography. Groups like Women Against Pornography and Women Against Violence in Pornography and Media adopted pornography as the quintessential symbol of a male sexuality assumed to be inherently violent and oppressive, then made that symbol the focus of a moral crusade reminiscent of the 19th-century social purity and temperance movements. Predictably, they have aimed their attack not only at male producers and consumers of porn, but at women who refuse to define lust as male or pornography as rape and insist without apol-ogy on their own sexual desires. While continuing to call itself radical feminist—indeed, claiming that it represents the only truly feminist position—the antiporn movement has in effect collaborated with the right in pressuring women to con-form to conventionally feminine attitudes.

Though there was surprisingly little resistance to the collapse of radical femi-nism, some movement activists did fight back. In 1973 Kathie Sarachild, Carol Hanisch and several other women revived Redstockings, which had disbanded three years before, and in 1975 they published a journal, *Feminist Revolution*. *FR* was an ambitious attempt to analyze the deradicalization of the movement and contained the first major critiques of cultural feminism and *Ms.* liberalism. Its publication was an important political act, especially for those of us who felt alienated from what was passing for the radical feminist movement—or, as it was coming to be called, the "feminist community"—and were trying to make sense of what had gone wrong without the help of any ongoing group. But the journal also revealed the limitations of Redstockings politics when carried to their logical conclusions. *FR*'s critique did not contain any second thoughts about the premises of radical feminist materialism, including its rejection of psychology. On the contrary, the editors blamed the devolution of radical feminism entirely on deviations from these premises. From this unreconstructed viewpoint they could explain the deviations only as deliberate sabotage by "Agents, Opportunists, and Fools" (a section heading). One article, which provoked brief but intense controversy in the "feminist community" and eventually led Gloria Steinem to threaten a libel suit, contained a detailed account of *Ms.*'s corporate connections and Steinem's past work with the Independent Research Service, an outfit that had received CIA funds, with Steinem's knowledge, to send students to European youth festivals. While the information provided useful commentary on *Ms.*'s and Steinem's political perspective, many of the implications drawn from it were tortuous at best, including the overall implication that Steinem's ascendancy as a feminist leader, and *Ms.* itself, were a government and/or corporate plot to supplant radical feminism with liberalism.[5]

The implicit heterosexual chauvinism of the original Redstockings became overt homophobia in *FR*. Like the dominant tendency in lesbian feminism, Redstockings talked about sexual orientation in terms of political choice rather than sexual desire. But where orthodox lesbian feminists defined heterosexuality as entirely political, a patriarchal imposition on women, Redstockings took heterosexuality for granted and argued that homosexuality, both male and female, was a product of male supremacy. For the *FR* editors, lesbianism was at best one of the many compromises women made with a sexist system, a substitute for the equal heterosexual relationships we all really wanted. At worst it was a copout, a futile attempt to escape from men and male supremacy instead of struggling. By the same logic, *FR* condemned male homosexuality as a form of male supremacy: it was misogynist in that it did not simply subordinate women as lovers and sexual partners but rejected them altogether; and it was a resistance to feminism in that it allowed men to evade women's demands for equality by turning to each other. In a sense, *FR* implied, men who did not need women were the greatest threat of all. Like their cultural feminist opponents the *FR* editors filled the gap in their understanding of sexual psychology with political reductionism on the one hand and biological determinism on the other. But their uncritical acceptance of the concept of a natural, normative heterosexuality was especially ironic for self-proclaimed materialists.

Feminist Revolution crystallized my opposition to cultural feminism and stimulated a long-dormant desire to think seriously about the state of the movement and its future. But it also reinforced my suspicion that simply reviving the old-time radical feminist religion was not the answer, that while we needed to affirm and learn from what we had accomplished, we also needed to move on—to what was still unclear. I had similar reactions to *Meeting Ground,* a radical feminist and socialist journal that Carol Hanisch began publishing in 1977. Though *MG* was intended as a forum for debate and hopefully an impetus to renewed organizing—Hanisch and her coeditors solicited readers' articles and comments—for the most part its content reflected Redstockings' orthodoxy and embattled isolation. And though it was concerned with exploring the connections between feminism and antiracist, anticapitalist politics—a concern I shared—its conception of socialist revolution was based on Marxist-Leninist-Maoist assumptions with which I had little sympathy.

During the last few years—dating roughly (and not coincidentally) from the start of the Reagan era—there has been a more promising resurgence of dissident feminist voices, coming from several different directions. Yet another attempt to reconstitute a radical feminist movement began in 1980, when Brooke, a radical feminist, a lesbian and one of the earliest critics of cultural feminism (her essay, "The Retreat to Cultural Feminism," appeared in *Feminist Revolution*), published an article in a feminist newspaper calling for a new radical offensive. Response to the piece led its author and several other women to form the Radical Feminist Organizing Committee, which set out to create a network of radical feminists by circulating a newsletter, *Feminism Lives!*, and inviting readers' responses. RFOC now has about 70 members and is starting a national organization. Its basic stance is materialist; besides opposing cultural feminism and lesbian vanguardism it has taken an explicit stand against heterosexual chauvinism (Brooke broke with Redstockings over its line on homosexuality). Otherwise the group does not have developed positions; it is at the stage where virtually everything but opposition to male supremacy is open for discussion. As a result, *Feminism Lives!* has been largely free of the sectarian, defensive tone that *Feminist Revolution* and *Meeting Ground* tended to fall into. The terms of the discussion—its vocabulary and underlying assumptions—are still those of 60s radical feminism. But if RFOC makes a serious effort to revive militant feminist activism in a political climate and social situation that have changed dramatically since the 60s, it may well end up questioning some of those terms and breaking new ground.

Another, more publicly visible challenge to cultural feminism, and to the antisexual strain in radical feminist thought that dates back to Ti-Grace Atkinson, has come from feminist opposition to the antipornography movement. The antiporn groups, which emerged as an organized political force in 1979, quickly captured the attention of the media and dominated public discussion of feminism and sexuality. Because their ideas resonated with the conservative social climate and appealed to women's fears at a time when real freedom and equality seemed increasingly remote, they exerted a strong influence on the liberal mainstream of the women's movement and on the public perception of feminism. I found these developments alarming, as did many other women who felt that feminists should be fighting the right's assault on women's sexual freedom, not reinforcing it. Our opposition has generated a fierce intramovement debate on the significance of sexuality for feminist politics.

The sex debate has recapitulated the old division between those radical feminists who emphasized women's right to equal sexual pleasure and those who viewed sex primarily in negative terms, as an instrument of sexist exploitation and abuse. But contemporary "pro-sex" feminists (as the dissidents have been labeled) are also doing something new—placing a specifically feminist commitment to women's sexual autonomy in the context of a more general sexual radicalism. Bound by its theoretical framework, the radical feminist movement analyzed sexuality as a function of sex class; it did not concern itself with sexual repression versus liberation as a problematic distinct from that of male power over women. Accordingly, most radical feminists in all factions equated women's sexual oppression with male domination and rejected the idea of sexual liberation for men as at best redundant, at worst a euphemism for license to exploit women with impunity. Within this framework there was no way to discuss the common elements in women's and men's (particularly gay men's) subjection to sexual repression; or to explore the extent to which men's sexual guilt, fear and frustration contribute to their sexism (and specifically to sexual violence); or to understand the complexities of lesbian sexuality; or to examine other variables besides sexism that influence sexual formation—such as the parent-child relationship, race, class, and anxieties shared by both sexes about the body, pleasure, emotional vulnerability and loss of control.

The pro-sex feminists are raising all these questions and others, provoking an explosion of intellectual activity and reintroducing the spirit of critical inquiry to a movement all but ossified by cultural feminist dogma. The emphasis has been on questions rather than answers. There is a good deal of ideological diversity within the pro-sex camp, a loose, informal network that consists mostly of lesbian dissenters from the lesbian feminist consensus, women with political roots in early radical feminism, and feminist academics influenced by Marxism, structuralism and psychoanalysis. We also maintain friendly relations and an ongoing exchange of ideas with parallel tendencies in the gay movement and the neo-Marxist left.

At the same time, black women and other women of color have begun to create the context for a feminist radicalism based on efforts to analyze the web of race, class and sex/gender relations. Like pro-sex theorizing, these explorations break with prevailing assumptions—in this case the competing orthodoxies of radical and cultural feminism, black nationalism and Marxist socialism. Each of these movements has insisted on hierarchies of oppression and primary causes, forcing women who suffer from racial and class oppression to subordinate some aspects of their identity to others or be political schizophrenics. While socialist-feminists have purported to address this dilemma, in practice their economistic bias has tended not only to vitiate their feminist analysis but to reduce racism to its economic component. Many women of color have shared this perspective and its limitations. What is novel and exciting about the current discussions is their concern with the totality of a culture and their recognition that sexism, heterosexism, racism, capitalism and imperialism intersect in complex, often contradictory ways. When this multidimensional analysis is applied to bedrock issues of sexual politics—marriage and motherhood, sexual repression and violence, reproductive freedom, homophobia—it does not simply correct for white middle-class feminists' neglect of other women's experience; it shows that whatever a woman's particular social vantage point, her experience of femaleness is charged with class and racial meanings.

Though the emergence of this tendency and the burgeoning of the predominantly white pro-sex coalition happened independently (a small number of black and Hispanic women have been involved in both) they end up raising many of the same questions from different angles. They also reflect a common impulse toward a decentered radicalism sensitive to difference, ambiguity and contradiction, and critical of all forms of hierarchical thinking. The same impulse informs contemporary cultural radical revisions of Marxist and Marxist-feminist theory. It seems to me that these convergences represent a first fragile step toward the creation of a multiracial left that will include feminism as a basic assumption. At the moment, helping this process along is my own political priority; I think a "new new left" is the prerequisite for a third feminist wave.

Still, the paradox posed by early radical feminism remains unresolved and may be unresolvable in any definitive way. An antisexist politics abstracted from a critique of familialism, a commitment to sexual liberation, and race and class struggle cannot sustain itself as a radical force; a movement that attempts such an abstraction is bound to fragment into bitterly opposed factions and/or turn conservative. Yet so long as sexist power relations exist there will be a need for an autonomous, specifically feminist women's movement. It is the legacy of radical feminism that makes it possible to talk even tentatively of a feminist left. And it would be naive to imagine that a left intellectually committed to feminism would automatically be free of sexism either in theory or in practice. In the foreseeable future, any feminist movement that aims to be radical will somehow have to negotiate this tension between the need to preserve its political boundaries and the need to extend them. It will help to remember that radical feminism named the boundaries in the first place.

Social Text, Summer 1984

NOTES

1. In this essay, as in common usage on the left, the term "socialist feminism" refers primarily to an activist tendency and "Marxist feminism" to a body of theory. There is of course some overlap between the two, but by no means a one-to-one correspondence. As a movement, socialist feminism has generally been more socialist than feminist, assuming that economic relations are fundamental, while sexual political questions are "cultural" or "ideological," i.e., epiphenomenal. Often socialist-feminists have adopted a cultural feminist view of these "ideological" questions and thereby reduced feminism to a matter of lifestyle.

Marxist feminism has displayed a similar weakness for economic reductionism, but it has also used Marxist methodology to expand feminist theory; in recent years, especially, Marxist feminists have both influenced and been influenced by the cultural radical critiques that have generated the "crisis in Marxism" debate. On the other hand, since Marxist-feminist theorizing has been carried on mostly in the academy, it has suffered badly from lack of contact with any organized feminist movement.

2. In any case, postrevolutionary China is hardly a model for those of us whose definition of liberation includes individual freedom. This does not invalidate the process of self-assertion by peasants against landlords, women against men and autocratic matriarchs that Hinton describes. But it does raise the question of whether the Maoist model of struggle can have more than limited success only in a revolution in which individual autonomy and cultural diversity are not important values.

3. Alice Echols, "The New Feminism of Yin and Yang," in *Powers of Desire: The Politics of Sexuality,* ed. Christine Stansell, Ann Snitow and Sharon Thompson (New York: Monthly Review Press, 1983).

4. Ellen Willis, "Toward a Feminist Sexual Revolution," *Social Text* 6 (Fall 1982).

5. Before publishing *Feminist Revolution,* Redstockings held a press conference on the Steinem-CIA connection and distributed copies of the *FR* article. At the time I was working part-time at *Ms.,* editing book reviews, and had just concluded that I ought to quit, having come to the limits of my tolerance for the constant (and usually losing) battles involved in being the token radical on a magazine with mushy corporate liberal politics. The Redstockings flap pushed me over the edge. I had mixed feelings about the article and was upset about the press conference, which by villainizing Steinem and implying a conspiracy could only undercut the credibility of Redstockings' valid critique of *Ms.'s* politics and impact on the movement. But I was incensed by Steinem's response, a disdainful who-are-these-people dismissal of Sarachild, Hanisch et al. as crazies and not real Redstockings. I resigned from *Ms.* and wrote an open letter to the movement press detailing my own criticisms of the magazine and its editor. Redstockings included it in *FR.*

In 1979, Random House published an "abridged edition with additional writings" of *Feminist Revolution.* The chief abridgement was "Gloria Steinem and the CIA," which Random House deleted in response to Steinem's threat to sue, although the facts of her involvement with IRS had long been public information and the article had already survived a libel reading. Though Redstockings organized a protest, this act of censorship provoked little interest outside of radical and cultural feminist circles, and cultural feminists mostly supported Steinem. In the end, the entire episode was a depressing defeat for radical feminism, albeit largely self-inflicted. Not only did Redstockings fail to provoke significant debate about *Ms.*-ism; most people who heard about the controversy at all were left with the impression that Steinem had been attacked by a lunatic fringe.

Escape from New York

For Americans, long-distance buses are the transportation of last resort. As most people see it, buses combine the comfort of a crowded jail cell with the glamor of a liverwurst sandwich. Though I can't really refute that assessment, I don't really share it, either. As a student with lots of time, little money, and no driver's license, I often traveled by bus. Un-American as it may be, I feel nostalgic about those trips, even about their discomforts. In my no doubt idealized memory, discomfort was the cement that bound together an instant community of outsiders, people who for reasons of age, race, class, occupation (student, soldier), handicap, or bohemian poverty were marginal—at least for the time being—to a car-oriented culture.

It is this idea of community that moves me now. Lately I've been feeling isolated, spending too much time hiding out in my apartment, wrestling with abstract ideas. What better remedy than to take a bus trip, join the transportation-of-last-resort community, come back, and write about what I've learned?

I am not immediately struck by the paradox: that in search of community I'm leaving home. Breaking out of my everyday web of connections—to my friends, my women's group, the man I've begun to think about living with—and going on the road.

On a long bus trip, the difference between a tolerable ride and a miserable ride is having two seats to yourself. Anyway, there are a limited number of games you can play on a bus, and scoring two seats is one of them. My technique for getting people to sit elsewhere is to take an aisle seat near the back, put something ambiguously proprietary on the window seat (a jacket, say, or a book, not something that's obviously mine like a purse), spread my body out as much as possible, and pretend to be asleep.

As I leave New York on Greyhound's express to Montreal I am self-consciously taking none of these precautions. I throw my backpack on the overhead rack, clasp my trusty Van Morrison tote bag between my knees, sit by the window, and try to look inviting. But the bus is half-empty and no one sits with me. Most of the passengers are older women traveling alone, Canadian students, and foreign tourists. A little Hispanic girl skips up the aisle, inspecting faces; she has on a sky-blue skirt and a T-shirt that says DANCE DANCE DANCE. My nearest neighbor sits across the aisle, a plump, dark, curly-haired woman who looks unidentifiably foreign and impenetrably self-contained.

Ten minutes out of the Port Authority terminal, a familiar sensation hits. I recognize it from childhood. Whenever I went to an amusement park I would make a point of going on the roller coaster. Every time, as soon as I was irrevocably trapped in my seat and we had started to move, the idiocy of what I'd done would overwhelm me. But why should I feel that now? I'm not trapped. I can get off the bus at Saratoga Springs and be back in New York by tonight.

Between Montreal and Toronto I watch a teenage couple neck, listen to a bunch of high school girls sing "One Hundred Bottles of Beer on the Wall," and read Doris Lessing's *The Marriages between Zones Three, Four, and Five*. The story is sucking me in despite my revulsion at its basic premise—that the rulers of a certain section of the universe have a benevolent grand design ungraspable by lesser beings, and so their orders must be obeyed however cruel and incomprehensible they seem.

In Toronto I have an hour's wait. Since there are no seats in the crowded waiting room I find a spot on the floor and open my book. A girl who looks about 16 sits down close to me and pretends to be absorbed in a pamphlet. A New Yorker to the core, I make sure I know where my wallet is. The girl has straight blond hair and metal-rimmed glasses; she is wearing a long navy skirt and a gray sweater with a hood. After about 30 seconds she asks me what I'm reading. I pass her the book.

"I've been reading this poem," she says, handing me her pamphlet. It's Kipling's "If." "My name is Joan."

I introduce myself. Joan turns out to be 27.

"Don't you think," she says, "that caring is the most important thing in life? So many people don't care. They sit next to each other the way we are doing and don't talk to each other. What do you think about Christ?" She speaks very fast in a high voice that's hard to hear over the noise of the terminal.

"Well—I don't. I'm Jewish."

"I don't know anyone of the Jewish race," Joan says. "I had a Jewish friend once. You don't believe Christ died for us?"

"Well, no."

"Christ is someone who picks you up when you stumble, you know? Like a little kid. He dries your eyes and helps you go on. I have a lot of bad experiences in my past. Sometimes I backslide, I go out and smoke pot, put Christ on the shelf. But then I call on him again, 'Christ, I'm sorry!' Some Christians can't stand moral flaws in other Christians. Piss on that!"

We cross the border after midnight and stop in Detroit. The atmosphere of the bus has changed completely; it's proletarian, young, funky, and two-thirds black. In the dark several portable radios play disco, though there's a rule against radios without earphones, and the bus begins to smell like marijuana. As it moves onto the highway someone behind me whispers, "*Shift gears,* motherfucker. Come on man, *shift,* man—ah!"

A red-headed college student asks if he can sit with me. "A woman just got on with her child," he apologizes, "and she asked if I'd move so they could sit together." He's a nice kid from a small town in Ontario, but almost immediately he begins encroaching on my rightful space. Men on buses always take up too much space. Sometimes it's hard to tell, when they fall asleep and sprawl all over you, whether they're really asleep.

During the '60s the men I met on buses used to ask if I was a hippie. During the '70s they asked if I was a women's libber. They almost always asked if I had a man in New York. On my first coast-to-coast bus trip in 1963, I was waiting in the Oakland terminal and got into a conversation with a young man. He was 18, he said, and engaged. But now his girlfriend was wanting him to do something he didn't want to do. What did I think, should he do it?

"Well, that depends," I said, with a touch of condescension. "What is it she wants you to do?"

"She wants me to kiss her *there,*" he said, jabbing a finger at my crotch. I jumped backward. He smiled innocently. "You got a man in New York?"

But this college student is perfectly okay, it's just that I'm scrunched against the window and resenting it. I consider a friendly confrontation. I'll tap him awake and say, "Excuse me, but this"—indicating the arm rest between our seats—"is really the boundary of your seat, and you're leaning way over on my side, and the seats are narrow enough as it is—" Oh, shit. It's only another six hours to Chicago.

The Greyhound terminal in Chicago is home to a huge, ornate Burger King with white trellises and fake vines. I eat something that passes for an English muffin, then walk a few blocks down deserted Randolph Street, past neon theater marquees flashing incongruously, to the Trailways station, where at 7:30 a.m. I will board the bus to Denver. Trailways stations, this one included, tend to be less crowded, less grungy, and more middle-class than Greyhound stations. It's hard to imagine a rapist lurking in the restroom of a Trailways station. Yet when I think about hitting the restroom to wash and change my clothes, I have a flash attack of urban paranoia. I will wait till the bus stops at some small town in Illinois.

In mid-morning the cooling system quits. The temperature on buses is never right; either the air-conditioning is efficient enough to chill beer, or it doesn't work at all. On this bus at least the windows have vents that can be opened to let in a sliver of air. Farm smells, hay and manure, drift in. The heat and the miles of cornfields, punctuated by gas stations and John Deere Tractor signs, are soporific. For a while the bus is almost empty, but then it begins filling again. It picks up a fat blind woman with hennaed hair and a loud, hearty voice. A young man, blond and bespectacled, wearing a button that reads Humanity Is One, takes her suitcase and heaves it onto the rack.

"Now where has that young man gone with my suitcase?" the blind woman jokes, waving her cane with dangerous exuberance. The young man has been on the bus since Chicago. I've already heard him tell an old lady who got on somewhere in Iowa that he's moving west to work in an organization devoted to persuading intellectuals and technical experts to think about their work in moral terms. Now he notices me looking at him. He asks me where I'm from, what I do. He wants to know how I go about communicating with a particular audience.

"Well, I'm sure my sense of who's reading me influences what I write," I say. "But I don't sit down and consciously think about how to communicate."

"But wouldn't you say," the young man persists, "that a lot of art these days is too obscure for people to relate to?"

For a moment I can't answer because I'm having a peculiar experience. The young man has become an alien creature, a different species. I can't imagine what to say that will communicate across this gap. Finally I get out some words that amount to "Yes and no." The young man becomes an ordinary passenger again, indisputably human. He is smiling; evidently he has noticed nothing strange.

In Omaha I buy some postcards to get change for the toilet. Bus stations are the last great bastion of the pay toilet, though they usually provide a few free cubicles with broken locks, no doors, or clogged bowls. One of my post-cards has a picture of the highway, captioned "Driving Beautiful Interstate 80." When we start up again the moon and clouds look like an El Greco painting. I fall asleep, and when I wake up around 3 a.m. the moonscape is gone, leaving nothing but black Nebraska night. The bus is silent; only a couple of reading lights indicate that anyone else is awake. At a rest stop in North Platte I wash down my potato chips with coffee that tastes like Styrofoam and liquid soybean extract.

This afternoon I will be in Colorado Springs, birthplace of my friend and ex-lover Paul, who now makes his home in New York. Paul is about to move in with the woman he's been seeing, and it feels like the end of an era. We lived together through the early '70s, and neither of us has lived with anyone since. Evidently one thing we have in common is ambivalence about creating such bonds. For a long time we couldn't quite let go of each other. For a long time after that I seemed to be attracted only to men who lived in other cities or were otherwise unavailable. For a year I cut myself off from men altogether. Perhaps I had to plunge so deeply into the negative side of my ambivalence in order to say good-bye to it, or try to. When I began to be with someone again it was a bit like moving to a strange country. In the intervening years aloneness had become my norm, my taken-for-granted context. And yet those same years had changed my sense of myself, of men, of the ground rules for relationships, making it impossible simply to pick up where I left off.

In spite of the coffee I fall asleep again. When I open my eyes the first thing that hits them is a store window advertising waterbeds. We've just pulled into Sterling, Colorado, and it's raining. A man in stretch pants and a sweatshirt, with a beard and twinkly eyes, leans across the aisle and offers me an apple.

Lee Ann and her husband Don meet me at the Colorado Springs bus station on Saturday afternoon. In her short shorts and sleeveless top Lee looks slim, brown, and, as always, beautiful. A clergyman's daughter from Michigan, she has an archetypal midwestern beauty with a counterculture overlay—fresh face, candid eyes, freckled nose, long, gleaming, and absolutely straight brown hair. Eleven years ago we converged on the Springs to help run Home Front, an antiwar movement center for soldiers from nearby Fort Carson. At the time Lee was a 20-year-old weaver who traveled light and toked heavily; I was 27 and an activist with ideas about building an alliance between women's liberation and the rest of the left. We shared a lot of history, lived and worked and demonstrated together, met Paul and his family, took LSD, fell in love with the Rockies. I consider our connection unbreakable, though we come from and have gone on (or in my case back) to different worlds, and hardly ever see each other.

I've met Don only once before. He is quietly friendly, but I feel shy with him. We have no history to mediate our different worlds. Then, too, perhaps I'm afraid of getting my loyalties confused. Though Lee and Don have been together for five years, their marriage has not yet shaken down. Lee hasn't been able to get Don to share the housework (though she usually works full-time and keeps the books for his roofing business besides), and she feels that he dominates their sexual relationship. Periodically she blows up and things change temporarily. She feels frustrated and ambivalent: she will have to leave if the situation doesn't change, yet she and Don love each other, "whatever that means," and she thinks he is a genuinely good person, which is more than she can say for certain former lovers.

"I've got to make a phone call," Lee announces as the three of us walk toward her red pickup truck. "We're supposed to pick up some dope."

"So what else is new?" I say, grinning. Whenever I set foot in the Springs I feel as if I've never left.

Lee and Don live several miles out of town; they've bought a roomy house still surrounded by woods, though that won't last long at the rate the city is growing. They are gradually fixing the place up; Don has put in wood paneling in the kitchen and the living room. They have handsome pine furniture, bought on time at Penney's; a fireplace; plants hanging in macrame holders Lee has made; a color TV; a truck and a van; two German shepherds. Lee confesses her yearning for an efficient dishwasher and one of those fancy refrigerators that make ice cubes.

"Lee, you've become an American," I tease. "You used to think it was immoral to own more than one dress." On the other hand, she has always had a taste for toys and gadgets; she kept our commune supplied with slinkies, pinwheels, and other amusements.

"It's this house," Lee says. "For the first time I really want to have nice things."

We take the red pickup over to Lee's friend Carey's place to get the dope. On the way Lee brings me up to date. She's still confused about what she wants—with her marriage, with her life. At the moment she has a temporary job painting, the only woman in the crew, and the men hassle her so much it's driving her insane. The previous winter she went up to Wyoming to take advantage of the construction boom; she got a job, but was fired on the grounds that she was "a distraction."

"I'd like to go back to school. But how would we live? We've got so many bills—for transportation, especially. I can't count on Don to make enough, consistently. And I haven't figured out what I want to do. I want work that's interesting, but I also want to make decent money. I've thought of becoming a fast food manager, but that takes capital, which I don't have." Then there's the question of whether to have a kid. Don wants to; Lee isn't sure. It's so ironic—Carey really wants to settle down and have a family, but her last lover was too unreliable, and this one is too young and uncertain.

Carey and Joe live in a little house with a flower and vegetable garden. I realize after an unsettling minute that I was there years ago, visiting one of Paul's brothers. My sense of déjà vu is accentuated by Joe's long hair and embroidered shirt. It's Joe who's selling the dope. When the transaction is done we sit and listen to Emmylou Harris and talk about friends from my Colorado days. An ex-GI, part of the Home Front crowd, agreed to marry his long-suffering girlfriend, then changed his mind at the last minute. A woman I liked, a Vietnam widow who over the years has been hooked on several different drugs, is in terrible shape—still a junkie, and now a prostitute as well.

When we get home Don orders a pepperoni pizza and we smoke. Since I rarely smoke dope anymore, one hit has me floating. I call my man in New York, but he isn't home, so I talk to his answering machine: "Hi. I'm in Colorado Springs, and I'm really stoned." Then we eat and watch *Chinatown* on the color TV.

I spend Sunday night with Paul's parents. Peg and Andrew have five children. They were also surrogate parents to the Home Front staff and, it often seemed, to the entire '60s generation of Colorado Springs. Peg was one of the town's leading peace activists; Andrew, a physician, took care of our bodies. We trooped in and out of their house—a sprawling, modern redwood and glass structure with a spectacular view of the mountains—talking politics, meeting out-of-town visitors, eating holiday dinners, confiding our troubles.

Peg is a vivid woman with a sexual vitality impervious to age. She has long since given up on politics—it all looks so hopeless—and turned her prodigious energy to other pursuits. She makes beautiful, intricate quilts in patterns with evocative names—log cabin, cathedral window, clamshell. She and Andrew are building a passive solar house on the adjoining lot. They will live there and sell their present home.

Peg takes me on a tour of the lot and shows me the plans for the house, which she designed. Then she reports on the marriages, breakups, babies, and other projects of various old acquaintances. She manages to combine a taken-for-granted acceptance of her surrogate children with a complete lack of inhibition about telling them when and how they've gone off the track: "Every time he came over here, he would give me the same rap about Maharaj-ji. Finally I said, 'Bruce, if that's all you have to talk about when you're over here—if you honestly think there's nothing else that's worthwhile—then there's no point in your coming, because you have nothing to say to me.'"

In the morning, after dashing up to the lot for a consultation with the contractor and the surveyor, Peg drives me to the bus. We are almost at the depot when she asks after a mutual friend. I tell her we've drifted apart, partly because of tension over his anti-Zionist politics.

"Well, I don't know, Ellen," Peg says. "I never discuss these things with Jewish people, because they get so defensive."

Oh no. We can't have *this* conversation in five minutes. "We get defensive," I reply, "because we feel threatened, and for good reason—there really is such a thing as anti-Semitism."

"I guess I've never really understood Jewish suffering and Jewish persecution that well, because Jews seem the same as everyone else. Not like blacks."

"If you're 3 per cent of the population, and you get a lot of hostility from the other 97 per cent, it makes you defensive."

Peg frowns, shaking her head. "The Jewish people I know are very aggressive, they're elitist, they look down on people who aren't geared to success, or this society's idea of success—"

"Like me, you mean?"

"Well, you're a little different, you come out of the '60s—"

"You're indulging in a stereotype. What about all the radical Jews? A big portion of the left is Jewish."

"Yes, I know. But the Jewish people I know in Colorado Springs aren't radicals."

I have to get on the bus. I feel schizophrenic, kissing Peg good-bye with the same affection as always, yet thinking oh no, not you too, I can't stand it. What's odd is that I'm not angry. I only wish I could stay and fight this out.

West of Denver the bus runs through gorgeous canyons and over two mountain passes. I feel nauseated from the altitude; my head aches. The weekend has been a respite, but now I'm running through another session of "What am I doing here?" This trip has not turned out as I expected. I thought I was rejecting my solipsistic impulses and getting out, as they say, among the people. Instead my solipsistic impulses keep flaring up like TB on the Magic Mountain.

The man sitting next to me is stocky, fortyish, rumpled. He was born in a tiny town in Denmark and has been shuttling between there and the San Francisco Bay Area for the past 30 years, unable to decide which place he likes better. He owns a farm in Denmark. He is vague about what he does in California. I mention that I'm thinking of stopping off in Reno to play a bit.

"Have you ever played the horses?" he inquires.

"No."

"Good. I know owners and trainers, and it's a crooked business. I once owned a horse myself. Won a harness race. It was a sloppy track and the horse was juiced up. It was what you would call a fixed race."

We move into Utah and the bus begins to fill up with men in wide-brimmed hats. Around 10 at night we stop at a grocery store with a snack bar. A man in a wide-brimmed hat is joking with the woman behind the counter: "I like my coffee the way I like my girls."

"How's that?"

"Fresh."

"Oh, I thought you were gonna say hot and black."

Fun and games! *"I like my coffee the way I like my men." "How's that?" "Sweet." "Oh, I thought you were gonna say strong and full of cream."* I buy some aspirin for my headache. As I walk back to my seat, Horse Race taps me on the shoulder and whispers, "Have you noticed that the old guy in front of you never gets off?" It's true; since Denver the tall, white-haired old man in front of me has stayed in his seat reading a book called *Spiritual Discipline*. I close my eyes and nap. When I wake up my headache is gone and Salt Lake City is emerging from the night, a soft glow on the horizon that turns into glitter and then glare.

By Tuesday morning we're in Nevada. Our driver is talking over his microphone, the one customarily used to warn, "No radios without earphones, no smoking except in the last four rows, no pipes or cigars, none a them *funny* cigarettes." A sign to the left of the driver's seat identifies him as YOUR HOST, JOHN DOE. "The government," he announces, "the U.S. government, that is, owns about 87 per cent of this state. It uses the land for wonderful things, like the atomic bomb and the MX missile." Behind me a middle-aged woman with dyed blond hair, pink lipstick, and sunglasses is exchanging medical horror stories—unnecessary hysterectomies, incompetent anesthetists—with a teen-age girl.

We stop for lunch at Flossie May's Country Cafe in Lovelock. The blond woman wins $10 playing the slot machine. Horse Race sits next to me and says, "The old guy didn't get off, did he?"

"He's reading a book called *Spiritual Discipline.*"

Horse Race shakes his head. "He's gonna need it."

As we continue across the desert, John Doe resumes his commentary. "Maybe you'll come back across here sometime during a wild storm. We'll go sideways to Reno, into ditches, it'll be a lot of fun." We pass some electrical installations. "The power company just put in for another raise. They won't use solar power—they use oil, which we have none of, natural gas, it's all imported, so you know whose hands are on it. I get real ticked off thinking of the old people on fixed incomes, who can't pay their bill." We pass Mustang Ranch, the legal whorehouse. "It's like a concentration camp over there," John Doe says cheerily. "All those guards and towers—that's to keep the mafia out." And how do *you* like your coffee?

Serious gamblers may sneer at slot machines, but for amateurs who just want to have a little fun without losing much, they're perfect. They entertain you with noise and colors and lights; they offer continual bits of reinforcement, even if it's only two nickels clattering into the tray; and if you play with nickels and dimes it takes hours to lose any real money. Slots are addictive; once you get into a good rhythm and win a few coins you start to feel rapport with the machine, and you know you can influence what comes up. And in fact I think there's something to the idea that winning streaks, even on nickel slots, are never just luck. In Reno I pass up an opportunity to gamble for krugerrands and stick to the slots. I win 13 bucks, mostly in one orgasmic cascade of dimes. After that I begin to sense that I'm losing rapport with my machine, so I quit and get on the 5:30 bus to San Francisco.

It's a local bus, dilapidated, cramped, and crowded with gamblers returning to Sacramento and the Bay Area. Many are black and Chicano, the first non-white passengers I've seen since Colorado. The bus is so small that every time the woman in front of me adjusts her seat back it bangs painfully against my knees; the woman next to me is eating a sandwich in my lap. After Sacramento I spot what I think are two empty seats in the back, but as I'm getting settled my seatmate returns from the john. He is a large black man, expansively drunk. In back of us is a young, fair, funky-hip couple. They've just gotten married in Reno and are expansively newlywed; the groom keeps hugging the bride and announcing, "Mmm, that's my mama!" My seatmate turns to me and says, "Hey, honey dear, my name's Coyle."

"My name's Ellen."

"Hey, how you doin', honey dear?"

"Fine."

"You got a boyfriend?"

"Yes."

"Hey, honey dear. Hey, honey dear. Hey—are you gonna talk to me? Are you mad with me?"

"No, I'd just rather be called by my name, that's all."

The groom leans over and puts his arm around Coyle. "Hey, man, why don't you change seats with my mama? I wanna talk to you."

The transfer is effected. "Hey, man," the groom begins, "you should let that lady alone. She just left her old man, and she hates the whole world. She don't want *nothin'* to do with men."

"What you mean she don't want a man? She *need* a man."

"You ain't lookin' at it from her point of view. She don't want nothin' to do with nobody. Forget it, man."

The newlyweds get off in Vallejo. I get off in Oakland. It's too late to see anything but the lights in the East Bay hills. I tell myself I'm in California. I call my friend Lou, an artist, well known in the lesbian-feminist community. She is stoned and bubbly. She is playing bridge with some women friends. She will come right over and pick me up.

I stand in front of the terminal with my pack. A long coffee-colored sedan cruises by. It slows down as it passes me, and a woman peers out; then it picks up speed and turns the corner. A minute later I see it coming around again. This time it stops and the woman gets out. She's Chicana, with long black hair and large black eyes; she's wearing tight black shorts, a magenta blouse, and bright pink lipstick; she is plump and very young.

"Are you alone?" she says, smiling.

"I'm waiting for a friend," I say, smiling back.

"Do you need a home?"

"No thanks, I'm fine," I say, conveying with my eyes that I know what she's asking and I'm not interested. "My friend is coming to get me."

"Are you sure? I can take you home if you want."

"No, really, thanks."

"Well, okay," she says, still smiling, and goes back to the car. It turns the corner and comes back again. The driver gets out, a tall, thin, light-skinned black man in a neat brown suit and a hat with a snappy brim.

"Look," I say. "I'm waiting for someone. Would you please?"

"Okay," he says politely. "I hope he comes soon."

They leave, and a minute later Lou's car pulls up. Or is it hers? I'm looking at it, trying to see who's inside, when she gets out and waves at me. I wave back.

It's unseasonably cold, and on the bus from Oakland to Los Angeles the heat isn't working. The woman next to me wraps herself in a woolen blanket. I huddle in my jeans jacket, which until this morning belonged to my friend Lou. I love the jacket, but what warms me is my friend's gesture. I hardly ever give my clothes away. I'm not an impulsive giver. A Marxist might say I've been infected with the what's-in-it-for-me commodity exchange ethic of capitalism. A feminist might say I've been preoccupied with the unequal struggle to take care of my own needs. Anyway I'm grateful to Lou for doing what I find hard to do. It's as if I've received not only a jacket but a vote of confidence that what I've received I will someday in some way pass on. I'd like to believe it because at the moment there's a glass wall between me and the rest of the human race. This wall has appeared periodically ever since I left New York. I don't know if I'm on the inside looking out or the outside looking in.

Nearly everyone on the bus is black, including the driver. It's a cheerful, talkative crowd. The woman in the blanket is going home for a visit to Bass Drum, Louisiana; the woman across the aisle was born in Baton Rouge, lives in Fresno, and has nine children; the man behind me is headed for Galveston. The woman in the blanket asks him, "You got a wife and kids?"

"I got 11 kids."

"I wouldn't want to be *your* wife."

"Ain't got no wife."

"All those children by the same woman?"

"I've had four wives."

"Buried 'em all, eh?"

We pass a house with a sign out front: FOR SALE $40,000. "In a few years," our driver remarks, "there ain't gonna be no more middle-class people like you and me. Everybody's gonna be either beggin' in the street the way they do in other countries, or they're gonna be rich. The big companies, the oil and gas companies are makin' it all."

In front of me a woman with a purple scarf calls out, "I don't want to be rich."

"I do," says the driver. "You gotta make heaven here in this life, 'cause there's nothin' after you die."

"What do you mean?" says Purple Scarf accusingly. "You an atheist?"

"No, I'm not an atheist. I just think for God to help us we gotta help ourselves."

The woman in the blanket grins. "He's gettin' himself in trouble. But I agree with him. We gotta do it ourselves. We're God's instruments. His hands, his feet. He can't do nothin' without us."

She resumes her conversation with the man who's going to Galveston. He tells an elaborate story about lending a woman some money to travel down to Louisiana to buy a home, but when she got there they refused to sell her the home, so she came back to Oakland.

"I don't believe it," says the woman in the blanket. "She ripped you off."

"No, she was okay. You can tell when somebody's honest."

"Well, you didn't tell this one. She was rippin' you off, if you ask me."

My strategy for facing LA without a car is to pretend I'm a foreign tourist, complete with street map and the names of cheap hotels copied from guidebooks. My first choice, the Beverly Vista, has a single room without bath. In the terminal parking lot I accost a young man with long blond hair: "Where do I get the number 5 bus?"

He shrugs, grins, stares at my pack and my map; he is drunk. "Where are you going?"

"Beverly Hills."

He bursts out laughing. "You've got a long trip ahead of you. A *long* trip."

The trip takes an hour. For the first part of it I'm the only passenger who is neither Chicano nor over 65. I change buses in a section of downtown LA that looks like Times Square. Near the bus stop a preacher out of *Wise Blood* is haranguing a sizable crowd. As the bus turns up Wilshire Boulevard, I'm standing near a Spanish woman in a dancehall costume. Next to her a man with a Hollywood-handsome face and a cheap bright blond wig entertains his fellow passengers by doing some card tricks, then turning an ordinary 50-cent piece into a huge silver coin. An extremely old lady totters onto the bus and falls in a heap. Two men help her up. She's wearing platform shoes with four-inch heels.

The Beverly Vista is plain, clean, and neat, like a European *pension*. Apparently many of the guests are permanent residents. The manager tells me her first name and asks mine. I'm lucky, she says, the hotel is usually booked months in advance. I feel lucky. In the morning my friend David picks me up and takes me home for breakfast. He and his new wife Karin live in a spacious, light apartment on a street with palm trees, not far from the hotel. The three of us and another friend of David's talk and eat omelets, chopped liver, whitefish, and bagels. We are interrupted by a neighbor, Milly, knocking on the back door.

Milly, a middle-aged blond woman who reminds me of Sylvia Miles, owns an enormous old silver-gray Cadillac, the source of the problem. She and David and Karin share a large parking space out in back of the house. By normal standards there is plenty of room for two cars to drive in and out, but Milly is a lousy driver who has trouble maneuvering her behemoth. Whenever she wants to leave she demands that Karin move her own car out of the way. Karin has begun to feel imposed on, and this time she politely insists that Milly try driving around her.

The argument does not stay polite. "You little bitch!" Milly shouts. "I'm a good neighbor—I'm quiet. You should be happy to have me for a neighbor!"

She leaves, but a few minutes later the phone rings. "All right, Benny," Karin says. "I'll move it this time, as a favor to you. But you're the landlord, it's your responsibility to talk to her. She has to learn how to drive her car. I can't be expected to move my car every day."

The obstacle removed, Milly eases her Cadillac out. Even with the whole space to herself she barely misses our back steps. "Am I okay?" she calls to us. Agitation has clearly not improved her control. "You shouldn't drive when you're so upset," Karin says. Milly gives her a Sylvia Miles glare. "*Don't* try to be my friend."

That afternoon I go to a party in Santa Monica, where I've been invited by

Diane, an expatriate journalist friend from New York. The host is also an old friend. Still I feel uneasy, as I always do at a party full of strangers. At a New York party it's all too possible to spend the whole evening standing in a corner, trying to marshal the courage to talk to someone or join one of those little groups that may as well have signs above their heads saying PRIVATE CONVERSATION. But this is California, and whenever I look as if I might be at loose ends, someone makes a point of coming to the rescue. I'm relieved, yet my uneasiness perversely flourishes. I feel I should respond to people's friendliness by being convivial, part of things, *on,* but I'm not up to it. It occurs to me that if this room were a bus I wouldn't have to worry about being conspicuous or invisible, a wallflower or a snob; I would have an automatic legitimacy and purpose.

Later Diane and I have dinner and talk about the usual subjects: work and love. Yes, I'm really involved with someone now, after a long period of being alone. (Of being a loner. The image that comes to mind is a huge NO TRESPASSING sign. I am painting out the letters and will write WELCOME.) Yes, it's certainly a big change. Yes.

The eastbound bus is nearly an hour late. I commiserate with the woman behind me on line, an 85-year-old widow. Her husband, a retired physicist, died 17 years ago. "We were very happy," she says. "He worshiped me. I understood how important his studies were to him."

"Do you have children?"

"No. It's just as well. He wouldn't have been able to shut himself up in the den and work."

She is moving from San Diego to Tulsa to be with her sister and help care for her sister's husband, who was recently disabled by a stroke. "People say I should stay in San Diego for the climate. Ridiculous! There's nothing there for me. The people were all unfriendly, except for the old women who were always asking me to do things for them. Drive me here, drive me there, and not one of them ever offered me carfare."

In San Diego she has been living alone. "I like the talk shows—Larry King and Ray Breen. You learn a lot, listening to them. When my husband died I used to listen to Ray Breen—it was like being with other people. He really helped me."

Around 11 p.m. we make our first stop, in Barstow. A bunch of us troop into the coffee shop and sit at the counter. A cute, punky-looking kid in a leather jacket and sunglasses strides in and calls out to the waitress, "Double cheeseburger and an order of fries." The waitress gives him an up yours, buddy, look. "You were the last one to walk through the door, you'll be the last one waited on." Whistles, cheers, laughs from the spectators at the counter. The offender looks abashed, amused; recovering, he attempts a sulk. "Bitch!" he says, unconvincingly.

I sleep and am awakened by a man's voice, somewhere to my rear, yelling and cursing: "Don't touch me, you cocksucker, I'll break your leg and break your head with it." He carries on like this for several minutes; as far as I can make out, someone has brushed against him, and he's construed this as a deliberate insult, an attempted theft, a pass, or all three. People begin yelling at him to shut up and let them sleep. "Hell, I won't shut up! When I have to stop talking, I'll move to Australia!" Finally the driver pulls over, stalks to the back of the bus, and threatens to throw him off at the next stop. He quiets down for a while, then starts in again, in a lower voice: "You're a dope addict! I can tell a dope addict if I hear two words out of his mouth!" By this time it's dawn, and I can see that our foul-mouthed paranoid is an elderly blind man.

In Gallup, New Mexico, in front of the restaurant where we're having lunch, a Navajo man in jeans and a white hat is sitting on a ledge. The blind man starts wandering off in the wrong direction; the Navajo goes after him, takes his arm, and turns him around. The driver shouts, in a voice loaded with contempt, "Hey! Don't you bother the people on this bus! Just leave them alone!" As I pass the Navajo on my way into the restaurant, I acknowledge the incident with an uncomfortable, I-know-that-was-racist half-smile. He responds, "Hey, sweetie!" and starts following me; I retreat into the cafe. When I return, he is panhandling. He approaches a teenager who has long, straight hair and a backpack and looks like a granola ad. "You're giving a bad impression of the Navajo people," she says primly. I feel depressed.

In the early '70s, when I lived with my then-lover Paul in a small town in upstate New York, we became close friends with our neighbors, a married couple about our age with a little boy. Jim, the husband, now lives in Albuquerque with his second wife Maya, her son and their daughter. I haven't seen him in years, but I've had news of him through Paul; I know that Maya is black, that both of them have become born-again Christians. In the old days Jim's attitude toward religion of any sort was actively hostile. Still his conversion doesn't really surprise me; it seems consistent with his need—which he also once denied, though less convincingly—for a stable, more or less traditional family structure.

When we first met, the counterculture was belatedly arriving in small-town America. Jim and his wife Gail had been straight-arrow schoolteachers, and she had quit her job when the baby was born. Jim began letting his hair grow. They both began smoking dope. Our households were increasingly intertwined; we wandered in and out of each other's apartments, ate communal dinners, and Paul and I did a lot of babysitting. Jim hated teaching and Gail hated staying home, so they switched roles. They had affairs and eventually split up. There were always tensions between Jim and me—over feminism, over our uneasy and ambivalent sexual attraction to each other—and there was always affection. Waiting in the Albuquerque terminal I feel a little tense, but mostly affectionate.

Jim picks me up in his truck on his way home from work. He looks pretty much the same—tall, thin, bearded, full of nervous energy. He has a job managing an employment service and hopes someday to start his own. "I wouldn't charge fees to people, only businesses. I can't see anyone having to pay for a job."

I ask him how he likes Albuquerque.

"I hate it. The people are lazy—what I call basic energy, they call 'the New York hype.' I've become a bigot—I'm not into Spanish culture at all, I'm not into adobe houses, I'm not into Indian beads and jewelry that all looks alike. We have a nice church, but that's about it." He's thought a lot about moving back east, but Maya, who grew up in Bedford-Stuyvesant, is worried it wouldn't be good for the kids. "Maybe we'll go to Colorado," he muses.

Albuquerque is flat, dusty, featureless except for the mountains on the horizon. The sun glares. Jim and his family live in a complex of two-story apartment houses next to a highway. Their apartment is unpretentious and full of children's clutter. Religious homilies hang on the walls, and over the dining room table a tile offers a Recipe for a Happy Home, with instructions like "Combine two hearts. Blend into one."

I meet Maya, a slender woman with light skin and freckles, a mass of black hair, a no-bullshit, this-is-me directness; her son Jeff, who is wearing a green shirt that says "Spirit Power" on the back; and plump toddler Penny. We sit in the living room and Jim asks me what's going on in New York. Automatically I start complaining about the women's movement—so much energy attacking pornography instead of defending abortion rights—then stop in confusion, realizing I can no longer assume agreement, or even sympathy, on such matters.

"I guess you might have a different point of view," I say.

Jim smiles. "Around here the anti-pornography thing comes from the churches—we don't want this in our community, it's immoral. I can get into that."

"Well, I've been curious, needless to say, about how you got into religion."

"I don't call it religion—I can't stand religion. I call it my faith," Jim says, looking nervous. Does he think I'm going to argue with him? We've had some fearsome arguments in the past; we're both capable of dirty fighting. There was a time when I might have tried to argue him out of his faith, but that was before my brother became an Orthodox rabbi. "It comes out of an experience of the holy spirit. It's hard to describe. I haven't intellectualized it, and I don't want to. I can shoot down Christianity logically, just the way I always did, but it's beside the point, because it's an experience of being a new person, looking at things in a different way."

"It sounds like the kind of experience I've had on acid," I say, trying to be helpful. Jim looks nervous again. "Satan is a good counterfeiter," he says gently. "I think that's what the drug movement was about."

I remark on the difference between his attitude toward Christianity and my brother's view of Judaism as above all a reasoned commitment. "You should read what scripture says about the Jews," Jim says. "The Christ-killer thing is a lot of crap. That never came from people of faith."

"What does it say?"

"The Jews are the chosen people of the Lord, and they've been repeatedly tolerated and punished for their disobedience. Culminating," Jim says, directing an affectionately exasperated look at me and the stiff-necked people I represent, "with their rejection of His son. Come Armageddon, there are going to be a lot of Jews hailing the arrival of the Messiah."

"You're involved with the women's movement, right?" Maya says. "Why is that crazy person, what's her name, against the ERA? I don't see anything wrong with it." Jim agrees that the argument that the ERA would destroy the family is bullshit. "If I thought it was against the family, I'd be against it."

"Well," I say, "it does challenge the traditional definition of the family. The traditional roles."

"The woman should stay home all the time and have 20 kids," Maya says scornfully. She's about to start work at McDonald's; Penny is in day care.

Maya makes dinner, and as we eat our spaghetti and green beans I tell them about Paul's present love life and my own.

"Do you have any plans for marriage?" Maya asks.

"I don't believe in marriage," I pompously reply, suddenly overtaken with an urge to declare myself, to draw lines. "But we may live together," I add, bracing for anxiety like a bad swimmer in rough surf.

By the time I get up the next morning Jim has left for an early men's fellowship meeting at the church. Maya and I sit and talk about New York, about the Village.

"I love New York, I love the urban atmosphere. But I worry about bringing Jeff up there. I know my kid. On the other hand, I grew up there, and I turned out all right." Racial prejudice is worse out here, she says. But then, she's gotten more prejudiced herself; she can understand where the Indians are coming from, but still she feels resentful having to pay for their publicly supported housing when it costs so much to feed a family.

I ask if Jeff ever sees his father, whom Jim describes as "a hustler and numbers runner." "No, we're not in touch, Jeff hasn't seen him in years. It's just as well—I don't know how I'd handle it if he wanted visitation. I don't know," Maya says, shaking her head. "The last time I saw him, I felt nothing. No love, no hate. I couldn't imagine us making love. It was strange, it was really strange to feel that way."

"Love stinks!" a radio in the back of the bus informs us as we pull out of Albuquerque, late again. I've just spent a few hours with Suzy McKee Charnas, a science-fiction writer and transplanted New Yorker, and she's given me a copy of her latest book, *The Vampire Tapestry.* It absorbs me all the way to Amarillo. Suzy's vampire hero is not the supernatural creature of legend but a predator at the top of the food chain. In order to survive he must mingle with his human prey, pretend to be one of us, yet at the same time maintain total objectivity; he cannot afford either to underestimate human beings or to get involved with them. In the course of the book he commits both sins and barely escapes disaster.

In Amarillo I wait in an almost empty, unnervingly quiet depot from midnight to 3 a.m. On the bus to Dallas I drift into sleep, but wake up as we pull into a station and the driver announces a 30-minute break without announcing the town. I have no idea where we are and can't find out from the timetable because my watch has stopped. This feels intolerable. I turn to an old couple sitting across the aisle and ask, "Where are we?" They look past me. Maybe they haven't heard; maybe they don't like my looks.

Rattled, I get off the bus and walk into the station looking for a sign or some other clue. The bus stations in this part of the country all look alike. They have metal contour chairs in standard colors, Muzak punctuated by arrival and departure announcements, rows of chairs with pay TV, lockers, signs that say "TV Chairs for TV Watchers Only" and "These Lockers Are for Use of Trailways Passengers Only," buzzer systems so that a clerk can check your ticket before letting you in.

I stop at the ticket counter. "Excuse me, can you tell me where we are?"

The woman at the counter looks mystified. "Pardon me?"

"What town is this?"

A long pause, a we-get-all-kinds carefully blank expression. "Wichita Falls, Texas."

I sleep again and dream that I'm a vampire who longs to be a human being, like the mermaid in Hans Christian Andersen.

The center of social life on a bus is always the back. People who want quiet and order sit near the driver, the authority figure. This is a rule we all learn around the age of five. On cross-country buses the gap between front and back is accentuated because of the no-smoking-except-in-the-last-four-rows rule. Though I am a nonsmoker, loyal to my tribe, there is no getting around the fact that the goody-goody quotient is higher among abstainers of all sorts. On the overnight bus from Shreveport to Atlanta, I head for the back. Still spooked from my dream, I've decided I need company.

My seatmate, Linda, is almost six feet tall and has long blond hair with dark roots. She's on her way from Oklahoma, where she lives with her fiancé and her three-year-old daughter, to visit her folks in Tuscaloosa. She and her fiancé lived in Colorado for a while, in a condominium in Steamboat Springs, but they couldn't make it economically. What with the construction boom Linda's fiancé was making $13 an hour as a carpenter, but the cost of living was impossible. "The population is mostly single men who raise hell all the time. There are some single women construction workers. The mountains were beautiful, but I couldn't stand it."

Across from us is a chubby kid with a baby face. She looks about 15 and I assume her name is Ann because that's what her T-shirt says. But from her conversation with the guy in back of her I gather that her name is Jeanie—the T-shirt was handed down from a relative—and she has a husband. She's from San Diego and likes country singers and TV. She also likes to talk. She tells a

Ellen Willis at her office at New York University in the midnineties. She founded the Cultural Reporting and Criticism Program there in 1995.

*Ellen in the late sixties,
in hippie mode.*

*Ellen's high school
graduation photo. She was
always mortified by the heinous
pre–Janis Joplin haircut options
for curly-haired girls.*

A sample of Ellen's reading material. Those flowered sheets were still around when Nona Willis Aronowitz, her daughter, was a kid in the eighties.

Ellen Willis in upstate New York in 1970.

Ellen was a meticulous and slow writer; her essay "Dylan" took seven months to write. She transcribed Dylan's lyrics by hand (and sometimes got them wrong).

Just Like A Woman

Nobody feels any pain
takes   Tonight as last night inside the rain
Everybody knows that baby's got new clothes
But lately I see her ~~ribbons~~ & her bows
?? Have fun from her ~~~~

Being married she's my friend
Yes, I believe I'll go see her again
takes   Nobody has to guess that baby can't be blessed
tell she finally sees that she's like all the rest
with her fog, her amphetamine & her pearls

It was rain' from the first & I was dying
of thirst so I came in here
And your long-time curse hurts but what's worse
is this pain in here
I can't stay in here
Aint it clear that

take   I just can't fit
Yes I believe its time for us to quit
When we meet again introduced as friends
Please don't let on that you knew me when
I was hungry & it was your world

The rest of the piece:

Dylan's evolution to less traditional, more personal & literary xxsongs
inevitable--similarities and contrasts with Guthrie--the importance of
politics in the folk music ethic and the impact on folk coterie of Dylan's
rejection--continues to write protest, but it is literary protest, concerned
with individual psychology, a pickup on anarchism of beats. His switch to
rock & roll, and its effects on folk and pop music--why the new rock & roll
is (no, was, it's getting too self-conscious now) authentic folk music for
our culture and why folk music world ignored it before Dylan. "Pop" culture
and its xxxx early manifestations in the beat generation, an anti-literary
literary movement--how Dylan combines folk and rock, traditional and pop
culture in his songs. Assessment of his verbally and musically: he is verbally
very gifted, but is not a poet. On the other hand, his voice, which everybody
puts down, is extremely effective. He is intelligent musically, derivative
but cleverly so, a mediocre technician. His genius is in the way he puts the
elements of his songs together into a total experience--this is a peculiarly
contemporary thing, yet in a different way, you can see the same thing in
folk tradition, Guthrie, for instance.   *Has created a new folk style*

I'm not sure exactly what note to conclude on, will depend on how it evolves.
Should run 10-12-even more? additional pages.

and, as innovator

(and not profoundly think)

If 2 insets are good, half for so do for much better

Last summer, Bob Dylan had a motorcycle accident. Reports of his condition were vague, and he dropped out of sight. Publication of his book, Tarantula, was indefinitely postponed. Gruesome rumors circulated: Dylan was dead; he was badly disfigured; he was paralyzed; he was insane. The cataclysm his audience always expected seemed to have arrived. Alan Lomax once remarked that Dylan might develop into a great poet of his time, unless he killed himself first. Pete Seeger believed Dylan could become the country's greatest troubadour—if he didn't explode. Topical singer Phil Ochs predicted a year ago that Dylan would be risking assassination by appearing on stage.

Now, images of James Dean filled the news vacuum. As the months passed, reflex apprehension turned to suspense, then irritation: "Have we been put on again?" There were stirrings—friends began to admit, with smiles, that they'd seen Dylan; he was rewriting his book; he was about to sign a contract with MGM Records. The new rumor was that Dylan had used his accident as an excuse to retreat. After Blonde on Blonde, his most intensive foray into the pop demi-monde, Dylan needed time to replenish his imagination. According to a less romantic version, his manager had advised him to disappear till his contracts expired. The put-on is intentional.

Not since Rimbaud said "'I' is another" has an artist been so obsessed with triumphing over identity. his masks hidden by other masks, he is the (celebrity-stalker's) ultimate antagonist. The disparity between his original public pose as rootless wanderer with southwestern drawl and the private facts of home and family and high school diploma in Hibbing, Minnesota—was a commonplace subterfuge, the kind that pays reporters' salaries. It hardly showed his talent for elusiveness; what it probably showed was naivete. But his attitude toward himself as a public personality was clear from the beginning. On an early recording, he used the eloquent pseudonym "Blind Boy Grunt." "Dylan" is itself a pseudonym,

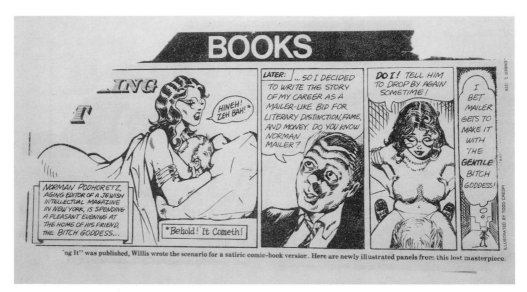

ILLUSTRATED BY TODD CRESPI

"ng It" was published, Willis wrote the scenario for a satiric comic-book version. Here are newly illustrated panels from this lost masterpiece.

Ellen created a satiric comic book series using stick figures, based on Norman Podhoretz's "Making It," in the late sixties. Some years later, the Voice gave it real illustrations.

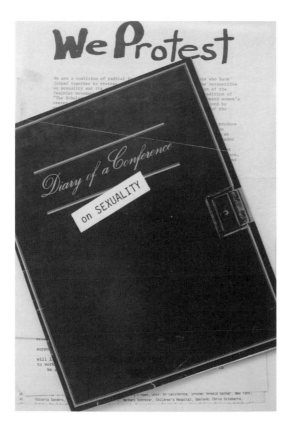

Pamphlet from a conference on sexuality at Barnard College in 1982.

Fragments from my commonplace book--

"these pleasures which we lightly call physical"
Colette, The Ripening Seed.

"love, which, sexual or non-sexual, is hard work"
George Orwell, "Reflections on Gandhi."
--Quandra Prettyman Stadler

The Scholar and the Feminist IX planning committee met steadily from
September 1981 to April 1982, during which time we reaffirmed that the most
important sexual organ in humans is located between the ears.

Carole S. Vance

Dear Barbara,
I just came back from a planning committee for the Barnard Conference. They
are doing sexuality this year. You'll love it. It should be a very exciting
event: a coming out party for feminists who have been appalled by the intellectual
dishonesty and dreariness of the anti-pornography movement. I am the conservative
on the committee. I mean, I understand the advanced position on porn, on s and m,
but I can't understand the argument for pederasty! Ellen says its because I am
a mother.
Love,
Judy

For me the planning committee meetings had a compelling, politically urgent quality,
I hadn't experienced in a long time — maybe not since the early years of the women's
liberation movement. I believe that as the sexuality debate goes, so goes feminism. The
tendency of some feminists to regard women purely as sexual victims rather than sexual
subjects, and to define the movement's goal as controlling male sexuality rather than
demanding women's freedom to lead active sexual lives, reinforces women's oppression
and plays into the hands of the new right. It is a dead end, a politics of despair.
Feminism is a vision of active freedom, of fulfilled desires, or it is nothing.
In these meetings we have been concerned with preserving and extending such a
vision. Given the current social atmosphere, this is a radical act! Ellen Willis

---

Ode to an Herbivore

Orange and grave,
Trembling beneath
Chicory and queen's lace
I smile for
Your mild embrace.
My grassy top
Spilts in the wind,
Flicking fragrance
To rabbits and
Flirting with
Herds of brown
Cows. Will I flower
At death?
Come then, gnaw me
Toward heaven.

Patsy Yaeger

---

endorsed the ~~~
laws that prohibit adults from sexually ~~~

over...

*Ellen's notes before the sex conference at Barnard, in which she echoes the pro-sex
sentiments she expresses in "Lust Horizons."*

Ellen at the 2004 March for Women's Lives, accompanied by her sister, Penny Froman (center), and cousin, Judy Oppenheimer (far right).

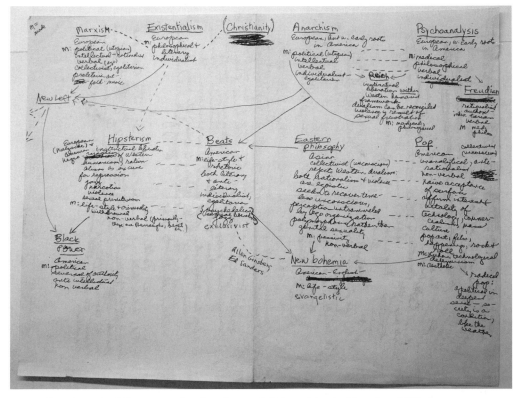

In 1967–68, Ellen created a flowchart of philosophies for Esquire. *Wilhelm Reich, a profound influence on her, gets major props.*

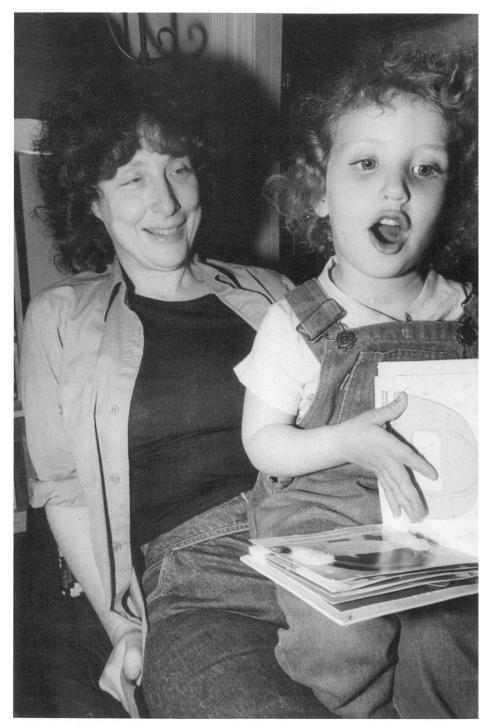

Ellen and Nona read a book at Nona's group day care in Park Slope. This photograph is one of the outtakes for "The Diaper Manifesto: We Need a Child-Rearing Movement."

long, detailed story about going to see Johnnie Lee at Disneyland and going backstage and getting her husband to take a picture of her and Johnnie and being rewarded with a kiss from Johnnie.

"Gee, all *I* have is a Johnnie Lee Looking for Love T-shirt," Linda remarks.

"—and this other singer in the show, he was tellin' me about once he was onstage with some musicians? And they were snortin' cocaine and smokin' marijuana? Not realizin' they're onstage! And suddenly the curtain goes up!"

We stop in Jackson for an hour, check out the pinball machines. Linda plays a machine with a Dolly Parton motif. She's a dynamite player and wins four free games.

We're approaching Fayetteville, where I can, if I like, get off the main route and catch a northbound bus to Fort Clare to look up my friend Richard. I haven't called to tell him I'm thinking of coming. Mainly, I tell myself, because I haven't been sure how my schedule would work out, whether I'd have time to make the detour. But also because of ambivalence—I'm not quite sure I ought to do this, I'm worried Richard will feel intruded on. Our friendship began during the same period as my friendship with Jim, when Richard and his lover Coral lived in upstate New York, 10 miles up the road from Paul and me. Richard is black, from a northeastern urban middle-class background; Coral is southern Jewish. The four of us were post-hippies together, enjoying or suffering a moratorium from figuring out what we were doing with our lives. Sometime after we had all moved on, and both couples had split up, Richard went to live in Fort Clare, in his grandmother's house, in a southern small-town world that could not have been more removed from the intellectually sophisticated, predominantly white, countercultural milieu he'd been plugged into even while he was holing up in the Catskills.

It was supposed to be a temporary retreat, but it's lasted about five years. A couple of years ago, when Richard was in New York for a friend's wedding, he told me he was feeling like coming back. I haven't seen or heard from him since. Coral talks to him periodically. Still, whatever it is that keeps him in Fort Clare, soul-searching, identity conflicts, comfort, or plain inertia, it seems to involve a need to cut himself off. So I worry about intruding, but at the same time I figure our bond has been strong enough so that I can presume on it. Better to err on the side of presumption rather than paranoia.

When we get to Fayetteville at nine Saturday morning I finally call, but Richard isn't home. Well, fuck it—the bus for Fort Clare leaves in 20 minutes, and it's only a three-hour ride, which by now seems like no time at all. As it turns out, the ride is a treat; I'm happy to get off the featureless interstate onto a country road that goes through woods, fields, small towns. But when I get to Fort Clare, Richard hasn't come back. I leave a message, explain I can't be reached anywhere, and promise to call back later. In the meantime I'll wander around, maybe find some real food. The bus station is on a highway, surrounded by fast food places, so I ask the ticket-taker where the center of town is.

"The center? What do you mean?"

"Well, the post office, stores—"

"The post office is just four blocks down, but most of the stores are out at the mall."

I walk in the direction of the post office and find the town's main street, or what's left of it in the area of the mall. It's very quiet; there are few people on the street and virtually no women. The only real restaurant is closed; I settle for a snack bar worthy of any bus station. After killing some time in the Christian bookstore, reading about how it's perfectly all right to choose to be single (so long as you also choose to be celibate), I walk down by the river, then back through residential streets to the bus depot, where I try Richard one more time.

Still out. Instantly I have an overwhelming craving to be done with all this. I've had enough. I feel ridiculous hanging around a strange town, three hours out of my way, making futile phone calls. Where is Richard, anyway? Does he want to see me? Do I want to see him? I know that since I've come this far I should be patient and hang around some more. I know if we connect it will be worth the effort. But I'm beyond patience, fed up with effort. Like a child I want to be home *now*.

I want to go straight north, instead of back to Fayetteville, but I'm informed this is impossible within the terms of my special discount ticket from the coast. Disgruntled, resentful, I board the Fayetteville bus. The three hours back feel a lot longer than the trip up. Then there's a long, boring wait till 11:15, when my bus to New York departs. It's the smallest, oldest, dirtiest bus I've been in yet. And crowded—another bus, on its way to Fort Bragg with a load of soldiers, has broken down, and our bus will be making an unscheduled stop there. A large woman with a baby on her lap is sitting next to me. Two soldiers are in the seat behind. One of them, a young guy with a mustache, asks me where I'm going, and we make the usual small talk. He keeps touching me on the shoulder for emphasis, which makes me nervous, and besides I'm in no mood for conversation. As soon as I can politely manage it I turn around and scrunch down in my too-small seat. Undaunted, he taps me on the shoulder.

"How long were you in California?" he inquires when I look up.

"A week." I scrunch down again.

Tap.

"What?" I say, exasperated.

"You know, almost everybody on this bus is gettin' off at Fort Bragg. You won't be crowded after that."

He keeps touching me and I keep trying to back off, impossible in such a small space. Finally I blurt, *"Will you please keep your hands to yourself?"* He immediately shrinks back and looks horribly offended. Though I consider that I am technically in the right, I feel like the blue meanie of all time. I also feel revulsion, for this man, the bus, everyone on it. I am out of place. I want to be home, with people I care about, who care about me. I want to be with my friends and especially my lover. To be welcomed and comforted and told I've been missed. The last time I talked to him I told him I didn't know when I'd be back, I'd call as soon as I knew. But it's after midnight now, and by morning I'll be so close to New York a call will be superfluous.

Somewhere around Richmond I blank out; when I wake up it's early morning and we're in Washington, D.C. Two men, not soldiers, are sitting behind me complaining about inflation. We progress too slowly up the New Jersey Turnpike, the world's ugliest road. Finally the New York skyline looms, and we touch down at Port Authority.

Home. I call the man I've come home to, anticipating pleased surprise. Instead the answering machine clicks on. Somehow, caught up as I've been in my obsession with reconnecting, this obvious possibility had not occurred to me. I feel irrationally betrayed and bereft; isolation clings to me like grime from the road. I reach for the phone again, to call a woman friend, but in the middle of dialing I change my mind. It's after all not so bad to be here alone, with no one knowing, no one expecting me, no one to take up half my seat or tap me on the shoulder. I start running water for a bath and take my phone off the hook.

Village Voice, July 1981

Coming Down Again
After the Age of Excess

Dedicated to the memory of Vic Dyer

"That Blake line," said my friend—for the purposes of this article I'll call her Faith, a semi-ironic name, since she is a devout ex-Catholic—"It's always quoted as 'The road of excess leads to the palace of wisdom.'"

"That's not right?" I said.

"It's 'The roads of excess *sometimes* lead to the palace of wisdom.' Very different!"

I looked it up. There it was in "The Marriage of Heaven and Hell," the "Proverbs from Hell" section, directly following "Drive your cart and your plow over the bones of the dead": "The road of excess leads to . . . ," etc. No matter, I realize the poet is playing devil's advocate; anyway I'm willing to concede that Faith is more of an expert on the subject than I (or, possibly, Blake). Not that I haven't had my moments, but Faith's are somehow more—metaphoric. I think, for instance, of the time that, drunk and in the middle of her period, she engaged in a highly baroque night of passion and woke up in the morning to find herself, the man, and the bed covered with gore, a bloody handprint on her wall.

Two years ago Faith joined Alcoholics Anonymous. When she told me, I was doubly surprised. First, because I had never thought of my friend as having "a drinking problem"—a condition I associated with nasty personality traits and inability to function in daily life, certainly not with the all-night pleasure-and-truth-seeking marathons that had seemed to define Faith's drinking style. The other surprise was that AA was evidently not the simpleminded, Salvation Army–type outfit I had imagined; somewhere along the line it had become the latest outlet for the thwarted utopian energies of the '60s counterculture.

Faith's AA group, which included cocaine and heroin junkies as well as alcoholics, functioned (or so I inferred) as a kind of beloved community. Within that community one's alcohol or drug problem was a metaphor for human imperfection, isolation, confusion, despair. True sobriety—not to be confused with compulsive abstinence or puritanical moralism, which were merely the flip side of indulgence—was freedom, transcendence. The point was not self-denial but struggle: confronting the anxiety and pain indulgence had deadened. AA, in short, was a spiritual discipline that, in its post-'60s incarnation, had much in common with that most secular of spiritual disciplines, psychotherapy.

Among the welter of feelings I had about Faith's new project was envy: I was frustrated by the lack of community in my own life. Having first begun living with a man and then decided to have a baby, I had plunged into the pit of urban middle-class Nuclear Familydom and its seemingly inexorable logic—an oppressively expensive apartment, an editing job (more lucrative than writing, less psychically demanding), a daily life overwhelmed with domestic detail ("moving sand," the therapist I was complaining to, a fan of *Woman in the Dunes,* called it), a Sisyphean struggle to keep a love affair from dissolving into a mom-and-pop sandmovers' combine, and a disquieting erosion of other human relationships. Those of my friends who did not have young children lived in another country, of which I was an expatriate, while other NFs of my acquaintance seemed either content to stay on their own islands or, like us, too exhausted from sandmoving to have much time for bridge-building.

My life as a mother did have a dimension of transcendence, marked by intense passion and sensual delight; yet while I'd always insisted that real passion was inherently subversive, my love for my daughter bound me more and more tightly to the social order. Her father and I had remained unmarried, as a tribute to our belief in free love, in the old-fashioned literal sense, and our rejection of a patriarchal contract. But the structural constraints of parenthood married us more surely than a contract would have done. If there was spiritual discipline involved, it had nothing to do with changing diapers or getting up at night—that was just putting one foot in front of the other, doing what one had to do—but rather with the attempt to maintain an ironic ("Zenlike," as I thought of it) detachment from our situation, to think of Nuclear Familydom as an educational experience, an ordeal, like Outward Bound.

It didn't help that I was going through all this during the worst orgy of cultural sentimentality about babies and family since the '50s. On the other hand, it seemed unlikely that the flowering of my own procreative urge—along with that of so many of my '60s-generation/feminist peers—had been a simple matter of beating the clock. The pursuit of ecstasy—in freedom of the imagination and a sense of communal possibility as much as in sex, drugs, or rock and roll—was no longer our inalienable right. Babies, however, were a socially acceptable source of joy.

At a time when anti-drug hysteria was competing with pro-family mania for the status of chief '80s obsession, the same logic could be applied to sobriety. So another of my reactions to Faith's detoxifying was uneasiness. Abstinence might not be the point, but it was the means (unless one somehow achieved the satori of genuinely being able to take a drink or drug or leave it alone). As a metaphor it was troublesome. And it was catching on: Faith pointed out with no little glee that the new aura of AA had lent cleaning up an unprecedented glamour. (As a rule it's still true that whatever my generation decides to do, whether it's cleaning up or having babies, becomes a cultural phenomenon. Ecstasy by association, as it were. Neoconservatives hate us more for this than for anything else.) I was less pleased than she to read Elizabeth Taylor's announcement that she had joined the ranks of the sober. Liz Taylor, whom I'd always cherished as one of the few famous women to barrel down the road of excess with a vengeance—eating, drinking, swearing, fucking, marrying, acquiring diamonds as big as the Ritz. . . . Faith had little sympathy for my discomfort, noting that Liz had scarcely been a happy boozer these last years, burying herself in all that weight: now she was, judging from the press accounts and especially the pictures, in better shape physically and emotionally than she'd been in a long time.

If I find sobriety as a pop ideal threatening, it's not for the obvious reason. I've never been a drinker, and except for a brief period when I took a lot of psychedelics and smoked marijuana more or less regularly, my forays into drugs have been sporadic and experimental—for the past decade or so virtually nonexistent. The point of drugs, for me, was always the eternal moment when you felt like Jesus's son (and gender be damned); when you found your center, which is another word for sanity or, I assume, sobriety as Faith understands it. But I never found a drug that would guarantee me that moment, or even a more vulgar euphoria: acid, grass, speed, coke, even Quaaludes (I've never tried heroin), all were unpredictable, potentially treacherous, as likely to concentrate anxiety as to blow it away. Context was all-important—set and setting, as they called it in those days. My emotional state, amplified or undercut by the collective emotional atmosphere, made the difference between a good trip, a bad trip, or no trip at all.

For me, the ability to get high (I don't mean only on drugs) flourished in the atmosphere of abandon that defined the '60s—that pervasive cultural invitation to leap boundaries, challenge limits, try anything, want everything, overload the senses, let go. Unlike the iconic figures of the era and their many anonymous disciples, I never embraced excess as a fundamental principle of being, an imperative to keep gathering speed until exhaustion or disaster ensued. (My experience of the '60s did have its—"dark side" is a bit too melodramatic; "rough edges" is closer. But more about that later.) Rather, since my own characteristic defense against the terror of living was not counterphobic indulgence but good old inhibition and control, the valorization of *too much* allowed me, for the first time in my life, to have something like *enough*.

Transcendence through discipline—as in meditation, or macrobiotics, or voluntary poverty, or living off the land—was always the antithesis in the '60s dialectic: in context it added another flavor to a rich stew of choices and made for some interesting, to say the least, syntheses. But its contemporary variants are the only game in town, emblems of scarcity. Another metaphor: runners by the thousand, urging on their bodies until the endorphins kick in. The runners' high, an extra reward for the work-well-done of tuning up one's cardiovascular system. What's scarce in the current scheme of things is not (for the shrinking middle class, anyway) rewards but grace, the unearned, the serendipitous. The space to lie down or wander off the map.

Of course, there's a moral question in all this: the Elizabeth Taylor question, or, to put it more starkly, the Janis Joplin question. If ever anyone needed some concept of sobriety as transcendence—not to mention a beloved community offering the acceptance and empathy of fellow imperfect human beings for whom her celebrity was beside the point—it was Janis. The embrace of excess strangled her: would I drive my cart and my plow over her bones? I think of Bob Dylan, avatar of excess cum puritanical moralist, laying into the antiheroine of "Like a Rolling Stone" for letting other people get her kicks for her. And I think of Faith again, of an incident that, unlike the Night of the Red Hand, doesn't make an amusing or colorful story: expansive on wine, wanting to be open to the unearned and serendipitous, she let a pretty boy she met in a club come home with her. Inside her door the pretty boy turned into a rapist, crazy, menacing; lust gave way to violence.

But I don't want to oversimplify in the other direction. It was not the '60s, after all, that caused Janis Joplin's misery; what we know about her years as odd-girl-out in Port Arthur, Texas, makes that plain. The '60s did allow her to break out of Port Arthur, to find, for a painfully short but no less real time, her voice, her beauty, her powers—her version of redemption. Had rock and roll, Haight-Ashbury, the whole thing never happened, I can't imagine that her life would have been better; it might not even have been longer. Nor does Faith regret her time on the road. Among '60s veterans in AA there is the shared recognition of a paradox, one that separates the "new sobriety" from its fundamentalist heritage: taking drugs enriched their vision, was in fact a powerful catalyst for the very experience of transcendence, and yearning for it, that now defines their abstinence. It's crucial not to forget that the limits we challenged—of mechanistic rationalism, patriarchal authority, high culture, a morality deeply suspicious of pleasure, a "realism" defined as resignation—were prisons. Still are.

The image of excess that bedevils the conservative mind even more than reefer madness is that of the orgy—anonymous, indiscriminate, unrestrained, guiltless sex. As contemporary mythology has it (and as the right continually repeats with fear and gloating) the sexual revolution of the '60s was an exercise in "promiscuity"; because of AIDS, promiscuity is now fatal; therefore the sexual revolution was a disastrous mistake. This syllogism, which takes the now-devastated gay sex-bar-and-bathhouse world as the paradigm for '60s sexual culture, says less about the actual habits of that culture than about the envious prurience of this one. But then, myths generally have more to do with imaginative reality than with the practical sort, and if the idea of AIDS as retribution (God's or nature's) wields power far beyond the constituencies of Pat Robertson and Norman Podhoretz, if the white, non-needle-using heterosexual population's fears of contagion have far outstripped the present danger, it's in part because the traditionalist's sexual nightmares are the underside of the counterculture's dreams. There was the dream of recovering innocence, dumping our Oedipal baggage, getting back to the polymorphous perversity of childhood and starting over; the dream of a beneficent sexual energy flowing freely, without defenses, suspicion, guilt, shame; the dream of transcending possessiveness and jealousy; the dream, at its most apocalyptic, of universal love: it was one thing to have sex with strangers, quite another if the strangers were your brothers and sisters, if you need not fear games, or contempt, or violence.

Few people tried seriously to live this vision, even in circles where LSD and hippie rhetoric flowed as freely as libido was supposed to; the New York writers and artists I hung out with were positively snarky about it all. Yet the dreams put their stamp on us.

Context, again, was crucial, and in these skittish days it bears repeating that the context of sexual utopianism was, in the first place, the near-universal revolt of young people against what are now nostalgically referred to as "traditional values": that is, women's chastity policed by the dubious promise of male "respect" and lifetime monogamy; by the withholding of birth control and the criminalizing of abortion; by the threat of social ostracism, sexual violence and exploitation, forced marriage and motherhood. Men's schizophrenia, expressed in hypocritical "respect" for the frustrating good girl and irrational contempt for the willing bad one, pride in their lust as the emblem of their maleness and disgust with it as the evidence of their "animal natures." Homosexuality unspeakable and invisible. By the end of the '50s the sexual revolution had begun, but the first version to gain ascendancy was a conservative one—it defined sex as a commodity, or a form of healthy exercise, that merely needed to be made more available. Furious at the moral code we'd grown up with—I knew no one of either sex who didn't feel in some way crushed by it—yet uninspired by the curiously antierotic liberalism proposed as an alternative, we were ripe for ways of imagining sex that might begin to heal our wounds.

Imagination was the key (as John Lennon was to claim, in a song too often misjudged as simpleminded). My own sexual behavior remained relatively conventional; during most of the years when the '60s sexual imagination was at its height, I was living with lovers for the most part monogamously. While I rejected monogamy as a moral obligation, it was mostly the sense of freedom I wanted, the right (after the years of not enough) to feel open to the world's possibilities, without prior censorship. I disliked the idea of the on-principle

Exclusive Couple; it was smug, claustrophobic. On acid trips I perceived that there was indeed another kind of sexual love, better than romantic love as we knew it, more profoundly accepting and trusting, free of the insecurity that demands ownership. I even left one man for another in pursuit, or so I thought, of that version of the dream. Of course, to be capable of translating such transient flashes of perception into my real, daily life, I (and he) would have had to be born again, into a different world, and my new relationship was soon as mired in coupledom as the other one had been.

Still . . . a couple of years later, this same man and I were sharing a two-family house with a married couple and their baby. I decided, for once, to act on my fantasies of extending sexual intimacy beyond the sacred dyad, and my initiative was enthusiastically received by all concerned. From the conventional point of view I got my comeuppance. It turned out that while the husband and I were pursuing an enjoyable experiment, expanding our friendship, transcending the nuclear family, and so on, our mates were doing something rather different— were infatuated with each other, in fact. It hurt, it was disruptive, it made me for a time feel like killing two people. Yet I could never honestly say I was sorry I'd started the whole thing. The power of that urge to stretch the limits could not cancel out jealousy and possessiveness, but it could compete. And, in a sense, win.

Though a respect for history compels me to add that my friend, the family man who also wanted more, later divorced his wife, remarried, and became a born-again Christian.

History and its convolutions. . . . The affirmation of love's body against the life-denying brutality of "traditional values" was at the heart of what made me a feminist. As a popular Emma Goldman T-shirt implied, if I couldn't fuck it wasn't my revolution. For me, for thousands of women, the explosion of radical feminism was a supremely sexy moment; we had the courage of our desires as we'd never had before. It was not only that we could make new demands of our male lovers or seek out female ones; not only that we were rejecting the sexual shame and self-hatred endemic to our condition. We were making history, defining our fate, for once taking center stage and telling men how it was going to be. Sisterhood was powerful therefore erotic.

And yet it was feminism—not the new right, certainly not the as yet-unknown AIDS virus—that first displaced the counterculture's vision of sex with a considerably harsher view. I don't mean only, or even primarily, the brand of feminism that has attacked sex as a form of male power, the sex drive as an ideological construct, and "sexual liberation" as a euphemism for rape. In the early radical feminist movement such polemics were regarded as eccentric (though I was not the only one who, with overt relish and unconscious condescension, admired them as rhetorical excess, a Dadaist provocation, part of the exhilarating racket of newly discovered voices transgressing the first law of femaleness: be nice). Most of us felt about the sexual revolution what Gandhi reputedly thought of

Western civilization—that it would be a good idea. There was, however, the little matter of abortion rights; there was the continuing legal and social tolerance of rape; there were all those "brothers" who spoke of ecstasy but fucked with their egos, looked down on women who were "too" free, and thought the most damning name they could call a feminist was "lesbian." And then—our new sense of ourselves might be aphrodisiac, but the rage that went along with it wasn't. Nor were men's reactions—ridicule, fake solicitude, guilt, defensiveness, hysteria, and, when none of that shut us up, what-do-you-bitches-want fury— much of a turn-on for either sex.

It was the best, the worst, the most enlightening, the most bewildering of times. Feminism intensified my utopian sexual imagination, made me desperate to get what I really wanted, not "after the revolution" but *now*—even as it intensified my skepticism, chilling me with awareness of how deeply relations between the sexes were corrupted and, ultimately, calling into question the very nature of my images of desire. For my sexual fantasies were permeated with the iconography of masculine-feminine, seduction-surrender, were above all centered on the union of male and female genitals as the transcendent aim of sex (not, surely not, one form of joining among others). Why did I want "what I really wanted," and did I really want it? And—oh, shit, forget about utopia— what were the chances of steering some sort of livable path between schizophrenia (or amnesia) and kill-joy self-consciousness in bed?

But there was one more convolution to come: feminism inspired gay liberation and with it a renewed vision of untrammeled sex as the key to freedom, power, and community. Ironically (at least from my point of view), it was a vision of sex among men. The lesbian movement of the '70s was not primarily about liberating desire (though there were, of course, plenty of individual and subcultural exceptions) but about extending female solidarity; for the gay male community solidarity was, at its core, about desire. To this version of the sexual revolution I was, of course, doubly an outsider. That aspect of the gay male imagination that most repelled and fascinated the straight world, the culture of anonymous, ritualistic sex and sensation for pure sensation's sake, repelled and fascinated me. It seemed the epitome of distance and difference—except when an evocative piece of fiction or theater, or more rarely a conversation about sex with a gay man, would awake in me some ghost of a forgotten fantasy, reminding me that otherness is at bottom a defensive illusion.

AIDS, paradoxically, has impressed this on me in a deeper and more lasting way. That's partly because the issues AIDS raises transcend sex, per se. The eruption of a massive plague-like epidemic, of a sort we were supposed to have "conquered" long ago, not only threatens to test our economic resources and social conscience in unprecedented ways, but attacks the fundamental faith of our scientific-technological culture—that we can dominate nature. And for this very reason, the sexual significance of AIDS transcends the demographics of high- and low-risk groups. On one level the sexual liberation movements embody the revolt of "the natural" against social domination, yet they are unthinkable without technology. Modern contraception, safe childbirth and abortion, antibiotics drastically reduced the risks of sex, and in doing so encouraged the heady fantasy of sex with no risk at all. AIDS is hardly the first challenge to that fantasy: women found out a while ago that the only truly zipless contraceptives, the pill and IUD, were dangerous—sometimes deadly—and in some parts of the world, resistant strains of gonorrhea are already out of control. I suspect that as we learn how to "manage" AIDS—with imperfect but workable vaccines, treatments that keep people alive and functioning, condoms, and other precautions—our sense of it as a dramatic watershed, a radical break with the past, will diminish (even, eventually, for gay men), just as condoms themselves will become an ordinary part of sexual culture instead of an emotionally charged symbol of (take your pick) all hated barriers to delight or rampant permissiveness. Still, our sexual imagination is bound to change. The idea of achieving safe sex through chemistry will come to seem a quaint piece of Americana, akin to the notion of abolishing scarcity through unlimited economic growth.

So does this mean the conservatives are right, the dream is over? A lot of erstwhile dreamers, gay men especially, are feeling a kind of rebellious despair as they contemplate the shadow of death between desire and act. What can sexual freedom possibly mean if not pleasure unconstricted by fear or calculation? Yet—and I speak as a woman who is passionately pro-abortion, who remembers nostalgically the ease and security of the pill—there is something muddled about a logic that equates freedom with safety. Freedom is inherently risky, which is the reason for rules and limits in the first place; the paradox of the '60s generation is that we felt secure enough, economically and sexually, to reject security. The risks people took were real and so were the losses: the deaths, breakdowns, burnouts, addictions, the paranoia and nihilism, "revolutionary" crimes and totalitarian religious cults, poverty, and prison terms. Though the casualties of drugs and politics have been more conspicuous, sex has never been safe certainly not for women and gay men: in a misogynist, homophobic culture suffused with sexual rage, to be a "whore" or a "pervert" is to "ask for" punishment.

In many post-AIDS elegies to sexual liberation lurks a sentimental idea of gay male culture as paradise lost, a haven of pure pleasure invaded by the serpent of disease. Yet the appeal of the gay fast lane on the road of excess surely had something to do with being outlaws, defying taboos, confronting and ritualizing danger, assimilating it to the marrow of a pleasure that was, in part, a triumph over fear. It could not be a coincidence that the sexual anonymity invested with so much excitement had historically been a survival strategy for gay men in the closet. At the same time, gay men's pursuit of sex without attachment reflected a widespread male fantasy—one that men who want sex with women must usually conceal or play down. For many men, freedom to separate sex from relationship without guilt or hypocrisy has always been what sexual liberation is about. But the conventionally masculine dream of pure lust is, I'm convinced, as conservative in its way as the conventionally feminine romanticism that converts lust to pure emotion—or, for that matter, as the patriarchal values that subordinate passion to marriage and procreation. All are attempts to tame sex, to make it safe by holding something back. For the objective risks of sex would not terrify us half so much if they did not reinforce a more primal inner threat. To abandon ourselves utterly to sensation and emotion—to give up the boundaries and limits that keep us in control—would be, for most of us, like cutting loose from gravity and watching the earth spin. Dissolution of the ego is the death we fear; the real sexual revolution, the one no virus can keep us from imagining, is the struggle to face that fear, transcend it, and let go.

My favorite statement about risk and excess is also my favorite '60s joke. It's a Fabulous Furry Freak Brothers comic strip in which one of the skanky protagonists gets busted for dope. At the police station he is granted his one phone call. The last panel shows him burbling euphorically into the phone, ordering one large with pepperoni, mushrooms, green peppers.

The road of excess is a roller coaster, the palace of wisdom a funhouse. Liberation is playful, useless, unproductive, for itself—too much. Like Little Richard's screams, Phil Spector's wall of sound, Dylan's leopard-skin pillbox hat, Janis's feather boa, the foxhunt on Sgt. Pepper. Or, to stick with our main metaphor, the custom cars Tom Wolfe immortalized, Ken Kesey's Pranksters' Day-Glo bus, the Byrds' magic carpet, Jefferson Airplane. The trouble is, the trip always ends up heading for somewhere, loaded down with all the tragic baggage of human deprivation and yearning. And when that happens, the vehicles start going off the track, over the edge, down the slippery slope from yes she said yes she said yes to just say no. Which is where irony comes in.

I'm a political person, a political radical. I believe that the struggle for freedom, pleasure, transcendence is not just an individual matter. The social system that organizes our lives, and as far as possible channels our desire, is antagonistic to that struggle; to change this requires collective effort. The moment a movement coalesces can be, should be itself an occasion of freedom, pleasure, and transcendence, but it is never only that. Radical movements by definition focus attention on the gap between present and future, and cast their participants, for the present, in the negative role of opposition. Fighting entrenched power means drawing battle lines, defining the enemy. In the '60s and after, the strains of radicalism I identify with have defined the enemy as all forms of domination and hierarchy—beginning but not ending with sex, race, and class—and from this point of view, as a French leftist slogan from the May '68 upheavals put it, "We are all Jews and Germans." Which doesn't mean that we're all equally victims and oppressors, or that the differences don't matter, just that there are few of us who haven't abused power in some contexts, suffered powerlessness in others. And that all of us, oppressors and victims alike, have had to make our bargains with the system—bargains often secret even from ourselves—for the sake of survival and, yes, for those moments of freedom, pleasure, and transcendence that give survival meaning.

So to be a radical as I've defined it implies self-consciousness and self-criticism, a commitment to (in the language of that segment of the '60s and '70s left most heavily influenced by feminist consciousness-raising) confronting not only our own oppression but the ways we oppress others. And since it's politics we're talking about, not therapy, this confrontation is of necessity a collective process . . . and already we're in very deep waters indeed.

In 1970 I was living with a group of people running a movement hangout for antiwar GIs. It was my first venture into the mixed left since becoming a radical feminist, and my sense of embattlement was acute. Predictably, I was angriest at the men I felt closest to, the ones I knew really did care—about me, about having good politics; so often they simply *didn't get it,* a solid, dumb lump of resistance masquerading as incomprehension of the simplest, clearest demands for reciprocity. At the same time, another woman in the project, a feminist from a working-class background, was confronting me and the rest of our group of predominantly middle-class lefties about the myriad of crude and subtle ways we were oppressing her and the mostly working-class soldiers we worked with. And I began to see it all from the other side: my good intentions; my struggle to see myself as my friend saw me, to change; my continual falling short; my friend's anger and hurt when I just *didn't get it*; my own dumb lump that, to me, often felt indistinguishable from the core of my identity. Male guilt made me furious ("Don't sit there feeling guilty, just get your fucking foot off my neck"), but now I was mired in guilt, resentful about having to feel guilty, guilty about being resentful, and so on.

In "Salt of the Earth," an ostensible ode to the "hard-working people," Mick Jagger suddenly blurts that they don't look real to him, they look so strange. On one awful acid trip I saw with excruciating clarity just how deeply and pervasively I experienced poor people as alien, how the very word "poor" embodied that implacable distance called pity. And of course I saw that from the other side too. I don't remember if this glimpse into hell-as-other-people made me any less angry at men, but it certainly made me more despairing: I didn't look real to them; the rest was commentary.

More and more it seemed that everything that gave me pleasure, kept me sane, soothed (or distracted from) the wound of female otherness was a function of my privileges—education, leisure, certain kinds of self-esteem, work I enjoyed that let me live like a bohemian, and most crucially the luxury of distance, therefore insulation, from certain kinds of human misery. I might agree, as an intellectual proposition, that only a violent revolution could break the power of the corporate state, but imagining what that meant filled me with revulsion and terror; I was glad there was no practical prospect of it. What my friend really wanted (I knew, because I wanted the same thing from men) was that I give up my blinders and live, no exit, with relentless awareness of her pain, as she had to do: only then would I be truly committed to revolution, whatever it entailed. To my shame I couldn't do this, couldn't bring myself to what I saw as a self-immolation at once necessary and intolerable.

Something was wrong, I realized dimly, something was out of whack. Political virtue equated with sacrifice, pleasure with corruption—how had I gotten back *there*? Yet seeing how class distorted my vision had shaken my faith in my judgment. Part of being oppressed was having one's perceptions negated; part of being an oppressor was doing the negating. I reminded myself of this when a soldier I didn't like or trust became my friend's lover and moved into our house. My friend thought I was cold to him for class reasons—he was uneducated, inarticulate, with a kind of bumpkin style. I accepted her analysis, suppressed my qualms, and tried to welcome the man as housemate and brother. Then it turned out that everything he had told us, even his birthday, was a lie.

I felt ambushed, but I'd done it to myself: pursuing revolutionary purity by handing someone else responsibility for my choices (yet another form of exploitation, she would have said if she'd known). Yes, there was something wrong, something sinister, even: I didn't have the words for it, didn't yet have Jonestown and Cambodia as reference points, but I smelled death. This was where excess led when fed by desperation and hubris instead of exuberance and hope. I was depressed for a long time. Many years and shrink sessions later it occurred to me that I was addicted to being right.

In an earlier, more innocent time I am sitting with friends in a coffeeshop in Toronto. We are New York rock critics in town for some festival or press junket. Our hair is very long, our dress ranges from East Village Indian to neo-pop. We have smoked some hash and are giggling with abandon. We order hamburgers and sundaes, then spaghetti, then, as I recall, more ice cream. The waitress smiles at us, inspiring a frisson of mock-paranoia around the table: *does she know*? Suddenly it strikes me very funny that the dope is illegal and the food is not.

Segue to the present, one of those days when conversation with my daughter, Nona, age four, goes something like this: "I want gum. I want a lollipop. I want ices. I want a cookie. I want another cookie, a *different* cookie. I want a Coke. I want candy. *That* candy. I want . . . ."

"You had ices today. No sweets till after dinner. No candy. No more cookies. You'll rot your teeth. You'll upset your stomach. You won't eat real food. NO!"

"I want—"

Once I answered by singing, "You can't always get what you want." That silenced her for a minute. I finished the verse. She looked at me thoughtfully. "But I *want* candy," she said.

This is no doubt the kind of exchange detractors of the '60s have in mind when they dismiss the counterculture as "infantile." I feel them looking over my shoulder as I play the part of repressive civilization frustrating limitless desire. I think they miss the point.

I love sugar. Controlling my craving for sweets is always a struggle, giving in to it an ambivalent, illicit pleasure. Sugar is my quick fix for anxiety or depression, an effortless and reliable consolation in a demanding, insecure world: the only problem is, a minute later you're hungry again. Determined to spare Nona this compulsion, I decided on a strategy even before she was born. I got her father to agree that we would treat sweets as casually as any other food, neither forbid them nor limit them nor insist that she finish her "real food" first. If we didn't give her the idea that sweets were evil/special/scarce, they would hold no fascination for her, and we could trust her to set her own limits. In short, we would put to the empirical test our cultural-radical faith in the self-regulating child.

Our strategy didn't fail; it never got a fair trial. Neither of us could stick to it. After a while I grasped the obvious: if I were capable of treating sweets as casually as any other food, I wouldn't have had to make an issue of it in the first place. And the anxious double messages I was transmitting were more likely to encourage an obsession with the stuff than if I'd followed the conventional advice, set limits I was comfortable with, and enforced them.

I do that now, but it's a matter of damage control. For Nona sweets are the object and the symbol of desire. Often the litany of Iwantcandygumcookies is code for wanting more from us. More time and patience and acceptance. More babying and reassurance. More freedom and power. We try to listen to what she's really saying, to give her what she wants when it's also what she needs. But we are parents in an age of scarcity and constraint, in the grip of family life, which is structured to ensure that no one gets enough time, patience, acceptance, babying, and reassurance, or freedom and power. In protest, Nona demands too much; we deny her for her own good; and so it begins again.

Village Voice, January 1989

The Drug War
From Vision to Vice

Wandering through the Brooklyn Botanical Gardens on the first expansively warm day of the year, snatching some time out from my work-ridden, pressured, scheduled dailiness, my daughter asleep in her stroller, I found myself thinking, "This would be a beautiful place to trip." A weirdly anachronistic thought—I haven't taken any psychedelic drugs in 15 years and have no serious desire to do so now. Even if I could negotiate the unencumbered 24 hours or so I always needed to go up, stay up, and come down again, it's the wrong time. The vibes, as we used to say, are not to be trusted—there's too much tension, anxiety, hostility in the air. Besides, right now I lack the requisite innocent optimism. Bogged down in material concerns I once managed to ignore, in thrall to New York's Great God Real Estate, I feel somewhat estranged from the Tao. "But what if something bad happened?" was my next unbidden thought that day in the park. "I have a child—can I afford that kind of risk?" Which of course answers its own question; a first principle of tripping as I remember it is that the main thing you have to fear is fear itself.

Whether or not I ever feel free to take psychedelics again, they remain, for me, a potent emblem of freedom. Somehow they disarranged the grids I'd imposed on the world, untied the Laingian knots I'd imposed on myself. They allowed me, for the moment, to see things freshly—the splendor in the grass, the glory in the flower, the ridiculous self-inflation in my self-hatred—and feel saner than I'd ever thought possible. This was an experience of intense pleasure, emotional catharsis, and enlightenment in its most playful, least solemn sense. My fellow trippers and I were always breaking out into what seemed to straight onlookers like maniacal laughter: sometimes we laughed because the people around us had turned into elegant giraffes and scared birds and angry terriers; sometimes because we realized how silly our most serious obsessions were; sometimes just because, like Lou Reed, we saw that *everything was all right*. If the vision and the feeling always faded, leaving glimpses, fragments, intimations behind, still they were real—or as real as anything else. They suggested what human beings might be if we grew up differently, if certain kinds of damage were not inflicted.

But that was in another country, or another language. If people still take drugs in search of transcendence, they don't talk about it in public. The one counterculture drug that's made it into the mainstream is marijuana, and its gestalt has changed radically in the process—where once it was valued as a mild psychedelic, now it's mostly used, like alcohol, to smooth out the rough edges. These days drugs are a metaphor not for freedom or ecstasy but for slavery and horror. It's the "hard" drugs—especially heroin and cocaine—that obsess the American imagination; rarely do we see the word "drug" without "abuse" or "menace" next to it.

On this issue the ideological right's triumph over '60s liberationism has been nothing short of a rout: it is now an unquestioned axiom of public discourse that drugs and drug taking of any but the purely medicinal sort are simply, monolithically, evil. Dope is the enemy that unites Ronald Reagan and Jesse Jackson, that gets blamed for everything from the plight of the black community to teenage alienation to America's problems competing in the world market. (Even Lyndon LaRouche features drug pushers in his paranoid cosmology, right up there with international bankers and Zionists.) In this climate, anyone who suggests that the question of drugs has real complexities, that some kinds of drugs and some kinds of drug taking are not a terrible thing and may even, under certain circumstances, actually be, well, a good thing, can expect to be as popular as Paul Krassner at a Women Against Pornography convention.

And yet the use of illegal drugs has never been more pervasive, visible, and socially accepted, especially among young people. As I write this, I'm looking at recent issues of *Time* and *Newsweek*: in the same week *Time*'s cover story was "Drugs on the Job," *Newsweek*'s "Kids and Cocaine: An Epidemic Strikes Middle America." How do you run a War Against Drug Abuse when Rambo is smoking crack?

The gap between ideology and behavior is increasingly filled with hysteria; while the cultural left has been busy combating various forms of sex panic, drug panic has come into its own. Frustrated by its inability to choke off the supply of drugs, the government has begun looking for ways to stifle the demand. The notorious campaign to spray paraquat on Mexican marijuana was a primitive version of this "demand side" strategy; the idea was not really to ruin the crop but to make people afraid to buy the stuff. Now efforts to deter and punish users have gone into high gear. The logic of such a mania to control the behavior of millions of individuals is totalitarian. And *totalitarian* is not too strong a word for the proposal of the President's Commission on Organized Crime that all companies test their employees for drug use, beginning with the federal government. Edwin Meese, true to form, commented that such a measure would not violate the Fourth Amendment, since testees would be consenting to a search in return for the "privilege" of applying for a job. (Listen, if you don't like it, my coke dealer has an opening.)

It's scary living in a time when a president's commission and a U.S. attorney general dare to talk this way so openly; scarier when you realize that many corporations—*Time* lists Exxon, IBM, Lockheed, Shearson Lehman, Federal Express, United Airlines, TWA, Hoffman-La Roche, Du Pont, and (!) the *New York Times*—are already requiring urinalysis for job applicants, without legal impediment or significant public opposition. Many other companies "merely" test suspected users; all branches of the armed forces now conduct random testing of servicepeople. And anything seems to go when checking on the purity of athletes, charged with the thankless burden of being wholesome "role models" for our nation's youth.

Yet this isn't simply a civil liberties issue; it's a question of cultural schizophrenia. I don't know of any polls on the subject, but sheer probability suggests that most of the miscreants insidiously wrecking our economic fiber by getting stoned on the job must have voted for Reagan. Perhaps the definition of an authoritarian society is one in which people won't stand up for or stand behind what they do, and prefer to think about the contradictions as little as possible.

Yes, the counterculture indulged in a lot of mindless romanticism about drugs, exaggerating their world-changing, soul-saving potential and minimizing their dangers. But there was also a thoughtful side to psychedelic culture, a salutary self-consciousness about the process of drug taking and what it meant. It was widely understood, for instance, that drugs were more the occasion or catalyst of "psychedelic experience" than the cause of it; that what shaped people's trips was their state of mind and their surroundings—"set and setting," as the then still professorial Alpert and Leary put it in their early LSD lectures. After all, for thousands of years people had been attaining similar states of mind through meditation and other non-pharmacological practices.

We took seriously the idea that drugs were good or bad depending on how you used them and whether they enhanced or restricted your freedom. It was probably best to take psychedelics in a spirit of curiosity and acceptance, leavened with an appreciation of the absurd, though on the other hand it was probably best not to make any rules about it. Drug abuse, in psychedelic terms, meant fetishizing the drug—looking to it as a solution rather than a pathway, or trying to repeat a particular good trip rather than following the serendipitous wanderings of one's mind. This fetishism could become the equivalent of addiction: it was a not insignificant risk along with the possibility that our minds would wander into hell rather than heaven, or that a drug powerful enough to knock our consciousness off its usual tracks might be powerful enough to do terrible things to our brain cells. We were willing to take these risks in the interest of seeing things differently—and this, ultimately, was the "menace" our cultural guardians were so determined to stamp out.

Of course, psychedelics were not the only '60s drug scene: speed, heroin, downers, and, to a lesser extent, cocaine also flourished. The ideological assault on drugs has conflated them all, making for a predictable irony: psychedelics and the idealism surrounding them have gone underground, while the hard drugs, which no one, including their users, ever defended in the first place, become more and more entrenched. In the '80s drugs are merely a vice, which is to say a covert and private rebellion that affirms the system, an expression of and hedge against boredom, impotence, and despair. They are also a mirror— coke embodies the compulsive nervous energy of the "opportunity society," smack the isolation of the excluded poor. Like Victorian pornography, dope in the Age of Meese shows us that every era gets the menace it deserves.

Village Voice, April 1986

The Drug War
Hell No, I Won't Go

At last the government has achieved something it hasn't managed since the height of '50s anti-Communist hysteria—enlisted public sentiment in a popular war. The president's invocation of an America united in a holy war against drugs is no piece of empty rhetoric; the bounds of mainstream debate on this issue are implicit in the response of the Democratic so-called opposition, which attacked Bush's program as not tough or expensive enough. (As Senator Biden—fresh from his defense of the flag; the guy is really on a roll—put it, "What we need is another D-Day, not another Vietnam.") To be sure, there is controversy over the drug warriors' methods. Civil libertarians object to drug testing and dubious police practices; many commentators express doubts about the wisdom of going after millions of casual drug users; and some hardy souls still argue that drugs should be decriminalized and redefined as a medical and social problem. But where are the voices questioning the basic assumptions of the drug war: that drugs are our most urgent national problem; that a drug-free society is a valid social goal; that drug use is by definition abuse? If there's a war on, are drugs the real enemy? Or is mobilizing the nation's energies on behalf of a war against drugs far more dangerous than the drugs themselves?

By now some of you are wondering if I've been away—perhaps on an extended LSD trip—and missed the havoc crack has wrought in inner-city neighborhoods. One of the drug warriors' more effective weapons is the argument that any crank who won't sign on to the antidrug crusade must be indifferent to, if not actively in favor of, the decimation of black and Latino communities by rampant addiction, AIDS, crack babies, the recruitment of kids into the drug trade, and control of the streets by Uzi-toting gangsters. To many people, especially people of color, making war on drugs means not taking it anymore, defending their lives and their children against social rot. It's a seductive idea: focusing one's rage on a vivid, immediate symptom of a complex social crisis makes an awful situation seem more manageable. Yet in reality the drug war has nothing to do with making communities livable or creating a decent future for black kids. On the contrary, prohibition is directly responsible for the power of crack dealers to terrorize whole neighborhoods. And every cent spent on the cops, investigators, bureaucrats, courts, jails, weapons, and tests required to feed the drug-war machine is a cent not spent on reversing the social policies that have destroyed the cities, nourished racism, and laid the groundwork for crack culture.

While they're happy to use the desperate conditions of the poor as a club to intimidate potential opposition, the drug warriors have another agenda altogether. Forget those obscene pictures of Bush kissing crack babies (and read his budget director's lips: money for the drug war is to come not from the military budget but from other domestic programs). Take it from William Bennett, who, whatever his political faults, is honest about what he's up to: "We identify the chief and seminal wrong here as drug use. . . . There are lots of other things that are wrong, such as money laundering and crime and violence in the inner city, but drug use itself is wrong. And that means the strategy is aimed at reducing drug use." Aimed, that is, not at solving social problems but at curbing personal freedom.

Of course, it's not all drugs Bennett has in mind, but illegal drugs. And as even some drug warriors will admit, whether a drug is legal or not has little to do with rational considerations such as how addictive it may be, or how harmful to health, or how implicated in crime. Bill Bennett drinks without apology while denouncing marijuana and crack with equal passion; heroin is denied to terminal cancer patients while methadone, which is at least as addictive, is given away at government-sponsored clinics. What illegal drugs do have in common is that in one way or another they are perceived as threatening social control. Either (like heroin and crack) they're associated with all the social disorder and scary otherness of the so-called underclass, or (like marijuana and the psychedelics) they become emblems of social dissidence, "escape from"—i.e., unorthodox views of—reality, and loss of productivity and discipline. Equally important, illicit drugs offer pleasure—and perhaps even worse, feelings of freedom and power—for the taking; the more intense the euphoria, the more iniquitous the drug. Easily available chemical highs are the moral equivalent of welfare—they undercut the official culture's control of who gets rewarded for what. And they invite subversive comparisons to the meager ration of pleasure, freedom, and power available in people's daily lives.

Illegal drugs, furthermore, are offenses to authority by definition. Users are likely to define themselves as rebels—or become users in the first place as a means of rebelling—and band together in an outlaw culture. The drugs are then blamed for the rebellion, the social alienation that gave rise to it, and the crime and corruption that actually stem from prohibition and its inevitable con-comitant, an immensely profitable illegal industry.

From this perspective, it makes perfect sense to lump marijuana with crack—while different in every other respect, both are outlaw, countercultural drugs. From this perspective, mounting a jihad against otherwise law-abiding citizens whose recreational drug of choice happens to be illegal is not a hugely expen-sive, futile, punitive diversion from addressing the real problems of our urban wasteland; it goes straight to the point. After all, hard-core addicts presumably can't help themselves, while casual users are choosing to ignore two decades of pervasive antidrug moralizing. The point is that the cultural changes of the '60s and '70s eroded traditional forms of authority, loosening governmental and corporate control over people's lives. And the drug war is about getting it back.

One means of achieving this is legitimizing repressive police and military tactics. Drugs, say the warriors, are such an overriding national emergency that civil liberties must give way; of course, laws and policies aimed at curbing dealers' and users' constitutional rights will then be available for use in other "emergency" situations. Another evolving strategy is to bypass the criminal jus-tice system altogether (thereby avoiding some of those irritating constitutional obstacles as well as the public's reluctance to put middle-class pot-smokers in jail) in favor of civil sanctions like large fines and the withholding of govern-ment benefits and such "privileges" as drivers' licenses.

But so far, the centerpiece of the cultural counterrevolution is the snowball-ing campaign for a "drug-free workplace"—a euphemism for "drug-free work-force," since urine testing also picks up off-duty indulgence. The purpose of this '80s version of the loyalty oath is less to deter drug use than to make people undergo a humiliating ritual of subordination: "When I say pee, you pee." The idea is to reinforce the principle that one must forfeit one's dignity and privacy to earn a living, and bring back the good old days when employers had the unquestioned right to demand that their workers' appearance and behavior, on or off the job, meet management's standards. After all, before the '60s, employ-ers were free to reject you not only because you were the wrong race, sex, or age, but because of your marital status, your sex life, your political opinions, or anything else they didn't like; there were none of those pesky discrimination or wrongful firing suits.

The argument that drug use hurts productivity only supports my point: if it's okay to forbid workers to get stoned on their days off because it might affect their health, efficiency, or "motivation," why not forbid them to stay out late, eat fatty foods, fall in love, or have children? As for jobs that affect the public safety, if tests are needed, they should be performance tests—an air controller or rail-road worker whose skills are impaired by fatigue is as dangerous as one who's drugged. Better yet, anyone truly concerned about safety should support the demands of workers in these jobs for shorter hours and less stressful working conditions.

In the great tradition of demagogic saber-rattling, Bush's appeal seeks to distract from the fissures of race, class, and sex and unite us against a common enemy: the demon drug. The truth is, however, that this terrifying demon is a myth. Drug addiction and its associated miseries are not caused by evil, irresistible substances. People get hooked on drugs because they crave relief from intolerable frustration; because they're starved for pleasure and power. Addiction is a social and psychological, not a chemical, disease.

Every generation has its arch-demon drug: alcohol, reefer madness, heroin, and now crack. Recently the *New York Times* ran a front-page story reporting that drug experts have revised their earlier belief that crack is a uniquely, irresistibly addictive drug; crack addiction, they assert, has more to do with social conditions than with the drug's chemistry. Two cheers for the experts; surely it shouldn't have taken them so long to ask why crack is irresistible to the black poor but not to the white middle class. Perhaps they will take the next step and recognize that so long as crack is the only thriving industry in the inner city—and integral to its emotional economy as well—there's only one way to win a war on drugs. That's to adopt the method the Chinese used to solve their opium problem: line every dealer and user up against the wall and shoot. And try not to notice the color of the bodies.

If the logic of the drug war for blacks and Latinos leads to a literal police state, for the rest of us it means silence and conformity. In recent years, much of the drug warriors' ideological firepower has been aimed at the '60s. Members of my generation who took any part in the passions and pleasures of those times—that is, most of us now between, say, 35 and 50—are under enormous pressure to agree that we made a terrible mistake (and even that won't help if you aspire to be a Supreme Court justice). Which makes me feel irresistibly compelled to reiterate at every opportunity that I have taken illegal drugs, am not ashamed of it, and still smoke the occasional joint (an offense for which Bush and Bennett want to fine me $10,000, lift my driver's license, and throw me in boot camp). I believe that taking drugs is not intrinsically immoral or destructive, that the state has no right to prevent me from exploring different states of consciousness, and that drug prohibition causes many of the evils it purports to cure.

According to the drug warriors, I and my ilk are personally responsible not only for the deaths of Janis Joplin and Jimi Hendrix but for the crack crisis. Taken literally, this is scurrilous nonsense: the counterculture never looked kindly on hard drugs, and the age of crack is a product not of the '60s but of Reaganism. Yet there's a sense in which I do feel responsible. Cultural radicals are committed to extending freedom, and that commitment, by its nature, is dangerous. It encourages people to take risks, some of them foolish or worse.

It arouses deep longings that, if disappointed, may plunge people into despair (surely one aspect of the current demoralization of black youth is the peculiar agony of thwarted revolution). If I support the struggle for freedom, I can't disclaim responsibility for its costs; I can only argue that the costs of suppressing freedom are, in the end, far higher. All wars are hell. The question remains which ones are worth fighting.

Village Voice, September 1989

The Diaper Manifesto
We Need a Child-Rearing Movement

The other day I ran into a woman I hadn't seen in a long time, a veteran feminist, and within minutes we were talking about child care problems. Her horror story reminded me, as if I needed reminding, of how precarious, really, are our arrangements, so crucial to a household's ecology, so vulnerable to changes—in the caretaker's situation, the parents', the child's—that we can never quite relax even when things are going well. The ironies were not lost on us: as feminist activists we, along with the thousands of other young, childless women who dominated the movement, had of course understood that sexual equality required a new system of child rearing, but the issue remained abstract, unconnected with our most urgent needs; as mothers in the political vacuum of the '80s, along with millions of other working parents, we pursue our individual solutions as best we can. The political has devolved into the personal, with a vengeance.

The influx of mothers into the work force has produced a child care crisis with radical implications—for the family, work, the condition of women. Yet except for the far right, virtually no one is discussing it on that level. For purposes of media agonizing, the problem has been defined in narrowly pragmatic, thoroughly sexist terms: how to get mothers enough help so they can keep doing their double duty, inside and outside the home. (This approach has recently nosed out the even more parochial idea that we need day care to get poor women off welfare.) If there is any issue that can revitalize contemporary feminism, this is surely it. But it's not simply a question of getting out there and organizing. We have to have a vision, to figure out what we really want. What is good child care, anyway? And what needs to change for us to have it?

Before I had a child, I had lots of opinions on the subject. Two years afterward, some of them have stuck with me: I'm still convinced that staying home full-time with a healthy, rambunctious kid would turn me into squirrel food, that child care should be as much men's job as women's, that communal child rearing in some form holds out the most hope of resolving the collision between adults' and children's needs, as well as the emotional cannibalism of the nuclear family. But for the most part, figuring out what kind of care best meets my daughter's needs has been—continues to be—a process of disentangling prejudice from experience.

In the beginning I hoped to avoid paid child care altogether. At best, I felt, it had to be inferior since it was done for money, not love. And in this society child care was a devalued occupation: without any serious public subsidy no one could afford to pay child care workers what they deserved, and the relations between workers, parents, and children were bound to be poisoned by class and racial exploitation. Since Stanley (my lover, Nona's father) had committed himself to equal sharing and we were both in the privileged position of having jobs with flexible hours, I didn't see why we couldn't do it all ourselves. Stanley, who had had children before, insisted that flexible hours or no, if we were going to do our jobs we would need help. Just like a man, I thought, or words to that effect.

Sometime during three months of total immersion (for the first two we were both home full-time) I grudgingly admitted he was right, and as I prepared to go back to work we started looking for part-time care. I still had fantasies of avoiding the class implications of being an employer. My idea was to find a student or artist or housewife who needed a part-time job, liked children, and hated office work—someone with educated-middle-class psychologically oriented attitudes toward child rearing and, equally important, someone who was not taking a child care job simply because she (probably, though of course I wouldn't rule out he) hadn't much choice.

We interviewed one such person who asked for more money than we could afford and hired another who quit after a couple of weeks to take a clerical job. I could hear Portnoy's analyst saying, "Now ve are to begin, yes?" and took the hint. In the end we hired a Haitian woman who, as a friend dryly put it, "fit the demographic profile for the job," and who quickly put to shame all my stereotypes. Without benefit of higher education, middle-class choices, or green card, Philomèse had all the psychological smarts I could ask for and tended to the baby with love and imagination. As I watched her relationship with Nona develop, I stopped thinking of her as simply a necessary (read necessary-evil) surrogate for us; she broadened Nona's world, added a whole extra dimension, a whole extra *person,* to Nona's life. Philomèse and the baby had their own games and routines and adventures and treats. In some ways, her role was more like an aunt's or a friend's than a parent's: its very limitations—its distance from the psychic entanglements of parenthood, the intense, global attachment and corresponding anxiety, not to mention the exhaustion—had their advantages. Quite aside from our own needs as working parents, Nona was clearly better off for having an intimate daily relationship with another adult.

The dilemmas of child care mediated by the market did intrude, though. For one thing the $5 an hour we were paying, meager as it was for the invaluable job Philomèse did, was nonetheless a big economic drain on us. And the relationship posed other paradoxes. At one point, for instance, Stanley and I were trying to figure out who would take the baby if we both died. It struck me that next to us, the person who was closest to Nona, who knew her rhythms and habits, the person she loved and felt comfortable with, was Philomèse; yet if I suggested her as Nona's guardian everyone, Philomèse included, would think I was crazy.

And then, when Nona was almost a year old, we were kicked out of our apartment. To get to our new place, Philomèse had a long trip on the subway rather than a short one on the bus. Around the same time there were complications in her personal life, another source of income lost, an immigrant relative to support. Unreliable trains made her arrival times erratic; she was unhappy, distracted, and strapped for money. So she quit, after staying longer than she wanted—we didn't mean to put pressure on her, but we did—and we were bereft. Nona had no visible reaction, but surely she must have felt something: her world had been doubly disrupted by our move and Philomèse's departure.

A friend introduced us to the woman who had once taken care of his children. Marion, who had had five children herself, ran a small, informal "family" day care operation in her house, with the help of her mother (known to the kids and parents as Grandma) and sometimes a third woman. I was instantly attracted to her and her place; the expression "good vibes" might have been coined to describe its atmosphere of warm acceptance and cheerful, controlled chaos. But I worried that Nona was too young to be displaced from the center of a dyadic universe. I had always believed that if you *had* to have paid care, it ought to be individual care, preferably in the child's own home, up to the age of two or maybe three. Abstract principles aside, Nona was a child who demanded, and clearly thrived on, lots of one-to-one attention.

Again Stanley disagreed. He thought group care was better for children past infancy, that it encouraged their social development and sense of self to spend their days in a world of equals. Since most urban kids no longer had lots of brothers and sisters or an active neighborhood street life, he reasoned, day care should fulfill that function. Another friend who had been sending her son to a day care center since he was Nona's age had expressed her enthusiasm for the center in much the same terms, but I'd suspected her of making a virtue of necessity, since she couldn't afford individual care. Stanley pointed out that we were both being loyal to our own past experience: his mother had always had a job and his life had centered around his peers; I had stayed home with my mother till I went to school. True, I thought; neither of us is objective. And where does that leave us?

Finally it was Nona who decided. Since we were going on vacation soon and it didn't make sense to hire a new person before then, I agreed to try Marion for a month. Nona walked in the next morning and never looked back. She returned the affection Marion and Grandma offered, yet didn't seem to mind that they couldn't be her personal slaves. (Once when I came to pick her up, I made the mistake of holding another baby. Nona howled: this was not part of the deal.) She loved being with the other kids, most of them older, and quickly found her place in the crowd. I looked on, somewhat bemused: not only had I lacked such social skills at her age, I was far from adept even now. (Stanley, on the other hand, was one of your gregarious prom king types. Was that what day care was good for?) A year later, Nona usually goes to Marion's five full days a week, and sometimes when we pick her up she's so involved in playing she doesn't want to go home.

Yet the number of hours Nona spends in day care is another source of anxiety. During her first year, especially the first nine months when I was nursing her regularly, I limited my work at the *Voice* to part-time editing, hardly wrote anything at all, and was rarely out of the house more than seven hours (one bottle) at a stretch; Stanley also curtailed his activities, though not as drastically as I did. Still my eye was always nervously on the clock; some ur-cultural inner voice, nagging that a parent should be there most of a child's waking hours, clashed with my observation that this child, at least, seemed quite content. Then, as Nona moved into toddlerhood and discovered her own world beyond the home, we started rediscovering ours. Without making any conscious decision, we gradually increased her time in day care.

When I'm in the mood to trust myself, I believe that the balance between my time with Nona and my time away from her is basically self-regulating. If I'm gone too much, Nona, who has never been shy about making her wants known, gets angry and cranky; I, needing her too, feel deprived and tense; and I find a way to make up for lost time as soon as I can. I've also learned that what she hates most is for me to be physically there but distracted, so it's better if I stay and finish the work, then come home and give her my full attention, rather than cut corners so my hours-away tally looks good. Stanley's relationship with her, while different from mine (though we've worked out a fairly equal division of child care, she's more dependent on me—but that's another article), has similar built-in monitors. And yet I'm still nervous. Is she really as happy as she seems? Do I read her as well as I think I do? Lately she's been getting aggressive, hitting us and other kids when she doesn't get her own way. Is this normal two-year-old behavior, or are we doing something wrong?

These are not questions I can ever really answer by myself. They reflect a social reality—that child rearing is no longer governed by a system, one that, however oppressive, assigned responsibilities and tasks in a coherent fashion and was supported by tradition and social consensus; instead we have a nonsystem, without institutional supports or a collective wisdom to guide us. Like most parents, I'm winging it. In the process I've come to entertain certain hopeful possibilities: that children are more open, earlier, to a wider variety of relationships, less dependent on constant bathing in oceanic parental love, than

I thought; that other, less intense forms of nurturing are not only okay but valuable; that collective care works. To know whether I'm really on to something, or whether Nona is atypical, or whether Stanley and I are self-serving or maybe just deluded, I need to check my perceptions, in some systematic way, with other people's—to give my private experience a public context. In the feminist movement we had a name for this process: consciousness-raising.

The only consciousness-raising sessions on children I can recall going to took up the question of whether we wanted children or not. The early women's liberation movement, which in so many ways set the agenda for feminism in general, did not make child care a primary organizing issue. And while a new vision of relationships between adults and children was implicit in the radical feminist critique of the patriarchal family, it mostly remained implicit, or at least on the level of generalities. There was a certain vagueness about goals. Did we want simply to abolish parental sex roles? Or did women's liberation require defining child rearing as a public, collective concern rather than a private, familial one? Were child care centers supposed to make family life more equitable—or were they to be a first step toward a different system entirely?

Individual feminists speculated on such questions (the best-known example is probably Shulamith Firestone's attack on the family model of child rearing and argument for children's liberation in *The Dialectic of Sex*), but the movement as a whole did not pick up on them. In a sense, they transcended the movement's categories. It was the counterculture that was most interested in communal child rearing, and its version was hardly feminist—usually the women in hippie communes took care of the kids and the housework, while the men often took off altogether.

Feminist thinking on the family centered on the relations between men and women, not parents and children. Those feminists who declared their opposition to the family usually meant they opposed marriage or monogamy. Others (probably the majority, even among the radicals) opposed the subordination of women within the present family structure while leaving open the possibility of an egalitarian nuclear family; some, outraged by the piggish behavior of bohemian men, could see opposition to the family only as a male plot to abandon any obligation to women and children. In any case, for many feminists the details of how child rearing would be organized in an egalitarian society were not specifically a feminist issue but rather a wider social problem to be taken up by men and women both: wasn't the whole point of women's liberation to *free* women from making these decisions alone? (Even Firestone prefaced her argument by urging women to take up the cause of children one last time.) The trouble with this logic was its *echt*–New Left distinction between challenging the old system and building a new one—a distinction that's always somewhat artificial, but especially so when you're talking about children. Workers rebelling against oppressive conditions can strike, but women can't simply stop taking care of their children till the society decides what to do with them.

Radical feminists were not incognizant of this dilemma—we did call for publicly funded, 24-hour-a-day child care centers staffed by both sexes. But we never actually worked for them. Part of the problem was demographic—the paucity of older women, the exclusion of black women, childless women's greater physical and psychological freedom to be politically active. Part of it had to do with the movement's culture: while it was far more sensitive to the situation of mothers than the society at large or the rest of the left—what group ever bothered to provide child care at political events before feminists started putting the pressure on?—the emphasis on rebelling against what women were supposed to do led, perhaps inevitably, to an antinatalist bias. As a result, many mothers who did join the movement felt inhibited about discussing a central aspect of their lives.

Yet these limitations were hardly the only, or even the primary, obstacle to tackling the institution of motherhood. We were, after all, facing a problem of enormous scope. Sexual equality in child rearing would require not only great changes in—perhaps a total transformation of—family life, but also drastic changes in the nature of work: not only would sexism in the economy have to end, but the concept of the full-time job, which assumed someone else was taking care of domestic business, would have to die. Changing the child-rearing system was, in short, a revolutionary project. How did you get there from here?

In 1971, a coalition that included liberal feminists got Congress to pass the Comprehensive Child Development Act, which mandated federal funds for community-controlled child care (it was vetoed by Richard Nixon, who cited its antifamily implications). As with the ERA, radical feminists created the political atmosphere that allowed such a bill to pass, but didn't get actively behind it: it wasn't revolutionary enough.

I saw the act as a necessary (that is, necessary-evil) stopgap reform. In retrospect, and from my vantage point as a parent, it seems to me that I was using my communal vision of child rearing to keep the issue at a distance. Actually, I was more confused about it than I knew. Intertwined with my radicalism was a kind of cryptotraditionalism: re-creating mother-at-home in a communal, nonsexist version was the only goal I felt comfortable with. In a way, the current view of child care as a quick fix (which will have to be provided by the private sector, since the government has no money for such things) for mothers' immediate problems is the logical extension of my attitude back then. I can see now that Nixon understood what was going on better than I did. Demanding a public commitment to child care—which is to say, a commitment to the principle that children are indeed a public and not simply a familial responsibility—is a crucial first step in moving from our present nonsystem of child rearing toward a real alternative.

Though it's not what people want to hear these days, there's an intrinsic conflict between sexual equality and the basic assumption of the family system: that children belong to their biological parents, who are legally and socially responsible for their own children—and no one else's. Women's position in this system is inherently different from men's, since a mother's parental responsibility follows automatically from pregnancy and birth, while a father's must be acknowledged or proved. This puts the burden on women to make sure their children have a social father and gives men a great deal of power to set the terms of their cooperation in child rearing. The fear that women will *go too far* and men will retaliate by abandoning responsibility for children has been a subtext of the debate on all sorts of sexual-political issues—ERA, abortion, divorce, single parenthood. Only when each child is considered a member of a larger community, automatically entitled to protection, support, and care, can women escape this bind.

Often, when I get this far in the argument I'm hit with the ultimate conversation-stopper: "You want to take kids away from their parents and give them to the state." Which implies not only that there are just two choices—when in fact there are many possible models of communal child rearing, even some that actually exist, like the kibbutz—but that any alternative to the family would have to be imposed, probably by totalitarian methods—when in fact the issue has arisen in the first place because the family as we've known it isn't working. People are already struggling to find alternatives. The political question is whether as a society we will lend economic and social support to those struggles.

To fight for this support we need a radical child-rearing movement that can operate on several fronts at once. Mothers, fathers, child care workers, others who are or want to be involved with children, need to get together to find out what their common interests are and work for them. Women also need to organize specifically as feminists, to make sure that the issue of child rearing remains firmly anchored in a larger antisexist politics; otherwise it could be all too easy to settle for public day care staffed by low-paid women, or to promote seemingly egalitarian "fathers' rights" measures that in practice discriminate against women who have been their children's primary parent.

In addition to demanding a national child care program, I think a child-rearing movement should immediately raise the issue of work. We could demand, for instance, a shorter work week with no loss of pay (the aura of inviolability that now surrounds the 40-hour week tends to make us forget that it's a recent product of long and bloody labor struggles). Not only does this demand speak to people's need for time to tend to their children and homes in a post-housewife era, it's also a radical response to the massive unemployment now being generated by new technology and deindustrialization.

So what's good child care, anyway? At this point, I think most feminists would agree on certain basic ground rules: child care centers should be set up and controlled by the parents, workers, and local communities who use them; they should be available and affordable to everyone; their staffs should be sexually and racially integrated and well paid; they should be run in accordance with democratic principles—with as much participation as is practical by the children themselves—and in a pluralistic, experimental spirit, so that people can try different models of care and discover what works best for them. I also believe that parents who want to stay home with their children should be entitled to economic support (not "welfare," but pay for doing a necessary job), since our immediate aim should be a child care policy that allows the widest range of choices, in the confidence that freedom is the best teacher.

In the long run, of course, we'll only find out what kind of child care we really want by working for it. It's in coming together to discuss the day-to-day problems of child rearing, observing lots of different kids, arguing over and hashing out differences, that parents and other caretakers will be able to lay claim to a genuinely radical vision of how to bring up children—one rooted in the concrete realities of daily life. Consciousness-raising, anyone? We have nothing to lose but our lonely and deadening privatism.

"Handle with Care," *Village Voice,* July 1986

NOTE

In more ways than one, this article was inspired by conversations with Beth Bush, an organizer and gadfly on this issue.

To Emma, with Love

Tyranny is joyless. Freedom is pleasurable. Liberation from tyranny is ecstatic. Pleasure, joy, ecstasy—all are forms of the erotic, which is to say the delight one's bodily, sensory being takes in freely moving toward, plunging into, engulfing the world. Freedom in pleasure, pleasure in freedom—dancing and fucking (yes, Emma), and having visions (with or without the aid of chemicals), and doing work that engages and matters to us, and living in an atmosphere of cooperation, friendship, and love among free, self-respecting people, and having the opportunity to be truly responsible for our own lives, to put our visions into practice—are at the core of all real revolution.

At the moment Eastern Europe is demanding freedoms Americans already have, at least in principle, but this democracy stuff has a way of getting out of hand. Where will it all end, and where else will it begin? As Czechs and East Germans take to the streets, their free movement overwhelming their static, joyless, bureaucratic states, I feel the thrill in my own nerve ends; I think, "Why not me? Why not us?" No wonder our own state bureaucrats are nervous. Revolution is contagious; it inspires a subversive anticipation of pleasure.

Indeed, a founding principle of our revolution was the inalienable right to pursue happiness. But these days, that pursuit is regularly slandered as irresponsibility, self-indulgence, and narcissism. Contempt for and terror of pleasure—along with frustrated and repressed longing for it—fuel today's intertwined mass hysterias about drugs and sex. The reluctance of leftists and feminists to wholeheartedly defend pleasure skewed the abortion debate, putting advocates of "choice" on the defensive, for the heart of the matter *is* women's sexual freedom, which is integral to freedom itself. It's less a matter of "the right to control our bodies" than the freedom to accept and relish our bodies, to explore our capacity for pleasure. Without that freedom we are divided selves, crippled in our capacity to move toward the world, trapped in the stasis to which women have historically been condemned.

But this revolution, the erotic revolution, the real thing not Playboy bunnies, has to begin with children. We are living in an era in which fear of children's sexuality is being displaced onto a series of highly publicized sex-abuse cases featuring bizarre allegations, a witch trial atmosphere, and a paucity of evidence; in which "experts" can seriously claim that children's sex play with each other shows they've been abused, while the use of brainwashing techniques to force them to "confess" they've been molested shows they're being protected; in which—as always—the stifling of children's sexual exploration is considered not abuse but moral guidance; in which laws requiring teenagers to notify parents before having abortions are hypocritically promoted as a way of giving parents a chance to help their children in a time of crisis, when the real motive is anger at teenage sexuality and the desire to resurrect parental wrath as a deterrent and punishment. Do we dare to make the radical demand that children's sexuality be affirmed and protected from both exploitation and inhibition by adults? That teenagers be entitled not only to birth control and abortion but to all the information, advice, and social, emotional, and medical support they need to express their sexuality safely and responsibly?

It's highly ironic that *prolife* has come to mean *antiabortion*. The phrase *prolife* was originally used by sexual radicals like Wilhelm Reich and A. S. Neill to mean pro-sex, pro-freedom, pro-pleasure. Of course, they saw life as synonymous with eros, the point and the essence of life as the active enjoyment of living. To the antiabortion movement, life is an absolute, a fetishism of biological existence for its own sake.

And in another context, it's important that living not be equated simply with surviving. What is devastating about AIDS is not only that it kills people, but that it threatens to kill desire; and this threat is part of what we have to fight. If we despair of freedom and pleasure—abandon the revolution—we won't have to worry about dying of AIDS; we will already be dead.

Village Voice, December 1989

The Nineties
Decade of Denial

INTRODUCTION
Cord Jefferson

I wish Ellen Willis were no longer relevant. That's not to knock the quality of her work, which is equal parts poignant, dynamic, scathing, and sharp like a scalpel. Rather, it is her targets that I find so contemptible—pernicious because of their resilience: sexism, racism, classism, craven politicians and journalists, greedy businesspeople, hypocritical liberals lacking in guts. The divisions in society continue to outlive those who have spent entire careers trying to destroy them, leaving us where we are today: without Willis yet still surrounded by her foes.

For a glimpse at how pertinent much of Willis's decades-old work is, one need only read this passage from "What We Don't Talk about When We Talk about *The Bell Curve*," her exploration of the infamous 1994 IQ hagiography:

> Companies are shedding managers and replacing engineers and computer programmers with machines. The job markets in the academy and the publishing industry are dismal, support for artists and writers are even scarcer than usual, the public and nonprofit sectors—hotbeds of cognitive elitism—steadily shrinking. Nor are card-carrying CE [cognitive elite] members exempt from the pervasive trend toward employment of part-time, temporary, and benefit-free workers. Wealth is increasingly concentrated at the top and, last I looked, still handily outstrips other sources of power.

Put that nearly fifteen-year-old paragraph into next week's *Village Voice* and nobody would bat an eyelash. Just because the Million Man March and the O. J. Simpson trial have faded from the headlines doesn't mean the lessons about race and gender roiling within them aren't as important in our era of stop-and-frisk policies and double-digit black unemployment. Like today, black communities in the '90s were being decimated by the rise in the prison industrial complex. The crack era was on a downswing, but young black men clashing with police was common and, as Willis argues in the accusatorily named "Rodney King's Revenge," the impetus for many African Americans to breathe a sigh of relief when O. J. Simpson was acquitted of murder.

Later in the decade, Willis would speak unflinchingly about the misogyny and sex-negativity inherent in the media's reaction to the Clinton-Lewinsky scandal—and the president's, too. In "Monica and Barbara and Primal Concerns," Willis notes that despite being relentlessly characterized by the right as a pot-smoking, countercultural radical, the president showed his true colors when backed into a corner built by a blowjob and a stained blue dress. "It was Mr. Clinton who cheapened their relationship with his angry denial, his 'harsh' and 'hurtful' reference to her as 'that woman,' his maligning her as a stalker and his eventual portrayal of their sexual contact as entirely one-sided," writes Willis. Meanwhile, the "eat-your-vegetables school of journalism" failed to see how the scandal had uncovered "primal human concerns." That doesn't sound so unlike our current status: while conservative lawmakers may be the ones stripping away women's rights, commentators across the political spectrum are complaining that we have spent too much time focusing on "social issues" and not enough time fixing the economy. That's an ugly little sleight of hand that's become a go-to grievance of both the right and the left.

One other essential bit of Willis worth stealing, no matter who you are, is her willingness to provoke and chastise her own left-of-center ilk when necessary. Many of Willis's nineties contemporaries, for instance, found it difficult to address the Million Man March's obvious sexism, and Louis Farrakhan's obvious anti-Semitism, because to do so could be perceived as antiblack or cynical about a march that was supposed to be peaceful and kind. Calling the event a shot at a "utopian moment," Willis nevertheless wrote, "It's a mistake to imagine that the good feelings generated by the Million Man March negate its political dangers." As a person of color, I'm not sure I can agree with Willis on this one. But as someone who loathes cowardice in the face of sanctimonious liberal tyrants and supports stepping on sacred toes in an effort to beat back bullshit, I surely do appreciate her.

CORD JEFFERSON is a writer and editor living in Los Angeles.

Selections from "Decade of Denial"

Don't Think, Smile!

High on my list of petty urban irritations are those signs posted by smug possessors of driveways: "Don't Even *Think* about Parking Here." I fantasize about plastering their premises with superglued bumper stickers that say "Down with the Thought Police" or "Don't Even *Think* about Telling Me What to Think." It occurs to me, though, that the signs are an apt metaphor for the one-way conversation carried on by driveway guards who call themselves journalists: "Don't even *think* about questioning the need to balance the federal budget." "Don't even *think* about workers getting a fair share of the wealth they produce." "Don't even *think* about the problems with the institution of marriage that punishing unmarried mothers won't solve."

Commentators are always inviting me to accept as a foregone conclusion conservative dogma on some issue I had foolishly imagined was debatable. Consider the *Wall Street Journal*'s obituary of Barry Goldwater, which assures the reader, "Today even liberal Democrats agree that some part of Social Security should be privatized." Or the Manhattan Institute's James Pinkerton, opining in *Newsday* about the high rate "among some groups" of unmarried childbearing, "leading, everyone now agrees, to the chaos and crime of the urban underclass." Or the *New York Times*'s classic "News Analysis" of the 1996 budget battle: the president, the reporter remarked, was disinclined to move because "he now can make the argument that Democrats . . . are the defenders of education and the elderly while all the Republicans care about is tax cuts. It is a flawed argument, especially on Medicare, for Mr. Clinton knows as well as the Republicans do that spending on such entitlements must be curbed eventually." Not "Mr. Clinton *believes*," which is undoubtedly true, but "Mr. Clinton *knows*."

Don't even *think* about the government raising revenue for social spending by restoring the progressive income tax, or making steep cuts in the post–cold war military budget. If you're the kind of crank who has to have irrational doubts about what everybody *knows,* go join the Flat Earth Society.

For the past few years, everybody has known that we are enjoying a terrific economy, with out-of-sight stock and real estate prices, jobs going begging, even the wages of bottom-tier jobs beginning to creep up. Never mind that the statistics don't measure involuntary part-time and temporary employment, or the steady flow of people (especially people over fifty) out of jobs with good pay and benefits to those offering neither, or the conversion of real jobs to sub–minimum wage "workfare" slots; that a minority has garnered most of the wealth, while real estate inflation has displaced all but the rich and the subsidized from boom towns like Manhattan; that the current growth rate depends on an unstable mountain of debt. Meanwhile, much of the world economy is in crisis. Sooner or later, Roadrunner will figure out that he's treading air, and Americans will rediscover their enduring reality: growing economic insecurity, a long-term decline in real wages, and fewer social benefits and public services. No doubt the gatekeepers of our collective wisdom will revert to their usual strategy of convincing people there's nothing much to be done about these miseries other than blaming themselves for not striking it rich as everyone else seems to have done, or blowing off steam at corrupt politicians, the undeserving poor, the immoral cultural elite, the unqualified blacks who are supposedly getting all the good jobs, and so on.

But there's a problem looming: call it the euphoria gap. If you can't get with the most marvelous expansion since the '60s, you're a sorehead. But when the bubble sags, your discontent will once again be worrisome to what might be called the "conservative center"—that is, the financial and corporate establishment, the "new Democrats," those Republicans whose antiliberal zeal stops somewhere short of radical right-wing anarchism or militant Christianity, and their countless flacks in the think tanks and mass media. For the CC, it's not enough that Americans "know" they have no choice but to accept a declining standard of living; it's essential that they accept this adversity with good grace. The ultra-right traffics in anger, which it hopes to enlist in behalf of its vision of counterrevolutionary change. But the CC wants to control the pace of change, and understands that popular anger is a wild card. While its main priority is avoiding a class revolt from the left, it is also leery of all-out culture war from the right: congressmen in league with white supremacist militias, or worse, Pat Buchanan, covering both bases with his rabble-rousing populism, nationalism, and fundamentalism, are a conservative centrist's nightmare. How then to get us to chill out?

I'd suggest reissuing Robert J. Samuelson's *The Good Life and Its Discontents: The American Dream in the Age of Entitlement, 1945–1995.* It was published in 1996, while memories of the right's government shutdown were still fresh and before the boom hype had taken hold, to enthusiastic reviews in the *New York Times* and the *Wall Street Journal*. *Newsweek* ran an excerpt as a cover story: "Cheer Up, America! It's Not as Bad as You Think." Americans are unhappy, Samuelson argues, not because we're really doing badly, but because we're hooked on unrealistic expectations. The post–World War II economic boom led us to envision a utopian future of ever rising incomes, stable jobs, personal freedom and fulfillment, and government solutions to all social problems. But the boom ended, and conditions reverted to what we ought to accept as normal but experience as betrayal and disillusionment. It's time to pull up our socks, relinquish our overweening sense of entitlement, and settle maturely for what we've got.

Samuelson has a point about the naïveté of American optimism. The extraordinary affluence of the postwar years and the liberal social compact that allowed most people to share it were the product of a unique set of circumstances. Not only did the United States emerge from World War II an economic superpower, but business, labor, and government were resolved, in the wake of depression and war, to save capitalism both from its own tendency to crisis and from the socialist threat represented most concretely by the Soviet Union. The translation of phenomenal economic growth into high wages, job security, and social benefits was a formula for buying people's loyalty to the system, neutralizing potential radicalism, making genuine economic equality seem unnecessary. For capitalists, who relinquished some of their profits but never their power, collaboration with labor and the welfare state was strictly a temporary marriage of convenience. For most Americans, it was a historical shortcut to the pursuit of happiness. As with our abuse of the environment in the name of growth, and our abuse of antibiotics in the quest to "conquer disease," the bill for that complacency is now coming due.

This, however, is not exactly the point Samuelson wants to make. For him, capitalism is a given, a natural fact. The economy is like "a vast river, where fish and plants flourish and perish and where occasional floods occur." Its inherent "instability, insecurity, and excess" may be hard to take, but without it we wouldn't have computers and microwave ovens. So absolute is Samuelson's assumption that there's no possible alternative to this system that he doesn't even bother to say so. (I mean, didn't the fall of Communism lay that one to rest forever? Don't even *think* about it.) During the '60s, when this now taboo subject was actually raised in public, defenders of capitalism used to argue that despite its inequities, it delivered the goods. Now they're reduced to arguing that you can't control a river. But what's happened to the economy over the past two decades has nothing to do with laws of nature; it's the product of conscious and deliberate social policy.

Prodded by competition from Europe and Japan, American capital invested in cheap third world labor markets and job-decimating technologies that undermined American workers' bargaining power; unconstrained by a left grown pitifully weak, business abrogated the liberal compact. Employers embarked on a concerted campaign to break the unions (which don't get even a token mention in Samuelson's account of the "forces" behind shrinking wages). Government obligingly deregulated, threw out progressive taxation, declared the austerity state, and is now taking an ax to those programs that represent the last vestige of the idea that markets ought to be subordinate to the needs of society, not vice versa. As computers allow companies to produce more and more with fewer and fewer workers, so that profits and stock prices go up with every round of layoffs, productivity is being decoupled from income as surely as sex from procreation. Yet the idea of plowing back some of the wealth generated in the process into support for the unemployed is sacrilege to the free-market ideologues who run the country. River? What we've got here is a steamroller.

There's a strong element of déjà vu in Samuelson's "Party's over, get used to it" message. The first concerted assault on "the age of entitlement" took place in the '70s, the decade of the energy crunch, the New York fiscal crisis, and the first wave of "pro-family" activism; it was the theme of the Carter administration. Then the strategy was moral intimidation: our greedy profligacy had led government to overspend; our narcissism (women's especially) had undermined the family; we were a bunch of lazy, morally flabby slobs who had better shape up. The main result of all this guilt-tripping was that Americans elected Ronald Reagan, who reassured the electorate that material aspirations were fine so long as they were channeled into private gain, and that it wasn't the American people who were lazy, morally flabby, and narcissistic, just feminists, gays, blacks, and welfare queens.

But by now, conservative centrists know better than to lecture people about tightening their belts when they're already doing so, willy-nilly. Instead Samuelson offers economic determinism: prosperity made us do it. It's not our selfish desires we must curb, but our overstimulated imaginations. Don't worry—it only hurts when you think.

Left Out

The morning after, November 1994: a dirty job, but somebody had to do it—assess the left's reaction to the congressional putsch. My problem, however, was finding a left to assess, at a time when conventional notions of the political spectrum were shifting to the right with a speed reminiscent of German hyperinflation in the '20s. One went to bed assuming Bob Dole was a bona fide member of the hard right, and woke up to find he'd become a moderate. Bill Clinton, on the basis of his feeble lurch toward health care reform, had been branded the next thing to a Marxist revolutionary, while the modest social liberalism that was one of his selling points in 1992 (and that he had been backing away from ever since) was equated with the ultimate in radfemqueerthink. The Democratic Leadership Council was hectoring him to "move toward the center," occupied, presumably, by Newt Gingrich. On Black Tuesday (though who knew what Wednesday might bring), it seemed that a leftist could be defined as anyone who didn't want to repeal the income tax, thought public schools were a good idea, and doubted that putting poor kids in orphanages was the solution to welfare dependency.

This ideological bracket-creep lent a certain absurdity to the right's determination to interpret the election results as an omnibus revolt against New Deal liberalism and '60s cultural radicalism. So enthusiastically did conservatives push this line that both the *Wall Street Journal* and the *New York Post* enlisted me in its behalf, quoting a comment I'd made in the *Village Voice* that the Clintons were "inescapably '60s figures." In fact, I was making precisely the opposite point—that Clinton's frantic attempts to distance himself from his image as a "counterculture McGovernik" (Gingrich's phrase) and his socially liberal impulses had, if anything, increased his political enemies' contempt, while confirming most people's impression that there was no there there. The 1994 election was not a repudiation of the left—you can't repudiate something that for all practical purposes doesn't exist. Rather, it demonstrated that the electorate abhors a vacuum.

By then the list of Americans' frustrations was long and growing: economic insecurity, overwork or not enough work or stultifying, regimented work at insultingly low wages, with no prospect of improvement and no margin for illness or retirement; recognition that the dream was over, that education and hard work guaranteed no reward whatsoever; crime, lousy schools, disintegrating public services, lack of community, racial and ethnic tension, conflict between the sexes, familial instability, no time for personal life and child rearing. All this had exacerbated people's sense of government as an alien institution that took their money for purposes decreed by arrogant bureaucrats and corrupt politicians, was impervious to their influence, and did nothing to address their problems.

The right put these grievances in the context of its own vision; it offered an analysis, a set of principles, a program. While much has been made of the divisions among Republicans—economic libertarians versus religious rightists, internationalists versus isolationists—from 1980 through the early Clinton years they subordinated their disagreements to a coherent overall message. Politically, they identified the cause of our problems as a government that neglects its primary duty to maintain law and order, discourages enterprise by taxing and regulating business, destroys individual freedom and opportunity by promoting special rights for groups, and confiscates the hard-earned money of productive citizens to support an out-of-control debt, a huge bureaucracy, and a parasitic, immoral, dangerous underclass. Culturally, they blamed the '60s— shorthand for the decline of traditional religious and moral authority, the demand for personal freedom and social equality, the revolt of blacks, women, and gays, the sexual revolution, the normalization of divorce and single parenthood.

In response, the "left" (see definition above) offered neither a competing vision of the good society nor an alternative analysis of our ills nor a believable strategy for tackling them. Its main activity was directing moral appeals for justice and compassion to a Clinton administration and a Democratic Party that paid it as much attention as a buzzing fly. On the cultural legacy of the '60s, leftists were divided. But few were willing to defend its radical libertarianism—as opposed to liberal platitudes about inclusion and diversity, or the authoritarian moralism that so often passes for militance on behalf of the oppressed—while the hostile and dismissive voices steadily increased in both number and volume. A significant portion of the left had always been uncomfortable with cultural politics, especially feminism and gay liberation. In the '70s, as the social atmosphere grew more repressive, many leftists, liberals, and even feminists decided that the politic course was to back away from any controversial criticism of traditional moral, sexual, and familial values, while some urged that the left court Middle America by actively embracing cultural conservatism. With the triumph of Ronald Reagan, a beleaguered, defensive, and thoroughly deradicalized left (which had taken to calling itself "progressive," a word that aptly conveys the righteous vagueness of the politics it describes) generated an outpouring of sentiment on behalf of the old-time economistic religion. In the interest of uniting to oppose the massive upward redistribution of wealth—so the line went—divisive social issues must be downplayed if not ignored altogether. And anyway, wasn't it time to admit that the defenders of work, family, and virtue had a point?

Some of us sharply disagreed. We argued that "progressives" who allowed the right's moral agenda to go unchallenged—thereby tacitly supporting its demand that people submit to authority and stifle their desires for freedom and personal fulfillment—could not expect to be taken seriously when they urged people to stand up to authority as embodied in the formidable alliance of corporate CEOs, public officials, economists, educators, and all manner of "experts" who had decreed that the new economic order, like it or not, was a permanent and non-negotiable fact of life. You could make a good case that the ensuing years, in which the corporate juggernaut rolled over abject unions and a quiescent public, more than validated this point of view. By 1994, you could also point out that the left's only recent claim (pathetic as it was) to making a dent in national politics had been electing a president who exuded the whiff (faint as it was) of sex, drugs, rock and roll, Vietnam, and feminism, amid widespread alarm about the Christian right's attacks on working women, single mothers, and gays at the 1992 Republican convention. But apparently neither fourteen years of almost unrelieved defeat nor the exception of Clinton's candidacy had inspired any second thoughts in the progressive camp.

As for the Democrats, from the start of the Reagan era they had responded to the conservative challenge in two characteristic ways: defending the status quo—mainstream social liberalism, the shrinking welfare state—or (increasingly) me-tooing the right on both fronts. Since most Americans were desperate for some kind of change and much preferred passionate conviction to halfhearted, opportunistic pandering, both Democratic strategies were basically losers. When Democrats won, it was usually because the ultra-right got carried away with itself and refused to temper its rhetoric with reassuring nods to tolerance and democracy. That had happened in 1992; it would happen again in 1996, after self-styled congressional "revolutionaries" shut down the government rather than compromise with the president on the budget. Nineteen-ninetyfour, on the other hand, presented the classic and predictable case of a party with energy and ideas smashing a sclerotic, demoralized operation that had nothing whatsoever to say. And if this event turned out to be the defining political moment of the decade—a moment that not only shaped national policy for the next four years, but set a tone that made it thinkable to impeach the president for illicit sex—it is largely because the opposition, such as it was, stubbornly refused to smell the coffee.

Was *anyone* out there, in the wake of the tsunami, countering the right's unleash capitalism–return to morality–get the poor off our backs offensive with a convincing alternative? Not so far as I could tell. As I made my dispirited way through the putatively leftist postmortems, the first thing that struck me was their unselfconscious similarity—references to current events and issues aside—to the postelection commentary of 1980. Once again the common theme was a call for economic populism, with or without an explicit invocation of New Deal liberalism (i.e., liberalism before 1968, when all those nasty social issues came along). While most of these proposals simply ignored cultural issues, or argued that an appeal to class would defuse them, some defined cultural conservatism as an integral part of the populism the left should embrace. In *Newsweek,* Joe Klein argued, "There *was* a subtle alliance between 'left-wing elitists' and the nascent black underclass in matters of personal morality in the 1960's." In the *New York Post,* Jack Newfield appealed to "fellow Democrats" to "Dump Bill": "Liberals ought to stand for traditional values like work, family, law, discipline, patriotism and individual moral responsibility."

Back at my home base, the *Voice,* our postelection cover was devoted to Michael Tomasky proclaiming, "Tuesday's returns were the final referendum on a left-liberal agenda that paid too much attention to its tiny narcissisms and too little attention to the needs of most Americans." "Narcissism," for any feminist or gay liberationist who had experienced the first round of cultural backlash in the '70s, was a fighting word. As popularized by the late Christopher Lasch's *The Culture of Narcissism,* it had been regularly invoked against those of us who argued that real radicalism was about affirming the right to freedom and pleasure, unmasking the repressive functions of institutions like Family and Work. But in the grim context of the '90s, this sort of narcissism, tiny or huge, was rarer than steak tartare.

That the left's problem was not an excess of self-love but a paucity of ideas was amply demonstrated by Tomasky's brand of belligerently anti-intellectual populism. "Most Americans," as he saw it, work, pay taxes, have children, want the trash picked up, go to school so they can get a secure job so they can "own a home and do the regular things Americans . . . want to do," and "think Fish and Jameson stand for a dinner of carp and Irish whiskey." Whereas the "liberal elites," who presumably don't work, pay taxes, have kids, or believe in garbage collection, and are off doing perverted rather than regular things, "sit around debating the canon at a handful of elite universities." Never mind that Tomasky's portrait of Average Joe was as condescending as anything the "liberal elites" could dream up. (In fact, the apathy about class that is indeed all too common on the academic cultural left is the flip side of this know-nothingism.) Even more telling was his assumption that academic debates were inherently trivial. Conservatives, in contrast, knew that it mattered what went on in universities, especially the elite kind. Decisions about what got taught there—what counted as bona fide knowledge—resonated through the educational system and the culture as a whole, which is why the right, *not* the left, had made changes in the canon and other aspects of academic culture a major public issue.

Tomasky did make one statement with which I entirely agreed: "There's no surer way to create new generations of conservatives . . . than to let the right take the lead on welfare, crime, immigration. . . . The left isn't offering [people] an alternative way of doing things that makes any sense in their lives." Exactly! And what might that alternative be? In a follow-up piece, he spelled it out: the left should combine a progressive economic program with a rethinking of the "categories of left and right" on social issues. Education, for instance: "Why is it wrong for the left to advocate higher learning standards, a longer school day, a longer school year?"

"Higher learning standards"—who could disagree? But what that meant was not as self-evident as Tomasky seemed to think. Conservatives had strong ideas about what should be taught, how, and to whom. They liked old-fashioned authoritarian pedagogy, indoctrination in morals, official inspirational versions of history, Great Books for the elite, vocational training for the masses. There were radical alternatives to this agenda, but developing and presenting them entailed the kind of discussion Tomasky would no doubt dismiss as elitist thumb sucking, on the grounds that Average Joe thought Dewey was Donald Duck's nephew. As for a longer school day and year, why should the left uncritically embrace this nose-to-the-grindstoneism, which also demanded that adults work longer and longer hours? My daughter, then in the fifth grade, had school six hours a day (less twenty minutes for lunch) plus homework time, ten months a year. Why wasn't that enough? What was wrong with having the time to play, to relax in hot weather?

Then there was welfare: "The left resisted welfare reform for years. Some of the left even argued, years ago, in favor of expanding welfare rights. . . . Well, those arguments were lost. The welfare laws are going to be rewritten. The point is to write them in a humane way." Aside from its Orwellian flavor—how do you "humanely" pretend there's a job at a living wage out there for any welfare recipient who tries hard enough, or "humanely" punish women for having children outside marriage?—this pronouncement suggested that there were only two positions you could take on welfare: defend the existing system or accept the assumption behind the present reform campaign, that people are poor because they are lazy or immoral. Yet '60s new leftists had criticized the welfare system as a means of pacifying and controlling poor people instead of attacking economic inequality. And given the economic and technological changes eliminating "good jobs" at an accelerating rate, it might be time to stop thinking in terms of relief for a discrete class of "the poor" and discuss what a universal guaranteed income might look like. If you wanted to talk about genuine left alternatives, those were good places to start. If, on the other hand, you were simply tired of losing and eager to come in from the cold, Tomasky's "If you can't beat 'em, join 'em" approach definitely had the edge.

While the message was familiar, on closer inspection there *was* something new about the way its 1994 version was being delivered—a note of angry aggrievement. Tomasky made explicit what the anger implied: rather than merely urging cultural leftists to back off and get with the program, he actually blamed them for the ascendancy of the right. This would be a recurring theme in the writings of progressives in the latter half of the '90s, in books like Todd Gitlin's *The Twilight of Common Dreams,* Richard Rorty's *Achieving Our Country,* nouveau liberal Michael Lind's *The Next American Nation,* and Tomasky's own entry, *Left for Dead,* as well as numerous polemics in *The Nation* and elsewhere.

It seems that a bunch of academics, tiny as their narcissisms may be, have nonetheless managed to take up all possible space left of center, leaving the people they turn off with no choice but to throw in their lot with the Republicans. But how is this possible, given that the left opponents of cultural politics have hardly been silent all these years? Why is the public not listening to the cultural left's progressive critics? If they are so much more in tune with the concerns of ordinary people, why do they have so little political influence, either as an independent voice or as a faction of the Democrats? Socially conservative leftists have long complained that it's in the interest of the elite that runs the Democratic Party and dominates the media to promote cultural liberation rather than class issues. But this charge can't explain why the right has been so much better at grassroots organizing than the economic-justice left, or (the same question, really) why the Democratic Party elite has not felt the need to appease its economic progressives the way the Republican elite (often to the detriment of its own class interests) has appeased its social reactionaries.

It's hard to avoid the conclusion that disgruntled liberals and leftists have projected onto the cultural left their own deep sense of failure—and furthermore that the real reason for their anger is not the supposed irrelevance of cultural radicalism but, on the contrary, its enormous and lasting impact. The

'60s liberation movements may have sprung largely from the middle-class "liberal elite," but their influence ultimately spread through all social strata: no American has been untouched by the changes in sexual mores and male-female relations, the breakdown of taboos on public expression, the demand for a cleaner environment and a healthier diet, the new centrality of paid work to women's lives, the increasing racial and ethnic heterogeneity of mainstream American life. Nor have three decades and more of ferocious backlash, actively supported by the federal government, accomplished the social equivalent of putting toothpaste back in the tube. On the contrary, the right has had far more success at consolidating its political power and promoting its economic program than at reversing the cultural tide.

Cultural conservatives have made the most headway when they have focused on targets who are already unpopular or suspect, like criminal defendants, black women on welfare, teenagers who flout adult authority, "feminists" coded as man-hating and career-obsessed killjoys, professors who think there are no absolute truths, artists who get government grants for trampling on conventional morality (or worse, conventional ideas about art). When they attack divorce, day care, and unmarried mothers they may succeed in raising the national level of guilt, but ultimately they run up against Americans' uncomfortable recognition that the enemy is them—or their relatives, friends, and co-workers. (Increasingly, homosexuals are moving from the category of despised minority into that of "people we know.") For much the same reason, the right was unable to mobilize public support to remove an adulterous president.

Conservatives have stigmatized and dangerously restricted access to abortion but have not been able to arouse popular support for outlawing it. Nor has rampant hysteria about teenage sex restored the old taboos. Despite periodic censorship campaigns, open sexuality, feminist assumptions, and the iconography of multiculturalism permeate the popular media, including TV programs watched by millions; Dan Quayle's attack on *Murphy Brown* made him look sillier than his spelling. What were once radical ideas and sensibilities have been selectively assimilated not only by liberals but by a wide and politically varied swath of the population: gay Republicans demand the right to marry in the name of family values; white suburban teenagers embrace rap music and hip-hop style; evangelical Christian women roll their eyes at the Southern Baptist convention's call for wifely submission to male leadership—and in some cases their churches even leave the convention. In short, American cultural values are in flux, and Americans, pulled in conflicting directions, are ambivalent—which is why the culture wars have gone on so long and been so inconclusive.

This is not to deny that the cultural reaction has had profound effects. If it has not restored the antebellum status quo, it has nonetheless curtailed hard-won civil rights and liberties, starting with attacks on the most vulnerable groups and culminating in a jihad against the president of the United States. It has had a chilling—no, freezing—effect on any further social experiment, or even talk about it: as work, family, and morality have become bywords across the political spectrum, the implicit boundaries of "relevant" debate have virtually silenced radical social criticism in mainstream public venues. (One irony of the populist left's attacks on insular academics is that the university is the only institution of any size that still provides cultural dissidents with a platform. As a result they talk mainly to each other except when given publicity by a right indignant that they should exist at all.) Yet even as the right appeals to the electorate's sexual guilt and fear of social disorder, it has simultaneously managed to play to the other side of Americans' ambivalence: in offering dreams of wealth and power and defining as heroic rebellion the sadistic release of bashing the government, the media, the black poor, and other scapegoats, conservatives have claimed the ground of freedom and pleasure that the left so readily abandoned.

In staking out all this territory, conservatives have been helped along by the cultural movements themselves. Pressure from the right long ago led many black, feminist, and gay activists to adopt a strategy of caution and appeasement, while others took refuge in moral posturing, guilt-mongering, and the celebration of group identity for its own sake. In the '80s and '90s, the ever dangerous mix of frustration and self-righteousness has propelled cultural leftists' egregious efforts to have the state and the university bureaucracies enforce their demands for political conformity, standards of sexual propriety, and attacks on free speech. Ironically, these "radical excesses" are far more in tune with the moralistic, antidemocratic temper of the conservative crackdown than with the '60s cultural radical vision, which put its faith in freedom above all. Yet both the right and anticulturalists on the left have invoked them to equate cultural radicalism with authoritarian "correctness." Since neither group has any use for the libertarians within the cultural movements, opportunism is a kind word for this maneuver, but it has played well.

Given that the culture wars have become such a one-sided affair, it's all the more remarkable that the liberatory impulse, however qualified and muted, remains a potent force in contemporary American life. What would have happened in 1994—or 1980—if desire had had a champion? Suppose—why should Charles Murray have a monopoly on "thought experiments"?—that from the '70s to the present, instead of echoing moral conservatives or changing the subject, the left had consistently argued that the point of life is to live and enjoy it fully; that genuine virtue is the overflow of happiness, not the bitter fruit of self-denial; that sexual freedom and pleasure are basic human rights; that endless work and subordination to bosses are offenses to the human spirit; that contempt for the black poor is the middle class's effort to deny that *we are next*; that mom is not going home again and so we need to rethink domestic life, child rearing, and the structures of work; that democracy is not about voting for nearly indistinguishable politicians but about having a voice in collective decision-making, not only in government, but at home, at school, at work? And suppose those arguments were coupled with a thoroughgoing critique of the new economic order and its accelerating class war, in a challenge to Americans to wrest control of their lives from the sex cops *and* the corporations?

I submit that the current political landscape would be quite different. At the very least the opposition would be on the map and able to draw some lines. The alternative is to stay in a rut so deep as to raise the bleakest of questions: is the left so afraid of freedom that it would rather lose?

Don't Think, Smile! Notes on a Decade of Denial, 2000

Editor's note: Again, you may ask, why is a piece from 2000 appearing in the nineties chapter? Not only was much of the material culled from 1990s writing, but it is plainly an assault on the decade itself.

Ending Poor People
As We Know Them

In the Sunday *Times*'s Week in Review, Jason DeParle points out a central contradiction in the discussion of welfare reform: "It is hard to imagine a less popular word than welfare. . . . But shift the conversation to the fate of 'poor children,' and the psychic landscape is transformed. . . . These twin forces—disdain for welfare, concern for poor children—are the seismic forces beneath the debate over public assistance. . . . It is the age-old conundrum of welfare reform: The more one seeks to punish the parent, the greater the risks to the child." He quotes last week's *New York Times*/CBS poll: 48 per cent of respondents supported cuts in "government spending on welfare," while 13 per cent called for an increase; yet asked about "spending on programs for poor children," 47 per cent advocated more spending, with only 9 per cent wanting less. DeParle (whose *Times Magazine* cover story profiling a former welfare recipient appeared the same day) clearly sees in this contradiction an opening to the left. He implies that if the debate can be reframed to focus on children rather than welfare, Americans might be convinced that the real issue is not how to end welfare but how to end poverty.

I wish it were true, but my own observation of the psychic landscape suggests otherwise. Americans are ambivalent about much of the right's program, yet are more and more influenced by the right's cultural imagination, in which the end of welfare means the return of domestic tranquility and order, the defense of Judeo-Christian morality against a dark outlaw class that represents all the heresies of the '60s. Filtered through that vision, compassion for poor children—inevitably mixed with fear of the teenagers and adults they will become—easily slides into fatalistic pity for damned souls who should never have been born, or into fantasies of somehow rescuing the kids from their hopeless parents.

The welfare debate needs to be seen in a larger context: ever since the election, the media have been promoting a right-wing myth of cultural counterrevolution that, despite its ambiguous connection to the voters' actual intentions, is fast becoming a self-fulfilling prophecy. This is not a question of partisanship. Conservatives are basically right about the press—it *is* an integral part of a cultural establishment that's essentially liberal and secular on social issues. For the most part, the mainstream media are nervous about the right, which keeps breaking their rules of Civil Discourse, i.e., noblesse oblige and multicultural politeness. Yet as their centrist self-definition struggles with the unconscious erotic attraction of energy and power, the center drifts steadily toward the vortex.

Time, for instance, recently ran a cover depicting a scowling Gingrich, in top hat, striped pants, and goatee, as "Uncle Scrooge." "'Tis the season to bash the poor," the cover type reads. "But is Newt Gingrich's America really that heartless?" No, the story inside argues: ". . . in their unbridled willingness to go after immigrants and the poor, the new House firebrands may be getting out ahead of the public mood." But forget about the words; the image melds Gingrich with an America embodied in a stubborn, cranky geezer raring to, in the machoid lingo of the day, kick some ass. Just as Bruce Springsteen's "Born in the U.S.A." persona became—contrary to its protagonist's conscious intention—a Reaganite icon, Uncle Scrooge is easy to imagine on a conservative bumper sticker.

The trajectory of welfare politics offers the most striking evidence of how the deep, unconscious appeal of the right's world view drives the framing of political issues, not the other way around. Consider *Newsweek*'s cover on "The Orphanage: Is It Time to Bring It Back?" A box next to the headline informs us that this question refers to "The Welfare Debate." The illustration is a photographed assemblage of short-haired, poignant-looking little white kids holding out their hands to the viewer and wearing what looks like white nightgowns, or are they choir robes? What do these cherubs have to do with the welfare debate? Not much, in practical terms; a lot, symbolically speaking.

As originally floated by Charles Murray and other conservatives, orphanages were simply an answer to the bleeding-heart question, "If you throw women off welfare and they can't find work, what happens to their kids?" If taking children away from their mothers seemed hard-hearted, well, ending welfare dependency was the greater good; and if these women knew their babies could be taken away, maybe they wouldn't have them in the first place. There were two problems with this formulation, however. It handed the Democrats a gold mine of righteous rhetoric about Dickens, and it seemed to contradict family values. So a new rationale began to surface: kids are better off in orphanages than in the chaotic, lawless culture of the underclass, with no fathers and abusive, neglectful, drug-addicted mothers incapable of giving them a moral foundation. *Newsweek*'s piece is dutifully balanced—on the one hand Oliver Twist, on the other, "the concern, now verging on panic, for the catastrophic decline of proper child-rearing practices among the poor." But its imagery—like Gingrich's bizarre, Reaganesque suggestion that Hillary Clinton watch *Boys Town*—promotes the subliminal fantasy that welfare reform can save civilization by transforming all those fearsome, unsocialized black kids into Mickey Rooney.

I don't think orphanages, group homes, or whatever we want to call them are inherently a bad idea for children whose parents are absent, abusive, or neglectful—as opposed to merely poor—and who are unlikely to be adopted. By giving kids the security of a place they can count on, long-term placement in a group home could be a lot better than foster care, with its assumption of impermanence—an assumption so basic to its definition that kids have actually been taken away from foster parents judged to be "too attached." Of course, to have a shot at meeting children's emotional needs, group homes would have to be small, with enough staff to give the kids (especially infants and toddlers) individual attention, and surrogate parents who saw their jobs as a long-term professional commitment. Though such homes do exist, making them widely available would cost a fortune. Since welfare reformers have no intention of spending that kind of money, any discussion of orphanages that pretends it's about helping kids, rather than demonizing parents, is frivolous and hypocritical.

But then, so is the whole discussion of welfare, which is less a debate in any meaningful sense than an argument among undertakers about how to dispose of the body. At bottom, the logic of the attack on welfare mothers—still taboo in Civil Discourse, though less so every day—is that the poor should stop breeding altogether, and solve the problem of the underclass by disappearing. In Charles Murray's latest screed on the subject ("What to Do about Welfare," December *Commentary*), he declares, "To bring a child into the world knowing that you are not intellectually, emotionally, or materially ready to care for that child is *wrong*." Leaving aside that obnoxious "intellectually" (Murray continues to be obsessed with poor people's IQs), who in good conscience can disagree? But consider the context. Murray is not only talking about teenage mothers here; he means that parents should have jobs and be married. Especially married. "Illegitimacy," he insists, "is the central social problem of our time." The most crucial purpose of welfare reform is to "generate a situation in which a young woman . . . is so scared at the prospect of getting pregnant that she will not have intercourse, or will take care not to get pregnant if she does." Having a child out of wedlock should be, as it once was, "so immediately, tangibly punishing that it overrides everything else. . . . Subtle moral reasoning is not the response that works."

With this tirade, Murray crosses the boundaries of welfare polemic into the classless terrain of patriarchal terrorism. Yet for the poor women who are its immediate targets, it poses a particular double bind: fear of unwed motherhood might give them an incentive to marry, but without any chance for the privilege and status that come with breadwinning, why would poor, unemployed men go along with the program? Nor do these same women have much prospect of *ever* earning enough money to support children adequately. Nor do Murray's politics allow for any kind of collective social commitment to alleviating the debilitating poverty and social demoralization that affect people's ability to care for their children. There is in fact no way for most indigent women to be responsible parents in Murray's terms. Nonetheless, most people, whatever their class, have a powerful desire to reproduce, and communities are unlikely to assent to their own annihilation on moral grounds. What happens when we cut the poor off welfare and they still won't go away?

Village Voice, December 1994

What We Don't Talk about When We Talk about *The Bell Curve*

Around the same time that an insurgent right-wing Congress was taking charge of American politics, a parallel cultural event occurred: the publication of Charles Murray and the late Richard Herrnstein's *The Bell Curve*. This massive work was really two books. One was a media event designed to fill a conspicuous gap in public discourse—while the figures on crime and "illegitimacy" had long served to release sensitive white people from their pesky inhibitions about calling blacks violent and hypersexual, in recent years there had been no comparable statistical outlet for the sentiment that blacks are dumb. The other, which lurked obscurely in the shadow of the public conversation, was a polemic about the intelligentsia or, as authors called it, the "cognitive elite." The first book presented IQ as the preeminent criterion of social worth; the second attacked intelligence as a means of allocating social power. Contradictory as they sounded, these arguments nonetheless converged in a paradoxical vision: invoking the authority of science. *The Bell Curve* rejected the whole enterprise of modernity.

Conservatives are perennially tempted by the illusion that vexing social conflicts can be settled by exposing radical aspirations to the dry air of "the facts." Twenty-five years ago, Steven Goldberg thought he could prove "the inevitability of patriarchy" by citing studies that linked aggression with testosterone and concluded that men were innately more aggressive than women. (As far as I can tell, this line of argument has had no effect on sexual politics except to inspire mock diagnoses of "testosterone poisoning.") Fifteen years ago, right-to-life activists imagined that the expansion of scientific knowledge about fetal development would have to change people's minds about abortion. Now *The Bell Curve*'s revival of decades-old claims about IQ—that there is such a thing as a quantifiable general intelligence; that IQ tests measure it accurately and objectively; that it is largely genetic, highly resistant to change, and unevenly distributed among races; that high IQ correlates with economic and social success, low IQ with the abject condition and aberrant behavior of the poor—is supposed to tell us what to do about social equality, namely abandon the idea as quixotic. Yet to argue about the meaning of IQ—as about the humanity of fetuses or the nature of sexual difference—is really a way of defusing anxiety by displacing onto impersonal "factual" dispute a profound clash of interests and worldviews, with all the yearning, hatred, and fear that clash entails. If I bought the authors' thesis, I would still be allergic to their politics. I don't advocate equality because I think everyone is the same; I believe that difference, real or imagined, is no excuse for subordinating some people to others. Equality is a principle of human relations, not Procrustes' bed.

In fact, the authors tacitly recognize that science is not the key issue here. Recounting the history of the IQ debate, they focus less on the substance of the argument than on the struggle to prevail as the conventional wisdom. As they tell it, their view of intelligence and IQ testing was taken for granted until it ran into the dogmatic egalitarianism of the '60s and '70s, when Herrnstein, Arthur Jensen, and others who correlated race and class differences with IQ scores were driven out of the public arena by intimidating demonstrations and intellectual antagonists like Stephen Jay Gould; but although the latter "won the invisible battle," discussion of the significance of IQ continued to take place offstage. The clear implication of this tale of exile is that, with the rightward shift in the narration's politics, it's time for the return.

In short, *The Bell Curve* is not about breaking new intellectual ground, but about coming up from underground. Murray and Herrnstein are convinced "that the topic of genes, intelligence, and race in the late twentieth century is like the topic of sex in Victorian England. Publicly, there seems to be nothing to talk about. Privately, people are fascinated by it." I can't quarrel with this point. The idea that black brains are genetically inferior to white brains did not fade from the public view simply because white people were convinced by Stephen Jay Gould's eloquent arguments. Rather, the gap between Americans' conscious moral consensus for racial equality and the tenacious social and psychic structures of racism was papered over with guilt and taboo. Many opponents of racism thought they were doing their political duty by shouting down the Jensens and Herrnsteins, driving them underground. But this literal enforcement of taboo was only a crude reflection of a much more widespread process of self-censorship.

I don't mean that the moral consensus of the post–civil rights era wasn't genuine. I mean that morality isn't enough, that it can't forever keep the lid on contrary feelings rooted in real social relationships that have not been understood, confronted, or transformed. Commenting on *The Bell Curve* in the *New Republic,* John B. Judis indignantly points out that the taboo Murray and

Herrnstein are so proud of violating was a reaction to Nazism: "It's not a taboo against unflinching scientific inquiry, but against pseudo-scientific racism. Of all the world's taboos, it is most deserving of retention." The problem, though, is that taboos can never truly vanquish the powerful desires that provoke them. For some decades after the Holocaust, there was a moratorium on open anti-Semitism in Europe and America: it didn't last. So long as hierarchy is a ruling principle of our culture, a basic fact of everyday life, the idea of black inferiority cannot be transcended, only repressed. And in an era when an ascendant global capitalism is creating a new, worldwide class structure—when the language of social Darwinism is increasingly regarded as simple description of reality—genetic determination of social status is an idea whose time has come back.

The media blitz began with Murray's picture on the cover of the *New York Times Magazine,* its headline a classic self-fulfilling prophecy: "The Most Dangerous Conservative." "Over a decade," the cover type continued, "Charles Murray has gained ground in his crusade to abolish welfare. But now, with his contentious views on I.Q., class and race, has he gone too far?" The accompanying profile was critical of Murray's views. But the real message of the article lay in its existence, its prominence, and the assumption embedded in its presentation—that *The Bell Curve* had pushed the American public debate to a new and daring frontier, with all the disreputable glamour such an undertaking implied (and incidentally had outflanked Murray's crusade to abolish welfare, which was now respectable—hadn't Clinton all but endorsed it?).

Subsequent coverage continued in this vein, proclaiming through sheer volume and visibility that *The Bell Curve* was a serious work whose thesis, however unpalatable, could not be ignored. *Newsweek*'s cover featured a Janus-like white face and black face turned away from each other (was it my imagination, or did the black face look a little like O. J. Simpson?) on either side of the headline, "IQ: Is It Destiny?" The front page of the *New York Times Book Review*—which reviewed *The Bell Curve* and a number of other books making biological-determinist arguments in the same issue—asked, "How Much of Us Is in the Genes?" (Note the ubiquitous question as ass-covering device. Is it destiny? Hey, we're not saying it is, we're not saying it isn't.) The *New Republic*'s cover, in huge type, simply read "Race & I. Q."; virtually the entire issue was devoted to an article by Murray and Herrnstein, based on material from the book, and nineteen (!) replies. Murray's TV appearances and countless op-eds hammered the theme home: attention must be paid.

Most of this commentary was hostile. Some of it noted that *The Bell Curve*'s thesis was not new but a rehash of ideas with a long and dubious pedigree. It would not have been an implausible reaction if editors had rolled their eyes at Murray's getting in bed with the IQ crowd, if they'd felt the kind of embarrassment one feels when, say, a respected intellectual joins a religious cult. Instead, it seemed that their dominant emotion was fear of being or being called a censor. I can't help suspecting that that fear had less to do with a healthy respect for debate than with the cultural unconscious of a white, educated middle class projecting onto an Evil But Courageous book its own tabooed racial feelings.

Not coincidentally, the media's treatment of *The Bell Curve* centered obsessively on race and virtually ignored class, which is the book's main subject (its subtitle is *Intelligence and Class Structure in American Life*). Murray and Herrnstein clearly invited this reaction, not only by including a section on race and repackaging it for the *New Republic,* but by devoting so much space to their dire view of the underclass—while they warn of an "emerging white underclass," elsewhere in the book, as in the public conversation generally, the word is code for "black." Still, it seems peculiar that journalists, certified members of *The Bell Curve*'s "cognitive elite," should have so little comment on its analysis of their own class status. Their silence is one more piece of evidence that even as economic restructuring makes class an issue in more and more people's lives, they stubbornly resist talking about it. It strikes me, in fact, that blackness has become as much a code for "underclass" as the other way around—that when whites treat middle-class black men in suits and ties like potential muggers and rapists, what they fear is being engulfed and tainted by lower-classness. It's a truism that poor whites embrace racism so they can see the lower class as safely Other. But in the new, anarchic world order, the specter of downward mobility haunts us all.

The Bell Curve's class analysis goes like this: at an earlier time, when social classes were sorted out by birth and there were many fewer specialized occupations that demand high intelligence, cognitive ability was distributed fairly evenly throughout the class structure. Now equal opportunity—particularly equal access to higher education—and the shift toward a high-tech, knowledge-based economy have made intelligence the main agent of class stratification. (If you're tempted to tune out right here—equal opportunity? What are they talking about?—bear with me. The argument gets more interesting.) As the brainy rise to the top and the dull-witted sink to the increasingly miserable bottom, social proximity makes people ever more likely to mate within their cognitive group (a tendency exacerbated by feminism, which encourages educated men in high IQ jobs to marry similarly situated women). That accelerates the process of IQ stratification, since (to quote one of the summaries for the cognitively impaired that precede each chapter) "as America equalizes the circumstances of people's lives, the remaining differences in intelligence are increasingly determined by differences in genes."

As a result, the authors worry, the cognitive elite is coalescing "into a class of its own." Smart people are socialized in similar ways and isolated from the TV/tabloid/talk radio culture of ordinary Americans. They have exploited the increasing reach of the federal government since the '60s to impose their values on the rest of society. And now, as the rich get brighter and the bright get richer, a scary confluence looms: "Do you think," Murray and Herrnstein ask rhetorically, "that the rich in America already have too much power? Or do you think the intellectuals already have too much power? . . . just watch what happens as their outlooks and interests converge." A probable consequence, in the authors' view, is that a large class of smart, affluent people (10 to 20 percent of the population) will wall itself off from the rest of society, particularly from the threatening underclass, withdrawing from public institutions and preferring to pay for its own private services. Still clinging to its belief in the welfare state, even as it loses faith that the poor can improve their condition, this class will most likely use its power to institute "the custodial state"—"an expanded welfare state for the underclass that also keeps it out from underfoot."

How to avoid this dystopia? What people need, *The Bell Curve* argues, is a "valued place" in the social order. In traditional societies, people across the cognitive spectrum attained this "valued place" through work, community, and family. As occupations that don't require a high IQ lose prestige and learning power, it is harder and harder for the dull to find a valued place at work. This makes community and family all the more important, yet these sources of valued place have also been undercut. And much of the blame for this situation rests on, you guessed it, the CE's misguided attitudes and values. For one thing, "the federal domination of public policy that has augmented the cognitive elite's political leverage during the last 30 years . . . has had the collateral effect of stripping the neighborhood of much of the stuff of life." This hasn't bothered the CE because its members aren't centered in a geographic community but are oriented to the nation and the world. Furthermore, the CE is now running American society by rules that people with low or even ordinary IQs find too difficult to follow. These rules are based on the idea that "complicated, sophisticated operationalizations of fairness, justice, and right and wrong are ethically superior to simple, black-and-white versions." Such rules "give the cognitive elite the greatest advantage," since "deciphering complexity is one of the things that cognitive ability is most directly good for."

In the crucial area of morality, for instance, society should make it easy for dullards to be virtuous by making simple rules about crime and punishment that everyone enthusiastically enforces. But the CE with its complicated rules and moral ambiguities has produced a confusing system where the bad guys don't always lose, and worse, people don't always agree on what's bad. Similarly, the CE's sexual revolution has made it more difficult for the dull "to figure out why marriage is a good thing, and, once in a marriage . . . to figure out why one should stick with it through bad times." Marriage is satisfying to the extent that society unequivocally upholds it as an institution; the CE supports the right to sex and procreation outside marriage and demands legal and social recognition of nonmarital relationships.

This broadside against the *clercs* has enough contradictions to keep the critics busy (for one thing, the increasing reliance of the affluent on private rather than public services, which the authors view with alarm, is a direct result of the governmental shrinkage they champion). But a more serious problem is the fanciful nature of its central conceit—the supposed ruling coalition of the rich and the smart, which lumps together the titans of the global marketplace and the people like me. Since I belong to the CE if anyone does (skipped a grade in junior high school, graduated from a Seven Sisters college, work in not one but two knowledge industries, managed to get through 845 pages of *The Bell Curve* with a minimum of cheating), how come I'm not running the World Bank?

In the real world, intellectuals and techies not directly tied into the production of wealth are fast following blue-collar workers into redundancy. Technology eliminates intellectual along with manual labor; white-collar jobs migrate to countries whose newly educated classes are willing to work at lower rates; obsession with the bottom line translates into suspicion of any intellectual work whose productivity can't be easily measured. Companies are shedding managers and replacing engineers and computer programmers with machines. The job markets in the academy and the publishing industry are dismal, support for artists and writers are even scarcer than usual, the public and nonprofit sectors—hotbeds of cognitive elitism—steadily shrinking. Nor are card-carrying CE members exempt from the pervasive trend toward employment of part-time, temporary, and benefit-free workers. Wealth is increasingly concentrated at the top and, last I looked, still handily outstrips other sources of power.

Still, I do have something in common with the Walter Wristons, the Rupert Murdochs, the venture capitalists in Eastern Europe—that deeply suspect tropism for locating the center of our lives outside the neighborhood. Like genetic theories of racial inferiority, antipathy toward intellectuals and capitalists on the ground of their rootless cosmopolitanism is a recurring theme among reactionaries whose loyalties are more aristocratic than bourgeois. And for all the authors' lip service to the American ideals of meritocracy and equal opportunity (as opposed to equal results), their vision of the good society is essentially feudal: it's that old chestnut the organic community, where there is "a Place for Everyone" (a chapter heading) and all cheerfully accept their place, while a kindly but firm, paternal ruling class runs things according to rules even the darkies can understand. Equality of opportunity unleashes the disruptive force of intelligence, deposes the organic hierarchy, and rends the social fabric. In effect, *The Bell Curve* restates a core belief of unreconstructed conservatives (not the free-market kind): that the Enlightenment ruined culture.

Yet Murray and Herrnstein, themselves part of the elite they decry, are nothing if not free-marketeers; despite their suggestion that the rich are too powerful, their targets are government and culture, not the economic system. On the surface, this doesn't make sense: do they seriously imagine that capitalism can somehow be divorced from its cosmopolitan character, and that if only the government and the CE would get out of the way, community and family would provide the underclass with a valued place? But a deeper logic is at work here. Murray and Herrnstein don't really object to the power of wealth; they're merely willing to appeal to resentment of the rich to bolster their argument against intellectuals and their subversive ways. Who, after all, is the *you* they're addressing with those rhetorical questions? Clearly, "the average American," whom the authors regard as "an asset, not part of the problem," and who, they imply, would do fine were it not for the oppressive power of the cognitive elite and the burdensome underclass its policies have nurtured. By this route, *The Bell Curve*'s aristocratic outlook merges seamlessly with right-wing populism.

The Bell Curve, with its dry academic tone and pages of statistics, is not in itself a powerful book. But it rides a powerful wave of emotion—the frustration of a middle class that, whatever its IQ scores, sees its choices narrowing, its future in doubt. Rejecting the moral taboos of the left to flirt with the shameless brutality of the right feels like a hit of freedom. But like all drugs it wears off, leaving the underlying problem untouched. The danger is that Americans will seek out more and bigger doses, while radicalism remains the greatest taboo of all.

Don't Think, Smile! Notes on a Decade of Denial, 2000

Rodney King's Revenge

Call me the last innocent in America, but the day the O. J. Simpson verdict came in, I thought a conviction was possible, even likely. Paradoxically, it was Detective Mark Fuhrman's lurid tape-recorded spew that made me think so. Here was this guy, the personification or nightmare caricature of the law gone rotten, the cop as racist vigilante (with a name from the same root as "führer," no less), and yet his exposure had failed—or so it seemed to me—to make a serious dent in the prosecution's case. Simpson's history of violence against Nicole was damning, even without the evidence Judge Ito had disallowed. There was simply too much physical evidence to be entirely invalidated by the bungling that had surrounded its collection; and deliberately falsifying that evidence would have required an elaborate conspiracy that required too much coordination and disciplined silence, among too many people with no discernible motive, to be remotely plausible. In any case, it didn't make sense that policemen who had protected Simpson in the past, and hesitated to arrest him for the murders, would want to frame him. And in the absence of such a plot, the Fuhrman tape, however shocking, was irrelevant.

Most juries, when it comes down to the wire, take their job seriously; surely, I thought, in a world-is-watching case like this, the jurors' pride in their role, their sense of the gravity and public import of their decision, will prevail. Wasn't it, in a genteel middle-class way, as racist as Fuhrman's rantings to assume that black jurors would act reflexively to free a black celebrity or stick it to the LAPD? And when the decision came back so quickly, I knew it had to be "guilty." True, quick verdicts were usually acquittals, but in this case it was inconceivable that twelve people could let their man off without a long and bloody argument. So I began mentally composing my *Village Voice* column, along the lines of how whites had been carried away by racial paranoia and blacks by dreams of Rodney King's revenge, but in the end the jury had chosen reality over fantasy and history over myth.

In the column I actually wrote, I told this story. In response I got an angry letter from a black woman who accused me of wanting the Simpson jurors to "rise above race" to reassure me that I had nothing to worry about. I was embarrassed to realize she was right. That moment of recognition didn't change my opinion of the verdict, but it made it clear that wherever one stood in relation to this Rorschach test of the century, there was little enough innocence to go around. Not that I had ever imagined my view of O. J. Simpson was unconditioned by my overall views of the world. In truth, the moment I knew he had beaten Nicole, I found him guilty. To me it was clear that the same mania for control that had led him to beat her had ultimately led him to kill her. I also thought he deserved to be put away whether or not he had actually committed murder. While various commentators, in the days after his arrest, suggested that people felt they knew O. J. and therefore wouldn't want to see him executed, I found Simpson's history of unpunished brutality so infuriating that I lusted to kill him myself (which I guess means I could hold my own in a presidential debate) and include a few cops, judges, and freeway cheerleaders for good measure. Of course, had I been on the jury, I would have made every effort to put my preconceptions aside and weigh the evidence; I believe in the principle of a fair trial. But that's what they all say (and what, in fact, jurors said). The point is, I knew my story had a gendered spin. I shouldn't have been surprised that it had a racial spin as well.

In view of the acquittal and its aftermath, it's easy to forget that racial fantasy was inseparable from the Simpson case long before Johnnie Cochran started spinning it—as early as the controversial *Time* cover with the "photo illustration" of O. J. that darkened his skin a few shades. The "American Tragedy" *Time* proclaimed on that cover referred less to Simpson's downfall, in itself, than to white Americans' continually thwarted quest for a painless solution to their Negro problem. O. J. the good, the friendly, the easygoing, the generous, the black man who transcended race, who "had it all"—have you ever heard that obnoxious concept applied to anyone not black and/or female?—was a deeply soothing figure. Simpson with a "dark" side was anything but. Indeed, he became fodder for a particularly insidious form of white paranoia: no matter how much one of "them" appears to be one of us, underneath they are all rampaging brutes. The *New York Post* blurted it best, in a front-page headline: "O. J. and Coke: Drugs Fueled His Rage." Or so "friends and acquaintances of Nicole" reportedly told columnist Andrea Peyser. An accompanying story cited "police sources in Buffalo" as claiming that "Simpson narrowly missed being nailed in two major drug raids in 1975." Note how this formulation transmutes the iconography from "man abusing woman" to "another crazed black guy on drugs."

Just as Simpson's beating of Nicole Brown, though a matter of public record, had no impact on his pristine image; just as the media indulged in weeks of maudlin Othello analogies before picking up on the domestic violence theme; so O. J.'s defense shifted the focus of his trial from violence against women and the way men get away with it to a classic black-man-versus-racist-police scenario. In the process, Nicole was demoted from a central character in the drama to its mere occasion. And as race became its main theme, while gender disappeared, a familiar lacuna was revealed: "race" referred entirely to the situation of black men in relation to white authority. Black women, who have no little experience of domestic violence, didn't count. In that respect, the trajectory of the Simpson trial recalled the Clarence Thomas hearings, where Thomas appropriated blackness with his "high-tech lynching" rhetoric, while Anita Hill was deracialized, defined by the media, Thomas's allies, and many black people as a surrogate white feminist.

The Rodney King case was the wrong gird to lay on O. J. Simpson. It didn't fit the crime, it diverted the jury from what should have been its job, and it led to a miscarriage of justice. But it's a misreading to equate the verdict, as some commentators did, with the South's old habit of routinely acquitting whites who committed crimes against blacks. The message of those acquittals was that whites had the right to kill blacks to keep them in their place. This jury did not act out of animus toward the victims because of their race, or Nicole because of her sex; it didn't imply that their deaths were a good thing for the social order; it simply ignored them, which was bad enough.

The southern comparison was the most overwrought position in a generally reductive debate. One side accused the jurors of nullification, pure and simple—of ignoring the evidence and freeing Simpson out of racial solidarity and/or to "send a message" to the LAPD. The other insisted that they had weighed the evidence, including the credibility of police witnesses, and had reasonable doubts—and furthermore, anyone who imagined otherwise was guilty of stereotyping blacks, especially black women, as "emotional" and "irrational." The problem with both arguments is their common assumption that evidence speaks for itself, or should. In reality, the way any jury perceives a body of evidence depends heavily on the stories the lawyers weave around it. And the Simpson defense wove a compelling story of police incompetence, mendacity, and racism. Told to a mostly black jury inclined to admire O. J. and believe the worst of LA cops, that story had the power to reduce the prosecution's mountain of evidence to a pile of tainted rubble. At the same time, in putting Fuhrman on trial and casting Simpson as his victim, it overshadowed the People's narrative: the story of the genial O. J. as Mr. Hyde, stalking, battering, and finally butchering the ex-wife he couldn't control.

Yet the card Cochran played had arguably been dealt by his opponents. Simpson was hardly a natural for the role of oppressed black man, given his wealth, celebrity, and raceless persona; the LA police, far from harassing him, had been all too indulgent of his "domestic disputes." It would seem to be the

D.A. who reinvented him in the mold of Rodney King, letting the fear that Simpson would be convicted by an all-white jury and touch off another riot dictate the downtown venue of the trial (though Marcia Clark insists that any case of such major proportions would have had to be tried there). The prosecution then conveniently delivered the racist cop, out of a baffling hubris—or perhaps a profound unconscious urge to replay the King movie with a different ending. Clark also admits, in her autobiography, that she saw her cause as basically doomed from the moment she confronted a jury pool she deemed so hopeless that she didn't bother to use all her peremptory challenges. I don't doubt that her chances of prevailing were slim; yet her attitude toward the jury blurs the line between rational pessimism and a defeatism that may have amounted to self-fulfilling prophecy. A lawyer blaming defeat on a closed-minded jury— especially before the fact—is a bit like a psychotherapist complaining that the patient doesn't want to get well: the charge may be true, but it's not terribly useful. Penetrating the psyche of a hostile jury, finding ways to make the elusive connection, is basic to a trial lawyer's skill. It follows that failure to connect reflects the lawyer's limitations as well as the jurors'.

Could the prosecution have done more to disrupt the defense's story and foreground its own? Clark and Christopher Darden knew almost from the start that Fuhrman was a dicey character. They didn't believe his professed innocence of racial slurs; Darden even wanted to declare him a hostile witness. Shouldn't they have investigated, found witnesses who would discredit him, and expressed preemptive shock and horror, rather than merely putting him on the stand and hoping nothing damaging would come out? Clark is impatient with such questions. As far as she's concerned, Cochran should not have brought race into his defense, and Ito should not have allowed it—enough said. But in the trial of a black male celebrity accused of murdering two white people, against the backdrop of post–Rodney King Los Angeles, race was going to be present in the courtroom; the only question was how openly or covertly.

As for the domestic violence story, Clark acknowledges that although "deep down I knew [it] lay at the center of the case," she pursued it halfheartedly. She was leery of being thought to "spout a feminist line" or condone "the culture of victimization." She recognized in herself an "emotional resistance" to the issue, apparently related to memories of being raped as a teenager and having shoving matches with her possessive first husband. And she doubted the jury would buy it—a sentiment that clearly reflected her own ambivalence as well as her corroding doubt that the jury would buy anything.

Among whites outraged by the verdict, and by the popular support it enjoyed in the black community, there was much apocalyptic talk about the damage it had supposedly done to race relations (in one of her more hyperbolic moments, Clark in effect blames Johnnie Cochran for the passage of California's anti–affirmative action proposition). Those who, like me, were more anguished than outraged were inclined to dwell on what seemed to be the separate and incommensurable realities that stared at each other from across the racial divide. In my column, I suggested that what we were seeing was something even more alarming: the breakdown of belief in any possibility of a good-faith struggle toward some consensual version of truth, a breakdown that did not start with black jurors but with mostly white intellectuals—talk about chickens coming home to roost! In retrospect, this observation, while not entirely false, strikes me as melodramatic. That even eyewitnesses tend to give wildly divergent accounts of the same event; that this endemically human problem is aggravated by social conflict; that some see it not as a problem but as an affirmation of difference—all this complicates our every endeavor from justice to politics to love. The Simpson trial is not the first nor will it be the last proof of that truism, though it may well be the best publicized.

My father, a retired New York City policeman, has his own take on the infamous Fuhrman tape: he thinks it was a put-on, a typical example of the way cops love to scandalize civilians with exaggerated accounts of their own badness. I like this idea; it appeals to my sense of irony as well as explaining why Fuhrman would confide in a stranger about conduct that was not only reprehensible but illegal. It doesn't absolve Fuhrman, whose racism and sexism are well-documented from other sources anyway; the purpose of such bad-cop tales, true or not, is to intimidate (as my father sees it, the more terrifying civilians' idea of what cops are capable of, the better for the crime rate). But it adds a new wrinkle to the question of those ever shifting, permeable boundaries between fantasy and fact that make up the stuff of how we live now. When I relayed my father's theory to my black male editor, he had his own story to tell: a cop had stopped him on the highway, supposedly for speeding but really for having a white female passenger. On the side of the road was a steel barrier. The cop kept ordering Joe to pull up closer and closer to the barrier, till finally he had no choice but to scratch his car. Fuhrman may have been fantasizing, but one person's fantasy can be another person's fact.

Marcia Clark should have kept that in mind. One of the more poignant passages of her memoir reveals that in the end she convinced herself that physical evidence was all she really needed. "Blood would tell the truth," she thought. How ironic that a woman who believed in the importance of her own story, urgently enough to write a book, should forget an elementary fact: blood doesn't talk—people do.

Don't Think, Smile! Notes on a Decade of Denial, 2000

Million Man Mirage

For the obvious antiseparatist, antisexist, anti–family values, antireligious, anti–moral uplift, antibootstrap, anticapitalist, antifascist, and anti-Simpson reasons, I hated the whole idea of the Million Man March. But as celebratory reviews kept coming in from marchers and onlookers—some of whom had been skeptical or even hostile beforehand—I had to conclude that either a sizable portion of the black community had been taken over by pod people, or something significant had happened that wasn't covered by my social and political categories.

What I kept hearing about was peace, love, connection, freedom from tension and suspicion. While the press insisted on making comparisons to the 1963 Martin Luther King march, the analogy that sprang irresistibly if somewhat queasily to my mind was Woodstock. On that occasion, half a million people had converted what looked like sure disaster into a spectacular exercise of collective will to live out a utopian moment. Amid the ecstatic accounts of the participants, sympathetically passed along by the media, it was considered impolite if not downright mean to mention certain other aspects of the festival—like the incompetence and dangerous irresponsibility of its promoters, or the enormous amount of work and taxpayers' money involved in making emergency provisions for food, water, and sanitation. On the other hand, to have focused on such complaints and ignored the utopian moment would have been to miss the story.

I don't want to push this analogy too far. Woodstock was the invention of affluent white kids with an expansive sense of entitlement, seeing themselves as countercultural missionaries to America. The marchers were middle-class and working-class black guys whose ordinary humanity is daily denied and challenged, coming together not to declare a cultural revolution but to contest their demonization as culturally alien, inferior, and criminal. The point, though, is that utopian moments are basically alike; there's the falling away of the convoluted layers of embattlement and mutual paranoia that stand in the way of simple human contact, the melting of the psychic fortress, the freedom from a loneliness more terrible than you knew; the knowledge that it's okay, really okay, to relax. At such a moment Louis Farrakhan, anti-Semitism, the carapace of masculinism would be irrelevant—concerns from another dimension.

But utopian moments have something else in common—transience. Insofar as they challenge cynicism and encourage the faith that it's possible to live differently, to be different, they do change people, but not in any predictable direction: the myriad utopian moments shared by psychedelic trippers in the '60s produced born-again Christians and Buddhist stockbrokers as well as anarchists. Only movements with particular social visions and practical goals can give faith a concrete, real-world shape. Which is to say it's a mistake to imagine that the good feelings generated by the Million Man March negate its political dangers.

Yet this is exactly what a lot of black and white liberals want to believe. Before the march, its defenders argued for distinguishing the message from the messenger. When feminists pointed out that part of the message was that women should stay home and men should resume their rightful place as head of the family, a subtle rhetorical shift occurred; skeptics were urged to endorse not the "message" but the "purpose" of the march. What was that purpose, exactly? Vague inspirational generalities ensued, along with a perceptible irritation. Since the march, its emotional power has become the focus of the discussion, inspiring paeans to brotherhood and unity and, on the flip side, what I think of as the let-a-hundred-flowers-bloom theory of the event. Shortly after the march, WNYC's "On the Line" aired a conversation between me and black sociologist Joyce Ladner, in which she laid out this perspective: Farrakhan and the Nation of Islam and their ideology have nothing to do with why the marchers were there or what the march meant to them; each man's view of the march reflected his own unique reality, and each will respond to this energizing experience in his own way.

Ladner also said that as "a womanist and a feminist" she had no problem with the men-only march. As she saw it, this wasn't about patriarchy but about men getting their act together so they could give black women some help. Some younger black women I talked to said they disagreed with the patriarchal paternalism stuff and couldn't take it seriously; black women weren't about to stay home and submit. Still, they supported the march. Black men, they argued, are so disconnected and demoralized, the first step is getting them to come back and get involved with women, with their kids—then we'll worry about equality.

All mass mobilizations have a life of their own. Almost by definition, they appeal to broad discontents rather than narrow ideological agendas; most people aren't ideologues. But this hardly means that who leads them, and what those leaders are saying, doesn't matter. The dismissal of Farrakhan's importance reminds me of the confidence with which Iranian and American leftists argued, during Khomeini's revolution, that the people were in the streets to oppose the Shah, not to support a religious fanatic. If Farrakhan is so incidental to the whole affair, how come it was Farrakhan and not someone else who pulled it off?

The answer, it seems to me, has everything to do with the bankruptcy of liberalism and the vacuum that gapes where a radical left should be. Faced with a deepening racial crisis and the right's relentless class war, beleaguered liberals and "progressives" haven't the least idea what to do beyond clinging to the shards of the New Deal. On the cultural front, the superiority of the two-parent family has become such an unquestioned assumption that it's taboo (except on the far right) to acknowledge the obvious: among whites as well as blacks, the institution of marriage is in trouble because its basic underpinning is women's subordination. The disengagement that black women—and more and more white women—complain of reflects men's resentment at being deprived of dominance in the family, whether because they're too poor to support a household or because of women's increasing economic independence and insistence on equality. And though most women want men to share their lives and parental responsibilities, they're not willing to put up with the old terms. Exhorting men to do the right thing is not going to resolve these conflicts. What we need is to imagine new ways of organizing domestic life and child rearing. But anyone who says so is accused of spouting hippy-dippy nonsense.

In the circumstances, it's hardly surprising that black men would flock to a Farrakhan march, or that black women would support it, any more than it's surprising that whites voted for the Gingrich Congress. Most blacks don't subscribe to Farrakhan's more extreme views, but then most whites don't subscribe to the Republican right's more extreme views. It's just that there's no one out there with a powerful alternative vision. Who among the assorted black politicians and civil rights establishmentarians currently passing for leaders is capable of organizing a militant mass movement, or even aspires to do such a thing? Even Jesse Jackson, the left's great black hope, could never quite decide who he was. He wanted to be progressive without alienating the nationalists, nationalist without alienating the Jews, socially conservative *and* feminist, a champion of self-help *and* an advocate of the welfare state. Last I heard, he was still arguing for a rainbow coalition, so what's he doing back on Farrakhan's platform? Who can trust the guy? Nor did he ever get serious about building a movement.

Farrakhan, in contrast, knows exactly who he is: a skilled organizer with a vision and a program. He isn't afraid of offending white people or Jews; on the contrary, he revels in giving offense. With his own powerful persona, he conveys the hope of power to black men, indeed to many black women as well. To assume that his appeal is confined to people who embrace the Nation of Islam's tenets is to deny everything we know about the unconscious and how charisma works.

In any case, the political impact of the march is not confined to the marchers themselves. White America respects success, and the media were clearly impressed with Farrakhan's achievement. He is a player now in a way he wasn't before, no longer a marginal antiwhite extremist but the leader of a massive peaceful demonstration in favor of family, self-help, spiritual renewal—in essence, the Republican program. Sure, he's anti-Semitic, but as many observers have noted, this hasn't kept Pat Buchanan and Pat Robertson out of the mainstream.

The most potent message the march transmitted was that blacks have come in from the cold, are ready to be part of the profamily solution instead of the problem. Though its moralism was for once aimed at men, it will inevitably reinforce the right's attacks on single mothers and "illegitimacy." Predictably, the *Wall Street Journal,* in a post-march editorial, crowed that the event showed Dan Quayle was right. When I brought this up on the radio, Joyce Ladner scoffed that most of the people who marched don't read the *Wall Street Journal* and aren't affected by it. This is silly: we're all affected by one of the most influential newspapers in the country whether we read it or not. But don't take it from the *WSJ*; take it from the president of the National Urban League, who told *Time,* "I think this may have been the largest family-values rally in the history of America." I listened for a hint of irony, but heard none.

Village Voice, November 1995

Monica and Barbara and Primal Concerns

From the day the Monica Lewinsky story burst from the recesses of the Internet into the mainstream press, it has been trailed by a Greek chorus of high-minded journalists and media critics lamenting the saturation coverage of the affair. In their eyes, it has displaced the O. J. Simpson trial as the ultimate symbol of a deplorable trend: the devolution of news into entertainment. As I watched Ms. Lewinsky's interview on "20/20," I could almost hear the chorus mutter: "It's bad enough we had to pay attention to That Woman when grave questions of state were involved. But now the political crisis is over. Do we have to tolerate not only the inevitable book, but two hours of That Face on television? And can she wipe That Smile off the face, at least?"

For members of the chorus, public fascination with Monica, O. J., Princess Diana, Lorena Bobbitt and their ilk is mere mindless prurience. That respectable news outlets should encourage this fascination signals a catastrophic breakdown of the barrier between serious news, which aims purely to enlighten, and sensational, sleazy tabloid gossip, which aims to titillate its audience and make money for its purveyors. Serious news is about government, business and war. Stories about sex and power, crime and punishment, fame and its pitfalls are "entertainment"—that is, most people find them more exciting than stories about fiscal policy—and therefore inherently trivial.

But these stories are compelling because they speak to primal human concerns. They are also newsworthy because they dramatize the central conflicts and obsessions of contemporary culture, especially issues of sexual morality and male-female relations. The Lewinsky scandal has prompted an impassioned national conversation on the relationship of the political to the personal, public authority to private behavior; on sexual privacy versus "family values";

on female sexual autonomy and victimization. Granted, the affair has also produced an outpouring of schlock with no redeeming social value. But far from vindicating the eat-your-vegetables school of journalism, the schlock suggests what's wrong with it. Arguably, just as Victorian repression produced a thriving pornography industry, the exclusion of sex from "serious" news media produced tabloidism. As this taboo passes into history, there should be more room for a public conversation on sex that is neither coy nor prurient, but simply frank.

In this respect, the Lewinsky interview was, for network television, an extraordinary event. Drawn out by Barbara Walters's alternately stern and sympathetic prodding, a vividly telegenic (plumpness notwithstanding) and self-possessed young woman firmly defends her sexuality and that of her former lover, who happens to be President of the United States. Despite the havoc, both national and personal, that ensued, she cannot bring herself to regret her passion, her pleasure or her boldness in pursuing the affair. She is still excited by the memory of Mr. Clinton's "energy" and "sensuality." She describes the progression from intense eye contact to first kiss as "a dance," the notorious thong-flashing incident as a "subtle, flirtatious gesture" that meant "I'm interested too. I'll play." She recalls her efforts to persuade the President to have intercourse. If her subtlety is in doubt, her exuberant lustiness is not. It's easy to see why Mr. Clinton was attracted.

At the same time, Ms. Lewinsky is in no sense tough, as the stereotype of the sexually aggressive woman would have it. Indeed, early in the interview, when she talks about her weight and attributes her penchant for married men to low self-esteem, I thought she had decided to run for the cover of pop-psychology clichés. Instead, she turns the clichés inside out. If she was needy and insecure, so, she suggests, was Mr. Clinton, who was lonely in his marriage and sucked in his stomach when he unbuttoned his shirt. Their mutual neediness was part of their bond. And sexual intimacy was, in part, a way of assuaging that neediness on both sides. Ms. Lewinsky's insistence that the connection was emotional as well as physical is entirely believable, if only because most of us know from experience that no relationship goes on for months without getting complicated.

Ms. Lewinsky's performance is an effective rebuke to the lip-curling television commentators who have portrayed her as a pathetic victim, a brainless groupie or both. She emphatically rejects sexual shame, telling Ms. Walters that her sexual acts never made her feel cheap or sordid. Rather, it was Mr. Clinton who cheapened their relationship with his angry denial, his "harsh" and "hurtful" reference to her as "that woman," his maligning her as a stalker and his eventual portrayal of their sexual contact as entirely one-sided. Ruefully, she avers that he was not the person she thought he was. She persuasively claims the moral high ground.

She also makes hash of the idea that a young woman cannot truly consent to sex with her powerful boss. This story is not about a sexual harasser and his victim, any more than it's about a stalker and her prey, nor is it simply about a

President and an intern. Once they were involved, Ms. Lewinsky says, she saw Mr. Clinton less as President than as a man. This was a naive and disastrous view, insofar as it impelled her to confide in her friends, including Linda Tripp, as if the President were just another guy. Yet it expresses an undeniable truth: if only for the moment, sexual pleasure can be a great equalizer and intimacy can strip people of their social roles. Ms. Lewinsky tells a convincing tale of two human beings who, however unsaintly and foolish, shared one of those moments. Heightened by the immediacy of the televised image, her story will stand as the definitive counter–Starr Report.

After the show, I received a delighted E-mail from my old friend Karen Durbin, the film critic for *Mirabella,* calling it "the most pro-sex piece of television I've ever seen in this country." On the other hand, there was Pete Hamill's reaction, expressed in his Digital City column: "Will Everybody Please Shut Up, Please?" Mr. Hamill speaks nostalgically of tight-lipped gangsters going silently to the electric chair. He might as well have come right out with what he meant: "Will all these women please shut up?"

Watching Monica, I couldn't help thinking about the other woman who had recently talked about Bill Clinton: Juanita Broaddrick. Her portrait of Mr. Clinton is starkly different from Ms. Lewinsky's. Her charge of rape is unproved and, absent tapes or DNA, almost certainly unprovable. Yet the two women have something in common: the high-minded press wishes they would go away. When women discuss sex in public, male prerogatives and male hypocrisy come under scrutiny. And that makes a lot of journalists (especially male journalists) nervous—not because sex is trivial, but precisely because it isn't.

New York Times, March 1999

Villains and Victims

When Marx amended Hegel to specify that history repeats itself, the first time as tragedy, the second as farce, he could have been talking about the history of American sexual politics from Anita Hill to Paula Jones and Monica Lewinsky. From the beginning conservatives used Jones's case not only to attack Bill Clinton but to accuse feminists of a hypocritical double standard. "Paula Stunned by Feminists' Silence," a headline in the right-wing *New York Post* observed, while in the *New York Times* Maureen Dowd offered such tidbits as that redoubtable neanderthal, Representative Bob Dornan, suddenly converted to the cause of fighting sexual harassment, sporting an "I believe Paula" button. While these complaints, however disingenuous, pointed to an uncomfortable truth—most publicly visible feminists had reacted to Jones's charges with reflexive avoidance, and some with inexcusable class snobbery—they had little impact, since Paula was perceived by most people to the left of Dornan as a tool of the sectarian right. But with the breaking of the Lewinsky story, conservative demands that, as *Post* columnist Steve Dunleavy put it, feminists "ravage Clinton the same way they ravaged Clarence Thomas" went into high gear.

Undeterred that Lewinsky had been over twenty-one during the (then still alleged) affair and had not complained of harassment or indeed complained at all, right-wing champions pronounced her a victim of at best exploitation, at worst child-molesting. Where they would ordinarily have been inclined to see Monica as a nutty/slutty temptress and condemnation of her male partner as a case of totalitarian sexual correctness, they had now evidently adopted the view of the correctniks that sex between a woman and her boss, or between a young woman and a powerful older man, is inherently abusive. Kathleen Willey's claim that she was groped in the White House, with its echoes of Bob Packwood, was a more plausible subject of indignation, but since Lewinsky was the focus of Kenneth Starr's inquiry and the public's attention, conservatives showed little interest in distinguishing her case from Willey's or even Jones's: the three were simply lumped together as "Clinton's women." In their zeal to portray the president as the worst serial abuser of women since Bluebeard, some even tossed Gennifer Flowers into the mix of victims, despite her publicly voiced admiration for Bill's talents as a lover (on a scale of 1 to 10, she rated him a 9). Feminists, they insisted, were duty-bound to support Starr's investigation: if they really believed that the personal is political, their partisan loyalties to Clinton and the Democrats would not deter them from defending their sisters.

Their own hypocrisy aside, the conservatives' logic was faulty. To assert that "the personal is political" is to claim that politics is not synonymous with government but extends to those sexual and domestic relations in which men exercise institutionalized power over women. It doesn't necessarily follow that "personal politics" should be feminists' chief criterion for judging a public official—that who he is as a sexual actor should outweigh who he is as an agent of the state. This is not to say that a male politician's personal relations with women are inherently irrelevant to his office (as many of Clinton's defenders have argued), but rather that except in cases clearly involving violence or abuse, there is no inconsistency in arguing that other issues—the politician's public stance and policies on women's rights, the motivation and political agenda of his enemies—are more important. Such trade-offs are, after all, the essence of electoral politics, which normally is not about purity of principle but about compromise and lesser-evilism. The last time this question came up for feminists was in 1980, when Ted Kennedy ran against Jimmy Carter in the Democratic presidential primary: the womanizer with a staunch pro-woman record in the Senate versus the apparently faithful spouse who had distanced his administration from the women's movement and opposed federal funding for abortion. My position then was "Marry Carter; vote for Kennedy."

Clinton's situation doesn't lend itself to one-liners. His reputation as a profeminist president is, on the level of policy, mostly myth. Though he has appointed women to high-level positions and defended abortion, he has also pandered shamelessly to the family-values sentiments of cultural conservatives—especially their campaign against "illegitimacy"—and signed a welfare "reform" bill whose essence is an attack on impoverished single mothers; nor does his fidelity to corporate economic priorities benefit women as a group. But as a cultural figure, he evokes the revisionist masculinity of his generation with his soft, sensual, semi-androgynous sexual persona, his avoidance of military service, and his egalitarian marriage. (Indeed, for most of his time in office criticism of his personal life centered less on his alleged affairs than on his refusal to put Hillary in her place.) The far right's single-minded hatred and determination to bring Clinton down have been driven not by his quasi-Republican program but by outrage that such a figure should have attained either the political power or the symbolic authority attached to the presidency. From this choleric standpoint, the Lewinsky scandal merely confirmed that the Oval Office had become, as Pat Robertson put it, "the playpen for the sexual freedom of the poster child of the 1960's."

The Lewinsky witch hunt was at its core an effort to crush the perceived cultural enemy by any means necessary and plant the flag of patriarchal morality on the corpse. It began with the victimization of Lewinsky, not by Clinton but by Linda Tripp, who illegally taped her phone calls, and by Starr, who used those illegally obtained tapes as an excuse to entrap her and threaten her with prosecution unless she delivered the goods. Starr went on to mobilize a terrifying array of hardball tactics, amplified by the independent counsel's virtually unlimited license to pursue a long-running, open-ended fishing expedition aimed at one suspect—in the process raising troubling questions about the independent counsel statute and the power of federal prosecutors even when directed at "deserving" targets like mob bosses—all to unmask a consensual affair between two adults and the lies meant to conceal it. It was hardly in the interest of feminists to sign on to a crusade that subverted civil liberties and turned the screws on a woman whose major "crime" was terminal lack of discretion (or woefully insufficient paranoia) in order to destroy a president for his real and imagined sexual liberalism.

As for Jones, there were reasons other than bigotry against trailer park residents to be skeptical of her story. One important way it differed from Hill's was simply that Hill's already existed: the Thomas-Hill affair had provided at once a model of how to make trouble for a political enemy and a means of embarrassing feminists—a doubly tempting motive for Clinton haters to prevail on Jones to invent, or more likely edit, her story of an encounter with the governor. Then there was the matter—intangible, to be sure, but assessing someone's credibility often hinges on intangibles—of one's sense of Bill Clinton as a sexual animal. I could imagine John F. Kennedy, who appears to have had a blanket contempt for wife and girlfriends alike, having the droit-du-seigneur mentality to behave as Jones alleged. But Clinton has never conveyed the impression of misogyny or unquestioned confidence in his right to dominate. On the contrary, he is insecure. He wants to please, to charm; and the drop-trou scenario is anything but charming. Although Jones may nonetheless have been telling the truth—as with Thomas and Hill, we will never really know—she did not compel belief.

Yet while most feminists intuitively understood that it was Starr's inquisition they should be worried about, not Clinton's libido, the efforts of the liberal feminist establishment to articulate that view were unconvincing. Like the rest of what passes for the left, feminist organizations and politicians had by January 1998 long since forfeited their claim to an independent voice and circled their wagons around the administration. Had they even once rebelled against Clinton—say, organized public protests and threatened to withdraw their support if he signed the infamous welfare bill—they would have been less vulnerable to the charge of knee-jerk partisanship in the Lewinsky crisis; but they hadn't. When the news broke, their first impulse was to make cautionary noises about rushing to judgment. But that response not only sounded fake— who, after reading the excerpts from Tripp's tapes, could say with a straight face that they believed Clinton when he denied having sex with "that woman"?—it seemed to concede that if he had, his behavior was indeed comparable to what Thomas was alleged to have done; and if that were true, why weren't feminists demonstrating in front of the White House, demanding that the president explain himself and cooperate fully with the independent counsel?

The next line of defense was to suggest that, as Gloria Steinem put it in a *New York Times* op-ed, Clinton's alleged actions fell within feminists' "common sense guideline to sexual behavior . . . no means no; yes means yes." The problem here was that so many feminists for so long had argued that in a male-dominated society, no meant no, but yes could mean something more ambiguous. In any case, this line applied better to Lewinsky than to Willey or (especially) Jones. Steinem argued that if Willey and Jones were to be believed, in both cases the president had simply "made a clumsy sexual pass, then accepted rejection." Willey's alleged groping might fit that description (though you would have to add the word "pushy," at the very least). But Jones's story? For the CEO to summon an employee he's never met and, without any preliminaries to speak of, ask her to kiss his dick is no more a "pass," a word that implies some vague connection to ordinary conventions of courtship, than the same request coming from a furtive, glassy-eyed guy in the subway—though it is, I would imagine, more intimidating.

In the wake of the firestorm after Clinton's August confession, many establishment feminists, sharing the political panic of the Democrats and worn down by constant criticism, denounced the president's behavior as morally reprehensible, while still refusing conservatives' demands that they repudiate him as a misogynist and call for his resignation. Trying to present themselves as independent yet judicious, they succeeded mainly in sounding ever more defensive and incoherent. For at bottom, liberal feminists' problem was not simply a matter of blind loyalty; it reflected deep confusions and contradictions in feminist thinking. The Lewinsky scandal had sprung a trap that was set when the dictum "the personal is political" devolved from a tool of social analysis to a weapon of moral condemnation. For its coiners, the idea was that the social rules governing sex, marriage, and motherhood were part of a system that enforced women's subordination, so that much of what appeared to individual women to be their own private unhappiness was widely shared and reflected their social inequality. Armed with that knowledge, women could demand changes in the rules. But over the years, the slogan has increasingly come to mean that all personal behavior is subject to political judgment, that there are now feminist rules both sexes should obey. Accordingly, feminism, insofar as it deals with personal life, has largely abandoned politics, which seeks to affect social structures, for moralism, which aims to control individuals.

Like all moral crusaders, the feminist kind are impatient with the argument that people can't simply change their sexual psychology at will. Nor does consent count: if a woman chooses to condone a man's bad behavior, she is either guilty of collaboration or a victim whether she admits it or not. By this logic, a president who fools around with a White House intern should be in big trouble. After all, such behavior replicates one of the culture's hardier sexist clichés: the powerful older man amusing himself with a sexy woman whose youth, inexperience, lack of worldly clout, and awe of him feed his ego. (In the bargain, one can't help suspecting Bill of seeking a little relief from having to live up to that egalitarian marriage—and of rebelling against Hillary's moral authority by being a bad boy.) But the logic is screwy. Given the president's importance as a cultural icon, it would clearly be nicer for feminism if he'd had an affair with, say, Barbra Streisand; but does it actually further the cause of sexual equality to define gender-stereotyped erotic tastes as an impeachable offense? Was watching the president's downfall supposed to inspire the millions of people in relationships based on the mutual lust (sometimes even love) of young women and powerful men to change their ways? Is it the business of feminism to condemn and where possible punish such couples? Perhaps we should get on the case of men who reveal their sexism *and* racism by their tropism for thin women with blond hair?

If feminist moralism were applied to any area other than sex—housework, for instance—its absurdity would be apparent: imagine trying to make a political scandal of the fact that most male politicians spend little time at home and dump all domestic responsibilities on their wives. But in fact its central purpose has always been sexual repression; it arose from certain feminists' conviction that sex is fundamentally a male weapon for subjugating women. The right understands all this a lot better than liberal feminists, who, having swallowed the moral reading of "the personal is political," found themselves groping for arguments about why it didn't apply in this case.

The right also knows what it thinks about sex, while mainstream feminism is thoroughly ambivalent and confused on the subject. Its dominant impulse—especially among academic and corporate bureaucrats—is, as feminist anthropologist Gayle Rubin once remarked, to presume that sex is guilty till proven innocent (and in our litigious era that's no mere metaphor). Not only has the antisexual strain in feminist politics—particularly as it has been expressed through antipornography and anti–sexual harassment activism—been a powerful influence; the pervasiveness of "pro-family" cultural conservatism, even in feminist circles, has spread the idea that any departure from monogamy is inherently antiwoman. Yet there is also a vocal contingent of feminists who oppose the sexual moralists, arguing that sexual freedom is integral to women's equality. And since liberal feminism, like liberalism in general, goes where it's pushed, the pro-sex influence has made itself felt, at least to the extent of prodding the movement's spokespeople to extend their "right to choose" rhetoric from abortion to sex itself. These competing sets of ideas float around in the thin gruel of an orthodox feminist conversation largely devoid of real political content, available to be fished out and brandished when they seem to fit the occasion. I don't mean that Steinem was insincere when she said "no means no; yes means yes." It's just that she acted as if large chunks of feminist history, in which she herself had been involved, simply didn't exist.

Still another dilemma for Clinton's feminist defenders, especially in the matter of Paula Jones, was squaring their stance with an entrenched item of conventional movement wisdom—that since men have notoriously gotten away with all manner of crimes against women by vilifying them as liars, feminists must redress the balance by assuming that men always lie and women always tell the truth. This assumption is silly; but because it has deep roots in women's collective experience of having their reality denied, it is not easily relinquished. Given the highly charged atmosphere surrounding Clarence Thomas's nomination, it was not unreasonable for his advocates to worry that an opposition about to lose the battle might resort to dirty tricks. Yet when Republican senators and other partisans attacked Anita Hill's credibility, many feminists were incensed not only at the misogynist and often bizarre character of the attacks—or at the lack of evidence for the feminist cabal that was darkly alleged—but at the fact that her truthfulness should be questioned at all. This precedent enabled conservatives to profess shock that feminists would not embrace Jones's tale, no questions asked—especially about the political agenda of her sponsors. One result, it seems to me, is the tortured reasoning in Steinem's piece. I suspect that she didn't believe Jones's account any more than I did, but that having accepted its truth "for the sake of argument," she felt compelled to deny its seriousness.

As the foregoing observations suggest, much of the murk that afflicted feminists' response to the Lewinsky scandal can be traced to precisely that larger-than-life episode that cast its shadow over Clinton's troubles: the Anita Hill–Clarence Thomas confrontation. Indeed, feminists' difficulty in answering the challenge, "Why go after Thomas and not Clinton?" ultimately has less to do with Clinton than with Thomas. The iconic status of the Thomas-Hill affair, and of Anita Hill as a feminist heroine, has discouraged second thoughts. It was, after all, the event that put sexual harassment on the political map. And as public opinion shifted toward Hill in the aftermath of Thomas's confirmation, feminists felt powerfully vindicated: this moral victory, in the face of political defeat, showed that a woman could be believed when she accused a powerful man of abuse, and that—in the face of Thomas's "high-tech lynching" speech and the accusation by many blacks that Hill was a tool of white feminists—a black woman could successfully challenge the idea that it was disloyal to the race to call an abusive black man to account. Yet the legacy of this triumphant moment has been decidedly ambiguous—and in some ways disastrous.

The original outcry on behalf of Anita Hill was not only, or even primarily, about sexual harassment. It erupted as it did for a simmering stew of reasons. There was feminists' desperation over the alliance of the Reagan and Bush administrations with the Christian right and the imminent appointment of a right-wing ideologue to the Supreme Court, at a time when it was widely assumed that one more antiabortion vote would topple *Roe v. Wade.* There was the smug protectiveness of the old boys in the Senate. And there was above all the decade-long, cumulative frustration of women in a political atmosphere that increasingly denied the legitimacy of their anger at men. The "they" in that iconic rallying cry, "They just don't get it!" did not refer simply to the misguided senators but to men in general; "it" was not just Hill's complaint but the sum total of unheeded, invalidated female complaints about the whole range of oppressive male behavior women had to put up with—in short, the culture of male dominance. At that moment "they" were the object not only of rage but of cynicism and even hatred: as feminist social critic Judith Levine suggested in a book published a year later, the unspoken coda to "They don't get it" is "and they never will, those hopeless assholes!"

Conservatives never did get this key aspect of the pro-Hill revolt. They insisted that the outpouring of female fury was a media campaign orchestrated by feminist organizations, and in a sense they were right. But feminists had not been able to foment such a reaction on other issues—abortion rights, for instance—and not for lack of trying. All the orchestration they could muster would not have produced a national obsession had Hill not hit a larger cultural nerve. (For this reason, the right's effort to promote Paula Jones as Anita Hill II was not only opportunistic but tin-eared. Even if organized feminism had been assiduous in coming to Jones's defense, the issue would not have ignited: aside from the second-time-around problem, the iconography was all wrong. Clinton's sexual persona and his general pliability—not to mention the diminished aura of the presidency in an age of corporate rule—made him an unsuitable figure on which to project free-floating rage at male power. Nor was it possible to make a convincing feminist heroine of a woman who was being used by right-wingers against a man they hated in large part because they saw him as a traitor to masculinist culture.)

Yet for those who were listening carefully, the reaction to Thomas-Hill exposed a troubling distortion in the public conversation about feminism. The thought that something about the furor didn't quite track first occurred to me in connection with Levine's book, *My Enemy; My Love.* Appearing at a time when Thomas and Hill were still the subject of hot and bitter emotion, it was a brave attempt to write honestly about man-hating, that taboo emotion—feared by men, anxiously denied by women, routinely projected onto feminists—that

was in fact a powerful if usually subt   strain in the female psyche, an
ongoing emotional protest against the   everyday life. The book's original subtitle was *Man-hating and Aml   n Women's Lives;* but when the
paperback edition came out, I noticed   been sanitized to *Women, Men,
and the Dilemmas of Gender.* Accordi   ne, The Word had been a total
conversation stopper: people either   go near the book (as if it har-
bored a contagious disease) or substituted their fantasy of what the author
must be saying for her actual, impeccably humanist perspective. Odd, isn't it?
An author dares to put the word "man-hating" on a book jacket and reviewers
and potential readers go berserk, convinced they are being stalked by some
killer dyke out of the movie *Basic Instinct*—even as a dramatic outburst of what
could reasonably be called man-hating, channeled through the issue of sexual
harassment, is taken quite seriously and acclaimed, not only by feminists but by
male commentators and editorial writers, as a long overdue national teach-in,
mass consciousness-raising session, and so on.

In fact, this schizophrenia had been a long time in the making. At a feminist
meeting I attended in the mid-'70s, a member of the group wondered, "Why all
of a sudden is the movement so preoccupied with violence? Why have feminists
stopped talking about mundane kinds of sexism, like your husband constantly
interrupts you or 'forgets' when it's his turn to do the shopping?" Someone else
pointed out that in feminist discussion about sex, the emphasis had changed
from confronting men with their petty tyrannies in the bedroom—the myriad
small acts of selfishness, ignorance, and egotism that interfered with women's
sexual pleasure—to denouncing rape as the paradigm for male power. In retrospect it's clear that we were witnessing a pivotal moment in the movement's
history: as the women's revolution hit a wall of reaction, many feminists' utopian hopes gave way to despair. From then on radical feminism, whose most
distinctive contribution had been critiquing the sexist patterns embedded in
male-female relations, was increasingly influenced by its separatist fringe and
came to connote, to the public as well as to many of the activists themselves, a
rejection of heterosexuality as inherently abusive. After all, you could demand
that your husband share the housework or be a more sensitive lover, but if he hit
or raped you, what was there to do but throw him out and have him locked up?

These observations are even more apt today. One of the great successes of
the antifeminist reaction is that there is now no socially acceptable public language in which women, particularly young women, can directly and explicitly
express anger at the "mundane kinds of sexism," or what I've called the sexism
of everyday life—that is, men's ubiquitous, culturally sanctioned, "normal" expressions of dominance. To be sure, such expressions are documented in a large
body of pop-psychological/sociological literature; but, as in Deborah Tannen's
best-selling *You Just Don't Understand,* they are presented as neutral cultural
differences that hinder communication between the sexes—not as strategies,
however reflexive or unconscious, for preserving male power. To suggest that

the source of chronic, common-cold-level male-female conflict is not misunderstanding but inequality is to invite the quarantine reflex that greeted Levine's
book. Yet women have been deeply influenced by feminism; they desperately
want men to "get it"; and they are furious. Where are these feelings to go?

At first it seemed that the eruption over Thomas-Hill might reopen a long-
suppressed discussion. Men reacted, for a while at least, with a degree of self-
consciousness, defensiveness, and worry about their own behavior ("Is it okay
to tell a woman she looks nice today?") unknown since the launching of radical
feminism some twenty years earlier. And sexual harassment is easily related
to more general patterns of sexism: the assumption that men have the right to
define the sexual norms women must conform to; the corollary assumption that
men's view of what goes on between men and women is reality, while contrary
views expressed by women are oversensitive, dishonest, vindictive, or crazy;
men's frequent predatory and manipulative behavior in pursuing sex and disregard of women's signals that their attention is unwanted; men's reluctance to
accept women's presence in the public world as workers, citizens, even mere
pedestrians, rather than as objects of their sexual assessment or desire.

To some extent that larger discussion did take place—especially in black
feminists' analyses of the case as a crossroads of racial and sexual politics—
but it was mostly confined to academic circles. In the mass media the taboo on
admitting how mundane, pervasive, and *normal* sexism is remained stubbornly
in force. Rather than stimulating a broad critique of male-female relations as
such, the hearings entered popular discourse as a riveting morality tale of Hill
the long-suffering martyr versus Thomas the sexual predator, encouraging
women to encode their anger in the limited vocabulary of sexual victimization
and abuse. In effect, the Thomas-Hill affair became the vehicle for bringing into
the mainstream the shift that had already occurred within radical feminism,
from understanding sexual violence and harassment as particularly blatant ex-
crescences of a sexist culture to seeing violence as the essential fact of sexism.

From this perspective, all manifestations of sexism are forms of violence,
and feminist consciousness-raising means combating public resistance to admitting the extent of violence against women. "Violence" is thereby robbed of
all concreteness and becomes a metaphor for a larger, and largely inexpressible, set of feminist concerns. The complexities of male-female relations—those
tensions of enmity and love that Judith Levine was trying to explore—are flat-
tened to caricatures of villains and victims; the radical demand for equality
in personal life is displaced onto a profoundly conservative appeal for law and
order. While daily grievances remain unanalyzed, uncontested, and unredressed,
women soothe their anger with the fantasy that men's refusal to "get it" can be
outlawed and punished.

So long as sexism remains the dominant culture—ingrained in the texture
of people's everyday behavior, language, imagery, thought, feeling—that fantasy is at once totalitarian and absurd. Yet it has had a serious political result:

campaigns to stretch the meaning of rape and sexual harassment to cover a wide range of male sexual behavior that a woman may find unwelcome or offensive. Antirape activists want to blur the legal line between physically forcing a woman to have sex, or threatening her with force, and subjecting her to verbal and psychological pressure. The term "sexual harassment" is increasingly used to refer not only to specific uses of sex that interfere with women's ability to work or inhabit public space, but to male-dominated or male-oriented sexual culture per se—which in turn is increasingly conflated with sex itself.

The agenda of sexual harassment politics, post Thomas-Hill, can basically be traced to one key figure: Catharine MacKinnon, the chief feminist architect of sexual harassment law, who is also a leading exponent of the idea that pornography is violence against women. Since the villain-victim model of sexual politics cannot, by definition, grant women any dimension of autonomy or pleasure in their sexual relations with men, it inevitably reduces those relations to rape: the antipornography movement takes this equation a convolution further, defining as violence not only heterosexual acts but sexual desire, fantasy, and representation. In a fateful convergence of MacKinnon's central concerns, the case that was to become, in the public mind, synonymous with sexual harassment happened to hinge on a woman's allegations of verbal smuttiness against a man who was reportedly fond of pornographic magazines, films, and videos. (Though Thomas's supposed taste for pornography was arguably germane to his credibility, since it contradicted his claim to share Hill's distaste for sexually explicit language, it proved nothing about how he had behaved toward her—a distinction rarely made by his detractors.)

As a result, the issue of sexual harassment has come to be viewed chiefly through the lens of the antiporn movement, with its assumption that any form of sexual expression in the workplace subjects women to the "intimidating, hostile, or offensive" environment proscribed by federal law. In universities, charges of sexual harassment have become a rubric for promoting censorship and undermining academic freedom: a male professor is accused of using a sexual comparison to make a point in class; a teaching assistant, supported by her professor, warns a student she considers him a harasser for handing in a paper containing an "inappropriate" sexual analogy; the State Board of Regents orders professors at the University of Iowa to warn students before exposing them to sexually explicit material. There is also a growing trend toward defining as sexual harassment consensual sex between men and their female students or subordinates and invoking that definition to justify banning or punishing such relationships. Indeed, current sexual harassment law admits a defendant's consensual affairs with subordinates as evidence of a pattern of behavior supporting the charge of harassment—which is how Bill Clinton came to be deposed about Monica Lewinsky in the first place. While it's not unreasonable to suggest that a boss's or professor's affair with someone whose work he (or she) is directly supervising can pose problems—conflict of interest, potential favoritism, and so on—it's another matter to infantilize women by claiming that they are incapable of choosing whether or not to sleep with more powerful men.

That Anita Hill's trauma has been put to such dubious uses raises a question most feminists would prefer to consider settled: assuming that Hill told the truth—and I too am inclined to believe she did—was Thomas's behavior sexual harassment? That is (and here I'll try to formulate my own definition of the slippery beast), was it a systematic effort to interfere with Hill's work by treating her as an erotic object or extension of his sexual fantasy world rather than as a colleague? Was it a way of punishing Hill for taking her job seriously, of putting her in her place by constantly reminding her in the crudest possible way that they were not only boss and subordinate but man and (mere) woman? Or was Thomas simply an obnoxious, angry guy who no doubt sensed Hill's vulnerability and enjoyed baiting her, but was not engaged in a campaign to sabotage her work?

Listening to Hill's rendition of Thomas's words and actions—abstracted from their original context, his tone of voice, his body language—I couldn't tell. Nor did it help to read the endless reporting and commentary on Thomas (including Jane Mayer and Jill Abramson's *Strange Justice,* which made the most convincing case for believing Hill's testimony). Had Hill been a plaintiff in a lawsuit, able to subject Thomas to cross-examination and call all relevant witnesses, would we have gotten a clearer picture? To some extent, perhaps; but in the end this kind of behavior is inherently ambiguous and subject to interpretation.

Am I then comfortable with the idea of a man with this level of sexual hostility, even if it's not legally actionable, sitting on the Supreme Court? Well, no, I'm not. But before Hill came into the picture, I was already opposed to Thomas's appointment on the grounds of his right-wing politics, which—despite his strategic refusal to answer questions about abortion—were not ambiguous in the least; and the same is undoubtedly true of every feminist who demanded that Hill be heard. How would I feel if a prospective justice with an expansive view of women's civil rights were similarly accused? Immediately the distinction I'd found so hard to make in Thomas's case would become crucially important. For if the man was a true sexual harasser—in the habit of using sex as a weapon to subvert women's right to equal treatment in the workplace—he was unfit to be a judge. But if he was just a sexist jerk, who managed like so many men to disconnect his noble public principles about women's equality from his piggish personal relations—or if it wasn't clear, as it probably wouldn't be, which category he fell into—I would be inclined to decide that it was in women's best interest to give the noble public principles the nod.

Similarly, I'm convinced that feminism would have been better served if the opposition to Thomas had remained focused on his legal and political philosophy. By becoming the dramatic center of the confirmation hearings, the Thomas-Hill confrontation legitimized and promoted the idea that feminists should judge public figures chiefly on their personal behavior toward women, even as the MacKinnonites' co-optation of the drama would promote a dangerously loose conception of sexual harassment and abuse. Furthermore, when Hill became the issue that would decide Thomas's fate, a battle over political ideas was supplanted by a clash between different versions of reality—compounded by uncertainty about what Hill's version might mean—that could never be definitively resolved. It is this history that has enabled the right to claim a feminist moral imprimatur for Starr's exercise. Worse, it has played a crucial part in creating the repressive climate that made such a travesty possible.

Postscript: this book was already in type when Juanita Broaddrick's allegation that Bill Clinton raped her in 1978 surfaced in the mainstream press. Ironically, though her story is the most serious charge of sexually abusive behavior yet leveled against Clinton, it will no doubt get the least attention. Perhaps that's as it should be, with charges that are twenty years old and probably impossible to prove. Yet the irony underscores how little the prevailing rhetoric about sexual harassment and abuse has to do with the thing itself. For a year the Republicans cried wolf, attacking Clinton on the basis of feminists' worst confusions between consensual and coercive sex. As a result, the public is in no mood to listen to further accusations, and anti-impeachment Republican Senator Jim Jeffords feels free to dismiss an alleged rape as a private matter. Progress, anyone?

Don't Think, Smile! Notes on a Decade of Denial, 2000

'Tis Pity He's a Whore

As Bill Clinton looked me straight in the eye, tightened his jaw, and denied having sexual relations with "that woman," I had a fantasy: suppose, on that historic *60 Minutes* episode in 1992, he had said, "Yes, I had an affair with Gennifer Flowers." And suppose Hillary had added, "Not every marriage is monogamous. Relationships are complicated, and ours is no exception."

Why is such candor unthinkable? After all, most of the voters who elected Clinton didn't believe his denial that he'd slept with Flowers, any more than they would believe his denial about Monica Lewinsky, five and a half years and a second victorious campaign later. There's a good chance that Americans would have supported the Clintons' right to set the terms of their marriage—even identified with it, considering the complications of their own lives. Yet declining to tell the lies that pay homage to virtue would indeed have been a daring political gamble and a shocking, radical act. It would instantly have shifted the debate from whether personal lapses from conservative sexual and familial values should disqualify a candidate for public office to a more basic issue: should public officials be required to conform to those values in the first place? Bill Clinton, who is neither a radical nor much of a political gambler, was not about to stake his candidacy on the outcome of such a debate. But by lying, he acceded to his opponents' moral framework. Had he challenged it and won anyway, he would have done himself and the entire country a favor by showing that politicians, even presidents, need no longer submit to the sexual blackmail of the right. Instead, he supplied the rope that has strangled his presidency.

My enthusiasm for radical candor won't sit well with those who argue that the worst feature of the presidential scandal was its contribution to a horrifying breakdown of the distinction between public and private life. Jean Cohen and

Andrew Arato—responding in *Dissent* to the article where I first made the foregoing suggestion—contend that the proper public response to intrusive sexual
questions is simply that they are "out of line and nobody's business." Of course,
Clinton shouldn't have to discuss his sex life with the media. Nor should he have
been questioned about a consensual affair in a sexual harassment lawsuit, any
more than a woman who complains of sexual harassment should have to testify
about her sexual relationships with other men in the office. Nor should Kenneth
Starr have been allowed to investigate Clinton's relationship with Lewinsky on
the pretext that his attempt to cover up an affair he shouldn't have been asked
about in the first place was relevant to the Whitewater inquiry. Nor should
Starr have forced Lewinsky to testify by threatening to prosecute her and her
mother on the basis of illegal tapes, or asked her questions about the minute
details of her encounters with the president, ostensibly to nail down Clinton's
perjury but actually to strip him naked before the world. Nor should the House
have voted to release this material to the public, with utter disregard for what
is supposed to be the confidentiality of grand jury proceedings (granted that
Starr's leaks to the press had long since made it a joke). Clearly what we have
witnessed is the frightening spectacle of right-wing zealots abusing the power
of the state to invade Clinton's—and Lewinsky's—privacy.

But public discussion of what to make of this invasion has displayed a persistent confusion—shared by queasy liberal commentators and ambivalent "ordinary Americans" alike—between sexual privacy and sexual secrecy. The
two are in fact very different in their meaning and purpose. Genuine sexual
privacy rests on the belief that consensual sexual behavior is a matter of individual liberty that need not and ought not be policed. Privacy will be consistently
respected only in a sexually libertarian culture, for repression inevitably gives
rise to a prurient preoccupation with other people's sex lives. And when privacy is respected, secrecy is unnecessary: as the actor and libertarian Orson
Bean once observed, if people were brought up in a culture where eating was
considered a shameful act, they might rebel against that social taboo, yet they
could never truly imagine the unselfconsciousness of Americans dining in a
restaurant.

Secrecy, on the other hand, is based on the need to hide one's behavior from
public scrutiny and judgment. What's at stake is not only moral respectability
but dignity, in a culture where sexual needs and appetites are still on some level
regarded as infantile, ridiculous, and an offense to our higher spiritual natures.
The widespread acceptance of secrecy ("everybody lies about sex") reflects the
recognition that people must protect themselves from others' prurience; but it's
also a way to avoid openly confronting the gap between our official standards
of morality and dignity and our actual behavior. While the defense of privacy
involves a critique of conservative sexual norms, the defense of secrecy serves
to enforce them by denying their ubiquitous violation. Refusing secrecy, and
the shame it implies, can paradoxically further the cause of privacy. A person's

sexual orientation, for instance, is surely nobody's business. Yet by choosing to come out of the closet, often in the most public of ways, gay and lesbian activists launched us on the path toward a society in which homosexuals may enjoy their private lives without constant fear of exposure and punishment.

When the Lewinsky story broke, media commentators indulged in such an outpouring of nostalgia for the good old days of "Don't ask, don't tell"—before those feminists decided that the personal is political and oral sex made it onto *Nightline*—that you would have thought judging politicians' private lives was something new. On the contrary, candidates, especially for the presidency, have always been vetted by the family-values cops for marital respectability. Until Ronald Reagan broke the taboo, no divorced man had ever become president. (I always admired Nelson Rockefeller for divorcing his wife to marry the woman he loved, though it probably meant the end of his presidential prospects.) Open homosexuality is still beyond the pale, as is heterosexual cohabiting out of wedlock. Presidential wives are supposed to be supportive mates, preferably mothers, domestic minded, and never openly sexual.

What *is* new is the end of the trade-off that allowed politicians, in return for outward conformity, to lead a secret sexual life on the side. This conspiracy of silence, joined by the press, served to maintain strict public norms and the illusion that authority figures exemplified the morality they preached, while cutting powerful men some slack. (Needless to say, the deal has never been available to female candidates or political wives.) It also mystified sex, keeping the gritty details of respectable men's disreputable desires and practices from compromising the enforced "innocence" (that is, ignorance) of respectable women and children. The undoing of this corrupt bargain is part of our society's continuing revolt against Victorian morality, sexual hypocrisy, and a sexist double standard. From this perspective, open discussion of the realities of people's sex lives—including the sex lives of public figures—is much to be preferred. If revelations of politicians' sexual proclivities cripple their ability to indulge in pious blather about the evils of "illegitimacy," I can only cheer.

Yet this assault on repression, however desirable in the long historical view, has given rise to an immediate and serious problem: while sexual secrecy has broken down, sexual privacy has yet to be achieved. In these circumstances, the readiness of the media to pass along sexual revelations becomes a weapon of outraged moralists bent on restoring the old sexual order. And ironically, the loudest defenders of secrecy are likely, once it has collapsed, to end up joining the hunt. For if the norms can no longer be upheld by concealment, then they must be upheld by punishment, and if necessary by purge. It is this imperative that explains the curious reversal of the nation's journalistic and political establishment, from its initial horror that the president's sex life should be exposed in the national media and investigated by the independent counsel to the outpouring of high moral indignation that followed Clinton's grudging confession of an "inappropriate relationship." The underlying theme remained the same:

the moral authority of the president and the presidency must be preserved—an authority presumed to require an acceptable facade of sexual dignity and "family values."

There was a surreal quality to the revulsion and, even more peculiar, the sense of betrayal that Clinton's speech unleashed among Democratic politicians, administration officials, and the standard-bearers of what I think of as "high journalism"—that is, the (mostly moderate conservative to neoliberal) commentators for the major dailies and TV networks, including the editorialists of the *New York Times*. In the weeks leading up to the president's grand jury testimony, the prevailing line in these circles was that Clinton should publicly admit and apologize for the Lewinsky affair; that the admission could not hurt him since hardly anyone believed him anyway; that the country simply wanted to hear the truth, after which it could achieve "closure" and "move on." But as it turned out, for this same crowd there was all the difference in the world between believing the president had lied and hearing him confirm the fact. The aides and politicians who had loyally echoed Clinton's denials now felt compelled, whatever the insult to everyone's intelligence, to declare their shock. Centrist Democrats in Congress—led by Senator Joseph Lieberman, whose last claim to fame had been a moral crusade against TV talk shows—saw yet another chance to "take the values issue away from the right." And the high journalists, who resented the saturation coverage of the sex scandal as the latest affront to their role as guardians of serious public discourse (in their worldview, sex is much too interesting to be legitimate news), turned that resentment from Starr and the tabloids toward the man whose behavior, by his own admission, had made the media orgy possible.

In short, the moment the secret was really out, the logic of preserving moral authority demanded that Clinton somehow manage to say something so powerfully redemptive that he would in effect be born again, shedding his tainted public persona for a new one worthy of the presidential mantle. The specific complaints against the president's speech—that he wasn't abject enough, that he attacked Starr, that he continued to weasel out of admitting perjury—reflected a larger frustration with his failure to accomplish what even for a gifted politician was an impossible task. No apology, made under extreme duress by an admitted liar with a long-term reputation for philandering, could have sufficed; and Clinton's subsequent attempts to juice up his repentance were merely embarrassing. Soon a chorus of voices—among them the *Times* and both Democratic congressional leaders—began suggesting that the president could yet appease his critics by giving up his last shred of cover (not to mention his legal right to defend himself against a criminal charge) and confessing that he lied under oath. If Clinton had fallen for that one, he would have been as pathetic as Charlie Brown perennially kicking the football because Lucy swears that this time she won't pull it away at the last minute.

The logical resolution of the demand that the president magically turn into someone else was resignation or impeachment. And indeed, even as Starr and the congressional Republicans were doing everything they could to ensure that Clinton's image was defined by cigar-fucking and dress stains, while Democrats cowered in fear of being associated with "immorality," growing numbers of high journalists and elder statespeople types hinted or openly suggested that the president spare our sensibilities by stepping down. The logic might have been irresistible, if it had not hit a major snag: the public's refusal to get with the program.

Commentators who have attributed Americans' lack of lynch-mob fervor to a "Who cares, the economy's good" attitude illuminate little but their own condescension (and their membership in that minority for whom the economy actually *is* good). Conservatives like William Bennett, who mourn "the death of outrage," are closer to the mark. In fact, the electorate's feelings about Clinton mirror the contemporary standoff in the culture wars, both on the issue of sexual morality and on the larger question of how we view authority. On the one hand, most people believe, or profess to believe, that Clinton's behavior with Lewinsky was morally wrong; yet they are also strongly influenced by the idea of a right to free sexual association between consenting adults. They are unhappy with his lies, but think the questions that provoked them should not have been asked. They would have preferred to fudge the contradictions with secrecy, but are reluctant to deny the president privacy—and on both counts are leery of the right's moral police.

Even more telling, perhaps, "ordinary" Americans clearly do not share the Washington elite's investment in the idea of the president as a moral exemplar, charged with validating the existing structure of (patriarchal) authority. They see him as a man elected to do a job, a politician in a political culture where lies are a taken-for-granted part of the game and sex is a perk of power. It's hardly news that the public's respect for the governing class and the establishment press is not at an all-time high. For those once accustomed to deference, its loss is an ongoing crisis, which the Lewinsky scandal exacerbated to an intolerable degree: as they see it, "cynicism" threatens to undermine democracy, unless the elite gets its house in order. Yet in fact Americans' refusal to put their "leaders" on a pedestal is not only eminently democratic, but altogether realistic, in an age when the nation-state is steadily weakening and the president, as Stanley Aronowitz has put it, is basically a trade representative.

Nor is this refusal merely cynical; it also involves an element of identification. The Republican strategy of bombarding the public with sexual details fizzled, not only because people saw it as gratuitous and hypocritical, but because it shifted the focus of moral disapproval from the fact of Clinton's sexual relationship with Lewinsky to the nature of their activities. In the wake of the Starr Report, the *New York Post* pronounced its revelations "kinky"; *Post* columnist John Podhoretz bragged of his superior character on the grounds that he had never used a cigar for sexual purposes or been sexually serviced while on the phone; Congressmen lamented the disgrace of it all; and even the president's lawyers, complaining about the report, called its sexual descriptions "lurid." All this huffing and puffing was bound to make people nervous, inspiring discomfiting thoughts about how lurid or kinky their own sexual impulses and quirks might look in front of an audience. Nobody, after all, is a moral authority while having sex, even with one's spouse in the missionary position under the covers. In any case, the Bill Clinton of the Starr Report does not come across as an arrogant exploiter, a Sadeian libertine, the creepy exhibitionist depicted by Paula Jones. Rather, he seems needy, affectionate, attracted yet painfully cautious and conflicted, and terrified of getting caught—in short, a neurotic middle-aged married guy, ordinary to the point of banality, except that he happens to be President of the United States. That most people saw no need to get rid of him on that account speaks well for their acceptance of their own sexuality.

If it's true that Dick Morris's poll results convinced Clinton he had to lie to the public about Lewinsky, this was a fateful miscalculation, seemingly at odds with his usual political instincts. But it's consistent with a long-standing contradiction in the president's modus operandi. Bill Clinton was elected in large part because of who he was: a member of the '60s generation, an embodiment of youth and eroticism. To be sure, he was on the clean-cut, respectable end of the spectrum of '60s types, a man who from the beginning had had mainstream political ambitions. Yet there were certain influences he couldn't help inhaling: his style and body language bore the imprint of shaggy hair, rock and roll, the sexual revolution, the blurring of racial and gender boundaries. While this made the right hysterical, it made for a bond with voters who shared these formative experiences, which is to say, a large portion of the "ordinary American" population. People liked him when he did things like playing the saxophone on Arsenio Hall's show, and arguably Gennifer Flowers added to his popularity more than she detracted from it.

Nonetheless, Clinton long ago bought into the idea that to win he had to live up to a presidential image that had little to do with who he really was. I suspect that consciously or not, this concern with appearances has had less to do with maintaining public support than with courting the same centrist elite that now resents his failure to slink quietly away. Clinton is a product of lower-middle-class Arkansas who despite his Yale and Oxford education will never be part of that elite. Instead, in the classic manner of climbers, he internalized both its corporate neoliberal agenda and its demand for moral rectitude. Yet predictably, his efforts to wrap himself in the family-values flag—from denouncing "illegitimacy" and signing the welfare bill to backtracking on gays in the military to the ridiculous firing of Surgeon General Joycelyn Elders for suggesting that masturbation is a legitimate topic of discussion in sex education classes—never for a moment appeased either the right's crazed hostility or the establishment's more subtle disdain.

The essential quality of that disdain was perhaps best articulated by then-*Newsweek* columnist Joe Klein in a 1994 piece on the Paula Jones case. Jones's accusations, he asserts, should be of no interest to the media. They are unprovable, backed by "despicable" enemies of Clinton with dirty motives, and in any case "it can be persuasively argued" that politicians' private lives (John F. Kennedy's, for instance) are irrelevant to their public performance. But, Klein continues, the issue won't go away, because there have been so many "previous allegations of misbehavior" against the president and because "it seems increasingly, and sadly, apparent that the character flaw Bill Clinton's enemies have fixed upon—promiscuity—is a defining characteristic of his *public* life as well." That is, the dictionary definition of "promiscuous," revolving around such concepts as "indiscriminate," "casual," and "irregular," fits the style and substance of Clinton's governing in both good ways (he is empathetic, skilled at bringing people together and finding common ground, able to disarm opponents and forge compromises) and bad (he lacks principle, wants to please everyone, has trouble saying no, fudges the truth, believes he can "seduce, and abandon, at will and without consequences").

In my reading, the not-so-deep structure of this argument unfolds more or less as follows: since JFK displayed a suitable, manly decisiveness in public ("acting in a sober, measured—and inspired—manner during the Cuban missile crisis"), we can assume that he was able to contain his sexual weakness, to confine it to the bedroom, where it belonged. His expenditure of bodily fluids did not corrupt, and so the press was right to keep it quiet. With Clinton, in contrast, the media may be forgiven for breaching the proper boundary between public and private, because his own libidinal boundaries appear to be alarmingly porous. He is charming and seductive, wont to "wheedle" and "cajole." "He conveys an impression of complete accessibility, and yet nothing is ever revealed. 'I've had blind dates with women I've known more about than I know about Clinton,' James Carville once complained." In short, Bill is not only too feminine; his femininity is of the unreliable, manipulative, whorish sort. He has let sex invade the core of his being, as we all know women do (this is why it's so much worse for a woman to be "promiscuous"); and it's this erotic spillover, this gender betrayal, that explains (or symbolizes) his moral squishiness in the public realm.

I can't argue with the charge that Clinton is unprincipled; it's exactly this trait that makes him so useful as a trade representative. You would think the corporate elite and their allies in government and media would be more grateful for services rendered. But then, just because you use a whore, it doesn't mean you want to marry her. Clinton put his faith in a protective culture of secrecy that was designed for the JFKs, not for the likes of him—a culture that in any case was dying (though it had protected George Bush and might still have closed ranks around a president deemed to be One of Us). Ironically, despite his "femininity," Clinton also apparently subscribes to a deeply ingrained axiom of masculine conventional wisdom—that the proper response to being caught at infidelity is to deny everything. So he did what reporters would once, in effect, have done for him: he lied. And the combination of a take-no-prisoners right and a spill-the-beans press—not to mention the miracle of DNA testing—did him in.

The Republicans insisted that the issue was not sex, but lies. Right, and what Clinton did was not sex, but whatever. Yet in a way it's true that falsehood was at the center of this crisis—not Bill's third-rate perjury, but the larger lie that he has tried desperately to preserve with his I-am-a-humble-sinner act. The president has behaved like a victim of hostage syndrome, embracing the moral dogma of his persecutors. As a result, although he managed to hang on to his job, he has nonetheless been defeated. For the rest of us, the war goes on.

Don't Think, Smile! Notes on a Decade of Denial, 2000

Is Motherhood Moonlighting?

News correspondent Meredith Vieira lost her job on *60 Minutes* recently after taking her doctor's advice not to work full time during her pregnancy. A few days later, the *New York Times* reported the story of a woman denied unemployment benefits on the grounds that she had been fired for misconduct—taking too many days off to care for her sick baby. Her case is now before the Minnesota courts.

Sexism? Or a valid single standard? Here and there you can still find feminists—along with traditionalists hoping to expose contradictions in feminism—who'll argue that equality in the workplace requires equal commitment to the job, that it's inconsistent to demand consideration for pregnancy or parenthood.

Yet increasingly the public recognizes that telling women "if you can't take the heat, get back in the kitchen" is a way of dismissing a problem rather than solving it. Forcing women to choose between working and childbearing is no more equality than forcing them to stay home. As for the sick-child dilemma, this is a feminist issue only because women are still the primary child rearers. If men did their share at home, it would be obvious that accommodating people who have jobs and children is not giving in to special pleading, but responding to practical necessity.

At this point, the real question is not whether such accommodations should be made, but how. So far, most proposals for reform, such as parental leave, flexible hours, more opportunities for part-time work, and the "mommy track" (or its more palatable, gender-neutral variant), have aimed to make employers' policies less rigid. I have a simpler and more radical idea: abolish the full-time job.

The assumption that work should be organized so that a real job takes at least seven hours a day, five days a week, is a relic. It fit a system in which, for most whites at least, a class of people called housewives devoted their lives to taking care of (male) workers' domestic needs. The system is gone but the assumption lingers on, along with its corollary—that "part-time" work is supplementary, marginal, and fundamentally frivolous. Defending his decision to fire Vieira, executive producer Don Hewitt explained that he had five *60 Minutes* correspondents, each doing 22 stories a year. "I can't afford any part-time people, man or woman," he said. Is it impossible to imagine *60 Minutes* operating with, say, 10 correspondents, each doing 11 stories a year? Is it fanciful to speculate that if the work were divided in this fashion, *60 Minutes* might have had more than two female correspondents in the past 23 years?

The current full-time work week is not a law of nature, but a fairly recent product of bitter labor struggles. Not so long ago, 16-hour days and seven-day weeks were considered normal. Today, automation and the flight of American industry overseas have been rapidly eroding the number of full-time jobs. Yet because full-time work remains the norm, part-timers are typically second-class workers with lower wages, benefits, and status.

At a time when more and more employees—mostly mothers but some fathers as well—have another major job at home, it makes sense not only to shrink the work week but to scrap the presumptuous notion that employers are entitled to our "full time" while other concerns should be confined to our "spare time." On the contrary, domestic work should be counted as real work, as time-consuming as a paid job and occasionally—as with sick babies or risky pregnancies—more so. The number of workers hired, and the way each job is defined, should anticipate these ordinary human contingencies. Individual schedules should reflect individual needs. And workers should not get "part-time" salaries but a living wage (no doubt Meredith Vieira, at $500,000 a year, could live with a substantial pay cut; not so most of the rest of us).

Absurdly expensive? Think of it this way: our present standard of reasonable labor costs depends on women doing housework and child care gratis. Equality means ending this free ride. Subsidizing domestic work indirectly, through wages, is the least complicated way to do it. Inefficient? Certainly, by conventional standards, which emphasize maximum productivity and strict management control. Reducing work time shifts power from employers to workers and subordinates efficiency to quality of life. As I said, a radical idea—a challenge to our most basic cultural values. But then, so is feminism.

With the largest participation ever of women soldiers in a war zone, the Gulf mobilization raised these issues in their starkest form. After all, the military is the ultimate inflexible, hierarchical employer; fighting a war is the ultimate full-time job. To contemplate changing this is to threaten the very underpinnings of war as we know it. Ironically, feminism may end up subverting militarism, not because women are natural pacifists—as the stereotype has it—but precisely because we aren't.

Newsday, March 1991

Say It Loud
Out of Wedlock and Proud

I'm an unmarried mother, one of those miscreants recently denounced in these pages by former education secretary William Bennett and Peter Wehner of Empower America. I am not and have never been on welfare; rather, I'm the sort of affluent Murphy Brown type Dan Quayle thinks sets a bad example for the lower classes. Nor am I functionally a single parent: I live with my daughter's father, my companion of 14 years. I've always hoped we would join or start a communal household, but it hasn't happened. As far as I can tell, our domestic routine is indistinguishable from that of married couples in our socioeconomic milieu—at least those couples who are making a self-conscious effort to share child-rearing. Our finances are equally intertwined, our problems no doubt equally banal.

Still, we've resisted marrying, partly in symbolic protest against the relentless drumbeat for "family values," partly because we feel no need to get the state involved in our relationship, and no irresistible economic or social pressure to do so.

Since "illegitimacy" does affect both baby's and father's rights, we went to court to have legal paternity declared. Ironically, in New York State there's no simple way to do this—you can't just sign a paper. One parent has to sue the other. Since it's usually the mother who sues the father, we did it the other way around. The judge asked me if this man was indeed the baby's father, and if I waived my right to a lawyer and blood test results. He then pronounced Nona and Stanley daughter and dad. "May we kiss now?" I asked.

To be sure, the image Bennett and Wehner mean to invoke when they call unwed childbearing the "road to economic poverty and social decay" is not white, middle class or coupled. Yet the current barrage of propaganda against unmarried mothers on welfare is also an attack on me, as surely as the Hyde

Amendment cutting off Medicaid funds for poor women's abortions is an attack on all women's reproductive freedom. The bottom line of this campaign is not saving the taxpayers money or keeping children from growing up in poverty, but restoring women's dependence on marriage and submission to a sexual double standard. "Having children out of wedlock," Bennett and Wehner sermonize, "is *wrong*—not simply economically unwise for the individuals involved or a financial burden on society, but morally wrong."

We haven't heard this kind of talk lately, not since Quayle's TV criticism and the Republican convention's crudely right-wing family-values pitch were widely seen as contributing to George Bush's defeat. In the Clinton era, cultural conservatives have shifted their ground to seemingly pragmatic arguments about why we need to stamp out unmarried childbearing: single-parent households are disproportionately poor; boys brought up by single mothers turn to crime for lack of a male authority figure. Such arguments get a better reception from the public. They exploit middle-class distaste for welfare. They come packaged in the "reasonable" language of social science and economic policy. And they are promoted not only by arch-conservatives like Charles Murray, but by "New Democrat" think tanks and centrist politicians like Sen. Daniel Patrick Moynihan.

Apparently, the success of this strategy has encouraged Bennett and Wehner to raise the rhetorical ante once again. Their bluntness is a public service, reminding us that what the right is pushing as welfare reform is moral fiat rooted in religious dogma. It is the churches that have made a moral issue of confining sex and procreation to marriage.

Historically, marriage has not been a moral but an economic arrangement in which men support women and children in return for women's domestic and sexual services. When women have means of support other than a husband, and aren't stigmatized for unwed motherhood, they can be a lot choosier about whom they marry, or if they marry or stay married, and under what conditions. This independence makes the moralists crazy. They can't do much about women like me—*yet*—so poor women, who can be punished through welfare policy, are taking the brunt of their anger. (Of course, given the poverty and social marginality of the men in their lives, many women on welfare have little prospect of marrying even if they want to; for them the right's "morality" amounts to the demand that they not have sex or children at all.)

The scariest aspect of this latest offensive is that the Clinton administration has embraced the right's agenda. Bennett and Wehner gleefully quote Donna Shalala, of all people, opining that "having children out of wedlock is just wrong." Can the Secretary for Health and Human Services possibly believe this, or is she mouthing what she thinks the zeitgeist requires? Either way it's a depressing portent. Some of us imagined that Clinton would, if nothing else, get the religious right off our backs. We'd better think again.

Bring in the Noise

Whenever the right and the left agree on some proposition about culture, I know it's time to grab my raincoat; and so it is with the incessant demonizing of popular culture and media. Everywhere they look—tabloid television, MTV, *Married . . . with Children, Pulp Fiction,* gangsta rap, saturation coverage of O. J. Simpson/the Bobbitts/Amy Fisher—politicians and high-minded journalists see nothing but sleaze and moral degradation.

The latest target is daytime TV talk shows. Rumblings began last year when Jonathan Schmitz murdered Scott Amedure, a gay man, after Amedure identified Schmitz as his "secret crush" on *Jenny Jones.* Since then, William Bennett and Democratic Senator Joe Lieberman of Connecticut have called on talk-show advertisers to withdraw their support, N.E.A. nemesis Donald Wildmon's American Family Association has joined the cause with a full-page ad in *the New York Times* and Phil Donahue's retirement has touched off a round of head-shaking at the contrast between the now-respectable pioneer of the talk show and his degenerate successors. Commentators reveal the stop-the-presses news that the talk-show audience prefers sex and violence to analyses of health care and foreign policy. Beyond this indisputable fact the legions of outraged moralists have little enlightenment to offer, since they rarely bother to pay much attention to the reviled genre, let alone try to understand what's going on in the imagination of people who do.

The popularity of popular culture is a problem for its detractors: it would be a breach of American democratic etiquette, not to mention an implicit rebuke to free-market platitudes about supply and demand, for journalists or (especially) politicians simply to claim that their own cultural tastes are superior to those of the barbarian hordes (though they come close to doing this when the subject is black music). The solution is to rely heavily on the assumption that the media are a species of addictive drug, pushed on a vulnerable populace by corporations out to make a buck and/or infiltrated by a perverse New York and Hollywood cultural elite. The audience is often referred to as "our children," even when the medium in question is aimed at adults. Lieberman indignantly cites a report that claims "children aged 2 to 11 comprise six percent" of talk-show viewers nationally. The other 94 percent? Don't ask!

In the case of talk shows, the critic-audience gap is even wider than usual. I doubt that Lieberman and his fellow attack dogs got the idea for their crusade by actually watching Ricki Lake or Richard Bey or Sally Jessy Raphael. But what's more interesting is the paucity of sympathetic popcult critics who are talk-show fans: Donna Gaines, with her *Village Voice* testimonial that *Jenny Jones* saved her life, is the conspicuous exception. Like McDonald's, these shows are genuinely lowbrow; unlike Quentin Tarantino or Snoop Doggy Dogg, they can't be said to appeal to the so-called cultural elite. They resist hip readings—it's hard to watch a talk show ironically, even when you're sure it's as fake as a wrestling match. Anyway, the shows come on at the wrong time for the critical classes, right in the middle of the sacred working day.

I first saw the Ricki Lake show because my daughter had mentioned it, and I thought I should check it out. We watched a show together; the subject, as I recall, was women whose boyfriends had impregnated other women. There were moments that made me squirm, but not because I was worried that, as Lieberman would later put it, "the constant confrontations and emotional violence" would teach my 11-year-old "a perverse way to solve personal problems" or give her the impression "that is the way normal adults behave." Leaving aside the absurdity of the idea that "normal adults" don't have nasty fights, it took little in the way of probing discussion to confirm that my daughter could tell the difference between real life and stage-managed psychodrama. Anyway, from my own childhood encounters with horror comics, soap operas, graphic sex manuals and other crypto-pornography of the fifties, I know kids have more complicated filters than adults tend to give them credit for.

The danger, it seemed to me, was exactly the opposite: that my child was seeing Ricki's guests, working-class people willing to spill the beans on TV, as alien and unreal. Or maybe I was afraid that's what I was doing.

Like other forms of popular culture, talk shows reflect the peculiar contradictions of today's social and political climate. While conservatives dominate the political system and control the terms of debate on economic issues, their drive to roll back the cultural changes of the sixties and seventies has had much more ambiguous results. The most telling success of the cultural right (and in that category I include social conservatives who are political liberals or leftists) has been the discrediting of the idea of a pro-freedom, pro-pleasure revolution in everyday life in favor of nostalgia for an idealized past: these days it's even harder to get a serious public hearing for a radical critique of the family than for a radical critique of capitalism. This repression of the utopian impulse has combined with economic insecurity to brew a protean anger that leaks out in various forms of sadism—physical, verbal, moral and vicarious. On the other hand, social conservatives have been notably unsuccessful at stemming the democratization of culture, the breakdown of those class, sex and race-bound conventions that once reliably separated high from low, "news" from "gossip," public from unspeakably private, respectable from deviant.

Talk shows are a product of this democratization; they let people who have been largely excluded from the public conversation appear on national TV and talk about their sex lives, their family fights, sometimes their literal dirty laundry. What's more taboo than the subject matter itself is the way it's presented—as personal revelation rather than social comment, and as spectacle mostly devoid of pretensions to redeeming social value: "In these shows," William Bennett complains, "indecent exposure is celebrated as a virtue. . . . There was once a time when personal or marital failure . . . and perverse taste were accompanied by guilt or embarrassment." Talk shows are meant to entertain, to excite the nerve ends. This in itself is anathema to social conservatives, for whom the only legitimate function of popular culture is instructing the masses in the moral values of their betters.

It's not that morality is absent from talk shows. True, some guests flaunt "deviant" behavior without being condemned for it; but others indignantly defend conventional moral standards against wayward lovers or children. Talk-show hosts often lecture guests, especially teenagers—Sally Jessy has perfected a stern school-principal style, Ricki a more maternal-therapeutic approach—while members of the audience or other guests (the parents, wronged girlfriends and so on) may subject the (usually defiant) miscreant to verbal stoning. The catch is that their very complicity in a public free-for-all undermines their moral authority. And though therapists may be called on to give "expert" commentary or do a bit of ad hoc family counseling, they are about as relevant to the action as those trailers that used to introduce porn movies with homilies on the need for sex education. At the dramatic center of talk shows are mostly black, Latino and low-rent white guests who, by their very willingness to expose intimate, "shameful" matters and yell and scream at each other on the air, assert their lack of deference to middle-class norms.

I mean "dramatic" literally; talk shows are theater. Like most kinds of popular entertainment, especially on television, they rely on formula. There's the trial scenario—an accusation ("My ex-husband's wife abuses my kid"), a rebuttal ("I hit her because she's disrespectful, but I don't abuse her") and a parade of witnesses: the alleged victim ("I don't have to obey you, you're not my mother and you threw me downstairs!"), the nervous father who hasn't seen anything and is totally out of it, the "expert" who lectures that it's abusive to hit a kid, even your own. The judge/host presides, asking questions and being fair to all sides. The jury/audience gets into the act, berating the stepmother for overstepping her bounds, the kid for being disrespectful, the father for being out of it. What's missing is a unanimous verdict or any semblance of courtroom decorum.

Then there's the increasingly popular "surprise" show, where a guest is tricked into appearing. This ploy makes explicit the basic appeal of talk-show formulas: however often repeated, they're never totally predictable, but offer the exciting possibility that a situation will get out of control. An argument can lead to an outburst of violence; the woman who is proposed to can say no. The talk show is a dangerous ritual like boxing or bullfighting, an improvisatory performance that seems to blur the boundary between actors and audience, yet leaves the larger audience safe behind the barrier of the screen. And since talk shows traffic in subjects that have universal resonance—from infidelity, incest and juvenile rebellion to clothes ("My mom dresses like a tramp!")—I suspect that few people are entirely impervious to their crude power.

As a distant graduate of youth culture and mother of a soon-to-be-teenager, I'm riveted by shows that feature generational collisions. On a recent *Sally Jessy Raphael* episode, "I'm Ready to Divorce My Children," kids of 12 (has sex and steals) and 13 (throws ashtrays), hiding behind their bad-seed fright masks to ward off who knew what terrors, sullenly confronted their desperate, baffled mother. There was Dantesque torment in that encounter; it stayed with me for days. I'm sure a lot of guests invent or exaggerate their torments, with or without the connivance of producers. But in this case, I could swear the emotions were real. If not, the acting was surely marvelous.

I don't mean to romanticize talk shows. If they reflect a democratizing impulse, they're also a symptom of today's anti-utopian and anti-political mood. While great popular art tends to bring disparate groups together—the way the Beatles reached teenyboppers and intellectuals, or Duke Ellington whites and blacks—talk shows are more likely to reinforce class and racial fragmentation. Though viewers from the same social milieus as the guests may identify with them and their problems, my hunch is that for many middle-class talk-show fans, the kick is feeling superior (or as my daughter put it when I posed the question, "lucky").

As for the guests themselves, in the absence of any other way to have an impact on history—which is to say, the absence of effective social movements— the opportunity to sound off on national television offers visibility, and therefore validation, to teenagers and people of color and working-class whites; in effect it's the culture's acknowledgment that they exist. But existence proved this way is existence on someone else's terms. Often guests are so vivid, or funny, or sure of their right to be who they are that they outflank the manipulative condescension of their producers and hosts. But often they don't, especially when the audience gangs up on them, or when they're set up to be surprised. The Schmitz murder is a disturbing commentary on talk-show tactics, not because "Jenny made him do it"—homophobia made him do it—but because the whole rationale of talk shows is bound up with risking such events. If a show becomes a flashpoint for the culture's free-floating sadism, or a conduit for politics by other means, is it truly an accident?

Finally, though, our problem is not the excesses of talk shows but the brutality and emptiness of our political culture. Pop bashing is the humanism of fools: in the name of defending people's dignity it attacks their pleasures and their meager store of power. On talk shows, whatever their drawbacks, the proles get to talk. The rest of the time they're told in a thousand ways to shut up. By any honest reckoning, we need more noise, not less.

The Nation, April 1996

Intellectual Work in the Culture of Austerity

On the crudest level, the lives of American intellectuals and artists are defined by one basic problem: how to reconcile intellectual or creative autonomy with making a living. They must either get someone to support their work—whether by selling it on the open market or by getting the backing of some public or private institution—or find something to do that somebody is willing to pay for that will still leave them time to do their "real work." How hard it is to accomplish this at any given time, and what kinds of opportunities are available, not only affect the individual person struggling for a workable life, but the state of the culture itself. This tension between intellectual work and economic survival is thoroughly mundane and generally taken for granted by those who negotiate it every day; but to look at the history of the past thirty years or so is to be struck by the degree to which the social, cultural, and political trajectory of American life is bound up with this most ordinary of conflicts. During that time, the conditions of intellectual work have radically changed, as a culture operating on the assumption of continuing—indeed increasing—abundance has given way to a culture of austerity.

In the 1960s, prosperity and cultural radicalism were symbiotic: easy access to money and other resources fueled social and cultural experimentation, while an ethos that valued freedom and pleasure encouraged people's sense of entitlement to all sorts of goods, economic and political. For many of us, the "excess" of the '60s meant the expansion of desire and fantasy, but also (and not coincidentally) of money and time. I (a child of the hard-working lower middle class) found it relatively easy to subsist as a freelance writer in New York. With a fifty-dollar-a-month rent-regulated East Village apartment, I could write one lucrative article for a mainstream magazine and support myself for weeks or even months while I did what I liked, whether that meant writing for counter-cultural publications that couldn't pay or going to political meetings. When I did have jobs, I didn't worry overmuch about losing them, and so felt no impulse, let alone need, to kiss anyone's ass. There was always another job, or another assignment. At one point, while I was living with a group of people in Colorado, the money I made writing (sporadically) about rock for the *New Yorker* was supporting my entire household.

Throughout this period, cheap housing was the cement of cultural communities. It allowed writers and artists to live near each other, hang out together. It invited the proliferation of the underground press and alternative institutions like New York's Free University, with its huge loft off Union Square, where just about all the leftists and bohemians in town congregated at one time or another. Prosperity also financed travel, and with it the movement of ideas; encouraged young people to avoid "settling down" to either careers or marriage; and even made psychotherapy, with its ethos of autonomy and fulfillment, a middle-class rite of passage subsidized by medical insurance. This climate of freedom in turn fomented dissident politics—which, contrary to much recent and dubious rewriting of history, included class politics. Although the distinctive quality of the '60s social movements, from ecology to feminism, was their focus on the kinds of concerns that surface once survival is no longer in question, economic issues were by no means ignored. Criticism of capitalism and economic inequality was part of mainstream public debate. There was significant liberal pressure to extend the welfare state, while at the same time the new left was challenging "corporate liberalism" and its social programs as fundamentally conservative, a way of managing inequality rather than redressing it.

Since the early '70s, however, the symbiosis has been working in reverse: a steady decline in Americans' standard of living has fed political and cultural conservatism, and vice versa. Just as the widespread affluence of the post–World War II era was the product of deliberate social policy—an alliance of business, labor, and government aimed at stabilizing the economy and building a solid, patriotic middle class as a bulwark against Soviet Communism and domestic radicalism—the waning of affluence has reflected the resolve of capital to break away from this constraining alliance. In 1973, as the United States was losing both the Vietnam War and our position of unquestioned economic dominance in the world, the formation of OPEC and the resulting "energy crisis" signaled the coming of a new economic order in which getting Americans to accept less would be a priority of the emerging multinational corporate and financial elite. By then the reaction against the culture and politics of the '60s was already in progress. With the end of cheap, freely flowing gasoline—the quintessential emblem of American prosperity, mobility, and power—the supposed need for austerity began to rival law and order as a central conservative theme.

For the cultural right, austerity was not just an economic but a moral imperative; not mere recognition of what was presented as ineluctable necessity but a new weapon against the "self-indulgence" and "hedonism" that had flowered as masses of Americans enjoyed a secure and prosperous existence. For the economic elite, whose objective was convincing the middle class that the money simply wasn't there, whether for high wages or for social benefits, this brand of moralism served a practical function: in diverting people's attention from the corporate agenda to their own alleged lack of social discipline and unrealistic expectations, it discouraged rebellion in favor of guilty, resigned acquiescence.

The determination of corporate capital to enforce a regime of austerity provoked a pivotal event: the New York City fiscal crisis of 1975. New York was not only the chief national center of intellectual and cultural activity but the proud standard bearer of a political ethos that reflected its history as a center of working-class activism. New Yorkers maintained a militant sense of entitlement to a high level of public services and social supports—including a free college education—unequaled anywhere else in the country. When the banks pulled the plug on the city's credit, this was not simply a financial decision—indeed, more than one analysis of the situation has concluded that it was unnecessary from a purely economic point of view (see, for example, Jack Newfield and Paul Du Brul, *The Abuse of Power: The Permanent Government and the Fall of New York,* or Eric Lichten, *Class, Power, and Austerity: The New York City Fiscal Crisis*). It was a political act motivated by the will to destroy New York's pro-worker, anticorporate political culture, with its immense symbolic importance as a flagship of resistance: if austerity could be imposed on New York, it could be imposed anywhere. In essence, the specter of bankruptcy was a pretext for breaking the power of the municipal unions and forcing the city to shrink its public sector, while successfully convincing the population that there was no point in taking to the streets. To this end, economic restrictions were coupled with a relentless moral attack on the city, particularly the supposedly greedy city workers who had gotten us into this mess. New Yorkers (so the next few years' worth of clichés would have it) had been selfish profligates living beyond their means, but now the days of wine and roses were over, and we would have to shape up, lower our expectations, tighten our belts.

The rhetoric of austerity, embraced by the Carter administration, quickly spread from New York to the rest of the country. By 1980 it appeared that Americans had had enough; rejecting the ascetic Jimmy "Moral Malaise" Carter, they opted for Ronald Reagan's vision of limitless opportunity and his up the rich, damn the deficit guns-and-tax-cuts policy. Yet paradoxically, it was in the so-called decade of greed that the culture of austerity became solidly entrenched. As public services and amenities were increasingly deemed an unconscionable extravagance, the very idea of a public life whose rules and values rightly differed from those of the private market came into disrepute. As personal morality was conflated with productivity and adherence to the work ethic, business was held to be the model for how all organizations, regardless of their purpose, ought to operate: tightly controlled from the top, obsessed with the bottom line, and "efficient," that is, uninhibited by sentimentality about the welfare of their workers or the surrounding community. Most ominously for the future of democracy, it came to be taken for granted that basic decisions about public spending, taxes, regulation, and economic policy generally would be made, not by our elected representatives, but by corporations prepared to withhold credit or move their capital and jobs elsewhere in response to any government foolish enough to defy their disapproval. Today all these propositions are virtually unquestioned axioms of economic, political, and cultural common sense.

The culture of austerity has had a profoundly depressing effect on intellectual life. Most obviously, its axioms reinforce and rationalize an actual material scarcity. It is harder and harder to find support for any sort of intellectual or creative work that can't be mass-marketed or subsidized by corporate-financed conservative foundations and think tanks: public funds for scholarship and the arts are drying up, book publishing and journalism are dominated by conglomerates, full-time faculty jobs are giving way to academic piecework at poverty-level wages. People work longer and more exhausting hours, often at more than one job, just to get by; they have little time, energy, or money with which to launch alternative publications, schools, and other cultural experiments. In New York and other major cultural centers, real estate inflation, spurred by tax giveaways to developers, disinvestment in public housing, and creeping deregulation (New York's co-op conversion movement, which went into high gear in the '80s, was essentially a scheme for property owners to "liberate" rent-stabilized apartments to be sold and in many cases re-rented at market rates), has led to prohibitive rents that chase writers, artists, and students out of convenient downtown neighborhoods while ensuring that discretionary income is an oxymoron. Nor can groups afford to rent large, easily accessible spaces for cultural and educational activities. (Under present conditions, the Free University would have to be on Staten Island.)

Austerity has also reinforced the characteristic anti-intellectualism of American culture, deeply rooted in a combination of business-oriented and populist attitudes, which takes thinking, imagining, and learning with no immediate instrumental object to be a useless luxury rather than work in any meaningful sense. After all, such activities are not quantifiable in terms of how much they add to the GDP, nor are they easily rationalized in terms of working hours. Furthermore, they are pleasurable; therefore it seems unfair that they should be economically rewarded. In fact, they are regarded not only as pleasure but as infantile narcissistic gratification, as one might infer from such locutions as "They're off contemplating their navels," or "thumbsucker" as a pejorative term for essay. Intellectual occupations excite suspicion because they are always at least potentially outside social control; at the same time, they are perceived and widely resented as a source of power and influence and as the preserve of an elite that is getting away with not putting its nose to the grindstone.

In the service of this *ressentiment,* it is the current fashion to insist that intellectual enterprises like publishing and education prove their mettle in the marketplace by embracing corporate goals, management techniques, and standards of cost effectiveness. The huge media companies that control trade publishing will not tolerate the traditionally low profits on so-called mid-list books, let alone subsidize worthy money-losers as the old independent houses did. At the same time, universities are reducing or eliminating subsidies to their own presses, whose decisions about publishing books and keeping them in print are increasingly dictated by market considerations. University presidents at both public and private institutions adopt the language of CEOs charged with reducing labor costs, increasing "productivity" (i.e., faculty workloads and class sizes), cutting and consolidating programs in the name of efficiency, and becoming more "accountable" to their "customers" (variously construed as the taxpayers who fund them, the employers that hire their graduates, or the parents who pay tuition—rarely the students themselves). Increasingly, they demand that faculty become entrepreneurs, raising outside money to support their programs.

Tax law and IRS policy reflect the same mentality. Writers and artists, who may have to live for years on an advance or the income from one major commission, are no longer permitted to average their incomes over several years for tax purposes, and the rules for deducting the cost of a home office are so strict few freelancers working in small apartments can qualify. The policy that allowed publishers to deduct the costs of warehousing their unsold inventory was rescinded on the grounds that a book is no different from any other product, a move that in effect penalizes companies for keeping slow-moving books in print. As a result, thousands of books that might have sold a few copies a year are remaindered or shredded. Postal subsidies for books and periodicals have been abolished. Shrinking the space for independent intellectual and cultural activity is no mere unfortunate byproduct of such exercises in corporatethink but their fundamental logic and purpose.

For some time my own working life was relatively insulated from the culture of austerity. During the '70s, I was a columnist or contributing editor at various magazines and in 1979 began working as a staff writer at the *Village Voice,* which had become a highly successful commercial enterprise while remaining, in crucial respects, a countercultural institution. Rupert Murdoch had bought the *Voice* two years earlier, much to the consternation of the staff, which promptly unionized. But after a few initial skirmishes—his first act was to fire the editor; a staff walkout forced him to back down—he had made no serious moves (at least in public) to change the paper's content or its freewheeling culture. By the time I joined the staff, he had managed to install his own appointee, David Schneiderman, as editor-in-chief. But Schneiderman (who hired me) proved to be a staunch defender of the *Voice*'s independence, staving off his boss's persistent complaints about the paper and demands to fire writers whose politics offended him or whose investigative zeal impinged on his and his friends' interests. Schneiderman was able to get away with this because the *Voice* was making huge profits at a time when Murdoch was financially stretched by his efforts to build his media empire.

In contrast to the hierarchical system typical of magazines and newspapers, the structure of authority at the *Voice* was loose and decentralized. Editing was a collaborative process in which a writer and an editor came to an agreement on the final version of a piece; the editor-in-chief might make objections or suggestions, but only in the rarest of cases were the writer or original editor overruled. Both writers and editors were militantly protective of their autonomy and notoriously contentious. Having come of age during the economic boom and cultural revolt, we still had a '60s sense of entitlement, were neither afraid of nor reverent toward authority, and believed that we who gave the paper its character were really its rightful owners. (This sentiment was not shared by the non-editorial employees, who were much more regimented.) Furthermore, the *Voice*'s identity as a "writer's paper" and its claim on the loyalty of its audience depended on its stable of writers, who knew they couldn't easily be replaced. As a result, management's sporadic and tentative attempts to rationalize the paper and bring the staff under more control met stiff resistance and were, in literal bottom-line terms, more trouble than they were worth. The trade-off was that we were paid much less than journalists in comparable positions at other publications (if no longer the ridiculous pittance of the underground-paper, pre-union days), a major reason the *Voice* was so profitable.

And so, through the first years of the Reagan era I still led a freelancer's life, controlling my own time. My income was small but adequate given my rent, which had gone up quite a bit since the '60s, but owing to rent stabilization was still pretty cheap. The *Voice* office, where I hung out a lot, was a short walk from my apartment (in the West Village now), and most of my friends lived nearby. I belonged to a lively community of journalists and to a feminist group; in these circles the ethos of sex, dope, and rock and roll was by no means passé. Though I felt the sting of the cultural backlash and worried, rather abstractly, about my economic future, my day-to-day habits were unaffected.

Then I met a man I wanted to live with and had a baby. Many changes ensued, not least my induction into the new economic order. My apartment was too small for three, and in Reagan's morning-in-America rental market, finding an affordable (i.e., rent-regulated) alternative in the neighborhood required both ace detective skills and large bribes. So we moved away from the Village and eventually bought a co-op in Brooklyn, forty-five minutes by subway from my old haunts and four times as expensive, in terms of monthly carrying costs, as my old rent. (As for its value as an investment, that collapsed with the stock market in 1987.) Since I needed more money—as well as some concrete reason to be in Manhattan regularly so as not to get totally sucked into domestic life—I asked the *Voice* for an editing job. I would only work part-time, though, and not simply because I wanted to spend time with my daughter; for me it was a matter of principle not to sign on to a forty-hour week unless I had no choice. I hadn't had a full-time job in fifteen years. My personal solution to the tension between earning a living and preserving my autonomy was institutional marginality. While I hadn't rejected institutions altogether, as many '60s bohemians had done, I liked to keep my distance.

This was not an issue at the *Voice,* where writers and editors had all sorts of idiosyncratic arrangements. So long as you did your work, no one much cared when you did it or where or on what terms. In fact we worked very hard—I certainly put in many more hours than I'd officially agreed to—but we were driven by passion and perfectionism, not subordination. Even as an editor, I preserved as much as I could of my freelance mentality: one summer, wanting to leave town, I estimated the extra hours I'd worked so far that year and announced that to make up the time I was taking an extra month's vacation. My boss, the editor-in-chief (a successor to Schneiderman, who had been promoted to publisher), acceded to my plan, albeit without great enthusiasm. For me, this kind of freedom was worth any amount of the money I might have made at an uptown magazine.

When birdseed tycoon Leonard Stern bought the *Voice* in the mid-'80s, it was clear that he and Schneiderman were impatient with an editorial culture that, from the viewpoint of conventional business practice, bordered on anarchy. To be fair, their perception of an impossibly unruly staff was not wholly unjustified. Freedom of expression at the paper was often indistinguishable from egomania and bullying, as certain writers were in the habit of throwing tantrums—at editorial decisions they disagreed with, editors' suggesting that their deathless words might be a tad fewer in number, or underlings' insufficient servility. The long-running culture war at the *Voice*—the old guard of straight male lefty politicos and "hard" newswriters (dubbed "the white boys" by their antagonists) versus the "thumbsucking" critics and essay writers, many of them feminist and gay activists (though only marginally less white)—kept erupting into vicious public fights. Trying to run a railroad in the midst of this constant fractiousness was no enviable task. And as the culture of austerity tightened its grip, the effort must have begun to seem not only anomalous but an exercise in antediluvian masochism.

Since moving to the business side of the paper, Schneiderman had hired two editors-in-chief, neither of whom had taken charge the way he'd hoped. In 1988 he settled on a third, who, unlike his ill-fated predecessors, was utterly disdainful of the *Voice*'s democratic tradition. Jonathan Larsen embarked on a systematic effort to centralize authority, relying on a small, loyal band of top editorial managers to carry out his decisions and limiting the control of individual writers and editors over the pieces they worked on. He was also determined to rationalize office time and space, ending the crazy quilt of individual arrangements that left computer terminals idle before eleven A.M. and most of Tuesday (the day after the paper went to press) while they became the object of fierce competition at more popular times.

The *Voice*'s content underwent parallel changes. The paper was rigidly divided into sections devoted to particular kinds of stories. As a result, there was no more room for the uncategorizable, serendipitous piece of great writing or idiosyncratic weirdness that had once been a *Voice* specialty. There was also less and less room for genuine thought. Even in its best days, the *Voice* had never truly transcended the conventional journalistic values whereby reporting was considered both more important and harder work than essay writing or criticism. *Voice* reporters were generally rewarded with higher pay and more prominence in the paper: there was the front of the book, which was supposed to be news, and the back of the book (or the bus) with the cultural sections. Still, this distinction was regularly violated, and major staff freak-outs could often be traced to a story on the arts or cultural politics that had made it onto the front page, scandalizing the "white boys." (There was, for instance, C. Carr's cover piece on the then obscure Karen Finley, which included graphic descriptions of her act and inspired an outraged column by Pete Hamill, months of letters to the editor, graffiti wars in the restrooms, and endless jokes about yams and where you could stuff them.)

Now the increasing balkanization of the paper, along with Larsen's own anti-intellectual bent, shored up the conventional mind-set. Once, my proposed head-line for a cover story I'd edited was rejected because "it sounds as if the piece is an essay"—evidently something to be avoided at all cost. Cultural politics didn't go away, but like everything else it was institutionalized and ghettoized. On Larsen's watch the paper that had been home base for the most radical and icono-clastic feminist voices instituted a column called "Female Troubles," as well as columns for various ethnic groups. On the other hand, to my great puzzlement one indubitably good thing did happen during Larsen's editorship—the flower-ing of a lively and diverse group of black writers. My admittedly jaundiced theory was that Jon was so eager to enhance his liberal credentials with black bylines that he printed interesting stuff by black writers he wouldn't have ac-cepted from white writers.

While individuals resisted the process of corporatization, it went forward without the concerted protest it would once have provoked. Though the *Voice* was still a highly profitable business—which is to say that the new regime was motivated more by ideology than by bottom-line concerns—changes in the sur-rounding economic and social environment had finally eroded the paper's in-ternal culture of opposition. The cost of living had risen while opportunities in journalism had shrunk, especially opportunities for paying jobs at publications that featured serious writing, left politics, or any sort of "alternative" outlook (the *Voice*'s last serious competitor, the weekly *Soho News,* had folded several years earlier). The ethos of austerity and the celebration of corporate values had permeated the culture for a decade or more. A younger generation of *Voice* writers and editors had grown up under these conditions. Not only were their economic prospects far dicier than ours had been, their character formation was different: however "progressive" their politics or bohemian their cultural proclivities, many of them lacked the self-confidence (or arrogance), visceral antiauthoritarian impulse, and faith in the efficacy of collective action that were second nature to those of us imprinted with the '60s.

It did not take long for my relationship with Larsen to devolve into total war. I had been on a leave of absence when he arrived; when I came back I found that my "office" (which like most *Voice* offices was actually a small cubicle) had been allotted to someone else. I kept pestering the managing editor to give me my office back or assign me a new one, till she finally admitted that the boss didn't think I needed the space because "You're not here all the time." It seemed that when I *was* there I was expected simply to tote my stuff around, using whatever space was vacant, and doing without such amenities as my own telephone extension, let alone a terminal. I filed a grievance with the union, since our contract did not permit management to unilaterally change our working conditions. Having won my point and inspected my new cubicle, I assured Jon, "It will be fine—all it needs is a window and a carpet." His face registered a split second of panic before he realized I was joking—a moment that foreshadowed an unbridgeable sensibility gap.

After innumerable clashes with Larsen—who respected neither my ideas, the traditional autonomy I had exercised over the projects I supervised, nor the established boundaries of my job (which had allowed me to concentrate on my areas of interest and expertise)—I knew I had to get out of there. The question was how, in the age of austerity, I could get what I needed—a job that fit my skills, was reasonably engaging, was not morally offensive, and offered a decent income plus a modicum of freedom to do the writing I wanted to do. So far as I could see, there were no suitable possibilities in journalism: I already had the best job available to someone of my inclinations, and it wasn't good enough. Book publishing looked equally unappealing (though I did consider starting a freelance editing and editorial consulting business; perhaps there was a market for the Maxwell Perkins figure publishing houses had long since dispensed with).

The alternative was the university: I had no advanced degrees, but perhaps with my credentials as a writer, an editor, and a feminist I could teach journalism or women's studies. The more I thought about it, the more I saw the academy—which I'd rejected nearly thirty years ago when I dropped out of graduate school—as my best shot. Whatever the realities at particular schools (and living with a professor, I knew a bit about those realities), at least in principle the university was an institution that supported the life of the mind, that considered one's "real work" part of one's job. In my experience, it was easier to maneuver by demanding that bosses live up to their professed principles than by insisting on principles they'd repudiated or never had in the first place.

In 1990 I left the *Voice* and joined the journalism faculty at New York University (of which more later). By my lights, the paper—which I continued to read assiduously, as if I were keeping a fever chart—became steadily duller and less influential. Its articles weren't talked about; hardly anyone I knew read it anymore. Apparently this defection was not limited to my friends; the *Voice*'s circulation dropped, even as costs, especially the cost of paper, were rising. By 1994 alarms were going off: although the *Voice* was still making money, it was increasingly marginal to the public conversation, widely regarded as the mouthpiece of a tired, outdated leftism at a time when conservatism and free-market libertarianism were hip. For the first time in years, the paper found itself pressed hard by competitors, the *New York Press* and *Time Out* (both offered extensive listings of cultural events; neither bore the leftist stigma). Jon Larsen quit or was fired. And then David Schneiderman did something that amazed and delighted me: he hired Karen Durbin as editor-in-chief.

Durbin was a cultural radical, a visceral democrat, passionate about ideas, a champion of the individual writer's voice. She had been nurtured on the *Voice*'s oppositional culture, having first become a *Voice* writer, and then an editor, in the early '70s. She was arts editor when Larsen was hired; when she saw that he had no intention of allowing her any power, she had left to be arts editor at *Mirabella*. She was also a longtime close friend of mine, and I felt much the way the FOBs must have done when their man ascended to the White House. I was ensconced at NYU and didn't want a staff job, but I accepted with gusto the offer of a column on media. It seemed to be one of those rare moments of vindication: evidently, Stern and Schneiderman had realized that corporatizing was not only bad for journalism, but bad for business, and were ready to try letting the *Voice* be the *Voice*. Two-and-a-half years later Durbin was gone, and so was I.

Score another for the culture of austerity. Larsen had destroyed the old *Voice* culture and left a timid, unimaginative bureaucracy in its place. There was no way one person could substantially change this without wholehearted support from management—especially the financial kind. Revitalizing the paper would have taken a huge investment in new writers and editors and an equally substantial outlay for firing people humanely, either by giving them large severance packages or keeping them on till they found other jobs (a necessity not only for ethical reasons, but to forestall a debilitating atmosphere of panic in the office). And then, having made big changes, management would have had to launch an expensive promotional campaign to make sure the public knew about them. But Stern, in *echt-*'90s fashion, was determined to cut costs, a resolve that was reinforced by a steep rise in the price of newsprint shortly after Durbin was hired. As a result, the *Voice* became a reverse roach motel—you could get out, but you couldn't get in. Durbin undertook a few highly publicized firings and faced down the inevitable controversy, only to be handed an ever-shrinking budget for new hires. Schneiderman also micromanaged the editorial budget in a way that repeatedly undercut Durbin's authority. The double whammy of hand tying and cost cutting was crippling. The *Voice* did improve, but not enough. And though circulation rose—especially after the paper instituted free distribution in Manhattan—the paper's aggressive competition kept its ad rates down, encouraging Stern to stick with his disastrous penny-wise strategy.

After Durbin's departure, Schneiderman strongly intimated that he wanted a young editor, on the assumption that such a person would attract a young readership, and his first offer went to Michael Hirschorn of *New York* magazine. But when Hirschorn didn't bite, he hired Don Forst, the former editor of *New York Newsday,* a sixty-four-year-old with a classic newsman's sensibility. Clearly the *Voice* has suffered a massive identity crisis: the Larsen-Durbin-Hirschorn-Forst trajectory evokes the image of a drunk lurching from one direction to another with only the vaguest idea of a destination. The glib explanation is that the *Voice*'s historic identity as the cultural left's newspaper of record is no longer commercially viable in a conservative climate, but I don't think that's the real issue. In New York there is still a sizable base of readers for such a publication—a base that eroded in the first place not because the *Voice* was too left-wing, but because it was too boring. Besides, I believe that if you publish a paper that's lively, iconoclastic, well written, and full of stories that can't be found elsewhere, people will read it even if they hate your politics—and that includes a lot of those panted-after young people, especially the ones who are drawn to the libertarian right not because they think Frederich Hayek was a genius but because they want to be where the energy is.

Anyway, the *Voice* in its shakiest moments has never been in danger of losing money. It's just that a *Village Voice* chastened by the new economic order and out of sync with cultural-political fashion can't be expected to *roll* in money, as it did when it was riding the economic boom and the countercultural wave. It's hardly surprising that a businessman with no personal stake in the matter would be reluctant to accept less profit for the sake of preserving the paper as an oppositional force—especially in an era when accepting less profit for any reason is regarded as effete if not downright perverse. Yet it would arguably have made good business sense to take advantage of the *Voice*'s distinctive character—which was, among other things, a marketing niche—to secure its core audience while appealing to others precisely by departing from the general trend to bland, editor-driven, and idea-free journalism. Instead, the apparent strategy has been to move the paper toward that "mainstream" where the (relatively) mass readership and its concomitant ad rates reside. But this strategy inevitably poses the problem of why anyone should read a publication that's so much like everything else out there it has no compelling reason to exist.

In quest of a solution to this dilemma, the *Voice* has inexorably transformed itself from an editorial vision seeking an audience to a marketing vehicle seeking a formula. Its feature articles are conspicuously shorter, simpler, and dumber, with that *Voice* signature, the first-person essay, purged in favor of conventional news reporting. But perhaps Forst's most symbolically resonant act was to get rid of Jules Feiffer, whose cartoons bore something of the same relation to the *Voice*'s persona as Eustace Tilley to the *New Yorker*'s, by informing him that the *Voice* would be happy to continue to publish his work—it just didn't want to pay his salary. Increasingly, the paper has taken on the denatured flavor of the glorified pennysavers that mostly pass for an "alternative press" these days. The irony, of course, is that the *Voice* was the original model for all its canned versions: imitating them, it has become a simulacrum of itself.

Meanwhile, Leonard Stern has acquired several alternative weeklies and designed suburban versions of the *Voice* for Orange County and Long Island. In the context of these purchases, management announced the imposition of a new contract that forces *Voice* freelancers to give up most rights to their work; among other things it allows pieces to be recycled to all the papers in Stern's chain. This was an open break with the *Voice*'s pro-writer tradition. Yet compared to the spontaneous outrage that would once have greeted such a move, an anticontract organizing campaign by the National Writers Union went nowhere; nor did the *Voice*'s own union make any significant fuss. Many of the freelancers affected must have sensed that the game is up, that once the individual voice has been radically devalued, so has the source of their power. In effect, they are becoming anonymous content providers, nearly as interchangeable as classified-ad takers. And if their jobs can't be exported to Bangladesh, there is always the army of hungry would-be freelancers—the ones who still imagine their individual voices matter, and for whom solidarity's just another word for nothing left to lose.

As I write this, I'm on break from my classes at NYU, finally getting the block of time I need to finish an essay I've been working into the interstices of my schedule. My present life in the academy is, as the hounds of austerity view it, scandalously privileged. I teach three courses a year and, in lieu of a fourth course, direct a concentration in the journalism department's M.A. program. I have tenure. I have spring break, winter break, and those "three big reasons for becoming a professor"—June, July, and August. I'm about to spend a yearlong sabbatical, at three-quarters pay, working on a book. I have considerable control over my courses, my working hours, and the administration of my program. My salary and benefits are better than they were at the *Voice,* and my family and I live in affordable, if cramped, faculty housing (back in the Village, after all these years!). I am one of a shrinking minority of academics who enjoy such working conditions, which in my view are not pampered but merely humane.

When professors defend their perquisites, they like to invoke the special nature of their work: tenure is not about job security (perish the thought) but about academic freedom; summers off and sabbaticals are not vacations but a recharging of intellectual batteries; and so on. This line of argument not only incites the hounds all the more, since they think our work is a boondoggle to begin with, but reveals the extent to which they've colonized our minds. The truth is that in a rich postindustrial economy like ours, everyone should have a job, or more to the point income, security; everyone should be able to speak their mind without being fired; and everyone should have time off to recharge their intellectual batteries, their sexual batteries, or any batteries they like. The university isn't Shangri-La; it's (for some of us) a decent workplace in a time when indecent is the norm.

On balance, academia has served my purposes well—or as well as I can reasonably expect at this unpropitious moment. Yet it has also subverted those purposes by plunging me into the kind of entangling institutional alliance I always tried so hard to avoid. In the first place, the classroom consumes much more of my energy than I naively imagined it would: unlike editing, which I experienced as a relief from the psychic demands of writing—an intellectual game of sorts—teaching makes intense demands of its own. It soon became important to me to teach courses that reflected my intellectual obsessions, and to have students who shared them—so I started a new concentration, which made me an administrator, involved me in department politics, led me to sit on certain committees and plot how to raise money. The voice of austerity at NYU tends to whisper of future problems rather than proclaim crises, but in one respect it's very loud: if faculty want their projects to prosper, they had better be entrepreneurial. In June I'll dive into my book, but for now I have a proposal I'd like you to read. . . . For me, the sabbatical that lies ahead is at once a great gift and a great paradox: for a year it will give me back what used to be my life. Imagine an antelope transported from the African veldt to a lovingly constructed, meticulously detailed simulated habitat in a state-of-the art zoo, while the hounds growl that in an age of austerity, a cage should be enough.

Don't Think, Smile! Notes on a Decade of Denial, 2000

The Aughts
Our Politics, Ourselves

INTRODUCTION
Spencer Ackerman

It was fitting that the terrorist attacks of 9/11 caused the Twin Towers to collapse on themselves, because the attack would make American intellectual culture perform a similar maneuver. The monolith of dread that defined the Cold War returned to destabilize America through an onslaught of historical analogy. The terrorists hated freedom and could not be reasoned with; this war required new methods and new recalibrations of the balance between liberty and security; and writing was the act delineating loyalty from treason. Poor Susan Sontag remembered that 9/11 took place in the context of "specific American alliances and actions"; and so she was denounced as a moral cretin. Graydon Carter more safely proclaimed that al-Qaeda brought about the death of irony, just as America was about to repeat many of its bellicose mistakes of the twentieth century while loudly declaring it was avoiding the mistakes of weakness.

Nor were the left's criticisms of the era immune to the same repetitions, including those of Ellen Willis. In "Dreaming of War," written days after the 9/11 attacks, Willis attacked not a rabid, warlike political consensus but the cosmopolitan writers who hoped something beneficial might come out of the disaster. The Frank Riches of the world were flirting with "purification of our national soul through war." And yet those who stood against such a destructive tendency were busy arguing with other writers over miniscule differences in their perspectives on the decade of war to come. It's a good thing Willis never used Twitter.

The left's familiar templates—the power of media, government, and corporate elites to distract the public from actual dangers—reasserted themselves as easily as the right's fixation on moral clarity. September 11 convinced both the right and the left that what mattered was restating first principles rather than attempting to reconcile them with the inconvenient complexities of an unfamiliar world. As Irin Carmon notes in this anthology, Willis considered "living in the past" to be "the worst insult" to writers of her generation, but the 9/11 era deployed the past like a leghold trap.

Yet Willis got more right than wrong—and, at important times, smashed those same templates. "Why I'm Not for Peace" confronts the "mantra" that desiring peace is an amulet against a predatory world—a powerful rejection of the post–9/11 fetish for first principles. "Is There Still a Jewish Question?" provokes the left to examine its rage at Israel. "The Mass Psychology of Terrorism" insightfully observes that anyone motivated to kill for a promise of penetrating virgins in heaven has taken sexual repression to its logical conclusion. "Three Elegies for Susan Sontag" resurrects one of the most vital American critics out of the nadir of her reputation, and in the process embraces the "political stand" that Sontag demanded from intellectuals while remaining cognizant of its limits: "Individuals bearing witness do not change history; only movements that understand their social world can do that."

That appropriately tragic sensibility runs through Willis's twenty-first century writing, and it helped her avoid many of the now-predictable intellectual mistakes of the era. She stumbled, as writers will: Willis ought to have distinguished legitimate rage at Israel's often-destructive policies from illegitimate rage at the idea of Israel. And *The Sopranos* self-indulgently reneged on the promise in "Our Mobsters, Ourselves" to hold up a dark mirror to the culture through soapy devices like putting Tony in a coma. But at least Willis's mistakes were not mistakes of cant, convenience, or cliché, which would become the balm of the 2000s for the violence they unleashed.

SPENCER ACKERMAN is the U.S. national security editor of the *Guardian*. He was previously senior writer for *Wired,* where he won the 2012 National Magazine Award for Digital Reporting.

Why I'm Not for Peace

During the war in Bosnia, in an attempt to express my impatience—if that's the word—with fellow leftists who opposed American intervention in the Balkans, I wisecracked, "Some people would oppose intervention if New York were invaded." Little did I know: this is an age when *absurdum* outstrips all efforts at *reductio*. Yes, my title is a provocation. I'm not really against peace; what I'm against is Peace as a mantra—Anti-Imperialism being another—that wards off thought. What I'm against is the illusion that by opposing military action anywhere at any time Americans can somehow avoid the moral ambiguities inherent in being citizens of the most powerful nation-state in a world largely shaped by the reality or threat of force.

Those ambiguities weighed heavily from the first moment of impact on September 11. The shock of the attack itself was compounded by the aftershock of realization that all the decisions about how to respond to it would be made by the most reactionary presidential administration in my lifetime, with any fallout from the stolen 2000 election now to be swept away by the deference and goodwill commonly accorded a wartime commander in chief. The immediate worry, given Bush's cowboy rhetoric and sentiments of Defense Department hawks (along with their cheering section in the press), was that we would reflexively launch an indiscriminate bombing campaign in Afghanistan, make preemptive war on Iraq, or declare most of the Middle East our enemy. I believed the situation called for military force. Not to retaliate for a massacre of Americans, clearly aimed at the United States as such, would be to abdicate our government's most basic function, providing for the common defense. But a measured, carefully targeted retaliation was one thing; the larger "war on terrorism" was a far more complex problem, not conducive to solution through sheer firepower.

So I was relieved when Bush stopped hyperventilating and settled, for the moment at least, on a limited war against Al Qaeda and the Taliban. The administration said the right things about minimizing civilian casualties, distinguishing between the Afghan people and their oppressive regime, and preventing mass starvation (granted that our token airlift of food was hardly a serious response to that threat). It even appeared to backtrack on its aversion to "nation-building," suggesting that it had learned from past mistakes and would devote money and energy to reconstructing a post-Taliban Afghanistan.

I supported, and still support, the basic outlines of this policy: as the saying goes, even a blind hen sometimes finds a pea. It's impossible not to be happy that a regime of totalitarian lunatics is gone; not to be moved by the photographs of women showing their faces on the Kabul streets—or, for that matter, not to get ironic satisfaction from our president's belated conversion on women's liberation. Cynical, to be sure: but that certain words are pronounced on the international stage is more important, in the long run, than the motives of the speaker.

The objections I have had from the beginning—and still have—are not to the fact of our war in Afghanistan but to the way we've conducted it. I object in general to our modus operandi of avoiding American casualties by depending on air power and using local troops as our proxies. If we have a legitimate stake in a war we should take responsibility for it by putting our own troops on the ground. Bombs, however "smart," inevitably hit civilians and should be kept to the absolute minimum necessary to destroy an opponent's military capacity—yet even after the Taliban's collapse, and under conditions of maximum confusion between soldiers and civilians, we kept on bombing. As for the decision to let the Northern Alliance fight our war, the predictable result is that the warlords are back in control, the provisional government has no means of enforcing its authority, and rampant banditry is once again the rule. In interview after interview with ordinary Afghans, they plead for an international presence to establish law and order. Yet for all its lip service to reconstruction, the United States refuses to send troops or allow other countries to send them in anything like the numbers needed.

My frustration, in other words, is not that we took action in Afghanistan but that we have not done *enough*. We should have fought the ground war and occupied Kabul; organized an international force to disarm the warlords, protect ordinary citizens, and oversee the distribution of aid; demanded that secularists be included in the negotiations for a new government and that basic women's rights be built into a new structure of law. If this is "imperialism"—in the promiscuous contemporary usage of that term—I am for it: I believe it is the prerequisite of a stable peace.

All this is by way of illustrating the chasm the size of Ground Zero that stretches between me and the antiwar movement that sprang up post-9/11. What caught my attention first was crowds of young people looking and sounding like preserved specimens of the sixties antiwar counterculture, with the same songs and peace-and-love slogans. Everything about this bothered me: that 20-year-olds were using their elders' language and style instead of inventing their own; that those blinky-eyed, reductive slogans had induced me and many other card-carrying members of the antiwar counterculture to roll our eyes even in 1967; and worst, that the demonstrators were invoking the moral authority of the Vietnam protests in an obscenely inapposite way.

The other main antiwar contingent came from my own generation of leftists and erstwhile Vietnam protesters, heavily concentrated on academia. Most were not pacifists, but rather took it as axiomatic that no assertion of military power by the United States could possibly be justified or have a good result. A war undertaken by the U.S. was by definition imperialist aggression; self-defense and the barbarism of the Taliban were merely excuses. After all, hadn't we engineered the fundamentalists' rise to power in the first place? Who were we, anyway, to be self-righteous about terrorism after the terrible things we had done or condoned in Iraq/Chile/East Timor/fill in the blank? Many in this camp were convinced beyond a doubt that we would carpet-bomb the civilian population, leveling what was left of Afghanistan; that in fact we refrained from doing this did little to stem the flow of impassioned rhetoric about mass violence and atrocity.

Watching these developments I flashed back to the Gulf War, a far more dubious proposition that nonetheless had me feeling a similar alienation from the peace movement. Then, too, the moral and conceptual assumptions of the Vietnam opposition were dusted off as if international relations had frozen in 1975. Demonstrations were notable for the simpleminded slogan "No blood for oil," as well as for a strain of vulgar pacifism amounting to little more than the conviction that war is a yucky nasty thing we shouldn't have to deal with. (I was particularly chilled by a news photograph of some young protesters holding up a sign that read "Nothing is worth dying for." What would Gandhi have thought?) That Saddam Hussein was a megalomaniac tyrant; that he clearly meant to establish himself as a regional superpower, with highly dangerous consequences; that his move on Kuwait was, among other things, a test to see if anyone cared to stop him—none of this was deemed relevant to the debate. Nor, a year later, did Slobodan Milosevic's "ethnic cleansing" campaign in Bosnia prompt any serious soul searching on the antiwar left about whether intervention to prevent genocide might be warranted. Nor did its reprise in Kosovo. Whatever the circumstance, the dogma remained constant: violence is bad; any military action by the United States is imperialist.

And so the arguments went after 9/11. Making war on the Taliban was revenge, not justice, and would only perpetuate the "cycle of violence." We could not win, because the Afghan people did not want foreign intruders and would reject us as they had the Soviet Union. Our cause would be seen by millions of Middle Easterners and South Asians as a war of the West against Islam and would incite a massive backlash in support of Osama bin Laden's *jihad*. It would destabilize the fragile government of Pakistan, with its nuclear weapons. Instead, we should address the root causes of anti-American terrorism, which lie in our misguided foreign policy. Meanwhile we should regard the attack not as war but as a crime, and seek to try the criminals before an international court.

These arguments raise political, moral, and practical questions that deserve to be addressed. Yet in the end it seems to me that they are debating points marshaled to support an a priori conviction, that to the extent they can be refuted—or have been refuted by events (the Taliban fell, to no apparent regret on the part of the Afghans; no massive Islamic backlash has occurred)—other points will hastily fill the gap. For at the heart of the matter is an unspoken meta-argument: that America is a sinful country, and must achieve redemption through nonviolence. Violence as committed against us is the wages of sin. To strike back in kind is to continue to collect the geopolitical equivalent of bad karma, inevitably provoking more "blowback." Sow the wind, reap the whirlwind.

The crudest expression of this attitude—the claim that terrorism is retaliation for specific U.S. policies—does not pass cursory inspection. It trivializes the Islamic fundamentalist movement, which has quite bluntly declared its dedication to destroying unbelievers and their morally corrupt societies, to imagine it would be mollified by the withdrawal of American troops from the Persian Gulf or the lifting of sanctions against Iraq. Even sillier is the idea that our route to safety is getting tough and imposing an Israeli-Palestinian settlement (the one cause in which throwing our weight around is okay, it seems). While such a settlement is devoutly to be wished, far from deterring fundamentalist terrorism it would probably cause a Palestinian civil war. The radical Islamists do not want a settlement; they want Israel to go away.

Yet the broader claim that we are responsible for our vulnerability has resonance because it's at least partly true. After all, it's incontestable that America's tunnel-vision cold war policy of building up radical Islamists to fight the Soviet Union has blown back on us. Overall, our government's commitment to the notion that the business of America is global business, its championing of neoliberal policies that exacerbate economic inequality, its alliances with "stable" autocratic regimes and allergy to any democratizing movement with a leftish tinge have done their part to foment the economic and political resentments that fundamentalist demagogues exploit.

Suppose, then, that this were the whole story: America's malfeasances unleashed a monster. Why would it follow that we should not fight back? On the contrary, wouldn't we have even more responsibility to confront the golem we created? In the years before World War II the Western Powers were clearly complicitous in Hitler's rise; they hoped he would attack the Soviet Union and solve their Communism problem. Furthermore, the Nazis exploited the economic misery and political humiliation of the German people, which stemmed from the crisis of capitalism and its most horrendous symptom, World War I: in these developments Britain, France, and the U.S. were thoroughly implicated. Hitler, in short, was blowback too. And at the time, many on the left insisted—especially before Hitler attacked Russia—that this was just another war among rival imperialists. Were they right?

Of course, it's simplistic to see Nazism as purely a product of capitalism and imperialism, and equally so to see Osama bin Laden as a product of the World Bank. Nazism was a revolt against modernity (notwithstanding its use of modern technology and media as mainstays of its power) and specifically against the liberal values of the Enlightenment. As a mass movement, it was an outbreak of collective irrationalism, impelled by the anxieties of a people caught up in the clash between the rigid patriarchalism of traditional German culture and the competing forces of globalization, liberalism, and democracy. It was in the context of such liberalizing forces that a populist movement like fascism could emerge. It was in the context of deeply rooted patriarchalism that the people's rebelliousness failed to take the form of a democratic movement aimed at improving their economic and political situation, but instead expressed itself in submission to an absolute authority that provided an outlet for their rage: the capitalist/communist/rootless cosmopolitan Jew.

Much the same can be said of the religious totalitarianism Al Qaeda represents. It is the latest flashpoint in the ongoing, worldwide culture war that began in the eighteenth century: intertwined with the spread of capitalism, though by no means synonymous with it, the ideas of freedom, equality, separation of church and state—and their more recent application to our sexual and domestic lives—have penetrated everywhere, eroding traditional patriarchal institutions and rigid social controls. And in the Islamic world as in Weimar Germany this erosion has had a paradoxical result, at once inciting a fundamentalist backlash and creating the conditions for mobilizing its supporters. There could hardly be a more vivid metaphor for this paradox than the success of the Al Qaeda hijackers in blending into American society and using our airplanes against us.

The United States is the world's most powerful exporter of liberal and secular values, just as it is the preeminent tribune of corporate globalization; yet neither global class conflict nor the culture war can be reduced to a question of American national power. The division between transnational corporations and their increasingly immiserated victims exists within America itself, as does the clash between secular modernity and patriarchal fundamentalism. Transnational capital may use the United States as its headquarters and dictate its economic policies, but it has no loyalty to any nation or national interest. Nor is the democratic secular impulse the property of America, or of the West. These global forces are fundamentally beyond American control.

Indeed, I would argue that the U.S. government has contributed to its present predicament not only by exercising but also by abdicating its power. Our bracketing of theocratic despotism and the persecution of women as non-issues in our international relations—a cultural-political blind spot as well as a matter of corporate realpolitik—has substantially strengthened the hand of radical fundamentalists no longer willing to confine their atrocities to their own population. (Consider our complaisance toward Saudi Arabia, or our tepid response to the death sentence pronounced on Salman Rushdie.) Which is to say that the old imperialism model does not hold, either economically or culturally—and that the left badly needs a new and more nuanced analysis of the role of the nation-state in world affairs.

But this assumes a left that's genuinely interested in politics—that is, in how to influence national and international policy to promote more freedom, equality, and democracy in the world. In fact, the animating impulses of the left's peace wing have far less to do with politics in this sense than with a quasi-religious moralism that conceives of the United States as a soul that needs saving: it is power-hungry, violent, greedy; it's a sinkhole of lies and hypocrisy, professing democracy while supporting dictators and selectively condemning terrorism; and so on. I could argue that this indictment is one-sided, that if you're appraising America's soul you also have to consider its passion for freedom and irreverence toward authority, its ability to inspire great social movements, its inventiveness, its appetite for pleasure and fantasy. I could claim that if you stack up our virtues and faults against those of other nations around the world, we actually come off as relatively well. I could point out that on 9/11 it was our virtues more than our faults that were under attack.

But really, it's the underlying premise of the argument that's wrong. The implication is there's such a thing as a morally pure state: one that abjures power, wealth, and violence and is sincere, truthful, and consistent. In fact, a morally pure state is an oxymoron. The state, including its liberal democratic version, is an inherently problematic institution, whose basic reason for being is to exercise power and protect its sovereignty, its physical integrity, and its wealth, by force if necessary.

It's certainly the province of a democratic left to critique that institution, to try to force it to be more accountable to its citizens and to international bodies and agreements—or, for that matter, to envision other forms of social organization more in keeping with the needs of free and equal people. And given that we are, willy-nilly, members of a nation-state that constantly acts in the world in our name, we must of course try to influence what it does. But our focus should be assessing the impact of U.S. policy, not taking its spiritual temperature and parsing its inevitably tangled motives. Ask not that your country be sincere; ask that its actions further democracy and promote the welfare of the people they affect.

From this perspective, 9/11 should indeed impel leftists to take a hard look at all aspects of America's relationship to the world; but that means asking if there is anything new to learn, not simply assimilating the event to preexisting dogma. On the most elementary level, what's new is an experience no living American has had before: American cities were attacked by a foreign force, and not just any cities, but our seat of government and our economic and cultural capital. Several thousand civilians died. What is to be done in such a case? Do we have the right to defend ourselves; or rather, does the impure American nation-state have the right and the responsibility to defend us?

Pressed on this question, war opponents have uncharacteristically tended to change the subject from rights and morality to practical consequences. Military action, they have argued, will not make us safe; on the contrary it will make matters worse, inviting further attacks, exacerbating anti-American hatred, provoking the Islamic "street," and playing into Osama bin Laden's desire for an apocalyptic East–West showdown. These worries are hardly baseless, even if at the moment their most lurid possibilities seem remote. War by definition is dangerous; neither safety nor victory is guaranteed. What this line of argument leaves out, though, is that there are also consequences for doing nothing for fear of inflaming one's enemies. There is ample historical evidence that appeasement never placates aggrooooro; quite the contrary. Bullies respect power and have contempt for weakness. The surest way to invite further attacks would have been to signal that they could be committed with impunity. Indeed, it could be argued that 9/11 might never have taken place were it not for our inaction in the face of a long line of provocations from the 1979 hostage taking in Iran to bin Laden's embassy bombings in 1998.

What of the international tribunal option? As an argument for an alternative to violence, this proposal is frivolous, since a military campaign would be needed to capture the would-be defendants in the first place. The real point is to allow the peace movement to condemn the massacre as a crime against humanity while refusing to condemn it, or even to recognize it as an attack meant to damage and demoralize the American polity: that is, a political crime, an act of war. Of course, there is no chance whatsoever of convening an international court that would be able to try this case as a purely "human" matter, appealing to a transcendent conception of justice untouched by the muck of international politics; but never mind. The peace left's ultimate answer to my question about self-defense is this: as abstract human beings we are entitled to seek theoretical justice; as (tainted) Americans we must turn the other cheek.

The politics of moralism and self-abnegation are an old story on the left. Among white middle-class radicals in the sixties there was always tension between those who believed that the purpose of a political movement was to transform society for everyone's benefit, including their own, and those who saw themselves as engaged in a moral mission on behalf of justice for the truly oppressed—poor people, black people, the Vietnamese, the Third World. The latter attitude eventually dominated the antiwar movement, and the results were not good. Denying the legitimacy of their own needs and desires, movement moralists ended by estranging themselves from their own identities, seeing nothing in their Americanness but unearned, corrupt privilege, and so radically isolating themselves from Americans in general. Some, brandishing their isolation as proof of their superior virtue, went so far as to set off bombs; a far greater number, not given to violence, merely stewed in alienated, depressed confusion. Either way, the movement as a force for change was destroyed.

These are different times, but if anything 9/11 underscores the point: if we aspire to change our society, we must be for ourselves as well as others. That doesn't mean embracing a facile, uncritical patriotism. It does mean resisting the equally facile temptation to declare peace and go home.

Radical Society, April 2002

Confronting the Contradictions

For me the event that most clearly represents the fecklessness of our hijacked government took place after the fall of Baghdad: the looting of Iraq's historic museum and burning of the national library in full view of American troops, who looked on and did nothing. The loss of life in war is terrible, yet the loss of a cultural legacy is arguably worse, for it negates the enormous amount of human energy devoted, over thousands of years, to the activities that make life meaningful—creating, preserving, remembering, passing on. We judge the loss of memory and consequent loss of self a calamity for the individual human being; how much more so, then, for a civilization?

This loss is doubly excruciating because it could so easily have been prevented. That the collapse of Saddam's regime amid the chaos of war would create a dangerous vacuum of authority was utterly foreseeable, yet the American military evidently had no plan to fill that vacuum and maintain law and order. Archaeologists and museum experts had warned the Pentagon about the danger of looting and provided information about what needed to be guarded; nothing was done. The oil ministry was protected; the museum and the library— and for that matter the hospital—were not. And afterward, where was the president's apology? Where were the calls for a congressional investigation? Where was our so-called opposition party—you know, the Democrats? Where was the media conglom—uh, the press? This should be a national scandal. Instead Donald Rumsfeld mumbled something rendered in family newspapers as "Stuff happens," and judging from their tepid reaction, the political class and the political-journalism elite agreed. Cultural critics were upset, but who cares about them?

On the Internet claims have circulated that the Pentagon, in league with rich collectors, deliberately allowed the looting. It says something about the nature of the Bush regime that I find myself unable to dismiss such charges out of hand. But larceny or criminal negligence, it hardly matters. The unbearable truth is that we are being governed by barbarians who have no compunction about sacking the world in the name of American supremacy (just as they sack their own country on behalf of its plutocrats). These are people unwilling to assume the most elementary responsibilities of an occupying power, even as they rush to claim the spoils. Witness their gleeful urgency to turn military victory into economic plunder: the contracts brazenly awarded to corporations like Bechtel and Halliburton; the plans to privatize and sell off Iraqi industries and use Iraqi oil to pay for reconstruction; the lies told about all of the above. But their behavior is not simply a matter of capitalist triumphalism or "the oil, stupid." It's also thuggish reveling in the power of brute force, with a millenarian tinge: history and culture are only in the way.

As I write, the main beneficiaries of the Bushite mentality appear to be the Shiite clergy, the only Iraqi force that's been organized enough to get moving on the task of restoring some semblance of normal daily life, and Baathist bureaucrats the Americans have kept in place, the better to facilitate our military's speedy exit (this maneuver has already generated protests by Iraqi doctors and professors). Which is to say that the aftermath of the war poses conundrums for the democratic left, as the war has all along.

I opposed the invasion of Iraq because I opposed the Bush Doctrine of preventive war and unilateralism; because I believed Afghanistan offered more of a clue to how the United States would behave after victory than Germany or Japan; because I feared open-ended adventurism abroad as a cover for ruinous economic and social policies at home. But I was uneasy in my opposition because I couldn't answer the question raised by Iraqi democrats like Kanan Makiya: how else, in a totalitarian society with a pervasive apparatus of state terror that had crushed all opposition, could the Iraqi people get rid of Saddam Hussein? I thought we owed the Iraqis for having failed to depose Saddam in 1991 and then failing to support the uprisings against him. Although I had no faith that the war would result in a democratic Iraq, I found it hard to argue that Iraqis would not be better off under virtually any kind of postwar government.

Shortly before the invasion, I attended a meeting addressed by Entifadh Qanbar, Washington director of the Iraqi National Congress (INC) and, like Makiya, a member of its democratic secular wing. Qanbar expressed his conviction, to much incredulity on the part of the academics and intellectuals in the audience, that George W. Bush and the Defense Department (unlike the State Department and the CIA) were committed to Iraqi democracy. Talking to him after the meeting, I remarked that for us, the Bush administration was a serious threat to American democracy, given the stolen election followed by the relentless pursuit of a hard-right agenda, assaults on civil liberties, abrogation of church-state separation, and so on. It was Qanbar's turn to be incredulous: I saw there was no way he could take seriously my complaints against the American government when the oppression the Iraqis were suffering was of a wholly different order. His skeptical look embodied the contradiction that bedeviled me: on the one hand, the impending Iraq war was about Iraq; on the other hand it was about the direction of world politics and of my own country.

The war's end has not resolved this conflict. In principle, it's clear what the left should stand for: multilateral supervision of security, peacekeeping, and reconstruction; handover as soon as possible to an Iraqi government; the rule of law; basic human rights—including, it always needs to be stressed, women's rights—and democratic institutions; and de-Baathification of Iraqi society. But applying these principles to the actually existing situation is at best a convoluted task. Pace those leftists who have moved seamlessly from "no war" to "end the occupation," the most immediate danger to the Iraqis is the Bushites' limited attention span. Having already demonstrated their boredom with the mundane task of policing, and ever unwilling to spend any money except on conquest itself, they are all too likely to pull our troops out prematurely, leaving behind a chaotic mess or whatever inheritors of power prove most convenient. If anything, we need more troops to establish and maintain security until an international force can take over.

Furthermore, if a liberal secular government is to emerge in Iraq, that project will require the active support of the United States. I suspect that, as Qanbar and Makiya claim, there is a significant constituency for such a government, given Iraq's large urban population. But the only indigenous organized group calling for a democratic secular state is the Communist Party, which is too small to hold its own against the Islamists. The other main force for liberal secularism is the dominant faction of the INC, headed by the much-maligned Ahmed Chalabi. From a left perspective it has two drawbacks: it's composed of exiles whose internal connections are uncertain, and it's sponsored by the Pentagon. Still, loath as I am to be aligned with Paul Wolfowitz on any matter, Chalabi and his people are good guys in this postwar context—democrats and insistent proponents of de-Baathification. Democratic leftists should support them, while also demanding that the Communists be included in negotiations to form a new government. At the same time, we should strongly oppose any effort by the State Department to make a deal with supposedly moderate, pro-democracy Shiite clergy, as urged by both the *New York Times* and the *Wall Street Journal*. Bush may well buy the conventional foreign-policy wisdom that we can be friends with good, pro-American fundamentalists who are easily distinguished from the evil terrorist kind. (As usual, the tradeoff of women's rights will not be seen as a problem.) That idea will be all the more tempting if the Iraqi Communists begin to be perceived as a threat. But in the current volatile situation it is doubtful that religious "moderates"—assuming they are not merely telling the Americans what they want to hear—would be an effective bulwark against the militant theocrats. The administration may want Turkey, but it could get Iran.

One last irony: to the extent that the war was about the future of the Iraqi people, the diplomatic establishment in the United States and Europe has been and continues to be a model of cynical, Metternichean unconcern. But to the extent that the war was about aggrandizing the Bush administration at the expense of international cooperation and American democracy, this same establishment—and the transnational corporations it represents—could be, for the moment, our best hope. The Bushites are a rogue regime, a runaway faction of capital. It's hardly in the interest of the mainstream of the global ruling class that international checks and balances on U.S. power dissolve, or that the American economy collapse under the weight of unemployment, reckless tax cutting, and huge military outlays. At a time when the American left is terminally weak and the Democrats reduced to a squeak, look to the corporate globalizers to rebel against the new American order.

Dissent, Summer 2003

The Mass Psychology
of Terrorism

The symbolism of the Twin Towers has been much remarked on: they are said to have represented the forces of modernity in general and global capitalism in particular. Yet oddly, it has been more or less ignored that the towers were also and quite obviously sexual symbols. What might it mean for men to commit mass murder by smashing symbols of desire—desire that in terms of their religious convictions means impurity, decadence, evil—and at the same time destroy themselves? Can it be that those symbols and the set of realities they represented were at the deepest level a source of intolerable attraction and temptation to these men, one that could be defended against only by means of total obliteration? Was the rage that such an act must entail directed solely against an external enemy, or was it also against the actors' own unfreedom? In short, was the hijackers' plunge a spectacular dual act of sadomasochism?

When I raised these questions at the conference from which this book arose, the audience responded with nervous tittering. Perhaps people thought I was trying to make some satirical point they didn't get; perhaps they thought I had gone off the deep end. Or maybe they were merely startled by the intrusion of sex into what was supposed to be serious leftist analysis of international politics. In any case, the reaction was not unfamiliar to me. For a brief period in the 1960s and '70s, a portion of the left concerned itself with the psychosexual dimension of politics; but even then such insights were rarely applied to the international arena. By now, in an era of anti-Freudian backlash and pervasive anxiety about changes in our sexual culture, they have been entirely purged from the political conversation.

This absence is, in my view, disastrous. Without understanding the psychosexual aspect of political violence and domination—and the cultural questions with which it is intertwined—we cannot make sense of what happened on September 11; indeed, we cannot make sense of the history of the 20th century. I don't propose that we discuss psychosexual politics *instead* of the very real, and certainly crucial, economic, and geopolitical issues that have shaped the Middle Eastern and South Asian condition, from oil to the legacy of colonialism and the Cold War to the ascendancy of neoliberalism to the Israeli-Palestinian conflict. Rather, my claim is that the particular kind of crisis Islamic fundamentalism represents erupts when economic and geopolitical issues converge with cultural and psychosexual conflict. Though one member of my restless conference audience accused me of anti-Arab racism for speculating on the hijackers' sexual motivation, I do not view this convergence and its consequences as peculiar to the Arab or Islamic world. Indeed, the paradigm of such crises occurred in Europe with Hitler's rise to power. "Ethnic cleansing" in Bosnia—in which Muslims were the victims—is a more recent European example, notable for, among other things, the mystified reaction of so many observers: how, in a modern European country and a cosmopolitan city like Sarajevo could such an outbreak of barbarism occur? Evidently they were unaware that a similar incredulity had followed the Holocaust.

In fact, the necessary condition for such outbreaks is "modernity"—catchall shorthand for the ongoing, worldwide cultural revolution that includes the assaults of capitalism, science and technology, Enlightenment liberalism, and democratic movements in the broad sense against the patriarchal authoritarian form of social organization that in one or another version has dominated human culture for the last 5,000 years or so. This revolution is only about 200 years old. In the United States and Europe, which are supposed to represent its vanguard, it is very much unfinished; and yet it has had an impact virtually everywhere in the world. It is also driven by contradictions: if capitalism and imperialism have propelled it, so have socialism, communism, and anti-imperialist movements. To add still another layer of convolutions, both capitalist and anticapitalist, imperialist and anti-imperialist forces have been counterrevolutionary as well—often upholding or opportunistically allying with patriarchal reaction and, more crucially, substituting their own versions of neo-patriarchal, anti-democratic tyranny for the traditional kind. Yet however contradictory and uneven, the cultural revolution has put freedom, equality, and democracy on the world agenda in an inescapable way; and the cutting edge of this project is a challenge to the structure of sexual life, the family, and male-female relations. Enormous psychological conflict, tension, and anxiety are the inevitable accompaniment of changes in this realm. And under certain circumstances those emotions get out of control.

Proponents of the "clash of civilizations" thesis are half right. There is such a clash, but not the kind Samuel Huntington has in mind; this is not a question of East versus West. The struggle of democratic secularism, religious tolerance, individual freedom, and feminism against authoritarian patriarchal religion, culture, and morality is going on all over the world. That includes the Islamic world, where dissidents are regularly jailed, killed, exiled, or merely intimidated and silenced by autocratic governments. In Iran the mullahs still have power, but young people are in open revolt against the Islamic regime. In Pakistan before the Afghan war, the urban middle classes worried that their society would be Talibanized. In Afghanistan the Revolutionary Association of Women of Afghanistan (RAWA) calls for a secular state. There are feminist movements in all these countries as well as in Egypt, Jordan, Turkey, Morocco. At the same time, religious and cultural reactionaries have mobilized to attack secular modernity in liberal democracies from Israel to the postcommunist countries of Eastern Europe to the United States. Jerry Falwell's view of September 11—that the massacre was God's judgment on an America that tolerates abortion, homosexuality, and feminism—mirrors Osama bin Laden's. Moreover, this clash—this culture war, if you will—exists not only within regions and within counties, but also within individuals. Social instability and personal ambivalence are its hallmarks.

When I speak of "patriarchal authoritarian" social organization, I refer to the historic institutions of the father-ruled family and monotheistic religion; to the ideology and morality perpetuated by these institutions, even as the institutions themselves weaken or break down; and to those aspects of all existing societies (such as corporate and state bureaucracies) that still model themselves on patriarchal institutions and replicate patriarchal ideology. The basic impulse of patriarchalism, in this sense, is the drive to dominate nature, a project that requires control over sexuality (nature within us), control of women and children (onto whom the anarchy of nature and sexuality is projected), and social hierarchies that assume people's inability to govern themselves. Desire is equated with unbridled selfishness, aggression, and violence. Morality is equated with self-abnegation, repression of desire, and submission to authority.

A traditional function of the family—now seriously challenged or compromised in many societies—has been to acculturate each new generation into this belief system and moral code by promising (if not always delivering) communal solidarity, economic security, love, and a degree of sexual satisfaction to those who obey its rules, while threatening violators with punishments ranging from physical force and violence to economic, social, or emotional isolation. Children characteristically internalize these promises and threats, identifying with their parents' morality and punishing themselves with guilt or shame for transgressing it. The patriarchal religions have served to reinforce this moral system with their conception of God as the ultimate parent; insofar as they retain social authority or political power, their appeal to the inner force of conscience is backed up by communal and legal sanctions. At the same time, religion has offered a pathway to freedom from the constriction and alienation that patriarchal morality imposes: not only the prospect of immortality as a reward for goodness, but access in the here-and-now to a spiritual realm where the constrictions don't apply, where one can make contact with the infinite and experience ecstasy or glimpse its possibility.

Of course, patriarchal morality and religion also condemn murder and other forms of predatory aggression. Their overriding claim to legitimacy even among unbelievers is their enforcement of such prohibitions, without which no society could survive. But here we run into a curious paradox, for in fact violence is endemic to patriarchal culture—violence that is outlawed and punished; violence that is overtly prohibited but covertly condoned; and violence that is sanctioned by state, familial, or religious authority. For defenders of the system, illicit violence is simply an unfortunate product of human nature, while licit violence is a necessary defense against unprovoked aggression and other kinds of anti-social behavior. Skeptics, however, might ask: can the high level of violence in patriarchal cultures be attributed to people's chronic, if largely unconscious, rage over the denial of their freedom and pleasure? To what extent is sanctioned or unofficially condoned violence—from war and capital punishment to lynching, wife-beating, and the rape of "bad" women to harsh penalties for "immoral" activities like drug-using and nonmarital sex to the religious or ideological persecution of totalitarian states—in effect a socially approved outlet for expressing that rage, as well as a way of relieving guilt by projecting one's own unacceptable desires onto scapegoats? Might religiously motivated violence, in particular, combine a longing for spiritual transcendence with guilt transmuted into self-righteous zeal and rage rationalized as service to God?

Most of the time, the ongoing violence of patriarchal cultures is contained and integrated into "normal" social functioning; but periodically it erupts into bloody wars, massacres, sadistic rampages, witch-hunts, the lesser of which make news and the more horrific, history. The 20th century—and now the beginning of the 21st—have been marked by a massive increase in the scale and frequency of such episodes, of which Al Qaeda's holy war is only the latest spectacular example. Not coincidentally, in the same period of history the destabilizing forces of cultural revolution have put traditional patriarchalism on the defensive to an unprecedented degree. This is an age in which mass media, mass migration, economic globalization, and the ubiquity of modern technology have vastly increased the points of provocative contact between modernity and its antagonists. Opponents of the cultural revolution have not scrupled to exploit its innovations—from modern mass communications, transportation, and weaponry to elections and civil liberties—while both the avatars of global capitalism and their anti-imperialist opponents have tried to enlist anti-modern movements in their struggles for dominance. As modernizing, liberalizing forces erode the repression that keeps rage unconscious and the social controls that keep violence contained, it becomes ever easier for a match of political grievance to ignite the gas of psychosexual tension, touching off a conflagration. Eventually, the fire is put out, for the time being. The gas remains.

In the 1920s Germany was a modern capitalist state with a liberal democracy that was, however, a fragile veneer over an authoritarian, sexually repressive culture; the patriarchal family ruled, subordinating women and youth—though the latter, stirred by new permissive currents, were growing restless. The Germans had no shortage of political grievances: a humiliating defeat in World War I, an economy crippled by unemployment and hyperinflation. The left offered an analysis of why the calamity of the war had happened and attempted to rally workers to fight for their concrete economic and political interests. Hitler instead offered a virulent backlash against Enlightenment values, centering on a racial myth *cum* paranoid fantasy: Aryan Germany had been "stabbed in the back" by the racially inferior Jews—the preeminent symbol of international capitalists, communists, cosmopolitans, sexual libertines, homosexuals, emancipated women, "race mixers," all the contaminating, alien influences of modernity. The majority of Germans, workers as well as the lower middle class, opted for Hitler's fantasy.

Right-wing industrialists supported Hitler because of his anti-communism, in the mistaken belief that they could control him; the Western powers abetted his rise in the hope that he would fight the Soviet Union (a strategy that set up a dramatic case of "blowback"). But Nazism was not a creature of the capitalist, imperialist right; it was a mass movement, of the kind that, ironically, was fostered by the very liberal democracy it despised. As radical psychoanalyst Wilhelm Reich put it in his classic work *The Mass Psychology of Fascism,* what defines a fascist movement is its "mixture of rebellious emotions and reactionary social ideas."[1] Political abjectness and economic ruin could explain why Germans wanted to rebel, but not why their rebellion took the form of support for totalitarian, genocidal sadism, or why they were so resistant to democratic and socialist appeals to rational self-interest.

It was in response to this conundrum that Reich and other psychoanalytically minded radicals, including the Marxist social theorists of the Frankfurt School, challenged the conventional economistic wisdom of the European left to argue that unconscious psychosexual conflict had played a central role in the triumph of Nazism. In the view of this Freudian left, the liberalism of Weimar had stirred up repressed longings for freedom—and rage at its suppression—that people whose characters had been formed by patriarchalism could not admit. While their anger was encouraged and legitimized by real political complaints, their underlying fear of freedom prevented them from contemplating real revolution.

For the mass of Germans, then, Hitler offered a solution to this impasse: he represented the authoritarian father who commanded submission—only in this case submission entailed the license, indeed the obligation, to vent rebellious rage by supporting and participating in persecution and mass murder. For young people caught between subservience to the family and guilt-ridden desires for freedom and sexual pleasure, this prospect had particular appeal: in the name of patriotic duty they could at once discharge and deny their unconscious hatred of the patriarch by directing that hatred toward the perceived enemies of the fatherland. At the same time, their repressed sexuality could find distorted expression in the sadistic pleasures of actual or vicarious cruelty, in the surrender to a charismatic leader, and in the quasi-religious ecstasy of mass rallies.

If this hypothesis of unconscious conflict allows us to make sense of the spectacle of an entire nation succumbing to a manifestly irrational ideology, it also sheds some light on the ubiquitous claim by Germans, Western governments, and Poles living in close proximity to Auschwitz that they didn't know the Holocaust was going on. I suspect that most *didn't* know, that such knowledge was blocked from consciousness along with a widespread emotional complicity in anti-Semitism. Indeed, the most disturbing implication of the Freudian left analysis is that Nazism was not a phenomenon peculiar to post–World War I Germany but, rather, had fulfilled a potential inherent in patriarchal culture, even in "advanced" societies—a potential that might be activated anywhere by destabilizing political events.

After World War II, the enormity of the Nazi catastrophe could no longer be denied, and so for a time blatant racism and anti-Semitism were socially unacceptable. Liberal Western governments preached tolerance while capital, chastened by the crisis it had barely survived and by the looming presence of the Soviet Union, cooperated with government and labor in curbing its most predatory features, fostering mass prosperity and with it social stability. The USSR and the communist dictatorships of Eastern Europe simply suppressed the culture war, imposing a modern secular regime (albeit without freedom or democracy) by fiat.[2] Meanwhile, moralists spoke of the Holocaust as an evil beyond comprehension, a confirmation of original sin, proof of the need for religion, and the futility of utopian projects. The culture that had produced the Nazis was not confronted; its overtly pathological aspects were merely re-repressed.

This détente did not last long. The 1960s and '70s brought a resumption of culture war in the United States and Western Europe, as a revolt from the left on behalf of racial equality, personal and sexual freedom, feminism, and gay liberation was soon followed by a backlash of religious and secular conservatives aimed at restoring traditional morality, social discipline, and white male dominance. In the '70s, American business reneged on its compact with labor and the welfare state, launching an era of renewed class warfare: while many factors contributed to this development, including the OPEC oil cartel, America's impending loss of the Vietnam War, and the rise of the transnational corporation, surely part of the story was that corporate investment in high wages and social welfare could no longer buy a compliant middle class—on the contrary, economic security had produced a generation with a subversive sense of entitlement.

The '60s revolt in the West was in turn a crucial influence on the democratic revolutions of Eastern Europe; yet the reality of the postcommunist era would turn out to be far darker than the euphoric expectations of 1989. With the collapse of communism, global capitalist triumphalism went into high gear. Neoliberal "shock therapy" and the abolition of communist social benefits devastated Eastern Europe's standard of living at the same time that fascists, nationalist fanatics, and religious reactionaries who had been silenced by communist regimes were once again free to operate. In Yugoslavia the combination proved lethal.

Not long after Francis Fukuyama declared "the end of history,"[3] the war in Bosnia would show that, if anything, history was taking up where it had left off in 1945. Yugoslavia was a poor country that had lived fairly well by borrowing from the West; but in the new era, Western banks were calling in its debt and Western governments were turning their back. It was also a country that was superficially modern and profoundly patriarchal, with a traditionalist, sexually repressed population. For a communist-apparatchik-turned-nationalist-demagogue like Slobodan Milosevic, or a fascist like Franjo Tudjman, these circumstances offered ample opportunity to mobilize people's rebellious emotions behind reactionary social ideas. The result was an insane genocidal war in which people turned their rage against neighbors who shared their language and culture— neighbors they had lived with, worked with, married without making ethnic distinctions. And again the world declined to look this irrationalism in the face or examine its roots, preferring to blame evil individuals and "ancient ethnic hatreds."

To examine Islamic fundamentalism through the lens of the last century's history is to discern a familiar pattern: psychopathology brought to the surface by the promise and threat of modernity and aggravated by political oppression. As with fascism, the rise of Islamic totalitarianism has partly to do with its populist appeal to class resentments and to feelings of political subordination and humiliation, but is at bottom a violent defensive reaction against the temptations of freedom. Islamic militants demonize the United States not simply because of its foreign policy—as so many American leftists would like to believe, despite the explicit pronouncements of the Islamists themselves—but because it exports and symbolizes cultural revolution.

In the wake of 9/11 it has often been noted that militant Islamism filled a vacuum created by the failures of secular leftist movements in the Middle East to improve the condition of the people or do away with corrupt regimes, from Egypt to Saudi Arabia, that collaborate with the West's neocolonial policies. And of course those failures are in no small part the result of relentless American opposition to leftism of any sort (in contrast to our support for Islamist fanatics we have deemed to be on our side, from the Saudi rulers to the Afghan mujahadeen). Yet none of this can really explain why so many people should be attracted to a movement that has no agenda for solving their real economic and political problems but, rather, serves up the fantasy that the answer is murder-suicide in pursuit of a holy war against infidels and the imposition of a draconian religious police state. The appeal of this fantasy cannot be understood without reference to the patriarchalism that governs the sexual and domestic lives of most people in the Islamic world. Osama bin Laden and his gang are themselves products of an ultra-patriarchal theocracy hardly less tyrannical than the Taliban's; if the catalyst for their rebellion was opposition to the Saudi regime, their ideology clearly derives from their upbringing within it.

Another clue to the psychopathology that drives the Islamist movement is its increasingly hysterical Jew-hatred, which has borrowed liberally from both Nazi and medieval Christian polemics. True to its characteristic evasions, the left has tended to dismiss Islamist anti-Semitism as a mere epiphenomenon of justified anger at Israel, which would presumably go away if justice were done. But is it not worth examining the strange mental processes that transmute a political grievance against Israel into a widespread delusion that the Jews masterminded the World Trade Center massacre? And what do we make of the execution of an American journalist who, before being beheaded, is forced to intone, "I am a Jew, my mother is a Jew, my father is a Jew"?

In any case, the war between Israel and the Arab and Islamic worlds has never been *only* about conflicting claims to a piece of land, the homelessness of the Palestinians, or the occupation of the West Bank; if it were, it would have been settled long ago. Rather, Islamist passion for Israel's obliteration has at its core revulsion at the perceived contamination of the holy land by an infidel nation; worse, a modern democracy; even worse, one populated by that quintessentially alien, blood-sucking tribe of rootless cosmopolitans, the Jews. Just as the Europeans once handed their unwelcome Jewish refugee problem to the Arabs, their genocidal anti-Jewish rhetoric has migrated to the Middle East; but the emotions that give the rhetoric its power are strictly indigenous. They are unlikely to be assuaged by an Israeli-Palestinian settlement; they are far more likely to be inflamed.

And if the worst should happen, the world will once again be shocked. We still don't know—and don't want to know.

In America it often happens that the lunatic right, in its feckless way, gets closer to the heart of the matter than the political mainstream, and so it was with Jerry Falwell's incendiary remark, and Pat Robertson's concurrence, about the cause of 9/11. There was a flurry of indignation in the media, but basically the incident was dismissed as an isolated moment of wretched excess. Most Americans, from George W. Bush to Noam Chomsky, resist the idea that the attack was an act of cultural war, and still fewer are willing to admit its intimate connection with the culture war at home.

That war has been a centerpiece of American politics for thirty years or more, shaping our debates and our policies on everything from abortion, censorship, and crime to race, education, and social welfare, to the impeachment of Bill Clinton and the 2000 election (with those ubiquitous maps of "blue" liberal coasts versus "red" heartland). Nor, at this moment, does the government know whether foreign or domestic terrorists were responsible for the anthrax offensive. Yet we shrink from seeing the relationship between our own cultural conflicts and the logic of *jihad.* We are especially eager to absolve religion of any responsibility for the violence committed in its name: for that ubiquitous post–9/11 cliché, "This has nothing to do with Islam," read "Anti-abortion terrorism has nothing to do with Christianity." Post-Enlightenment, post-Reformation, post-feminist, post-sexual-revolution, liberal democratic nation though we are, the legacy of patriarchalism still weighs on us: our social policies on sex and the family are confused and inconsistent, our psyches more conservative than the actual conditions of our lives. We are deeply anxious and ambivalent about cultural issues, and one way we deal with this is to deny their importance, even sometimes their existence.

For the most part Americans speak of culture and politics as if they were two separate realms. Conservatives accuse the left of politicizing culture and see their own cultural-political offensive against the social movements of the '60s as an effort to restore to culture its rightful autonomy. Centrists deplore the culture war as an artifact of "extremists on both sides" and continually pronounce it dead. The economic-justice left regards cultural politics as a distraction from its efforts to win support for a populist economic program. Multiculturalists pursue the political goal of equality and respect for minority and non-Western cultures, but are reluctant to make political judgments about cultural practices: feminist universalists have been regularly attacked for "imposing Western values" by criticizing genital mutilation and other forms of female subjection in the Third World.

The artificial separation of politics and culture is nowhere more pronounced than in the discourse of foreign policy and international affairs. For the American government, economic, geopolitical, and military considerations determine our allies and our enemies. Democracy (almost always defined narrowly in terms of a freely elected government, rather than as a way of life) and human rights (only recently construed as including even the most elementary of women's rights) are invoked by policy makers mainly to justify alliances or antagonisms that already exist. While the Cold War inspired much genuine passion on behalf of freedom and the open society, there's no denying that its fundamental motive was the specter of an alternative to capitalism spreading across the globe and encouraging egalitarian heresies at home. The one cultural issue that seems genuinely to affect our relationship with foreign states is our mania for restricting the international drug supply (except when we ourselves are arming drug cartels for some strategic purpose). The left, meanwhile, criticizes the aims of American foreign policy; yet despite intensified concern with human rights in recent years, most leftists still share the government's assumptions about what kinds of issues are important: the neoliberal economic agenda and struggles over resources like oil, the maintenance of friendly client states versus national self-determination, and so on. And like the United States, leftists have often displayed a double standard on human rights, tending to gloss over the abuses of populist or anti-imperialist regimes.

Given these tropisms, it's unsurprising that the absence of religious and personal freedom, the brutal suppression of dissent, and the extreme oppression of women in Islamic theocracies have never been serious subjects of foreign policy debates. Long before the Taliban, many feminists were upset by U.S. support for the mujahadeen; yet this never became a public issue. Even now the Bush administration, for all its self-congratulatory noises about Afghan women's liberation, refuses to lead or even allow an international peacekeeping force in Afghanistan that could stop fundamentalist warlords from regaining power.

Back in the 1950s, in pursuit of its Cold War aims in Iran, the United States overthrew an elected secular government it judged too left-wing and installed the tyrannical and deeply unpopular Shah, then dumped him in the face of Khomeini's 1979 revolution. Except for feminists, the American left, with few exceptions, supported the revolution and brushed off worries about the Ayatollah, though he had made no secret of his theocratic aims: the important thing was to get rid of the Shah—other issues could be dealt with later. Ten years later, on the occasion of the *fatwa* against Salman Rushdie, the Bush I administration appeared far more interested in appeasing Islamic governments and demonstrators offended by Rushdie's heretical book than in condemning Khomeini's death sentence, while an unnerving number of liberals and leftists accused Rushdie and his defenders of cultural imperialism and insensitivity to Muslim sensibilities. Throughout, both defenders and detractors of our alliance with "moderate" Saudi Arabia have ignored Saudi women's slave-like situation, regarding it as "their culture" and none of our business, except when it raises questions about how Americans stationed in the Gulf are expected to behave. It's as if, in discussing South Africa, apartheid had never been mentioned.

There are many things to be learned from the shock of September 11; surely one of the more important is that culture is not only a political matter but a matter of life and death. It follows that a serious long-range strategy against Islamic fundamentalist terrorism must entail open and emphatic opposition to theocracy, to authoritarian religious movements (including messianic Jewish fundamentalists in Israel and the West Bank), and to the subjugation of women. The corollary is moral and material support for the efforts of liberals, modernizers, democratic secularists, and feminists to press for reforms in Middle Eastern and South Asian societies. Yet to define the enemy as fundamentalism—rather than "evil" anti-American fundamentalists, as opposed to the "friendly" kind—is also to make a statement about American cultural politics. Obviously nothing of the sort can be expected from George W. Bush and John Ashcroft, but our problem is not only leaders who are fundamentalist Christians. More important is the tendency of the left and the center to appease the right and downplay the culture war rather than make an uncompromising defense of freedom, feminism, and the separation of church and state. It remains to be seen whether fear of terrorism will trump the fear of facing our own psychosexual contradictions.

Implicating Empire, 2003

NOTES

This essay originally appeared in *Implicating Empire: Globalization and Resistance in the 21st Century World Order,* ed. Stanley Aronowitz, Heather Gautney, and Clyde W. Barrow (New York: Basic Books, 2003).

1. Wilhelm Reich, *The Mass Psychology of Fascism,* first English ed., trans. Theodore P. Wolfe (New York: Orgone Institute Press, 1946).

2. While this chapter focuses on fascism and religious fundamentalism, a comprehensive discussion of the mass psychology of terrorism would also have to address communist totalitarianism, including such episodes as the Stalin terror, the Chinese Cultural Revolution, and the mass killing in Cambodia. Communism has its own distinctive psychopolitical dynamics, whose most striking feature is the Orwellian disconnect between professed values—freedom, justice, peace, etc.—and actual behavior.

3. Francis Fukuyama, "The End of History?" *National Interest* (Summer 1989).

Dreaming of War

You don't have to be Sigmund Freud to surmise that war has a perverse appeal for the human race, nor is the attraction limited to religious fanatics committing mass murder and suicide for the greater glory of God. Among the so-called civilized it takes many insidious and sublimated forms. In the week after September 11, one of the more disturbing themes to surface in the press was the suggestion that as devastating as this attack has been, something good may come of it: an improvement in the American character or, at any rate, a salutary blow to our purported complacency and self-indulgence.

An editorial in the *New York Times* opined, "There has been a sense that whatever comes next must naturally be diminished. That need not be true. . . . Americans desperately want to commit to something greater than themselves. That was the secret of what we admired in the World War II era, and it is what this new war against terrorism will require as well. The awful week of death and destruction that has just ended might be the invitation to create a great new generation and a finer United States." The *Financial Times* gave us Francis "End of History" Fukuyama: "As with individuals, adversity can have many positive effects. Enduring national character is shaped by shared trauma. . . . Peace and prosperity, by contrast, encourage preoccupation with one's own petty affairs." Americans have been allowed to "wallow in such self-indulgent behaviour as political scandal or identity politics." (Of course, a terrorist attack by Islamic militants is identity politics carried to its logical extreme, but never mind.)

And then there was *New York Times* Op-Ed columnist Frank Rich, who concluded that any event with the power to force shark attacks off *People*'s cover can't be all bad: "Not all of what's gone may be a cause for mourning. . . . This week's nightmare, it's now clear, has awakened us from a frivolous if not decadent decade-long dream . . . that we could have it all without having to pay any price, and that national suffering of almost any kind could be domesticated into an experience of virtual terror akin to a theme park ride." Gary Condit, Lizzie Grubman, overblown fears of school shootings, Elián González, the California blackout that wasn't, *Survivor,* a Hollywood-sanitized Pearl Harbor—all are breathlessly invoked as horrible examples of ersatz catastrophe now swept away by the real cleansing thing. President Bush, Rich declares, must prepare us for sacrifice, "something many living Americans, him included, have never had to muster"—as though that gap in experience were self-evidently to be deplored.

Have we come to this? Purification of our national soul through war? It has a ring to it, all right; an unnervingly familiar ring at that. The authors of these commentaries cannot be accused of war fever, exactly. They are not, after all, among the ranters venting their anger by demanding that we wipe most of the Middle East off the map. They merely hope to use a lemon to make lemonade, as it were. But if that hope resonates with enough people—if Americans are seduced into going for the secret erotic payoff of sacrifice, discipline and submergence in the collective will—the effect will be more repressive than a crude crackdown on civil liberties could ever be.

To begin with, the premise that this country ("That fat, daydreaming America," in Rich's words) has been corrupted by prosperity is a lie. The "prosperity" of the past decade has mainly consisted of the dramatic concentration of wealth among 20 percent of the population. Most people have continued to struggle economically; their daydreams, if any, were about the riches they were told they were supposed to have, but that had somehow eluded them. In any case the boom was already over, without any help from terrorists.

It's true, as Fukuyama argues, that in recent years "many Americans lost interest in public affairs, and in the larger world . . . others expressed growing contempt for government." True too, as the *Times* suggests, that most Americans have been disinclined to commit themselves to any larger cause. But this is not because we are too well fed. Rather, a triumphalist corporate capitalism, free at last of the specter of Communism, has mobilized its economic power to relentlessly marginalize all nonmarket values; to subordinate every aspect of American life to corporate "efficiency" and the bottom line; to demonize not only government but the very idea of public service and public goods.

Will putting the country on a war footing do anything to change this, other than getting the free marketeers to tone down their antistatist rhetoric? On the contrary, things have just gotten infinitely more difficult for the nascent rebellion against "globalization," which is to say world domination by transnational capital. The mass demonstration that was to have taken place in Washington September 29–30 has been canceled. Few would have had the stomach for it anyway. And though some smaller groups are still going, how can the public possibly hear them the way they wish to be heard? A serious effort to put public affairs back on the American agenda, to revive people's sense that they have a stake in the way our society is run, would require a national debate on privatization, deregulation, income redistribution, the rights of workers, the share of our national wealth that should be devoted to subsidizing healthcare, childcare, education, support for the aged. Implementing such an agenda would require massive infusions of public funds. Does anyone believe this crisis will stimulate such a debate or encourage public spending for anything other than the military, law enforcement, the national security infrastructure, relief for the airlines and other stressed industries? Will Congress, in the interest of national solidarity, rush to repeal Bush's tax cut for the rich?

As for the obsession with violence and scandal that so exercises Frank Rich, its source is not an excess of contentment but chronic anxiety, at times blossoming into full-blown panic. The day the frame froze, it was on a culture that had become ambivalent to the point of schizophrenia: caught between the still-potent hype of the boom and the reality, for most, of a stagnant and increasingly insecure standard of living; enmeshed in our ongoing, seemingly intractable tensions between the impulse to freedom and the fear of it; between desire and guilt, secular modernity and religious moralism (here too this latter conflict breeds violent fundamentalists). The boundaries of political debate had steadily narrowed, not because we were fat and happy but because it was taboo to challenge in any serious way the myth that we were fat and happy. The notion that there might be any need for, or possibility of, profound changes in the institutions that shape American life—work, family, technology, the primacy of the car and the single-family house—is foreign to the mainstream media that define our common sense. And so conflicts that cannot be addressed politically have expressed themselves by other means. From public psychodramas like the O. J. Simpson trial, the Lewinsky scandal and Columbine to disaster movies, talk shows and "reality TV," popular culture carries the burden of our emotions about race, feminism, sexual morality, youth culture, wealth, competition, exclusion, a physical and social environment that feels out of control.

Will this confrontation with real terror kill our taste for the vicarious kind? Perhaps; but it does not follow that we will be less susceptible to illusion. As many have pointed out, if this is war it is a mutant variation: a war in which the enemy is protean and elusive, and how to strike back effectively is far from clear. Yet for a decade Americans have been steeped in the rhetoric of "zero tolerance" and the faith that virtually all problems from drug addiction to lousy teaching can be solved by pouring on the punishment. Even without a Commander in Chief who pledges to rid the world of evildoers, smoke them out of their holes and the like, we would be vulnerable to the temptation to brush aside frustrating complexities and relieve intolerable fear (at least for the moment) by settling on one or more scapegoats to crush. To imagine that trauma casts out fantasy is a dangerous mistake.

Similarly, while the need to focus on our national crisis will no doubt supplant the excruciating triviality of our usual political conversation, it will if anything reinforce the denial of our deeper social problems. In emergencies—and war is the ultimate emergency—such long-range concerns are suspended. This may be unavoidable, but it is never desirable, except to tyrants. I'm not a pacifist—I believe that war is sometimes necessary—but I agree with pacifists that there's nothing ennobling about it. I accept that in this emergency, national defense must be our overriding concern. But let's not compound our losses with deluded bombast about what we have to gain.

The Nation, September 2001

Freedom from Religion

George W. Bush's creation of a federal office to coordinate public financing of euphemistically labeled "faith-based" social services is a bold assault on the separation of church and state; it is also, ironically, a triumph of bipartisanship. During the presidential campaign, the religious right's long-running crusade against "secular humanism" achieved its Nixon-in-China moment. Rushing headlong from the mythical anti-Clinton backlash, Al Gore and Joe Lieberman did their best to outdo the Republicans at religiosity. Gore made a point of his born-again Christianity, rejected "hollow secularism" and declared his support for "charitable choice," a policy that would loosen the rules for allotting public funds to faith-based programs. Lieberman was even bolder: he responded to what he called the "miracle" of his nomination with repeated public professions of faith in God, along with declarations that religion is the basis of morality and that the Constitution provides "freedom of religion, not freedom from religion." In a speech at Notre Dame, he linked secularism to a "vacuum of values" that had been filled by—what else?—"our omnipresent popular culture."

As a Jew and a Democrat, Lieberman was able to say things no Christian Republican could get away with. While the ACLU and a few other usual suspects voiced objections, the overall response from liberals was distinctly muted. Non–Orthodox Jewish organizations are normally staunch defenders of secularism, yet the only major spokesperson to criticize Lieberman's rhetoric was Abe Foxman of the Anti-Defamation League. No doubt the dearth of protest had something to do with reluctance to hurt the Gore campaign, appear hostile to a noble experiment in diversity or, in the case of Jewish groups, rain on the parade of the first Jewish vice-presidential candidate. But it's also true that Lieberman's views are common among centrist Democrats and have gained increasing legitimacy in progressive circles. Eleanor Brown, a fellow of the neo-liberal New America Foundation, defended him on the *New York Times* Op-Ed page. E. J. Dionne, Garry Wills and Christian minister and antipoverty activist Jim Wallis were among the left-of-center commentators who concurred.

For a year we had been hearing that cultural politics were passé. The flame-out of the ultraright's crazed jihad against Bill Clinton left chastened conservatives gearing up for a presidential campaign in which abortion would be relegated to a footnote and the Republicans' most loyal supporters would be the Christian who? On sexual issues we seemed to have arrived, for the moment, at a standoff (not to be mistaken for a resolution). But the battle for the culture never really subsided, only shifted its rhetorical ground. The use of "family" as a metaphor and catalyst for cultural conservatism is now being rivaled by a newly popular catchword: "faith." And just as "pro-family" ideology is not confined to the political right but has influenced liberals, leftists, even feminists, what might be called "pro-church" sentiment cuts across the political spectrum.

This is bad news. I believe that a democratic polity requires a secular state: one that does not fund or otherwise sponsor religious institutions and activities; that does not display religious symbols; that outlaws discrimination based on religious belief, whether by government or by private employers, landlords or proprietors—that does, in short, guarantee freedom from as well as freedom of religion. Furthermore, a genuinely democratic society requires a secular ethos: one that does not equate morality with religion, stigmatize atheists, defer to religious interests and aims over others, or make religious belief an informal qualification for public office. Of course, secularism in the latter sense is not mandated by the First Amendment. It's a matter of sensibility, not law. Politicians have a right to brandish their faith and attack my secular outlook as hollow. That they have such a right, however, does not mean exercising it is a good idea. Politicians also have a right to argue that Christ's teachings are essential to public morality, but few would dare devalue the citizenship of Jews in such a fashion. Why is it more acceptable to marginalize the irreligious with appeals to God and faith?

The issue for the left is not religious participation in politics per se. As anti-secularists are fond of pointing out, churches have played a significant role in left movements for peace, civil rights and abolition of the death penalty. But for the most part, religious liberals and leftists have allied with their secular counterparts on matters of common concern, rather than working to promote the power of religion itself or taking issue with the secular left on specifically religious grounds. In fact, many religious progressives, including some whose community organizations would be eligible to receive public funds, oppose the erosion of secularism in general and measures like "charitable choice" in particular.

There has been one important, if numerically small, exception to this community of interests: the antiabortion movement among liberal and left Catholics and some religious pacifists. There has also been a good deal of tension within the secular left between feminist and gay activists committed to abortion rights, equal protection for gays and sexual liberalism generally, and progressive organizations unwilling to take stands that might jeopardize alliances with Catholics or black evangelicals on labor, poverty or racial issues. Moreover, since the 1970s, when the anti-'60s cultural backlash took hold, a significant portion of the left has argued that criticizing traditional values—whether familial or religious—abets the right by alienating middle America.

But what's happening now is new: some liberals and leftists, both religious and secular, are defending or actively supporting efforts to dilute the separation of church and state and increase the power and influence of religion in American life; and those efforts increasingly invoke the language of multiculturalism, tolerance and concern for the poor. In a *Nation* article last year, Dennis Hoover endorsed charitable choice: "Progressives can't afford to ignore realistic opportunities to help poor people," he argued, and so long as government funding does not discriminate in favor of Christianity or directly support religious activity, it "advances social justice and a robustly impartial pluralism in the relationship between religion and public life." Similarly, advocates of vouchers that can be used at parochial schools, such as former Atlanta mayor and UN ambassador Andrew Young, have contended that nit-picking about church and state should not stand in the way of educational opportunity for poor black and Latino kids.

Beyond specific policy issues, pro-church arguments aim to shift progressive sympathies from secularists battling the political power of churches toward the claims of churches and believers that they are victims of a biased and rigid secularism. In part, those claims reflect the anger of religious intellectuals who feel marginalized in the secular cultures of the academy and the media and personally insulted by stereotypes that assume Catholics mindlessly take orders from the Pope, evangelical Christians are superstitious ignoramuses and "religious intellectual" is an oxymoron. Believers have also complained of protests that go beyond targeting church officials and their politics to take aim at worshipers themselves, like ACT UP's widely (and in my view rightly) criticized disruption of services at St. Patrick's Cathedral.

But charges of discrimination have also taken far more problematic forms. Consider the 1989 crisis over the publication of Salman Rushdie's *The Satanic Verses,* which depicted Mohammed in a manner that scandalized the Islamic world. Censorship, book-burning and riots in Islamic countries reached a climax in Iranian dictator Khomeini's call to Muslims around the world to execute Rushdie for blasphemy. A clearer case of religious oppression would be hard to come by; yet the writers and civil libertarians who protested on Rushdie's behalf (myself included) were criticized from the left—by columnist Juan Gonzalez and liberal theologian Harvey Cox, among others—for their supposed cultural imperialism and insensitivity to devout Muslims' feelings.

Most such sentiment probably had more to do with reflexive pro–Third World attitudes than with concern for religion as such. But parallel arguments have surfaced in home-grown controversies about art deemed sacrilegious and offensive to Christians—such as Andres Serrano's notorious depiction of a crucifix immersed in urine, *Piss Christ,* and Chris Ofili's elephant-dung-encrusted Virgin Mary in the 1999 "Sensation" exhibit at the Brooklyn Museum of Art. These works have repeatedly been characterized as expressions of anti-Catholic bigotry; that Serrano received a grant from the National Endowment for the Arts and the Brooklyn Museum gets support from New York City have been cited as evidence of state-sponsored hate. As liberal Catholic and *Commonweal* editor Margaret O'Brien Steinfels put it in a *New York Times* Op-Ed, "Elephant dung smeared on a church, synagogue or mosque would get the perpetrator arrested."

Yet both these artists have chosen to engage with their own religious tradition, through images that to my secular eye are designed not to insult believers but to question the disgust with the body and materiality embedded in orthodox Christianity and endemic to our culture. In *Piss Christ,* the radiant, sensuous liquid that surrounds the cross is not identifiable as urine unless you read the title. It seems clear—especially in the context of other Serrano works involving equally gorgeous, abstracted images of blood and semen—that the artist is invoking the idea of piss as desecration to challenge it with another possibility: that bodily fluids are holy. Similarly, Ofili's sweet-faced Madonna, with its dung (which is not "smeared") and little pornographic cherubs, is an earthy rather than ethereal figure. If these images are bigoted, then so by implication is any art that refuses a conventional reverence toward religious icons or invests them with idiosyncratic meanings that contradict orthodox beliefs.

Critics of organized religion who call attention to its history of persecuting dissenters have also been charged with bias on the grounds that modern secular regimes have committed even more murders. In his Notre Dame speech Lieberman recalled, as an illustration of antireligious intolerance, that when Jim Wallis gave a talk at Harvard on religion and public life, a member of the liberal audience asked, "What about the Inquisition?" Is it then intolerant of anti-Communists to bring up the gulag, since after all Christianity hardly has clean hands? Some commentators have even implied that opposition to the sexual politics of conservative churches is tantamount to discrimination. In the *Times,* religion columnist Peter Steinfels, also on the Catholic left, scoffs at Democrats' criticism of Bush for speaking at Bob Jones University; as he sees it, Bob Jones's anachronistic version of anti-Catholicism is innocuous compared with the way Catholic Democrats have been made to feel like "pariahs" by their party's "unqualified support for abortion rights." (It's not as unqualified as all that, but never mind.) On his list of anti-Catholic prejudices held by America's supposedly enlightened opinion-makers, he includes the notion that the Church's sexual standards are "unnatural, repressive, and hypocritical." I concede that "hypocritical" is a presumptuous judgment, and "unnatural" a philosophical can of worms. But the belief that proscriptions on sex outside marriage, homosexuality, masturbation, birth control and abortion are repressive (and, I would add, sexist) is not a prejudice—it represents a basic disagreement with the Church about the conditions of human well-being.

Just as the family issue migrated from the precincts of the Christian right into the political mainstream via neoconservatives, communitarians and New Democrats, the faith issue has followed a similar route. The Moral Majority and the Christian Coalition, with their influence on the Republican Party—a Justice Department run by John Ashcroft would be their biggest prize yet —opened up political space for attacks on secularism. But the biblical rhetoric of right-wing evangelicals, with its invocations to a "Christian nation" and sectarian campaigns like the fight against teaching evolution in the public schools, have little popular appeal outside the South; nor do they speak to the centrist elites in the media and the governing class, let alone the left. Ashcroft is the nose-thumbing choice of an accidental President; if confirmed (as this issue goes to press the Senate has not yet voted) he will no doubt do real damage, but he will also excite constant opposition, and his influence on the larger culture will be minimal. Before pro-church views could make real headway, they had to be translated into a less parochial language.

Two Christian intellectuals have been key figures in developing that language. Richard John Neuhaus, now editor of the "theocon" journal *First Things,* wrote what might be considered the pro-church movement's canonical work, *The Naked Public Square,* which appeared in 1984; Yale law professor Stephen Carter published his influential book *The Culture of Disbelief* in 1993 and recently came out with a new polemic, *God's Name in Vain.* While their politics are different—Neuhaus is firmly on the right, Carter a cautious mixture of socially conservative and liberal impulses—they agree that a public role for religion is essential to American democracy. Both argue that secularism thwarts the will of the great majority of Americans who believe in God, that there needs to be a prominent place for institutional religion as a check on state power and that the main purpose of the First Amendment's establishment clause is to protect the church from the state, not vice versa. Together they have changed the debate by challenging secularism on its own moral ground, as the defender of democratic values.

The Naked Public Square was Neuhaus's response to the emergence of the evangelical Christian right and the resulting liberal panic: he agrees that the movement is dangerously authoritarian but proclaims it an inevitable reaction to the relentlessly antireligious program of the secular elite. Secularism, he maintains, is itself an antidemocratic, indeed potentially totalitarian pseudo-religion whose institutional form is an ever-expanding state that confuses its own aims with transcendence. Carter's complementary view is that secularists, in opposing any government accommodation to religion, trivialize people's religious convictions by treating them as a matter of choice rather than an absolute commitment. (His examples range from the Supreme Court decision that Native Americans cannot violate drug laws by using peyote in religious rituals, to rulings that Jehovah's Witnesses cannot prevent hospitals from giving their children transfusions, to the voiding of a law that denied civil divorces to Orthodox Jewish men who refused to give their wives religious divorces so they could remarry.) As he sees it, defining religious freedom as purely a matter of private conscience rather than public recognition forces the believing majority to suppress the most essential part of themselves in their public lives. This trivialization, he argues, hinders the church's proper role as an independent, prophetic voice challenging the hegemony of the state.

These arguments confuse democracy with populism and show little concern for the rights of the minority of unbelievers, who are regarded not as dissidents but as powerful agents of the state. For the neoconservative Neuhaus, what's oppressive about the state is precisely its intervention on behalf of individuals—like homosexuals objecting to discrimination or opponents of publicly sponsored Christmas trees—who do not want to be subjected to "the beliefs, symbols, and rules of the majority culture." Carter, meanwhile, proclaims religion to be the source of movements of the oppressed: in a rewriting of history characteristic of antisecularists he equates the civil rights movement with Martin Luther King Jr. and the black church. (What about A. Philip Randolph, Rosa Parks, Ella Baker, Bob Moses, John Lewis, Julian Bond, Jim Forman—secular activists all—and such non–church-run organizations as the NAACP, CORE and SNCC?)

But in demanding that state and society defer to the absolutism of religious devotion, Carter gives the game away, for as many devout believers will admit, there is an inherent tension between religion and democracy. The authority of the biblical religions—which are the main subject of this debate—is embedded in sacred texts, religious laws and ecclesiastical hierarchies that claim to transmit absolute truth and serve the will of a Supreme Being. Democracy, in contrast, depends on the Enlightenment values of freedom and equality, which are essential to genuine self-government. In a democracy, truths are provisional and subject to debate—which doesn't mean arbitrary, only arguable. A society grounded in democratic principles can neither restrict people's choices because they don't conform to religious truths nor give them privileged treatment because they do.

The democratic spirit does encourage respect for acts of conscience—whether by recognizing them legally, as with conscientious objection, or by limiting penalties for nonviolent civil disobedience—but it can't extend respect only to acts mandated by a belief in God or condone acts that violate others' rights (like denying one's child life-saving medical treatment). Nor, even with the laudable intention of helping desperate Jewish women, can it threaten men with loss of their civil right to a divorce because they refuse to participate in a religious ritual. As for laws that capriciously interfere with personal freedom, the answer is to fight the law, not to carve out a religious exception: members of the Native American Church should be permitted to alter their consciousness with peyote, but so should everyone else. (In this regard, Carter makes a valid point: it's usually minority religions whose pleas for exemption from burdensome laws get brushed aside; laws that would burden mainstream religious practice don't get passed in the first place.) If believers feel that their faith is trivialized and their true selves compromised by a society that will not give religious imperatives special weight, their problem is not that secularists are antidemocratic but that democracy is antiabsolutist.

Insofar as religion is a matter of personal conscience and identity, a means for individuals and congregations to pursue life's ultimate questions and their vision of a transcendent reality, religious freedom is not only compatible with democracy but essential to it. Among those who favor a secular society, many are believers. Many other secularists, in an age influenced by psychedelic drugs and Eastern spiritual disciplines, value the freedom to pursue their own versions of transcendence, which they may or may not define as religious. The conflict with democracy arises when organized religion pursues its interests as a social and political institution.

Apart from its relationship to the state, the church is an independent source of social control, exercising authority through the culture and first of all through the socialization of children. Like the church itself, the family is not a democratic institution, and freedom of religion in this society applies only to adults; parents have a taken-for-granted right to impose on their children their own religious beliefs and associated moral—especially sexual—prohibitions (the Jehovah's Witnesses case is the rare exception). While some people choose their religion, in "*free* acknowledgment of that by which we are bound," as Neuhaus puts it, most absorb it at an age when parental authority is what counts. In fact, it's doubtful that adults who reject religion can truly escape the influence of a religious upbringing—a proposition that explains a lot about Americans' ambivalence on moral and cultural issues.

So long as American society preserved relatively clear boundaries between public and private and applied democratic ideals to a narrowly defined political realm, conflict between secularism and religion was kept to a minimum. (Even a notorious incident like the Scopes trial had more to do with the conflict between mainstream Protestantism and fundamentalism.) But the movements of the '60s destabilized that détente. Now issues of sexual morality, male-female relations, childrearing and education—the very issues on which the institutional authority of religion is most at stake—are politicized. The democratic quest for individual autonomy, equality of political power and a strict interpretation of the establishment clause now extends to all cultural institutions and norms, challenging religious orthodoxy on issues that range from school prayer to censorship, nonmarital sex and childbearing, abortion, divorce and same-sex marriage. Secularists tend to see religious opposition to social liberalism purely as an attempt to impose church doctrine on unbelievers, but this is too simple. Believers' complaint against a secular culture is above all that it exposes their own children to powerful—and as they see it disastrous—temptations to choose a different way of life.

One need not trivialize the fears of religious parents to recognize that this is at bottom a complaint against democracy itself. The devout cannot have it both ways. Pro-church arguments have made headway on the left by purporting to defend the democratic rights of the religious, but this is not really a debate about rights. Rather, what pro-church militants are demanding is exemption from challenge to, or even criticism of, their claim to a privileged role in shaping social values. With no sense of contradiction, they presume the right, even obligation, to attack secularists' worldview while feeling entitled to unquestioned "respect," which is to say suffocating reverence, for their own beliefs. In a democracy, however, organized religion has no more right to be shielded from opposition than the state, the corporation, the labor union, the university, the media or any other institution.

Pro-churchers will object that religion is different, that even those who reject its truth need its morality. But the conflation of morality with religion is exactly what secularists contest. The secular stereotype of the devout as irrational has its counterpart in the pro-church assumption that secularists are devoted to a "value free" relativism and derive whatever morality they happen to retain from vestigial religious influence. Into this "vacuum," it is supposed, enter the nightmare inversions and perversions of morality that characterized the totalitarian secularisms of recent history. It's true that the basic moral proposition of secularism—that social norms should be grounded in the imperatives of earthly, human happiness—can lead to morally obnoxious ideas, depending on one's understanding of happiness. (Of course, so can the proposition that social norms must be grounded in God's will, depending on one's understanding of that will.) But a *democratic* secularism, which regards personal freedom and social equality as underpinnings of the good society, offers an alternative moral vision that coincides with religious morality in many respects, yet sharply departs from it in others—particularly in matters of sex.

Antisecularists argue that left critics of religious intrusion into politics have a double standard: we don't mind when churches take a stand against racism or poverty, only when they oppose legal abortion, homosexual rights and related sexual-political causes. But racial and economic issues do not provoke a clash between competing religious and secular moralities; believers and nonbelievers can be found on all sides of these debates, and religious as well as secular liberalism has been shaped by Enlightenment principles. Conservative sexual morality and antifeminism, on the other hand, are rooted in premodern, patriarchal religious ideology, while the logic of secular morality supports gender equality and a view of sexual fulfillment as a human right.

Unlike parochial-school vouchers, charitable choice and George W.'s new federal office, the right's sexual-political agenda, however religiously motivated, does not violate the establishment clause; religious morality and religion itself are not the same thing. But it does undermine the spirit of secular democracy. Although there are atheist right-to-lifers, the militant leadership, organization and financial sponsorship of the antiabortion and "pro-family" movements are religious. Without the conservative churches, those movements would not exist. Furthermore, these churches display a unique passion and commitment when it comes to sexual politics: the Catholic Church attacks Catholic politicians who stray from Church teachings on abortion—not capital punishment. For in fighting to enforce sexual orthodoxy, organized religion is also fighting to salvage its own authority. Sexual guilt, instilled at an early age, makes people feel sinful and reinforces their need for the church. Belief in their right to sexual freedom drives them away.

For democrats, it's as crucial to defend secular culture as to preserve secular law. And in fact the two projects are inseparable: when religion defines morality, the wall between church and state comes to be seen as immoral. This is what we're facing now—not only from Bush and the Christian right, but from the earnest centrists and liberals who are doing their dirty work.

The Nation, February 2001

Our Mobsters, Ourselves

Midway through the first season of *The Sopranos,* the protagonist's psycho-therapist, Jennifer Melfi, has a not-exactly-traditional family dinner with her middle-class Italian parents, son and ex-husband Richard. She lets slip (hmm!) that one of her patients is a mobster, much to Richard's consternation. An activist in Italian anti-defamation politics, he is incensed at the opprobrium the Mafia has brought on all Italians. What is the point, he protests, of trying to help such a person? In a subsequent scene he contemptuously dismisses Jennifer and her profession for purveying "cheesy moral relativism" in the face of evil. His challenge boldly proclaims what until then has been implicit: the richest and most compelling piece of television—no, of popular culture—that I've encountered in the past twenty years is a meditation on the nature of morality, the possibility of redemption and the legacy of Freud.

To be sure, *The Sopranos* is much else as well. For two years (the third season began March 4) David Chase's HBO series has served up a hybrid genre of post-*Godfather* decline-of-the-mob movie and soap opera, with plenty of sex, violence, domestic melodrama and comic irony; a portrait of a suburban landscape that does for northern New Jersey what film noir did for Los Angeles, with soundtrack to match; a deft depiction of class and cultural relations among various subgroups and generations of Italian-Americans; a gloss on the manners and mores of the *fin-de-siècle* American middle-class family; and perfect-pitch acting, especially by James Gandolfini as Tony Soprano; Edie Falco as his complicated wife, Carmela; Lorraine Bracco as Dr. Melfi; and the late Nancy Marchand as the Sopranos' terrifying matriarch, Livia.

Cumulatively, these episodes have the feel of an as yet unfinished nineteenth-century novel. While the sheer entertainment and suspense of the plot twists are reminiscent of Dickens and his early serials, the underlying themes evoke George Eliot: The world of Tony Soprano is a kind of postmodern Middlemarch, whose inhabitants' moral and spiritual development (or devolution) unfolds within and against the norms of a parochial social milieu. This era being what it is, however, the Sopranos' milieu has porous boundaries, and the norms that govern it are a moving target. In one scene, the family is in mid-breakfast when Tony and Carmela's teenage daughter, Meadow, apropos a recent scandal brought on by a high school classmate's affair with her soccer coach, declaims about the importance of talking openly about sex. Yes, Tony agrees, but not during breakfast. "Dad, this is the 1990s," Meadow protests. "Outside it may be the 1990s," Tony retorts, "but in this house it's 1954." It's wishful thinking, and Tony knows it. What 1950s gangster would take Prozac and make weekly visits to a shrink—or, for that matter, have a daughter named Meadow?

In fact, contemporary reality pervades the Sopranos' suburban manse. A school counselor tries to persuade them that their son, Anthony Jr., has attention deficit disorder. Meadow hosts a clandestine party in her grandmother's empty house that gets busted for drugs and alcohol. Tony's sister Janice, who years ago decamped to Seattle, became a Buddhist and changed her name to Parvati, shows up at his door flaunting her postcounterculture reinvented self. And while Tony displays some of the trappings of the stereotypical Italian patriarch—he is proud of supporting his family in style, comes and goes as he pleases, leaves the running of the household to Carmela, and cheats on her with the obligatory *goomah*—his persona as fear-inspiring gangster does not translate to his home life. Carmela is his emotional equal; she does what she likes, tells him off without hesitation and, unlike old-style mob wives, knows plenty about the business. Nor, despite periodic outbursts of temper, is Tony an intimidating father. Caught between empathy for their children and the urge to whip them into line, the Sopranos share the dirty little secret of nineties middle-class parenthood: you can't control teenagers' behavior without becoming full-time prison guards. "Let's not overplay our hand," Tony cautions after Meadow's party caper, "'cause if she finds out we're powerless, we're fucked."

In Tony's other "house"—represented by his office in the Bada Bing strip club—1954 is also under siege. Under pressure of the RICO laws, longtime associates turn government witness. Neophytes chafe at their lowly status in the hierarchy, disobey their bosses, take drugs, commit gratuitous freelance crimes and in general fail to understand that organized crime is a business, not a vehicle for self-expression or self-promotion. The line between reality and media image has become as tenuous here as elsewhere: Tony and his men love *Goodfellas* and the first two *Godfathers* (by general agreement *III* sucks) and at the same time are objects of fantasy for civilians steeped in the same movies. Tony accepts an invitation to play golf with his neighbor Dr. Cusamano, who referred him to Melfi, and finds that his function is to titillate the doctor's friends; during a falling out with Jennifer he tries to connect with another therapist, who demurs, explaining that he has seen *Analyze This* ("It's a fucking comedy," Tony protests). Tony's fractious nephew Christopher, pissed because press coverage of impending mob indictments doesn't mention him, reprises *Goodfellas* by shooting an insufficiently servile clerk in the foot. He aspires to write screenplays about mob life, and in pursuit of this dream is used for material and kicks by a Hollywood film director and his classy female assistant. Meanwhile Jennifer's family debates whether wiseguy movies defame Italians or rather should be embraced as American mythology, like westerns. *The Sopranos,* of course, has provoked the same argument, and its continual reflection of its characters in their media mirrors is also a running commentary on the show itself.

Self-consciousness, then, is a conspicuous feature of Tony Soprano's world even aside from therapy; in fact, it's clear that self-consciousness has provoked the anxiety attack that sends him to Jennifer Melfi. It's not just a matter of stressful circumstances. Tony's identity is fractured, part outlaw rooted in a dying tribal culture, part suburbanite enmeshed in another kind of culture altogether—a split graphically exemplified by the famous episode in which Tony, while taking Meadow on a tour of colleges in Maine, spots a mobster-turned-informer hiding in the witness protection program and manages to juggle his fatherly duties with murder. Despite his efforts at concealment, his criminal life is all too evident to his children (after all, they too have seen *The Godfather*), a source of pain and confusion on both sides. Tony's decision to seek therapy also involves an identity crisis. In his first session, which frames the first episode, he riffs on the sad fate of the strong and silent Gary Cooper: once they got him in touch with his feelings, he wouldn't shut up. "I have a semester and a half of college," he tells Dr. Melfi, "so I understand Freud. I understand therapy as a concept, but in my world it does not go down." In his wiseguy world, that is: Carmela thinks it's a great idea.

Richard Melfi's charge of moral relativism is highly ironic, for Jennifer finds that her task is precisely to confront the tribal relativism and cognitive dissonance that keep Tony Soprano from making sense of his life. He sees his business as the Sicilians' opportunity to get in on the American Dream, the violence that attends it as enforcement of rules known to all who choose to play the game: gangsters are soldiers, whose killing, far from being immoral, is impelled by positive virtues—loyalty, respect, friendship, willingness to put one's own life on the line. It does not strike Tony as inconsistent to expect his kids to behave or to send them to Catholic school, any more than he considers that nights with his Russian girlfriend belie his reverence for the institution of the family. Nor does he see a contradiction in his moral outrage at a sadistic, pathologically insecure associate who crushes a man with his car in fury over an inconsequential slight.

In its original literal sense, "moral relativism" is simply moral complexity. That is, anyone who agrees that stealing a loaf of bread to feed one's children is not the moral equivalent of, say, shoplifting a dress for the fun of it, is a relativist of sorts. But in recent years, conservatives bent on reinstating an essentially religious vocabulary of absolute good and evil as the only legitimate framework for discussing social values have redefined "relative" as "arbitrary." That conflation has been reinforced by social theorists and advocates of identity politics who argue that there is no universal morality, only the value systems of particular cultures and power structures. From this perspective, the psychoanalytic— and by extension the psychotherapeutic—worldview is not relativist at all. Its values are honesty, self-knowledge, assumption of responsibility for the whole of what one does, freedom from inherited codes of family, church, tribe in favor of a universal humanism: in other words, the values of the Enlightenment, as revised and expanded by Freud's critique of scientific rationalism for ignoring the power of unconscious desire. What eludes the Richard Melfis is that the neutral, unjudging stance of the therapist is not an end in itself but a strategy for pursuing this moral agenda by eliciting hidden knowledge.

Predictably, the cultural relativists have no more use for Freud than the religious conservatives. Nor are the devotees of "rational choice" economics and of a scientism that reduces all human behavior to genes or brain chemistry eager to look below the surface of things, or even admit there's such a thing as "below the surface." Which is why, in recent years, psychoanalysis has been all but banished from the public conversation as a serious means of discussing our moral and cultural and political lives. And as the zeitgeist goes, so goes popular culture: though a continuing appetite for the subject might be inferred from the popularity of memoirs, in which psychotherapy is a recurring theme, it has lately been notably absent from movies and television. So it's more than a little interesting that *The Sopranos* and *Analyze This* plucked the gangster-sees-therapist plot from the cultural unconscious at more or less the same time and apparently by coincidence. In *The Sopranos,* however, therapy is no fucking comedy, nor does it recycle old Hollywood clichés about shaman-like shrinks and sudden cathartic cures. It's a serious battle for a man's soul, carried on in sessions that look and sound a lot like the real thing (at least as I've experienced it)—full of silence, evasive chatter, lies, boredom and hostility, punctuated by outbursts of painful emotion, moments of clarity and insights that almost never sink in right away. Nor is it only the patient's drama; the therapist is right down there in the muck, sorting out her own confusions, missteps, fantasies and fears, attraction and repulsion, as she struggles to understand.

The parallels between psychotherapy and religion are reinforced by the adventures of the other *Sopranos* characters, who are all defined by their spiritual state. Some are damned, like Livia, whose nihilism is summed up in her penchant for smiling at other people's misfortunes and in her bitter remark to her grandson, "It's all a big nothing. What makes you think you're so special?" Some are complacent, like the respectable bourgeois Italian-Americans, or the self-regarding but fatally unself-aware Father Phil, Carmela's young spiritual adviser, who feeds (literally as well as metaphorically) on the neediness of the mob wives. The older, middle-level mobsters see themselves as working stiffs who expect little from life and for whom self-questioning is a luxury that's out of their class. (One of them is temporarily jolted when Tony's nephew Christopher is shot and has a vision of himself in hell; but the crisis passes quickly.) Charmaine Bucco, a neighborhood girl and old friend of Carmela's who with her husband, Artie, owns an Italian restaurant, is the embodiment of passionate faith in the virtues of honesty, integrity and hard work; she despises the mobsters, wishes they would stop patronizing the restaurant and does her best to pull the ambivalent Artie away from his longtime friendship with Tony. And then there are the strugglers, like Christopher, who inchoately wants something more out of life but also wants to rise in the mob, and Big Pussy, Tony's close friend as well as crew member, who rats to the Feds to ward off a thirty-year prison term, agonizes over his betrayal and ultimately takes refuge in identifying with his FBI handlers.

Carmela Soprano is a struggler, an ardent Catholic who feels the full weight of her sins and Tony's and lets no one off the hook. She keeps hoping Tony will change but knows he probably will not; and despite the many discontents of her marriage, anger at Tony's infidelity and misgivings about her complicity in his crimes, she will not leave him. Though she rationalizes her choice on religious grounds ("The family is a sacred institution"), she never really deceives herself: she still loves Tony, and furthermore she likes the life his money provides. Nor does she hesitate to trade on his power in order to do what she feels is a mother's duty: she intimidates Cusamano's lawyer sister-in-law into writing Meadow a college recommendation. Guilt and frustration drive her to Father Phil, who gives her books on Buddhism, foreign movies and mixed sexual signals, but after a while she catches on to his bullshit, and in a scene beloved of *Sopranos* fans coolly nails him: "He's a sinner, Father. You come up here and you eat his steaks and use his home entertainment center. . . . I think you have this MO where you manipulate spiritually thirsty women, and I think a lot of it's tied up with food somehow, as well as the sexual tension game." Compromised as she is, Carmela is a moral touchstone because of her clear eye.

But Tony's encounters with Melfi are the spiritual center of the show. The short version of Tony's psychic story is this: his gangster persona provides him with constant excitement and action, a sense of power and control, a definition of masculinity. Through violence rationalized as business or impersonal soldiering he also gets to express his considerable unacknowledged rage without encroaching on his alter ego as benevolent husband and father. But when the center fails to hold, the result is panic, then—as Melfi probes the cracks—depression, self-hatred, sexual collapse and engulfing, ungovernable anger. There are glimmers along the way, as when Tony sees the pointlessness of killing the sexually wayward soccer coach, calls off the hit and lets the cops do their job (after which he feels impelled to get so drunk he passes out). But the abyss always looms.

Tony's heart of darkness is personified by Livia Soprano, who at first seems peggable as a better-done-than-usual caricature of the overbearing ethnic mother but is gradually revealed as a monstrous Medea. Furious at Tony for consigning her to a fancy "retirement community," Livia passes on some well-chosen pieces of information—including the fact that he's seeing a shrink—to Tony's malleable Uncle Junior, who orders him killed. When the hit is botched, she suddenly begins to show symptoms of Alzheimer's. Jennifer Melfi puts it together; worried that Tony's life is in danger, she breaks the therapeutic rule that patients must make their own discoveries and confronts him with her knowledge. He reacts with a frightening, hate-filled paroxysm of denial—for the first time coming close to attacking Jennifer physically—but is forced to admit the truth when he hears a damning conversation between Livia and Junior, caught on tape by the FBI.

This is a turning point in the story, but not, as the standard psychiatric melodrama would have it, because the truth has made Tony free. The truth has knocked him flat. "What kind of person can I be," he blurts to Carmela, "where his own mother wants him dead?" Afraid that Junior will go after Jennifer, he orders her to leave town; when she comes back she is angry and fearful and tells him to get out of her life. He is lost, his face a silent Munchian scream. Later Jennifer has a change of heart, but things are not the same: the trust is gone. And yet, paradoxically, her rejection has freed him to be more honest, throwing the details of his gang's brutality in her face, railing at her for making him feel like a victim, at himself for becoming the failed Gary Cooper he once mocked, at the "happy wanderers" who still seem in control. Jennifer encourages him to feel the sadness under the rage, but what comes through is hard and bleak. He tells anyone who mentions his mother, "She's dead to me," but it's really he who feels dead. During this time, Anthony Jr. shocks his mother by announcing that God is dead; "Nitch" says so. (At its most serious, the show never stops being funny.) Tony mentions this to Jennifer, who gives him a minilecture on existential angst: when some people realize they're solely responsible for their lives, and all roads lead to death, they feel "intense dread" and conclude that "the only absolute truth is death." "I think the kid's on to something," Tony says.

As if to validate Richard Melfi's contempt, he uses what he's learned in therapy—that you can't compartmentalize your life—to more fully accept his worst impulses. Against his more compassionate instincts, he allows an old friend who is the father of a classmate of Meadow's and a compulsive gambler to join his high-stakes card game. When David inevitably piles up a debt he can't pay, Tony moves in on his business, sucking it dry and draining his son's college fund. Amid a torrent of self-pity, David asks why Tony let him in the game. Tony answers jocularly that it's his nature—you know, as in the tale of the frog and the scorpion. In the last episode of season two Tony whacks Pussy, whose perfidy has been revealed, choosing his mob code over his love and sorrow for the man. He then walks out on Jennifer, as if to say, this is who I am and will be.

Jennifer's trip is also a rocky one. In her person, the values of Freud and the Enlightenment are filtered through the cultural radical legacy of the 1960s: she is a woman challenging a man whose relationship to both legitimate and outlaw patriarchal hierarchies is in crisis. It's a shaky and vulnerable role, the danger of physical violence an undercurrent from the beginning, but there are also bonds that make the relationship possible. Tony chooses her over a Jewish male therapist because "you're a paisan, like me," and she is drawn to the outlaw, no doubt in rebellion against the safe smugness of her own social milieu. Predictably, Tony loses all sexual interest in his wife and girlfriend and falls in love with his doctor (if there is any answering spark, it stays under the professional surface), but after the initial "honeymoon" of therapy, trouble, as always, begins. Tony gives Jennifer "gifts" like stealing her car and getting it fixed; it's his way of assuring her, and himself, that his power is benevolent, but of course she only feels violated. Wanting to find out about her life, he has her followed by a corrupt cop who harasses her boyfriend, thinking he's doing Tony a favor; she can't help but be suspicious. By inviting her family to object to her criminal patient, she gives voice to her own doubts: perhaps she *is* not only endangering herself but abetting evil. Her conflict intensifies when she tells Tony she must charge for a missed session, and he throws the money at her, calling her a whore. It explodes in the aftermath of the attempt on his life. But then the other side of her ambivalence reasserts itself; she feels she has irresponsibly abandoned a patient and takes him back against the advice of her own (Jewish male) therapist. Now it is Jennifer who is in crisis, treating her anxiety with heavy drinking. She is frightened and morally repulsed by Tony's graphic revelations, yet also feels an erotically tinged fascination (it's like watching a train wreck, she tells her shrink). She still cares about Tony but seems to have lost faith in her ability to exorcise the demonic by making contact with the suffering human being. In the last episode, with Tony closed as a clam, she admits that she blew it, that she stopped pushing him because she was afraid. But he can't hear her.

No false optimism here. Yet it's no surprise that by the second hour of the third season premiere Tony is back in Jennifer Melfi's office. The requirements of the show's premise aside, his untenable situation has not changed. Having glimpsed the possibility of an exit from despair, it would be out of character for him simply to close that door and walk away. For the same reason, I suspect our culture's flight from psychoanalysis is not permanent. It's grandiose, perhaps, to see in one television series, however popular, a cultural trend; and after all *The Sopranos* is on HBO, not CBS or NBC. But ultimately the show is so gripping because, in the words of Elaine Showalter, it's a "cultural Rorschach test." It has been called a parable of corruption and hypocrisy in the postmodern middle class, and it is that; a critique of sexuality, the family and male-female relations in the wake of feminism, and it's that too. But at the primal level, the inkblot is the unconscious. The murderous mobster is the predatory lust and aggression in all of us; his lies and cover-ups are ours; the therapist's fear is our own collective terror of peeling away those lies. The problem is that we can't live with the lies, either. So facing down the terror, a little at a time, becomes the only route to sanity, if not salvation.

In the tumultuous last episode of *The Sopranos'* first season, another informer is killed. Tony finds out about his mother and sends Jennifer into hiding. Uncle Junior and two of his underlings are arrested, arousing fears that one of them will flip. Artie Bucco nearly kills Tony after being told—by Livia—that Tony is responsible for the fire that destroyed his restaurant (the idea was to help the Buccos by heading off a planned mob hit in the restaurant, which would have ruined the business—this way they could get the insurance and rebuild), but Tony swears "on my mother" it isn't true. Carmela tells off Father Phil. At the end, Tony, Carmela and the kids are caught in a violent storm in their SUV; they can't see a thing but suddenly realize they're in front of the Buccos' (rebuilt) restaurant. There's no power, but Artie graciously ushers them in, lights a candle and cooks them a meal. Tony proposes a toast: "To my family. Someday soon you're gonna have families of your own. And if you're lucky, you'll remember the little moments. Like this. That were good." The moment feels something like sanity. The storm, our storm, goes on.

The Nation, March 2001

Is There Still a Jewish Question?
Why I'm an Anti-Anti-Zionist

Early '90s, post-Bosnia conversation with a longtime political friend I've met by chance on the street: "I've come to see nationalism as regressive, period. I can't use phrases like 'national liberation' and 'national self-determination' with a straight face anymore."

"You know, Ellen, there's one inconsistency in your politics."

"What's that?"

"Israel."

I'm not a Zionist—rather I'm a quintessential Diaspora Jew, a child of Freud, Marx and Spinoza. I hold with rootless cosmopolitanism: from my perspective the nation-state is a profoundly problematic institution, a nation-state defined by ethnic or other particularist criteria all the more so. And yet I count myself an anti-anti-Zionist. This is partly because the logic of anti-Zionism in the present political context entails an unprecedented demand for an existing state—one, moreover, with popular legitimacy and a democratically elected government— not simply to change its policies but to disappear. It's partly because I can't figure out what large numbers of displaced Jews could have or should have done after 1945, other than parlay their relationship with Palestine and the (ambivalent) support of the West for a Jewish homeland into a place to be. (Go "home" to Germany or Poland? Knock, en masse, on the doors of unreceptive European countries and a reluctant United States?) And finally it's because I believe that anti-Jewish genocide cannot be laid to rest as a discrete historical episode, but remains a possibility implicit in the deep structure of Christian and Islamic cultures, East and West.

This last point is particularly difficult to argue on the left, where the conventional wisdom is that raising the issue of anti-Semitism in relation to Israel and

Palestine is nothing but a way of stifling criticism of Israel and demonizing the critics. In the context of left politics, the dynamic is actually reversed: accusations of blind loyalty to Israel, intolerance of debate, and exaggeration of Jewish vulnerability at the expense of the real, Palestinian victims are routinely used to stifle discussion of how anti-Semitism influences the Israeli-Palestinian conflict or the world's reaction to it or the public conversation about it. Yet that discussion is crucial, for there is no way to disentangle the politics surrounding Israel from the politics of the Jewish condition. Anti-Semitism remains the wild card of world politics and the lightning rod of political crisis, however constantly it is downplayed or denied. My anti-anti-Zionism does not imply support for Ariel Sharon's efforts to destroy the Palestinians' physical, political, and social infrastructure while expanding Jewish settlements in occupied territory; or the disastrous policy of permitting such settlements in the first place; or the right-wing nationalism cum religious irredentism that has come to dominate Israeli politics; or, indeed, any and all acts of successive Israeli governments that have in one way or another impeded negotiations for an end to the occupation and an equitable peace. Nor do I condone the American government's neutrality on the side of Sharon. But I reject the idea that Israel is a colonial state that should not exist. I reject the villainization of Israel as the sole or main source of the mess in the Middle East. And I contend that Israel needs to maintain its "right of return" for Jews around the world.

My inconsistency, if that's what it is, comes from struggling to make sense of a situation that has multiple and at times contradictory dimensions. Israel is the product of a nationalist movement, but it owes its existence to a world-historical catastrophe. The bloody standoff between Israelis and Palestinians is on its face a clash of two nationalisms run amok, yet it can't be understood apart from the larger political forces of the post–1945 world—anti-colonialism, oilpolitik, the Cold War, the American and neoliberal triumph, democracy versus authoritarianism, secularism versus fundamentalism.

Indeed, the mainstream of contemporary political anti-Zionism does not oppose nationalism as such, but rather defines the conflict as bad imperialist nationalism versus the good liberationist kind. Or to put it another way, anti-Zionism is a conspicuous feature of that brand of left politics that reduces all global conflict to Western imperialism versus Third World anti-imperialism, ignoring a considerably more complicated reality. But even those who are anti-Zionist out of a principled opposition to nationalism (including Jews who see the original Jewish embrace of nationalism as a tragic wrong turn) must surely recognize that at present, an end to nationalism in Israel/Palestine is not on either side's agenda. The question is what course of action, all things considered, will help in some way to further the possibilities for democracy and human rights as opposed to making things worse. I support a two-state solution that in effect ratifies the concept of the original 1948 partition—bracketing fundamental questions about Jewish and Palestinian nationalism—out of the non-utopian yet no less urgent hope that it would end the lunacy of mutual destruction and allow some space for a new Middle Eastern order to develop.

It looked for a while as if this might actually happen, and during that period, not coincidentally, there was a surge of discussion among Jews inside and outside Israel on the limits of nationalism and its possible "post-Zionist" transcendence. Now it's almost as if those years were a hallucination. Until recently, when a few fragile tendrils of sanity have surfaced in the form of the "road map" talks, the irredentists on both sides have been firmly in control, engaged in a deadly Kabuki dance whose fundamental purpose is to make a peace agreement impossible. Whatever the shortcomings of Ehud Barak's ill-fated Camp David proposal, it did move Israel onto previously non-negotiable territory, especially in its offer to share Jerusalem. In my view, the negotiations collapsed not because they had reached an impasse but, on the contrary, because they had finally become serious in a way that threatened Yasir Arafat's ability to walk the line between peacemaking and appeasing his rejectionist flank. Sharon set out to provoke violence by visiting the Temple Mount; the Palestinians gave him exactly what he wanted. The intifada, the suicide bombings, and Arafat's complicity in them basically destroyed the Israeli left, while aside from a few intellectuals there seemed to be no serious Palestinian peace party. Meanwhile Sharon has used the need to defend against terror as an excuse to brutalize the Palestinian population. Any peace initiative must withstand this formidable collusion of enemies.

Nonetheless, leftists tend to single out Israel as The Problem that must be solved. That tropism is most pronounced among those for whom the project of a Jewish state is inherently imperialist, or an offense to universalist humanism, or both. (A young professor of brilliant intellect and anarchist inclinations, whose development I've followed since graduate school: "Why don't the Israelis just leave? Walk away from the state?" and in the same conversation, "Israel is the biggest problem I have as a Jew.") But it is also widespread, if often unconscious, among people who have no ideological objection to the Jewish state as such, including Jews who care deeply about the fate of Israel and are appalled by government policies they deem not only inhumane but suicidal. I've received countless impassioned e-mails emphasizing how imperative it is to show there are Jews who disagree with the Jewish establishment, who oppose Sharon. There is no comparable urgency to show that Jews on the left as well as the right condemn suicide bombing as a war crime, a horrifying product of totalitarian religious brainwashing, and a way to ensure there is no peace. At most I hear, "Suicide bombing is a terrible thing, but . . ." But: if Israel would just shape up and do the right thing, there would be peace. Would that it were so.

Along with this one-sided view of the conflict, the left has focused on Israeli acts of domination and human rights violations with an intense and consistent outrage that it fails to direct toward comparable or worse abuses elsewhere, certainly toward the unvarnished tyrannies in the Middle East (where, for

instance, is the divestment campaign against Saudi Arabia?). No, I'm not saying it's reasonable to demand that critics of Israel simultaneously oppose all
the violence, misery, and despotism in the world, or that complaints against
Israel are invalid because Arab regimes are worse. Inevitably, at any given time
some countries, some conflicts will capture people's imagination and indignation more than others—not because they are worse but because they somehow
hit a nerve, become larger than themselves, take on a symbolic dimension. But
that is exactly my point: left animus toward Israel is not a simple, self-evident
product of the facts. What is the nerve that Israel hits?

Underlining this question are the hyperbolic comparisons that animate the
anti-Israel brief, beginning with the now standard South Africa comparison—
the accusation that Israel is a "settler state" and an "apartheid state"—which
has inspired the calls for divestment and for a boycott against Israeli academics. The South African regime, of course, was one whose essence was a proudly
white racist ideology, a draconian system of legal segregation, and the denial
of all political rights to the huge majority of people. To see Israel through this
grid is to ignore a great many things: that Israel was settled primarily by refugees from genocide in Europe and oppression in Arab countries; that while
Palestinian Israelis suffer from discrimination they are nevertheless citizens
who vote, organize political parties, and participate in the government; that the
occupation, while egregious, came about as a result not of aggressive settlement but of defensive war; that it continues because of rejectionism on both
sides; that there is a difference between the nationalist and ultra-Orthodox
militants who dream of a greater Israel and the majority of Israelis who once
supported peace but turned to Sharon out of fear and cynicism. As for Israeli
academics, they are independent and disproportionately active in opposing government policy, which leaves the boycott movement with no plausible rationale.

Even more fantastic is the Nazi comparison, often expressed in metaphors
(Israeli soldiers as SS men, and so on). I imagine that most perpetrators of this
equation, if pressed, would concede that Israel is not a totalitarian dictatorship
with a program of world domination, nor has it engaged in the systematic murder of millions of people on the grounds that they are a subhuman race. But why
do these tropes have such appeal? Where does it come from, the impulse to go
beyond taking Israel to task for its concrete misdeeds, to lump it with the worst,
most criminal states in history? That Israel is seen as a Western graft in the
Arab Middle East (a view Israelis themselves would contest, given that most of
the population comes from the Middle East and North Africa) and a surrogate
for American power contributes to its symbolic importance as a target, as does
an unconscious condescension toward Arabs that leads to a double standard of
moral expectations for Israel and its neighbors. But it's impossible not to notice
how the runaway inflation of Israel's villainy aligns with ingrained cultural fantasies about the iniquity and power of Jews; or how the traditional pariah status
of Jews has been replicated by a Jewish pariah state. And the special fury and

vitriol that greet any attempt to bring up this subject in left circles further suggest that more is at stake here than an ordinary political dispute—just as more is at stake in the Israel-Palestine clash than an ordinary border dispute.

At present, the Middle East is the flashpoint of a world ironically destabilized by the end of the Cold War, a world in a more volatile and dangerous state than at any time since the 1930s. And Jews are once again in the middle of the equation—in a vastly different position, to be sure, from the Jews of 1930s Europe; in a vastly different position because of what happened to those Jews; and yet the discourse about this set of Jews echoes certain familiar themes. The anti-Jewish temperature is rising, and has been for some time, in Arab and Islamic countries and in the Islamist European diaspora. I am speaking now not of the intemperate tone of left anti-Zionist rhetoric but of overt Jew-hatred as expressed in continual public denunciation of Jews and Zionists (who are assumed to be one and the same), ubiquitous propaganda tracts inspired by or imported directly from Nazi and medieval Christian sources, mob violence and vandalism directed against Jews, the execution of *Wall Street Journal* reporter Daniel Pearl, conspiracy theories like the widely believed tale that Jewish workers at the World Trade Center stayed home on September 11 because they had been warned.

Many on the left view this wave of anti-Semitism as just another expression, however unfortunately couched, of justified rage at Israel—whether at the occupation and the escalating destruction of the West Bank or at the state's existence per se. In either case, the conflation of "Zionists" and "Jews" is regarded as a misunderstanding of the politically uneducated. Which is to say, again, that Israel is The Problem—not only for Palestinians but for Jews as well. This is a serious failure of imagination, for in fact Israel's conflict with the Arab world owes more to the peculiar role played by the Jews in history, culture, and the Judeo-Christian-Islamic psyche than vice versa.

Half a century ago, Israel was supposed to have put a period to the long sordid history of Christian, European anti-Semitism, with its genocidal climax. Instead it turned out that the Europeans had in effect displaced their "Jewish problem," which Hitler had failed to "solve," onto new territory. This was true literally, in that Jewish refugees were now the problem of the Arabs, who didn't want them any more than the Europeans had, and worse, would be pressed, as Europe had never been, to deal with Jews not as a minority but as a sovereign nation in their midst. It was true geopolitically, in that Israel was slated to be a Western ally in a region struggling to overcome the legacy of colonialism—an alliance that would put Israel in the classic position of the Jew with a ruling-class patron, who functions as surrogate and scapegoat for the anger of the ruled. And it was true ideologically, in that the new state would become, for its neighbors, what the Jews had been to Europe—an unassimilable foreign body; a powerful, evil, subversive force; a carrier of contaminating modernity.

These developments exposed the core Zionist belief, that an end to the Jews' stateless condition would "normalize" Jewish life, as tragically naive. For those on the Zionist left who believed that Jewish nationalism was a necessary but temporary expedient on the way to an international proletarian revolution, the post–World War II landscape offered little support: in Western Europe, the revolution did not happen; the Third World revolutions were nationalist ones; and the Soviet Union proved to be, among other things, virulently anti-Semitic. For right-wing Zionists of the Jabotinsky stripe, the embattlement of the Jews in Palestine justified a ruthless terrorism that in turn validated Arab violence, in adumbration of the present vicious cycle. Of course, the Israeli right has had no monopoly on regressive anti-Palestinian policies, but it has expressed most clearly and consistently that strain of bitter pessimism about the intractability of Jew-hatred to which few Jews, I suspect, are entirely immune. All right-wing nationalism (perhaps all nationalism) is rooted in paranoia, but in the case of the Jews, the paranoids indeed have real enemies; and the Zionist right's glorification of the Jewish warrior must be seen at least in part as a reaction to the stereotype of the soft, bookish Jew who went passively to the Nazi slaughter.

If Israel's conflict with the Palestinians and the Arabs generally cannot be understood without reference to the larger question of relations between Jews and the rest of the world, what of its audience—that is, the international community, including the American left? I'd argue that no one, Jewish or not, brought up in a Christian or Islamic-dominated culture can come to this issue without baggage, since the patriarchal monotheism that governs our sexually repressive structure of morality, and all the ambivalence that goes with it, was invented by Jews. The concept of one transcendent God has a double meaning: it proclaims the subordination of all human authority to a higher reality at the same time that, codified as "God the Father," it affirms the patriarchal hierarchy. The Jews, in their mythic role as the "chosen people" destined to achieve the redemption of the world through their adherence to God's law, embody a similar duality: they are avatars of spiritual freedom on the one hand, patriarchal authority and the control of desire on the other. In relation to Christianity and Islam, the Jews are the authors of morality but also the stubborn nay-sayers, setting themselves apart, refusing to embrace Jesus or Mohammed as the fulfillment of their quest.

In the patriarchal unconscious Jews represent the vindictive castrating father and the wicked, subversive tempter, the moral ideal we cannot attain and the revolution we dare not join. As such, Jews are an object of our unconscious rage at repressive authority as well as at those who tease us with visions of (evil) freedom; a subterranean rage that is readily tapped by demagogues in times of crisis. The ambiguous role of Jews also has a social shape: for complex reasons having to do with their outsider status and efforts to overcome or embrace it, Jews have been overrepresented in the ranks of the privileged as well as among political and social rebels. As a result, Jews are a free-floating political target, equally available to the right or the left, sometimes to both at once. This is why Jews are likely to surface as an issue in some way whenever the political climate heats up (American examples range from the anti-Communist crusades of the '50s, to the energy crisis and consequent debates over Middle East policy in the '70s, to the racial conflicts of the past several decades). Typically, attacks on Jews invest them with far more power than they possess—a tribute to their power as emotional symbols, but a distortion of social reality. In the end, the anger that collects around Jews is anger deflected from its real sources.

My point here is not that Israel should be exempt from anger. Israel is a nation-state. As such it has military, political, and social power. In the exercise of its power, it must be held accountable for its actions. Its misuses of power must be censured and opposed. The victims of its power can hardly be expected to be other than enraged. Yet as a Jewish state, Israel is also subject to layers of irrational anger, whether from antagonists who will not settle for a negotiated peace but demand that the foreign body be expelled, or from political critics who conjure up a monster that rivals Hitler. Israel's power, too, has been exaggerated, contingent as it is on the support of the United States: in the period of economic troubles, foreign adventurism, and revived protest we have entered, who knows what America will look like a few years from now, what our aims in the Middle East will be, what trade-offs we will make?

In the debates over Zionism and anti-Zionism, the situation of Jews is by no means the only question. But it is a question. Is it possible that Jews could once again be massacred? Given the rise of Islamic fundamentalism, the ubiquity of anti-Semitism in the Arab world, the anti-Jewish subtext in much anti-Zionist polemic along with the denial that any such sentiment exists—and given that in an increasingly murderous world the unthinkable takes place on a daily basis—I have to argue that the possibility cannot be dismissed. If there should be a mass outbreak of anti-Jewish violence it will no doubt focus on Israel, but it will not, in the end, be caused by Israel, and the hatred will not disappear if Israel does. Nor will it disappear with an Israeli-Palestinian settlement. Still, from this point of view as from so many others, an internationally brokered peace agreement is the first line of defense. And that agreement must allow Israel to retain its character as a haven for Jews, not as a validation of nationalism but as a gesture of international recognition that the need for such a haven has not yet been surpassed. It's not inconsistent to hope that this will not always be true.

Wrestling with Zion, 2003

NOTE

This essay appeared in *Wrestling with Zion: Progressive Jewish-American Responses to the Israeli-Palestinian Conflict,* ed. Tony Kushner and Alisa Solomon (New York: Grove Press, 2003).

Ghosts, Fantasies, and Hope

For most of my politically conscious life, the idea of social transformation has been the great taboo of American politics. From the smug 1950s to the post-Reagan era, in which a bloodied and cowed left has come to regard a kinder, gentler capitalism as its highest aspiration, this anti-utopian trend has been interrupted only by the brief but intense flare-up of visionary politics known as "the sixties." Yet that short-lived, anomalous upheaval has had a more profound effect on my thinking about the possibilities of politics than the following three decades of reaction. The reason is not (to summarize the conversation-stopping accusations routinely aimed at anyone who suggests that sixties political and cultural radicalism might offer other than negative lessons for the left) that I am stuck in a time warp, nursing a romantic attachment to my youth, and so determined to idealize a period that admittedly had its politically dicey moments. Rather, as I see it, the enduring interest of this piece of history lies precisely in its spectacular departure from the norm. It couldn't happen, according to the reigning intellectual currents of the fifties, but it did. Nor—in the sense of ceasing to cast a shadow over the present—can it really be said to be over, even in this age of "9/11 Changed Everything."

That the culture war instigated by the 1960s revolt shows no signs of abating thirty-some years later is usually cited by its left and liberal opponents to condemn it as a disastrous provocation that put the right in power. Yet the same set of facts can as plausibly be regarded as evidence of the potent and lasting appeal of its demand that society embrace freedom and pleasure as fundamental values. For the fury of the religious right is clearly a case of protesting too much, its preoccupation with sexual sin a testament to the magnitude of the temptation (as the many evangelical sex scandals suggest). Meanwhile, during the dot-com boom, enthusiastic young free marketeers fomented a mini-revival of sixties liberationism, reencoded as the quest for global entrepreneurial triumph, new technological toys, and limitless information. Was this just one more example of the amazing power of capitalism to turn every human impulse to its own purposes—or, given the right circumstances, might the force of desire overflow that narrow channel? If freedom's just another word for nothing left to lose, as Janis Joplin-cum-Kris Kristofferson famously opined, this could be a propitious moment to reopen a discussion of the utopian dimension of politics and its possible uses for our time. After all, the left has tried everything else, from postmodern rejection of "master narratives" and universal values to Anybody But Bush.

Russell Jacoby, one of the few radicals to consistently reject the accommodationist pull, has been trying to nudge us toward such a conversation for some time. *Picture Imperfect* is really part two of a meditation that Jacoby began in 1999 with *The End of Utopia,* a ferocious polemic against anti-utopian thought. Both books trace the assumptions of today's anti-utopian consensus to the thirties and forties, when liberal intellectuals—most notably Karl Popper, Hannah Arendt, and Isaiah Berlin—linked Nazism and communism under the rubric of totalitarianism, whose essential characteristic, they proposed, was the rejection of liberal pluralism for a monolithic ideology. In the cold war context, Nazism faded into the background; the critique of totalitarianism became a critique of communism and was generalized to all utopian thinking—that is, to any political aspiration that went beyond piecemeal reform. As the logic of this argument would have it, attempts to understand and change a social system as a whole are by definition ideological, which is to say dogmatic; they violate the pluralistic nature of social life and so can only be enforced through terror; ergo, utopianism leads to mass murder. Never mind that passionate radicals such as Emma Goldman condemned the Soviet regime in the name of their own utopian vision or that most of the past century's horrors have been perpetrated by such decidedly non-utopian forces as religious fanaticism, nationalism, fascism, and other forms of racial and ethnic bigotry. (Jacoby notes with indignation that some proponents of the anti-utopian syllogism have tried to get around this latter fact by labeling movements like Nazism and radical Islamism "utopian"—as I write, David Brooks has just made use of this ploy in the *New York Times*—as if there is no distinction worth making between a universalist tradition devoted to "notions of happiness, fraternity, and plenty" and social "ideals" that explicitly mandate the mass murder of so-called inferior races or the persecution of infidels.)

In the post-communist world, Jacoby laments, the equation of utopia with death has become conventional wisdom across the political board. *The End of Utopia* is primarily concerned with the impact of this brand of thinking on the left; it attacks the array of "progressive" spokespeople who insist that we must accept the liberal welfare state as the best we can hope for, as well as the multiculturalists who have reinvented liberal pluralism, celebrating "diversity" and "inclusiveness" within a socioeconomic system whose fundamental premises are taken for granted. With *Picture Imperfect,* Jacoby takes on larger and more philosophical questions about the nature of utopia and of the human imagination—too large, actually, to be adequately addressed in this quite short book, which has a somewhat diffuse and episodic quality as a result. Still, the questions are central to any serious discussion of the subject, and it helps that they are framed by a more concrete project: to rescue utopian thought from its murderous reputation as well as from the more mundane charge that it is puritanical and repressive in its penchant for planning out the future to the last detail.

To this end, Jacoby distinguishes between two categories of utopianism: the dominant "blueprint" tradition, exemplified by Thomas More's eponymous no place or Edward Bellamy's *Looking Backward,* and the dissident strain he calls "iconoclastic" utopianism, whose concern is challenging the limits of the existing social order and expanding the boundaries of imagination rather than planning the perfect society. While he does not simply write off the blueprinters—fussy as their details may be, he regards them as contributors to the utopian spirit and credits them with inspiring social reforms—his heroes are the iconoclasts, beginning with Ernst Bloch and his 1918 *The Spirit of Utopia,* and including a gallery of anarchists, refusers, and mystics ranging from Walter Benjamin, Theodor Adorno, and Herbert Marcuse to Gustav Landauer and Martin Buber.

The iconoclastic tradition is mainly Jewish, and Jacoby, in an interesting bit of discursus, links it to the biblical prohibition of idolatry. Just as the Jews may neither depict God's image nor pronounce God's name, so the iconoclasts avoid explicit images or descriptions of the utopian future. Further, Jacoby argues, in the Kabbala and in Jewish tradition generally, the Torah achieves full meaning only through the oral law: "The ear trumps the eye. Alone, the written word may mislead: it is too graphic." Similarly, the future of the iconoclasts is "heard and longed for" rather than seen. Here, Jacoby's analysis intersects with a fear he has long shared with his Frankfurt School mentors—that a mass culture obsessed with images flattens the imagination and perhaps destroys it altogether. From this perspective, the iconoclasts' elision of the image is itself radically countercultural.

Is it also impossibly abstract? "The problem today," Jacoby recognizes in his epilogue, "is how to connect utopian thinking with everyday politics." Even as utopianism is condemned as deadly, it is at the same time, and often by the same people, dismissed as irrelevant to the real world. Jacoby will have none of this; he rightly insists, "Utopian thinking does not undermine or discount real reforms. Indeed, it is almost the opposite: practical reforms depend on utopian dreaming." Again, the sixties offers many examples—particularly its most successful social movement, second wave feminism, which achieved mass proportions in response to the radical proposition that men and women should be equals not only under the law or on the job but in every social sphere from the kitchen to the nursery to the bedroom to the street. (As one of the movement's prominent utopians, Shulamith Firestone, put it, the initial response of most women to that idea was, "You must be out of your mind—you can't change that!") Yet it seems likely that the relationship of the utopian imagination and the urge to concrete political activity is not precisely one of cause and effect; rather, both impulses appear to have a common root in the perception that something other than what is is possible—and necessary. We might think of iconoclastic utopians as the inverse of canaries in the mine: if they are hearing the sounds of an ineffable redemption, others may already be at work on annoyingly literal blueprints, and still others getting together for as yet obscure political meetings. So the formulation of the problem may need to be fine-tuned: what is it that fosters, or blocks, that sense of possibility/necessity? Why does it seem so utterly absent today (you're out of your mind!), and how can we change that?

These questions are an obvious project for a third book, though it's one Jacoby is unlikely to write: he is temperamentally a refusenik, like the iconoclasts he lauds, more attuned to distant hoofbeats than to spoor on the ground that might reward analysis. It is perhaps this bias that has kept him from seeing one reason why the anti-utopian argument has become so entrenched: although there is perversity in it, and bad faith, there is also some truth. Jacoby is no fan of authoritarian communism, but he is wrong in thinking he can simply bracket that disaster or that there is nothing to be learned from it that might apply to utopian movements in general. The striking characteristic of communism was the radical disconnection between the social ideals it professed and the actual societies it produced. Because the contradiction could never be admitted, whole populations were forced to speak and act as if the lies of the regime were true. It is not surprising that victims or witnesses of this spectacle would distrust utopians. Who could tell what even the most steadfast anti-Stalinists might do if they actually gained some power? Who could give credence to phrases like "workers' control" or "women's emancipation" when they had come to mean anything but? Jacoby persuasively analyzes *1984* to show that it was not meant as an anti-socialist tract, yet he never mentions the attacks on the misuse of language that made Orwell's name into an adjective.

Communism was corrupted by a scientific (or more accurately, scientistic) theory of history that cast opponents as expendable, a theory of class that dismissed bourgeois democratic liberties as merely a mask for capitalist exploitation, and a revolutionary practice that allowed a minority to impose dictatorship. Similar tropes made their way into the sixties' movements, in, for instance, the argument that oppressors should not have free speech or that the American people were the problem, not the solution, and the proper function of American radicals was to support third world anti-imperialism by any means necessary, including violence. A milder form of authoritarianism, which owed less to Marxism than to a peculiarly American quasi-religious moralism, dis-figured the counterculture and the women's movement. If the original point of these movements was to promote the pursuit of happiness, too often the empha-sis shifted to proclaiming one's own superior enlightenment and contempt for those who refused to be liberated; indeed, liberation had a tendency to become prescriptive, so that freedom to reject the trappings of middle-class consumer-ism, or not to marry, or to be a lesbian was repackaged as a moral obligation and a litmus test of one's radicalism or feminism. Just as communism discredited utopianism for several generations of Europeans, the antics of countercultural moralists fed America's conservative reaction.

But it's not only corruption that distorts the utopian impulse when it begins to take some specific social shape. The prospect of more freedom stirs anxiety. We want it, but we fear it; it goes against our most deeply ingrained Judeo-Christian definitions of morality and order. At bottom, utopia equals death is a statement about the wages of sin. Left authoritarianism is itself a defense against anxiety—a way to assimilate frightening anarchy into familiar pat-terns of hierarchy and moral demand—as is the fundamentalist backlash tak-ing place not only in the United States but around the world. Jacoby links the decline of utopian thought to the collapse of communism in 1989, and that is surely part of the story, but in truth the American backlash against utopianism was well underway by the mid-seventies. The sixties scared us, and not only because of Weathermen and Charles Manson. We scared ourselves.

How did the sixties happen in the first place? I'd argue that a confluence of events stimulated desire while temporarily muting anxiety. There was wide-spread prosperity that made young people feel secure, able to challenge au-thority and experiment with their lives. There was a vibrant mass-mediated culture that, far from damping down the imagination, transmitted the sum-mons to freedom and pleasure far more broadly than a mere political movement could do. (Jacoby is on to something, though, about the importance of the ear: the key mass cultural form, from the standpoint of inciting utopianism, was rock and roll.) There was a critical mass of educated women who could not abide the contradiction between the expanding opportunities they enjoyed as middle-class Americans and the arbitrary restrictions on their sex. There was the advent of psychedelics, which allowed millions of people to sample utopia as a state of mind.

Those were different times. Today, anxiety is a first principle of social life, and the right knows how to exploit it. Capital foments the insecurity that impels people to submit to its demands. And yet there are more Americans than ever before who have tasted certain kinds of social freedoms and, whether they admit it or not, don't want to give them up or deny them to others. From Bill Clinton's impeachment to the Terri Schiavo case, the public has resisted the right wing's efforts to close the deal on the culture. Not coincidentally, the cultural debates, however attenuated, still conjure the ghosts of utopia by raising issues of personal autonomy, power, and the right to enjoy rather than slog through life. In telling contrast, the contemporary left has not posed class questions in these terms; on the contrary, it has ceded the language of freedom and pleasure, "opportunity" and "ownership," to the libertarian right.

Our culture of images notwithstanding, it cannot fairly be said that Americans' capacity for fantasy is impaired, even if it takes sectarian and apocalyptic rather than utopian forms. If anxiety is the flip side of desire, perhaps what we need to do is start asking ourselves and our fellow citizens what we want. The answers might surprise us.

Dissent, Fall 2005

Escape from Freedom
What's the Matter with Tom Frank (and the Lefties Who Love Him)?

The American left loves Thomas Frank's latest book. A few quotes from the jacket of *What's the Matter with Kansas?* capture the general adulatory tone. Barbara Ehrenreich: "The most insightful analysis of American right-wing pseudo-populism to come along in the last decade." Michael Kazin: "The second coming of H. L. Mencken, but with better politics." Molly Ivins: "A heartland populist, Frank is hilariously funny on what makes us red-staters different from those blue-staters (not), and he actually *knows* evangelical Christians, anti-abortion activists, gun-nuts, and Bubbas." Janeane Garofolo: "Over the last 30 years, the Right has managed to agitate and frighten the citizens of the heartland into consistently voting against their own best interests. It's about time someone started telling the truth about it—kudos to Tom Frank." No left meeting or conference, it seems, is complete without a speech by Frank or a panel on the book. Trying to think of another piece of backlash-era social commentary that had had a comparable impact in left circles, the closest I could come up with was Christopher Lasch's *The Culture of Narcissism,* which articulated an emerging strain of left cultural conservatism and added "narcissist" to the lexicon of anti-'60s-liberationist putdowns. These two books could hardly be more different, yet in regard to their audience the comparison is oddly instructive. For throughout the tumultuous political changes of the past three decades, one theme has remained constant: the mainstream left's desperate wish that the culture wars would disappear. As Lasch appealed to that wish in 1978, so does Frank today.

What's the Matter with Kansas? is fun to read. It is vividly written. It is witty. It is blunt. It paints a depressing and infuriating picture of what globalization, which is to say transnational corporate suburbanism, has done to Kansas and by extension to America. It attacks with ferocity and eloquence the stereotyping of authentic heartlanders vs. latte liberals from which lightweights like David Brooks have fashioned careers. It gives earnest lefties permission to pause in their handwringing efforts to "understand" the proles of the ultra-right and vent their frustration instead: since Frank was born in Kansas, he's allowed to voice un-pc thoughts about the "derangement" of its inhabitants. All this would be enough to attract attention. But the book is also grounded in a compelling and unassailable observation: that a large chunk of the working class—enough people to set the tone of local and regional politics in much of the country as well as to swing national elections—has displaced its anger at class oppression from the corporations and allied politicians who actually rule us to the cosmopolitan, secular "cultural elite," whose offenses range from rejection of conservative sexual morality to epicurean habits of consumption. So long as these class wires remain crossed, changing the direction of American politics is not possible. The question of course is how to undo the tangle, and to answer that we first have to understand what it means. Frank does a first-rate job of describing the inversion of class politics and making savage fun of it. Analysis, alas, is not his strong point.

Frank's thesis is this: politically, what the right-wing cultural backlash amounts to is a ploy by Republicans to trick working-class voters into supporting them so they can carry out their pro-business, anti-worker economic program. It's pure bait and switch: "*Vote* to stop abortion; *receive* a rollback in capital gains taxes. *Vote* to make our country strong again; *receive* deindustrialization. . . . *Vote* to stand tall against terrorists; *receive* Social Security privatization." The "backlash leaders" know they can't change the culture; indeed, they have no intention of doing so: "Abortion is never halted. Affirmative action is never abolished. The culture industry is never forced to clean up its act." On the contrary, they need the cultural issues, so they can continue to be elected to wreak their economic havoc. The culture war, in short, is not real. It is a "never-ending" series of "forgettable skirmishes." It is an exercise in triviality whereby "because some artist decides to shock the hicks by dunking Jesus in urine, the entire planet must remake itself along the lines preferred by the Republican Party, U.S.A."

Why has this right-wing strategy succeeded so well? Beyond the non-explanation that millions of ordinary people have gone off the deep end, Frank offers a couple of suggestions. Part of the blame goes to mass media: "The corporate world . . . blankets the nation with a cultural style designed to offend and to pretend-subvert: sassy teens in Skechers flout the Man; bigoted church-going moms don't tolerate their daughters' cool liberated friends; hipsters dressed in T-shirts reading 'FCUK' snicker at the suits who just don't get it." When *People* magazine features celebrities who raise money for animal rights or tell us not to say mean things about the handicapped and "beautiful people of every description [who] don expensive transgressive fashions, buy expensive, transgressive art," and so on, it gives the impression that "liberalism is a matter of shallow appearances, of fatuous self-righteousness; it is arrogant and condescending." From this perspective it is perfectly understandable that people should vote for backlash politicians who at least "stand there on the floor of the U.S. Senate and shout *no* to it all" (though of course the *no* is entirely hypocritical since "the assaults on . . . values, the insults, and the Hollywood sneers are all products of capitalism as surely as are McDonald's hamburgers and Boeing 737s").

Mostly, though, the problem as Frank sees it is that liberalism, which is to say the Democratic Party (he makes no distinction between the two), has lost its way. "For us," he declares, "it is the Democrats that are the party of workers, of the poor, of the weak, and the victimized." But the Democratic Leadership Council "has long been pushing the party to forget blue-collar workers and concentrate instead on recruiting affluent, white-collar professionals who are liberal on social issues." Under such influence, Democrats "explicitly rule out what they deride as 'class warfare' and take great pains to emphasize their friendliness to business interests. . . . by dropping the class language that once distinguished them sharply from Republicans they have left themselves vulnerable to cultural wedge issues like guns and abortion and the rest whose hallucinatory appeal would ordinarily be far overshadowed by material concerns."

Does this polemic sound familiar? It should, if you follow *The Nation, The American Prospect, Dissent, The Progressive, Mother Jones,* and other left publications, or the work of such writers as Richard Rorty, Michael Tomasky, Michael Lind, and Eric Alterman. Since Ronald Reagan's victory in 1980, variants of Frank's argument and calls for the political strategy it implies have been endlessly repeated in the precincts of the liberal left. There is widespread agreement that the left must concentrate its energies on promoting a populist economic program, and that the Democrats, if they want to win elections, must stop being identified as the party of "upper middle class" feminists, gays, and secularists, preoccupied by what Lind calls "inflammatory but marginal issues like abortion." Unlike Frank himself, many of the writers in this camp directly attack the cultural movements: they demand that feminists, gay rights activists, cultural left academics, and other inflammatory marginals cease and desist from waving red flags at the right by pressuring Democrats to stand firm on abortion and other social issues or making silly claims that popular culture has its subversive aspects or engaging in elitist debates about curriculum or defending artists who dunk Jesus in urine. Libs to cultural rads: shut up.

These writers also tend to share the dubious assumption that the Democrats are at heart the party of the downtrodden, and that the neoliberal economic agenda they have pursued since the Carter administration is a temporary aberration induced by bad strategic thinking (Frank attributes it to a lust for corporate money, along with the mistaken belief that workers will continue to vote

Democratic because they have nowhere else to go). But let me bracket that line of thought for the moment and take up their conception of cultural politics. Cultural conflict, so the argument goes, has no real political meaning in its own right and, in itself, no real social consequences—yet for millions of people it takes precedence over real, concrete interests. Cultural concerns, however "hallucinatory," are so potent as to override workers' doubts about Republicans' economic policies—but their effect would vanish in an instant if Democrats' economic policies were better. Furthermore, cultural issues are a slam-dunk for the Republicans since most Americans basically share the right's cultural values and only an affluent minority has any actual or potential interest in supporting feminism, gay rights, the sexual revolution, artistic freedom, or the separation of church and state. (Applying this rap to race, the first "social issue" to provoke a right-wing backlash and the reason the south defected to the Republicans, gets a bit complicated, since no one on the left can deny that the condition of blacks is a "real" problem—a dilemma solved by downplaying the cultural aspects of racism and arguing that it's basically a function of class.)

All these propositions are false. They make hash of the past 40 years of American history and, indeed, of the history of the 20th century; they are absurdly provincial, for the culture war in its various forms is a global phenomenon. If the question of why the right has come to dominate national politics, and how to reverse its ascendancy, is the first and most urgent question anyone on the contemporary left must ask, coming close behind is the puzzle of why so many liberals and "progressives" have signed on to a chimerical view of the relationship of politics, culture, and class.

The first great wave of cultural radicalism in Europe and America, beginning toward the end of the 19th century and lasting into the 1920s, built the framework of cultural modernity: feminism, sexual reform and birth control movements, youth movements, self-conscious homosexuality, psychoanalysis, avant-garde art and its associated bohemianism, the Russian Revolution with its short-lived burst of sexual, domestic, and educational reforms, the social and cultural ferment of the Weimar Republic. The first great right-wing-populist backlash movement was Nazism. Hitler's *kulturkampf* mobilized the population against the traitorous cultural elite: the rootless cosmopolitans both capitalist and communist, the sexual perverts, the degenerate artists, the race mixers, and above all the iconic representative of all these groups—the Jews. Unlike their contemporary American counterparts, German workers could have voted for communist and socialist parties speaking to their economic interests, yet many supported the Nazis. Then as now, the left saw right-wing populism as purely a tool of corporate interests. For their part, the corporate interests thought they could control Hitler for their own purposes. Both were wrong. In the end, the murder of six million Jews could not be explained by class analysis. If you aimed to understand it, you would have to try to understand the *kulturkampf*: what was the profound appeal of Hitler's world view? Then as now, the mainstream of the left resisted this question, uncritically sharing the general tendency to attribute the Holocaust to an inexplicable outbreak of "evil."

The renewed cultural revolt known as "the '60s" had its epicenter in the United States, but its impact was felt worldwide. Feminism is a global movement, American mass culture with its invitations to sexual and other material pleasures is everywhere, and the vast increase in all manner of transnational interchange attendant on globalization ensures that almost nowhere on earth are people insulated from the challenges of secular cosmopolitanism to traditional religious and patriarchal authority as well as to nationalism and the preservation of local culture. The reaction, in turn, has not been confined to the United States and its Christian right. Militant fundamentalism in the Islamic world and its European diaspora is the most conspicuous, violent form of global backlash, but there is also right-wing Catholicism in Eastern Europe, ultra-orthodox Judaism in Israel (and its Brooklyn diaspora), evangelicalism in Latin America and South Africa, Hindu and Sikh fundamentalism in India. The role of capitalism in encouraging both cultural revolt and the reaction against it is complex—more on this later—but it should be clear that the latter is not a Republican plot. The American Christian right may be in bed with capital; the Islamists of the Middle East are not. Indeed, this has been very confusing to an American left that can't understand religion and culture as real issues: the great majority of leftists, feminists excepted, supported the Iranian revolution and are ignoring the incipient disaster of theocracy in Iraq; as for Osama bin Laden, those who do not buy the argument that 9/11 was simply motivated by revenge, however misguided, for American Middle East policy have again resorted to "evil" as a convenient non-analysis.

The cultural radical impulse is rooted in the core elements of the democratic ideal: equality and freedom. There is a clear logic in the progression from affirming that all men are created equal, with the right to choose their government, enjoy freedom of speech and religion, and pursue happiness, to demanding that these rights apply to racial minorities, women, homosexuals, young people, atheists, and other groups in one way or another denied them; that the challenge to repressive authority extend beyond government to institutions like the corporation, the family, and the church; that the pursuit of happiness include freedom from sexual restrictions dictated by patriarchal religious norms; that free speech include explicitly sexual and anti-religious speech. Such demands, however, challenge not only deep structures of social privilege and subordination but our very definition of morality. All of us living in Judeo-Christian or Islamic cultures have imbibed from infancy a conception of sexuality—and desire more generally—as dangerous and destructive unless strictly controlled, of repression and self-sacrifice as indispensable virtues. Movements that encourage us to fulfill our desires are bound to arouse conflicting emotions, to intensify people's yearnings for freedom and pleasure, but also their anxiety and guilt about such primal rebellion. An outpouring of social experiment and innovation liberates creative energies, but also rage—at oppression, at losses of status and privilege, at the sources of anxiety and confusion. Cultural radical demands immediately question and disrupt existing social institutions, yet building democratic alternatives is a long-term affair: this leaves painful gaps in which men and women don't know how to behave with each other, in which marriage can no longer provide a stable environment for children but it's not clear what to do instead. Is it really surprising that cultural revolution should cause conflict?

To argue that this conflict has no political significance is to say that democratic values have none—never mind the blood and passion expended by Democrats and their enemies. To argue that one's "material interests" have only to do with economic class is to say that sexual satisfaction or frustration, bodily integrity and autonomy or the lack of same in the sexual and reproductive realm, the happiness or misery of our lives as lovers and spouses, parents and children are ethereal matters that have no impact on our physical being. (If abortion is a marginal issue, what about contraception, which was illegal in Connecticut until the Supreme Court's *Griswold* decision of 1965?) To dismiss as "hallucinatory" people's embattlement about what moral and cultural norms will govern their everyday lives and intimate relationships is to say that people (at least working-class people) do not, under normal circumstances, care deeply about anything beyond the size of their paychecks. Nor does this view consider that culture and economics are deeply intertwined: the family, after all, is an economic as well as a cultural institution. (Is sexist bias in divorce settlements a cultural or an economic issue? What about women's "second shift" in the household?)

A similar disregard for history, and for the concrete realities of American life, is embedded in another of Frank et al.'s assumptions: that cultural liberalism is entirely an artifact of the upper classes, while most Americans are social conservatives, essentially uninfluenced, except in a negative direction, by the cultural upheavals of the past 40 years. In fact, though the countercultural movements of the '60s came largely from the educated middle class, their influence soon spread far beyond those origins, especially among young people. Rock and roll—invented by black people, taken up by white teenagers, combined with folk music and blues by white bohemians—became the rebellious lingua franca of a generation. Marijuana and countercultural styles in dress, hair, and speech migrated from the cities to the provinces and up and down the class ladder (certain '60s styles—like long hair for men—have remained widespread in the white working class, long after the middle class abandoned them). Young Detroit autoworkers and working-class Vietnam veterans were conspicuous participants in the dissident culture and its political disaffection. Feminism mutated, emphasizing or playing down different issues, as it arrived in black neighborhoods, union halls, Catholic and evangelical churches, Colorado and Mississippi, but no stratum of society or section of the country was untouched by it. Attitudes toward openness about sex, female sexuality, single motherhood, divorce, women's right to equal education and jobs changed across the board. Abortion is now commonplace (ending one out of five pregnancies, according to the *New York Times*) among women of all classes. Homosexuality is increasingly accepted, queasiness about gay marriage notwithstanding.

A telling indication of these widespread changes is the very social permissiveness of contemporary pop culture that Frank charges with contributing to the backlash. Like many critics of capitalism, Frank makes the mistake of imagining that mass culture is a pure reflection of the corporate class that produces it and has nothing to do with the tastes or values of the mass audience that consumes it—as if it were the habit of corporations to pursue profits by offending most of their customers, rather than trying to appeal to their desires and fantasies. No doubt some readers are offended by the liberal "beautiful people" in *People,* but what about the three million or more who buy the magazine each week? Conservatives may be scandalized by Skecher's ads, or hip-hop, or pornography on the Internet, but their audience is hardly limited to the rich. In the course of purveying culture the corporations have committed many sins against art, against thought, against human decency and the public good—but blowing off Middle America is not one of them.

Of course, many people who are drawn to the hedonistic world of mass culture may at the same time feel guilty or repelled; which is to say that on such matters Americans are ambivalent. There is clearly a large gap between what people say to pollsters about cultural issues and how they actually live. Surveys in which 40% of Americans claim to attend church regularly have been contradicted by studies that measure actual attendance (the most famous such study, published in the *American Sociological Review* in 1993, put the figures at 20% for Protestants and 28% for Catholics). A recent *New York Times* article on an abortion clinic in Little Rock, Arkansas, interviewed 26 patients, some of whom had had more than one abortion: several said they believed abortion was wrong, selfish, or against their religion, but nonetheless felt they were too young or poor or alone to take care of a child. The American public has also shown on numerous occasions that it is leery of the sexual Robespierres of the theocratic right. Their antics at the 1992 Republican convention, where Pat Buchanan declared "a religious war . . . for the soul of America" and Marilyn Quayle disparaged working women (husband Dan had earlier made his notorious attack on the single motherhood of TV character Murphy Brown), were widely considered to have contributed to Bush *pere*'s defeat. Americans were not happy about Bill Clinton's affair with Monica, yet they refused to join the right's crusade against him; they reacted to the Starr Report's prurient details with hostility toward Starr, opposed Clinton's impeachment, and punished the Republicans for it in the next Congressional election. (This recalcitrance was bitterly frustrating to right-wing activists, prompting William Bennett to lament "the death of outrage" and Paul Weyrich to advocate abandoning electoral politics in favor of building separatist Christian institutions.) Nor did the majority of Americans support the right's most recent wretched excess of cultural grandstanding—its orchestrating of federal intervention in the Terri Schiavo case. Assuming for the sake of the argument that "moral values" were a significant factor in the last two presidential elections, their closeness is yet another rebuke to the notion that the mass of the working population supports the cultural right's agenda. Bush lost the popular vote in 2000 and won it by only 2.5% in 2004; Kerry received over 26,000,000 votes in "red" states, including 420,846 in Kansas.

The public's continuing ambivalence about cultural matters is all the more striking given that the political conversation on these issues has for 30 years been dominated by an aggressive, radical right-wing insurgency that has achieved an influence far out of proportion to its numbers. Its potent secret weapon has been the guilt and anxiety about desire that inform the character of Americans regardless of ideology; appealing to those largely unconscious emotions, the right has disarmed, intimidated, paralyzed its opposition. From the time the evangelical right's "pro-family" movement arose and joined forces with Catholic right-to-life organizers in the mid-'70s, the broad left, including liberal feminists, adopted a strategy of appeasement rather than militant defense of feminism and abortion rights. Many men on the left had supported the women's movement only reluctantly and in response to tremendous political pressure at the height of the feminist surge; they jettisoned this baggage with relief. But plain sexism was only part of the story. It could not explain why Betty Friedan attacked feminist radicals and proclaimed herself "pro-family"; why feminist leaders insisted that the Equal Rights Amendment had nothing to do with abortion or lesbian rights or a critique of traditional sexual roles; why advocates of legal abortion began apologizing, praising the moral commitment of their opponents, and talking about "choice" in the abstract rather than the procedure that dare not speak its name. The appeasers argued that they needed to soften their stands to avoid alienating traditionalist voters from the ERA campaign, the "pro-choice" movement, and the Democratic Party. But in truth their lack of conviction that a majority of Americans could be won over—if not immediately, then in the long run—to a politics of equality, freedom, and pleasure reflected their own deep doubts about the legitimacy of those values. They were appeasing themselves as much as anyone else.

Predictably, the strategy of pandering to the right was an abject failure: Reagan was elected; the ERA lost. If an ambivalent public hears only one side of a question, the conservative side, passionately argued—if people's impulses to the contrary are never reinforced, and they perceive that the putative spokespeople for feminism and liberalism are actually uncomfortable about advancing their views—the passionate arguers will carry the day. Why would anyone support a movement that won't stand behind its own program? But the left did not learn the obvious lesson—that to back away from fighting for your beliefs on the grounds that you have no hope of persuading people to share them is to perpetrate a self-fulfilling prophecy. On the contrary, the appeasers could see in their defeats only a confirmation of their pessimism. This scenario has been repeated countless times as the country has moved steadily to the right, yet it appears to have inspired no second thoughts. The stubborn failure to rethink a losing strategy can't help but suggest that its proponents on some level do not really care to win.

If despite this abdication the cultural right has met considerable popular resistance—if most people today, including many who profess to be conservatives, are reluctant to give up certain social freedoms or deny them to others—suppose the left had consistently stood up for the principle of a feminist, democratic culture? Can anyone doubt that the political landscape would be different? It follows, surely, that if the left were now to push back on cultural issues, it would find Americans more receptive than it imagines. But for Tom Frank, the fact that the right has not decisively won the culture war leads to a different conclusion, reminiscent of Vermont Senator George Aiken's position on Vietnam—that we should say we won and go home. According to him, nothing has changed culturally, and nothing will change, because our corporate rulers don't want it to.

It's at this point that Frank crosses the line from merely being wrongheaded to committing the intellectual equivalent of criminal negligence. For a great many people, especially women, have suffered, and continue to suffer, from those practical effects of the cultural backlash that he insists do not exist, and therefore need not detain us. True, the corporate wing of the Republican Party (which is to say the dominant wing, ideologically and financially) sees the religious right mainly as a key constituency that is essential to a winning coalition and useful for such purposes as providing a moral rationale for laissez-faire policies. For much of the party leadership, including Reagan and both Bushes, cultural issues have indeed been a handy demagogic tool rather than a serious priority. But this is not to say the Republicans are averse to rewarding their evangelical allies whenever feasible. They have first of all given what used to be the lunatic fringe the prestige and legitimacy accorded to players in the nation's ruling party, as well as an ongoing national platform for their propaganda and for psychodramas like the Schiavo affair. They have treated as patronage for the Christian right numerous judicial appointments that will shape the courts for years to come, along with executive appointments that affect policy in areas ranging from criminal justice to women's health. Myriad laws and executive orders have financed religious activities and sanctioned religious discrimination in publicly funded jobs, banned all federal funding for abortion, required promotion of abstinence as a condition of supporting domestic sex education programs or international AIDS prevention organizations, restricted stem-cell research, blocked over-the-counter sale of the morning-after pill, denied federal grants to artists who don't meet religious right standards of decency (a very partial list). Nor should it be forgotten that the radical right nearly brought down a president out of cultural animus (Clinton's neoliberal economic policies could hardly have been the motive).

But the impact of the backlash transcends its role in the federal government. Christian right activists are a major force in local and state politics, from school boards to legislatures, especially but not exclusively in the south. They have also profoundly influenced the political climate—including, as I've noted, the behavior of their supposed opponents—and thereby the informal social norms and pressures that, far more than government action, dictate what people feel free to do, say, or even think. On all these levels they have pursued a war against secularism whose effects range from the planting of religious monuments in public buildings and efforts to teach religious pseudo-science in public schools to a new unofficial requirement for presidential candidates—that they not only believe in God but feel comfortable making public professions of faith.

Frank's cavalier pronouncement that "Abortion is never halted" is literally correct—abortion was never halted even when it was illegal all over the country—but entirely misses the point: the goal of the right is not to stop abortion but to demonize it, punish it, and make it as difficult and traumatic as possible. All this it has accomplished fairly well, even without overturning *Roe v. Wade*. Current legal restrictions include bans on funding abortion for Medicaid patients, parental consent requirements, regulations that make abortion clinics prohibitively expensive to operate, waiting period and counseling requirements that force women to make more than one trip to the clinic. (Evidently, for all his class consciousness Frank is unaware of how heavily these restrictions weigh on poor and working-class women, who can't afford to travel or take time off from their jobs, and must often delay their abortions beyond the safest period to save enough money for the fee.) And then there are the extra-legal tactics—the right's relentless stigmatizing of abortion (helped along by apologetic liberals), its harassment of clinic patients and staffs, its hit-list websites posting "murderers'" names and addresses, and its terrorist assassinations of doctors.

As a result large sections of the country have few or no abortion providers. Many clinics close because they can't afford to comply with regulations, can't get insurance, or are kicked out by landlords. Fewer and fewer doctors are willing to perform abortions, and most medical schools do not even teach the procedure. Increasingly, women who exercise their legal right do so in an atmosphere that encourages guilt, shame, and fear. At the Little Rock abortion clinic women worried about being ostracized were their secret to be known. "I'd lose my job," one said. "My family's reputation would be ruined. It makes me nervous even being in the waiting room." Nor should we imagine that such sentiment is confined to the likes of conservative Arkansas (where, nevertheless, Kerry got 45% of the vote). What are we to make of the recent cases of high school girls in the northeast, bastion of the cultural elite, who could find no solution to their unwanted pregnancies but to kill their newborn infants? Tom: is this real enough for you?

The idea that cultural radicalism is antithetical to egalitarian class politics—that it is at best a divisive distraction, at worst a weapon of the bourgeoisie—is not new. It has been floating around the socialist and communist movements since the 1880s and has been predominant on the left for the past century (except, perhaps, for a brief period during the 1960s). One strand of the argument rests on a populist identity politics that associates conventional morality with "working-class values." For most of history, only aristocrats had the power to avoid work, pursue pleasure, and flout with impunity the moral norms that applied to their inferiors; sexual rebellion in particular has been identified with domination (see the writings of the Marquis de Sade). In the modern era, feminist and other cultural radical movements have typically been founded by people who are economically secure enough to be free of day-to-day worry about survival and so able to focus on what's wrong with the quality of their lives. At the other end of the class hierarchy, since the emergence of the "lumpenproletariat" in the 19th century, "vice" has also been associated with social outcasts who have nothing to lose. It is therefore supposed to be a point of working-class pride, solidarity, and salt-of-the-earth status to reject the "decadence" of the rich and the upper middle class as well as the fecklessness of the very poor. The contemporary right's incitement of working people to direct their class anger against the "cultural elite" was in fact anticipated by the venerable and still prominent left tradition of charging cultural radicals with trespassing on the values of workers. Its exponents do not see—because they are blinded by their own guilt and fear of freedom—that subjection to sexual conformity and bromides about the "dignity of work" is if anything part of working-class oppression; that sexual happiness and freedom from alienated labor are universal goods to which everyone is entitled.

Another left rationale for rejecting cultural politics is rooted in the historical connection of cultural movements to the marketplace. The rise of capitalism, which undermined the authority of the patriarchal family and church, put widespread cultural revolt in the realm of possibility. Wage labor allowed women and young people to find a means of support outside the home. Urbanization allowed people the freedom of social anonymity. The shift from production- to consumption-oriented capitalism and the spread of mass media encouraged cultural permissiveness, since the primary technique of marketing as well as the most salient attraction of mass art is their appeal to the desire for individual autonomy and pleasure and specifically to erotic fantasy.

Accordingly, left cultural conservatives have argued that feminism and cultural radicalism, in weakening traditional institutions like the family, have merely contributed to the market's hegemony over all spheres of life. Many leftists, including Frank, see the cultural movements through the lens of their hostility to consumerism: observing that commercial exploitation of sex is ubiquitous and that rock and roll, feminism, and other countercultural artifacts have been used to sell everything from cars and fashions to credit cards and mutual funds, they conclude that cultural liberation, like the backlash against it, is a tool of capitalist domination. That capital is promiscuous in its zeal to reduce human impulses to selling points—willing to dish up feminism or family values, sex or religion as the occasion demands—is interpreted to mean that there is no real opposition between cultural left and right.

Again, this mindset puts a progressive political gloss on what is really a form of puritanism, offended by the fleshpots of the market, not just the profits. What it ignores, or denies—as Marx never did—is the paradoxical nature of capitalism. In destroying the old patriarchal order, in making all that was solid melt into air, in fomenting constant dynamism and change, capital made space for the revolutionary ideas that would challenge its own authority. In letting loose the genie of desire in the service of profit, consumer culture unleashes forces that can't reliably be controlled. Frank and his fellow anti-culture-warriors sneer at the idea that there can be anything subversive about popular culture, and indeed, these days the process of channeling potentially rebellious impulses into safe activities like shopping seems to be working well. Yet in the very different political and social context of the '60s, the invitation to pleasure that pervaded mass culture, from its advertising to its music, played an important role in the cultural revolt: it peeled off the repressive, security-oriented surface of post–World War II America and suggested to young people that another way of life was possible.

A crucial ingredient of that '60s context was unprecedented mass prosperity. In the post-war years the great majority of the white population had attained a middle-class standard of living; they produced a generation of children—a particularly large one, at that—who had never known the Depression and grew up taking economic security for granted, greatly expanding the pool of people likely to notice their cultural discontents. Though black people remained poor relative to whites, they too benefited from the general prosperity, enough so that a critical mass of students, clergy, and other middle-class activists was available to start the civil rights and black power movements (which in turn became a template for feminism and a major influence on the white left and counterculture). At the same time, the success of the post-war economy muted class conflict. Although '60s radicals did raise class issues, they did not gain much traction; most people were satisfied with their economic status, while liberals regarded the persistence of poverty and racial discrimination as occasions for a cleanup operation rather than evidence of any systemic problem. In contrast, cultural issues—feminism especially—tapped into widespread dissatisfaction and quickly became the signature of the time.

As I've suggested, the very nature of the cultural rebellion provoked a backlash; it was well underway by 1968—even as the radical feminist movement was getting off the ground—and four years later George McGovern sank under the weight of the slogan "Acid, Amnesty, and Abortion." But the reaction accelerated and intensified after 1973, when the economy contracted amid the first conspicuous domestic symptoms of what would come to be called globalization. Just as economic security had encouraged cultural experimentation and dissidence, economic anxiety had the opposite effect. In addition the renewed class warfare that marked this period was presented as a cultural offensive. Politicians and corporate spokespeople justified lower wages, layoffs, and assaults on public goods and social welfare programs as moral correctives to Americans' hedonism, profligacy, and excessive expectations.

Until 1980 this offensive was bipartisan (it reached its height under Jimmy Carter) and targeted the American people in general. It was the Reagan administration that began scapegoating the cultural elite (Spiro Agnew's "effete snobs" and "nattering nabobs") along with the "welfare queens" of the underclass. But Reagan also did something the left, to its great misfortune, has never understood: with his paean to "morning in America" and call for an "opportunity society" he co-opted the yearnings that had been aroused by the '60s movements and stifled by the nonstop pull-up-your- socks lecture of the Carter years. Freedom, as recoded by the Reagan right, meant pursuing unlimited wealth, at least in one's dreams, and so identifying with the rich, their desire for low taxes, and their aversion to "big government"; it meant embracing America's mission to make the world safe for democracy; it meant license to express rage. Pleasure in sex might be restricted, but pleasure in aggression was encouraged, including uninhibited bashing of black people, poor people, criminals, deviants, and liberals. The cultural elite, on the other hand, was portrayed as not only immoral and unpatriotic but repressive, what with its guilt-mongering attacks on greed and its allergy to guns and its lectures about bigoted language. Ever since, the right has won elections with some version of this formula. Its success has depended on convincing working-class swing voters not only that liberals are their class enemy, but that their own aspirations for "opportunity" and "ownership" are best expressed by policies that favor the rich. It's true that during this time American workers have not been offered a serious alternative to the right's plutocratic program. But neither have they been offered any alternative to the right's conception of freedom. The disastrous trajectory of American politics should long since have made clear that this second lacuna is as ruinous as the first—if not more so.

What little intra-left debate there has been on *What's the Matter with Kansas?* has centered on the question of "false consciousness." Does it exist? And do working-class cultural conservatives really suffer from it, or have they just figured out that there's no significant difference between the parties on economic issues so they may as well vote to defend their privileges as white people or men or Christians? I find the latter view reductive and not very interesting. On the other hand, I can't go along with Frank's implicit judgment that the right is more deluded than the left. I've already argued that leftists' refusal to take on the culture war has more to do with their own conservative impulses than with any rational strategy for a progressive revival. But what of the other trait the anti-culture-warriors appear to have in common—their mystifying attachment to the Democratic Party? Consider that the last Democratic administration to profess the philosophy of the New Deal—Lyndon Johnson's—held office before Tom Frank was born. A few years later, capital pulled out of the business-labor-government coalition that in response to the Depression and the Cold War had committed itself to maintaining a prosperous, stable middle class with high wages, social benefits, and government regulation. From now on, Americans were told, we would have to submit to the discipline of the free market. Carter embraced the neoliberal order with its mantra of austerity; he presided (with the help of Ted Kennedy) over decontrol of oil prices and deregulation of the airline, trucking, and banking industries. Clinton supported the pro-corporate program of the Democratic Leadership Council and abolished the entitlement to welfare. The Democratic establishment is firmly center-right, as its last two presidential candidates have been. The party has no economic-populist faction with any organization or influence; in any case the party of Roosevelt was the product of a particular set of conditions that are gone and will not return. Ironically, the Democrats do exactly what Frank accuses the Republicans of doing: they use cultural issues to get the base to swallow their economic policy ("We have to keep to the center or those swing voters will elect the lunatics, and there goes the Supreme Court"). *Vote* to protect *Roe v. Wade*; *receive* NAFTA.

Is the fantasy of the Democrats' renaissance just a matter of naivete, or is something deeper going on? I suspect it's of a piece with the denial that culture is important—a defense against the terror of radicalism that must be warded off at all costs. For some, there is also nostalgia for a time when white liberal men like Tom Frank were heroes, before they were robbed of the spotlight by blacks, women, and gays, forced to confront private conflicts as public issues, and ultimately pushed aside by the right. There is something poignant about this, given the political bleakness of the day, but it's an indulgence the American left cannot afford. We need to look not to the New Deal but to a new politics, one that recognizes equality and freedom, class and culture, as ineluctably linked. That we're so far from this recognition makes Kansas the least of our problems.

Situations, 2006

Three Elegies for Susan Sontag

Art

When I was finding my voice as a writer in the thick of the sixties, Susan Sontag loomed large: she was among the relatively few literary intellectuals who were seriously trying to grapple with a new, rich, and, for many, disconcerting cultural situation. The title essay of her first collection, *Against Interpretation,* combined a formidable erudition about the avant-garde with a manifesto-like plea that critics end their one-sided emphasis on teasing out the meaning of art and embrace their pleasure in it. "What is important now," she wrote, "is to recover our senses. We must learn to see more, to hear more, to feel more . . . . In place of a hermeneutics we need an erotics of art."

The arch-interpreters of the modernist canon, Marx and Freud, had in Sontag's view outlived their usefulness. Film, she declared, was "the most alive, the most exciting, the most important of all art forms right now" because its vivid immediacy discouraged interpretation. The reason, in part, was "the happy accident that films for such a long time were just movies; in other words, that they were supposed to be part of mass, as opposed to high, culture, and were left alone by most people with minds." Another essay in the same volume, "One Culture and the New Sensibility," argued that the distinction between high and low culture was breaking down and that the hallmark of the "new sensibility" was its orientation toward non-literary forms. "Sensations, feelings, the abstract forms and styles of sensibility": this was the stuff of contemporary art. Sontag also lauded the psychoanalytic radicalism of Norman O. Brown, who, unlike Freud or the bland Freudian "revisionists" of the day, insisted on the primacy of the body and on utopia as Dionysian ecstasy. And then there was the essay that made her famous, "Notes on Camp," which put all these strains of thought, or sensibility, together in a form that by abandoning linear exegesis for a series of epigrammatic "notes" embodied her point and was fun besides.

These essays were highly iconoclastic works in the context of Sontag's milieu. At the time they were published, literary intellectuals had two major preoccupations—defending high art against mass art, which, in Dwight Macdonald's inimitable formulation, was considered not art at all but merely a commodity like chewing gum; and rescuing civilization from, as they saw it, the barbarians and antinomian nihilists of the radical counterculture. Those few who tried to relate to, say, pop music, did painful things like analyzing Beatles songs to show how much like high art they were. In our turn, writers of my generation who were cultural and sexual radicals and had passionate mass-cultural loyalties—to movies and even more to rock and roll—regarded literary intellectuals as uncomprehending dinosaurs; our models were journalists like Pauline Kael and Tom Wolfe.

I don't remember how Sontag first came to my attention. It could have been through an article about her: she was something of a star, after all. In those days I didn't read avant-garde quarterlies like *Partisan Review,* and it had never occurred to me to write for them. Looking back, I see that it could easily have been otherwise, were it not for the fifties' gender politics that still prevailed in my college years. I was an English major at Barnard around the time that budding critics like Marshall Berman and Morris Dickstein were across the street studying with the likes of Lionel Trilling; but the Columbia English department would not allow Barnard women in its classes. Instead, I won the competition to become a summer guest editor at *Mademoiselle,* as Sylvia Plath had done some years before. (Like its masculine equivalent *Esquire, Mademoiselle* was once an important venue for literary journalism; in fact, Sontag's essay "One Culture and the New Sensibility" was originally published there.)

Later, the advent of the "new journalism" convinced me that writing for popular magazines could be more than a lark, that it had potent aesthetic and intellectual rewards; and this path also appealed to my interest in mass cultural forms. But Susan Sontag presented me with another possibility, which I must have taken in, though I don't remember consciously doing so: that one could write in her tone of high seriousness, and draw on high-cultural references, and still engage with contemporary pop culture and cultural radicalism on their own terms.

As the sixties' cultural upheaval gave way to seventies cultural austerity, Sontag retreated to a more conservative stance on aesthetic issues. Her prime concern was no longer achieving an erotics of art, but parsing the morality of art. Or rather, the erotics of art—the pleasure we derived from it—became something to be questioned and inspected for its darker, often sadomasochistic aspects. In *On Photography,* it was the potential for aggression, manipulation, and bad faith that caught Sontag's imagination (as it had done Walter Benjamin's): photographer, viewer, and the multifaceted object that lay between them were always guilty until proven innocent. "Fascinating Fascism" eloquently attacked the readiness of critics to abstract the beauty of Leni Riefenstahl's films and photographs from the moral implications of an aesthetic that validated and promoted the Nazis' world view—"the force of her work being precisely in the continuity of its aesthetic and political ideas." The essay implied some rethinking of Sontag's own past standpoint: "Art which evokes the themes of fascist aesthetic is popular now, and for most people is probably no more than a variant of camp. . . . Art that seemed eminently worth defending ten years ago, as a minority or adversary taste, no longer seems defensible today, because the ethical and cultural issues it raises have become serious, even dangerous. . . . Taste is context, and the context has changed."

The changed context was American society's aggressive repudiation of sixties utopianism. In 1996, in the preface to a new Spanish translation of *Against Interpretation,* Sontag wrote that while she still agreed with most of the positions she had taken, "The world in which these essays were written no longer exists. . . . The ever more triumphant values of consumer capitalism promote—indeed, impose—the cultural mixes and insolence and defense of pleasure that I was advocating for quite different reasons." Her once-dissident enthusiasms had become widespread, owing to forces she had not at the time understood. "Barbarism," she declared, "is one name for what was taking over. Let's use Nietzsche's term: we had entered, really entered, the age of nihilism." I imagine a smiling Theodor Adorno, welcoming Sontag home. This is the Frankfurt School's language of profound pessimism, a language that most of Sontag's peers never relinquished. I suspect it came more naturally to her than her moment of openness to a short-lived current of hope.

The truth is that the process of assimilating the counterculture to the mainstream—a process to which mass consumption was central—was already going on in 1966, when *Against Interpretation* was published and my rock critic friends and I were trying to make sense of what was happening as the Beatles sold millions of records while announcing they were more popular than Jesus. The culture was complex then as it is complex, if much scarier, now. The question remains: what of human possibility? Do we simply abandon the idea?

A few years ago, listening to Sontag speak at a panel discussion sponsored by the NYU journalism department, where I teach, I was startled by her wholesale, contemptuous dismissal of American popular culture. There was an enormous gap between her critique of Riefenstahl's defenders—which represented high-culture moral indignation at its most cogent and pointed—and this kind of free-floating animus: Sontag, it seemed, had ended up, well, a curmudgeon. Yet her early work remains a testament to boundaries that could be crossed, worlds that could come together in new ways. "Camp taste," she wrote, "is a kind of love, love for human nature. It relishes, rather than judges, the little triumphs and awkward intensities of 'character' . . . . Camp is a tender feeling." Yes.

Politics

Susan Sontag believed that intellectuals should, must, take political stands. She was active in the movement against the Vietnam War. She tried, with passion and persistence, to awaken American and European consciences to the genocidal catastrophe in Bosnia. And yet I would not call Sontag a political thinker. For Sontag, politics was an arena for practicing the high moral style. It was about the individual bearing witness. It was, in another of its aspects, about the writer defending literary values, the values of civilization, when they were under siege, as they were in Sarajevo. It was a question of will. Politics, however, is preeminently about social structures, collective behavior—or mass psychology—and the relation between the two. It is a question of understanding, and a question of power.

If Marx and Freud were enemies in the quest for an erotics of art, they were even more clearly antagonists of a politics of personal morality. They regarded morals as the product of social and psychic structures, respectively: this was why moralists' lofty values were never achieved in real life. For Marx, understanding the social structure was key to political revolution; for radical Freudians if not for Freud himself, understanding the libidinal structure made possible a revolution in culture.

Sontag's attitude was more in line with the strain of American liberalism that, in the years after 1945, regarded morality as the antidote to totalitarianism of the right and left: it was this stance that impelled her to statements like "Communism is fascism with a human face"—though in fact fascism and Communism, while having certain features in common, are fundamentally different in social structure and mass psychology both. This has also been the ethos of dissident Eastern European intellectuals, which characterizes the post-Soviet era. My own approach to politics owes much to Marx and Freud. In my view, Eastern Europe has suffered gravely from the refusal of its intellectuals to think seriously, in a political way, about structures like class, gender, and religion. I believe Bosnia was able to happen, and people who should have known better were able to ignore it, because we have never really come to terms with the confluence of historical, power-political, cultural, and psychological forces that produced the Holocaust. Moral condemnation alone will not keep these atrocities from happening again and again.

Individuals bearing witness do not change history; only movements that understand their social world can do that. Movements encourage solidarity; the moral individual is likely, all unwittingly, to do the opposite, for bearing witness is lonely: it breeds feelings of superiority and moralistic anger against those who are not doing the same. Sontag often succumbed to this temptation. Frustrated that the Bosnian cause did not arouse intellectuals as the Spanish Civil War had done, she accused them of middle-class selfishness and complacency. That there might be reasons other than personal moral turpitude that others did not share her urgency—a depoliticized time, the confusion and despair of the left, the lack of a social analysis that could put the Balkan events in context—did not occur to her, or so it seemed.

Still, I do not dismiss Sontag's moral challenge. For along with understanding, there must after all be will. It is one thing to understand how our conscience is formed; yet since we can't, except in the most marginal ways, undo the twists and turns of our formation, conscience is what we are stuck with—if we are lucky. Conscience may be a false front, but its absence is deathly. Individuals bearing witness cannot do the work of social movements, but they can break a corrosive and demoralizing silence. It was, then, a good thing, an important thing, that Sontag went to Sarajevo, and kept going there, and wrote about it, and wouldn't shut up. Her voice was hectoring, irritating, cranky, on-her-high-horse superior. But what it said was true.

Death

Although Sontag lived for many years with the disease that finally killed her, she never wrote about that experience, except obliquely. "Illness," she declared in one of her more famous polemics, "is not a metaphor . . . the most truthful way of regarding illness—and the healthiest way of being ill—is one most purified of, most resistant to, metaphoric thinking." Disease, as Sontag conceived of it, was a brute, dumb fact. The cultural baggage that produced the imagination of cancer as a "ruthless, secret invasion" or the expression of a sexually inhibited, emotionally resigned character was an artifact of mystery; just as the romanticism that had once surrounded tuberculosis lost its potency with the advent of antibiotics, so would the myths that defined our fear of cancer, once "its etiology becomes as clear and its treatment as effective as those of TB have become." In the meantime, metaphor merely served to terrorize and stigmatize the sufferer, on whom the public's anxiety-ridden fantasies were projected.

"Illness as Metaphor"—which originated as a lecture, became a *New York Review* essay, then a small book, and eventually acquired a companion essay, "AIDS and Its Metaphors"—is, like so much of Sontag's work, at once bold and problematic. It is also, in a sense, out of date. Since 1978, when it first appeared, both the ubiquity, which is to say familiarity, of cancer and improvements in its treatment have robbed the disease of much of the mythological aura that Sontag railed against. At the same time, the backlash against psychoanalysis has banished from the public conversation the theory, advanced by the radical psychoanalyst Wilhelm Reich, that most excited Sontag's indignation: that cancer has its genesis in sexual and emotional repression. The conventional wisdom now tracks Sontag's own views, in some measure, perhaps, because of her influence. Yet as a Sontag document "Illness" retains its fascination, in part because it is her only commentary on this fateful passage in her life, but more, perhaps, because of the conundrum it poses: this is the work of a writer whose passion was language rejecting metaphor as a means of understanding; a critic whose central subject matter was aesthetics, morality, and the relation between them stating categorically that illness has no aesthetic or moral meaning.

It makes sense to resist metaphors that aim to punish or control, reduce or falsify experience—indeed to acknowledge that even the aptest metaphor is a flawed prism, that we see through a glass darkly. But it does not follow that metaphoric thinking can simply be purged in favor of a "healthy" transparency. I am not of the school of thought that regards all human experience as reducible to language; the body, in my view, is not simply a discourse; but describing the body and its relation to the mind and the world is another matter. What Sontag does not seem to grasp is that the allopathic medical model of disease, as an entity entirely external to the person, with an objective cause and cure, is as metaphorical as any other, based on the larger metaphors of Cartesian philosophy and Newtonian science. And as a description, it's at best incomplete. We float in a sea of pathogens, microbial and chemical, natural and artificial, yet only some of us, sometimes, become seriously ill; or more precisely, our bodies falter and die at different rates, on different timetables, in different ways, despite the shared hazards of our condition. So too with our ability to recover. As a way of recognizing these facts, the psychoanalytic metaphors of libido and repression, conflict and defense may be closer to the mark.

Disease takes hold when the immune system fails, when external agent meets internal vulnerability. What makes us vulnerable? Today's common sense says "genes"—yet we know that genes represent the potential rather than the actual, and that the relation between genetic potential and its expression is complex and obscure: what mediates is our environment, but also our experience. We know that emotion affects the body—its heart and respiration rates, its hormone flow, its muscle tensions. Surely it is conceivable that disappointments we cannot bear to acknowledge or express directly might express themselves in physical form.

That this idea has so often been crudely translated into blame—as if the ill deliberately and perversely choose their disappointments, and their denials, and so their diseases—is the result of people's tendency to conflate it with yet another (and in our culture far more powerful) metaphorical system, a system dedicated to the idea of the abstract, disembodied will: Judeo-Christian morality. The New Testament tells us "the wages of sin is death"; the Jewish formulation is *mida k'neged mida* (measure for measure). If the concept of psychosomatic illness is regularly misused to add to the misery of the ill, is this justification enough to discard it altogether? What might sufferers themselves lose by doing so?

Shortly after I was asked to write an obituary for Sontag—a woman whose writing and public statements always made me feel as if we were enmeshed in an ongoing conversation, usually an argument—my ruminations on her and "Illness as Metaphor" took a more personal turn: I received my own cancer diagnosis. Caught early, amenable to the latest advances of allopathic medicine—still, the disease did not strike me as a brute, dumb fact. A life-threatening illness, it seemed to me, was a spiritual crisis by definition. Unanswerable questions about etiology were the least of it (though in truth I was instantly swamped—I imagine the ghost of Susan stifling a smirk—by a wave of superstitious terror and guilt, produced by the fantasy that every mean-spirited thought, let alone act, I'd ever committed had somehow converged in an unlikely spot on my non-smoker's lung). The real questions were about the future.

When clichés (that is, stale metaphors) about the precariousness of life suddenly present themselves as nothing less than the simple, compelling truth, it concentrates the mind. How best to further one's recovery, and how to live in the meantime? Exert all one's energies toward forging on, so as not to be dominated by the disease? Or revise one's priorities, focus on what's most important, and jettison the rest? (And what is most important—love? work? attention to the precious sensations of living?) Make health a central project, or refuse to be obsessed? What to put on the soundtrack—the Clash or John Fahey? Mahler or Arvo Pärt? And if it is not possible to do without metaphor, what metaphors suit? "You are in a war," a friend wrote me: the military metaphor being the most common of all and another for which Sontag has no use. Was I in a war—a civil war, perhaps, against my own rogue cells? Who was the enemy, exactly? Or was my ordeal more like a marathon swim against an undertow?

Interestingly, "Illness" begins with a metaphor. "I want," Sontag tells us, "to describe not what it is really like to emigrate to the kingdom of the ill and live there, but the punitive or sentimental fantasies concocted about that situation: not real geography but stereotypes of national character." This is a book without a protagonist, set in a terrain without inhabitants; or rather they are opaque, their presence revealed only by the tropes that surround them, as black holes are detected by a bent gravitational field. It is a somber silence, befitting the author's funeral; for death is truly the kingdom where metaphors come to an end.

New Politics, Summer 2005

Coda

Selections from
"The Cultural Unconscious
in American Politics:
Why We Need a
Freudian Left"

INTRODUCTION
Stanley Aronowitz

Shortly after the publication of her essay collection *Don't Think, Smile!* in 2000, my partner, Ellen Willis, began working on a book-length project tentatively called "The Cultural Unconscious in American Politics." The central argument was that our understanding of cultural and political crises would be incomplete without a psychoanalytic dimension. The three draft chapters she wrote integrate many of these elements with a nuanced and persuasive account of the salience of radical psychoanalytic thought. Freud's ideas about the force of the unconscious on human behavior, especially the compelling power of libido, is her starting point. But she also found the basis for her claims about radical psychoanalysis in Erich Fromm's early work, Herbert Marcuse's seminal *Eros and Civilization,* and especially in the many writings of Wilhelm Reich. As well as being a legendary radical feminist, she turned to her cultural radicalism as the most comprehensive framework of her thought.

In these excerpts from her unfinished project, Ellen takes unfashionable positions: that biology is ultimately the basis of character structure and human relations, and that there is a cultural unconscious—as opposed to purely economic or political forces—that illuminates the striking ability of the right to mount a successful counterrevolution against the most important gains of the sixties. She focuses on the sixties youth generation's important attitudinal shift about sex, its critique of the numbing and exhausting nature of much paid work, the beginning of a massive skepticism about marriage, and a Second Wave feminist movement that challenged the role of women in society by insisting that the personal is the political. Freed from Freud's insistence that humans must tolerate their inescapable subordination to the imperatives of labor, we were at the brink of a qualitatively new moment in history when pleasure could, for the first time, be realized in everyday life. She acknowledges the importance of the fight for women's economic equality with men, but stresses the potentially life-changing demands for sexual equality in the bedroom and in child rearing. Ellen reminds us that the sixties decade was marked by a new passion for politics produced by raised consciousness of the radical possibilities of a postscarcity epoch.

But as she points out, the passion didn't last: the conservative ripple throughout the white middle class seemed to occur "overnight." The astounding rise of the right—its attack on abortion, its pro-family conservatism, its resolute and successful campaign to defeat the Equal Rights Amendment, its implosion of conventional sexual morality—was greeted by many liberals and leftists with submission rather than scorn and opposition. Rejecting the good/evil mantra ascriptions that rely on concepts such as cowardice, Ellen instead invokes her category of the cultural unconscious. Many left and liberal folks were still ensconced in the old ways, and their recently adopted cultural radicalism was still too fragile to withstand the withering assault from the right. And many were aware of their backtracking. Some argued, as Ellen once reminded us, that "we can't let the conservatives capture family values." Others who drifted to the center or to the right held on to support for the social welfare benefits of the New Deal yet fell into the trap of blaming the victim for their distress, a moral argument that is often the last refuge of bad faith. Above all, Ellen analyzes the perfidy of the liberal feminists who, in order to "rescue the women's moment from the stigma of cultural radicalism," concentrated their efforts on economic issues and embraced many of the right's signature values.

Ellen's treatment of the defeat of cultural radicalism is not a rant against its detractors. In these pages, the reader will find a cool, levelheaded genealogy that traces the key events and attitudes conditioning the retreat from a bold feminism and, more broadly, radicalism. Among her claims is that the left has become prone to its own isolation by refusing to confront the essence of the right's appeal, even as its social justice program is virtually irrefutable.

The heart of the right's attack was the reinsertion of conventional sexual morality. In this respect, she devotes some space to the contributions of Reich. She cites his efforts, first in Austria and later in Germany, to arouse the interest of Communists and Socialists to the imperatives of the sexual question—especially among youth and the necessity for the left parties to address their issues—and draws the parallels to our own time. She points to Germany in the thirties, when it was in the grip of a profound economic crisis. Ellen argues that cultural conservatism became a basis of the rise of fascism there, just as cultural conservatism thrives in our own time of economic depression. Insecurity reinforces cultural conservatism because people seek solace in the past; they want to return, if possible, to their own childhood or to a mythological past when the family was together and prosperous, whether accurate or not. She writes: "Moral arguments have been [an] important part of persuading people to accept lower standard of living, harder, longer hours of work, for lower wages, cutbacks in social welfare benefits." Keep in mind that these lines were composed at the end of the past century, when the popular view was that all was well with the U.S. economy, despite a depression that was eight years in the offing.

The last chapter of her project, "The Flight from Libido," addresses the appearance and growth of the so-called neo-Freudian revisionists like Karen Horney, then later Erich Fromm, both of whom, while having disagreements among themselves, opposed one major aspect of Freud's theory: they rejected the biological basis of human mental functions in favor of "variable, mutable culture." Ellen opposes the social construction thesis that forms the foundation of these views as well as Jacques Lacan's reliance on language to ferret the vicissitudes of the unconscious. In her account, Ellen encounters one of the thorny debates in the philosophy of science: must any proposition that claims validity be subject to experimental falsifiability? If the unconscious is not visible, it cannot, according to this view, be subject to rigorous test.

While Freud was aware of this conundrum, he developed a method that inferred propositions from symptoms rather than direct observation. Ellen acknowledges the problem raised by its detractors, but she says it is a mistake to deny psychoanalysis of its analytic rigor. In this regard, she argues that any psychological theory must recognize the interplay between biological constitution of the subject and all aspects in which the personal and the social intersect. Moreover, "the analytic observer cannot stand outside the field of observation but must take into account how his or her own unconscious wishes affect the analytic process." Just as psychoanalysis encourages the subject to examine herself, so the analyst must engage in self-examination.

The chapter is a stunning series of examples of how sexuality and its cultural implications can help shed light on history as well as social life. Ellen unflinchingly tackles neuroscience, the antipsychiatry movement, biological reductionism, and other contemporary debates. Throughout her discourse is a serious commitment to represent contrary perspectives accurately and fairly. But she always stands her ground.

The reader might notice a distinct tonal difference between the introduction and the other two chapters. The introduction is vintage Ellen Willis style. But she believed that unless she wrote "scientific" or academic prose, the book would not be taken seriously. I tried to persuade her otherwise, but she insisted on this approach.

I witnessed Ellen's path to researching and writing this book. She accepted no shortcuts and immersed herself in most of the extant literature. But this supremely talented writer remained, throughout, self-doubting, although not about whether she could master the subject. As a journalist and essayist she remained somehow awed by the prospect of producing a full-length treatise. I urged her to regard each chapter as an essay rather than submitting to the fiction that a book must contain airtight coherence. She listened and ostensibly agreed. She was on the way to resolving her uncertainties, but the struggle with mortality cut her quest short.

STANLEY ARONOWITZ, a veteran political activist and cultural critic, is distinguished professor of sociology and urban education at the Graduate Center of the City University of New York. He is author or editor of twenty-five books, including *Taking It Big: C. Wright Mills and the Making of Public Intellectuals, Against Schooling: For an Education That Matters,* and *How Class Works: Power and Social Movement,* and he is the founding editor of *Social Text.* He was married to Ellen Willis.

The Cultural Unconscious in American Politics
Why We Need a Freudian Left

Prisoners of Sex

Slouching toward the end of the 20th century, American society is in a state of economic upheaval, political paralysis, and cultural panic. After 50 years of domestication by the corporate liberal state, laissez-faire capitalism has revived with a vengeance, on an unprecedented worldwide scale. The emergence of a global labor market, combined with the wholesale replacement of human labor by computers, has transformed the American economy, steadily eliminating the well-paid, secure jobs on which a solid middle class depends. As wealth is concentrated in fewer and fewer hands, the "underclass" is thrown off welfare to compete with the growing numbers of poor people already working at rock-bottom wages. No longer forced by the threat of Communism to maintain Americans' standard of living, indifferent to the fate of any one nation or polity, capital has declared war not only on the welfare state and the very idea of public goods, but on the power of government to regulate the economy at all. Elected officials hardly even pretend to make economic policy based on what their constituents need or want; they see no choice but to obey "the laws of the market"—that is, the economic and political agenda of transnational corporations ready to withhold investment and credit from any community that defies their will.

These economic winds blow through a cultural landscape dominated by the unfinished social revolutions of the 1960s. The housewife as institution and emblem of middle-class aspiration is obsolete, a transformation set in motion by feminism and accelerated by the loss of "family wage" jobs. The exodus of mothers from the home has disrupted the fabric of domestic life, child rearing, male-female relations. Men resist taking up the slack, burdening women with the infamous double shift. Employers who used to discriminate against women by operating as if their workers all had wives to take care of business at home have "progressed" to equal-opportunity contempt for the notion that workers need lives outside their jobs. Child care is treated as an individual problem, to be resolved by luck and money; the resulting arrangements are too often haphazard, inadequate, or nonexistent. Home may still be defined as the "working mother's" special project, but her time is short, her psychic resources stretched, her will perhaps compromised by suppressed resentment; the decline of the family dinner becomes a metaphor for a more general domestic shrinkage.

Americans agonize endlessly about these problems, yet seem incapable of any sustained, creative effort to solve them. Evidently we can't bear to decide that since Alice doesn't live here anymore, we have to figure out how to redistribute the physical and emotional work she used to do. Instead we scramble to cover the bare necessities, while berating her for leaving, pretending we're doing fine without her, or fantasizing that she's coming back.

At the same time the institution of marriage is unraveling. The old marriage contract, which traded male economic support for female sexual and domestic service, is, like Alice, a relic; but instead of a new, egalitarian contract, the main result seems to be the breakdown of marriage as a permanent partnership, the normalizing of divorce and single motherhood. The sexual and feminist revolutions have made it easier (if by no means easy) for single women and their children to survive, made marriage less attractive to men by eroding their traditional entitlements, and legitimized for both sexes the choice of personal happiness over familial obligation. The economy has also played a part; just as poverty has always weakened marriage, since poor men can't offer women economic security in return for patriarchal privilege, the general decline of male wages has had the same effect.

With growing consternation Americans have come to see that marriage based on the vagaries of personal choice rather than economic and social compulsion is unstable, that it makes children vulnerable, that families with a single female breadwinner are likely to be poor. Few people seriously imagine it's possible or desirable to restore the old order, yet even fewer raise the obvious question: if the family as we've known it isn't working, don't we need to invent forms of domestic life and child rearing more suited to a free, postpatriarchal society? No, it has long since been agreed that such talk is silly leftover hippiespeak. Instead we feel guilty, scapegoat single mothers on welfare, oppose no-fault divorce. Or else we declare that the crisis of the family is a myth—it's just that there are different kinds of families. Aren't gays clamoring to join the marriage club? My compliments to the Emperor's tailor: we are all pro-family now.

As wages fall, benefits evaporate, insecurity spreads, inequality worsens, people work harder and longer for less, domestic comforts and public amenities disappear, children fend for themselves, and democratic government becomes ever more oxymoronic, something is strangely missing: there's an eerie quies-cence where an opposition ought to be. To be sure, there is stirring in the labor unions and among intellectuals, dike-plugging by advocacy groups, occasional right-wing populist agitation by a Buchanan or a Perot; but no critical mass of rebellion against the new economic order or the cultural stasis, no sustained public critique of the system as a whole, no collective vision of an alternative—in short, no movement.

Quiescence, however, does not imply tranquility. On the contrary, the anger of working-class whites, poor blacks, middle-class taxpayers, antipornography feminists, antifeminist men, Christian conservatives, radical right-wing anar-chists has become the stuff of the daily news and pop cultural cliché. More and more this anger is laced with sadistic excitement, which finds expression not only in spectacular eruptions of shooting, bombing, rape, black/gay/Jew-killing, abortion-clinic terrorism, but in the culture's mundane background noise—the reveling in racist invective, the guest-baiting on talk TV, the ongoing drumbeat of contempt for the undeserving poor, government bureaucrats, the press, the "cultural elite" (but never the corporations). At the same time sexual anxiety, verging on hysteria and permeated with nightmares of violence, social disinte-gration, and the corruption of children, floats from one controversy to another, now simmering, now flaring up.

This stew of emotion pervades what passes for public discussion of un-married childbearing, divorce, gay marriage, teenage sex, AIDS, condoms, abortion, sexual harassment, date rape, child sexual abuse, pornography, art, sex and violence in television/pop music/cyberspace, race relations, welfare, crime, drugs, immigration, education. Beyond its impact on this or that policy or bill, it has a chaotic life of its own. The dominance of free-market ideology has foreclosed any significant debate on economics; the shrinking of public space and the tyranny of the bottom line are more and more accepted as inexo-rable laws of nature; yet the conflicts popularly referred to as the "social issues" or the "culture wars" remain unsettled after three decades of cultural revolt and crackdown.

The cultural radical impulse that emerged during the mid-'60s reached the peak of its influence around the turn of the decade. Large segments of the middle class, and millions of young people of all classes, regarded freedom, pleasure, and self-expression—sexual and otherwise—as important personal and social values. Popular culture, especially pop music, celebrated those val-ues. Psychedelic drugs and the idea of consciousness expansion were a defin-ing influence on youth culture, while marijuana use was a middle-class rite of passage. In loco parentis rules on college campuses had collapsed. Criticism of conventional family life, authoritarian education, and joyless, routinized work was part of mainstream public discourse. The welfare state was routinely attacked—from the left—as a corporate Leviathan that controlled people's lives and managed inequality to avoid abolishing it. The black movement had gone beyond civil rights to contest the social and psychic structures of racism. Feminism was challenging the ground rules of male-female relations everywhere from the bedroom to the kitchen to the office. In the wake of the 1969 Stonewall rebellion, the gay liberation movement burgeoned. Through the '70s the cultural shock waves continued to be felt, in everything from the *Roe v. Wade* decision legalizing abortion to the rising divorce rate to the influx of women into the professions and mothers into the workforce.

Yet the reaction had already begun. In 1968, Richard Nixon was elected on a law-and-order platform; George Wallace's right-wing populist campaign picked up 13 percent of the vote. By 1970, intellectuals who defined themselves as liberals but opposed the new left, the counterculture, black nationalism, feminism, and the cultural-left wing of the Democratic Party were regrouping in what would become the neoconservative movement. In 1972, George McGovern's presidential bid was crushed in what was widely regarded as a referendum on "acid, amnesty, and abortion." The following year, even as it became feminists' most conspicuous legal victory, *Roe v. Wade* galvanized the nascent antiabortion movement.

The latter half of the '70s was a period of accelerating backlash against feminism, tacitly supported by the White House; Jimmy Carter, a Democrat with a left-populist image, was nonetheless a born-again Christian, antiabortion cultural conservative. The right-to-life troops won passage of the Hyde Amendment outlawing Medicaid funding of abortion, while the pro-family movement, a coalition of conservative Catholics and evangelical Christians, mounted such a successful offensive against the Equal Rights Amendment—which had breezed through Congress in 1972—that only a few states ratified it after 1977. The movement went on to play an instrumental role in Ronald Reagan's presidential campaign. With Reagan's election in 1980, the religious right, which liberals had dismissed just a few years before as a lunatic fringe, achieved national legitimacy and became one of the most powerful interest groups in American politics.

Even more striking than the right's political victories was the change in the social atmosphere. Helped along by the puritanical tone of the Carter administration, antiabortionists seized the moral offensive, shifting the focus of the abortion debate from women's self-determination to fetal life. The dominant iconography of the "pro-life" movement depicted the fetus as a vulnerable infant floating in space (the pregnant woman's body literally and metaphorically out of the picture), the antiabortion crusader as protector of this innocent creature from its destruction for mere "convenience." This argument, or image, had a broad impact, hitting a nerve even with abortion-rights advocates, who became steadily more defensive and apologetic. Feminists stopped talking about abortion in terms of sex and freedom, and instead focused their arguments on rape, incest, health problems, and dire poverty. The very word *abortion* became taboo, replaced by euphemisms like *choice* and *reproductive rights*.

As the pro-family Christian right agitated for government intervention in support of traditional sexual roles and morality, the predominantly Jewish neo-conservatives launched a broadside against the "hedonism" and "narcissism" of '60s liberationist politics, invoking self-discipline and social stability rather than the Bible and aiming to change consciousness rather than laws. This proved to be a far more effective strategy for influencing the secular, educated upper middle class that dominated the country's opinion-making apparatus and had provided the shock troops of the '60s revolt. Like the antiabortion propaganda whose themes it echoed, neoconservatism had a chilling effect on the very people who led, and in most cases continued to lead, the postcounter-culture, post–sexual revolution, postfeminist lives it was criticizing. A mood of guilt and self-doubt began to erode the '60s generation's sense of entitlement to freedom and fulfillment.

Much of the new left had always been hostile to cultural radicalism, regarding it as frivolous, morally dubious, and/or disrespectful of most Americans' cherished values; and while open opposition to the feminist and gay movements had by the mid-'70s become unacceptable in left circles, covert resistance remained strong. As the new right and neoconservative reaction gained momentum, leftist cultural conservatives found their voices and an increasingly receptive audience. Unlike the neocons, who were staunchly pro-capitalist (though still, for the most part, defenders of the liberal welfare state), they blamed capitalist individualism and consumerism for the "excesses" of sexual and cultural liberationists. While neoconservatives charged that the cultural radicals represented an elite "new class" out to undermine the structures of social authority in order to gain power for themselves, left conservatives argued that the "elitist" concerns of affluent feminists and gays distracted the left from addressing the "real" (i.e., economic) needs of the working class, blacks, and the poor. As they saw it, the left had lost credibility through being unfairly tainted with cultural radical attacks on the family and traditional values. It was time to "take the family issue away from the right."

Despite the left conservatives' barely disguised antifeminism, many mainstream liberal feminists endorsed this defense of the family and sought to rescue the women's movement from the stigma of cultural radicalism. By promoting equal rights, they argued, feminism made the family stronger; mothers worked outside the home not for "individualist" reasons like independence or ambition but because their families needed their income. The leaders of the ill-fated ERA campaign insisted that the measure had no bearing on abortion rights and implied no changes in the family or sexual morality. In contrast, most feminists on the left attacked the traditionalism of left conservatives and demanded that the definition of family be expanded to give full recognition to single-parent and gay and lesbian households. Yet in the name of pluralism and tolerance they too distanced themselves from earlier feminist and cultural radical critiques of marriage and the nuclear family as institutions. As the family values issue moved to the center of the national political conversation in the '80s and early '90s, a bland "My family's OK, your family's OK" stance became the left wing of the debate.

By 1975, even as momentous changes in consciousness about sex and gender were still penetrating layer after layer of American culture, the feminist radicals who had launched those changes were thoroughly marginalized in an increasingly conservative political environment. Something called "radical feminism" still existed, but what had been a vital political movement to abolish sexism was now little more than a moral counterculture that celebrated "female values" and marched against male violence. While feminists had previously analyzed rape and the myths and rationalizations surrounding it as part of a larger male-supremacist social structure, the neoradical feminists defined rape as the essence and purpose of male power, which was assumed to be intractable and all-pervasive and implicitly resided in maleness itself. Their rhetoric did not distinguish between male sexual aggression and male sexuality or, for that matter, sexuality per se: in opposition to feminist sexual radicals, for whom sexual freedom was an integral part of women's liberation, they regarded sex purely as a male weapon and the so-called sexual revolution as a euphemism for unrestricted antiwoman violence. Following the logic of these assumptions, their focus soon shifted from rape and other acts of violence to sexually violent or "degrading" media images and, toward the end of the '70s, pornography.

The antipornography movement was founded by women who called themselves radical feminists at a time when radicalism was in disrepute and women who were feminist on the issues were backing away from the label. Yet the movement, with its claim that "pornography is violence against women," had substantial public impact. It was covered sympathetically in the popular media, embraced by mainstream women's organizations, and taken up by young women on college campuses. The Christian right, which had been seeking to ban pornography on traditional moral grounds, quickly appropriated the argument that porn hurts women. In the mid-'80s, feminists and Christian fundamentalists collaborated in campaigns for local ordinances aimed at subjecting purveyors of pornography to civil penalties for sex discrimination. Antiporn feminists testified at the otherwise impeccably right-wing hearings on pornography held by Reagan's attorney general. In truth, this "radical feminist" movement, with its pessimism, its sexual conservatism, its embrace of gender difference, and not least its preference for law and order over free speech, was fully in accord with the spirit of the cultural backlash.

In other respects, as the '90s began, organized feminism as a vital social movement was all but dead. The Supreme Court's 1988 decision in *Webster v. Reproductive Health Services* had fallen short of overturning *Roe v. Wade*, but was widely regarded as a temporary reprieve. It was in this context that Clarence Thomas's nomination to the Court became a national psychodrama. The outpouring of female anger on behalf of Anita Hill at first seemed to herald a larger feminist revival: besides making sexual harassment a visible public issue, it expressed women's intense frustration at the efforts of Reagan and Bush to pack the Supreme Court with abortion opponents, the Senate's initial readiness to brush off Hill's allegations without a hearing, and the culture of male dominance in general. The Thomas-Hill affair also inspired a wave of organizing by black feminists and renewed discussion of the intersection of race and gender.

But in the end these sparks did not ignite; instead Thomas-Hill became a vehicle for further popularizing the sexually conservative politics of neoradical feminism. The heightened awareness of sexual harassment has evolved into a campaign to prohibit any form of sexual expression or representation in the workplace, the assumption being that sex and its representation are inherently offensive and harmful to women. A parallel campaign has proposed to define as rape any situation in which a woman engages in sex she doesn't want, whether or not she is physically forced or threatened—the assumption being that women are powerless to resist men's sexual demands and cannot be held responsible for making their wishes clear.

From its early stages, the cultural reaction was intertwined with a gradually accelerating movement away from the economic ground rules that had prevailed in the United States since World War II. During the '60s, widespread prosperity and its attendant optimism encouraged cultural rebellion. In an economy awash with money and a seller's labor market, a generation of young people unscarred by the economic insecurities of their elders had little incentive to subordinate themselves to work or social authority and plenty of time to devote to political activism and cultural experiment. In response, publishers, record companies, and other cultural entrepreneurs were willing to invest in all manner of innovative and risky countercultural projects, many of which proved highly profitable. Conversely, the '60s freedom-and-pleasure ethos reinforced Americans' sense of entitlement to a decent standard of living and a high level of public goods and services.

But in the early '70s this economic-cultural symbiosis began working in reverse: a steady decline in Americans' standard of living has encouraged political and cultural conservatism, and vice versa. In 1973, as the United States was losing both the Vietnam War and its unchallenged dominance in the global economy, the formation of OPEC and the resulting "energy crisis" signaled the coming of a new economic order in which getting Americans to accept less would be a priority of the emerging transnational corporate elite. With the end of cheap, abundant gasoline—the quintessential emblem of our prosperity, mobility, and power—austerity began to rival law and order as a conservative rallying cry. For the cultural right, austerity was not just an economic but a moral imperative, a new weapon against the "self-indulgence" and "hedonism" of the affluent '60s. For the economic elite, whose objective was convincing the middle class that the money wasn't there, whether for high wages or for social benefits, moralism served to divert people's attention from the corporate agenda to their own supposed unrealistic expectations and lack of discipline.

Corporate determination to impose austerity led to a pivotal event: the New York City fiscal crisis of 1975. New York had the most militantly left-wing political culture, the strongest municipal unions, and the most extensive public services in the nation. When the banks proclaimed their intention to cut off the city's credit unless its finances were radically restructured, this was not merely a business decision but a political showdown of immense symbolic importance: if New Yorkers could be induced to swallow austerity without taking to the streets, the rest of the country would be easy pickings. The ensuing economic cutbacks were coupled with a relentless moral attack on the city, especially the supposedly greedy unions: New Yorkers, the lecture went, had been selfish profligates living beyond their means; they had better lower their expectations and tighten their belts. Solemnly the governor of New York State opined, "The days of wine and roses are over."

Though the *Daily News*'s "Ford to City: Drop Dead" headline elected him, Jimmy Carter nonetheless made it his mission to spread the gospel of economic and cultural austerity on the national level. And then an apparent reversal occurred: Ronald Reagan won the presidency on an antiausterity platform. While the dour, ascetic Carter preached limits and sacrifice, a sunny, optimistic Reagan promised growth and opportunity; where Carter's inability to resolve the Iranian hostage crisis symbolized America's lowered expectations in the world arena, Reagan's military buildup promised a resurgence of American power. Carter exhorted Americans to curb their self-indulgence and spoke ominously of a pervasive moral malaise; Reagan championed the average American as a righteous defender of traditional moral values against the depredations of blacks, feminists, gays, welfare queens, and pointy-heads.

What was happening, almost imperceptibly at first, was a radical shift in the terms of American political debate. The conservative counteroffensive against the values of the '60s had been bipartisan, with Carter taking up what was essentially a Republican program of cultural conservatism and economic retrenchment.

> [*Editor's note*: What followed here was a collection of disjointed notes about the Bush/Clinton/Gingrich era—"Clintons as McGovernik/Carterite; Gingrich and radical right as recapitulation of '60s radicalism"—then a conclusion that "this is a society marked by irrationality and contradiction." That is, "people's desires as expressed in the ways they choose to live clash with their ideological assent to social conservatism."]

The contradictions of contemporary American politics and culture are the product of a profound and largely unconscious psychic struggle: an ongoing clash of powerful desires for freedom and pleasure with guilt-ridden fear that such desires lead straight to license, chaos, and destruction. These contending impulses do not respect conventional divisions of right and left. Their battles are fought out not only among individuals and groups of opposing worldviews, but within individuals and superficially like-minded groups. The imprint of what I call the cultural unconscious is stamped all over the present agonies of the American people: a citizenry buffeted by events, seemingly incapable of taking decisive collective action on serious social problems, passive in the face of an economy being transformed before our eyes, ambivalent to the point of schizophrenia on cultural issues.

My claim is not that our problems are caused by, or can be reduced to, states of mind. The ascendancy of global capital, the lack of social provision for the child care and domestic services and comforts once provided by the vanishing housewife, the instability of the family, and the decline of traditional social controls in the absence of practical alternatives—such developments are all too concrete and material. Rather, it's in our responses to them (responses that themselves become concrete social facts, to be responded to in their turn) that the cultural unconscious wields its power.

Mustering the imagination, courage, and stamina to fight for real solutions to the dilemmas that beset us requires first of all that people believe they have the ability and the right to actively shape their lives. This necessary confidence is undermined by the widespread unconscious conflation of self-determination with selfishness, the pursuit of personal and sexual happiness with moral corruption. Under this unconscious burden, people fear and mistrust their desires as invitations to catastrophe. The uncertainties, mistakes, defeats; the destructive maneuvers of ideologues and opportunists; the blind alleys and unforeseen obstacles that attend all serious efforts to change social conditions come to be regarded not as problems to be solved and spurs to further effort, but as the inevitable wages of sin, punishment for daring to depart from the old ways. At the same time, frustrated desire generates rage and resentment, which are readily incited by demagogues against targets that represent the repudiated longings—immoral and criminal blacks, licentious gays, a permissive "cultural elite." A political movement that aspires to have an impact on our deepening economic and cultural crises cannot succeed simply by appealing to moral principle or rational self-interest; it must speak to the cultural unconscious, address the hidden conflict. The story of contemporary American politics is that the right intuitively understands this, while the left, by and large, has no clue.

For a brief historical moment in the 1960s, segments of the new left and the black student movement, along with feminists, gay liberationists, and a dissident youth culture, became the party of freedom and pleasure. Overnight, or so it seemed (in fact, rebellion had been a long time in the making), a coherent, if repressive, white middle-class culture was destabilized, all forms of social authority were guilty till proved innocent, and male-female relations were up for grabs. Despite the short life of its radical phase, the '60s revolt and the various social movements it inspired have made enduring changes in the ground rules of Americans' daily lives. Those changes have produced a freer, more sensual, more heterogeneous, and more democratic culture. Yet they have also been disruptive, scary, confusing, and sometimes malign: the loosening of controls liberated destructive as well as creative energies, and in any case it is always easier to break down established social structures than to build new and better ones.

In the ensuing years, conservatives have fought the legacy of the '60s by appealing to fear and guilt, arguing that "hedonism," "narcissism," "baby-killing," and so on amount to moral anarchy, while brandishing the disruptions, confusions, and malignities as proof that God and nature will not be mocked. Their moral attack has largely succeeded in discrediting the '60s revolt on the level of ideology; there would seem to be a solid public consensus in favor of sexual conservatism, strong families, and social order at almost any cost. Yet in terms of people's actual behavior, the relentless agitation against divorce, abortion, day care, teenage sex, and single motherhood has had little effect; TV shows, movies, and pop music have no trouble attracting a mass audience with open sexuality and socially liberal values; and acceptance of homosexuality has progressed to the point where openly gay Republicans advocate same-sex marriage (albeit in the name of family values). If the language of freedom has been muted, its lure remains strong.

Paradoxically, the right has also managed to turn this unacknowledged yearning to its advantage by championing freedom in the guise of government bashing, unleashed capitalist "opportunity" (i.e., vicarious identification with tycoons like Bill Gates), relief from the onerous moral and economic claims of the poor, and permission to vent "politically incorrect" racial and sexual hostilities. Indeed, far from resolving unconscious conflict, the conservative reaction has intensified it.

Trapped in its contradictions, the American cultural unconscious is highly volatile, anxious, and susceptible to authoritarian snake oil. Under these conditions, the right will continue to thrive unless its opponents confront the contradictions, bring the unconscious conflict into the open, and unambiguously defend desire. Yet from the standpoint of most inhabitants of the broadly defined left—liberals, populists, socialists, communitarians, assorted "progressives"—such a suggestion would seem to be eccentric at best. Indeed, I sometimes think that except for a small minority of feminist, gay, and cultural radical intellectuals, it's the left that has most solemnly taken to heart the right's polemics against frivolous and immoral self-indulgence. While conservatives manage their moralist-libertarian two-step without appearing to suffer overmuch from cognitive dissonance, most leftists are rationalists who feel compelled to be consistent; and so they have increasingly become the party of unrelieved guilt. Not only has the mainstream left either seconded the right's demonizing of '60s cultural radicalism or conspicuously avoided contesting it; segments of the left have made their own distinctive contributions to the anti-pleasure ethos, from antismoking and general health-and-fitness fanaticism to the idea that any open sexual expression in the workplace is tantamount to sexual harassment. (Predictably, left puritanism of this sort has been gleefully and effectively attacked by conservatives, their own antidrug, antisex campaigns notwithstanding.)

Even more telling, leftists tend to promote their central project, economic and social equality, not as a freer, happier way of life but as a moral obligation. Loath to let the right monopolize the moral regeneration racket, they define their mission as vanquishing greed, callousness, aggression, and hate in favor of justice, compassion, peace, and respect. In the process they set themselves against precisely those "freedoms" the right has designated as acceptable compensation for repression—economic selfishness, name calling, general churlishness toward the downtrodden. With no alternative vision of freedom, only relentless exhortations to self-improvement, it's hardly surprising that they lose their audience to Rush Limbaugh. To be sure, the left supports real needs for economic survival and security, while arguing, logically enough, that people's anger is more profitably directed toward the rich and powerful than toward welfare mothers and "feminazis." Yet its own cultural conservatism undercuts its program. In the grip of unconscious moral intimidation, most people imagine that they will survive better by going along with the system than by rebelling against it in any but small, symbolic ways.

The unconscious is, of course, a psychoanalytic concept. By invoking it, I am arguing that there is a crucial psychoanalytic dimension to politics. More precisely, in this book I have set out to demonstrate the contemporary relevance of the Freudian left that emerged in Europe between the World Wars. Faced with the converging disasters of mass support for Hitler, the inability of the socialist left to comprehend fascism or fight it effectively, and the rise of totalitarianism in Russia, radical psychoanalysts and psychoanalytically minded Marxist cultural critics turned their attention to social psychology. The result was a body of theory with a bold and ambitious aim: understanding authoritarianism, its persistence in putatively democratic societies, and its perpetuation through social irrationalism, destructiveness, and apathy.

Freud's early sexual theory defines erotic energy—"libido"—as a dynamic, biological force that when blocked from direct expression or consciousness emerges in myriad indirect and disguised forms. On this fundamental claim rests his argument that the key to the transmission of culture is parental repression of infantile sexuality: love for and fear of the castrating parent (especially the father) transforms the pleasure-seeking, amoral infant into the civilized adult, who directs a portion of libido into the narrow channel of marriage and procreation, the rest into identification with the moral values of the frustrating parent, constructive cultural activity, and—if thwarted desire is insufficiently repressed—neurotic symptoms or antisocial behavior. In characterizing the edifice of civilization as nothing other than a congelation of alienated libidinal impulses—founded on the renunciation of our deepest desires and therefore on enormous human misery—this theory is revolutionary in its implications. Inescapably it raises the question, is what we call civilization necessary?

It was, however, not Freud himself but Wilhelm Reich, Erich Fromm, Herbert Marcuse, and other psychoanalytic radicals who pursued that question, arguing that sexual repression is not the condition of civilization per se but of a historically specific culture—authoritarian, hierarchical, and in its modern version subject to bureaucratic and technological means of mass manipulation. Where Freud saw libido as inherently aggressive and antisocial, the Freudian radicals contended that the natural erotic impulse is benign, life-enhancing and self-regulating, while repression gives rise to sexual rage and therefore to the very aggressive and antisocial tendencies, including predatory and violent sexuality, that are then invoked to justify the repression that produced them in the first place. The twin psychic engines of authoritarian culture, Wilhelm Reich argued, are rebellious sadism and reactive, guilty, masochistic submission to authority: by appealing to these sadomasochistic impulses, Hitler had won over much of the German working class despite a program inimical to its rational economic and political interests. As for Russia, as Reich saw it the profound patriarchal conservatism of the population, shared by most of the Communist leaders, had crushed efforts at radical sexual and educational reform, leading to the consolidation of dictatorship and ultimately to Stalinist terror.

The clear lesson of the European crisis, in the radical Freudian view, was that no program for democratic social transformation can succeed without a sexual and cultural revolution. That lesson was not lost on American cultural radicals. A number of key Freudian left figures, including Reich, Marcuse, and Fromm, ended up in the United States, where their ideas came to the attention of the small but prescient minority of sexual and cultural dissidents in the 1940s and '50s. Their work and that of Reichian-influenced social critics like Paul Goodman (also a founder of gestalt therapy) and A. S. Neill (the English educator and author of a classic account of his "free school," Summerhill), as well as more idiosyncratic thinkers like Norman O. Brown, had a strong impact on the '60s counterculture and the cultural radical wing of the new left.

Today, however, this once-powerful intellectual current is missing from the American public conversation, except as the occasional target of attack or ridicule. Indeed, the Freudian left has apparently achieved what in America is the most devastating status of all: it is utterly unfashionable, deemed not merely wrong but quaint, the artifact of a less sophisticated era. In part, this disdain reflects the widely and uncritically accepted commonplace that we have nothing in common with Freud's Victorian world of stern patriarchal families and repressed women, that for better or worse we are already a sexually liberated society; therefore, since utopia is as elusive as ever, sexual freedom clearly has no significance for any larger political program. Among left intellectuals, however, the Freudian radicals' loss of cachet follows from the prevailing view that any invocation of biology to explain social phenomena is by definition naive, "essentialist," and reactionary.

Ironically, from my perspective, the ascendancy of this view can largely be traced to the influence of the feminist and gay movements. Those movements anathematized Freud, not only for his belief that male dominance is ineluctable and homosexuality a product of arrested development, but for his more basic claim that sexual psychology has a biological foundation. Many feminists, especially in recent years, have argued against the grain of this hostility that psychoanalysis offers vital insights into sex and gender in a patriarchal culture; but they have tended to embrace versions of Lacanian and object relations theory that depart radically from Freud's view of sexual energy as the fount of human motivation.

From the beginning, skepticism and outright hostility toward the idea of sexual freedom have been prominent themes in second-wave feminist politics: many 1960s feminists regarded radical Freudianism (not without some justification) as the ideology of a male-oriented sexual revolution espoused by a male-dominated counterculture, while the movement's early separatists denounced the idea of a biological sexual need as a male invention and a rationale for rape. Yet feminism has always had a sexual-liberationist wing, which, along with the more radical strands of gay liberation, might have appropriated the Freudian left tradition. Instead, feminist and gay sexual radicals have been among its firmest detractors. Most reject as repressive the assumption of both orthodox and radical Freudians that the sexual impulse is a biological drive in conflict with culture. In their view, the concept of "natural" sex inevitably leads to norms that stigmatize unconventional sexual practices. (Reich, they note, defined natural sexuality as heterosexual and coital.) It follows that freedom depends on understanding sex as an infinitely varied social construction.

Obviously, I disagree with these assessments. Our society may be more sexually permissive than Freud's, but it is far from free. Nor do I think it's contradictory to ground the case for freedom in biological need. On the contrary, if there is no inherent need for freedom—if all desire is purely a social construction—then a free society is, arguably, merely a matter of taste, one possibility among others. This isn't to imply that radical Freudian thought can be seamlessly joined to the present situation. It should go without saying that any serious psychosocial interpretation of American politics has to take into account the convolutions and contradictions of post-'60s American culture, as well as contemporary feminist and gay analyses of sex and gender. Like any body of thought viewed from a historical distance, the writings of the Freudian radicals suffer from their immersion in their own culture and their failure to anticipate the future. Yet in reading those writings—particularly Reich's tales of his quarrels with culturally conservative liberals and Marxists about the family, sex, and youth—I'm struck by an almost uncanny sense of familiarity. After three-quarters of a century of political and cultural turmoil, from World War I and the Russian Revolution to the present worldwide upsurge of right-wing religious and nationalist movements, the underlying issues have never been resolved—only repeatedly "forgotten" and rediscovered. It seems to me that the present sweeping rejection of radical Freudian ideas is itself part of that larger story.

In the past decade, not only Freudian radicalism but Freudian thought in general has been increasingly dismissed as irrelevant; like Marxism, psychoanalysis is undergoing a crisis of legitimacy. Cultural conservatives seek to rescue the metaphysical pretensions of Judeo-Christian morality from Freud's brilliant deconstruction, reviving the concept of good and (especially) evil as abstract essences beyond the reach of human understanding. The scientific establishment attributes all human behavior to genes, hormones, and neural pathways in the brain, while pronouncing psychoanalysis unscientific because its propositions cannot be falsified by experiments. And cultural critics and scholars of both the right and the left have largely abandoned psychoanalysis as an intellectual framework.

This ecumenical turn away from Freud comes at a time of widespread disenchantment with the systemic, "totalistic" explanations of the world characteristic of the great modernist thinkers. It is now commonly assumed that to perceive an overall logic in a social system, or certain unities underlying the complexities of human life, is to squeeze that life into an ideological mold. Since the 1930s, conservatives and anti-Communist liberals and leftists have argued that Soviet totalitarianism was the inevitable consequence of a Marxism that proclaimed itself a comprehensive theory of revolution in all areas of social and cultural as well as economic life. In the '60s and '70s, the black, feminist, and gay movements challenged the Marxist designation of class as the primary social division, arguing that it subordinated their concerns with race, gender, and sexuality to a false white-straight-male-dominated universalism. More recently, cultural left intellectuals, influenced by these social movements as well as by postmodernist and poststructuralist theory, have contended that Marxism and other "master discourses" or "master narratives" that purport to make sense of reality are less tools of knowledge than weapons of social domination.

For the postmodern left, the alternative to the master discourse is a multicultural, pluralist "micropolitics" of diverse movements focusing on particular groups or issues. For the Christian right (and many left cultural conservatives), the problem is not totalism but secularism, and the answer is a cultural counter-revolution rooted in religion. On the other hand, neoconservatives (many of them anti-Communist liberals or leftists in an earlier incarnation) argue that politics and culture should be separated altogether; and most of the mainstream left openly or tacitly agrees. From this perspective, American politics is about liberal democratic government, whose proper domestic responsibilities are maintaining social order, enforcing contracts, providing such public goods and services as the electorate deems necessary, and, for the left, promoting legal and economic equity. Culture is the supposedly apolitical sphere of private life and communal custom and tradition; efforts to subject it to an alien political framework can lead only to tyranny or its less dramatic relative, "political correctness."

In reality, to accuse radicals of politicizing culture is like accusing unions of engaging in class warfare. Social institutions like the family and the church enforce rules, establish social hierarchies, police behavior, and parcel out rewards and punishments just as government does (though with far fewer liberal democratic pretensions). And in any case, just as government sets innumerable ground rules for the supposedly private economy, it also enforces cultural norms, through agencies like public schools and laws regulating such matters as marriage, divorce, abortion, obscenity, and drugs. In practice, "depoliticizing culture" means accepting or actively supporting those norms—heterosexual marriage, say, or the two-parent family, or the ethic of self-sacrifice—while declaring dissent out of bounds, a frivolous or dangerous diversion from serious matters of state.

For the left, decoupling culture from politics is a losing game. Since cultural coercion is disproportionately aimed at subordinating or marginalizing women, racial and ethnic minorities, homosexuals, and social dissidents, refusal to confront it poses an untenable contradiction for an egalitarian movement; inevitably, the result has been a disabling fragmentation of the left into separate and often competitive social groups. Furthermore, as I've argued, that refusal dooms "legitimate" left politics to defeat, since a left with no sense of the stakes in cultural political issues can never compete with the right's ability to exploit them. (Leftists often advocate me-tooing the right on culture in order to take it off the table and focus people's attention on economics; or else they declare that the answer to the right's "distracting" white male workers with cultural issues is a populist economic program. That neither of these strategies ever gets anywhere does not deter the left from continually reinventing them, which suggests that something other than pure pragmatism is at work.) Equally unpromising is the postmodern multiculturalist approach; aside from trying to make a virtue of the left's crippling divisions, the advocates of micropolitics have as little to say about class or the political economy as the rest of the left has to say about culture. In either case, the dogmatic rejection of systemic theory—in effect, the denial of any structural links between the political system, the economy, and people's personal and sexual lives—seems to me to reveal a terrible weariness, a longing to be free of the burden of trying to understand.

The problem with Marxism as social theory is not its effort to understand the social system as a whole, but the failure of Marxists, with few exceptions, to understand a crucial factor in that system—human subjectivity. A product of scientific rationalism, Marxism in most of its versions has no concept of unconscious or irrational motivation and assumes that the motor of human activity is material need, not the pleasure principle. The basis of freedom, in Marxist terms, is the progressive domination of nature. From a Freudian standpoint, however, the whole idea of "dominating" or "conquering" nature expresses a need for control closely linked to the struggle to control and repress our sexual natures. This idea suggests that the basic problem with Marxism as a political movement was not its call for total revolution but its sanction of the will to power disguised in the language of emancipation. The Orwellian disjunction between rhetoric and meaning characteristic of Communist regimes follows the logic of the cultural unconscious: as the psychoanalytic radicals concluded, to explain what went wrong with Marx, you need Freud.

Granted that psychoanalysis too has been wielded as a weapon of power (often using the language of biological destiny or, more insidiously, sexual fulfillment), whether in public discussion or private therapy session. Nor, more generally, are the critics of systemic theories wrong in believing they're peculiarly susceptible to misuse. The very power of a social theory to explain people's experience, and therefore to persuade, is a temptation to absolutism, both for those who crave a quasi-religious certainty and those who would exploit that craving for their own ends. Yet the perversion of theory into tyrannical dogma doesn't happen automatically; it requires an active effort to protect the theory—through punishment, if necessary—from question, challenge, and revision. Resisting this effort requires an equally active defense of skepticism and free debate. But rejecting the whole enterprise of critical social theory on the grounds that it's too dangerous merely protects the existing structure of power.

Recently, a number of leftist intellectuals have called for a return to the values of the Enlightenment, by which they seem to mean liberal democracy, economic justice, and a rejection of "cultural divisiveness" in favor of "universalism." Their arguments feature a rhetorical slippery slope in which criticism of parochialism and dogmatism on the black/feminist/gay/multicultural left slides into blanket aversion to social movements and their associated ideas and issues, and finally into dismissal of cultural politics per se. "Universalism," on closer inspection, does not refer to principles that, from the standpoint of the Enlightenment, are valid for all human beings—surely feminism or racial equality is as universal in that sense as the right to a fair share of the wealth one's work has helped to produce—but rather means something like, "Let's not raise controversial questions that offend the culturally conservative majority." Predictably, the attack on cultural divisiveness has not been extended to left conservatives who defend the right of communities to impose religiously based moral and familial values on their dissident members.

To many in the cultural movements, universalism is inherently a lie, a synonym for white male Western dominance: all values, in this view, are culturally specific. Again, the implicit assumption is that biology plays no significant role in psychic or social life. I would argue rather that for all its immense variety, the human species has certain bedrock needs and desires in common. That universal human values have been falsely proclaimed, selectively practiced, and invoked as rationales for oppression does not prove there's no such thing. I subscribe to the basic values of the Enlightenment, by which I mean individual autonomy, equality, democracy; freedom to pursue, disseminate, and act on knowledge; freedom from the tyranny of religion and tradition. However honored in the breach, I believe these Enlightenment values do in fact represent universal human aspirations, that they are not simply a cultural peculiarity of white male Europeans but have inspired subordinate peoples around the world. Liberalism in itself cannot fulfill those aspirations, which require a much more ambitious conception of democracy as an economy and culture based on individual freedom and collective self-government. But liberalism made that conception possible. Without the Enlightenment, cultural radicalism could not exist, nor, of course, could Freud.

And yet the Enlightenment—as I am hardly the first to observe—was disastrously naive about the human condition. In love with science and reason, it had no inkling of the capacity of murderous passion to overwhelm reason—or bend it to such purposes as scientific racism, apocalyptic weapons, and technology that threatens the earth's ecological balance. In undermining the traditional culture that kept both passion and reason under tight control, liberalism ignited a democratic social revolution that continues to this day; but it also unleashed the rage that provided the psychic underpinnings of Nazism and Stalinism—the first a barbaric revolt against the Enlightenment, the second a monstrous caricature of it.

For cultural conservatives, those nightmares prove the intractability of evil and the need for traditional curbs on freedom. For me they show that liberalism and socialism don't go deep enough, don't touch the core of human misery and the longing for happiness. They are also a warning: in ignoring the cultural unconscious, we risk a reprise of the European horror, this time on a global scale and in a postnuclear age, while the left wrings its hands and moralizes all the way to the grave. By looking at American cultural conflict and its international context through a radical Freudian lens, I mean to revive a long-neglected question: suppose a radical democratic politics that affirms freedom and pleasure is not a summons to moral corruption, not dangerous utopian nonsense, not even simply an ethical or spiritual possibility, but an expression of needs anchored in the body and, in the long run, a condition of human survival? In grappling with this question—or so I will contend—lies Americans' best hope of reversing the passive drift toward disaster in favor of active struggle over our social and political fate.

Freudian Radicalism in Europe and America

The Freudian left arose in tandem with what German historian Detlev Peukert has called "the crisis of classical modernity" that unfolded in Central Europe in the wake of World War I.[1] By the turn of the century Europe had undergone a process of modernization marked by the dominance of large-scale industrial production, urbanization, a decreasing birth rate, a first wave of feminism, and the easing of Victorian sexual morality, all of which were eroding the authority of the patriarchal family and causing no little anxiety. Hysteria, the malady that inspired psychoanalysis, had attracted the attention of the European medical establishment because it was reaching epidemic proportions among the middle and upper classes, including the prominent Viennese families that would supply so many of Freud's (mostly female) patients. The fin de siècle and prewar years were a period of technological innovation and social and cultural ferment, of avant-garde art, and the beginnings of what would be the revolutionary force of mass media and mass culture. At the same time the unconscious—the under-side of modern rationalism and technological progress—was a prominent theme in art and philosophy as well as the subject of Freud's investigations.

The war and its attendant social disruption further destabilized traditional forms of authority. In its aftermath the monarchies in Germany and Austria were replaced by liberal democracies; restrictions on women and young people loosened; the sexual revolution proceeded, with a robust movement for sexual freedom, birth control, and abortion reform developing in the Weimar Republic during the 1920s.[2] Reverberations from the Russian Revolution's early phase of sexual, educational, and cultural experiment were felt throughout Europe. Sexual reformers like Havelock Ellis and Bertrand Russell were prominent in-tellectuals. Yet for all these changes, modernity in Central Europe had shallow roots, especially outside the cosmopolitan centers of Berlin and Vienna. People who had grown up in strict patriarchal families in authoritarian states—in coun-tries that still had a significant agrarian population—could not easily assimilate new freedoms. To complicate the picture further, modernity had generated its own contradictions, with its subversive emancipatory impulse shadowed by the rise of technocratic scientism and the potential of mass media as a means of social manipulation and control.

If the cultural ambivalence that afflicts all postenlightenment societies was already acute in the newborn German and Austrian democracies, it was exacer-bated by a dismal economic and political climate. The war that had shattered the optimism of the new century had also wrecked Europe's economies, especially those of the defeated parties: in Germany and Austria economic stagnation was compounded by the ruinous hyperinflation of 1922–23 and mass unemployment in the wake of the global depression that began in 1929. The Weimar Republic had been founded on a series of shaky compromises: the cautious leadership of the dominant working-class party; the Social Democrats, casting a nervous eye on the upheavals in Bolshevik Russia, looked to its right rather than its left for alliances and collaborated in putting down the radical socialist uprising of January 1919; the trade unions negotiated wage protections and social benefits for workers with industrialists who were profoundly hostile toward democracy and the welfare state. Under conditions of increasing conflict over a shrinking economic pie, those compromises could not hold.

The German socialist left was bitterly divided between a Social Democratic majority supporting republican constitutionalism and the revolutionary Communist Party; in the end the Communists refused to ally with the Social Democrats, whom they characterized as "social fascists," to defend the republic against the Nazis. The liberal and centrist parties were weak and indecisive in the face of a dynamic radical right, while the traditional authoritarian right, which hoped to restore the monarchy, imagined it could use the Nazis on behalf of its own antidemocratic agenda. The big employers abrogated their wage agreements with the unions and pushed for cutbacks in social benefits. Meanwhile, the National Socialists, as their oxymoronic name signified, blurred conventional categories of left and right. They were not the product of the German elite but a popular movement that took up the banner of the unemployed and the impoverished middle class at the same time that it championed nationalism, anti-Semitism, anti-Bolshevism, and the cult of the charismatic leader with an emotional and erotic intensity that the economistic left and the timorous liberals and centrists could not match. This proved to be a potent formula for attracting not only the Nazis' core constituency—a lower-middle class that felt betrayed by the Weimar government, resentful of big business and hostile to foreigners, Jews, and communists—but unemployed youth and a significant portion of the working class as well.

During the 1920s, Austrian politics was defined by escalating tensions between the Social Democrats who controlled "Red Vienna" and the clericalist Christian Social Party, which represented rural Catholics and was the dominant force in the conservative central government's ruling coalition. The conservatives by turns overlooked and actively abetted the illegal arming and terrorist activity of the Heimwehr, the fascist militia supported and funded by Mussolini, in the hope of achieving through thuggery what could not be accomplished through elections—the destruction of the socialist opposition. The Social Democrats, unable to count on the police, had their own paramilitary arm, the Schutzbund, to protect them against fascist violence, though its (equally illegal) caches of weapons were regularly confiscated by the authorities.

There is wide agreement that the turning point in the struggle between left and right occurred in Vienna on "Bloody Friday"—July 15, 1927. Earlier that year the Heimwehr had fired on a socialist meeting and killed two people; on July 14 the killers were acquitted. The following day, thousands of workers marched to the Parliament building. When police barred the way and charged into the crowd on horseback, a peaceful demonstration turned chaotic and violent; the nearby Palace of Justice was set on fire and destroyed. The police fired indiscriminately into the crowd, killing at least 100 people, and, according to the British journalist G. E. R. Gedye, went on a shooting binge in other parts of the city as well.[3] Nonetheless, the official version of events branded the workers criminal instigators of a "bolshevist" plot. Neither the police nor the Heimwehr were in any way held to account. From then on the right was increasingly bold in its antisocialist assaults.

If the Schutzbund had intervened in the face-off between demonstrators and police, it could no doubt have prevented the confrontation from getting out of control, but inexplicably it did not show up in force. In the aftermath the workers responded nonviolently with a general strike, which was easily broken by the Heimwehr. Perhaps history would have been different had the socialists mobilized an aggressive military response to the fascists' campaign of intimidation; instead they continued to maintain their faith in a parliamentary system that was more and more beside the point until the Christian Social chancellor Engelbert Dollfuss, with the backing of the Heimwehr, abolished it in 1933. Less than a year later the Heimwehr mounted a full-scale war against the Vienna workers. This time the Schutzbund fought back, but it was too late. The only question remaining was whether Austria's homegrown fascists would be able to resist a German takeover. It was answered soon enough.

For Wilhelm Reich, who witnessed it, the July 15 debacle was a profoundly affecting and formative experience. His firsthand account (ironically titled "A Practical Course in Marxist Sociology") is the launching point of *People in Trouble,* an episodic narrative—thought to have been mostly written in the late 1930s, though not published till much later—that interweaves his observations on the political situation in Austria, his own sexual-political activism, and his efforts to formulate a theory of the origins and purpose of sexual repression.[4] With great emotion, Reich describes his overwhelming sense of the gap between abstract ideas about class struggle and the reality of violence in the streets, the spectacle of "thousands and thousands of workers, in and out of uniform," of police "warring here with their own kind." He was struck by the mechanical bearing of the police who shot into the crowd, the passivity of onlookers who did nothing to stop them, the sight of Schutzbund troops walking away from the scene as the demonstration was careening out of control.[5]

July 15 propelled Reich toward radical activism even as it led him to doubt the adequacy of the left's categories. He was frustrated by the Schutzbund's abdication of responsibility and the failure of Otto Bauer, the leader of the Social Democrats, to confront the growing power of the right: instead, he observes ruefully in *People in Trouble,* "Bauer appealed to the reason of the Christian Socialist government and to its statesmanlike insight." Why, he asks, "did Bauer, a powerful man with thousands backing him, not have the streets closed off immediately?" Determined "to avoid civil war at any cost," Bauer did not understand that civil war was already happening.[6] The vacillation of the Social Democrats drew Reich to the more militant Communist Party; yet he found the Viennese Communists—who unlike their German counterparts were little more than a fringe group—largely removed from social reality. (He makes some savage fun of himself and his erstwhile comrades, who once embarked on a grandiose "revolutionary" attempt to disrupt a Heimwehr march and Social Democratic counterdemonstration, only to fall into a predictable police trap.)

Looking back, Reich concludes that a basic problem of the left's leaders and activists was an unadmitted fear of their own constituency—a suspicion that the masses of workers were too dependent on authority to take responsibility for their own lives, that popular power could only lead (just as the reactionaries warned!) to replacing authoritarian institutions with anarchy. This heretical suspicion, so contrary to the parties' utopian rhetoric, was in Reich's view amply justified; but it could not be openly—or perhaps even consciously—acknowledged. His analysis here only hints at what he lays out more explicitly in other political writings, particularly *The Sexual Revolution*—that unconscious guilt and ambivalence about freedom on the part of the leftist leaders themselves also affected their political judgment. In any case, for the Social Democrats the result was indecisiveness and an impulse to appease the right; for the Communists, an out-of-touch sectarianism (or, in countries where they had some actual power, a manipulative and authoritarian style of politics). In Reich's retrospective view, the issue was not this or that political mistake but the irrationality of politics as such. So long as working-class police were willing to shoot at workers like themselves; so long as workers expressed their anger at injustice by burning down a symbolic building, yet could not organize themselves to disarm the greatly outnumbered police; in sum, so long as the question of people's inability to seize and make use of freedom was not addressed, the right would exploit their fear and dependency, while the left would be neutralized.

As he got more involved in politics, Reich decided that he could be most useful in his role as a physician and psychoanalyst, and in 1928, along with some of his medical colleagues, he founded the Socialist Society for Sex Counseling and Sex Research. Its objective was to provide for the people of Vienna, especially working-class women and youth, "free counseling on sexual problems, the rearing of children, and general mental hygiene to those seeking advice."[7] The counseling included information on birth control and abortion, and a gynecologist associated with the group provided contraceptives. Reich advocated legal abortion, taking an uncompromising position on the right of women to end a pregnancy for any reason. (This was yet another issue on which left politicians were useless: the Social Democrats were worried about the Catholic vote, while the Communists equated abortion reform with population control and saw it as a distraction from class politics.) He was initially hesitant when approached by teenagers asking about birth control—adolescent sexual activity was (as it still is) even more controversial than abortion—but ultimately became a firm advocate for the right of children and adolescents to sexual gratification. Bringing up children to affirm their sexuality was, for Reich, the key to preventing neuroses. He saw puberty, in particular, as a critical turning point, a time when bodily changes and soaring hormone levels instigate a kind of "derepression," reviving the desires and emotional conflicts associated with the Oedipus complex. At that point, Reich contended, adolescents who are able to find an outlet for this surge of libidinal energy in a sexual relationship have a far better chance of emotional health and happiness than those who, in response to social taboos, struggle to rearmor themselves against their sexual feelings.

In 1930 Reich moved to Berlin, where he met other analysts with leftist sympathies, among them Erich Fromm and Karen Horney. He started new sex counseling clinics on the model of those he had run in Vienna, joined the Communist Party, and became an activist in the larger sex reform movement, simultaneously promoting Marxism among the sexual reformers and challenging the left parties' resistance—which in Germany as in Austria was considerable—to embracing sexual issues that offended the Catholic Church and social conservatives in general.[8]

Throughout, the aim of Reich's "sex pol" activities, as he called them, was not only to help individuals but to call attention to the social factors that promoted sexual misery and to integrate sexual concerns with the overall socioeconomic program of the left. The impact of sexual ignorance, terror of pregnancy, and fear of society's—especially parents'—disapproval was compounded by inadequate housing and lack of privacy. Most teenagers were forced to live with their sex-negative parents, while women's economic dependence trapped them in unsatisfying marriages. Some of these problems could be alleviated through immediate practical measures, like defying law and custom to distribute contraceptives or make space available to young lovers. But attacking the roots of sexual unhappiness would require major changes in the economy, the status of women, the upbringing and education of children, marriage, and family law. At that, even a social revolution of major proportions would have a limited impact on the sexual fulfillment of the adult population, given that ingrained characterological inhibitions were difficult to overcome even with intensive therapy.

Still, Reich insisted on the importance of sexual education and counseling, since making people—including left activists—aware of the issues was a prerequisite for doing anything about them. Myron Sharaf, Reich's biographer, astutely compares this insistence to the efforts of the contemporary women's liberation movement to "politicize the personal . . . one 'raised consciousness' about the problem."[9] In making women aware that what they thought were private troubles were actually the shared product of social inequality and could be challenged by collective action, the process of sharing personal experience in consciousness-raising groups was a powerful political organizing tool; my own experience in the movement convinced me that it was equally powerful on a psychological level. For many of us, realizing our subordination was rooted in a social system that could be changed aroused repressed hopes that, in psychoanalytic terms, rearranged our libidinal economies: our balance of ambivalence tilted in favor of recognizing, legitimizing, and pursuing our desires. In this sense, politics could be therapeutic. That Reich was well aware of this is suggested in his response to colleagues who questioned what sexual education could accomplish in the absence of some means of mass therapy: "If [a sexually inhibited woman] . . . is present . . . at a rally at which sexual needs are discussed clearly and openly in medical and social terms, then she doesn't feel herself to be alone. Her individual moralistic inhibition is offset by a collective atmosphere of sexual affirmation. . . . Secretly, she herself has mourned her lost joy of life or yearned for sexual happiness. The sexual need is given confidence by the mass situation. . . ."[10]

Much of Reich's writing during this period is similarly focused on melding a Marxist perspective with psychoanalytic thought and the particular insights of his own character-analytic work. In *The Invasion of Compulsory Sex-Morality* (1931) he attempts to refute Freud's equation of repression and civilization with a historical-materialist account of the origins of sex-negative culture. Friedrich Engels, in *The Origin of the Family, Private Property and the State,* had theorized that private property and class society were rooted in the transition from a hypothesized matriarchy characterized by "primitive communism" to the patriarchal family; Reich applies Engels's framework to the work of the British anthropologist Bronislaw Malinowski, who had come to public attention with a 1926 paper denying the universality of the Oedipus complex, and more recently had published his groundbreaking study of the Trobriand Islanders, *The Sexual Life of Savages.*

Malinowski's Trobrianders enjoy, in the main, a sex-affirmative way of life with complete sexual freedom in childhood and adolescence (and a corresponding lack of "civilized" neurotic misery). But they are a people in transition, a matrilineal society—women, their children, and their male relatives are the primary social unit; most goods are communally shared—invaded by patriarchal elements, in the form of marriage customs that involve gifts to the wife's brothers. And with these changes have come sexual restrictions: most strikingly, children designated for "cross-cousin" marriages, which consolidate economic power in the hands of men whose sons marry their sisters' daughters, are denied the freedom of their peers. The reason, Reich argues, is that children whose sexuality is self-regulated will not grow up into adults willing to subordinate their desire to others' economic or political interest. Sexual repression, then, develops as a weapon of class hierarchy.

As a tale of origins, this scenario is less than convincing; it does not explain why a matrilineal society would evolve toward patriarchalism in the first place, or—what is perhaps the same question—how people first come to value economic accumulation over sexual happiness. (It is not until much later that a post-Marxist Reich seriously confronts such questions.) Furthermore, Malinowski's rendition of the Trobrianders' sexual culture is controversial among anthropologists.[11] Reich's book nonetheless stands as a provocative and not implausible effort to provide historical and cultural context for his fundamental political claim: that sexual inhibition reproduces the submissive character the socioeconomic system requires.

[*Editor's note*: This section was followed by a timeline of the late 1920s, early 1930s, and Nazism, the last of which "brought out the two-sidedness of sexual repression: the submission on the one hand, the expression of the secondary layer on the other." Willis also included various notes on early Freudianism and the United States; Herbert Marcuse's *Eros and Civilization*; and the basic questions of Reich and the Frankfurt School.]

The Flight from Libido

While Reich's technical innovations of the 1920s were incorporated into mainstream psychoanalytic practice—among psychotherapists *Character Analysis* is still considered a canonical text—that acceptance did not extend to his orgasm theory, which he considered inseparable from his therapy, or its radical implications. Freud, in ascribing aggression to a death instinct, was taking psychoanalysis in a distinctly conservative direction: in the context of a fatalism that envisioned repression as a leaky seawall containing the anarchic tide, Freud's theory of sexuality came across not simply as a powerful description of the individual's submission to culture, but as an implicit justification of moral and sexual conformity. Meanwhile, new currents in the psychoanalytic movement were deemphasizing libido theory or rejecting it altogether.

As early as 1911, Alfred Adler had broken with Freud and psychoanalysis to formulate his "individual psychology" attributing human motivation to feelings of inferiority rather than sexual desire. In 1939, Heinz Hartmann established the framework of modern ego psychology with the publication of a series of his lectures as *Ego Psychology and the Problem of Adaptation*. By then, Freud had shifted his focus from the repressed instinctual drives to the repressing forces of the ego; Anna Freud (clearly influenced by Reich's work on character defenses and resistance) had elaborated on the subject in *The Ego and the Mechanisms of Defense*. While Hartmann saw himself as building on this work and disclaimed any affinity with Adlerian or other "surface psychologies," his major innovation was delineating what he called the "conflict-free ego sphere." In Hartmann's formulation, this is the aspect of a given individual's ego that is not forged by repression and management of libido, but develops from the human organism's inborn capacities for adaptation to its environment. Implied if never openly stated is the rejection of Freud's claim that civilization is the product of repression. Rather, Hartmann speaks of "average expectable envi-

ronmental conditions," conducive to normal development and adaptation, as opposed to "atypical" conditions, which presumably make adaptation more difficult
and foster pathology. Where libido theory regards neurotic symptoms as especially dramatic markers of a more general unfreedom, ego psychology makes
a conventional distinction between the normal and the pathological, based on
the degree of successful adaptation. Although Hartmann emphasizes that adaptation does not mean passive submission but includes the ability to act on
one's social world and even transform it, the nature of the "average expectable
environment" is not subjected to scrutiny beyond the banal suggestion that it
involves a mother caring adequately for her child. The social critique embedded
in Freudian thought has been stripped away.

Also during the late 1930s, the so-called neo-Freudian revisionists, of whom
the most prominent were Karen Horney and (a more complicated case, as the
previous chapter suggests) Erich Fromm, reacted against Freudian conservatism by rejecting libido theory altogether as biologistic and arguing for the primacy of cultural factors in neurosis. In their view, the underlying conflict was
not between biological drive and culture but between the individual personality and social authority in a specific cultural context.

The revisionists' emphasis on variable, mutable culture as opposed to universal biological destiny presented itself as a critique of Freudian pessimism
from the left—Horney was a feminist, Fromm a passionate critic of capitalism.
But in fact the neo-Freudians reinforced the psychoanalytic movement's flight
from radicalism, for in eliding biology, they divorced psychoanalysis from its
material foundation. Reverting to the abstract, spiritual conception of self that
Freudian psychoanalysis had challenged, they took as a given the "personality" whose formation Freud had traced to libidinal repression; their social criticism was firmly lodged in a conventional ethical framework, as if Freud's account of civilized values as the tragic product of alienated desire did not exist.
Paradoxically, the human being as represented by the neo-Freudians is far less
a creature of culture than its Freudian counterpart, whose personality is not
merely deformed by the social order but formed by it in the first place.[12]

In its early years, psychoanalysis had scandalized the public, which immediately recognized the "pansexuality" of libido theory as a threat to conventional
morality and religion; the turn away from its subversive core propositions made
it respectable. Both Freud's resort to that mythical entity, the death instinct,
and the efforts of the ego psychologists and neo-Freudians to distance psychoanalysis from its roots in bodily desire ultimately contributed to the view that
psychoanalysis may offer literary insights but has no relevance to concrete, material reality. Freudian conservatism, imported to America, congealed into a
vulgarized, dogmatic antifeminism that eventually became a prime target of
the women's liberation movement.[13] Overall, the rejection of radicalism within
psychoanalysis laid the groundwork for the backlash against psychoanalysis as
such—or more precisely was its first manifestation.

In devoting the next two chapters to examining that backlash, I do not propose to write yet another brief in the ongoing debate about Freud's intellectual
honesty and therapeutic methods. Nor will I engage, except incidentally, the
line of argument that focuses on analysts' authoritarian misuses of their power
over patients or on their circular attempts to deflect criticism by attributing
it to the critic's neurosis. Those issues are worthy of discussion in their own
right (even if polemics in this vein too often feature a conversation-stopping
insistence that the entire fabric of psychoanalytic thought is a more or less deliberate hoax, whose defenders are either knaves or dupes).[14] But they are peripheral to my concern here, which is the range of substantive objections to the
fundamental concepts of psychoanalysis—that libido theory is not scientific,
that it is naively "physicalist" or biologistic, and that it serves to rationalize,
depending on the ideological bent of the critic, either amorality and relativism
or male supremacy and sexual conservatism.

The contention that psychoanalysis is not a science is based, overtly or implicitly, on Karl Popper's definition, which holds that scientific claims must
be subject to experimental falsification.[15] On those restricted terms, the argument can only be conceded. There is no way either to confirm or to rule out the
content or dynamics of the unconscious through controlled experiments; one
cannot observe unconscious feelings, fantasies, or conflicts, only infer them
from people's words and behavior. The question is whether psychoanalytic
method can be said to fit an older, broader view of science as an effort to attain
some systematic knowledge of the material or social world through the use of
observation and reasoning, rather than fantasy, myth, religious authority, or
mystical revelation. (From this standpoint, the element of imaginative speculation in the psychoanalytic corpus, including Freud's metahistorical and anthro-
pological writings, might best be regarded as elaboration on its theory rather
than evidence for it.)

The crucible of psychoanalysis was the problem of hysteria: how to explain
disabling emotional suffering and physical symptoms with no perceptible
organic cause. The proposed solution was to systematically investigate mental life. That project in turn took as its working assumption that subjectivity
is not wholly individual and idiosyncratic, but has objective characteristics,
in the sense of common elements and patterns, of which we are unaware—
patterns that can be discerned through particular methods of close observation. Following on this assumption, the evidence for libido theory is derived
from phenomena of everyday life such as dreams, jokes, and slips; the words
and behavior of people with mental and emotional problems or inexplicable
physical complaints; the associations of analysands and the ways they express
their failure or refusal to produce associations. In the public realm, the evidence
consists of constant or recurrent patterns of social and political irrationality (by
which I mean ideology or policy that is self-contradictory, supported by masses

of people who are hurt by it, and based on fantasies that bear little or no relation to reality—especially fantasies that rationalize domination, murder, and war).

Antagonists deny the value of this evidence on the grounds that there is no reliable way to distinguish one's own subjective associations and fantasies from the actual meaning of dreams or other psychoanalytic "material" one is interpreting; or to tell whether a patient's productions are spontaneous or in some way suggested by the therapist. Arguing that psychoanalytic data can mean anything the analyst wants it to mean, Frederick Crews writes, "Freud left us with no guidelines for perceiving whether a given expression should be taken literally or regarded as a compromise formation shaped by this or that unconscious defense against a wish or fantasy."[16]

It's true that there is no way to set up a subject-interpreter or analyst-patient relationship completely free of "contamination" by the interpreter's expectations—which may color interpretations as well as unwittingly influencing the subject's "expressions"—or for that matter by the subject's own prior embrace of psychoanalytic concepts. As I've already noted, psychoanalysis did not develop in a vacuum; its context was the identification of hysteria as a social problem, itself a reflection of Victorian Europe at a historical moment when the seams of patriarchal morality were beginning to rip. Freud had to have suspected from the outset that what ailed his patients had something to do with sex (certainly he was impressed by Charcot's pronouncement that "it's about the genitals, always!"). And of course clinicians who were drawn to psychoanalysis by Freud's findings could hardly approach their own cases as blank slates. But then, it has long been recognized that there is no such thing as a scientist, be it in physics or any other discipline, whose empirical research is devoid of theoretical expectations. Indeed such expectations—inevitably shaped by the social climate and what scientists or people in a position to influence them most urgently want to know—determine the direction of scientific research and why particular experiments are constructed in the first place.[17] The issue is not whether such expectations exist, but how to judge their validity.

From this perspective, it's one thing to recognize the potential for error when psychoanalysts interpret ambiguous material, another to dismiss analytic interpretation as inherently arbitrary. The latter claim implicitly accepts the view that only falsifiable experiments can produce legitimate knowledge. It does not refute but simply rejects out of hand the psychoanalyst's thesis—that it's possible to gain "objective" knowledge of someone else's internal reality through "subjective" investigation. If one adopts that thesis, at least tentatively, it suggests a strategy for evaluating interpretations: consistently applying the analytic method, which means treating everything that goes on in an analytic session as "material" to be scrutinized.

To this end, there are two principles analytic observation must follow. First, a particular piece of material cannot be understood in isolation, only in the context of the larger web of information—other "expressions," the history and social situation of the subject—in which it is embedded. The meaning of a dream, for example, will likely be unclear until other dreams or remarks point to a particular theme; it is not a matter of mechanically interpreting symbols. (Indeed, it is possible to pack several different layers of meaning into a dream.) Over time the analyst—not unlike other kinds of detectives—can also judge whether the patient's expressions confirm or contradict each other, and how they fit into the overall picture. When Wilhelm Reich expanded the field of the analyst's attention to include forms of communication like body language and tone of voice, which are far less subject to conscious censorship and a priori intellectual convictions than words, he was able to significantly refine his interpretations: if, for instance, a patient described castration fantasies without emotion or with what Reich called the "inward smile," this meant something different from the same fantasies related with enormous anxiety. In interpreting the disparity between the patient's words and his manner as an expression of, say, contempt for the analyst, and observing how he reacted, Reich would elicit more information that would give further clues to the patient's inner life.

Equally important, the analytic observer cannot stand outside the field of observation, but must take into account how his or her own unconscious wishes affect the analytic process; therefore that process must always include self-examination. As Reich noted, analysts who do not recognize their own erotic impulses or fear of aggression or desire for unchallenged authority will fail to distinguish between patients' genuinely positive feelings toward them and hatred masked as friendliness or seduction. Similarly, insecure analysts who need to have patients confirm their theories can develop a comfortable symbiotic relationship with patients who prefer to turn therapy into an intellectual exercise rather than confront their feelings.

In *Character Analysis,* Reich makes a compelling case for consistently interpreting the form of his patients' communication before its content, and interpreting those aspects of patients' stories, fantasies, or dreams that clearly refer to their present situation (that is, to realities that can be checked) before tackling seeming allusions to deeply buried unconscious wishes. Through this technique one avoided making interpretations that whether true or not were analytically useless because the patient was not ready to accept them, but was inviting them to distract the analyst from more obvious, more immediately painful material. The result was an analysis that unfolded in a more or less orderly fashion, in which the unconscious sexual source of the patient's problem became clearer as associations referring to it repeatedly surfaced with more and more vivid emotion and conscious understanding. Each time this happened, moreover, the patient would then "forget" what he or she had just learned and temporarily revert to earlier characteristic forms of defensive behavior, which would have to be interpreted once more. In other words, though each analysis was as individual as a fingerprint, analyses that Reich conducted according to character-analytic methods turned out to have certain predictable patterns in common. It is not possible to explain these similarities, occurring in the treatment of many patients with different presenting symptoms, life stories, and personal characteristics, as the result of "suggestion."

In applying psychoanalytic theory to social criticism, the same basic principles hold. Particular events must be regarded in light of what we know about the overall social context and about history; critics must include in their examination the psychic predispositions that may influence their own social views. If such investigations reveal certain predictable patterns—if, as I've been suggesting, the insights of psychoanalytic radicalism make intelligible much that is otherwise mysterious about our social arrangements and conflicts—then they deserve serious consideration. It is up to the antagonists of psychoanalysis to show that its apparent explanatory power is illusory or to point the way toward more convincing alternatives.

This is not the same as saying that psychoanalysis can prove its central propositions. Yet it's also true that the prevailing dismissal of the very idea of a biological energy associated with sexuality, as if it were self-evidently absurd, is an item of conventional wisdom, not a conclusion of science. Freud's appropriation of terms from physics to describe the movements and effects of libido has typically been derided as "hydraulics" and an extension of 19th-century positivism rather than considered in context as an effort to find a vocabulary for discussing phenomena previously undescribed. And when Reich claimed to have verified the physical existence of libido through experimental science, he was promptly labeled a quack and a lunatic. To this day, so far as I know, there has never been a systematic attempt by mainstream scientists to replicate his experiments and confirm or falsify his data. In truth, the issues raised by Reich and other Freudian radicals about the nature of the sexual drive and its relationship to emotional, social, and political life have not been high on the scientific establishment's agenda. It is necessary to address them nonetheless.

Libido theory challenges the most basic ideological underpinning of civilization as we know it: the belief that human beings can and must dominate nature. If the human animal is part of the natural world, this belief is a contradiction in terms; nonetheless it unites the symbiotic institutions of religion and science. The Abrahamic religions resolve the contradiction by proclaiming a dualism of nature and the supernatural, matter and spirit, body and soul; the struggle against nature takes the form of a struggle to keep the body in its place, to subordinate the insistent claims of our "animal nature"—above all, sexuality—to the spiritual demands of the soul and the will of a transcendent God. The vocabulary of that struggle is one of abstract moral and ethical values, of good and evil as essences that precede any concrete act, of idealism, in the philosophical sense, as opposed to materialism. Freudian psychoanalysis proposes instead that our animal nature may be repressed but is never surpassed, and that the very idea of a transcendent God or a disembodied morality derives from sexual energy.[18]

Psychoanalysis serves the quest for a secular materialist understanding of, among other things, religion. For the believer such a project is not only unnecessary but dismissive: religion exists because God does. It follows that the resurgence of the religious right that began in the United States in the 1970s is an antipsychoanalytic backlash by definition. But the influence of religious morality is hardly confined to fundamentalist Christians, or even to believers. In the most secular precincts of the West, morals and ethics as they are commonly understood bear the unspoken prefix "Judeo-Christian," and the left as well as the right tends to express its aims in moral terms that have religious roots, acknowledged or not. Those who raise the banner of morality in behalf of socially progressive causes have nevertheless embraced a way of thinking that from a Freudian perspective is a product and constituent of unfreedom.

This is not to say that psychoanalysis implies no moral vision. The psychoanalytic worldview (pace Freud, who claimed there was no such thing) espouses self-knowledge, assumption of responsibility for the whole of what one does, freedom from the reflexive codes of family, church, tribe—in short, the values of the Enlightenment as inflected by Freud's critique. In its radical version, psychoanalysis gives unequivocal moral affirmation to the pursuit of happiness. But this morality derives its substance and conviction from the needs of the body. For moral conservatives, of whatever political stripe, it is no morality at all, but on the contrary represents a nihilistic relativism. (In defending this view, they often cite the neutral, unjudging stance of the analyst, failing to realize that that neutrality is not an end in itself but a strategy for pursuing the psychoanalytic moral agenda by eliciting hidden knowledge.) On the other hand, liberal or libertarian moralists—who can also be found on both the left and the right—may sympathize with psychoanalytic values, but like the neo-Freudians they elide the body in favor of a dematerialized ethics, in which the ghost of religion hovers.

In the end there can be no serious debate between religious doctrine or religion-based idealist morality and libido theory, only a clash between opposed and incommensurable cosmologies. In contrast, attacks on psychoanalysis from the standpoint of experimental science would seem to meet their target on secular ground—if anything it is psychoanalysis that, in this context, stands accused of mysticism. But this is a superficial view. Science—that is, science as an institution, driven by the promise of technological innovation—turned the war against nature outward from the self to the world. The constant equation of our ability to manipulate the natural environment with the "conquest" of nature itself entails an unacknowledged but no less potent acceptance of the religious premise that human agency is in some sense outside nature and above it. Nor is the rhetoric of conquest merely metaphorical; it has played out in practice in a stubborn disregard for the unintended consequences of our scientific-technological interventions in the world. The dominant response to ecological crises like global warming or the resurgence of infectious disease despite its supposed "conquest" by antibiotics has ranged from denial to new technological fixes (more powerful antibiotics!) rather than a rethinking of the techno-scientific project. Although the "uncertainty principle" of quantum physics proposes that the process of observation changes the object observed,[19] and that observer and observed exert a mutual effect on one another, these ideas and their implications have yet to seriously undermine the conventional technoscientific assumption that we can examine nature from a position that transcends it.

The mainstream biological sciences implicitly depend on that assumption; yet many biologists and psychologists who study human behavior paradoxically conceive of the body and the brain by way of analogy to machines, as if there were no essential difference between living beings and inanimate objects. ("The brain is a physical system. It functions as a computer. Its circuits are designed to generate behavior that is appropriate to your environmental circumstances," as a characteristic piece of scientific-psychological literature informs us.)[20] One might say that the war against nature is redirected once again, from the world back to the self, but the self is split: in its guise as observer it is implicitly defined as pure spirit; as the object of observation, pure matter, which is to say brain circuits or chemicals or DNA.

There is no way to understand subjective experience within this mechanistic framework. At its most reductive, as in various genres of behaviorism, it simply does away with subjectivity as a phenomenon worth investigating and assumes that human beings, like rats, respond predictably to pleasurable and painful stimuli. Alternatively, mental and emotional states, whether "normal" or pathological, are said to have organic causes—aggression, for instance, has been attributed to testosterone, schizophrenia and depression to biochemical imbalances, autism to scrambled hard-wiring in the brain. But what the relevant studies show is an association between psychological and physiological conditions, not causality. Might emotions manifest themselves in organic changes, rather than the other way around? Might chemical or neurological factors make people more or less susceptible to being overwhelmed by traumatic experiences, or influence how, or with what intensity, emotions and emotional conflicts are expressed? There is compelling evidence that particular areas and structures of the brain are associated with various capacities for cognition, perception, and feeling, but what factors influence whether and how those capacities are activated?

However intricately scientists may trace neural and chemical influences and the relationships among them, the role of experience in forming the psyche remains to be explained. Research on the way brain activity produces memory is often brandished as proof that psychoanalysis is worthless; but while it may suggest that particular psychoanalytic formulations are reductive or naive, it does not contradict the basic psychoanalytic claim that memory is influenced by unconscious desire and anxiety, because it does not, and by its nature cannot, examine that claim in the first place. Memory studies show, for instance, that what one remembers is not a literal snapshot of what happened and may indeed be entirely false, or the product of someone else's suggestion. But psychoanalysts, beginning with Freud, figured that out long ago. On the issue of what subjective experience a memory represents (or is arguably designed to censor); or what it might mean when a memory intrudes into consciousness that was absent before; or how, in the case of a memory implanted by suggestion, that mysterious thought-transfer called "suggestion" actually works, the studies have little of interest to say. (Adolf Grunbaum, the most prominent anti-Freudian philosopher of science, provides an unwitting example of the problem with invalidating psychoanalytic evidence on the grounds that memory is unreliable. In the course of making this argument, he cites a well-known experiment whose subjects were shown a picture of a subway car in which a white man holding a razor was arguing with a black man; when asked to describe what they had seen, many "remembered" the black man brandishing the razor.[21] Yet this result would seem to undermine rather than bolster Grunbaum's point. Where, after all, did the racist distortion of memory come from if not the unconscious of the subjects? The transposition was suggested not by the picture itself but by an internal impulse, inviting a psychoanalytic interpretation: that fantasies of black people as violent or hypersexual are a screen for the fantasists' anxieties about their own forbidden desires—a disguise that both reflects and perpetuates institutional racism.)

Similarly, the discovery—also regularly invoked by Freud debunkers—of REM sleep and the brain patterns that activate dreams tells us nothing about the content of dreams or their psychodynamic significance. The most sophisticated research in the fields of cognitive neuroscience and neuropsychiatry adopts a multicausal framework for understanding thought, memory, and emotion, in which experience and interpersonal relations are acknowledged to play a part.[22] But these latter categories remain unanalyzed; as with the neo-Freudians, they are uncritically based on conventional, commonsense definitions.

The preoccupation with genetics that has dominated biology since the discovery of the double helix—and the propensity of researchers to suggest to credulous popular media that there are genes for everything from impulsiveness to homosexuality—invites similar objections. At most, genetic factors can be shown to have some statistical correlation with certain forms of behavior, cognition, or emotion; they cannot in themselves explain human experience. Nor, by and large, do scholars and clinicians mining this terrain disagree. Nonetheless genetics has spawned a neo-Darwinian ideology, embodied in the field that used to be called sociobiology and has now been revamped as evolutionary psychology: it regards human behavior as the product of natural selection, which has resulted in the development of brain structures (see the quotation on brain function, above) conducive to passing on our genes.[23] Underlying this view is a conception—simply assumed rather than justified—of the life process as governed solely by the imperative to survive and reproduce.

In the end, because it offers no satisfying account of subjectivity, biological reductionism reinforces the claims of religion and moral and ethical idealism. The same can be said of the rationalism underlying the currently ascendant ideology of free-market economics—that is, the claim that individuals, unimpeded by an intrusive government, will act in their economic self-interest, and in doing so will promote the general interest by maximizing both freedom and prosperity. This claim is grounded in a wholly unreflective view of individual choice. Do people always choose what's in their interest? Is their perceived interest and their actual interest the same? Might individuals' irrational behavior produce irrational social arrangements, and vice versa? For economic libertarians, such questions are irrelevant or worse, a cover for the totalitarian urge (equally unanalyzed) to tell people what's best for them. It is taken as axiomatic that the individual is wholly autonomous and that society is nothing other than an aggregate of individuals. On its face, neoliberal or libertarian rationalism is opposed to the determinism of mechanistic science; it emphasizes free will and assumes freedom and individual responsibility as primary ethical values. Yet the reductio ad absurdum of libertarianism, rational choice theory, reconciles it with scientism by generating mathematical models that purport to chart individual preferences as a function of rational cost-benefit analysis. (Spawned by economists, this approach has been enthusiastically taken up by political scientists and philosophers.) Whether people's perception of costs and benefits is rational in the first place, or how those perceptions are formed, does not figure in the equation. Such considerations are regarded as outside the bounds of science.[24]

Again, taken at face value the libertarian ethic clashes with traditional religious morality, which emphasizes altruism and sacrifice. Indeed, this clash inspired the novelist and "objectivist" philosopher Ayn Rand to envision a countermorality in which selfishness is exalted as the source of all human creativity, entrepreneurs in the mold of the Nietzschean superman are the moral equivalent of God, and evil is personified by "looters," i.e., all those who would force the supermen to bow to the totalitarian concept of the common good. Paradoxically, however, the writings of free-market libertarians often seek a rapprochement with religion-based morality: for many, evidently, what the libertarian and religious worldviews share—the assumption of an abstract, disembodied moral will—is more telling than their differences. Libertarians have argued that free-market economics will restore virtue to society by rewarding the work ethic; making families rather than welfare programs responsible for supporting children, the old, and the sick; and allowing landlords and employers free rein to discriminate against anyone they consider undesirable. They have demonized taxation and regulation of private property as, in effect, a violation of the commandment "Thou shalt not steal."[25] Alternatively, some see the free-market ethos as governing a public realm assumed to consist of men doing the world's work, while they regard the domestic sphere of women and children as the proper domain of patriarchal morality.[26] This philosophical miscegenation explains why libertarians and moral conservatives can maintain an alliance within the Republican Party; it's also a tacit recognition that rationalism is alien to most people's "structure of feeling"—even, perhaps, among the libertarians themselves.

On the other hand, some libertarian rationalists have made a serious effort to address psychological issues. A notable example is the psychiatrist Thomas S. Szasz, whose influential book *The Myth of Mental Illness* was first published in 1961, at the height of Freud's prestige and influence in America.[27] Szasz argues against assimilating psychiatry to medicine, whether by attributing psychological complaints to organic causes or by equating such complaints, including those that are expressed through the body, with physical illness—he pointedly makes hysteria, with its paralyses, seizures, and pains, his primary example. From this perspective, he rejects libido theory with its vocabulary of *biological drive, energy, neurosis, symptoms,* and so forth. Rather he defines psychological disturbances as "problems in living" best addressed in terms of communications analysis and the theory of games—that is, of interpersonal relations as structured by sets of mutually accepted rules. (Game theory also figures prominently in "rational choice" analyses of politics.)

Hysterics, in Szasz's view, are enacting a simulation of illness in what amounts to a nonverbal message, "I'm disabled," designed to appeal to our solicitude for invalids. This tactic, employed to escape social demands or to be cared for, would once simply have been condemned as malingering; but at a key historical juncture in 19th-century Vienna, certain doctors agreed to accept faked illness as real and join the hysteric in playing the doctor-patient game. The psychiatrist's alternative, as Szasz sees it, is not to revert to condemnation, but to understand the life situation encoded in the specific contents ("symptoms") of a hysteric's nonverbal language, in order to make "patients" aware of the game they are trying to play and why, and what other, more satisfying games they might choose to play instead. For these purposes, Szasz finds the techniques of psychoanalysis useful even as he jettisons its theoretical apparatus.

Szasz contends that psychiatry, conducted as a systematic inquiry into people's game-playing behavior, is a scientific enterprise. But when he turns to the inevitable question of subjectivity—why people play the games they do and how they feel about it—he falls back on the language of ethics, which, like the neo-Freudians, he regards as a product of culture. Hysteria, he argues, conforms to the ethics of organized religion, particularly Christianity, which in exalting humility, meekness, and faith rather than competence fosters "irresponsibility and childish dependency"; this ethic, in turn, is rooted in the desire of slaves during the Roman Empire to change "the rules of the game of life" to favor them rather than their oppressors.[28] In contrast, the ethic on which

Szasz bases his own life and approach to his work is one of individual autonomy, personal responsibility, and interpersonal equality—values rooted in democracy. (He stresses the need for psychiatrists to talk about their ethical presuppositions with their patients—or more precisely, students, since he regards the psychiatrist's role as properly that of an educator, not a doctor.)

This narrative of competing moralities leaves a good deal unexplained. Why did the slaves, who far outnumbered their masters, not overthrow their oppressors, rather than invent a morality that glorified their own helplessness? Why would this "slave morality" have such power that it not only spread all over the world but is still thriving in modern liberal democracies 2,000 years later? If hysterics are malingerers, imposing their irresponsible, dependent attitude on others, why not condemn them and demand that they shape up? If, on the other hand, they are simulating disability, yet are convinced of its reality and so unable simply to decide to give it up, how do we apply ethics—which assumes free will—to this odd state of affairs? Szasz does not exactly deny the unconscious; he acknowledges that the hysteric's simulation is self-deceiving as well as purposeful. But he evades the issue libido theory explores: what is it about the human organism that allows this profound split in the self, between conscious will and unconscious motive, to come about?

It is arguably possible (and certainly entertaining) to translate the "moves" of the libido into Szasz's game model of behavior. Szasz distinguishes "object games"—directed toward such biological goals as survival or release of tension—from "metagames," whose rules refer to the rules of other games. It is metagames that, for him, are the subject matter of psychology; biology merely sets the limits within which metagames can be played. But suppose one of humanity's earliest and most universal metagames distinguishes between two kinds of object games—one consisting of games whose rules are directed toward survival, the other governed by a single rule, the pleasure principle—and specifies this basic rule: to be allowed to play the survival games successfully, one must give up or drastically restrict participation in the pleasure games. This is a rule that is at once impossible to follow and impossible to reject (in the parlance of communications theorist Gregory Bateson, whom Szasz cites as an influence, it sets up a double bind). I'll leave aside for the moment the key question, which I touched on in the previous chapter, of why human beings would invent such a self-torturing game. Regardless, the result is a host of metagames that allow libidinal energy to express itself by disguising, displacing, and repressing consciousness of its aims. Games of this kind, by definition, can only be played by cheating. "Religious morality" is such a game (guilt is, among other things, a recognition of the cheat). Hysterics may make use of its rules, but not simply to achieve the practical goals of the malingerer. Rather, hysteria, like all "neurotic" metagames, can be seen as a strategy designed to resolve but also to protest the double bind: ultimately, the responsibility hysterics aim to avoid is responsibility for their desire.

The problem with my "translation," from a Szaszian standpoint, is that it blurs the categories of object games and metagames by suggesting that biological need, in the form of sexual energy seeking an outlet, shapes the rules of the latter: the body becomes a subject, or an agent, not simply a machine that provides a substratum for the nonmaterial mind. In this way, Szasz comes full circle to accept the biological reductionism of mechanistic science, and so, like the religious moralists he disdains, he must also accept morality or ethics as a thing apart from the material world. So long as scientific and rationalist thought keep perpetuating this dualism, they will also perpetuate religion as the only game in town.

NOTES

Editor's note: Given the unfinished nature of this manuscript, the reader will see that these notes still reflect Willis's own jottings to herself as she was formulating the arguments in the book. They have been left in that work-in-progress state.

1. Peukert, *The Weimar Republic.*

2. See Atina Grossmann, *Reforming Sex.*

3. For a particularly detailed and vivid account of the July 15 events, see Gedye's *Betrayal in Central Europe* (New York and London: Harper & Brothers, 1939), 21–25.

4. Wilhelm Reich, *People in Trouble* (New York: Farrar, Straus, & Giroux, 1976), 22–47. As Reich's biographer Myron Sharaf notes, it can be hard to sort out exactly when Reich wrote what, as he would often revise or add to his work after the fact, without bothering to mention that he had done so: see Sharaf's *Fury on Earth: A Biography of Wilhelm Reich* (New York: Da Capo Press, 1994), 123. In addition, *People in Trouble* contains a bracketed running commentary on the text by the author's 1950s self, whom he calls "the Silent Observer."

5. *People in Trouble [PIT],* 24.

6. *PIT,* 39–40.

7. *PIT,* 107. For an overview of Reich's "sex pol" work in Vienna and Berlin, see also Sharaf, 129–44, 158–59 (in galleys, check w. book).

8. Check relevant passages in Grossmann.

9. Sharaf, 133.

10. Wilhelm Reich, *The Mass Psychology of Fascism* [from Higgins/Raphael edition; check the other one], 187.

11. Cite critiques of Malinowski here.

12. Cite Marcuse's polemic against revisionists in *Eros and Civilization*; also Russell Jacoby, *Social Amnesia,* and Paul Goodman essay on revisions of Freud in *Psychological Essays.*

13. Cf. Bergler, Farnham, and Lundberg et al. Viewed women's aspirations to transcend the wife and mother role as pathological.

14. A number of the more influential anti-Freud polemics are collected in *The Unauthorized Freud,* ed. Frederick Crews. See also Jeffrey Masson, *The Assault on Truth.*

15. Grunbaum, Crews's book, etc.

16. *Unauthorized Freud,* xxv.

17. Cite sources on theory-laden nature of experimental science.

18. Brief comment on Eastern religion in this regard. Buddhism—matter is an illusion. Status of idea of "life energy" in Eastern religion is correspondingly different. Psycho-

analysis—religion dialectic primarily refers to Judeo-Christian-Islamic cultures: these are my central concern. Expanding discussion a whole other book.

19. Explain difference between Heisenberg and Bohr: one says it's the act of observation, the other that it's the instrument of measurement.

20. Leda Cosmides and John Tooby, "Evolutionary Psychology Primer," Center for Evolutionary Psychology, UC Santa Barbara, 1997.

21. "Made to Order Evidence," chapter from *The Foundations of Psychoanalysis,* excerpted in Crew, 83. Look up original citation: Adolf Grunbaum, *The Foundations of Psychoanalysis: A Philosophical Critique* (Berkeley: University of California Press, 1984).

22. Cite D. Siegel, etc.

23. Cite relevant sociobiology/evolutionary psychology works.

24. Cite examples of books on r.c. [rational choice] theory.

25. Cite Boaz and Murray books.

26. Cite George Gilder.

27. T. Szasz, *Myth of Mental Illness.*

28. *Myth,* 196–200. For a similar argument from a neo-Freudian perspective see Erich Fromm's essay "The Dogma of Christ" in *The Dogma of Christ and Other Essays on Religion, Psychology and Culture* (New York: Holt, Rinehart, & Winston, 1963).

ELLEN WILLIS (1941–2006) was a groundbreaking radical leftist writer whose true loves were rock music, feminism, pleasure, and freedom. She was the first pop music critic for *The New Yorker* and an editor and columnist at the *Village Voice,* and she also wrote for *Rolling Stone,* the *New York Times, The Nation,* and *Dissent.* She was the founder of the Cultural Reporting and Criticism Program at New York University. Her other essay collections published by the University of Minnesota Press are *Beginning to See the Light: Sex, Hope, and Rock-and-Roll* (2012), *No More Nice Girls: Countercultural Essays* (2012), and *Out of the Vinyl Deeps: Ellen Willis on Rock Music* (2011).

NONA WILLIS ARONOWITZ is a journalist and editor who has written for the *Washington Post,* NBC News, *The Atlantic, The Nation, The American Prospect, Elle* magazine, and Rookie. She is cofounder of *Tomorrow* magazine and a former fellow at the Roosevelt Institute. She is the coauthor of *Girldrive: Criss-crossing America, Redefining Feminism* and the editor of *Out of the Vinyl Deeps: Ellen Willis on Rock Music* (Minnesota, 2011).